Business Ethics

RICHARD T. DE GEORGE

THE UNIVERSITY OF KANSAS

·

Business Ethics

SECOND EDITION

MACMILLAN PUBLISHING COMPANY

NEW YORK

Collier Macmillan Publishers

LONDON

Copyright © 1986, Macmillan Publishing Company, a division of Macmillan, Inc.

Printed in the United States of America

All rights reserved. No part of this book may be reproduced or transmitted in any form or by any means, electronic or mechanical, including photocopying, recording, or any information storage and retrieval system, without permission in writing from the publisher. Earlier edition copyright © 1982 by Macmillan Publishing Co., Inc.

Macmillan Publishing Company
866 Third Avenue, New York, New York 10022

Collier Macmillan Canada, Inc.

Library of Congress Cataloging in Publication Data

De George, Richard T.
  Business ethics.

  Bibliography: p.
  Includes index.
  1. Business ethics.   2. Business ethics—Case
studies.   I. Title.
  HF5387.D38   1986   174'.4   85-4974
  ISBN 0-02-328010-7

Printing: 1 2 3 4 5 6 7 8   Year: 6 7 8 9 0 1 2 3 4 5

ISBN 0-02-328010-7

Preface

Courses in ethics have long been standard fare in American colleges and universities. Courses in business ethics are of more recent vintage. The latter took root in the post-Watergate era, and were nurtured by successive exposés involving bribes and kickbacks, illegal political contributions, airplane disasters, and the sale of defective tires, automobiles, and other products. Consumerism, the cry for increased governmental control, and a changing attitude of large numbers of people toward business and its social responsibility have made questions of business ethics topics of general and current concern.

This book is an attempt to cover the field in a systematic and reasonably comprehensive way. It deals first with the techniques of moral reasoning and argumentation that are needed to analyze moral issues in business. It then raises basic questions about the morality of economic systems, especially that of the United States. It next discusses a variety of current and pressing moral issues in business, from worker's rights to trade secrets. Finally, it discusses the moral obligations of nations to other nations, of peoples to other peoples geographically distant from them, and of one generation to later generations.

Because business ethics is a comparatively new field of scholarly endeavor, I should make clear some of my presuppositions and aims from the start.

This is not a book on general ethics, one that simply takes its examples from the business world. Ethics as a discipline has a long and venerable history. But students do not need to know that history, nor do they need to know the numerous disputed questions with which that discipline abounds in order to engage in moral thinking. Moral issues are pressing, and people must grapple with them, using the best tools available to them. I try, therefore, to introduce the student to as much of the technical aspect of ethics as is necessary for him or her to approach moral issues intelligently, and to take part in the ongoing

v

debate about the morality of certain social and business practices. The aim of my initial chapters is a practical one, and to achieve this end I either ignore, or pass over lightly, some of the theoretical issues on which much of contemporary professional ethical thought is focused. Students, I assume, come to classes in business ethics with a good deal of moral baggage. They are not nonmoral beings who must be made moral; they are moral beings who can be helped to think through moral issues, and to argue cogently and effectively for their moral views.

The traditional approach to ethics is an individualistic one. Our notions of morality, moral worth, and moral praise and blame have derived primarily from consideration of the human person as a moral agent. We know what it means to call a person moral, or his or her actions morally praiseworthy. Economic systems do not act in a way comparable to the way human individuals act; corporations and nations act only figuratively—through the agency of human intermediaries. Moral language must therefore be used with care and caution when applied outside of the realm of human individuals and their actions. Special problems arise when considering the morality of corporations, nations, and people—problems that concern the meaning of moral terms, and problems that must be faced and clarified if we are to be clear about our moral judgments in these areas.

I assume that there is little need to argue that murder is wrong, that stealing and lying are in general wrong, or that discrimination on the basis of sex, race, or creed is immoral in business as well as in other areas of life. There is no need for a course in business ethics to arrive at, or justify, those conclusions. But many of the answers to questions in business ethics are not clear-cut, including reverse discrimination, truth in advertising, whistle blowing, and disclosure, among others. These require careful analysis, and a weighing of appropriate facts and applicable principles in order to arrive at justifiable answers. The viewpoint of our society is clearer on some of these issues than on others. I have tried to present the complexities of each problem, and to weigh the opposing views on each issue. When I have taken sides, I have given my reasons for doing so; if an argument is inconclusive, I have indicated where and why. On broad social issues, no argument will be the final one, and my hope is that students using this text will, by reading it, be encouraged and emboldened to continue the public debate on these issues.

I do not think it is sufficient simply to identify moral problems in business, to determine what actions are right and wrong, and to demand that people be moral heroes. If practices are immoral, and if people are faced with the obligation of sacrificing their jobs and their security to fulfill their moral obligations, then those practices should be changed. I therefore attempt not only to discuss what is morally required of a person in a business (a worker, a manager, or a member of the board of directors), but also what structures are conducive to a person's accepting moral responsibility and fulfilling his or her moral obligations. The question of how to reorganize firms so as to preclude the necessity for whistle blowing is as pressing (if not more pressing) a question as asking when a person is morally obliged to blow the whistle.

Business is a social activity, and, like all social activity, cannot function unless certain moral prerequisites are fulfilled. An analysis of these prerequisites, and of the social and business structures conducive to morality, are, I believe, an important and frequently neglected aspect of business ethics. At each stage of investigation, therefore, I raise and attempt to answer not only the question of whether a particular practice is moral or immoral, but also the question of what alternative can and should be pursued with respect to immoral practices. The morality of individuals should not be separated from the morality of business procedures and institutions; in this book, I handle them together, to the extent possible.

The daily newspapers carry ample current materials for analysis, for those who want case studies and specific, timely examples of moral issues in business. I have incorporated into my discussion some actual and some fictitious case studies, to illustrate specific principles, to exemplify ways of analyzing moral problems, and to contrast varying approaches to an issue. Although the book is written so that it develops a total view through successive chapters, each chapter can be studied apart from the others. Those who wish to omit the analysis of some issues and to concentrate instead on a selected few can do so without a loss of intelligibility. Those wishing to read further on a topic will find suggestions for doing so listed at the end of each chapter. The reading lists include the books or articles mentioned in the chapter, and represent both sides of controversial questions.

· · ·

During the four years since the first edition of this book appeared, business courses have proliferated and the field of business ethics has expanded. It is now a firmly established field. Two book-length bibliographies document the many books and articles in the field, two journals of business ethics have appeared, and a professional Society for Business Ethics is thriving.

Business ethics as a field is defined by the set of interrelated problems with which it deals. The field is developed by research. The second edition of this book attempts to take into account the significant research that has appeared during the past four years, as well as the pertinent developments in American business and society. Three new chapters have been added, one on workers' rights, one on whistle blowing, and one on moral issues related to the use of computers in business. Most of the original chapters have been significantly revised or enlarged. But the book's aim, approach, and theme remain the same: American business can be made more moral. This book is an attempt to help its readers think about how this might be accomplished.

R. T. De George

Contents

CHAPTER THREE
Utility and Utilitarianism

44

CHAPTER FOUR
Formalism and Justice

64

CHAPTER FIVE
Moral Responsibility and Corporations

82

MORAL ISSUES IN BUSINESS

CHAPTER SIX
Justice and Economic Systems

103

CONTENTS

CHAPTER SEVEN
American Capitalism: Moral or Immoral?

126

CHAPTER EIGHT
Corporate Responsibility and the Social Audit

151

CHAPTER NINE
Workers' Rights: Employment, Wages, and Unions

177

CHAPTER TEN
Workers' Rights and Duties Within a Firm

202

xi

CHAPTER ELEVEN
Whistle Blowing

221

CHAPTER TWELVE
Discrimination, Affirmative Action, and Reverse Discrimination

239

CHAPTER THIRTEEN
Marketing, Truth, and Advertising

265

CHAPTER FOURTEEN
Trade Secrets, Insider Information, and Corporate Disclosure

291

CHAPTER FIFTEEN
Computers, Ethics, and Business

313

CHAPTER SIXTEEN
Professions, Business, and Ethical Codes of Conduct

335

CHAPTER SEVENTEEN
*The International Free-Enterprise System,
Multinationals, and Morality*

354

CHAPTER EIGHTEEN
Famine, Oil, and International Obligations

381

CONCLUSION

Introduction

Ethics and Business

"Business and ethics don't mix," is the old adage. "Nor do heaven and businessmen," is the wry reply. This adage, a piece of American folk knowledge, forms part of a popular view, which I shall call the *Myth of Amoral Business*. The myth, as is true of most myths, has several variations. Many people believe the myth; at least, they more or less believe it. It expresses a partial truth and accounts for a surface phenomenon. At the same time, it conceals a good deal of reality. The myth is to some extent descriptive. It describes how American business and American business men and women perceive themselves and are perceived by others; that they are concerned with profit, with producing goods and providing services, and with buying and selling. According to the myth, people in business are not explicitly concerned with morality—they are *amoral*. This does not mean they are *immoral*. Rather, they feel that moral considerations are inappropriate in business. They are opposed to moralizing. They dislike being preached to by moralists, and they are very reluctant to throw stones at the glass houses of even their fiercest competitors. Most people in business do not act immorally or maliciously. They think of themselves, in their private lives as well as in their business lives, as moral people. They simply feel that business is not expected to be concerned with morality. Even when a firm acts according to a moral principle, it rarely boasts about it in moral terms, or presents its action as such.

One of the interesting variations on the theme is that because businesses are not concerned with morality, they often act immorally. Think of the many unsavory scandals that make newspaper headlines—accounts of bribery, misrepresentation, white-collar crime, kickbacks, unsafe products, and insider manipulation of markets. And then there is business's lack of concern for the environment, for company towns where the local plant has closed, and a gen-

3

eral lack of concern for the common good. According to the myth, businesses act immorally not because of a desire to do evil, but simply because they want to make a profit and therefore disregard some of the consequences of their actions.

The Myth of Amoral Business not only represents the way many people in and out of the business world perceive business, but also the way many would like to continue to perceive business. It is much easier to deal with dollars and cents than to deal with value judgments. It is more comfortable to discuss a problem in terms of a bottom line, which represents profit or loss. It is easier for those in business, and also easier for those not in business, to judge a firm by its financial status. The bottom line is what concerns investors, what directly affects the workers in a company. This is what consumers expect.

As with most popularly held myths, the Myth of Amoral Business captures a popular truth. Yet it also conceals a good deal. This book, and the general topic of business ethics, concerns what has for a long time been concealed or ignored. Scandals, environmental problems, and energy problems have all helped the reality to surface now and then, but no *Myth of Moral Business* has resulted. What, then, is the hidden reality? What is the true relation of ethics and business, which is now slowly emerging? What are the indications of its emergence?

Let us address the last question first. The breakdown of the Myth of Amoral Business has been signaled in three fairly obvious ways: by the reporting of scandals and the concomitant public reaction to these reports; by the formation of popular groups, such as the environmentalists and the consumerists; and by the concern of business, as expressed in conferences, magazine and newspaper articles, the burgeoning of codes of ethical conduct, and so on. How does the reporting of scandals in business, and the popular reaction to them, signal a breakdown of the myth? Consider what the myth implies, if it is taken seriously. If it is true that business is viewed as amoral, that it is not expected to behave according to moral rules, and that it is appropriate for it to do whatever is necessary in order to increase its profit, then there would be no surprise, shock, or uproar when a business acts immorally. The uncovering of bribes and kickbacks would not be news. Revelations about unsafe products and white-collar crime would be routine—expected and unexceptional. The fact that such events *do* make news, that they *do* cause public reaction, that they *do* adversely affect a company's image, and *do* cause scandal is an indication that the Myth of Amoral Business is not unambiguously held.

Many more people now expect companies to act morally, at least in certain instances and within certain limits. It is no longer true that anything goes. (Even though the myth does not say that anything goes, some of its variations imply this.) Contemporary reactions provide evidence that, if the myth does describe the way things are, many people think that things should be otherwise, that is, that business should behave morally. At least two groups—the environmentalists and the consumerists—articulate their demands and try to force businesses to consider values other than those that are reducible to sales figures and ledger sheets. The issues raised by these groups are not stated in terms

4

of dollars and cents but in terms of other values, such as the beauty of the land, the preservation of certain species of animals and fish, and the right of people to adequate information about the goods they purchase. These demands have a new moral dimension, which has forced even those firms reacting negatively to the environmentalists and consumerists to consider the claims that these groups and others are making. If the Myth of Amoral Business were the whole story, the environmental and the consumer movements would make no sense, and business would not respond to them. Because the movements do make sense, and because business does respond, the myth is only part of the story.

The reaction of business to the aforementioned movements has been significant. Sometimes the reaction has been one of annoyance and puzzlement. Some businesses have tried to ignore the claims made in the name of the environment, consumers, and morality, and have acted in conformity to the Myth of Amoral Business. Others have seen that ignoring demands will not make them go away. Another reaction has been to seek counsel and to share their perplexity about how to respond to the increasing public demands. A result has been the convening of a surprising number of conferences, meetings, and symposia, sponsored by business or attended by those in business. The theme is most frequently related to values, to questions of business ethics, and to ways of handling what has become known as the *social audit*. Business is not structured to handle questions of values and morality, and its managers have usually not been trained in business schools to do so. Experience has supplied even less training along these lines. Hence, many businesses have faced a new dilemma. They are now beginning to feel they should respond to demands involving social values, and should take moral issues into account in their deliberations, but do not know how to do so. Nonetheless, the conferences, meetings, and new ethical codes in business prove that the Myth of Amoral Business is slowly waning.

The American Business Value System

The Myth of Amoral Business in part reflects, and in part ignores, the fact that American business is embedded in American society and shares its values. The myth focuses on the rugged individualism emphasized in a free-enterprise approach to business, on the negative aspects of competition, and on the pragmatism characteristic of the American approach to abstractions. It recognizes that freedom is necessary to the system. But the line between freedom and license in business is not always sharp.

The American business system is often described as a free-enterprise system. In contrast with socialism, American business claims to be free from government ownership and domination. It is, of course, not totally free of government intervention, nor of government support and protection. But freedom *is* a value that forms an important basis for business activity in the United States.

5

On the positive side, freedom in American business extends not only to the owners and managers of business but also to the employees and consumers. Those who defend the free-enterprise system against critics typically emphasize the value of individual freedom as opposed to planned, directed, state-owned, and state-dominated economies. The argument in defense of free enterprise trades heavily on the maturity, intelligence, and responsibility of those operating within the economic system. The value of free enterprise, though taken to be self-evident by Americans, is not so perceived by all people. Our system assumes that each person wishes his own good, and knows better than anyone else what he wants. The system allows each adult person to make his own decisions, to follow his own way of life, and, within the limits set by the rights of others, to choose the other values he or she wishes to pursue. This freedom tends to mask the common values held by most people, and to promote a wide tolerance of different life-styles and ways of acting. The Myth of Amoral Business reflects this tolerance.

The system presupposes the value to each of us of entering into transactions of our own choosing, of pursuing our own good, and of satisfying our individual needs and desires. Because each of us differs to some extent in what we want and need, each of us is free to use our own resources to obtain what we want. Some spend comparatively more on housing than others; some spend more on food; some spend more on clothing or transportation or entertainment.

The possibility of acting freely puts a premium on the social and geographic mobility of individuals, as well as on the mobility of money and resources. The freedom of the manager to hire and fire is matched by the freedom of the worker to choose his kind of work, and, within limits, his employer. Freedom, however, carries with it the risk of failure, and frequently tends to favor the business more than the individual employee or prospective job applicant.

Those who enter the marketplace carry on transactions with an eye toward advancing their own good. The system itself holds promise of producing goods in great abundance, of allowing people to satisfy their needs and wants, and of providing them with a higher standard of living than was previously imagined possible. If freedom is central to free enterprise, however, the value of profit, money, and goods cannot and should not be overlooked. The free-enterprise system places a premium on profit, because it is for profit that profit-making enterprises are established. Together with the desire for profit goes the desire for goods, and for the kind of life that money can buy. The desire for a good life, and the value placed on a good life are not unique to the free-enterprise system. But they are central values in it. These values do not necessarily lead to the overemphasis on possessions and on materialistic values that many of its critics claim, but a tendency in that direction certainly exists. The Myth of Amoral Business frequently focuses on the desire for profit rather than on the freedom to choose one's good. Both are part of the system.

Even to characterize the system as one of free enterprise, however, is to accept a somewhat idealized view of it, because the freedom has always existed within the limits imposed by a political framework. In that context, freedom in business is limited by two traditional values that have been held as ideals— the values of fairness and of equal opportunity. The notion of fairness is a typically American value; business transactions are expected to be fair. Both sides enter a transaction in order to achieve their own good, and both achieve this if the transaction is fair. Fairness, in turn, assumes the additional values of honesty and of truthfulness on the part of those who take part in the trans-action. Fairness is, of course, not always realized, but it does exist as an ideal. Similarly, there is a tacit assumption that talented people who are willing to work can advance and succeed. The ideal of equal opportunity thus forms a backdrop against which reality is measured.

Competition at all levels makes the free-enterprise system work. It operates on all levels. The laws of supply and demand regulate the cost of goods and the allocation of resources. Consumers vote with their dollars for the products of their choice, selecting from competing brands. There is competition among makers of goods, who compete for workers; there is competition among workers for better jobs, more pay, and more rapid advancement. The Myth of Amoral Business assumes that the competition is not only fierce but cut-throat. In fact, competition involves both benefits and costs, and though sometimes ruthless, it is not always ruthless.

Although everyone expects to benefit from the system, inequality is built into it. Some will succeed in a competition, and others will fare less well. Wealth is an attractive impetus for people to develop their creative, productive powers, but differential reward is part of the system. There is also a premium on risk-taking: those who take the greatest risks are offered the prospect of the greatest reward, but there is also the possibility of failure. The system does not prevent failure; it requires it. Competition weeds out the weak and the less productive, the overly cautious and the less skillful.

Two other values of the American business system are pragmatism and efficiency. Pragmatism evaluates reality in terms of results. The pragmatic approach of Americans emphasizes the practical over the theoretical; it dis-trusts abstractions, and looks continually for results. Pragmatism coheres well with efficiency—a value identified with American business and a value that it embraces. Fair competition rewards the most efficient—those able to pro-duce, at a lower price, commodities of a quality equal to or better than a competitor's. As machines multiply the productive output of human labor, and as microchips replace machines, more better-quality goods can be pro-duced more quickly, and frequently at a lower cost. Efficiency enables busi-nesses to increase their productive capacities, and to receive the greatest return for the energy expended. The efficiency of the machine, advances made pos-sible by technology, and the genius of American organization and ingenuity enabled Americans to produce the wealth, and to achieve the standard of living that we collectively enjoy.

Those who believe the Myth of Amoral Business tend to ignore some of the vices of the American business system. Inadequately restrained freedom in the marketplace tempts some to seek their own goals at the expense of others. Greed often blinds people to the requirements of fairness. Many people succumb to the temptation to win by whatever means available, fair or not. We know the history of the robber barons, and of the many with power and wealth who exploited those without either. We also know that many transactions into which people enter are not fair and free, but are forced and manipulated. Competition, moreover, leaves behind many who cannot compete, as well as those who fail. How are they to be cared for?

Some commentators characterize the American system as materialistic and morally soft. They claim America's wealth has undermined the industry and thrift exemplified in the Protestant work ethic, and replaced it with profligacy and the desire for the easy life. The reverse side of efficiency and rapid development is extravagance, and the waste created by built-in obsolescence. Products are not made to last forever because to do so would undercut productivity. Short-term considerations—reflected in quarterly reports by corporations—dominate long-term ones. The optimism characteristic of American society is reflected in the belief that things will always get better, that the abundance we enjoy will continue into the foreseeable future, and that the long run will take care of itself if we take care of the short run. But we buy such optimism at a price, and the "future," when it comes, is not always as good as we had hoped.

The American business value system is, consequently, a mixture of good and bad. Should freedom be emphasized more than security, or competition more than equality? How can we limit the negative aspects of some values and check the undesired consequences of pursuing others? Is the value system changing? Are some of the values, for instance, those based on abundance, obsolete? Many people ask these questions, as our society struggles with the realities of limited resources, a growing demand for economic as well as political equality, increasing pressures from foreign competition, the aging of many of our industries, and the pollution of the air, water, and land. Which values are morally justifiable? And is the system of free enterprise per se morally justifiable? If so, under what conditions? Business ethics studies these issues.

The Relation of Business and Morality

Business and morality are related in a number of significant ways that are ignored by the Myth of Amoral Business. Some of these relationships are obvious. They are so obvious that we take them for granted, and hence we tend to ignore them. Others are subtle. They are so subtle that, again, we tend to ignore them. But whether obvious or subtle, they are part of our daily lives and experience. We can illuminate them, focus on them, bring them into the open, and so articulate the relationship of business and morality. We shall consider five aspects, under the following headings: The Moral Background of Business; The Business of Business; Business and the Law; The Changing Mandate for Business; and The Foundations of Property.

The Moral Background of Business

Business is an important part of contemporary society. It involves all of us, in one way or another. We all purchase goods that we need for survival and comfort. We all rely on the availability of electricity and gasoline. We buy food, clothing, and services. People supply these for us. Manufacturers make goods that we need and want. Other people transport them to stores, where others sell them to consumers. Business is not something separate from society, or imposed upon it—it is an integral part of society and its activities. Morality consists of rules of human behavior, and specifies that certain actions are wrong or immoral and that others are right or moral. We can take the moral point of view to evaluate human action. Some actions, such as murder, are considered immoral. Others, such as helping one's neighbor, are generally considered moral. Still others, such as tying one's shoe, are, at least in the abstract, morally indifferent. These assume moral character only in particular circumstances, for instance, when used purposefully to annoy someone, or to cause someone harm. Any action can be viewed from a moral perspective. Hence, it is difficult to imagine what people mean when they say that morality and business do not mix, or are antithetical.

Because business activity is human activity, it can be evaluated from the moral point of view, just as any other human activity can be so evaluated. The relationship of business to morality goes even deeper than this. Business, like most other social activities, presupposes a background of morality, and would be impossible without it. For instance, employers expect their employees not to steal from the firm; parties to a contract each expect the other to honor an agreement; those who buy a product expect it to be as advertised, when they take it home and unpack it. People who work with others expect their co-workers to generally tell the truth, to respect rather than to assault them, and to do the job for which they are paid. In most cases, these expectations are met. If everyone involved in business—buyers, sellers, producers, management, workers, and consumers—acted immorally or even amorally (i.e., without concern for whether their actions were moral or immoral), business would soon grind to a halt. Morality is the oil as well as the glue of society, and, therefore, of business. It is only against the background of morality that immorality can be not only possible but profitable. Lying would not succeed if most people were not truthful and did not tend to believe others. A breach of trust requires a background of trust. Business does not operate according to the dictum "let the buyer beware." Business generally values its reputation. We therefore really do not live in a "dog-eat-dog" business world. Such a world would be intolerable.

People, of course, do act immorally in business, just as they do in other spheres of life. There are numerous cases of fraud, misrepresentation, and inflated business accounts, but there is no proof that people are more immoral in their business lives than in their private lives. The structures of business are no more prone to immorality than the structures of government, family, education, or religion. Nor are large, impersonal businesses

9

either more or less moral or immoral than small, individually owned businesses.

Business is a part of society, and, therefore, the actions of people in business are subject to moral rules. The point is probably so obvious as to be generally forgotten. Most adults do not need to be told that lying and stealing are wrong, or that murder is wrong. These are wrong whether done in or out of business. It is because the ordinary person does not need to be told that these things are wrong that they form part of the background of business. In other words, this is an assumption made by those in business. The propositon that business and morality do not mix, consequently, cannot be convincingly maintained. The point of business ethics is not necessarily to change anyone's moral convictions but, to build upon them.

The Business of Business

A famous cliché maintains that "the business of business is business." The business of business is not government, charity, or social welfare. Nor, the cliché implies, is it morality. But what does "the business of business is business" mean? Who is to decide what this cliché means? To get some perspective on the question, we must look beyond our own society. What we find is this: what is considered to be business and its business varies from society to society. In Japan, the business of large corporations is not only to produce goods but to care for the firm's employees—in effect, to guarantee them lifetime employment. Paternalism is thus part of the business of business in Japan, in a way that it is not in the United States. In the Soviet Union, private ownership of the means of production, that is, of companies and factories, is prohibited by law. Nevertheless, there are in Russia factories, offices, stores, and goods. But business there is a state affair, not a private affair. What constitutes business varies from society to society. The question of what business per se is, and what its proper concern is, is a social question, one that must be answered in a social context.

In the United States, the mandate to business was initially rather simple. People wanted goods to be as plentiful, as good, and as cheap as possible. Those interested in producing them were given relatively free rein under competitive conditions. Some businesses succeeded and grew; others failed. As problems developed, regulations were introduced by law. These laws regulated working conditions, protected children, prevented monopolistic practices, and preserved the environment. The regulations frequently represented the moral concerns of the American people. The business of business was, and is, decided by the people of each society. What practices are or are not to be tolerated are not eternal givens; nor are the determinations of what is or is not acceptable to a society. To some extent, the mandate to business also sets the limits to its proper activity, and to what is not socially tolerable. The limits are not set by business or by those who run business, even though some of them act as if they were. The limits imposed on business and the demands made upon business by society are frequently moral ones. A business may ignore the moral demands of an individual, but it can hardly ignore the moral demands of a whole society, because it is both part of that society and dependent on it, even though it serves society.

There is increasing evidence that the mandate to business in the United States is changing, and that businesses are increasingly expected to weigh more than financial factors in their actions. What the business of business is, in fact, is itself a moral decision, and one that is socially made and implemented. Insofar as business is a part of society, it rightfully has a voice in arriving at the social determination of what its business is. To do so effectively, it must be able to enter into the moral social discourse which is debating its future. Business ethics helps to clarify some of the issues and provides the techniques for effectively entering into the debate.

Business and the Law

Business is a social enterprise. Its mandate and limits are set by society. The limits are often moral, but they are also frequently written into law. The history of the development of business in America is an interesting one, as is the history of the relationship of business and morality, and business and law. In the early days of our history most American businesses were small. The Protestant work ethic was a strong influence; it provided both motivation and justification for the businessman's activity. According to this ethic, the good and the hardworking were blessed with riches; the lazy and incompetent suffered. Rugged individualism was both an ingredient in the work ethic and a secular moral value.

In contemporary society the work ethic has changed, to some extent. Society, through welfare, attempts to take care of some of the poor and needy. Small businesses have for the most part given way to giant corporations. Individuals who own their own businesses are relatively rare. The large firms are owned by stockholders, and are run by managers who are paid wages, but very handsome wages. The feeling of private ownership is no longer appropriate for those who run a business, and the old virtues are also no longer appropriate. Hired managers run the companies not for themselves but for the stockholders. They manage the company not necessarily as they choose, but to some extent as they must. They are subject to a board of directors. They cannot impose their own morality on company policy and therefore run it in a somewhat neutral way.

The dissociation of management from ownership took place at the same time that laws regulating business proliferated. As a result, it was natural, for those who were managing firms, to feel that what society and stockholders of their company required of them was compliance with the law. If they complied with the law, they fulfilled their social obligations. As a result, they began to feel that morality was personal, that it varied from person to person and from group to group, and that all that could be expected of the managers of business, as well as of business itself, was fulfillment of the law. The law prohibits theft, enforces contracts, sets limits to advertising, and reinforces many moral norms.

Equating what is required of business with what is required by law became a convenient and easy norm to adopt. It made clear one's duty and limited what one had to consider. It provided a convenient rationale for ignoring moral demands and for living by the Myth of Amoral Business.

This view fails to consider carefully the relation of law and morality. Many laws prohibit immoral practices; immoral practices, for the most part, are socially harmful practices. Some, such as murder, stealing, and perjury, are so harmful that to moral sanction is added the sanction of law. Hence, one of the ways to argue that a law should be passed is to argue that the conduct the law governs is immoral and seriously harmful to society. For instance, discrimination was immoral before it was made illegal.

But not all laws are morally defensible. Laws requiring racial segregation and discrimination are a case in point. To abide by the law in practicing discrimination was, in fact, to act immorally. It is dangerous to equate law with what one is morally, as well as legally, required to do, because this denies the possibility of arguing, from a moral point of view, that either a law should be passed or a bad law repealed. Finally, not everything that is immoral can be made illegal. If, for instance, it is immoral to lie, this does not mean that all lying should be made illegal. Such a law would be unenforceable. Nor would it be worth the time and effort to try to enforce it to any considerable extent. Yet it does not follow—even for those in business who claim that they are only bound by law—that it would be right for business people to lie whenever they feel like it, either to those within the company or to those with whom they do business. In most cases it would be considered bad business, as well as immoral.

The retreat to law as the sole norm by which to guide business is in part a reflection of the fact that most managers do not know how to handle many moral issues in business. Having equated morality with personal opinion, they understandably find it difficult to defend their moral judgments in objective terms. A correct perception of the status of morality and a knowledge of the techniques of moral argumentation are necessary to handle moral values and moral issues in business. Part of the task of business ethics is to supply the appropriate perception and knowledge.

The Changing Mandate for Business

The social mandate to business is not only given in law. The general mandate to provide a plentiful supply of high-quality goods at a cheap price is in fact a social mandate. It arises from the need of the general public, and is expressed in many ways. The mandate to business today is more complex. Demands are made on it from many quarters. Businesses have responded to some and not to others. Frequently, they do not know how to evaluate conflicting demands (we have already noted the retreat to law on the part of some firms). Some businesses choose to ignore the background of morality with which, and in which, they operate.

The retreat to law, together with a disclaimer concerning moral demands, is frequently not a reflection of bad will, or of a desire to be immoral. Rather, it often reflects the lack of internal structures within a firm to consider and weigh moral as well as financial considerations, as well as a lack of confidence in the ability of those within a firm to engage in public, moral reasoning. Even those firms that are exemplary, from a moral point of view, are reluctant to defend their positions in moral terms.

This is in part a reflection of the Myth of Amoral Business. The economic system is thought by some to be value-free: each person within it seeks his or her own good; and buyers contract with sellers to the mutual benefit of both. The marketplace thus becomes the neutral ground of common activity, and general good is achieved without its being intended by anyone. This view, which is a simplified form of how the free-enterprise system is sometimes presented, does not correspond to the way any economic system works. But it is certainly clear that it corresponds even less to the economic system of America today than it did in nineteenth-century America.

The nation and the world have come to see that there are limits to available natural resources, that industrialization has been purchased at a considerable price, and that the ecosystem is so delicately balanced that each change we produce in it triggers other, sometimes deleterious changes, which we do not necessarily intend. As a result, we now collectively know that many of our actions involve value judgments. For instance, do we want more electricity? If so, are we willing to risk the dangers involved in nuclear reactors? When oil is scarce, we know that we must sometimes choose between having gas for our cars or fuel for heating our homes. If we want a strong military force, we cannot have it unless we raise, through taxes, the money required to support it.

Individuals in business can no longer act as they choose. Government regulations, decisions, and guidelines temper the moves of the marketplace. In addition, corporations are asked, if not forced, to consider the impact of their decisions and actions on the environment, the public, and on the common good. Air and water are no longer resources to be freely used. The safety of workers and consumers of products is no longer something any manufacturer can ignore. Most businesses, however, are not structured to handle moral demands, or to weigh values in nonmonetary terms. How can they do this? They can do so by considering what structures promote moral responsibility and facilitate the weighing of moral and other values, topics that are appropriately raised in business ethics.

The Foundations of Property

Private property is a cornerstone of capitalism and of the free-enterprise system, and socially owned property is the cornerstone of socialist economic systems. But what is property? What makes property private? By what right do I call property mine? These are not economic questions. Legally, property is defined in terms of rights. If something is mine, I have the right to use it, to destroy it, to sell it, or to protect it from your taking it or using it. But rights may be moral as well as legal. The question of property can therefore be put in terms of morality as well as legality. In order to produce, human beings need raw materials with which to work. Who then owns nature? John Locke, the British philosopher whose theory influenced the American Founding Fathers, argued that every man is allowed to use what nature provides. He may make it his own if he can use it and if other people have as much, and as good, remaining for their use as well. The initial partition of the earth is a fact. Some people own the diamond mines, others the oil fields; others own the iron and coal mines. By what right do certain people claim the exclusive right to the earth's resources simply because they were fortunate enough to have been born in the country where the resources existed? Do some people have a right to resources and the riches they bring whereas others, who happen to inhabit barren land without resources, are doomed to poverty and starvation? Can one argue plausibly that the resources of the world are for the benefit of all people and not just for the lucky few? The less developed countries of the world are asking Americans these questions. Eight percent of mankind uses 40 percent of the earth's natural resources; the other 92 percent ask what right we have to do so.

Similar questions are raised within our own country. Can we justify the wealth and opulence of a few together with the poverty of large numbers of others? Those who claim not demand the transfer of wealth from those who have wealth to those who do not. The transfer of some wealth in the United States is achieved primarily through taxation. Taxation, therefore, is a means of transferring property—namely money—from one person or group to another. By what right is this done? The answer requires not only legal reasoning but also moral reasoning and argument.

Business Ethics

Thus far we have referred to business ethics but we have not seen, in any detail, what it is. Because business ethics is part of an ongoing philosophical enterprise, we can start with a general notion of philosophy, proceed to that portion of philosophy which is called ethics, and then finally proceed to business ethics. These three notions are closely related. Philosophy in its broadest meaning is a systematic attempt to make sense out of our individual and collective human experience. Unlike theologians, philosophers use only reason to interpret experience, and do not rely on divine revelation. Traditionally, philosophers have engaged in two types of rational activity. One is analytic. The philosopher analyzes or investigates in detail the meaning of terms, the validity of arguments, and the nature and status of presuppositions by discerning their components. The philosopher looks at basic questions, such as the nature of reality, the meaning and reliability of knowledge, and the foundation of values. He differs from the scientist in a number of ways. The questions he asks are sometimes broader than those of the scientist, and the techniques he uses are not laboratory techniques. But if he examines the theoretical

14

foundations of physics or the foundations of induction he does something that some scientists also do. The philosophy of science is therefore a meeting point for philosophers and scientists.

Synthesis is the second type of rational activity in which philosophers engage. They construct a unified view that brings together, integrates, and makes as intelligible as possible all the parts of our experience. They attempt to relate the findings of the sciences, the arts, and human experience in general into a comprehensible whole. The endeavor is an ongoing one, which has been perceived more favorably in some periods of history than in others.

Ethics is a branch of philosophy. Those who study ethics engage in analysis and synthesis, just as those in other branches of philosophy do. The two activities, moreover, are related, and it is not always easy to separate them. Ethics, as a part of philosophy, is related to the other parts. Whether we can have knowledge of the subject matter of ethics and how sure that knowledge can be are questions related in general to the question of what human knowledge consists of, the limits of such knowledge, the laws of valid reasoning, and also the status of values and norms. Yet, though related to philosophy, ethics is usually considered to have at least a relative independence because it can be pursued in its own right.

The object that ethics studies is morality. *Morality* is a term used to cover those practices and activities that are considered importantly right and wrong; the rules that govern those activities; and the values that are imbedded, fostered, or pursued by those activities and practices. The morality of a society is related to its mores or the customs accepted by a society or group as being the right and wrong ways to act, as well as to the laws of a society that add legal prohibitions and sanctions to many activities considered to be immoral.

Ethics in general can be defined as a systematic attempt, through the use of reason, to make sense of our individual and social moral experience, in such a way as to determine the rules that ought to govern human conduct and the values worth pursuing in life. The attempt is systematic and therefore goes beyond what each reflective person tends to do in his daily life in making sense of his moral experience, organizing it, and attempting to make it coherent and unified. Because it uses reason and not revelation, ethics can be distinguished from a religious or theological approach to morality. Insofar as it attempts to ascertain what rules and values *ought* to be followed and pursued, ethics can be distinguished from anthropology, psychology, and sociology. Those disciplines describe how people behave, but they usually do not prescribe how they should or ought to behave. Ethics concerns itself with human conduct, taken here to mean human activity that is done knowingly and, to a large extent, willingly. It does not concern itself with automatic responses, or with, for example, actions done in one's sleep or under hypnosis.

Despite the accuracy and usefulness of this definition of ethics as the study of morality, the term *ethics* is used in a variety of ways by different people. Sometimes *ethics* is used synonymously with *morality*; for example, an action that is morally right is called an ethical one. We referred earlier to the work ethic, because that is the common phrase, though we could have called it the work morality. Codes of moral conduct adopted by professions are frequently called ethical codes. Although philosophically speaking business ethics is a branch of general ethics, some people interpret the phrase business ethics to mean business morality. They interpret this either descriptively, that is, as the morality followed in business, or normatively, as the morality which ought to be followed. We cannot legislate the use of terms, therefore, it is wise to be conscious of divergent uses.

Those engaged in ethics as a branch of philosophy do analysis and synthesis. There are three related phases of ethical study, which are commonly known as descriptive ethics, normative ethics, and metaethics. The three constitute what is sometimes called general, as opposed to special, ethics.

Descriptive ethics is closely related to anthropology, sociology, and psychology, and leans heavily on them. It consists in studying and describing the morality of a people, culture, or society. It also compares and contrasts different moral systems, codes, practices, beliefs, principles, and values. Descriptive ethics provides basic material that normative ethics must account for, and it provides a touchstone of the considered morality of a people or society with which the normative theory must more or less coalesce.

Normative ethics systematically attempts to supply and to justify a coherent moral system. Typically it seeks to uncover, develop, and justify the basic moral principle or principles, or the basic moral values, of a moral system. The system itself consists of both the basic moral principle(s) and values and the particular moral rules that govern people's behavior, in the sense of prescribing those actions that are right or moral and proscribing those that are wrong or immoral. These rules and values constitute the moral norms of the society. The task of normative ethics is threefold. First, it attempts to form into a related whole the various norms, rules, and values of a society's morality. It tries to render these as consistent and coherent as possible, with perhaps some hierarchical arrangement of norms. Secondly, it attempts to find the basic principle from which the particular norms can be derived. Thirdly, it attempts, in a variety of ways, to justify the basic principle of morality.

A society can hold various moral norms that may or may not be consistent. In forming a system the moral philosopher attempts to make the various norms consistent with one another. This system constitutes a theory of morality. If the basic principle is powerful enough, it should provide the means for deriving the set of consistent norms accepted by a society, as well as for making explicit norms that were previously held only implicitly. The basic principle should also provide a procedure by which conflicting norms can be adjudicated and particular cases decided. A moral theory interacts dynamically with the norms of a society in that both remain open to correction. A moral theory that resulted in injunctions to murder, steal, lie, or commit other actions a society considered immoral would be properly suspect. It is difficult to imagine why a society would accept or adopt such a theory. In general, a society is more certain of the bulk of its traditional norms of morality than it is of any theory of morality. Exceptions are possible, however. For instance, a society may undergo a conversion and adopt a religion along with that religion's moral code. But this is not the general rule.

Metaethics, the third portion of general ethics, is closely related to normative ethics. Metaethics is the study of normative ethics, and, to some extent, both normative and descriptive ethics involve some metaethical activity. It is sometimes called *analytical ethics* because it is concerned with analysis. Metaethics deals with the meaning of moral terms and with the logic of moral reasoning. It asks, for instance, what the terms *good* and *bad* mean in the moral sense; what *moral responsibility, moral obligation,* and other similar phrases mean. Meaning, of course, is closely related to linguistic usage. Some people think meaning is identical with such usage. To say what *good* means may be distinct from saying what things or actions are good. The former is generally considered a metaethical concern, the latter a normative ethical concern.

The analysis of moral reasoning involves clarifying and evaluating presuppositions and investigating the validity of moral arguments. A famous, and still not completely resolved, metaethical dispute concerns the question of whether a moral ought or duty can be derived logically from a statement of what is, exclusive of normative premises. General ethical theory provides a careful and systematic approach to morality, one which finds parallels in ordinary life and discourse. It develops and analyzes the kinds of moral arguments that are used in ordinary language and in everyday life, in newspapers and magazines, and in books and articles on moral problems. Hence, it is a practical discipline with practical import. Like science, ethics constitutes a continuing social endeavor. It is not a completed discipline, but a developing one in which there are a number of disputed issues. The presence of these disputes, however, does not indicate that there is no agreement, nor does it indicate that ethics has produced no usable results. Some results are negative: certain theories that were initially plausible have been shown to be mistaken, and some popular approaches to morality have proved untenable. The last word has yet to be written, but this is to be expected of an ongoing enterprise. Mastery of ethical theory, however, provides the necessary tools to engage intelligently in personal and social analysis of moral issues.

Special ethics first applies general ethics (which, as we have said, includes descriptive, normative, and metaethics) to solving particular problems, and second, to investigating the morality of specialized areas of human endeavor. The first of these is sometimes called casuistry. *Casuistry* is the art of solving difficult moral problems, cases, or dilemmas through the careful application of moral principles. Casuistry uses the principles and norms that have been developed and justified in general ethics. It is an important art or skill, but one which has sometimes been held in low repute. It can easily degenerate into the technique of seeing how close one can come to the line that separates a moral from an immoral action. Moral people, its critics maintain, are more interested in pursuing a moral course of action than in seeing how they can minimally fulfill what is morally demanded. The attempt to determine the latter has frequently led to all-too-subtle rationalizations of questionable actions.

The second area of special ethics involves the application of general ethics to specialized fields. This yields business ethics, medical ethics, engineering ethics, professional ethics, social ethics, and so on. Business ethics obviously deals with business. We shall take business to include any and all economic transactions between individuals, between individuals and profit-making organizations, and between profit-making organizations and other such organizations. It will include the various activities carried on in producing, selling, and buying goods and services for profit. This is broad enough to include the business activities of people in the professions and therefore includes part of what is considered professional ethics. The delimitation of these domains, however, is not at all sharp and great precision in delimiting them is not necessary.

Business ethics typically involves four kinds of activities. The first is the applying of general ethical principles to particular cases or practices in business. Deciding whether the actions involved are immoral or morally justifiable is important. But the analysis of cases does not end there. Solving cases frequently involves the development, as well as the application, of special, rather than general, moral principles, which can nonetheless be made universal. Cases sometimes suggest moral issues that need attention, clarification, and discussion. Cases also challenge us to consider imaginatively how we can prevent similar cases from arising in the future, and to develop suggestions that business, if it wishes to be moral, might implement, or that government, if necessary, might adopt. Some questions are, what changes in organization, managerial techniques, social structures, programs, or approaches are required? And would moral imagination, care in assessing future development, or changes in attitude help preclude moral dilemmas?

Business ethics, however, involves more than just applying moral principles to business. The second kind of activity is metaethical. We shall investigate, for instance, whether moral terms that are generally used to describe individuals and the actions they perform can also be applied to organizations, corporations, businesses, and other collective entities. For instance, are corporations artifacts to be controlled, or moral or quasi-moral entities with rights, or do they have some other status? Do they have consciences in the same way individuals do? Does moral language appropriately apply to them, and if so, does it apply in the same way as it does to individuals? The answers to these questions are not supplied by general ethical theory, which traditionally has been concerned with the actions of human individuals. The meaning of responsibility must be changed, if it is to be appropriately applied to corporations as well as to human persons. The analysis of this type of problem in business ethics cannot take place in abstraction from general ethical theory. There is a reciprocal relation between business ethics and general ethics. But those involved in business ethics often engage in metaethical inquiries that their work demands and which general theory does not provide.

A third activity of business ethics is the analysis of the presuppositions— both moral presuppositions and presuppositions from a moral point of view— of business. Because business operates within an economic system, part of the proper task of business ethics is to raise questions about the morality of economic systems in general and about the morality of the American economic system in particular. In evaluating structures of business we must also analyze the meaning and justification of such nonmoral terms as *property, exploitation, competition,* and the presuppositions and uses of cost-benefit analyses, accounting procedures, and so on.

Fourth, those in business ethics are sometimes led by embedded problems to go beyond the field of ethics into other areas of philosophy and into other domains of knowledge, such as economics or organization theory. But when they go beyond their own areas they usually do so to resolve some problem in business ethics, or to investigate in some other area what appeared, initially, to be a problem in business ethics. This activity becomes especially important in dealing with macro-moral issues, such as whether rich countries have any moral obligations to poor countries, or multinational corporations to host countries. Here our ordinary moral intuitions are less clear than they are in our personal dealings with individuals. Hence, there is a special need to carefully sort out the issues, to see which are moral and which are not, and to clarify the language and the level of moral discourse. Sometimes the task concerns reducing moral problems to managerial, organizational, or economic problems, or vice versa.

Business ethics can help people approach moral problems in business more systematically, and with better tools than they might otherwise use. It can help them to see issues they might normally ignore. It can also impel them to make changes they might otherwise not be moved to make. But business ethics will not, in and of itself, make anyone moral. Business ethics, just as ethics in general, presupposes that those who study it already are moral beings, that they know right from wrong, and that they wish to be even better, more thoughtful, more informed moral beings. Business ethics will not change business practices unless those engaged in the practices that need moral change wish to change them. Business ethics can produce arguments showing that a practice is immoral, but obviously, only those in a position to implement the changes will be able to bring them about. Business ethics is a practical discipline with practical import, but it is up to those who study it to put what they learn into practice.

The Case of the Collapsed Mine

The following fictitious case illustrates the sorts of questions that might arise in business ethics, and various ways to approach them. Consider the case of the collapsed mine shaft. In a town of West Virginia, miners were digging coal in a tunnel thousands of feet below the surface. Some gas build-up had been detected during the two preceding days. The director of safety had reported this to the mine manager. The build-up was sufficiently serious to have temporarily stopped operations until it was cleared. The owner of the mine decided that the build-up was only marginally dangerous, that he had coal orders to fill, that he could not afford to close down the mine, and that he would take the chance that the gas would dissipate before it exploded. He told the director of safety not to say anything about the danger. On May 2, the gas exploded. One section of the tunnel collapsed, killing three miners and trapping eight others in a pocket. The rest managed to escape.

The explosion was one of great force, and the extent of the tunnel's collapse was considerable. The cost of reaching the men in time to save their lives would amount to several million dollars. The problem facing the manager was whether the expenditure of such a large sum was worth it. What, after all, was a human life worth? Who should make the decision, and how should it be made? Did the manager owe more to the stockholders of the corporation or to the trapped workers? Should he use the slower, safer, cheaper way of reaching them and save a large sum of money, or the faster, more dangerous, more expensive way, and possibly save their lives?

He decided on the latter way, and asked for volunteers. Two dozen men volunteered. After three days, the operation proved to be more difficult than anyone had anticipated. There had been two more explosions and three of those involved in the rescue operation had already been killed. In the meantime, telephone contact had been made with the trapped men, who had been fortunate enough to find a telephone line that was still functioning. They were starving. Having previously read about a similar case, they decided that the only way for them to survive long enough for any of them to be saved was to draw lots, and kill and eat the one who drew the shortest straw. They felt it was their duty that at least some of them be found alive; otherwise, the three who had died rescuing them would have died in vain.

After twenty days the seven were finally rescued, alive; they had cannibalized their fellow miner. The director of safety, who had detected the gas before the explosion, informed the newspapers of his report. The manager was charged with criminal negligence, but before giving up his position, he fired the director of safety. The mine eventually resumed operation.

There are many issues in the foregoing account. The tools for resolving them are part of what we shall develop in later chapters.

The director of safety is, in some sense, the hero of the story. But did he, before the accident, fulfill his moral obligation when he obeyed the manager, instead of making known to the miners, to the manager's superior, or to the public the fact that the mine was unsafe? Did he have a moral obligation, after the explosion and rescue, to make known the fact that the manager knew the mine was unsafe? Should he have gone to the board of directors of the company with the story, or to someone else within the company rather than to the newspapers? All these questions are part of the phenomenon of worker responsibility. To whom is a worker responsible, and for what? Does his moral obligation end when he does what he is told? Going public with inside information such as the director of safety had is commonly known as "blowing the whistle" on the company. Frequently those who blow the whistle are fired, just as the director of safety was. The whole phenomenon of whistle blowing raises serious questions about the structure of companies in which employees find it necessary to take such drastic action, and possibly suffer the loss of their jobs. Was the manager justified in firing the director of safety?

The manager is, of course, the villain of the story. He sent the miners into a situation he knew was dangerous. But, he might argue, he did it for the good of the company. He had contracts to fulfill and an obligation to the owners of the company to show a profit. He had made a bad decision. But every manager has to take risks. It just turned out that he was unlucky. Does such a defense sound plausible? Does a manager have an obligation to his workers as well as to the owners of a company? Who should take precedence, and under what conditions does one group or the other become more important? Who is to decide this, and how?

The manager decided to try to save the trapped miners even though it would cost the company more than taking the slower route. Did he have the right to spend more of the company's money in this way? How does one evaluate human life in comparison with expenditure of money? It sounds moral to say that human life is beyond all monetary value, and in a sense it is. But there are limits to what society and people in it can place on the amount they will, can, and should spend to save lives. The way to decide, however, does not seem to be to equate the value of a person's life with the amount of income he would produce in his remaining years, if he were to live to a statistically average age, minus the resources he would use up in that period. Then how does one decide? How do and should people weigh human lives against monetary expenditure? When building roads, designing automobiles, or making many other products, there is a trade-off between the maximum safety one builds into the product and the cost of the product. Extremely safe cars cost more to build than relatively safe cars. We can express the difference in terms of the number of people likely to die driving the relatively safe ones as opposed to those driving the extremely safe ones. Should such decisions be made by manufacturers, consumers, or government, or by some other group?

The manager asked for volunteers for the rescue work. Three of these volunteers died. Was the manager responsible for their deaths in the same sense that he was responsible for the deaths of the three miners who died in the first mine explosion? Was the company responsible for the deaths in either case? Do companies have obligations to their employees and their employees' families, in circumstances such as these, or are the obligations only those of the managers? If the manager had warned the workers that the level of gas was dangerous, and if they had decided that they wanted their pay for that day and would work anyway, would the manager have been responsible for their deaths? Is it moral for people to take dangerous jobs simply to earn money? Is a system that impels people to take such jobs for money a moral system? To what extent is a company morally obliged to protect its workers and to prevent them from taking chances?

The manager was charged with criminal negligence under the law. Was the company responsible for anything? Should the company have been sued by the family of the dead workers? If the company were sued and paid damages to the families, the money would come from the company profits and hence from the profits of the shareholders. Is it fair that the shareholders be penalized for an incident with which they had nothing to do? How is responsibility shared and/or distributed in a company? And can companies be morally responsible for what is done in their name? Are only human beings moral agents, and is it a mistake to use moral language with respect to companies, corporations, and businesses?

The decision of the trapped miners to cast lots to determine who would be killed and eaten raises a number of moral issues. Because this case is not an ordinary one, our moral intuitions can provide no ready answer as to whether their decision was morally justifiable. The question of how to think about such an issue raises another question: how are moral problems to be resolved? And this emphasizes the need for a moral theory by which we can decide unusual cases. A number of principles seem to conflict: the obligation not to kill; the consideration that it is better that one person, rather than eight, die; the fact, noted by the miners, that three persons had already died trying to rescue them. The issue here is not necessarily relevant to business ethics; it has been posed because it involves a moral dilemma that requires some technique of moral argument to solve.

In the narration of the case we are not told what happened to either the manager or the director of safety. Frequently, the sequel to such cases is surprising. The managers often get off free, and are ultimately rewarded for their concern for the company's interest, but the whistle blower is often blackballed throughout the industry. The immorality of such an outcome seems obvious: justice does not always triumph. What can be done to see that justice triumphs more often? This is a question that involves restructuring the system.

Business ethics is sometimes seen as conservative, and is used as a defense of the status quo. Sometimes it is seen as an attack on the status quo, then it is viewed as radical. Ideally, it should be neither. It should strive for objectivity. Where there are immoral practices, structures, and actions occurring, business ethics should be able to show that these actions are immoral, and why. But it should also be able to supply the techniques with which the practices and structures that are moral can be defended as such. The aim of business ethics is neither defense of the status quo nor its radical change. Rather, it should serve to remedy those aspects or structures that need change, and should protect those that are moral. It is not a panacea. It can secure change only if those in power take the appropriate action. But unless some attention is paid to business ethics, the moral debate about practices and principles central to our society will be conducted poorly.

Further Reading

BAUMHART, RAYMOND, S. J. *Ethics in Business.* New York: Holt, Rinehart and Winston, 1968.
Business and Professional Ethics Journal, Vol. 1 (1981–).

CAVANAGH, GERALD F. *American Business Values in Transition.* Englewood Cliffs, N.J.: Prentice-Hall, Inc., 1976.

DAM, CEES VAN, and LUND STALLAERT, eds. *Trends in Business Ethics.* Boston: Martinus Nijhoff Social Sciences Division, 1978.

DE GEORGE, RICHARD T., and JOSEPH A. PICHLER, eds. *Ethics, Free Enterprise and Public Policy.* New York: Oxford University Press, Inc., 1978.

DWORKIN, GERALD, GORDON BERMANT, and PETER G. BROWN, eds. *Markets and Morals.* New York: John Wiley & Sons, Inc., 1977.

JONES, DONALD G. *A Bibliography of Business Ethics, 1971–1975; 1976–1980.* Charlottesville, Va: University Press of Virginia, 2 vols., 1977; 1982.

Journal of Business Ethics, Vol. 1 (1982–).

McGUIRE, JOSEPH W. *Business and Society.* New York: McGraw-Hill Book Co., 1963.

POWERS, CHARLES W., and DAVID VOGEL, *Ethics in the Education of Business Managers.* Hastings-on-Hudson, N.Y.: The Hastings Center, 1980.

PURCELL, THEODORE V., S. J. "Do Courses in Business Ethics Pay Off?" *California Management Review*, XIX (Summer, 1977), pp. 50–58.

Moral Reasoning
in Business

TWO

Conventional Morality and Ethical Relativism

$\mathbf{M}$any people in business, as well as in other areas of life, feel that morality is personal, that each person has his or her own moral views and that no one should force such views on others. According to this position, each person is entitled to his or her own moral opinion. All members of a society must abide by the law, but beyond that, each is to be guided only by his or her own individual conscience. Many people hold a similar position with respect to different countries and cultures. Each, they maintain, has its own views of what is moral and immoral. No one country or culture is better than the other. If someone is doing business in a different culture, then that person should adopt the local ways. If bribery is the common practice in a given society, then it is proper to engage in bribery in that country. It is arrogant, they say, to think that the morality of one's own country is better than that of another country, or to think the morality of one's own country is binding when doing business in another country.

This view is a popular form of moral and ethical relativism. It is a popular position, and deserves careful attention. Is morality simply a matter of individual choice? Is it culturally determined? Is the claim that there is a universal morality, applicable to all people and all times, defensible? This chapter will deal with these questions.

The Levels of Moral Development

An American psychologist, Lawrence Kohlberg, has done extensive work on moral development and has generalized the findings based on his studies.

The results of his investigations coincide with what many people experience in their own moral development, and therefore his position, at least in its broad general outlines, is widely accepted. Kohlberg identifies three major levels in the moral development of an individual. Not everyone advances to the third level; and no one operates only on the third level. Most people operate sometimes on one level and sometimes on another. Yet the levels of development are characteristics of the moral development of individuals and serve as handy classificatory devices.

Kohlberg not only identifies three levels but subdivides each of the levels into two stages. He calls Level I the *preconventional level*. As infants start to grow up, they go through a phase of development that is not yet moral. In the first stage of the first level of their moral development, they react to punishment. Toddlers do not have any sense of moral right and wrong, but they soon learn that if they write on the living room wall with a crayon they will get spanked or scolded. What keeps them from writing on the wall is their desire to avoid a spanking, a scolding, or whatever other punishment they have come to associate with the action. The second stage of this level reflects their desire to receive a reward. Here they seek the praise of their parents. They act so as to maximize their pleasure, though of course they do so unwittingly. This reaction to punishment and reward teaches children that certain behavior is undesirable and other behavior is permissible. Children thereby learn what to do and what not to do. But they do not yet understand that they are obeying rules or performing an action *because* it is right; they do not yet have a developed sense of what morality means.

All of us to some extent react to pleasure and pain and reward and punishment. Hence all of us sometimes act on the preconventional level.

Kohlberg calls the second level of moral development, or Level II, the *conventional level*. The morality practiced here is the morality of conventional role-conformity. He calls the first stage of Level II "Good Boy/Nice Girl Morality." In this stage, a person reacts to the expectations of parents or peers. We conform to the norms learned at home, in school, or in church. The motivation for action is more subtle than in Level I—we come to understand what moral norms and rules are. We learn how a good boy or a good girl is supposed to act. The norms we get from our family, school, and peers may not all coincide. In a homogeneous society they will probably coincide more than in a less homogeneous one; they will also tend to coincide more closely in a traditional society than in a dynamic one. But in all cases, the morality we accept is a morality that we learn from others. We learn what is expected of us in our role as a devoted child, as an adolescent, and as a student. Conventional role-conformity in its first stage is a reaction to peers, parents, or other similar persons or groups. In its second stage, it usually develops into conformity with the laws of one's society. Kohlberg calls it the "law and order" stage. The individual becomes acculturated; he or she understands what a good citizen is supposed to be and do, and lives in accordance with the role he or she has in society, and with the conventional rules that govern that role.

Most adults live at the level of conformity morality. Some, probably many, never get beyond this level. All of us spend a good part of our lives on this level. Murder is wrong, lying is wrong, stealing is wrong. Why? Because everyone knows those actions are wrong. And, though it is impractical to have laws against all lying, lying in important circumstances is illegal (e.g., perjury), and murder and theft are both against the law.

Many adults never reach the third level of moral development, but some do. The third level shall be of most interest to us. Kohlberg calls Level III the *postconventional, autonomous,* or *principled level.* This is the level of self-accepted moral principles. At this level, one accepts moral principles not because society says they are right and acceptable, but because one knows what it means to say that principles are right, and understands what makes them right. The first stage of Level III is that of contract and individual rights. One speaks of, and understands, morality based on the rights of individuals and on agreements made between consenting adults. At the final and highest stage of Level III, one is able to give a rational defense of the moral principles that guide one's actions. The moral agent is conscious of the moral law and acts in accordance with it, not because of reward or punishment, and not because others say he should, but because he understands why the moral law is binding on him. The individual accepts the principles as his own, not as a foreign constraint imposed by others.

The third level is the most interesting to us, because at this level one raises questions about the justification of the moral norms one holds. Most people simply accept the morality of their society. But it is possible to ask: Is what my society holds to be right *really* right? Might the people of my society be mistaken? Why should I accept what my parents told me is right or wrong, or why should I accept what legislators tell me is right and wrong? How do they know? They certainly cannot *make* actions right or wrong; or, if they can, so can I. If none of us can, then there must be reasons why some actions are right and others are wrong, other than because people classify them in this way. What are those reasons?

These are the questions that ethics seeks to answer; and it is at this third level that moral theory operates. Of course, what conventional morality holds to be immoral may well be immoral. The difference between Levels II and III is not necessarily their content; rather, the difference is in the reasons for considering actions to be right or wrong.

Kohlberg's description of the levels of development helps us to understand a good deal about business ethics. We noted earlier that people in business frequently claim that they are bound only by the law and not by moral norms, which they see as personal. Most people like to operate at the second level of morality, so it is not surprising that most businesses operate at this level, too. Certainly some business practices are held to be moral and proper and others are held to be improper. It is possible simply to accept these conventional norms. But it is also possible to ask whether these norms should be held, whether some of them may in fact be improper, and whether there are other activities in which businesses *should* engage, but do not.

Thus at one time in the United States large numbers of people in the

29

South accepted slavery. Now, most people think that slavery is immoral. Was it always immoral? We might answer that according to the conventional morality that was held in the South at that time slavery was moral. But if one were to operate on Kohlberg's third level, slavery would be seen to have been immoral then as well as now. In fact, many did argue that it was immoral, despite the fact that it was part of conventional morality.

Let us take an example somewhat closer to our own time: Significant numbers of Americans held that the Vietnam War was immoral, despite the belief of the majority (at least in the beginning of the war) that it was moral. Critics of the war attacked conventional morality from the vantage point of Kohlberg's Level III.

Subjective and Objective Morality

When we speak of morality we refer to our judgments of right and wrong, good and bad. Three characteristics are usually associated with such judgments. First, moral judgments about the rightness or wrongness of an action are held to be universally applicable. If an action is right for me, it is also right for anyone else in the same circumstances. If it is wrong for you, it is also wrong for anyone else similarly placed. Something of the notion of universality is captured in the injunction, do unto others as you would have them do unto you.

A second characteristic of morality is that moral judgments are important. They are so important, in fact, that they override other considerations. We are morally bound to do what we sometimes may not want to do. For instance, it is wrong to steal, even when we would like to steal. If we say that it is our moral duty to perform an action, that means we have an obligation to do it, and this can only be overridden by a stronger moral consideration. Convenience, personal gain, and even legal requirements fall before moral obligations.

The third characteristic is that moral praise can properly accompany the doing of morally right actions, and moral blame can properly accompany acting immorally. If we say that someone in a business transaction acted immorally, this means that, from a moral point of view, it is appropriate for us to blame him. For instance, if taking bribes is immoral, then those involved in bribery deserve moral blame or censure.

The vocabulary of morality is rich, and it is applied to a variety of objects in a number of ways. We can make clear our meanings if we keep separate the various uses of the terms. We call individual persons moral or immoral; we call actions moral or immoral; and we call economic systems, social institutions, and business practices moral or immoral. What we mean in each of these cases is not identical, though each has something to do with conformity, or lack of conformity, to the moral law or to morality.

When we speak of persons being moral or immoral we may mean at least three different things. It is not always clear which meaning an individual has in mind when he describes someone as being moral. In one sense, a person may be considered moral if he habitually acts in accordance with his conscience. We may speak of him as more or less moral, depending on how frequently, within tolerable levels, he acts contrary to his conscience. What we mean is that he tries to do what he thinks is right. Here, sincerity is the keynote of morality. Although each of us knows our own conscience, we do not know the conscience of others, and so cannot be sure when they are acting in accordance with their beliefs.

In another sense, if we hold that certain actions are immoral, then we might call someone a moral person if he acts in conformity with the moral law; if he does what the moral law requires; or if he does not do what the moral law forbids. The third sense in which we mean moral is a combination of the other two. We may reserve the term moral to describe only that individual who acts in conformity with the moral law, and does so because he knows what that law requires. He acts in accordance with his conscience, which is correct in its judgments of right and wrong.

The meaning of moral in this third sense is the one to which a moral individual aspires. He knows that he should do the right thing, and that he should act in accordance with what his conscience dictates. Only then is his action fully praiseworthy, from a moral standpoint. But none of us can be sure we know, in all situations, what is right. We are all fallible. Hence, we can only try to determine, as carefully as possible, what is right, and so act. We can follow our conscience, and hope that our efforts to form a correct conscience have been successful. The distinction between what one believes to be right and what is actually right is an important one. We can make the distinction by referring to *subjectively* right (and wrong) and *objectively* right (and wrong) actions. What we are judging now, from a moral point of view, is actions, not persons. An action is subjectively right if a person believes that the action is moral. An action is objectively right if the action is in conformity with the moral law.

If I believe that telling the truth is right, and it is right, then telling the truth is both subjectively and objectively right. An action may be subjectively right and objectively wrong. If I am mistaken about the morality of bribery, for instance, I may believe it to be moral for me to take a bribe, even though it is actually (objectively) immoral. Conversely, an action can be subjectively wrong and objectively right. This again involves a mistake on my part about the morality of the action. Suppose that in taking candy from a box I think that I am stealing; in fact, however, the candy is part of a display and is there for anyone who wants to take it. I did not objectively steal, even if I thought I was stealing. Finally, an action may be both subjectively and objectively wrong; for instance, when I believe bribery to be wrong, and, in fact, it is immoral.

One of the pitfalls in the study of morality is that we typically operate on two levels: the personal level, in which we wish both to judge the action and to act in accordance with our conscience; and the third-person level, in which we wish to judge the actions of others from an objective point of view, but do not wish to know, or cannot know, the subjective state of the one performing the action.

Some people are reluctant to judge the internal state of others and this sometimes results in their refusing to judge the actions of others. The two judgments, however, can be kept distinct. We can judge the crimes of Hitler without knowing whether or not he *thought* he was doing something morally right when he performed, or ordered others to perform, immoral acts. Attitudes and intentions constitute a part of what is properly the object of moral evaluation. However, many actions can be considered in their own right, in abstraction from the intent of the agent, and can be evaluated from a moral point of view. This in fact is how we usually judge such actions as stealing, bribery, murder, lying, and so on. Obviously, when we speak of an economic system as being moral or immoral, or of business practices as being immoral, we are also judging them without reference to whether those involved in them believe them to be moral.

Some people adopt a moral tolerance toward others for these reasons: because we are fallible in our moral judgments; because we sometimes believe an action to be right when it is objectively wrong; because people disagree in their moral judgments; and because, in a pluralistic society, the norms of conventional morality are sometimes not clear. They not only refuse to judge others; they also refuse to judge their own actions. Because they cannot give reasons why actions are right or wrong, they often take this position: "there is no objective morality," or, "morality is purely subjective." They consider themselves to be personally moral when they act as they believe they should. (But others may act differently and still be moral, if they believe they are acting morally.) This position confuses subjective guilt and blame with objective guilt and blame. Pushed to its conclusion, it denies the objectivity of moral judgments; it claims that whatever anyone considers to be moral is thereby moral. It therefore abandons the universal characteristic of morality. When made explicit, this position is known as *ethical relativism*.

Cultural Relativism

Anthropologists and sociologists have documented the fact that people in different cultures, as well as people within a given culture, hold divergent moral views on particular issues. The ancient Greeks believed that infanticide was not immoral, although we believe that it is. Some members of our society believe that abortion is immoral, and others believe that it is morally permissible. These differences are examples of transcultural and intracultural relativism. We should, however, distinguish descriptive cultural relativism from normative cultural relativism, and distinguish both of these from normative ethical relativism.

Given the fact that a practice is held to be moral in one society at one time, and wrong at another time or in another society, and given the fact that people within a society in a given time differ in their moral views, we can draw no conclusions about cultures or about a society, except that the differences just described do exist. Consider a class of 20 third-graders who have been given a long-addition problem. Suppose that each child in the class comes up with a different answer to the problem. Because of our knowledge of mathematics, we can say that no more than one of the children has the right answer. (Of course, none of them may have the right answer.) But we would be mistaken if, on the basis of the reported differences, we concluded that there was no right answer to the problem.

Anthropology and sociology supply data to be considered and explained. Starting with the differences between societies concerning what is viewed as moral, we can appropriately ask about the extent of the disagreement and about the bases for the disagreement. Actually, it may be more interesting to inquire about the extent of the agreement rather than the disagreement, for surely the agreements as well as the disagreements deserve consideration and explanation.

Differing views regarding the morality of a given action or practice may be the result of a number of factors. Two societies may basically and ultimately disagree on moral principles. But the disagreement may also be on many other levels. For instance, two societies may adhere to this basic principle: what helps the society flourish is moral, and what hinders it is immoral. But if one society lives in a warm climate and has an abundance of water, it will have a different view of clothing and of the use of water than a society that lives in a very cold climate and has little water. A country with many men and few women will probably not look upon monogamy in the same way as a society with an approximately equal number of men and women. Differing conditions, therefore, provide a reason for holding differing actions to be moral or immoral. A society's beliefs also affect what it holds to be moral or immoral. A society that believes in volcano gods which demand human sacrifice will consider this practice to be moral, one that is demanded by higher authority and therefore necessary for the preservation of the society. A society that does not believe in volcano gods will not consider the practice to be either necessary or morally justifiable. Factual beliefs are an important ingredient in the morality of any society, and differences in the beliefs about facts lead to differences in what is considered moral or immoral.

Some societies believe what is false. To some extent, this is probably true of all societies. However, most societies are aware that they obtain more and more factual knowledge as they develop and progress. Just as a society may be mistaken about facts, so it may be mistaken about some of its moral judgments. From history, we know that members of a society frequently believe that one or more of the moral beliefs of that society are erroneous. There is no reason, in principle, why members of another society cannot make and defend similar claims about a society other than their own.

Descriptive transcultural relativism describes the differences between cultures. In some cases, the differences are such that the terms right and wrong or better and worse are not applicable to the differences noted. All cultures have a language, and some languages are more complex than others. But it makes little sense to say that one language is, in some absolute sense, better than another. Similarly, many aspects of one culture will differ from aspects of another, but both can be equally good.

Many people dispute the accuracy of anthropological reports of the morality of primitive tribes and foreign cultures, because they consider that what the anthropologist describes as a society's morality may be simply an imposition of his own categories of morality, resulting in faulty interpretations of unfamiliar practices. Yet there are clear cases: the ancient Greeks believed that infanticide was morally permissible, and we do not. And, once again: in the South, before the Civil War, many people thought slavery was morally permissible, whereas many in the North held it to be immoral. Do the differences in beliefs show that morality is relative? Does either descriptive cultural relativism or normative cultural relativism imply normative ethical relativism?

Ethical Relativism

Normative ethical relativism claims that when any two cultures or any two people hold different *moral* views of an action, both can be right. Thus an action may be right for one person or society, and the same action, taken in the same way, may be wrong for another person or society, and yet both persons or societies are equally correct. What exactly is meant by these claims? A first form involves saying that neither of two conflicting moral judgments is right and neither is wrong because moral judgments are not right or wrong—they are simply statements of opinion or of feeling. The defense of this form of relativism usually depends on a metaethical view of moral language and the logic of moral discourse. A second form holds that judgments of right and wrong are culturally determined, and that transcultural judgments make no more sense in questions of morality than they do in judgments about whether one language is better than another. Those who maintain this position claim that normative cultural relativism is applicable in the area of morality as in other cultural areas, and defend normative ethical relativism on anthropological grounds. A third form claims that we should not say that either of two competing judgments is right or wrong because we have no way of deciding which is which. One may be right and the other wrong; but because we have no way of proving this, it is better, more prudent, and more cautious not to claim either is right or wrong.

These forms of relativism deserve some attention because they bear directly on such questions as which morality a businessman in a foreign country should follow—his own or that of the country in which he is conducting his business. Their importance also becomes clear if we are to be able to judge the actions of businesses. Whose morality are they to follow? The various forms of moral relativism all hold that there is a close connection between the fact of moral diversity and the claim that there are many moralities, each equally valid or good. The connecting link between cultural relativism and normative ethical relativism is a theory or view about morality.

The obvious forms of normative ethical relativism, however, do not stand up well to analysis. Consider the first view, that moral judgments are neither true nor false, right or wrong, because they are simply statements of feeling or emotion. From this position, a number of consequences follow which do not cohere well with the moral experience of most people. One of the results of adopting this view is that a moral judgment about an action, the judgment that stealing is immoral, for example, is not a judgment about stealing at all. It is simply the expression of one's feeling about stealing. Suppose A feels negatively about B's taking his wallet and A says that B's taking A's wallet is immoral. B replies that B feels no guilt about taking A's wallet; therefore, according to B, his action is moral. If both are simply reporting or expressing their feelings, then each is speaking about himself. If each is speaking about himself, they are not speaking about the *action* of B taking A's wallet. That they have different reactions is perfectly possible and involves no disagreement between them. Hence, they each express their emotions, and if the emotions happen to differ, they differ. Nor does it change matters to say that when someone makes a moral judgment he not only expresses his emotions or feelings, he also adds that others should feel as he does. For once again, different people have different emotions. Each can feel that others should feel as he does. It may be said that each is simply saying something about himself, and neither of them is judging the action.

A second consequence is that we can never disagree with anyone about the morality of an action. For if a moral judgment is simply a statement about myself, my reactions, or my expression of my emotions, when someone expresses his emotions and they happen to differ from mine, we appropriately say that we have different emotions or are expressing differing emotions. But emotions are not true or false; therefore, because we are making no claims of truth or falsehood, no claims of right or wrong, we are not disagreeing with each other.

A third consequence is that, in this view, people can never be mistaken in their moral judgments. This is so because if someone feels negatively about an action today, and tomorrow feels positively about the same action, then he will have had, or expressed, different emotions. But expressing one emotion today is not incompatible with expressing a different one tomorrow. In neither case does the individual make a factual statement or claim, so there is nothing to be right or wrong about, and hence no way to be mistaken.

A fourth consequence is that people can change the morality of an action by expressing a different emotion concerning it. If a moral judgment is only the report of an emotion or the expressing of an emotion, then by changing his emotion a person changes the morality of the action.

These four consequences of normative ethical relativism do not correspond well with the moral experience of most people, because people do make judgments about actions—at least that is what they intend to do. They do find that, in some cases, they disagree with others about the morality of an action. People do change their minds, and often conclude that they were mistaken in the past in judging an action to be right, whereas today they know it is wrong. And they do not think they can change the morality of an action simply by changing their emotions or by expressing different emotions. What reason do they have for giving up these common-sense beliefs that form part of their experience? So far, we have not been given any evidence that is stronger than ordinary experience. What we have been given is a theory of what moral judgments supposedly are. But why accept that theory? We certainly do express our moral feelings when we make moral judgments. We do wish people to have feelings similar to ours when we express our emotions relative to an action. But that is not all we do. We also judge the action, disagree with those who judge it differently, and so on.

Consider next the view of the defender of normative ethical relativism who argues that judgments of right and wrong are culturally determined. The claim may be that one society holds some act to be right whereas another society holds a similar act to be wrong because the circumstances in which the act is performed make the acts different. What appears to be brutality in one society may appear as kindness in another. For instance, in a society where it is the custom to have the aged leave the society, to die alone, this might appear heartless to someone from a society where the moral thing to do is care for the aged, keeping them alive for as long as possible, and by whatever means possible. Both actions might be construed as showing respect for the aged, although the respect is shown in very different ways. In this instance, however, we do not have normative ethical relativism; we simply have differing instantiations, on the level of practice, of a similar higher moral norm, which is shared by both societies.

Another interpretation of normative ethical relativism might be to maintain that what each society means by the term *moral* is that the action is held to be right in that society. *Moral* then means, "is approved by this society." In this case it would follow that no two societies disagree on the morality of an action, for what each means by the term *moral* is different. By judging an action to be moral, a member of society *A* is reporting that the people of his society believe it to be moral. By judging the same action to be *immoral,* a member of society *B* is reporting that the members of his society believe it to be immoral. Each report can be correct. But a consequence of this view is that no two societies can disagree on the morality of an action. All anyone can do is report what one's own society thinks about the action. A second consequence is that no member of the society can disagree with his society about the morality of an action. According to this view, when saying that an action is immoral, the individual is really only saying that his society *believes* it to be immoral. And if this society actually believes the action to be moral, then one is simply mistaken when asserting what the society does not believe. Yet it is a fact of moral life that people do sometimes disagree in some instances with what the other members of the society believe regarding moral matters; and societies do disagree with one another on moral matters. Hence once again there is more reason for denying the doctrine of normative ethical relativism than there is for holding it.

Some cultural differences are matters of taste, which offer no basis for deciding that one is right and another wrong. Nor is there any need to do so. For instance, if one culture likes fried food and another dislikes it, each can have its own way, without harm. If one person likes chocolate ice cream and another strongly dislikes chocolate but likes vanilla ice cream, we are not tempted to say one is right and the other is wrong. Cultural and individual differences exist. There is usually no claim of truth or falsehood, and no basis, or need, for deciding one is right and the other wrong. Why is this not so in the moral realm?

The argument from moral experience claims that we do judge actions to be moral or immoral, and that in making these judgments we are saying something about the actions and not just something about ourselves. The argument also claims that people do disagree on moral issues. Because they believe they are making statements that are true or false, right or wrong, they are not satisfied if they are told that they are *not* doing this. Their protest is not sufficient to show that they are correct in their assertion. But more is needed to show them that they are mistaken than simply someone's theory which asserts the contrary.

A closer look at what many people think they are doing when they make moral judgments will show us, in part, why moral disputes occur. For instance, when making the judgment that murder is immoral, the ordinary person means that the act of murder is immoral for everyone. He is not making the judgment that it is immoral only for him, but that others, if they feel differently, may be acting morally if they kill him arbitrarily. He is claiming that the action is immoral for everyone. Nor is he restricting his judgment only to the members of his society. Murder is immoral in his own country and in other countries as well, whether or not the people of that country realize or admit it. In making his moral judgment, therefore, he is making a claim about the nature of an action, and it is a claim with universal import. This is what he means by saying murder is immoral: that no one should do it, and that it is wrong for anyone to do it.

A society may morally judge the actions of only its own members because it ignores all other societies, or because it considers all other people barbarians and not worthy of respect. The domain of a society may be restricted because of that society's beliefs about other people. But in making a moral judgment in such a society, the judgment still has universal import because it applies to all those within the moral community. If one's view of the moral community includes all human beings, then the moral judgment of an action is made in the name of all. If, in addition, one's moral community includes animals, then the judgments also apply to them.

Yet it does not follow that because people make universal moral judgments they do so correctly. Nor does it follow that simply because people disagree in their moral judgments it is therefore possible to determine which one is correct.

The third interpretation of ethical relativism stated that we should not say that disagreements on moral issues are right or wrong, because no one can show he himself is right and someone else wrong. There is no way of deciding such disputed issues. According to this view, it is arrogant to claim that one is right and another wrong in moral disputes. At best, we can discuss our differences to determine whether they rest on differing facts. If this is the case, then we can try to determine which facts are correct. We can also try to find out if we have different beliefs. Once again, we can try to adjudicate our differences. If we finally find, however, that we agree on the facts, and have the same beliefs, but still differ on the morality of an action, according to this view, there is then no way to show that one of us is right and the other wrong. The view implies that moral principles are not right or wrong and cannot be rationally defended; yet moral principles frequently have been given rational defense, and disagreements on moral issues are argued in rational as well as in emotional terms. It is worthwhile looking at these debates. But we should be clear what can and what cannot be claimed for them.

If the arguments presented here against normative ethical relativism are valid, what follows? What follows is not a complete moral system, and we do not claim that somewhere there is a complete moral system, waiting to be found. The fact is that moral judgments are judgments that can and should be defended, but that the arguments given are sometimes good and sometimes not so good. If we are faced with contradictory judgments about an action, only one of them can be right. The way to determine which one is right is to see which judgment is best supported by the facts, and by the arguments presented in its defense. We may eventually arrive at high-level, abstract, moral principles. If they clash, we will then have to decide which of the alternative principles or approaches has been best defended. Upon investigation, we may conclude that no theory that has been investigated is completely defensible or completely satisfactory. In that case, more work is necessary. The conclusion that there is no satisfactory theory is not a valid conclusion based on the evidence. We do not conclude that there is no satisfactory unified theory of physics because we have not yet found one. In both cases the appropriate response is to continue the search, to continue to make improvements, and to continue to use what we presently have available, despite the deficiencies.

Moral Absolutism

One alternative to ethical relativism is *moral absolutism*. A moral absolutist holds that there are eternal moral values and eternal moral principles which are always and everywhere applicable. There are different versions of absolutism. Some absolutists, for instance, hold that the most general principle of morality is absolute, but that, as it is applied in differing circumstances, certain lower-level norms may vary. Other, more extreme, absolutists claim that all moral norms are everywhere and always the same. Between the two positions is a third position, which holds that the most general principle of morality is everywhere and always the same, and that the moral norms are everywhere and always the same, but that these norms have exceptions, which are also everywhere and always the same.

There is a difference between holding that the principles of morality are universal and eternal and holding that one knows with certainty what the principles are. A person might hold that there are eternal moral principles without being able to produce them. Instead, he might produce various approximations of those principles, which he is willing and ready to modify when he sees they are not exact in their formulation.

There is an alternative to absolutism, however, which does not fall into the category of relativism. This position claims that morality is not eternal. It is an attempt by human beings to adopt principles to govern human society, and the lives of those within society, principles that will help them live together and abide by rules that all of them, in their reasonable and objective moments, would accept. Unlike the absolutist, someone holding this position need not claim that some final, ultimate, eternal moral principle exists somewhere, for instance, in the mind of God. He need only claim that the idea of such a principle forms an ideal toward which ethics strives. He is then content to examine the various moral principles that have been suggested during the history of mankind, and the various ethical theories that human beings have produced. He can see which ones stand up best to rational scrutiny, which ones are most helpful to him, and which ones correspond most closely to the values he perceives. This is not only an individual endeavor, but a collective one, for we can build on the accomplishments of others as well as on their mistakes. We shall follow this alternative in the succeeding chapters. No claim to infallibility or privileged eternal knowledge shall be made. Rather, we shall explain the most successful traditional approaches to morality, and the types of moral arguments currently used in our society.

Moral Pluralism

American society is diverse, a combination of various cultures and traditions. It is heterogeneous in composition, with many ethnic and racial groups. Dynamic and changing, it is pluralistic in many ways. It is culturally pluralistic. It is also, to some extent, morally pluralistic.

We can distinguish four levels of moral pluralism: radical moral pluralism, the pluralism of moral principles, the pluralism of moral practices, and the pluralism of self-realization. *Radical moral pluralism* describes that state of affairs in which people hold mutually irreconcilable views about morality, such as what the terms *right* and *wrong* mean, and which actions are right or wrong. People who hold such radically divergent views, however, do not form a society. To be a society, a group must accept certain fundamental practices and principles. At a basic level, for instance, there must be general agreement that life is worth living, that the lives of the members of the society should be respected, or that people will respect existing differences to the extent that they do not interfere with each other. If someone does not care whether he lives or dies, and also believes it is his moral duty to kill others, it may not be possible to convince him he is mistaken. But people with such a view cannot form a society.

To the extent that society and morality go together, the morality of a society must be a shared morality, not a radically pluralistic set of opposing moralities. Yet a society may be morally pluralistic on the other three levels.

A plurality of moral principles within a society does not necessarily mean irreconcilable diversity. Pluralism on the level of moral principles is compatible with social agreement on the morality of many basic practices. Such agreement does not necessarily involve agreement on the moral principles different people use to evaluate practices. The vast majority of the members of our society, for instance, agree that murder is wrong. Some members of our society operate only at the level of conventional morality, and do not ask why murder is wrong. Some may believe it is wrong because the God in whom they believe forbids such acts; others because it violates human dignity; others because murder has serious consequences for society as a whole, and so on. Each of these involves a different moral principle. These different principles are compatible with similarity of moral judgments.

On the level of specific actions, we encounter a variety of moral opinions about some of them. This pluralism regarding moral practices may stem from differences of moral principles, but it may also stem from differences of fact or of perception of facts, differences of circumstances, or differences in the weighing of relevant values. Even when there is basic agreement on principles, not all moral issues are clear. In a changing, dynamic, developing society there is certainly room for moral disagreement, even if there is unanimous agreement that what helps the society to survive is moral. New practices might be seen by conservatives as threatening the society's survival, and the same practice might be championed by others as the necessary means for survival. Pluralism of practices, however, is compatible with areas of agreement, and this is usually the case.

The fourth level of moral pluralism is that of self-realization. So long as the members of a society abide by the basic moral norms, they are allowed, in such a pluralistic society, to choose freely their other values and their life-styles. This constitutes a kind of moral pluralism, because self-development and fulfillment, according to some views, are moral matters. A society that allows divergence of self-development within the basic moral framework tolerates a great many differences that would not be allowed (or found) in a homogeneous society.

Moral pluralism of the second, third, and fourth kinds is found in the United States. These varieties of pluralism do not imply normative ethical relativism, and in fact they presuppose a wide common background of moral practices. The diversity of moral practices that we encounter is often so striking that we forget the similarities. But respect for human beings, respect for truth, and respect for the property of others are all commonplaces found in America, making business possible. With this background of moral pluralism, we have adopted laws to enforce common moral norms, to define proper areas of toleration, and to provide adjudicatory functions in cases of moral disputes on socially important issues.

If one considers the cohesiveness of American society, despite its pluralism, and then thinks about the diversity of the rest of the world, one should understand the difficulty of making some moral judgments on the international level. There are certainly some basic similarities in all the moral codes and views held in each country of the world. In every country, the murder of members of the society is prohibited, otherwise no society would exist. In all of them, lying is immoral; otherwise there would be no secure social interaction. There is respect for property, however defined; if this were not so, no one would be able to count on having what he needs to live. Yet the way in which the nations of the world form a society is at best a tenuous one. National sovereignty limits the extent to which any nation wishes to abide by a tribunal higher than itself. For instance, on the international level, law cannot always play the same mediating and adjudicating role it does in the United States, because there is no generally acknowledged body to enforce such law. The differences that divide nations are much more profound than the differences that divide members of the same society. The notion of a common morality for everyone in the world—pluralistic in nature but providing a basic framework within which all can work—is a goal still to be achieved, not a present reality. There is, however, sufficient agreement among societies to allow business to be carried on internationally. But even in business there are a host of unresolved problems. The moral intuitions, feelings, and beliefs of most people have been primarily focused within their own society, and on the level of personal morality. Their moral views on an international level of obligations among nations are less well formed, partly because people in general have not given it much thought. We find, therefore, few ready answers to questions on this level.

Before leaving the topic of moral pluralism, however, we can put to rest the question some people raise when speaking of morality in business. The question is: Whose morality? This is a bogus question. Moral pluralism presupposes a society, and if a society is to function, it must have a large core of commonly held values and norms. These norms form the common morality of the society. They are yours, mine, and ours. We hold them as applicable to everyone. In areas of serious differences (which I described as the third level of moral pluralism) the clash of moral views must be decided by public debate, and perhaps by legislation. Moral arguments are raised and countered until clarity emerges, or until a way of resolving the problem, while recognizing differences, is worked out. It is not true, therefore, that when faced with moral claims against me or my business practices I can dismiss them as being your moral views and not mine. Moral claims are universal.

Approaches to Ethical Theory

In describing the plurality of moral principles we saw that though people may all agree that murder is immoral, they may arrive at that judgment on the basis of different moral principles. Ethics is a theory of morality that attempts to systematize moral judgments, and establish and defend basic moral principles.

We need not describe here the many different ethical systems that have been developed in the history of philosophy. But through the centuries, two basic approaches to moral reasoning have prevailed. One approach argues on the basis of consequences. This approach to ethical reasoning is called a *teleological* approach. It states that whether an action is right or wrong depends on the consequences of that action. A common form of teleological ethics that is very strongly represented in our society is utilitarianism, a theory we shall examine in the next chapter.

The second basic approach is called the *deontological* approach. This states that duty is the basic moral category, and that duty is independent of consequences. An action is right if it has certain characteristics or is of a certain kind, and wrong if it has other characteristics or is of another kind. The traditional Judeo-Christian approach to morality is deontological. The German philosopher, Immanuel Kant, gave a classical philosophical statement of the deontological approach, which is currently influential in our society. Most of the discussion on questions of business ethics, as well as on questions of social ethics (e.g., welfare, the morality of governmental practices or of laws) is conducted by people who use—knowingly or unknowingly—a utilitarian, a Judeo-Christian, or a Kantian approach to ethics.

Philosophers, and others who wish to be consistent, often attempt to use only one of the ethical approaches to questions. Those interested in ethics as a theoretical pursuit attempt to construct their approach so that it can handle difficulties and objections, and can be defended and rationally justified. Those who are willing to mix their approaches are sometimes called *ethical pluralists.* They hold one primary approach or set of principles but join them with another approach or set of principles. One charge often brought against utilitarianism, for instance, is that it cannot provide a satisfactory account of justice. Hence, some philosophers join a deontological notion of justice to their utilitarian ethical views. The mixing of approaches has advantages. It also obviously has disadvantages, because one needs some rule to decide when to use one principle rather than another.

While philosophers argue, both they and other members of society must act. In the absence of definitive ethical theories we make do with the best we have. In our society, the moral arguments are basically the three types previously named. We therefore need to be familiar with them, we need to know how to employ them, and to be conscious of their strengths and weaknesses. To a large extent, our country is ethically inarticulate. The members of our society make moral judgments and hold moral values, but most are poorly trained in the art of defending their moral views, and fail to use moral reasoning in a focused way when debating public policy, social issues, and business practices. That art of moral reasoning is an important part of business ethics.

Further Reading

AYER, A. J. *Language, Truth and Logic*, 2nd ed. New York: Dover Publications, Inc., 1946. Chap. 6.

BLANSHARD, BRAND. "Subjectivism," in *Reason and Goodness*. New York: Macmillan Publishing Company, 1961. Chap. 5.

FOOT, PHILIPPA. *Moral Relativism*. Lindley Lecture, Lawrence, Kans.: The University of Kansas, 1978.

GINSBERG, M. *Essays in Sociology and Social Philosophy*, Vol. I. *On the Diversity of Morals*. New York: Macmillan Publishing Company, 1957.

HARE, R. M. *Moral Thinking*. Oxford: Clarendon Press, 1981.

KOHLBERG, LAWRENCE. "The Claim to Moral Adequacy of a Highest Stage of Moral Judgment." *The Journal of Philosophy*, LXX (1973), pp. 630–646.

MOORE, G. E. *Ethics*. London: Oxford University Press, Inc., 1912. Chaps. 3 and 4.

PIAGET, JEAN. *The Moral Development of the Child*. Glencoe, Ill.: The Free Press, 1948.

STACE, W. T. *The Concepts of Morals*. New York: Macmillan Publishing Company, 1937. Chaps. 1 and 2.

STEVENSON, CHARLES L. *Ethics and Language*. New Haven, Conn.: Yale University Press, 1944.

SUMNER, W. G. *Folkways*. Boston: Ginn & Company, 1907.

WELLMAN, CARL. "The Ethical Implications of Cultural Relativity," *Journal of Philosophy*, LX (1963), pp. 169–184.

WESTERMARCK, E. *Ethical Relativity*. New York: Harcourt Brace, Inc., 1932.

THREE

Utility and Utilitarianism

Businesses seek to make a profit. They engage in accounting and attempt to have their income exceed their costs. This is a rational procedure, one we all understand; it is a procedure we all use in our own lives. For instance, a family has an income, and it sets limits on what it can spend. The members of a family need a great many different kinds of goods. People also want things that they do not absolutely need. Typically, a family apportions its funds to take care of immediate needs first and then decides how to allocate the remainder, taking into account both present and long-range needs and desires. A budget helps a family plan the wise use of its money. Though it is difficult to weigh the desirability of a music lesson as opposed to a movie, and to weigh that against one's desire for new clothes or a vacation, we know that people make these comparisons and choices. We also know that occasionally people forego earning more money in order to have more leisure time, or more time to devote to members of their family. Although we can put a price tag on many things that we desire, we cannot calculate the value of all of them in terms of money.

This common practice of calculating what we want, balancing our wishes with our resources, and comparing present versus long-range desires, forms the basis of the utilitarian approach to ethics. *Utilitarianism* is an ethical theory that holds that an action is right if it produces, or if it tends to produce, the greatest amount of good for the greatest number of people affected by the action. Otherwise the action is wrong.

Utilitarianism does not force on us something foreign to our ordinary rational way of acting. It systematizes and makes explicit what its defenders believe most of us do in our moral thinking, as well as in much of our other thinking. It is reasonable for rational beings, who are able to foresee the consequences of their actions, to choose those actions that produce more good than those that produce less good, other things being equal. Businesses traditionally reduce *good* to money and calculate costs and benefits in monetary terms. Because the aim of a business is to make money, those actions that tend to help it make money are considered good, and those that tend to make it lose money are considered bad. A rationally operated company tries to maximize its good and minimize its bad so that when income and costs are balanced out, there is a profit. The bottom line of the ledger sheet, which shows a profit or a loss, is the final accounting in which business is traditionally interested.

This cost-benefit analysis is a form of utility calculation. People in business theory use utility curves to plot the results of various actions, choosing those that maximize whatever it is that they wish to achieve. This utility approach is not foreign to most people. It is widely used in many forms of general decision making and can be applied to moral issues as well as to strictly business issues. A defense of utilitarianism as an ethical theory is that it describes what rational people actually do in making moral decisions. It explicitly formulates for them the procedures they intuitively and spontaneously use in moral reasoning. The theory renders explicit what is implicit in the ordinary moral reasoning and argumentation that we ourselves use; we see it displayed in newspapers, we read it in discussions of public policy and in the opinions of the Supreme Court, and we encounter it in debates with our friends on moral issues.

There is a significant difference, however, between utilitarianism and a utility analysis as used by business. When a firm uses a utility, or a cost-benefit analysis, it weighs the good and the bad consequences of performing a certain action (usually in monetary terms) as it relates to *itself*. A utilitarian analysis, as a moral analysis, weighs the good and bad results of an action on *everyone* affected by it.

Utilitarianism adopts a teleological approach to ethics and claims that actions are to be judged by their consequences. According to this view, actions are not good or bad in themselves. Actions take on moral value only when considered in conjunction with the effects that follow upon them. Actions by themselves have no intrinsic value. They are simply means to attain that which has value. But what has value? To answer this we must distinguish what has value as a means toward something else, and what has value in and of itself. A few examples might help.

Businesses seek to make a profit. But what is the point of having money? Is there anything intrinsically valuable in the pieces of paper that we use as money? The paper in itself is not intrinsically valuable. But it can be used to buy goods that we want. It is valuable as a means to an end. The more money we have, the more goods we can buy. But are goods valuable in themselves? Food, shelter, books, and clothing are, in turn, only a means to satisfy our needs and wants. The stopping point in this progression seems to be ourselves and others. People are the centers of value, and what satisfies their needs is what they consider valuable. Basically, then, it is human satisfaction that is valuable in itself; money and goods are means to produce this satisfaction. Dissatisfaction, harm, pain, or unhappiness are examples of disvalue.

According to utilitarianism, we should evaluate an action by looking at its consequences, weighing the good effects against the bad effects on all the people affected by it. If the good outweighs the bad, it tends to be a good action; if the bad outweighs the good, it tends to be a bad action.

In trying to state what utilitarianism is, and when trying to use it, a number of complications arise; these have been discussed at length in the philosophical literature. We need note only a few. One question that surfaces immediately is: how can we calculate consequences that are radically different one from another? In a business calculation everything is typically reduced to dollars and cents. This makes calculation relatively easy. But how are we to evaluate actions from a moral point of view? Is there some least-common denominator, in terms of which we can and do calculate? A number of answers to this question have been proposed. One, which is called *hedonistic utilitarianism*, holds that the basic human values are pleasure and pain (sometimes defined simply as the absence of pleasure). According to this view, everything that people desire, want, or need can be reduced in one way or another to pleasure. Hence the calculation, though not easy, is possible, because we are dealing with units of the same kind.

The advantage of this approach has been challenged by those who claim that not all intrinsically valuable goods can be reduced to uniform pleasure and pain. What is intrinsically valuable, they maintain, is not simply pleasures—which may differ in quality as well as quantity—but happiness. This second view is called *eudaimonistic utilitarianism*, since the basic value in terms of which the calculation is made is happiness, not pleasure.

A third approach is called *ideal utilitarianism*. This position maintains that what has to be calculated is not only pleasure or happiness but all intrinsically valuable human goods, which include friendship, knowledge, and a host of other goods valuable in themselves.

The differences among these utilitarians are subtle; there are interesting and strong arguments on all sides. But we need not settle the dispute here because the debate does not actually call into doubt whether such things as knowledge, beauty, or friendship are valuable; rather, it questions whether they are valuable for their own sake, or because they produce pleasure or happiness. Most calculations will come out the same, whether we use the ideal utilitarian approach, which allows a plurality of intrinsic values, or the hedonistic approach, which reduces all values ultimately to pleasure, or the eudaimonistic utilitarian approach, which reduces them to happiness. The hedonistic calculation may seem to be more straightforward than the others, because we deal with the same units—that is, pleasure and pain. But the problem of trying to reduce the multiplicity of goods and values to pleasure and pain is not an easy one. How do we decide the amount of pleasure we receive from drinking our favorite beverage when thirsty, compared with the amount of pleasure we receive from learning a new theorem in geometry, or reading an exciting novel, or giving a gift to a friend? Whether we face the problem of comparison as we weigh the various goods and values, or whether we face it in attempting to reduce each to a common denominator of pleasure, face it we must. Thus, the dispute about the differing approaches to the interpretation of good in the utilitarian formula, though interesting, is not as crucial in deciding actual cases as it may seem.

Several assumptions of utilitarianism should be made explicit. In carrying out the calculation of good and bad consequences of an action, the utilitarian rule tells us to consider all the persons affected by the action. The assumption is that our good counts for no more than anyone else's good, and no one else's good counts for more than ours. The approach is neither egoistic nor altruistic—it is universalistic. The defense of this approach is that it captures the essence of what we actually do when we make moral judgments. Moral judgments are judgments that we make concerning actions, and we believe that the actions are right, not only for ourselves but also for anyone else similarly situated. From the moral point of view, which is impartial, my good counts no more than anyone else's. Nor does anyone else's good count more than mine. Each person is equal, and each person's good is as important and worthwhile as each other person's good. Our moral calculation, thus, is a calculation made from an impersonal point of view. It should come out the same whether made by me or by you, or by any other rational person adopting an objective point of view. What is weighed is the good or bad resulting to each person affected by an action. This is an objective state of affairs. Though pleasure, happiness, or other goods may be subjectively experienced, the experiences are considered and weighed objectively, with each given its due.

Jeremy Bentham (1748–1832), who was a hedonistic utilitarian, argued that in attempting to evaluate the pleasure or pain produced by an action there are various aspects of the pleasure and pain that we should consider. We can generalize his analysis to any value or good we are taking into account. We should consider the intensity, duration, certainty or uncertainty, propinquity or remoteness, fecundity, and purity of the value in question for each person affected. A more intense pleasure, for instance, might have to be weighed against a less intense but longer-lasting pain. In making our calculation, we give greater weight to the pleasure or other value we are more certain of attaining, and less weight to less certain values. Similarly, we weigh differently those goods that we will get immediately and those we will acquire at a more distant time. Frequently we are willing to undergo immediate discomfort and unpleasantness because we know these are necessary in order to achieve something worthwhile in the future, which makes the present unpleasantness worth suffering through. Fecundity refers to whether the action will produce more of the same kind of value we achieve in the first instance. The pleasure we get from learning a new skill, for instance, may be followed by other instances of pleasure as we utilize that skill. If a value is followed by its opposite, then it is impure. For instance, the pleasure of a glass of beer that makes one intoxicated is frequently followed by the pain of being sick or having a hangover.

In each case we consider the good and the bad produced by an action in the first instance, and also in later instances, for those most directly affected by the action. We then sum this up. Then, we consider all the others who will be affected less directly by the action. The number of others may be very large, but the intensity of the effect quite small. The good and the bad done to all these people must be totaled.

Many of our actions affect society as a whole. When I break a contract, I affect not only myself and the person with whom I made the contract; I also affect a great many other people—for instance, all those who hear about it. Many will be more cautious in making contracts, not only with me but with others. Some will worry more than they otherwise would have. Still others may refuse to make contracts for fear of others breaking the contract, as I did. All these are real consequences, and must be included in the calculation. After considering all the persons affected, we sum up the good and the bad. We then add this, together with the calculation we made concerning the effects on those more directly affected by the action. The final result of our calculation determines the morality of the action. If the action produces more good than bad, then it tends to be a morally right action.

But our calculation is not yet over. For the utilitarian principle tells us that in order for the action to be right, it must produce the greatest good for the greatest number of those affected by it. To know whether the action produces the greatest good, we need to compare it with alternative actions. In some cases the comparison will be simply that of the opposite action. If we are considering the morality of breaking a contract, we should calculate the effects of breaking it; but we should also ask what the alternative action is. In this case, it is not breaking the contract. Hence, we should sum up the results of that alternative in a way comparable to the way we did the first sum. When we compare the two, the morally right action is that which produces the greatest net amount of good.

We can add several dimensions to the calculation. For purposes of determining whether a certain kind of action is moral or immoral, we need only calculate the action and its opposite. If the action in general produces more good than harm, whereas its opposite produces more harm than good, then the action is generally a moral action. If more than one action and its opposite are available to us, we can calculate the results of all the alternatives. A stringent application of utilitarianism would lead to the conclusion that, among all the alternatives, the action that produces the greatest amount of good is the moral action in the situation in question.

A less stringent interpretation of rule utilitarianism would simply require that I choose one of the actions that tends to produce more good than harm, but would not require that I always choose only the best action among good actions. In any interpretation of utilitarianism, if two actions produce equal net amounts of good, then, from a moral point of view, both are equally moral, and we may do either. If we have only two alternatives, and both of them produce more bad than good, then we are morally obliged to do the one that produces the least bad. We thereby choose the lesser of two evils.

Act and Rule Utilitarianism

Two versions of utilitarianism are compatible with the utilitarian principle just stated. They are known as act utilitarianism and rule utilitarianism. *Act utilitarianism* holds that each individual action, in all its concreteness and in all its detail, is what should be subjected to the utilitarian test. When faced with the temptation to break a contract, we are always concerned with a particular contract in a particular set of circumstances. To determine the morality of the action we should calculate the effects of breaking this particular contract. The effects will be, in part, similar to breaking any contract, but they will be somewhat different. If we believe that what is true of breaking contracts in general will not be true in this case, we should investigate the effects.

When faced with the temptation to break a contract, we may know that the bad consequences will outweigh the good ones; this is based on our knowledge of what the results of breaking contracts are, and also on our knowledge that this case has no special qualities such that the consequences might be different from other cases. The act utilitarian knows that the vast majority of past cases of breaking contracts have resulted in more bad than good. We hence arrive at a rule of thumb about the morality of breaking contracts. The rule of thumb, however, is a generalization about past instances, and some particular future instance may prove an exception to the rule. In that particular case, the act utilitarian claims, breaking the contract is morally permissible.

Those who defend rule utilitarianism object to the act utilitarian approach. *Rule utilitarians* hold that utility applies appropriately to classes of actions rather than to given individual actions. Thus, by looking at the general consequences of breaking contracts in the past, we can determine that breaking contracts is immoral. It is immoral because the bad consequences outweigh the good consequences. We thus arrive at a rule which states that it is morally wrong to violate contracts. By a similar analysis a rule utilitarian determines that people should not lie, steal, or murder. Each of these injunctions is the result of having observed the consequences of those acts as performed in the past, together with an assumption that the consequences in the future will be similar.

Why favor the rule utilitarian rather than the act utilitarian approach? The answer is that we cannot know all the consequences of a particular act, nor can we know in advance, and with certainty, many of the specific consequences of such an act. Always present in act utilitarianism is the temptation to think that the instance we are considering will be the exception to the rule. If we are the primary beneficiaries of breaking a particular contract, we may tend to discount the harm done to others; we diminish its seriousness, and guess that the consequences will not be as serious for them as they usually are for those affected by broken contracts. And if finding out is what will cause others to be reluctant to make contracts, we will be inclined to assume that no one will find out. We will be tempted to project what we would like to have happen, because we cannot know what will happen. The rule utilitarian

49

maintains, therefore, that more harm is done by breaking a moral rule than any good that can supposedly be achieved by doing so. The rule utilitarian approach does not require guesswork as to what will happen. The history of mankind provides the sourcebook. If we wish to see the results of murder, lying, stealing, or breaking contracts, we can easily recall the consequences in many past cases. We know that most criminals think that they will get away with their crime. We also know that many, if not most, do not; and we know that even some of those who are not caught suffer pangs of conscience. We need not be prophets to foresee that the consequences of certain kinds of actions are on the whole bad rather than good. We can learn from human experience why people have come to hold the general moral rules they do.

Rule utilitarianism provides a technique for determining the moral value of actions—both those on which society has already made a moral determination and those on which it has not. It encourages us to determine whether conditions have changed to such an extent that what was once immoral because it produced more bad than good is now moral because, in changed circumstances, the action produces more good than bad. It also enables us to see whether we have been mistaken in our past calculation concerning certain practices. If we miscalculated as a society, we can now recalculate, and correct our past error. By making explicit the utilitarian principle that we implicitly used before, we have the means to check our prior moral judgments, challenge those that are mistaken, and evaluate actions, the moral values of which change because of new circumstances.

In our own society there are a number of disputed moral questions. In part, the disputes hinge on consequences, which are foreseen as likely by one group and denied as likely by another. To some extent business faces questions that are truly new, and for which we have no easy way to determine the real consequences. We have seen that both act and rule utilitarianism are used to decide the morality of actions. They may also be used to decide the morality of laws, social practices, social structures, political systems, and economic systems. For instance, does the adoption of free enterprise produce more good than bad? Compared with socialism, does it produce more total good than bad? The answer is not easy to determine because the consequences are so complex; there is no way of knowing what the consequences of adopting an economic system really will be. The adoption of an economic system is not like the performance of particular acts that are very similar to one another, and for which we have an abundance of information as to the consequences.

When dealing with legislation, utilitarian arguments are also frequently used. A moral political system is one that produces an abundance of good over bad for the members of the society. A policy is morally justified if it produces more good than bad, and it is optimally justified if it produces more good than any other alternative would. But because we cannot know that we have considered all the alternatives, and because we cannot know what all the consequences of any alternative will be, we cannot have certainty on the morality of policies. Sometimes we can foresee that they will produce more harm than good, and we can attack them on moral grounds. In some instances we think they will produce more good, and only after they are implemented do we find that we are mistaken. In still other instances, we may choose what appears to be the better alternative, only to find out that it may not be better, but that sticking with it may produce more good than trying to start all over. These are all part of our ordinary experience, and utilitarians are not surprised that they are. For, they claim, utilitarianism is simply the result of making explicit the ways in which we ordinarily think and argue about policies, laws, and actions.

Because some immoral actions seem at times to produce more good than bad, utilitarians promote penal legislation. A thief who sometimes gets away with his action may come to believe that theft produces more good consequences than bad. If, however, theft is made illegal, and if the penalty is serious, then the fear that accompanies stealing is increased; therefore the pain from stealing is made greater than the pleasure. One purpose of legislation, according to this view, is to attach legal sanctions to crimes so that any calculation of the consequences of committing a crime will obviously not be to the advantage of the perpetrator. Society protects itself by passing laws against those acts that tend to harm society and the people in it. By imposing sanctions, society reinforces the bad effects of those actions for the one who commits them.

The application of this approach to business activities is no different from its application to actions in general. If we adopt the utilitarian perspective, we can evaluate certain business practices on the basis of their consequences. If they tend to produce more bad than good, they are immoral. If the harm done to society by these practices is sufficiently serious, then legislation might be passed, subjecting the action to legal as well as moral sanctions. To be effective, the sanctions must outweigh the good that the perpetrator of the action hopes to gain. For example, the usual punishment imposed on a corporation for breaking a law is a fine. If the fine is to serve as a deterrent, the amount of the fine should be greater than the amount the company would gain by doing the action. Law is used to protect the members of society when moral means do not suffice. The justification for such law is utilitarian, just as the evaluation of the action is. Law can provide an incentive to act morally for those who would not otherwise do so.

Utilitarians also consider moral and other nonlegal sanctions in their calculations. If an action does more harm than good to society, the members of society can impose various sanctions on the wrongdoer, short of legal measures. If a merchant overcharges, people can stop patronizing him and spread the word to others to do the same. They can stop speaking to him, exclude him from various social activities, chastise him, vent their moral indignation on him, and so on. These sanctions should be expected by those who perform certain actions. The reason for imposing them is to prevent people from performing the actions to which the sanctions are attached.

Some people claim that act utilitarianism, properly applied, is reducible to rule utilitarianism. The argument hinges on the broad consequences of adopting the act utilitarian approach. If an action that violates a rule can be justified by act utilitarianism, it tends to do damage to the good of having the rule. Without rules, many people will no longer know how a moral individual will act, or should act. From an act utilitarian point of view, this is a negative consequence, one that should always be taken into account in any calculation. And this consequence will tend to outweigh the marginally good consequences of supposedly justifiable violations of a rule. The argument goes: in the vast majority of cases, if not demonstrably in all cases, the person who adopts the act utilitarian approach will end up justifying the same thing as the person who adopts the rule utilitarian approach. If we use the act utilitarian approach, we must be scrupulously certain that we are not giving ourselves any undue advantage; that the results we calculate are not simply wishful thinking; and that we consider all the results of the action, including the effect that it will have on society. To be morally justifiable, moreover, the results must be such that the action is right not only for me but for anyone in similar circumstances. If the results are, then we already have the basis for generalizing an exception to the rule, or for changing the rule to include the exception, which results in a slightly different rule. Hence the result is equivalent to adopting a rule utilitarian approach.

Objections to Utilitarianism

One of the classic statements of utilitarianism was given by John Stuart Mill (1806–1873) in his work *Utilitarianism,* first published in 1861. In it he answers a number of arguments against utilitarianism. One objection claims that utilitarianism is ungodly, because it proposes utility, rather than the Bible or God, as a basis for moral judgments. Mill's reply was, in some ways, a charming one. He indicated that because God was benevolent and loved His creatures, He would wish them to be happy. Hence, what He commands are those actions that tend to produce the greatest amount of good or happiness for the greatest number. What He forbids are those actions that tend to produce more harm than good or happiness. Hence, Mill argued, the actions commanded and forbidden by utilitarianism are the same as the actions commanded and forbidden by God. The advantage of adopting utilitarianism is that we have a technique for deciding moral questions on which we have no direct information from God. Even the Ten Commandments require interpretation. Utilitarianism gives us the tool necessary for deciding those acts of killing (e.g., self defense) that are compatible with the commandment "Thou shalt not kill," and those that are not.

A second objection frequently brought against utilitarianism is that no one has the time to calculate all the consequences of an action beforehand. This is frequently true. But utilitarianism does not require that we actually calculate all the consequences before we act, any more than the religious person must reread the Bible before he acts. As we saw with rule utilitarianism, we have the history of mankind on which to build. We know that murder is wrong and need not calculate the results of murder every time we get angry at someone. We know that the bad results of murder outweigh the good. This is obvious, and is a part of our general knowledge. But if we are ever questioned as to why murder is wrong, or if we ever seriously want to consider whether murder is wrong, we have in utilitarianism the means for arriving at a decision about the morality of murder, together with knowledge of why it is wrong. This also holds regarding other actions. If ever we are uncertain about the morality of an action, we know how to think about resolving the issue; we are not always in a moral quandary. But when we are faced with very difficult moral choices, we should stop and consider the consequences, weigh them, and arrive at the best possible conclusion. Moreover, the calculation is usually a fairly simple one. For instance, when lying *seems* advantageous, we focus on the advantage to ourselves and play down the harm done in the long run to either ourselves or to others. We can resist the temptation to lie by quickly producing a more accurate calculation of the consequences, which means using a rule utilitarian approach, in which the disadvantages are more clearly set out.

A third objection to utilitarianism is that we cannot know the full results of any action, nor can we accurately weigh the different kinds of good and evil that result. The calculation is artificial and not practical.

The reply to the first part of the objection is twofold. First, as we have already seen, in judging most actions we have the benefit of the consequences of similar actions done in the past. Second, we can frequently foresee a large number of possible, if not actual, consequences; among these are some consequences so important that they dominate the calculation. This observation also applies to the second part of the objection. For instance, the utilitarian approach does not require mathematically precise calculations; it is not possible to get mathematical precision in most calculations dealing with the morality of actions. But in the more standard cases the consequences are sufficiently obvious; the good or the bad predominates so clearly that great precision is not necessary. In difficult cases, where the calculation is not clear, we cannot be sure we are correct in our moral assessment, and we should be ready to revise it if we find our calculation is mistaken. This is not a defect of the theory but a statement of the human condition and the nature of morality. To those who claim that we cannot compare different values and weigh them, we can simply reply that all of us make such calculations everyday; we weigh present against future good, and one value against another, all the time. The claim that it cannot be done is false, and contrary to our ordinary experience.

A fourth objection concerns the interpretation to be given to the utilitarian principle itself. The principle claims that an action is right if it tends to produce the greatest good for the greatest number of persons affected by it. But, the objection goes, the formulation is ambiguous. Are we to put our emphasis on the greatest aggregate of good, or are we to concern ourselves with the good of the greatest number? Suppose, for instance, we had to choose between two cases. Action A results in 1,000 units of good for 100 people and 10 units of good for 9,900 people. Action B results in 19.9 units of good for each of the 10,000 people. In both cases we have a total of 199,000 units of good. If the resulting good at issue is the standard of living of a community, utilitarianism would have us conclude that there is no moral difference between the two cases. A society in which a few live at a very prosperous level, and the many live at a very much lower level, is no better than another society in which all the people live at a level almost twice as high as the latter group in the first community. Such a result, to the critics, seems clearly mistaken. To make the case even stronger, we can add one unit of good to the privileged group in the first society; because that society now has more good than its alternative, action A is morally better than action B. This, the objection continues, runs counter to our moral intuitions. Nor can we remedy the situation by putting the emphasis on the number of people rather than on the greatest good, because the problem will still remain.

The utilitarian counter to the objection takes two forms, usually offered jointly. The first is that the objection, though theoretically possible, is in real life implausible. The case is fabricated, the product of a philosopher's imagination; the case cannot be filled out in any concrete, historical detail. If one ever had such a choice, we should choose what produces good for more people rather than maximizing the greater good of a small number, because this choice maximizes good in the long run. This fact has to be added to the calculation. The foregoing case trades on an obvious discrepancy between the few and the many. And this discrepancy has negative consequences that the calculation does not take into account. The case seems to work because it is manipulated in such a way that the bad consequences, which result from the great discrepancy between the two groups, are not fully considered. If our moral intuitions tell us the calculation is mistaken, this is an indication that we have miscalculated, and that we are ignoring some negative component in the case. Once this has been said, the utilitarian is then content to claim that there may well be cases in which equal good is produced by two different actions, and that in such a case one may choose either alternative. This was made clear earlier, in the explanation of utilitarianism. Hence, this observation is not a criticism of the position; it is a result that is accepted by the utilitarian.

Utilitarianism and Justice

Even if the utilitarian's answers to the previous objections are accepted, some critics claim that the theory cannot account for justice and, in some instances, runs counter to it. The claim is not a new one, because it was raised and answered by Mill in *Utilitarianism*. But the criticism has persisted and remains a live issue today. The typical argument is as follows: Suppose we consider a small town in the western United States, during the nineteenth century. Law and order are newly established. Jim James is caught with a stolen horse and accused of being a horse thief. He claims he bought it from a passing stranger. The penalty for stealing horses is hanging. The judge in the town, unbeknownst to anyone, happened to have been passing by and actually witnessed the purchase. He was hidden by trees and was therefore not seen by Jim. The judge, it turns out, was in the vicinity only because he was buying some illegal whiskey. The town is outraged by the horse theft and wants an example made of Jim. If the judge comes forward as a witness he will have to say what he was doing out in the woods; he will then be dismissed by the town, another judge will not be available for some time, and the town will suffer. In addition, the people of the town are so convinced that Jim is guilty that they will probably hang him anyway. Innocent people may well be killed in trying to prevent this. Taking all this into account the judge decides it is better for him not to come forward with his information. He should condemn Jim and have him hanged. Jim will be killed no matter what. And more harm than good will come to the town if he tries to defend him.

The utilitarian calculation, its critics maintain, would result in saying that the right thing to do is to condemn an innocent man. But condemning an innocent man is obviously unjust. Hence it might be said that utilitarianism results in saying that to do what is obviously unjust is the morally right thing to do. The conclusion is that utilitarianism cannot be an accurate account of morality, nor can it be an appropriate way to make moral judgments.

In its generalized form the argument maintains that justice does not depend on consequences. Justice consists in giving each person his due, or treating people equitably. Such considerations do not depend on consequences. It is unjust to condemn an innocent person regardless of whether doing so produces better consequences than not doing so. Because consequences are irrelevant, justice is not based on utility, and utilitarianism is therefore inadequate as a foundation of justice.

The objection has not convinced all utilitarians. The standard reply is that in the foregoing example, or in any other situation like it, the objection is plausible only because not all the results are considered. The case does not end with the hanging. We must consider the consciences of the judge, and of the people of the town. What will the reaction be when the truth is discovered? What happens to the notion of justice if the judge continues to try to guess the consequences in each case that comes before him? When we consider all these effects, then we see that, in the long run, more harm than good is done by condemning an innocent man than by not condemning him. We must consider the results of this practice, not those of some isolated, hypothetical action whose results are arbitrarily cut off at a convenient point for the objector.

Many critics have not been satisfied by the reply. Nor have they been convinced by attempts to give a utilitarian account of justice. As a result, some people have advocated using two conjoint principles in moral evaluation: the principle of utility and the principle of justice. In most cases the principle of utility will take precedence, but in those cases in which the principle seems to go against justice, then the principle of justice takes precedence. The justification for this approach is itself utilitarian, namely, that it produces the best results or the greatest amount of good on the whole.

Despite the debate between the utilitarians and their opponents on the issue of justice, *in most cases* both sides will agree on which actions are just. If a case involves condemning an innocent man, most utilitarians will admit that such an action is morally wrong, and will show how such an action is not in fact required by utilitarianism. For practical purposes, this observation is important. It indicates that whether or not utilitarianism can be so formulated as to give an adequate theoretical account of justice, both sides can frequently agree on which actions are just. Because, from the practical point of view, we are interested in rendering moral decisions about cases, we can do so without having to resolve fully the theoretical issue. It is only when the two approaches—the utilitarian and the deontological—actually result in divergent moral judgments that we will have to choose between them. But if such cases exist, they can be treated separately, as special cases. In most instances, the utilitarian and the deontological approaches to justice, as well as to the moral evaluation of actions and practices, will result in similar moral judgments. This conclusion should not be surprising, because both utilitarianism and deontological theories are attempts to systematize, and provide the reasoned ground for, our moral judgments. Both have as their starting points the large number of actions that we agree are morally right, and those that we agree are morally wrong.

Applying Utilitarianism

Having seen the arguments in favor of utilitarianism, and the answers to some objections, we can now draw the various threads of the description of the technique together, and review the method of carrying out a utilitarian analysis.

The first step is to specify, clearly, the action that one wishes to consider. Identifying the action is not always easy. One should avoid the temptation to characterize the action too quickly as being one that has the connotations of either morality or immorality. If an analysis is required it is because the morality of the action is unknown, or questioned, or challenged. In a complex situation, clarifying which action one is to analyze is an essential first step. The action, once determined, is best described in morally neutral language. For example, the phrase "killing human beings" is a neutral description, compared with "murdering human beings." The latter phrase characterizes the killing as unjustifiable. And the addition of the term self-defense to either phrase characterizes the act as being justifiable.

How specific do we have to be in characterizing the action? Act utilitarianism, as we explained, demands that we guess all the consequences of a particular act—something we cannot possibly do with any degree of accuracy. Rule utilitarianism asks us to consider the general consequences of the kind of act in question, and this is usually possible because of the accumulated store of social information concerning kinds of actions. The action should be described not as unique, but as capable of being subsumed under a general rule.

Now to the second step. Having once clarified the act we wish to evaluate, we must carefully specify all those affected by the action. There is often a strong temptation to ignore some of those affected, and to ignore, as well, the general effects of the action on society. Someone who is tempted to falsify a record, for instance, might consider only his personal gain versus the harm done to other persons immediately affected by the falsification. Those immediately affected must certainly be considered, but rarely are the agent and victim the only ones affected. This might be the case on a desert island inhabited by only two people who would never leave it. But morality, as a social practice, is not properly tested in this way. Acts are usually performed in social contexts, and it is these acts with which we are most concerned in business ethics. Even those who are remotely affected, including business and society as a whole, should be specified, and they must all be considered in the evaluation of an action.

The third step is to formulate carefully and objectively the good and bad consequences for all those persons who would be affected. The calculation need not proceed immediately to a detailed examination of the good and bad for each individual. At this point, one should look for the salient features. Is there a dominant consideration? Are certain consequences so serious that we do not need to carry out a detailed analysis of all the consequences? Suppose, for example that someone is causing us difficulty in business and we wish that person were out of the way, so we consider killing that person. We should not need to weigh all the consequences of killing him. We know that the practice of eliminating annoying people by killing them does an overwhelming amount of harm, not only to those killed but to society as well. A brief moment's reflection tells us the action is wrong. And the social harm is a dominant consideration. To entertain the possibility of some instance being a general exception to this consideration would require very extraordinary circumstances. Unless we had such extraordinary circumstances—as in the case of self-defense—we need not calculate further. However, if we wished to prove to someone that killing a competitor is immoral, we would carry out the calculation. It is very clear that we do not have to review similar cases each time. Were we to pursue the morality of the action further, we need consider only briefly whether the good done the perpetrator, or one's company, can possibly justify the harm done to the individual killed and to society—remembering that if it is right for me, it will be right for all others to kill their competitors (including us!). The answer is clearly that the action is immoral.

In more complicated cases, however, we shall have to consider all the good and bad consequences of the action under consideration, starting with the consequences on those principally affected. But even in these cases we should look for both the dominant aspects of the case and the outstanding consequences. These will help to guide us in our analysis.

There is sometimes disagreement about the consequences of some actions. There are also possible disagreements about the dominant considerations in a case, and whether they are in fact overridden by other consequences. The application of utilitarianism is a not an automatic procedure. It requires thought, analysis, and serious impartial consideration of facts and consequences. When utilitarians argue among themselves about unclear cases, the arguments sometimes hinge on the description of the action, the facts, and the consequences; sometimes on the choice of the dominant consideration; sometimes on the relative weight given to some important conflicting factors.

We have already seen that we cannot expect mathematical precision. Talk of relative weights, and of summing up good and bad and comparing them, is appropriate only on a gross level. We can make approximations, and we should make these as explicit as we can. We know how to weigh the pain of going to a dentist against the pain of a toothache, and how to weigh the future pain of not going, and the pleasure of going to have a tooth fixed. That is a simple model of what the calculation is like. If we are making the analysis for ourselves, we must try to be objective; but we probably do not have to convince ourselves of the objectivity of our analysis. If we are using the method to convince others of the morality or immorality of an action, we should state, as clearly as possible, not only our evaluations but also why we make them as we do.

Once we have determined all the good and all the bad results for those primarily affected by the action, we compare the results. If the bad is over-whelming, further calculation may not be necessary. But even if the good is overwhelming, we should consider the results of the rule's being generally followed. This may be the dominant consideration. Whether or not it is, the good and the bad of adopting the rule is added to the good or bad results for those primarily affected; this is then summed. If the calculation produces overwhelming good or bad, further calculation may not be necessary. If the calculation is close, then we should consider, in as much detail as is reasonable, those indirectly affected by the action. The analysis gets wider and wider and more and more detailed, depending on how close the good and bad are, how far-reaching the action is, and what other considerations seem appropriate. Reasonableness is the guide as to when to end the calculation.

Once we have summed all the good and bad, having considered the consequences on all those affected by an action, we know whether that kind of action is morally good or bad. If it produces more harm than good, it is in general immoral. If it produces more good than harm, it is in general moral. But one more step is required.

We must now ask about the action as it takes place in the given context. What are the other choices, given this context? Is the choice simply to do the action or not to do it? Is it to kill my competitor or not to kill him? If that is the only question, then, in normal circumstances, we know what to do. Killing is wrong because it produces more harm than good. Not killing is morally right because it produces more good than harm. Hence, we should not kill our competitor.

Frequently, however, our choices are more complex, and we are faced with not only giving in or not giving in to an immoral temptation, but also with a number of alternative actions. If the choice is not simply doing x or not doing x, then we can and should evaluate the various alternatives in the same way that we did the original action. The action that produces the most good is the best one. Morally, we are not allowed to choose an act that produces more bad than good, if we have the alternative of choosing one that produces more good than bad. As we saw earlier, if faced with a choice between two actions, both of which produce more bad than good, we should choose the lesser of two evils. But often, if we use our moral imagination, we may find that there is another alternative: z; this z produces more good, or less bad, than the alternatives we originally considered. Utilitarianism encourages us to look for these other, better alternatives, because it encourages us to choose the best action available. The temptation to limit one's choices, or to consider too few alternatives, or to entertain false dilemmas, frequently obscures the fact that, correctly applied, the utilitarian technique does not preclude moral imagination; it demands it.

To sum up, in applying the utilitarian approach to evaluating the morality of an action, we should

1. Accurately state the action to be evaluated.
2. Identify all those who are directly and indirectly affected by the action.
3. Consider whether there is some dominant, obvious consideration that carries such importance as to outweigh other considerations.
4. Specify all the pertinent good and bad consequences of the action for those directly affected, as far into the future as appears appropriate, and imaginatively consider various possible outcomes, and the likelihood of their occurring.
5. Weigh the total good results against the total bad results, considering quantity, duration, propinquity or remoteness, fecundity, and purity for each value (kind of good and kind of bad), and the relative importance of these values.
6. Carry out a similar analysis, if necessary, for those indirectly affected, as well as for society as a whole.
7. Sum up all the good and bad consequences. If the action produces more good than bad, the action is morally right; if it produces more bad than good, it is morally wrong.
8. Consider, imaginatively, whether there are various alternatives other than simply doing or not doing the action, and carry out a similar analysis for each of the other alternative actions.
9. Compare the results of the various actions. The action that produces the most good (or the least bad, if none produces more good than bad) among those available is the morally proper action to perform.

Utilitarianism and Bribery

Most people in the United States readily acknowledge that bribery is immoral. Bribery in business is an interesting kind of action to examine from a utilitarian point of view, because those who engage in bribery frequently justify their actions on something similar to utilitarian grounds.

Consider an airplane manufacturer who has spent enormous amounts of money developing a new airplane. The company badly needs cash because it is financially overextended. If it does not get some large orders soon, it will have to close down part of its operation. Doing that will put several thousand workers out of jobs. The result will be not only disastrous for the workers but also for the town in which they live. The president of the company has been trying to interest the government in a large purchase. He learns that one of the key people in charge of making the final decision is heavily in debt because of gambling. He quietly contacts that person and offers him $100,000 in cash if he awards the contract to his firm. The contract is awarded, the money is paid, and the business is saved.

When justifying his action, the president of the firm points out all the benefits that result from the bribe: an important government official is much better off financially than he would be otherwise; the government purchases planes that are of good design and workmanship; the airplane company gets the contract and stays in business; and the workers at the plant do not lose their jobs. The town in which they live also benefits. The president therefore concludes that the results are, on the whole, positive. The only negative aspect is that an action, which some people would not approve of, took place. But that is the way of business, he claims.

The argument appears to be a utilitarian one in that it seeks to evaluate the results of the action, weighs the good against the bad, and argues that the good outweighs the bad. The alternative would have been not to give the bribe. But if it had not been given, then the contract may not have been awarded. If it had not been awarded, then all of the bad consequences indicated here would have taken place. No good would have been achieved, and the result would clearly have been worse.

The argument may sound plausible. Nevertheless we believe that bribery is immoral. Is it that utilitarianism does not work in this case? The reply is that it works, but it has not been properly used here. The foregoing account is obviously a one-sided version of the situation. It describes the thinking of the president of the company, his point of view, and his concerns, which, here, is not the moral point of view. The moral point of view is objective and considers all the consequences of an action on all of the people affected by it. We must therefore take into consideration much more than we have so far. We must broaden the picture, look more closely at the effects on the people already mentioned, and then open our vision to those whom we have so far ignored.

Our first step is to state precisely what we wish to evaluate. The president used a truncated *act-utilitarian* approach. Try to state the rule that he is implicitly advocating. Is it that all firms should be allowed to bribe government officials when they have the oportunity to do so? The president puts great emphasis on the negative consequences of not getting the contract, therefore perhaps the rule is that only firms in financial difficulty should be allowed to bribe government officials. If the company is in financial difficulty as the result of poor management, perhaps the rule is that only poorly managed companies should be permitted to bribe government officials. None of these rules sound plausible. The dominant consideration in evaluating all of them is the harm done to the *system* of doing business, to the notion of fair competition, to the equality of opportunity assumed in business, and to the integrity of government officials. If the action is clearly described as a rule for all firms similarly placed, we immediately see that we do not need a detailed analysis.

Even if we accept the president's approach, however, a full examination of the consequences of his action will show the action to be morally unjustifiable. First, what are the consequences of the bribe on the public official? The only consequence we have considered so far is that he gets the money he needs and gives a contract to the company in question. What are the chances that the bribe will be discovered, and what will the consequences be if it is discovered? Bribery is illegal. If the public official's action is discovered, he would in all likelihood be charged with a felony, lose his job, and, if convicted, be heavily fined and/or go to jail. Will his life be better? If he is not found out, he may be blackmailed. He may also be tempted to live beyond his means and end up in a similar situation again. He will have to explain where he got the money to his wife, and perhaps to others. He will not report it on his income tax and will thus be liable for not reporting income. We can continue to consider what might happen to him, and try to evaluate how likely these things are to occur, how seriously they will affect him, and so on.

The good done to the workers, plant, and town have to be given their due weight. But the story does not mention competing firms. What is their situation? Will their workers be out of jobs? Will their towns be depressed? Consider the president of the company. How will he manage to pay $100,000? Where will it come from? How will he pay it without its being recorded and reported to the Internal Revenue Service and to the company auditors? For this project to succeed, it is clear that the president will have to break more laws than the law against bribery. All of his actions will have their effects. If his actions are found out, he will be held liable, may lose his job, and may be imprisoned.

Consider next the effects on the general public. The government official is spending their money. If he is not buying the best equipment at the best price he can get, then he is misusing public funds, and hence harming the taxpayers. If the airplanes he contracted for were the ones he would have purchased anyway, then what was the point of the bribe? But even if he would have placed the order with that firm without a bribe, the $100,000 he received had to come from somewhere. Either it was added to the cost of the planes he purchased, and thereby came from the taxpayers, or it came from the company's profits, and thereby came from the shareholders. In either case the money was taken from those who had legitimate claim to it, and they will be negatively affected to that extent.

The bribe also had an effect on the general system of bidding, on the practice of competition, and on the integrity of those engaged in these practices. Once bribery is an accepted way of doing business, people will no longer get the best value for their money. Does the good done to the person who receives the bribe and to the person who gives it outweigh the possible harm done to them if they are caught? What about the certain harm done to those who must pay more, or who receive less profit, and to the system as a whole?

If we doubt whether the practice of bribery does more harm than good, we need only consider why it is not carried on openly. Why is the giving of a bribe not considered a legitimate part of doing business? The obvious reason is that a few people benefit from the practice but at the expense of a great many other people, including society and business in general.

The argument is a utilitarian one. We did not attempt any exact quantitative evaluation of good and bad results. But in our reasoning we did consider consequences to all those involved, and we avoided arbitrarily cutting off the consequences to be considered.

The president's account did not consider all those affected by the action. He ended his investigation of the consequences at the point most suitable to him. Obviously, the use of the utilitarian calculation does not provide an automatic guarantee of morality. To produce a morally justifiable result, it must be used by someone who truly wishes to find out what is right, and who impartially takes into account the immediate and future consequences for all concerned.

Someone might object that we omitted some important considerations in our analysis. If we have overlooked something important, then we should take that into account and see whether considering what we omitted changes the final outcome. In questions of public policy and public morality, the debate among utilitarians frequently takes place in just this way. Opposing sides may point to omitted considerations, such as the further consequences of an act, or they may argue that insufficient weight is given to one of the consequences discussed, or that a supposedly unlikely outcome can very likely occur.

The mid-1970s witnessed major international scandals concerning bribes, kickbacks, and illegal campaign contributions, both in the United States and abroad. Lockheed Corporation, among others, was involved in giving $12.5 million in bribes and commissions in connection with the sale of $430 million worth of TriStar planes to All Nippon Airways. Carl Kotchian, who later defended his payments in an article in the *Saturday Review*, was forced to resign from his position after the news of the payoffs broke. Defenders of the payments claimed that the practice was not only common in Japan but was expected. Nonetheless, the news rocked Japan even more than it did the United States. The Prime Minister of Japan, Kakuei Tanaka, and four others were forced to resign from the Government and were brought to trial. Legislation attempting to control bribery was proposed both in the United States and Japan, and some of it passed. The results of the bribery were far-reaching. But the Lockheed case was not a simple one. Lockheed did not offer a bribe; rather, the Japanese negotiator demanded it. Are those who accede to bribery as guilty as those who demand bribes? Do the same moral obligations exist in dealing with a corrupt government as in dealing with an honest one? If the people of a country tolerate bribery among their officials, do they in effect consent to the system? If the paying of such commissions is the *sine qua non* of doing business with the government, is it morally justifiable? These are complex questions, the answers to which are not deducible from the general claim that bribery is immoral. Some attempts have been made to control bribery by such legislation as the Foreign Corrupt Practices Act. Other forms of payment made abroad sometimes approach extortion and are not under the control of American laws. How should American companies react? Some, such as Gulf Oil, having once been stung, decided not to make any such payments. To the surprise of many, Gulf's new policy did not decrease its sales or lead to the threatened nationalization of its plants. Many fears were unfounded, and we have learned that the people of some nations have less tolerance for questionable practices than was thought. Firms in many countries have attempted to bring order into the international marketplace by demanding that companies compete on the merit of their products rather than on their skill at secret payments. All these facts must be taken into account in a utilitarian approach to the questions we have raised and left unanswered.

Utilitarianism, far from being a self-serving approach to moral issues, demands careful, objective, impartial evaluation of consequences. It is a widely used—but also an often misused—approach to moral evaluation. A powerful tool of moral reasoning, it is a technique well worth mastering.

Further Reading

BENTHAM, JEREMY. *An Introduction to the Principles of Morals and Legislation.* London: Athlone Press, 1970. (First published, 1789.)

BRANDT, RICHARD B. "Toward a Credible Form of Utilitarianism," in *Morality and the Language of Conduct.* Ed. by H. N. Castaneda and G. Nakhnikian. Detroit: Wayne State University Press, 1963, pp. 107–140.

HARE, R. M. *Moral Thinking.* Oxford: Clarendon Press, 1981.

JACOBY, NEIL H., PETER NEHEMKIS, and RICHARD EELLS. *Bribery and Extortion in World Business.* London: Collier Macmillan Publishers, 1977.

KOTCHIAN, A. CARL. "The Payoff: Lockheed's 70-Day Mission to Tokyo." *Saturday Review,* July 9, 1977, pp. 7–12.

MILL, JOHN STUART. *Utilitarianism.* New York: The Liberal Arts Press, 1957. (First published, 1863.)

MOORE, G. E. *Ethics.* London: Oxford University Press, 1972. (First published, 1912.)

——— *Principia Ethica.* London: Cambridge University Press, 1951. (First published, 1903.)

RAWLS, J. B. "Two Concepts of Rules." *Philosophical Review,* IXIV (1955), pp. 3–32.

SHAPLEN, ROBERT. "Annals of Crime: The Lockheed Incident." *New Yorker,* (January 23, 1978), pp. 48–50; (January 30, 1978), pp. 74–91.

SIDGWICK, H. *The Methods of Ethics.* Indianapolis: Hackett Publishing Company, 1981. (First published, 1874.)

SMART, J. J. C. *An Outline of a System of Utilitarian Ethics.* Melbourne: Melbourne University Press, 1961.

FOUR

Formalism and Justice

The deontological approach to ethics denies the utilitarian claim that the morality of an action depends on its consequences. Deontologists maintain that actions are morally right or wrong independent of their consequences. Moral rightness and wrongness are basic and ultimate moral terms. They do not depend on good and the production of, or failure to produce, good. One's duty is to do what is morally right and to avoid what is morally wrong, irrespective of the consequences of so doing.

The deontological position is a commonly held position, with a long history. In contemporary American society it is associated both with the Judeo-Christian tradition and with a philosophical tradition that goes back to the Greek Stoic philosophers. It includes the formalistic theory of the German philosopher, Immanuel Kant (1724–1804), as well as the theories of many contemporaries, who present moral arguments in terms of justice and rights.

Judeo-Christian Morality

The Judeo-Christian tradition has nurtured the morality of the West for centuries, and of our country since its inception. It is still an extremely potent force. Judeo-Christian morality includes not only a body of moral rules but also a view of what it means to be a human being and to have a set of values. These moral rules, the view of human beings, and their values have, to a large degree, been absorbed into the secular life of the West in general, and of the United States in particular. The morality taught in the pulpits is fairly close to the morality taught in the public schools and in the conventional morality found in our society.

Those aspects of the Judeo-Christian moral heritage that refer explicitly to religion and with man's duty to God can be distinguished from other aspects of morality, those that involve man's relations to his fellow men. Primarily the latter have been taken over by Western society—absorbed, and to a large extent secularized.

The Ten Commandments, at least the last seven, are still widely held to sum up that, morally, we should do (e.g., honor thy father and mother) or not do (e.g., thou shalt not kill). To these are joined the Christian injunction to love your neighbor, together with all that it implies. The Christian virtue of charity is thus added to the Hebraic virtue of justice. The other virtues follow. Because the morality of the Judeo-Christian tradition rested for so many centuries on a foundation of faith, there was great fear that as religious faith diminished, immorality would increase. However, what has tended to happen is that, as religious faith diminished, the virtues and commands that it had sustained found different underpinnings, both secular and philosophical. We have already seen how utilitarians have been quite ready to accept and explain Christian morality, using the utilitarian approach. Philosophical deontologists have also provided a secular foundation for the content of Christian moral norms and virtues.

A *theological* ethics, or theory of morality, is based on theology and hence on the acceptance of divine revelation. There are two dominant positions in this approach. One holds that *divine inspiration* took place not only in ages past through the prophets, Christ, and the authors of the *New Testament*, but that it continues even now, and is available to all believers. According to this view, conscience is God's word, and those who are in tune with Him know what is right and what is wrong. Viewed as an ethical theory, it claims that what is right and what is wrong is determined by God, and that He communicates knowledge of right and wrong directly to His followers. The second position holds that God determines what is right and what is wrong, that He revealed it through His prophets, Christ, and the authors of the *New Testament*, but that this revelation requires interpretation. In some Christian religions the interpretation is done by each individual; in others it is done by either the church collectively or by special persons in the church, who speak authoritatively about the morality of actions.

According to these interpretations, morality rests ultimately on God, and is held because of revelation. Though members of our society frequently guide their lives by such an ethic, a religiously based moral argument is frequently discounted by those not practicing the same faith as the person who puts forth the argument. Because the argument has as a central feature belief in God and in a certain kind of revelation, those who do not believe in God, or who believe in a different kind of revelation, are not logically compelled by such an argument.

Ever since the ancient Greeks, some people have asked whether an action is right because God says it is, or whether God says an action is morally right because it is morally right. In the former case, God could make murder, theft, or lying moral if He chose to do so. In the latter case, He could not. God knows those actions are morally wrong, and helps us know this through His revelation. But the rightness or wrongness of the actions are not subject to His whim. Because He made us in a certain way, the moral rules by which we should live have been built into our nature as human beings. Ultimately they depend on God; but we need not constantly ask or wonder whether He has changed His mind, and whether what He once said was immoral is today moral.

Three points should be made clear. First, if one believes that he knows, through direct divine intervention, which actions are right and which are wrong, then he has no need of a philosophical ethical theory, unless he wishes to defend his moral judgments to those who disagree with him or to those who do not believe in God's direct intervention.

Second, those who do not believe in God's direct personal moral communication to each person must interpret the Ten Commandments and the injunction to love one's neighbor. What specific actions do these prescriptions and proscriptions command or forbid? Is killing in self-defense a justifiable form of killing? Is killing in defense of one's property defensible? Both actions are forms of killing. The Commandment, "Thou shalt not kill," does not come with any exceptions built into it. How, if at all, do we justify exceptions? The rules by which we arrive at and justify exceptions make up part of a theory of morality, and are therefore part of an ethical system. If these rules are defended only on the basis of scripture, then the defenses are designed for the religious believer.

The third point is that what is demanded by a religious-based morality might also be justifiable on nonreligious grounds. The content of religious morality might be acceptable, at least in large part, to nonreligious people. Both they and religious believers might find philosophical grounds adequate to support at least the portion of morality that is not specifically religious. Many in the history of philosophy have defended this position, including such a major figure as Aquinas. Both Mill and Kant thought they were supplying a philosophical ethical theory that could support a Christian morality.

Churches have been effective in inculcating moral norms and in teaching and preaching morality in the marketplace as well as in other areas of life. They have emphasized the development of virtue and of a virtuous character, and have provided their members with role models. They have also developed and preached religious ideals, and ideals of virtue to which the faithful could, and should, aspire. Individual people engaged in business may of course be religious, and their religious convictions may govern the practices in which they engage. Moral individuals who live up to their religious and moral values in their business lives help make and keep businesses and their practices moral. Nonetheless, moral defenses of business practices are not usually made in religious terms to those not practicing one's own religion; nor are most public-policy questions that involve business argued convincingly only in religious terms. If arguments are intended to be convincing to large segments of the population, they are, characteristically, put in such terms that the premises are acceptable to all human beings, and not only to believers.

The Ten Commandments and the commandment to love our neighbor are deontological in form: They are commandments to do certain actions and to refrain from others. The commands do not instruct us to look at the consequences of the actions before deciding whether or not they are right. Hence, they command without concern for consequences. Whether they could be derived by looking at consequences, as utilitarians maintain, is another issue. The present point is that the form they have is not consequentialist, but deontological.

Ethical Formalism

The standard deontological approach in contemporary philosophical ethical theory received its classic formulation in the writings of Immanuel Kant. Both the contemporary deontological approach and Kant's are compatible with the Ten Commandments. But why should we obey these commands? Why should we do what our parents, peers, or society tell us to do? It may be that God, our parents, our peers, and our society inform us correctly about what the right thing to do is. But the reason that the actions are right is not because they command them. Morality and moral obligation cannot be imposed upon us by others; we are the only ones who can impose them on ourselves. If we are moral, we impose a certain way of acting on ourselves because we understand what it means to be a moral being, and understand what sorts of actions are appropriate for such a being. For someone in the Kantian tradition, to be moral is the same as being rational. Just as no one can force us to be rational, no one can force us to be moral. In this view, if we choose to be rational, we also choose to be moral. No reason can be given as to why we should be rational prior to our deciding to be so; to give reasons, to ask for them, or to be convinced by them are all rational activities and so presuppose the acceptance of reason.

If we wish to see more clearly what it means to be moral, and what morality demands, we must analyze closely what it means to be rational and what the implications of being rational are for our actions. Because morality consists in acting rationally, it only applies to rational beings. The source of morality is to be found in ourselves and in our reason, not in anything external to us. Reason is the same in each of us, therefore what is rational and moral is the same for all of us. According to this view, we act morally when we knowingly choose to act in the way reason demands. The statement of what reason demands in the realm of action is the moral law. By analyzing reason as applied to action, which we can call practical reason, we find the key to morality.

The deontological tradition holds that what makes an action right is not the sum of its consequences but the fact that it conforms to the moral law. The test of conformity to the moral law which an action must pass is a formal one. An action is morally right if it has a certain *form;* it is morally wrong if it does not have that form. The moral law at its highest and most general level states the form that an action must have to be moral. But the moral law at this level, or the highest principle of morality, does not state what content an action must have to be a right action. It states only the form the action must have. Such an approach is therefore called a *formalist ethical approach.*

What is the form an action must have to be moral? How can we state the moral law? The answer lies in the nature of reason. Because being moral is the same as acting rationally, we can determine the moral law by analyzing the nature of reason itself, by analyzing rational activity, and by analyzing what it means to be a rational being.

Consider what we know about reason by examining the reasoning we engage in when we do mathematics. Take the simple process of adding two plus two and getting four. Two plus two do not equal four because our teachers said so. Two plus two equal four independently of our teachers. Two plus two equal four for everyone—for all rational beings—even if they do not know it and even if they add two plus two and get a number other than four. If we uncover the foundations of mathematics we come to understand why two plus two equal four. But even without such an understanding we know that two plus two equal four for everyone, and that the validity of this addition does not depend on our experiencing two things and two other things equaling four things, but on the self-consistency of the mathematical operation.

Because the moral law is the statement of the form of a rational action, we should make explicit some of those characteristics that are central to reason. One of these is *consistency.* Moral actions must not be self-contradictory, and, to the extent that we have a system of morality, moral actions must not contradict one another. A second characteristic is *universality.* Because reason is the same for all, what is rational for me is rational for everyone else, and what is rational for anyone else is rational for me. A third characteristic of reason, which we found exemplified in mathematics and which we also find characterizing the moral law, is that it is a priori, or not based on experience. It applies to experience but it is not derived from it, nor is its truth dependent on it. This is the reason why the morality of an action does not depend on consequences.

Because the moral law is a law, it issues a command or states an imperative—something which must be done. The imperative is an unconditional one. It states what everyone is to do because it is a command of reason. Following the somewhat technical terminology of Kant, the moral law commands *categorically,* not hypothetically. A hypothetical imperative states that an action should be done if, or on the hypothesis that, one wishes to achieve a certain end. Thus, "If you wish to do well in school, study!" is a hypothetical imperative. Not everyone is required to go to school and not everyone is required to study. The moral law, however, is not stated in hypothetical form. It is not something we can choose to follow or not, depending on whether we wish to achieve this or that end. We are bound by the injunction to be moral no matter what else we wish to do. The moral law binds unconditionally. Kant called the statement of the moral law, or of the supreme principle of morality, the *Categorical Imperative.* We noted that the Ten Commandments are also stated in categorical form. "Thou shalt not kill" states a moral norm or principle, applicable to all and binding on all unconditionally. But it is an imperative with content. Therefore it is, according to the formalist approach, not the highest moral principle; it is a principle, an imperative, a norm that is *a* moral principle because it is in accord with the moral law, but it is not *the* principle of morality. It is a second-order or second-level principle. The highest moral principle—the Categorical Imperative—states the *form* moral actions have, and provides the criteria against which we can test whether an action or a second-order principle is moral. Kant gave three formulations of the Categorical Imperative. These state three aspects of it, or three formal conditions that an action must have if it is to be a moral action.

For an action to be a moral action: (1) it must be possible for it to be made consistently universal; (2) it must respect rational beings as ends in themselves; and (3) it must stem from, and respect, the autonomy of rational beings. These three conditions are all derivable from an analysis of reason and of what it means to be a rational being.

Universalization

Actions, strictly speaking, are specific intentional bodily movements that human beings do in a context and for a purpose. An action itself, therefore, is individual and not universal. It is what it is. Similarly, an action cannot contradict another action. We can avoid this difficulty, however, by speaking of a description of an action, of a rule or principle of action, or of the maxim of an action. It is the rule, principle, or maxim of an action that we test when we wish to determine whether an action is moral. The maxim of an action is a careful statement or description of its essential features. If the maxim is put in imperative form, it is a rule of action. The content of the rule can be considered a second-order principle of action telling us what we ought to do.

The a priori products of reason are universal and self-consistent. If an action is to be a moral action, it must have a rational form. This means that the rule, principle, or maxim of the action must be capable of being consistently universalized. If an action is moral for me it must be moral for everyone. We are all commanded to do what is morally right, therefore any action we are all commanded to do must be such that in doing it, none of us interferes with or precludes the other's doing it. An action that does not have this form is an immoral action. Note, moreover, that in asking whether the action can be consistently universalized we are not asking, as we would from a consequentialist point of view, what the results of everyone's doing that action would be. We need not suppose that everyone would do the action. We are inquiring whether the rule, principle, or maxim of the action is internally consistent when made universal.

Let us consider some examples, to see how we can test the morality of an action. Is murder wrong? Is lying wrong? Murder is the killing of a human being without a justifying reason. Defining it in this way, of course, characterizes it as unjustifiable from the start. So let us consider instead the action of killing, in anger, another human being. Stated as a rule it would read: "Kill others whenever you are angry at them." Can this rule be made consistently universal? The test is whether there is internal consistency within the rule when applied to everyone. Because it is likely that everyone gets angry at someone at some time, and because it is likely that everyone has had someone angry at him at some time, if everyone followed the rule we would kill each other off. But it is not this consequence that makes the action immoral, for if we all followed this rule none of us would be alive to continue following it. The rule, therefore, when made universal, leads to its own demise, and therein lies its inconsistency. On the other hand, consider the action of respecting human life. The rule reads: "Respect human life." If the rule were made universal, everyone would respect everyone else's life. The rule is consistent, for we can all go on respecting human life indefinitely. Following the rule does not lead to the rule's demise.

Now consider lying. The rule is: "Lie!" Can it be made universal, consistently? The answer is that it cannot. If everyone lied, then no one would believe anyone else. But if no one believed anyone else, the possibility of lying would disappear. Hence lying cannot be made consistently universal. "Tell the truth!" however, is a rule everyone can always follow. If we all tell the truth we can all believe one another. We can go on telling the truth indefinitely. There is no inconsistency in the rule when made universal. Hence, it is a moral rule.

The formulation of the Categorical Imperative that Kant gave concerning this condition of consistent universalization was, "Act only according to that maxim by which you can at the same time will that it should become a universal law."[1]

Respect for Rational Beings

A rational being can understand the need for consistency in action. A rational being is also conscious of himself as a person, as an entity who is valuable in himself, and as a being that is an end in itself. Because of this a rational being is worthwhile, has dignity, and is worthy of respect. Hence each person should be treated by every person as an end, with respect and dignity.

We all use objects for our own purposes, as means to our own ends. We also use people as a means to an end when, for instance, they serve us in a store or restaurant or when we hire them to do what we want done. But even when we treat people as means we should not forget that they always remain ends. Thus, Kant formulated a second version of the Categorical Imperative: "Act so that you treat humanity, whether in your own person or in that of another, always as an end and never as a means only."[2]

This formulation of the Categorical Imperative, according to Kant, is simply a different statement of the supreme moral law contained in the first formulation. Consequently, it commands and forbids the same actions as the first

---

[1] Immanuel Kant, *Foundations of the Metaphysics of Morals* (Indianapolis: Bobbs-Merrill Co., Inc., 1969), p. 44.
[2] Ibid., p. 44.

formulation. Consider the two actions we examined earlier. If we kill people in anger, or to get them out of our way, we clearly do not treat them with respect. We use them exclusively as means to what we want and not as ends in themselves. When we lie to them we intend to deceive them, we are denying their right to the truth, and are attempting to achieve our own ends at their expense. We treat them as the means to get what we want, or to avoid unpleasantness or punishment. Lying, theft, and murder all involve treating people only as means, not as ends, and therefore we do not treat them with the respect they deserve as rational beings.

The kind of treatment that rational beings deserve, as ends in themselves, is sometimes put in terms of rights. People thus have the right to life, and this right imposes obligations on others not to take their life, and, in certain conditions, to help them preserve it. A person's right to his property imposes the obligation on others not to take that property. This approach to rights maintains that people have rights because of the kinds of beings they are, and denies that rights are dependent on consequences.

Autonomy

Because being moral is the same as acting rationally, morality is not imposed on persons from the outside. It is part of their nature. The moral law is recognized by them insofar as they recognize that they are rational beings and belong to the kingdom of beings who are ends in themselves. The moral law is self-imposed and self-recognized. This position does not deny either that people act immorally or that many people act only on the level of conventional morality. When they act in conformity with conventional morality, they may act in conformity with what the moral law commands. But to have true personal moral worth, their actions should not only conform with the moral law; their actions should be done with consciousness of the moral law, and of the fact that they are obeying it.

There are three aspects of morality that are captured in the notion of autonomy: freedom, the self-imposition of the moral law, and the universal acceptability of the moral law.

Rational beings are the only entities that can be full-fledged members of the moral community because morality requires both the possibility of conceiving and understanding the moral law, and the possibility of knowingly and willingly acting in accordance with it. Animals are not moral beings because they fail in both these respects. They are not able to conceive of the moral law, and they are not able to choose whether to act in accordance with it. Animals act from instinct and in reaction to immediate sensations. Human beings are able to inhibit and control their instincts, passions, and drives, and are able to examine their actions before performing them. Their reason enables them to do so. The ability to so act carries with it the obligation to do so, and constitutes the freedom of the rational being. Nonrational entities that act only instinctively and in response to present stimuli are not free. They are determined by their instincts and stimuli. The ability to override instincts and stimuli constitutes the freedom of the human being. This freedom, which we can call the rational freedom of self-determination, becomes moral freedom when we choose to act in accordance with the moral law. This moral freedom can be called the rational freedom of self-perfection. The first type of freedom is a human being's ability to choose to act morally or immorally. But he acts morally only when he acts in accordance with the demands of reason. When acting in this way, he exercises his moral freedom, and, from the moral point of view, perfects himself.

The second aspect of autonomy emphasizes the fact that moral beings give themselves the moral law. As ends in themselves, moral beings are not subservient to anyone else. Each determines the moral law for himself in accordance with reason. Each imposes it upon himself and accepts its demands for himself. This is simply a function of the rational being's freedom and of his dignity as an end in himself. But though each person gives himself the moral law he cannot prescribe anything he wants. He is bound by reason and its demands. Because reason is the same for all rational beings, we each give ourselves the same moral law. The Categorical Imperative is the same for all of us, though imposed by each of us and recognized by each of us for ourselves. Kant's third formulation of the Categorical Imperative is, "Act only so that the will through its maxims could regard itself at the same time as universally lawgiving."[3]

The third aspect of autonomy, the universal acceptability of the moral law, is a function of the fact that each moral being gives himself the moral law. This aspect provides a third test of moral rules or principles. If we wish to see whether a rule, principle, or maxim is moral we should ask if what the rule commands would be acceptable to all rational beings acting rationally. Hence in considering murder, lying, theft, and so on, we must consider the action not only from the point of view of the agent of the action but also from the point of view of the receiver, that is, the person who is murdered, lied to, stolen from. Rational beings will all see that they do not want murder, lying, and theft to be universal laws applied to themselves as well as to others. They do not want to be murdered, lied to, stolen from. It is not simply a matter, however, of their own good being violated, though it is also that. As rational beings they also accept limitations on what they permit themselves to do, for they understand that they live in a community. Each sees the necessity of restricting his own actions, just as he expects others to restrict theirs. The test of the morality of a rule is not whether people in fact accept it. The test is whether all rational beings, thinking rationally, would accept it regardless of whether they were the agents or the receivers of the actions.

Application of the Moral Law

The Categorical Imperative, or the ultimate principle of morality, according to the dominant deontological position, requires that any second-order moral

---

[3] Ibid., p. 59.

rule or principle must be capable of being consistently universalized, must respect the dignity of persons, and must be acceptable to rational beings. Any action ruled out by one of these criteria should be ruled out by the other two. But sometimes one of the tests is clearer and leads more obviously to a moral evaluation than another. In testing whether the principle of an action is moral, therefore, it is prudent to apply all three tests. If the principle passes all three, it is moral; if it fails any one of the three, it is immoral.

There are two difficulties in attempting to apply this test to actions. One involves determining the level of generality of the principle on which we are acting; the second involves a clash between the actions that two second-order moral principles command.

The Level of Generality

Consider once again the case of the airplane manufacturer who wishes to save his company and feels that in order to do so he must bribe a potential foreign purchaser. What is the rule on which he is acting? We might consider the rule to be, "Bribe!" If we attempt to universalize the principle involved, we quickly see that it is self-contradictory. If bribery were made a universal principle it would no longer be bribery but a universal way of doing business. Bribery only works with a background of nonbribery, for it is a way of gaining special advantage. If everyone always gained advantage in this way, the advantage would no longer be special. Universal bribery is self-contradictory. Hence it is immoral. Bribery also fails the second and third tests. However, one failure is enough to make clear its immoral status.

The airplane manufacturer, however, might protest that he was not acting on the rule, "Bribe!" He would not advocate everyone always bribing everyone else. Rather, he advocates bribery only in certain select circumstances. The rule might be, "Bribe only when necessary to keep your company from going bankrupt!" Hence the test of universality requires only that all companies threatened with bankruptcy engage in bribery, not that all companies do so. Because the other companies do not engage in bribery, they form the necessary background for the bribery to be successful. But consider this principle more carefully. Would rational beings accept this principle as reasonable? Would everyone agree that a company facing bankruptcy should act in this way? Why should a company that is so managed as to be facing bankruptcy be allowed to gain special advantage? No company competing with other companies is likely to accept such a principle; nor are the people of a society, who will eventually pay for the bribe in higher prices. The principle clearly fails the third test, and hence is immoral.

The point of the airplane manufacturer, however, is partially correct. We can construe the principle of actions more or less broadly. When we considered the injunction, "Kill other human beings!" we saw that it could not be made universal without contradiction. But does this mean that self-defense is immoral? Most people would argue that it is not. The principle of self-defense is, "Kill an unjust attacker if that is the only way you can defend innocent life, whether your own person or that of another!" This can be made universal. It respects innocent life above that of our unjust attacker, and, upon rational consideration, would be accepted by everyone. It is an exception, therefore, to the general injunction, "Do not kill!" The injunction we should ultimately test is the injunction not to kill, together with all its exceptions. That would be a full statement of the principle concerning killing. It is sufficient, however, to test portions of it when considering particular cases. It is not always easy to state accurately the principle of an action, or to test it. It is also not always easy to be completely honest with oneself in stating the principle on which one is really acting. We are frequently tempted to fabricate a maxim that will allow us to do what we wish, rather than stating the maxim or principle on which we are actually acting.

The Clash of Moral Rules

The Categorical Imperative, or the supreme principle of morality, in itself involves no conflict, and principles or maxims of actions that are in accord with it can each be made universal without contradiction. But there are circumstances in which two second-order moral rules or principles, each of which is self-consistent, clash. Such clashes pose a moral dilemma. If we cannot follow either of the rules without violating the other rule, we necessarily violate one of them. We do what we should not do. Are we, in such cases, forced to do what is immoral? We cannot have a moral obligation to do what is immoral. This would be a contradiction, for we would have the moral obligation to do, and to refrain from doing, the action. How can we escape the dilemma?

Suppose that in a slaveholding society we are hiding a runaway slave. The slaveholder comes to the door and asks if we are hiding the slave. Should we lie, and oppose the immoral institution of slavery? or tell the truth, and co-operate in that immoral institution?

In attempting to resolve this and similar cases we should first make sure that we are really facing a dilemma. Is there some third way of acting by which we can avoid performing any action that violates the Categorical Imperative? Could we, in response to the question, not answer but faint instead? Would fainting preclude the necessity of answering the question and still protect the slave? If it would not solve the problem, and no other strategy would, then we must face the dilemma head-on and attempt to resolve it.

There are two standard ways of resolving such dilemmas, both of which should produce the same outcome. One is to construct the principle of our action in such a way that it allows for the exception needed in the resolution of the given case. Just as we construct the rule allowing one to kill as a last resort in the case of self-defense, we can attempt to construct a universal rule about lying which includes certain exceptions, and, in particular, an exception that fits this case. But how do we know we should seek an exception to the prohibition against lying rather than an exception to the prohibition against slavery? Unless the answer is obvious, we can attempt to construct principles allowing an exception to each rule. We then ask which action can be made universal, which respects human beings, which would be universally acceptable to rational beings? The answer is not always clear, hence arguments must be given. For instance, lying to the slaveholder in this case respects human beings; if slavery does not respect human beings, why is it permitted? Someone might argue that the slaveholder has no right to knowledge of where his slave is because slavery is immoral. Hence, in not giving him the information he requests we are not denying him anything he rightfully deserves as a person. We are thus not denying him respect and so are not treating him only as a means. This line of reasoning claims that although the statement made to the slaveholder is false, it is not a lie, because it does not violate anyone's legitimate right to information. Hence, one in effect reconstrues what lying is and the immoral aspect of making false statements. Another line of reasoning admits that the false statement is a lie but argues that it is permissible because all rational persons would accept as a rule the telling of a lie when necessary to protect someone against the unjust violations of human freedom that slavery involves.

A second approach to a clash of second-order rules views each of the moral rules as a prima facie moral rule. A prima facie rule is one which is in general binding. If in a given case only one prima facie moral rule applies, that states our actual duty. But when several prima facie moral rules apply, and when we cannot fulfill all of them, then they cannot all be morally binding. Our actual moral duty in such a case is to obey that prima facie moral rule which is appropriate in the given case. How are we to decide which prima facie duty is our actual moral duty? One answer, defended by some philosophers, is that when we carefully compare conflicting duties we come to see which takes precedence. However, reasons can and usually should be given as to why one rule takes precedence over another. These reasons constitute the justification for breaking a prima facie moral rule. In doing so we are not acting immorally, because prima facie rules do not express absolute moral obligations.

In the example of our hiding the runaway slave we are faced with two prima facie moral rules. One is, "Do not lie." The other is, "Do not engage in or abet slavery." Each rule is one we should follow. But if they conflict, and if we cannot follow both, then we must decide which one takes precedence in this case. The one that takes precedence states our actual moral duty. In weighing the two rules we can argue that slavery is a greater evil, and does more violence to the respect due to human beings than does lying. Hence, using the criterion of respect for persons in evaluating both rules, we see that our obligation to prevent someone from being a slave is greater than our obligation not to lie to a slaveholder seeking his slave.

If we use the notion of prima facie obligations, we can incorporate much of utilitarianism into a deontological ethical position. The command, "Produce the greatest amount of good for the greatest number of people affected by an action" can be considered a prima facie moral obligation. It states a rule or principle that can be universalized, one that respects people as ends, and can be rationally accepted by all. However, from a deontological point of view, this rule or principle is not the highest moral principle. Hence, if what it commands comes into conflict with some other moral principle (e.g., that of justice), it might have to give way. This approach will not satisfy the utilitarian, because he argues that utilitarianism states the highest moral principle. Yet this approach does satisfy many people who feel that utilitarianism states a moral principle, but admit that there are others as well.

When moral principles clash, it is often difficult to decide which takes precedence. In these cases both individuals and society should very carefully and objectively consider the various arguments in support of opposing positions. When a clear decision is not available and we are forced to act, we should act on the basis of the strongest arguments available.

The Ten Commandments can be considered prima facie moral obligations. They and other prima facie moral obligations can also be considered second-order moral principles. Once established, second-order moral principles can be, and most frequently are, used to solve particular cases. Hence one need not apply the Categorical Imperative on every occasion. But we can do so, and, if we ever have reason to doubt the validity of second-order moral principles, it is very important that we submit them to the tests required by the Categorical Imperative. It is in this sense that the Categorical Imperative supplies the basic criterion of morality, even though in ordinary life we tend to solve moral problems by using second-order moral principles.

Justice and Rights

Deontologists claim that justice and rights are not derivable from a utilitarian calculation, and that they do not depend on weighing the consequences of actions. Giving people what they deserve, or what is their due, may not be the best use of resources, from the point of view of utility; however, this fact does not lessen their right to what they deserve, or change the justice of giving them what they deserve.

Justice

Justice, in one of its formulations, consists in giving each person his due, treating equals equally, and unequals unequally. There are various ways of construing what each person is due, however. Individuals might be given what they are due according to their work, their ability, their merit, their need, and so on. Each criterion might be appropriate for certain purposes and in certain conditions. When the male head of a household was the typical wage earner in society, it was generally considered just to pay him more than a single male or a female for the same work. The rationale was that the male head of the household had more mouths to feed and therefore needed more money. But as the social structure changed and women entered the work force in greater numbers, the just thing to do became to pay people equally for equal work, regardless of their personal obligations to support a family.

76

There are different kinds of justice. Compensatory justice consists in compensating someone for a past injustice, or making good some harm he or she has suffered in the past. Retributive justice concerns punishment due a law-breaker or evil-doer. Procedural justice is a term used to designate fair-decision procedures, practices, or agreements. Distributive justice involves the distribution of benefits and burdens, usually by the state.

The contemporary American philosopher, John Rawls,[4] has formulated an influential theory of justice. The technique by which he defends it is Kantian in its approach. He attempts to arrive at principles of distributive justice that are acceptable to all rational persons. The principles would thus be universal, would respect all persons, and would be rationally acceptable to all. In order to find such principles, he suggests we perform a thought experiment. Let us imagine that all people are behind a "veil of ignorance." Behind that veil we would know that we are rational human beings and that we value our own good. But we would not know whether we are rich or poor, members of the upper or lower class, talented or untalented, handicapped or physically and mentally fit, white or black, or a member of some other race, male or female, and so on. This is the question we are to ask ourselves: What principles would we call just or fair if we did not know what place we would have in society? This technique is useful if we wish to achieve objectivity in our moral judgments. It is a technique that we can generalize beyond the way Rawls uses it. It can help us apply the test of autonomous acceptability to any principle or rule we wish to consider. To determine our answer, however, we must, for those behind the veil of ignorance, sometimes build in more knowledge than Rawls allows in his consideration of the basic principles of justice.

Rawls argues that, behind the veil of ignorance, people would agree to two principles of justice. In their simplest formulation in *A Theory of Justice*, Rawls states the two principles as follows:

- First: each person is to have an equal right to the most extensive basic liberty compatible with similar liberty for others.
- Second: social and economic inequalities are to be arranged so that they are both (a) reasonably expected to be to everyone's advantage, and (b) attached to positions and offices open to all.[5]

The first principle guarantees the equal liberty of each person, at a maximal level compatible with the same liberty for everyone else. Individuals want as much freedom as possible to achieve their ends; freedom is a function of rationality, and respect for it is respect for persons. Each person under this rule is to be treated equally. Hence, the first principle fulfills the requirements of the moral law, is morally justifiable, and would be accepted by all rational people. In the political realm, this principle guarantees each person equal political freedom, protection by law, and equal treatment before the law.

[4] John Rawls, *A Theory of Justice* (Cambridge, Mass.: Harvard University Press, 1971).
[5] Ibid., p. 60.

The second principle is more controversial. It has an egalitarian thrust, which some critics deny justice requires. The second part of this principle requires equality of opportunity and access to positions and offices. This is generally accepted. The first part allows for inequalities of wealth and income, influence and prestige. But it claims that such inequalities are acceptable to all only if the least advantaged group is better off as a result of them. For instance, consider the choice between two societies: in Society *A*, all members of the society have a standard of living of 100; in Society *B*, the standard of living of the members of the society varies, ranging from 150 to 200. It would be rational for everyone to choose Society *B*. Although all are not equal in that society—some live better than others—all are better off than in Society *A*. Though the second part of the principle demands equal opportunity, the first part allows for inequalities of success, providing all are better off because of it. The justification for capitalism is sometimes framed in this way. Because all are free to compete, some fare better than others, but the competition increases productivity, raising everyone's standard of living. Hence all are better off than they would otherwise be.

The second principle is attacked both by those who claim that the condition is too strong and by those who claim it is too weak. The former say that as long as there is equal opportunity, there is no injustice in some benefiting from their skill, work, and ingenuity, or from the risks they take. They deserve more than others, and their benefit need not be conditioned by its also producing benefit for the least advantaged group in society. Those who claim the principle is too weak argue that the inequalities allowed may be so great as to be obviously unjust. The principle, they argue, allows the very, very rich to get very much richer as long as the very, very poor get only a little less poor. This, they claim, is unacceptable.

Exactly which principles or practices people would agree to behind the veil of ignorance can be, and is, disputed. But there are some principles rational people would agree to; and using the behind-a-veil-of-ignorance technique is useful for choosing principles with detachment and objectivity.

Rawls's two principles of justice do not handle all questions of justice; in his theory, his principles serve to determine whether the contents of a society's constitution are just. Yet Rawls's theory does suggest an approach to, and provides a framework for, a fruitful social discussion of the justice of various institutions.

If we are faced with the question of whether discrimination in hiring is just, we can step behind a veil of ignorance and ask: if we did not know whether we would be male or female, black or white, would we prefer a system in which there was discrimination or in which there was none? The strategy is, if we were to be assigned our place in society by our worst enemy, would we pick the one or the other system. The point does not hinge on whether or not we are gamblers and risk-takers; it is whether we would all accept the chosen system or structure as just, prior to knowing which place we occupied in it. If all rational people would accept the system or practice, then it would be just.

Rights

The notion of moral rights is another important topic in the deontological approach to ethics. A good many social issues and business ethics topics are discussed in terms of rights. Moral rights are important, normative, justifiable claims or entitlements. The right to life (or the right not to be killed by others) is a justifiable claim, based on our status as rational beings and ends-in-ourselves. Does our status as rational beings confer other rights on us? What are these, and how can they be defended? In the *Declaration of Independence* the American Founding Fathers spoke of the natural rights of life, liberty, and the pursuit of happiness. John Locke had earlier spoken of the natural right to property. Today we speak of human rights, rather than natural rights. Some of these are rights vis-à-vis government, some vis-à-vis other people. Legal rights are rooted in law and protected by it. Moral rights are rooted in morality and in the nature of the members of the moral community. In a just society moral and legal rights overlap to a considerable degree.

Whether rights can be successfully defended by a utilitarian approach is debated. But whether or not they can, an important aspect of "rights talk" is that basic human rights cannot be overridden simply by considerations of utility. A right can only be overridden by another, or other, more basic rights. The purpose of designating certain claims as human rights is to underline their importance so that they will not be treated merely as one more claim among all those that might enter into a case. If we acknowledge the human right to life, for instance, we are precluded from considering whether to murder someone so as to produce more good for others. Similarly, if one has a right not to be discriminated against, it would be improper to argue that discrimination against someone produced more good than nondiscrimination and therefore was morally justified. (It is doubtful whether in real life one could ever successfully argue for either murder or discrimination on utilitarian grounds.) Both utilitarians and non-utilitarians acknowledge rights as important claims that should be respected, even if they ground the claims differently.

Rights are sometimes divided into negative and positive. Negative rights require others to forebear acting in certain ways, and to allow the bearer of the right to act without impediment. The right to life precludes others from killing the bearer of the right. The right to freedom of speech precludes others from preventing one from speaking in the normal circumstances in which speech is appropriate. Negative rights protect an individual from interference both by the government and by other people. Positive rights, on the other hand, require either the government or other individuals to provide the bearer of the right with certain positive goods or opportunities. Economic rights are frequently positive rights. The right to subsistence requires not only that the state and others not prevent one from getting what is necessary for subsistence, but that the state or others provide what is necessary for subsistence if one is unable to do so for oneself. The right to education requires not only that children not be prevented from going to school, but that they be provided with schooling by their society. The line between positive and negative rights is not always clear. The state may, for instance, have to take positive measures to protect the negative right of its citizens to life. Because the right to life entails the positive right to subsistence, this is considered by some the right to life in its positive form. Nonetheless, so long as it is not pushed too far, or made to bear too much weight, the distinction of positive and negative rights can serve some useful purposes.

The language of rights is frequently abused. People have claimed a wide variety of rights. Whether they can be justified is the crucial question. The way moral rights are justified is by presenting moral arguments of the kind we have seen in this and the preceding chapter.

Moral argumentation and reasoning are frequently difficult, and our conclusions on particular disputed issues are often tentative. The process of moral reasoning is a continuous individual and social endeavor, applicable to business as to all other spheres of life. The tools applicable in this endeavor are knowledge of ethical principles and mastery of the techniques of utilitarian and deontological moral argumentation. For most practical issues of business ethics, we need not resolve all the philosophical disputes between the utilitarians and the deontologists. Despite their differing approaches in the great majority of cases, either method, if carefully, subtly, and conscientiously applied, will produce the same moral conclusions with respect to the morality of the practice or act. This should not be surprising, because there is general agreement on the morality of most acts. Many of our moral judgments, moreover, are based on second-order moral principles, which can be grounded both by a utilitarian calculation and by a deontological approach. For practical purposes, the way we choose to ground the second-order principles is irrelevant. Sometimes one approach is easier to apply than another, or yields clearer results. Some people prefer one approach to another. When different approaches lead to different moral evaluations or to conflicting second-order principles, care should be taken to review the accuracy and completeness of each analysis. If the conclusions still diverge, we must ultimately decide on the basis of which argument is stronger or clearer, and which result coheres better with our other moral judgments. If forced to act, we should do so with the realization that we may be mistaken. Despite possible disagreements, both a deontological approach and a utilitarian approach to moral issues provide powerful and widely used techniques of moral argumentation which are useful in resolving an individual's moral problems and in reaching a consensus on public policy.

Further Reading

ARISTOTLE. *The Nicomachean Ethics.* Trans. by Sir David Ross. London: Oxford University Press, Inc., 1961.

DANIELS, NORMAN, ed. *Reading Rawls: Critical Studies of "A Theory of Justice."* New York: Basic Books, Inc., 1974.

DWORKIN, RONALD. *Taking Rights Seriously.* Cambridge, Mass.: Harvard University Press, 1978.

KANT, IMMANUEL. *Foundations of the Metaphysics of Morals: Text and Critical Essays.* Ed., Robert Paul Wolff. Indianapolis: Bobbs-Merrill Co., Inc., 1969.

MARTIN, REX, and JAMES NICKEL. "Recent Work on the Concept of Rights." *American Philosophical Quarterly,* XIX (1980), pp. 165–180.

NOZICK, ROBERT. *Anarchy, State, and Utopia.* New York: Basic Books, Inc., 1974.

OLAFSON, FREDERICK A., ed. *Justice and Social Policy.* Englewood Cliffs, N.J.: Prentice-Hall (Spectrum Books), 1961.

PATON, H. J. *The Categorical Imperative.* Chicago: University of Chicago Press, 1948.

RAWLS, JOHN. *A Theory of Justice.* Cambridge, Mass.: Harvard University Press, 1971.

ROSS, W. D. *The Right and the Good.* Oxford: Clarendon Press, 1930.

FIVE

Moral Responsibility and Corporations

Obligation and responsibility are closely related. In general, we have an obligation or a duty to fulfill our responsibilities, and we are responsible for fulfilling our obligations. Yet duty and responsibility are not the same.

There are many kinds of responsibility. Parents are responsible for their children—for raising them, feeding them, and caring for them. Hence, we speak of parental responsibility. There are responsibilities of citizenship—the responsibility that goes with public office and positions of trust. Certain responsibilities also go with one's job and with one's place in an organization. Some of these responsibilities are legal responsibilities and some are moral responsibilities; some are both, some are neither.

In a general sense each of us is responsible for all of his or her actions. For instance, if I drop and break a friend's expensive vase, I am responsible for having broken it. If, while I am driving a car, a child suddenly dashes out in front of me and I hit him before I can apply the brake, I am responsible for having hit him. In neither case may I be morally responsible; yet if someone asks who broke the vase or who hit the child, the answer is that I am responsible. In what sense am I responsible? I am *causally responsible* in each case. I was the cause of the broken vase and I was the cause of the injured child.

Causal responsibility is an ingredient in both moral and legal responsibility. The causal chain sometimes is a long one. If I give a command and a number of people transmit that command until it is finally carried out, both the ones who carry out the action and I (the one issuing the command) are responsible for it, though each is responsible in a different way in the causal chain. Usually we are most concerned with the proximate cause in the chain, with the person doing the action in question. Yet, especially in questions of agency, the originator of the chain also bears responsibility for the action.

For an action to be a moral action it must be done knowingly and willingly. For instance, though I am causally responsible for things I do in my sleep, I am not morally responsible for them. Actions I do in my sleep are neither moral nor immoral. When we say that I am *morally responsible* for an action, then, we mean both that I did the action (i.e., I am the cause of the result of the action), and that I did the action knowingly and willingly. Instead of saying that I did the action knowingly and willingly, we might say that I did it intentionally. The important point is that I was not forced to do it, that I had a choice, that I knew what I was doing, and that I did it deliberately. I can also be morally responsible for failing to do what I was morally obliged to do; but here too my failure must be intentional. A person who assumes his responsibilities is frequently called a responsible person, and such people are said to act responsibly. There are degrees of knowledge and degrees of deliberation; there are, accordingly, degrees of moral responsibility also.

Excusing Conditions

Moral responsibility may be lessened or mitigated in a number of ways. The conditions that diminish moral responsibility are known as *excusing conditions*. These conditions provide the reasons for lessening or cancelling moral responsibility, and they are related in one way or another to the conditions necessary for a moral action. Excusing conditions fall into one of three categories: those conditions that preclude the possibility of the action; those conditions that preclude or diminish the required knowledge; and those conditions that preclude or diminish the required freedom.

Conditions Precluding the Possibility of Action

To be morally obligatory, an action must be possible. We do not have an obligation to do what is impossible. Likewise, we cannot be morally responsible for doing what is impossible. We are relieved of moral responsibility in those cases in which we cannot fulfill what is demanded of us. The impossibility of doing an action may be a function of the type of action in question, of particular circumstances, or of lack of ability. We are excused from moral responsibility if (a) the action in question is an impossible one to perform; (b) we do not have the ability required in the given case; (c) the opportunity for our performing the action is absent; and (d) the circumstances are beyond our control.

For instance, assuming that I had been driving carefully, with due attention and observing the speed limit (i.e., assuming that I had been driving responsibly), I am not morally responsible for running over the child who darts in front of my car if it was impossible for me to stop the car before hitting him.

83

If I do not know how to swim, I cannot be morally responsible for letting someone drown if the only way I could possibly have saved him was by swimming out to him. Nor, if I knew how to swim, could I have the moral responsibility for saving him if I were not at the scene of the drowning and if there was no reason why I should have been there. Likewise, if, as I swam out to him, he was attacked and killed by a shark, that is a circumstance beyond my control, and it excuses me from moral responsibility for his death. These are just four examples of excusing conditions related to the possibility of performing the action.

Conditions Precluding or Diminishing Required Knowledge

Because knowledge and will are necessary for moral actions, moral responsibility is lessened or removed when these aspects are less than fully present or when they are entirely absent. With respect to knowledge, we can distinguish two excusing conditions: (a) excusable ignorance, and (b) invincible ignorance. Both are failures of knowledge. We are morally responsible for our actions and for the consequences of the things we do. But we cannot possibly know all the consequences of our actions. Which ones are we morally responsible for? We are morally responsible for the immediate and obvious consequences of our actions, as well as for the other reasonably foreseeable consequences of them. Our lack of knowledge may be either about the circumstances giving rise to a particular responsibility or about the consequences of our actions. Lack of knowledge is excusable if through no fault of our own we did not know the circumstances or the consequences. Ignorance, however, does not excuse us from moral responsibility if we could have and should have known of the circumstances or consequences. A common test of whether ignorance is excusable is whether the average person of good will would have known the circumstances or considered the possibility of the consequences in question. Invincible ignorance, or ignorance that we cannot overcome and for which we have no blame, is an excusing condition because we cannot be expected to know what it is impossible for us to know.

Is everyone who was involved in the production of the atomic bomb responsible for it and for the uses to which it has been and might be put? The atom bomb was developed in the United States in such a way that many people did not know what they were working on. Different people were responsible for working on different portions of its development, frequently without any knowledge of the nature of the project as a whole. Many people working in laboratories were responsible for only particular portions of the bomb. They were told that their work was secret and that they would not know the type of end product to which their work was contributing. In many cases they had assurances that what they were working on would help the United States win World War II. Though we can say they were partially responsible for producing the atom bomb in a causal sense, they were not responsible in a moral sense. Adequate knowledge was lacking, and its absence was morally acceptable. What about the leaders of the project? Should we hold the scientists who developed the atom bomb responsible for its use? Could they reasonably have foreseen the uses to which it would be put? They certainly knew that once developed it could be used to destroy both cities and the people in them. Assume that during World War II use of the bomb might have been legitimate. But suppose tomorrow some country that has developed the bomb uses it to attack and destroy a neighboring country, or uses it as a means of extortion. Were the scientists who originally developed the bomb responsible for its immoral use by others later on? Could they, and should they have foreseen such uses? These questions are not easy to answer. Many scientists have pondered their moral responsibility in this area. We can say that those who were ignorant of the nature of the project are free of moral responsibility for its production. We can also say with some confidence that no one could have foreseen all the uses to which the development of atomic bombs would be put. The moral responsibility for the use of these weapons in immoral ways is much greater for those who decide to use them immorally than for those who originally developed them. We do not hold those who invented gunpowder morally responsible for all the harm that has been done with it, most of which they could not possibly have imagined. The degree of moral responsibility is a function of our knowledge, and an absence of knowledge may diminish or remove our moral responsibility.

Conditions Precluding or Diminishing Required Freedom

The third set of excusing conditions has to do with impairments or impediments to our freely choosing the action in question. We can distinguish four: (a) the absence of alternatives; (b) lack of control; (c) external coercion; and (d) internal coercion.

(a) If there is only one possible action that I can perform, and there are really no other alternatives, not even that of nonperformance of the action, I cannot be said to have chosen the action, though I may or may not consent to it. By extension, if there is no reasonable alternative to the action that I perform, then my moral responsibility for it is lessened.

(b) Lack of control extends to a number of different kinds of cases. In some instances, it removes all moral responsibility; in others, it diminishes it. For instance, actions that I do in my sleep are actions over which I have no control and for which I am not morally responsible. Similarly, if I faint, and in the process knock over a lamp, which starts a fire, I am not morally responsible for starting the fire.

(c) External coercion or compulsion either diminishes moral responsibility or removes it, depending on the coercion and the alternatives. If I am a bank teller and a bank robber puts a gun to my head and tells me to hand over the money in my cash drawer, I give him the money under compulsion, and I am not morally responsible for giving away the bank's money. There are various, more subtle kinds of compulsion, however, which pose difficult problems. Suppose my boss tells me to falsify a report and also tells me that unless I do so, I shall be fired. Suppose, further, that I am deeply in debt because of the illness of my wife, and that I am unlikely to be able to find another job that pays as well as this one. Because of the coercion applied by my superior, am I morally relieved of my responsibility not to falsify documents? The details of the case must be more fully examined before we can answer the question satisfactorily. But even with this sketchy information, if I do sign, as commanded, I am less morally guilty than if I had falsified the documents without any outside compulsion. External compulsion may involve the use of physical force, the threat of death or violence to one's self or to others, or the threat, or use, of other kinds of pressures. Not all such pressures constitute excusing conditions. The kind and degree of external compulsion must be carefully considered, and the criterion of what the ordinary rational person of good will would expect and demand of himself is the best we sometimes have to work with.

(d) Internal compulsions can be divided into two kinds. One is the clinically abnormal, and the other is the normal. Let us suppose that a kleptomaniac is forced to steal because of some inner compulsion over which he has no control. If he is actually forced to steal, and has no choice, he is not morally responsible for his action. Other abnormal psychological conditions that drive a person to do what he does diminish his responsibility. Normal people are also sometimes overcome by passions that they say they cannot, or could not, control, such as sorrow or rage, lust or hate. Each person is morally obliged to control his passions and dominate them. But possibly there are cases in which, through no fault of the person in question, passions dominate him and lead him to perform some immoral action. Such internal compulsion provides an excusing condition and mitigates the agent's moral responsibility. The law also recognizes such conditions as excusing to some extent; for instance, a murder of passion is a less serious crime than a premeditated one.

Excusing conditions supply reasonable ways for lessening or precluding moral responsibility. But they must be used with care if we wish to assess accurately the moral responsibility of ourselves and of others. For instance, if I drive recklessly and I run over a child, does the fact that I was drunk lessen my moral responsibility for hitting the child? If I got drunk knowingly and willingly, the answer is no. For, although in my drunken state I had less control over the car than I would have had otherwise, and although, in a sense, I could not help hitting the child, I should have foreseen, when I decided to both drink and drive, that one of the possible consequences might be such an accident. I am morally responsible for the foreseeable results of my actions. How far people are expected to foresee the results of their actions in business, and to foresee the use to which their products might be put, is not always an easy question to answer. Many engineers and scientists have, appropriately, worried about the possible bad uses to which their research, discoveries, and inventions might be put. They are responsible for the products they create, even though they will not control the uses to which they are put. The problem of how much moral responsibility a manufacturer has for the use to which his product is put is a similar question. If a handgun is used to kill a shopkeeper during a robbery, the gunman is responsible for the death. Is the person who sold him the gun, the company that manufactured the gun, and the person who designed the gun also responsible? How far back do we go in the causal chain? What about the steel company that provided the metal to the gunmaker, and the iron ore company that provided the iron to the steelmaker? Obviously, the further back we go, the more remote the cause and the less likely that the person could have reasonably foreseen a particular consequence, or could reasonably be held responsible. The drug thalidomide caused a large number of birth deformities, and many parents sued the manufacturer. We assume that the doctors who prescribed the drug did so in ignorance of the drug's bad consequences; the druggists who sold it and the women who took it were also ignorant of this fact. If they acted in invincible ignorance, they are absolved of moral blame. Whether the drug company could have and should have known of the bad effects is a question we cannot answer without detailed investigation, though the company was liable for the effects of the drug.

The doctrine of excusing conditions is used by some people in a way that removes moral responsibility entirely for certain immoral acts, or entirely removes moral responsibility from everyone. In defense of those accused of murder, for instance, some argue that anyone who commits a murder must be at least temporarily insane. They are not responsible for their actions because they did not know what they were doing, or they had no control over their actions. Others, who believe that people are completely determined in all their actions, sometimes argue that all of us act from internal compulsions, and, because of the nature of these compulsions, we never really choose between actions. According to this view, we are compelled to do whatever actions we perform; our feeling of choice is an illusion; and we are truly compelled to do whatever we do, just as the kleptomaniac is compelled to steal. Such a view does not take adequate account of our common human experience, and of our ability to distinguish between acts of the kleptomaniac and acts of purposeful stealing. Such distinctions are sufficient to sort out different kinds of cases, varying degrees of consent and knowledge, and hence, varying degrees of moral responsibility.

Liability and Accountability

Moral responsibility is closely connected to several other concepts besides duty and obligation, possibility, knowledge, freedom, and choice. These include liability, accountability, agency, praise, blame, intention, pride, shame, remorse, conscience, and character. Liability for one's actions means that one can rightly be made to pay for the adverse effects of one's actions on others. Automobile liability insurance for drivers, for instance, is intended to cover the costs of damage to other persons or property. We are liable for such payments as long as we are causally responsible for the damage. If we accidentally run into another car, we do not do so intentionally. Yet we are liable for the damage we do. Liability, therefore, does not necessarily involve moral responsibility for the action. We may be morally (as well as legally) liable to make good the damage we do to others, even if we are not morally responsible for the action. In many cases, however, the excusing conditions that apply to moral responsibility also apply to moral liability. We may be liable to punishment, blame, or censure for an action we do knowingly and willingly, but not for similar consequences that we produce unwittingly or accidentally.

Legal liability can be fitted into a similar pattern of analysis with respect to individuals. Businesses, however, are often bound by laws of *strict liability*. Strict liability means that no excusing conditions are accepted or applicable. For instance, several people recently died of food poisoning. The cause was botulism that developed in cans of seafood which had tiny holes in the can cover. The packer did not intend to poison anyone, and no one intentionally punctured the can covers. Yet, under rules of strict liability, the packer was held legally liable and was successfully sued for damages by the relatives of those killed. Corporations are formed, among other reasons, to limit the liability of owners or shareholders to the amount represented by their shares. The personal assets of the shareholders are not liable to seizure. The extent to which strict liability should be applied to corporations for damage done by misuse of their products is a controversial topic. Should the manufacturer of a single-control shower faucet be liable if someone turns on only the hot water and gets scalded? The Fifth U.S. Court of Appeals upheld a jury's affirmative answer, even though this seems counter to common sense. The debate about liability concerns where the line should be drawn when assigning strict liability.

Accountability is the obligation of giving (or of being prepared, if called upon to give) an account of one's actions. The account should explain the reasonableness, appropriateness, correctness, legality, or morality of the action. Accountability might be moral or legal. One is accountable for one's actions and the consequences thereof. One is accountable to oneself, and one is properly accountable to others for actions that affect them. An agent acting for others is also accountable for the actions, and failures to act, with respect to the domain covered by his agency. Financial accounting is one familiar way in which an agent justifies or accounts for his actions with respect to a business.

Moral accountability consists in being prepared to render a moral account of an action done either for ourselves or as agents for others. We appropriately give an account of those things for which we are responsible. A moral account of our actions is not always given explicitly in moral terms. For instance, we might give an account in financial terms, through a financial report in which we list income and expenditures (which we justify if called on to do so). The report is an account of our handling of the funds, on the assumption that it is accurate, contains all income and expenditures, and balances properly.

Within a firm or organization, moral accountability may be structured or unstructured. Organizational accountability is frequently structured hierarchically, with those below accountable to those above, but not vice versa. Moral accountability is not determined only by organizational structure, however. Each person is morally accountable to those whom one's actions affect and only rarely will a person be called to account, for most actions fall within an acceptable range. They need no special justification because they form part of the large class of generally acceptable actions.

We are morally responsible in the sense of being liable, and in the sense of being accountable for our actions and failures to act. Broadly speaking, we are morally responsible for all our actions; more narrowly, we are responsible for fulfilling our obligations. We are responsible to ourselves, because we are rational agents and follow the moral law. Hence we appropriately hold ourselves morally responsible, and if we wish to be moral we appropriately assume moral responsibility. We may also take on particular moral responsibilities as a result of contracts, agreements, special relationships, prior commitments, or when we occupy certain positions. If we act immorally, we appropriately feel moral guilt. When we act immorally we do not act in accordance with our true ends, and, appropriately, we feel moral shame. Moral remorse is the feeling of sorrow for our immoral actions, together with an intention not to perform similar actions in the future. These emotions result from self-evaluation, whether or not prompted by the evaluation of others.

Because we all belong to the moral community, we can also ascribe moral responsibility to others; we hold them morally liable, and appropriately demand a moral accounting of their actions insofar as they affect us, the organization or group to which we jointly belong, or society as a whole. Although we can ascribe moral responsibility, it may not be assumed by the one to whom we ascribe it, and he or she may not agree to render an account. We can ascribe moral praise and blame for the actions of others, and attempt to induce moral guilt, shame, or remorse.

As human beings develop, they tend to adopt patterns of actions, and dispositions to act in certain ways. These dispositions, when viewed collectively, are sometimes called character. A person who habitually tends to act as he morally should has a good character. If he resists strong temptation, he has a strong character. If he habitually acts immorally, he has a morally bad character. If despite good intentions he frequently succumbs to temptation, he has a weak character. Because character is formed by conscious actions, in general people are morally responsible for their characters as well as for their individual actions.

Conscience is the ability to reason about the morality of an action, together with a set of values, feelings, and dispositions to do or to avoid doing certain actions. Conscience is something that every rational being has, insofar as he or she is rational. But we can act against our conscience, and stifle it, just as we can act in accordance with it. Though we give ourselves the moral law, we are all fallible, and so conscience must be informed, developed, trained, and corrected. We are morally obliged to act in accordance with our conscience; but we are equally obliged to develop an objectively correct conscience.

Failure to fulfill one's responsibilities sometimes leads not only to blame, shame, and remorse but also to punishment. We are liable to punishment if we do certain actions and are not able to provide any sufficient excusing conditions. The threat of punishment is a means of motivating people to act mor-

89

ally and responsibly, and to accept their responsibility. Yet justice demands that punishment be meted out only to those responsible for the actions in question. The innocent, or those not responsible for actions, should not be punished for them. Those who are more responsible deserve more punishment than those who are less responsible. Diminished responsibility because of excusing conditions rightfully diminishes the severity of the punishment appropriate for an action.

Agent and Role Moral Responsibility

We saw earlier that the causal chain in an action may sometimes be a long one. If one person acts for another person, we can often correctly say that the second person is acting as an agent for the first person. We can, accordingly, speak of *agent responsibility*. Such responsibility is frequently found in business; it is often complex, and it raises a number of special types of problems.

Consider first the simple case of agency, in which one person acts for another. A lawyer draws up a contract for a client. He acts as agent for the client, and does what the client wants done but is unable to do himself. The lawyer draws up the kind of contract the client wants, with the provisions he desires. The client is morally responsible for the contents of the contract, because they represent his desires. The lawyer is simply an agent for the client. But the lawyer has a moral responsibility for his actions, which he cannot dismiss simply because he acts as an agent for another. He cannot morally do what is immoral simply because he acts for another.

In a large organization the chain of agency frequently involves many people who are hierarchically related to one another. This raises problems of moral responsibility, both for those at the top and for those lower down the chain.

Suppose the president of a corporation tells his vice-president that costs have to be cut in a certain division of the corporation. He does not say how or where the cuts are to be made; he leaves that up to the vice-president. The vice-president, in turn, decides that the cuts have to come from a certain section of his operation, and tells the manager below him that certain cuts have to be made. This continues until finally, at the end of the line, corners are cut, endangering people's lives. Those near the end of the line feel that they are forced to do what they do. They have received their orders and the options open to them are limited. They may not have wanted to cut the corners that they cut; they feel that the responsibility for their actions belongs to those above them. They did not initiate the action or the practice; they are just following orders. The president of the company does not see the specific results of the order he gave to the vice-president because he is far removed from its concrete implementation. He feels that those below him should be given the authority to make decisions, and, so long as they perform well, he does not feel he should second-guess them. He did not intend to cause the particular dangers to which people at the receiving end might be exposed. He did not intend that anything immoral or unjust take place. Hence, at both ends of the chain, the people involved feel that the actions are actions for which they are not morally responsible. Those at the bottom claim they had no other choice, and were simply following orders; they did not initiate the policy, and hence are not responsible for its effects.

The absence of the feeling of moral responsibility, however, does not indicate an absence of moral responsibility. The delegation of authority to carry out a command or policy does not relieve the delegator of the moral responsibility for how the command or policy is carried out. We are morally responsible both for our actions and for the foreseeable consequences thereof. The diminished feeling of moral responsibility is psychologically understandable, but it is not therefore excusing. Similarly, those near the bottom of the chain may find themselves forced to do what they, on their own, would not choose to do. They may wish to deny moral responsibility for their actions, and feel that they are not morally responsible for them. Yet they remain moral agents and so cannot deny moral responsibility for their actions.

Agent moral responsibility, especially in large organizations, poses a variety of problems, some of which we shall investigate in later chapters.

Closely related to agent moral responsibility, and often overlapping it, is *role responsibility*. Role responsibility is usually a corollary of assuming a certain position, function, or role in society or in an organization, or by becoming a member of a certain profession, class, or group that assumes special obligations. Not everyone has the obligations of a parent, but when individuals become parents they take on the obligations of that position or role. They are responsible for their children in a way that others are not. Similarly, when one assumes a position in a firm, that person takes on the responsibility of performing the functions and tasks of that position. The president of a corporation takes on the responsibility of acting as president of the firm. Managers take on the responsibility of doing the job for which they were hired, as do all other workers. In each case one is expected to subordinate one's own desires and wishes to that of the role that one fills. An individual in a position within a corporation should properly distinguish between his responsibility and that of the corporation. He should distinguish between his goals and those of the corporation; and he should not inappropriately substitute the one for the other. Typically, a firm generates rules that are to govern the tasks done by the various members of the firm and that outline one's function and tasks within the firm. The more specific and inclusive the set of rules, the less discretion employees have in their work. In general we can say that a person fulfills his moral obligations to his employer by following the rules and carrying out the tasks that go with his role or position. In doing so he acts impersonally, in the sense that he does what is prescribed by the position, or what he is ordered to do by those above him. "I followed the rules," or, "I did what I was told," are perfectly acceptable defenses for someone called to account for his actions in a rule-governed position, unless the rule requires one to act immorally or if one is commanded to do what is immoral. For although each person has the moral obligation to fulfill the tasks for which he is hired, the assumption must be that the task is not itself immoral. Those who establish roles or give orders are morally responsible for the tasks assigned each role or position, and for the orders they give. But this does not excuse those who hold roles from the immorality of actions they commit in fulfilling those roles.

Members of a profession and of certain groups (e.g., religious groups) frequently take on special moral obligations of the profession or group. Because of the special training and knowledge a doctor has, for example, a doctor has a greater obligation to help the injured in an emergency than does the ordinary person. As a member of a profession with a role in society, moreover, the doctor shares in the responsibility of the medical profession to care for the health of the members of the society and to help see that the other members of the medical profession, and the profession as a whole, live up to their responsibilities. When professionals, such as doctors, lawyers, or engineers accept roles in organizations, they carry with them their professional role responsibility in addition to their role responsibility within the firm. Such dual-role responsibility should pose no moral problems because role responsibility is always subordinate to general moral responsibility. We can never justifiably do in a role what is immoral. But not all of our responsibilities in a role are moral responsibilities, and loyalty to one's role in a firm may conflict with one's loyalty to one's profession, or to one's role as a family member. If there is a clash of moral responsibilities, it must be resolved in the same way that clashes of other prima facie obligations are resolved.

The Moral Responsibility of Corporations and Formal Organizations

Moral responsibility is usually both ascribed to and assumed by individuals. Does it make any sense to speak of the moral responsibility of nations, or corporations, and of other formal organizations? If it does make sense to do so, do we mean the same thing by the term *moral responsibility* in these cases as we do when referring to human individuals?

If we start from ordinary usage, people clearly do refer to the actions of some nations as immoral; they speak of the moral responsibilities of rich nations vis-à-vis poor ones; they claim that corporations that sell unsafe or harmful products act immorally. Yet a strong position has been adopted by people like Milton Friedman, and by organizational theorists like John Simon, who seem to hold that corporations and other formal organizations are not moral entities. According to this view, they are legal beings, at best. They can be held legally liable, and they can be bound by laws, but only human beings are moral agents and only human beings have moral responsibility. Some people may speak as if corporations or businesses had moral obligations, but they are simply confused. Moreover, the view continues, when individuals work for a company, they act for the company and in the company's name. When so acting, their actions are part of the actions of the firm, hence, they should not be evaluated from a moral point of view. When they act contrary to the interests of the firm or when they break the law, steal from the company, or embezzle funds, then they act in their own right and are properly judged from a moral point of view. The conclusion is that businesses are not moral agents, have no moral responsibilities, and should not be morally evaluated.

This view, which I shall call the Organizational View, is a variant of the Myth of Amoral Business. It was developed in part as a reaction to a number of moral demands made by environmentalists and consumer groups concerning the social responsibility of business. Milton Friedman's reaction to such claims is to assert that the business of business is to make profits and that social reform, welfare, and the like are the proper concern not of business but of government.

The Organizational View has been widely attacked, yet it cannot be dismissed out of hand. It makes the valid point that organizations, corporations, and nations are not moral entities in the same sense as individual human beings. Therefore, if we are to consider them as moral agents we must be careful how we use our terms, and make clear what we mean by them.

The argument against the claim that formal organizations are not moral beings is fairly simple. Morality governs the action of rational beings insofar as they affect other rational beings. Formal organizations, for instance corporations, act. Ford Motor Company produces cars; it also builds factories, hires and fires people, pays them wages, pays taxes, recalls defective models, and so on. Not only do businesses act, they act rationally according to a rational decision-making procedure. Their rational actions affect people, hence these actions can be evaluated from a moral point of view. If it is immoral for an individual to discriminate, it is also immoral for a corporation to discriminate. If it is praiseworthy for an individual to give to charity, it is praiseworthy for a business to give to charity. If it is wrong for people to steal, it is wrong for businesses to steal. Actions, whether done by an individual or by an entity such as a company, a corporation, or a nation, can be morally evaluated. The alternative would be to say that though murder is wrong for individuals it is not morally wrong for businesses, or that although exploitation of one person by another is morally wrong, exploitation of a person by a corporation is morally neutral. This is clearly unacceptable, because murder, stealing, exploitation, and lying are wrong whether done by a human being, a corporation, or a nation; the action is wrong whoever the perpetrator of the action is.

The dispute does not end here, however, for part of the point of the Organizational View is that formal organizations do not act. Neither do corporations, clubs, companies, or nations. People within them act, but the organization itself is nothing more than a formal structure. It does not do anything. People within it do whatever it is that gets done. Obviously there is something correct about the assertion that only people act and that formal organizations do not act. Yet, as we noted previously, we often speak of firms and nations as acting. Who is correct? How do we decide?

The answer to both questions can be found through a closer analysis of our use of language. When we say, "Ford makes cars," we do not mean that the cars are made by magic; we know that no car will get made unless someone makes it. A great many people, using a variety of tools and machines, contribute to making a Ford car. Yet we can use the name *Ford* to mean all of the people and their relations and activities together. We know that there are workers and managers, a president of the firm, a board of directors, and shareholders. Yet without any knowledge of who does what within the firm, we can speak of Ford making cars. This is a perfectly understandable statement, made from outside the corporation and referring to it as a whole. If Ford recalls defective cars, someone must make the decision to recall them, and either the same person or other people must send out the notices. They act not in their own names but as employees or agents of the firm.

In our ordinary use of English it is proper and common to use the name of a firm to refer to all those associated with it, to refer to the products that those associated with it produce, or to refer to the entity that is liable to suit. Therefore, when we make a moral judgment about the actions of a firm or of a nation, we need not know who within the firm is the person or persons responsible. We can hold the firm as such responsible, from a moral as well as from a legal point of view. But granted that we can make moral judgments about the actions of a firm or nation, why should we? The answer can be found in what we wish to accomplish by such judgments. In making moral judgments about the actions we attribute to a firm or nation, we do many things. We express our emotions, evaluate an action, and encourage other people to react to the action as we do. In expressing our moral evaluation we either praise or blame. When we morally condemn an action, we might wish to encourage others to impose moral sanctions, or bring pressure to bear to rectify the wrong, or to change the policy in question.

A case in point is the seven-year Nestle Boycott, which ended in January, 1984. The Nestle Company was charged with causing a great deal of misery by promoting, in a number of questionable ways, the use of its powdered milk product for infants in underdeveloped countries. The charge was that the powdered milk was being mixed with polluted water, under unhygienic conditions, resulting in disease and death in large numbers of infants. In order to bring pressure to bear on the company to change what was seen as an immoral practice, a coalition was formed, which asked people to boycott all Nestle products. The point of the boycott was to produce a change in the company's policy. Those who called the boycott may not have known who within the company was responsible for the questionable practices, and they may not have cared. The boycott might have resulted in a cutback in production by the company, with a consequent laying off of workers who were not involved in setting policy or implementing it in any way. The boycott was called, however, not to lay off particular people but to change the company's policy. From the outside, it was a matter of indifference who was responsible for the practice and who carried it out. The intent of the coalition was to identify the practice as immoral, call it to people's attention, and unite them to create moral pressure to stop the practice.

Whether the attribution of an action to a corporation is, strictly speaking, correct, or whether it should be more appropriately attributed to the person or people within the corporation who make the decisions in question and carry them out, attribution of an action to a corporation is intelligible and, from a practical point of view, may be effective.

A similar analysis can be applied to nations. When the United States condemned the Soviet invasion of Czechoslovakia and the intervention in Afghanistan, spokesmen for the United States did the condemning. Although we say that the Soviet Union invaded Czechoslovakia, we obviously mean that Soviet soldiers invaded it. We see them as agents receiving orders from the heads of government. But the heads of government do not themselves physically invade. In some cases, we distinguish what the leaders of a country do from what the ordinary people do; in other cases, we do not. If one country blockades another, members of the armed forces of the one country prevent the exportation or importation of goods from or to the other country. One country may declare war on another, and does so through its government; but war is not declared only against certain people in that country. Just as in talking about a business, the collective term serves many functions, and no nation acts unless people act for it.

From within a formal organization or a nation, actions may also be ascribed by an individual to the organization or nation as a whole. Actions are more usually seen, however, as being done by certain people. The workers on an assembly line know that the cars they produce will not be produced unless they or others like them perform certain tasks, and policy will not be changed unless those capable of changing policy take the actions necessary to produce the changes. Moral responsibility may be assumed by various members within a firm. It may be assumed by the members of the board of directors, the president, various levels of management, or by the workers. Each person may hold himself morally responsible for doing his job, and he may hold others morally responsible for doing theirs; or moral responsibility may be refused by some or all of them.

Moral charges made from the outside, and moral responsibility ascribed to a corporation or nation from the outside, may be rejected, rebutted, refuted, or ignored. This happens when no one within the corporation or nation accepts the responsibility ascribed to it.

Corporations are not human beings. The differences between human individuals and corporations, other formal organizations, and nations are significant from a moral point of view and from the point of view of moral responsibility. A corporation as such has no conscience, no feelings, no consciousness of its own. It has a conscience only to the extent that those who make it up act for it in such a way as to evince something comparable to conscience. Because a corporation only acts through those who act for it, it is the latter who must assume moral responsibility for the corporation. It may not always be clear who within the corporation should assume this responsibility.

When harm is unjustly done to an individual by a firm, the firm has the moral obligation to make reparation to the individual. For example, it matters little whether the particular person who systematically paid women employees less than men for the same work is still with the firm. If the women deserve compensation for past injustice, the firm has the moral obligation to make it good. Someone who had nothing to do with perpetrating the past injustice but who is now employed by the firm may have the moral obligation to take action to make up for past wage discrimination. If a firm is morally responsible for wrongs done, it is morally obliged to make good those wrongs. But exactly who must do what within the firm can often only be appropriately decided by an analysis of individual cases.

We can and do use moral language with respect to the actions of businesses, formal organizations, and countries. But in any analysis, as we shift from individual human beings to organizational entities, we should be aware of the differences in meaning and application of the terms we use.

Corporations are not ends in themselves. Although they can be held morally accountable for their actions, they are not human beings. Hence, they cannot claim the moral rights of human beings—the right to life or continued existence, for example. The attempt to attribute all the rights of human persons to corporations results from a confusion about the moral status of corporations. Because corporations are not ends in themselves, we can morally evaluate the ends for which a corporation is established. The fact that it does exist, and has been established for certain purposes, is no guarantee that it should exist, or that its purposes are morally justifiable. Conversely, so long as the ends for which they are formed are not immoral, and so long as the means by which those ends are pursued are not immoral, corporations are not bound by the large range of moral rules that bind natural persons. An obligation to be charitable, for instance, might bind individuals but, because of their limited sphere of activity, would not be applicable to corporations. The showing of compassion might be an obligation of individuals but not of a corporation qua corporation. As we have seen, it does not follow from the fact that corporations are not human persons that they cannot be held morally accountable, nor that they can be regulated only by law. They can, moreover, be the bearers of legal rights, and one must consider the moral rights of those who formed the corporation and those who are part of it. Corporations are neither machines nor animals. They are organizations run by human beings, and as such, have a moral status that makes them amenable to moral evaluation, even though they are not moral persons per se.

Corporate Culture and Moral Firms

In dealing with human individuals we speak of their moral character. Do firms, other formal organizations, and nations have moral character? There are some people who maintain that a firm that takes its moral responsibilities seriously tries to be fair in dealing with its employees and customers, takes into consideration the effects of its actions, and so on, is correctly called a moral firm. It can be said to have a moral character, in a sense analogous to that used with respect to individuals. Its character is formed by its habitual actions in the past. It develops within it certain structures and patterns of acting. It molds those who join it into thinking and acting in certain ways. Tradition develops; pride in the policies of the firm takes root, and each member of the firm helps to form and to mold the others in the firm in conformace with its tradition. In this sense, then, a firm or a nation can be called moral or immoral, can be said to have a moral or an immoral character, and can be thought of as having, or as not having, a conscience. But the sense is only analogous; it is not identical with the meaning of these terms when used with respect to individual persons.

We can, however, properly speak of a *corporate culture*, and this may either foster or inhibit moral action on the part of its members. Corporate culture is analogous to the culture of a society, people, or nation. It includes the ambiance of the corporation, its values, beliefs, and practices; the relation of the people within the corporation to one another, and their feelings toward the firm; the history of the corporation; and the extent to which the present members identify with the history and tradition of the corporation in the past and present. Some firms have a strong corporate culture, unique and distinctive. Employees who join the firm are inculturated into it when hired by the firm. Such inculturation—which can take several years—may involve learning something of the firm's history, becoming familiar with its ideals and practices, and perhaps taking part in special activities of the firm. Some firms go so far as to have company songs; many have formal and informal meetings to discuss the firm's outlook, problems, or ideals. A company's culture may be consciously formed or may develop spontaneously. And part of a firm's culture may include a positive or a negative approach to moral issues and moral actions, both by individuals in the firm and by the firm itself, when dealing with employees, customers, and other firms.

Although a firm's corporate culture is established over time, it is both initially and continuously responsive, especially to direction from the top. Top management sets the tone that the rest of the firm follows. Those who do not agree with the tone and do not fit in usually do not stay long. It is possible for the top management to insist on morality throughout the firm. It can expect moral conduct on the part of all its employees, and establish a pattern— eventually a tradition—of moral action on the part of the firm and its officers. Not surprisingly, there is great loyalty and job satisfaction among employees who work for a firm that does not fire employees in times of cyclical downturns, and employees take pride in a firm that operates morally. Corporate excellence is not identical with corporate morality, because competent management is also necessary. But it is doubtful that corporate excellence is compatible with corporate immorality, or with a corporate culture that condones or encourages its employees to act either immorally or amorally in their roles for the firm.

Collective Responsibility

Assigning or assuming responsibility within a firm or within a nation can properly raise questions of collective responsibility. There are differences, however, between speaking of the collective responsibility of a random group of individuals, a non-freely joined group or organization such as a nation, family, or race, and a freely joined organization. One cannot dissociate oneself from one's family, race, or country in the same way that one can from freely joined organizations, including corporations and other businesses.

We can describe five models for assigning collective responsibility. In the first model, each member of the collective is assigned and/or assumes full responsibility for an action. Cases of collusion or of conspiracy are typical of this model. All the members of a conspiracy are fully responsible for the actions of any one of them. If a group of armed bandits robs a bank and one of them kills a bank guard, all the bandits are guilty of murder. For, in forming the conspiracy, they all intend the same end and are guilty of the results that any one of them produces in attempting to achieve it. If a firm decides to close down a plant without regard for the workers who will be let go, and if the action is immoral, then all those who decided the action have responsibility for it. If the action was decided by the board of directors, all the members of the board are equally responsible, even though each had only one vote.

The second model assigns only partial responsibility to all members of a firm or country, or as a variant, to those involved in any decision or action taken by the firm or country. Joint actions frequently require the participation of many people; some play a larger role than others, though all contribute to the total act, and therefore all are partially responsible.

The first two models break down collective responsibility into individual responsibility. The third model holds the firm or nation fully responsible, with responsibility assigned to individuals, as in the first model. Thus, for instance, a worker who had no part in making a decision that leads to the immoral action of his company judges the firm to have acted immorally and imputes responsibility to those who made the decision. Does he have a moral obligation to leave a firm that acts in this manner? Should he assume responsibility for the firm's actions simply because he works for it and thus helps it to act immorally?

The fourth model assigns full responsibility to the firm or nation, with individual responsibility assigned as in the second model.

The fifth model assigns responsibility for the firm's or nation's action only to the firm or nation as such, not to any of its members individually. Each member within the firm or country may have acted morally, but the outcome of their joint actions may be morally wrong.

Other models are possible, including mixes of the models just described. One view might place on the board of directors moral responsibility for all the actions a firm took. Another might place it on management, even though neither the members of the board nor the managers did anything immoral.

A third view might put the responsibility on the shareholders, who are in fact penalized if a firm is fined and cannot pass on the fine to either the public, in the form of higher prices, or to the workers, in the form of lower wages.

Which of these models is correct? How should we assign or assume moral responsibility when dealing with corporations or nations? Who really has responsibility for their actions? The answer is that moral responsibility may be appropriately assigned and assumed in all of these ways. The proper way cannot be decided a priori, but only after examining a particular case. The idea that a part-time janitor should be held fully morally responsible for the immoral actions of the firm he works for might sound extreme; in most cases it undoubtedly would be an extreme view. But in others, if the actions of a corporation were truly morally heinous, and if working for the firm in any capacity might be viewed as condoning its actions, then the janitor might be held morally responsible for the firm's actions. Obviously we would want to know what to condone its actions means, and whether the janitor's responsibility was of a lesser or greater degree than others in the firm. We would want to know what difference it makes to hold him partially or fully responsible, and the considerations that lead us to one or the other view. If the janitor is morally responsible, we might expect him, upon realizing it, to quit. If the president is morally responsible, we might expect him, upon realizing this, to change the firm's policies, assuming it is possible for him to do so. Ascribing responsibility and assuming it might imply responsibility to act in differing ways, depending on one's position.

To hold an entire nation or race morally responsible for what some of its members did, and in which the others have had no part, is unjust. And if guilt by association is taken to be an integral part of collective responsibility, then we should not adopt the notion. But neither of these interpretations of what it means to speak of collective responsibility forms a necessary part of the concept.

The notion of collective moral responsibility is vague because it can be interpreted in so many different ways. Our moral intuitions are frequently not clear when we are asked to decide who really is responsible for some actions taken by a firm or country. In many cases, there is room for disagreement. When we encounter such cases we must do our best to analyze the situation, see the results of adopting this rather than that interpretation of responsibility, take into account the consequences of using one rather than another of the models, see which can best be justified in the given case, which makes more sense, whether any make sense at all, and what difference it makes if we adopt or employ one rather than another.

The nature of the internal collective responsibility of a firm or nation should be pursued by those within each, attempting to clarify, assign, and assume responsibility as appropriate. Only when all those within such entities assume appropriate moral responsibility can the full moral responsibility of a firm, formal organization, or country be met. Ultimately, moral responsibility, and morality itself, must be self-imposed and self-accepted.

Further Reading

BLAU, PETER M., and W. RICHARD SCOTT. *Formal Organizations*. San Francisco: Chandler Publishing Co., 1962.

FEINBERG, JOEL. *Doing and Deserving: Essays in the Theory of Responsibility*. Princeton, N.J.: Princeton University Press, 1970.

———— "Collective Responsibility." *The Journal of Philosophy*, XLXV (1968), pp. 674–688.

FRENCH, PETER A., ed. *Individual and Collective Responsibility: The Massacre at My Lai*. Cambridge, Mass.: Schenkman Publishing Co., 1972.

FRENCH, PETER A. "The Corporation as a Moral Person." *American Philosophical Quarterly*, 3 (1979), pp. 207–15.

FRIEDMAN, MILTON. "The Social Responsibility of Business Is to Increase Its Profits." *The New York Times Magazine*, September 13, 1970.

GLOVER, JONATHAN. *Responsibility*. New York: Humanities Press, Inc., 1970.

GOODPASTER, KENNETH E., and JOHN B. MATTHEWS, JR. "Can a Corporation Have a Conscience?" *Harvard Business Review*, 60 (January-February, 1982), pp. 132–41.

LADD, JOHN. "Morality and the Ideal of Rationality in Formal Organizations." *The Monist*, LIV (1970), pp. 488–516.

LEWIS, H. D. "Collective Responsibility." *Philosophy*, XXIII (1948), pp. 3–18.

MYLES, BRAND, ed. *The Nature of Human Action*. Glenview, Ill.: Scott, Foresman and Company, 1970.

PETERS, THOMAS J., and ROBERT H. WATERMAN, JR. *In Search of Excellence: Lessons from America's Best-Run Companies*. New York: Warner Books, 1982.

SILVERMAN, DAVID. *The Theory of Organizations*. New York: Basic Books, Inc., 1971.

SIMON, HERBERT A. *Administrative Behavior*, 2nd ed. New York: The Free Press, 1965.

WALSH, W. H. "Pride, Shame and Responsibility." *The Philosophical Quarterly*, XX (1970), pp. 1–13.

Moral Issues in Business

SIX

Justice and Economic Systems

Consider two neighboring slaveholders in the American South before the Civil War. The first slaveholder treats his slaves reasonably well. He beats them only when they do not do the jobs they are supposed to do, or when they break the rules he sets. He feeds them fairly regularly. He does not expect them to work more than twelve or fourteen hours a day. He knows them by name and speaks to them on occasion. The other slaveholder beats his slaves whenever he gets angry at his wife or children. He gives his slaves swill to eat, and does not worry if sometimes they are not fed. When there is work to be done, he is not above making them work sixteen or eighteen hours a day. He is capricious in his dealings with them, arbitrary in the punishment he metes out, and surly in his attitude toward them.

Of the two slaveholders, which is the more moral? The temptation to call the first slaveholder the more moral is a strong one. For clearly he is kinder, fairer, more just in his dealings with his slaves. Yet to call either one moral has an odd ring to it. If holding slaves is immoral (if it is wrong to own another human being) then there is a fundamental injustice in the practice. A slave-owner's treating his slaves kindly is better than his treating them unkindly, but such treatment does not justify, or make up for, his engaging in slavery. Both slaveholders are involved in an immoral practice, even if one is kinder than another. Yet, we may reflect, probably neither of the slaveholders believes slavery is immoral. That may be true. But their believing slavery is moral does not make it objectively right. It is immoral whether or not, subjectively speaking, they believe it is.

Now, we can approach our own society in a similar way. Consider two employers. One discriminates against women and blacks, does not care about the safety of his employees, pays them subsistence wages, and replaces them as they wear out, just as he would replace his machines. The other employer does not discriminate, introduces safety devices where possible, pays his employees well above the subsistence level, and has a retirement plan. Which of the two is more moral? The answer is obvious and simple. But we can ask the question that we do not often ask: Are the employers in our system comparable to the slaveholders in the slave system? Is something wrong with the economic system in the United States today, just as there was something wrong with the economic system in the Southern United States before the Civil War? The fact that most of us do not feel that there is anything wrong with the wage system or with the economic system in general says something about us, although it does not necessarily say anything about the morality of the system in which we live. But is our system moral? We struggle with the questions of whether reverse discrimination is the proper way to make up for past discrimination, whether whistle blowing is morally defensible, and whether advertising aimed at small children takes unfair advantage of them, but are we questioning the morality of practices within a system when we should be questioning the system itself? Is the system basically just?

The Immorality of Slavery

Usually we speak of people or of actions being moral or immoral. Can we also describe an economic system as immoral? The answer seems to be clearly yes, because the overwhelming majority of Americans—as well as most other people—would readily admit that slavery is immoral. And slavery constitutes an economic system. Yet we would do well to look a little more closely at the question and at our answer.

In characterizing the system of slavery as immoral we use the term *slavery* in two different senses. In the first sense we mean the practice of slavery. This defines a relation between people and a way of treating people. We can analyze both the relation and the actions that follow as a result of the relation. In the second sense, by slavery we mean that economic system in which the slave relation is the fundamental productive relation. Because it is fundamental, we characterize the system by that relation. The system would not be that particular system if that relation were not present in a fundamental, constitutive way. If, for instance, we had an economic system that was basically capitalist or socialist, but a few people within the system had slaves, we could say that the practice of slavery was immoral. But that would not mean that the system within which it was found was immoral, because slavery was not a fundamental or defining relation of the system.

We can evaluate the economic system of slavery in two different ways. One involves evaluating the morality of the fundamental economic relation on which it is built, and by extension analyzing the actions that follow as a result of that relation. This is a structural analysis. It involves looking at the basic structures and practices of the system, because the system is defined by its structures and practices. These are necessarily seen as relations among people, and as practices that involve transactions among people. Are these fair and just? The second way of evaluating economic systems is an end-state approach. It involves looking at what the system as a whole does to the people affected by it. Does the system help them fulfill themselves and realize their potential as moral beings? Does adoption of the system produce a kind of human society that exemplifies or fulfills the moral aspirations of human beings? Both the structural and the end-state evaluations may be made from either the utilitarian or the deontological point of view.

Let us consider the economic system of slavery. We define it as a system in which the fundamental productive relation is the owning of one human being, the slave, by another, the master. The slave works for the master and produces the basic goods needed by the society. These include the food that the members of the society eat, the clothes they wear, the utensils they use, the tools they employ, the buildings they inhabit, and whatever else is necessary for their way of life. The masters may produce art, literature, philosophy, or other human products that typically require leisure and time for reflection. The slave not only works for the master but belongs to the master, as property belongs to a property owner. The slave, insofar as he is a slave, is not considered a person with rights, or worthy of moral consideration. He or she is an object to be used, much as animals are objects to be used. The primary function of slaves is work, even if some slaves may not be used for work but for other purposes, just as the primary function of work animals is work, though some may be kept as pets or for breeding, or for other purposes.

As we have described it, this fundamental productive relation may be defined by and circumscribed by law. But it is the economic, not the legal relation that is the center of our concern. We can look at the moral quality of the relation itself. We can also morally evaluate the actions that usually follow as a result of the relation.

First, let us consider the moral quality of the relation itself. Is it a moral relation? The obvious answer, from the deontological point of view, is clearly that it is not. The relation denies that the slave is an end in himself, worthy of respect. The maxim implied in the relation, namely, "Treat human beings who have the status of slaves as possessions," is in direct opposition to the second formulation of the categorical imperative, which requires that we treat all rational beings as ends in themselves, not only as means. If we were to go behind a veil of ignorance, not knowing whether we would end up as a slave or as a master when we emerged, and if we wished to protect ourselves in case we were assigned our place by our worst enemy, would we choose a slave society or one in which all were free? Clearly we would choose the latter. Slavery violates the first principle of justice, as developed by John Rawls, and hence, according to that criterion, it is unjust. A utilitarian approach would require that we examine the results of actions, and not only relations. Yet even from the utilitarian point of view it does not take much imagination to realize that the status of the slaves is such as to cause them great harm, regardless of how well they are treated. They will necessarily suffer loss of dignity, in their status as slaves—a loss for which they cannot be compensated, even by kind treatment. Because a slave society is one in which the slaves dominate numerically, the pain they suffer as a result of their status is enormous, and clearly greater than the pleasure or good of the slaveholders. In general, therefore, the relation in itself has a tendency to produce, in those affected by it, more harm than good.

Second, let us consider the actions that follow as a result of the slave relation. Are they moral or immoral? The answer, of course, depends on which actions we choose to evaluate. The productive work of the slave is not immoral, nor, necessarily, is the giving of commands by the master. But work and giving commands are not peculiar to slavery. Are there actions that follow from slavery as such? We need not deny that slaves might be treated kindly by masters. But if in all ways they were treated by masters as masters treat free men, then we would not in fact have the practice of slavery. The actions we must morally evaluate are those in which masters treat their slaves as property, as animals, as beings who are not ends in themselves. The analysis from both the deontological point of view and the utilitarian point of view would parallel the ones we just gave, except that the utilitarian analysis would include actions, the results of which one could evaluate. And the results would be similar. The conclusions we can draw are that the practice of slavery is immoral, and that an economic system which is dependent on the practice of slavery is inherently immoral. It cannot be made moral without changing the fundamental practice of the slavery on which it is based. A slave system might be more tolerable to the slaves in one society than in another, and one master might be kinder to his slaves than another, but neither of these considerations changes the moral character of slavery.

The results are similar if we take an end-state approach to slavery. The deontological evaluation will not differ significantly from the previous analysis. Slavery will still exist, and because that is the central ingredient in the system, the system remains immoral. But might slavery be only prima facie immoral? Might it be unjust but preferable to the other real alternatives? From the utilitarian perspective, might it not be possible that the results of adopting slavery are actually better than adopting some other system?

Suppose that as a result of a worldwide nuclear war the population of the world is decimated. The great majority of those who survive have been affected by radiation poisoning of a type that affects their brains, making them dull-witted and devoid of initiative. There are a few lucky people who were shielded by lead walls in bank vaults, or who were deep underground. When they emerge and assess the situation they realize that if the human race is to survive, they must reproduce. Meanwhile, they cannot handle all of their needs. But the masses can be corralled and forced to work. In being so forced they will each be better off than they would otherwise be, because the alternative is that they would die. By being forced to work they will both keep themselves alive and keep alive those who have the capacity to develop the human race again. Hence the fortunate few institute what we call slavery. They argue that all the people in the society will be better off with slavery than any of them would be without it; the alternative is death for all. Therefore, though slavery is prima facie immoral, when compared with the even worse alternative of the extinction of mankind and the dreadful suffering those who die would go through, it is the lesser of two evils and so morally justifiable.

What are we to say of the argument? The first reply is that it is a flight of fancy—a philosopher's puzzle, not a real state of affairs. Morality, we can insist, is concerned with real alternatives. We have little basis for judging what might be right or wrong in the conditions described, which are far beyond our ordinary experience. But we need not stop with this reply. Take the example on its merits: it states that the people affected by the radiation are dull-witted and without initiative, and if left alone would die. How dull-witted are they? Can they think enough to consider consequences? Are they rational and able to decide between alternatives? Do they have a desire to live, and do they see life as worthwhile? How can we explain the fact that they can be forced to work under slavery but not otherwise? How can the claim be defended that there is really no other alternative? Who decided that? The example makes too many vague and dubious claims. It concludes, if all the claims are admitted, that slavery, though prima facie immoral, is the least of the possible evils and therefore morally justifiable. Given our knowledge of human history, it is difficult to believe that there are really no other alternatives; that the few who become the masters do so for the good of all; and that the slaves are better off than they would be if some other means of impelling them to action were employed. Nor is there much reason to think that the system of slavery, once adopted, would not tend to degenerate, that people would be treated worse instead of better, and that, as the practice continued, the masters would be more and more reluctant to give up slavery. Because it is speculative, we cannot settle the argument. But we should not be forced to admit more than is plausible.

History might provide a better example. We know that, as a great many societies emerged from primitive tribal conditions, they developed slavery. The great pillars of Western civilization, Greece and Rome, were built on slavery. If slavery was historically necessary for us to emerge to the state of society in which each person is free, was not ancient slavery justified by its necessity, as well as by its results?

It is very difficult to settle counter-factual issues. How can we know what other alternative to slavery was available in early Greece and Rome, and what would have happened had slavery not developed? To say that slavery was a reality in ancient societies is not to say that it was unthinkable that there be ancient society without slavery. To claim it was historically necessary is to make an ambiguous claim. Certainly it was not logically necessary. It may have developed because of a natural inclination on the part of some people to dominate, or because of the weakness of others in comparison with the strength of the few, or because of the desire for luxury or ease on the part of those who would be masters, or for any number of other reasons. None of these is a justification for slavery, although in a sense they provide an explanation of why and how it arose. Historical necessity, if it is taken to mean simply that whatever happened historically happened necessarily, renders everything moral. More accurately, it renders everything morally neutral. Because if everything that happened happened necessarily, then one of the conditions for morality is denied, namely, the possibility of choosing freely. If Hitler's murder of millions of Jews in our century was historically necessary simply because it happened, then we can justify anything. The result would be that there is no basis for evaluating anything, and all we can do is state what happened.

The other historical rationale is to claim that slavery was necessary, but only up to a certain time; thereafter, it was no longer necessary and should have been given up. According to this argument, slavery in the United States was not necessary. Mankind had found ways to organize society productively without slavery. It was an anachronism, which was finally uprooted by the Civil War. But ancient slavery, the argument contends, was a step on the road to feudalism, which in turn led to the development of the world as we know it. We could not have developed our productive capacities unless we had gone through the stage of slavery. Hence it was justifiable then, even though it is not justifiable now.

Even if this argument is taken to be a type of utilitarian argument, it still remains questionable. The central issue is whether there was no real alternative to ancient slavery. How that claim can be substantiated is the crux of the issue. We can concede that *if* there actually was no better alternative, then slavery was justifiable as the least bad of bad alternatives; but this is different from accepting the claim that actually there was no alternative available.

Whatever our conclusion about ancient slavery, we can be certain that in today's world slavery is immoral. Clearly, there are alternatives, and there is no justification for choosing an immoral system when moral systems are available.

We can generalize on the basis of our analysis, however. Because we have been able to argue conclusively that slavery is immoral, and that today it is an immoral alternative, we have shown that it is possible, at least in the case of slavery, to give a moral evaluation of an economic system. We have seen how the question of the morality of economic systems can in general be approached and how specific arguments can be advanced. What of contemporary systems?

The Moral Evaluation of Contemporary Systems

In considering slavery we discussed an economically homogeneous economic system, characterized by the dominant productive relation of master and slave. We did not investigate the kind of political system to which it was joined. The political system of the Greek city-states was different from that of the Roman Empire, and both systems were different from the political system of ancient Egypt. But whatever the political system, it could not make up for the immorality of slavery. Nor was there any way that slavery could be changed internally so as to be moral and still be slavery.

The moral status of contemporary economic systems is not so easily settled. It is tempting to think simplistically about two great contending economic systems: capitalism and socialism. But we should remember the differences between nineteenth-century capitalism in England and capitalism as it exists in the United States today. If we consider contemporary capitalism, we should consider not only its structure in the United States but also that of other countries, such as Japan and South Africa. In the latter case it is joined with apartheid, a radical form of racial segregation and discrimination; in the former two it is not. In Japan, capitalism is joined with a kind of paternalism absent from its American counterpart. All socialistic systems are not identical, either. Socialism in the Soviet Union is closely linked with a centralized and dominant Communist Party. In England, socialism is mixed with a democratic form of government. In Yugoslavia, socialism exists with a Communist Party that allows a great deal of decentralization. Capitalism and socialism in each case is changed to some extent by the kind of political system and structure within which it operates. Moreover, pure capitalism and pure socialism do not exist in any country. Every country has something of a mixed kind of economic system, though some can be characterized as more clearly capitalistic and others as more clearly socialistic. Communism, as an economic system, has yet to be achieved, though countries with communistic governments claim to be developing toward it.

Because apartheid is present in South Africa but not in the United States, apartheid is not a constituent of capitalism. It is something added to capitalism, an ingredient in a particular kind of capitalism. Socialism in the USSR, under Stalin, existed together with totalitarianism, but socialism in England is not totalitarian. Hence, totalitarianism is not a necessary part of socialism. Though economic and political systems are intertwined, we can distinguish them to a considerable degree for purposes of analysis. The way in which any specific contemporary economic system actually works, however, cannot realistically be separated from a consideration of the political and legal system with which it is found. Some of the moral deficiencies of an economic system, for instance, might be compensated for by the political system. Conversely, the political system might interfere in an immoral way with the workings of the economic system.

For purposes of analysis, let us briefly consider capitalism and socialism as economic systems, floating free from any particular political system. The analytic technique useful for this purpose is the construction of a model. We can develop a model of capitalism and a model of socialism, and we can then investigate the models to determine their necessary components. Once we have isolated the necessary components, we can evaluate them from a moral point of view. If we find any structural immoral elements, then we can see if we can change those elements and still retain a system that we wish to call capitalism. If we do not find any structurally immoral elements, we can see if adoption of the system would result in an end-state product we would describe as either moral or morally neutral. We can do the same with socialism. The conclusions we reach as a result of this analysis will pertain only to the model. Then we need to see what degree, if any, the model is actually instantiated in any really existing society. Obviously we are interested in models that bear some relation to existing societies. To the extent that we find the model defective or deficient from a moral point of view, we should see whether it can be made moral while retaining its basic structure. If this is not possible, then the system is inherently immoral. If we find such a system in a particular country, the appropriate approach is to replace the system with a moral one. Whether that can be done while retaining the existing form of government is a question we cannot decide without investigating particular cases. Such replacement frequently involves a drastic and dramatic social change, usually called a revolution, whether it be violent or peaceful.

Economic Models and Games

Some people consider economics a kind of game. By pursuing the analogy to games we can see some of its strengths and weaknesses. Consider chess. To play chess you need a chess board and a number of pieces of a certain kind. The pieces can be considered to constitute two sides, or two armies. Each side has a king and a queen, two knights, two bishops, two rooks, and eight pawns. Is the game fair? One obvious reply is that it is fair because both sides have the same number and kind of pieces, and both sides are bound by the same rules. But this is evaluating the fairness of the game from the point of view of the players. What if we looked at it from the point of view of a pawn? Think of the pawn standing in front of the queen. In the game, the queen can make many different kinds of moves, but the pawn moves one square at a time. Is that fair? The reply is that it is inappropriate to look at the game of chess from the point of view of the pieces. If you want to play chess, then you must follow the rules of the game. Fairness consists in following the rules, not in changing the possible moves.

If you prefer equality, you might prefer the game called Chinese checkers. In it all sides have the same number of marbles. All the marbles are of equal value, and all can make the same moves. Therefore there is equality among the marbles as well as fairness for the players.

Consider now the game of economics. In one system we have slaves and masters. In another we have rich owners of industry and factory workers. In another we have commissars and workers. If each one of these is considered a type of game, with its own rules, we can describe how each operates. If each, taken as a whole, were considered a model, we could describe it in detail. We could talk of the place and role of each person in the economy. We could describe how prices rise and fall; how supply meets or fails to meet demand, and what this does to prices; what happens when taxes are increased, when the money supply is diminished, or when interest rates are raised; and how full employment might be achieved. We could describe all this with some precision, in our model, and possibly we could predict with some certainty the reactions of certain parts of the economy to certain actions in other parts of it.

According to this approach, economics is not something we morally evaluate. It is a game. Chinese checkers is one game and chess another. But it is silly to try to say that one is more moral than another. The rules are different; the players are different. Chess is more complicated and interesting because of the different kinds of pieces and moves allowable. Chinese checkers is less complicated; all the pieces are equal, and playing the game is comparatively dull. Some people prefer chess because of the skill it requires; others prefer Chinese checkers because of its simplicity. Similarly, some people feel that a free enterprise system is more challenging and interesting than a system of radical equality. From an economic point of view, different systems can be described; the laws or rules governing the variables within the system can be detailed. Each can be modeled. But models are not moral or immoral, just as most games are neither moral nor immoral.

Though economics might be considered a game, when actually implemented, economic systems are not games. Frequently, economics is studied as if it had nothing to do with people, as if it was simply the study of abstract concepts, such as supply and demand, money, price, and profits. Ultimately, however, economic systems are ways in which people are related. Their relations are mediated by money and commodities, by prices and wages, by supply and demand. And all of these relations, in the end, are descriptions of how people interact. Their lives are shaped and seriously affected by the system in which they find themselves, and by the rules according to which that system operates. Hence, economic systems are not, ultimately, morally neutral; they should be closely examined from a moral point of view. A chess piece is not a person. But a soldier fighting for a king is a moral being, an end in himself, and not simply a pawn to be used. We can therefore plausibly evaluate an economic system by an end-state evaluation, as well as by an analysis of the fairness, justice, or morality of its structures and operative rules. What is interesting in the analogy with games, however, is that we consider them fair when all players start out equally and abide by the same rules. We allow one to win and the others to lose. In fact, that is the object of the game. Do we feel the same about the game of life? Should all start out the same and abide by the same rules? If they do, is it right that some win and some lose?

A Capitalist Model

A model may not correspond to any social reality. A model of capitalism may also not correspond to any economy existing in a society. But a model can help us get conceptual clarity on some issues.

Capitalism, in its long history, has gone through a number of phases and stages. What is called classical capitalism is a model that is frequently both attacked and defended. It does not exist in its pure form anywhere in the world today, and may never have represented an actual economy. Yet its main features are commonly used and understood.

Most economic systems produce and exchange commodities, use money as a medium of exchange, and pay labor. What are the specific defining features of the model of classical capitalism? We shall consider three that are necessary to it. Although each of the three features may be found in other kinds of economic systems, it is the combination of the three that makes the model different from other models. The three are, an available accumulation of industrial capital; private ownership of the means of production; and a free-market system.

Available Accumulation of Industrial Capital

Capitalism derives its name from the fact that it is a system based on accumulated industrial capital. In a barter economy there is no accumulation of capital. Goods are exchanged for goods of equal value; there is no residue. Capital, which we can think of in terms of large amounts of money that can be put into the production of goods, must be accumulated. Before capitalism, kings might accumulate fortunes, but they did not usually use their fortunes for the production of goods. Merchants and tradesmen might accumulate some wealth (though rarely in very large quantities) but usually did not use their wealth for the production of goods.

Several features that correlate closely with its historical development are built into our model of capitalism. The accumulation of large amounts of wealth available for productive purposes is one such feature. Large sums of money alone, however, are not enough. We must also have industrialization. Capitalism did not exist prior to the industrial revolution. Hence industrialization on a large scale is a necessary element of our model.

Neither the availability of wealth for productive purposes nor large-scale industrialization is unique to capitalism. Any large, modern society, whatever its economic system, needs both of these. But inherent in industrialization are certain problems, one of which is pollution. Industrialization involves the use of machines, which in case of accidents can be dangerous. Also, machines wear out, become obsolete, and need replacing. Industrialization typically demands a large degree of division of labor. Some of the work required in using machines efficiently is routine and dull; some requires great specialization and training. All of these aspects and functions of industrialization are not peculiar to capitalism. Any industrial society faces these potential problems and difficulties. But industrialization also has definite advantages, the greatest being that it multiplies human productive capacity and so makes possible a much larger amount of goods than would otherwise be the case.

The model of classical capitalism includes industrialization and capital. It does not question where capital comes from or how it was developed. Because the model is not an historical account but an analytic tool, the presence of capital is a given, a prerequisite of a capitalist model. The same is true of models of other contemporary economic systems, which include capital and industrialization. Where did the capital present in that system come from?

The question of how capital was initially accumulated, as well as the question of how it is increased within a system, raises moral considerations. Although from a moral point of view we can examine the transactions within the model of the system, we cannot examine the process of the antecedent capital formation and accumulation if the presence of such capital is assumed by the model, and if such formation and accumulation are not part of the model.

Private Ownership of the Means of Production

The distinguishing characteristic of capitalism is sometimes said to be private ownership of the means of production. This is a distinguishing feature, however, only when joined with the first and third components of the model. In a slaveholding society or in a feudal society there may also be private ownership of the means of production. The characteristic feature of capitalism is that there is private ownership of the means of large industrial production.

Private ownership of the means of production should not be confused with private ownership of property. Personal property, for instance, might be privately owned in a socialist economy. Personal property is owned by an individual and is not generally used for the production of commodities, though personally owned tools may be so used. But personally owned tools are not the dominant type of productive instrument in capitalism. In speaking of private ownership of the means of production we mean private ownership of factories, plants, corporations and businesses, transportation and communication facilities, raw materials, and large, commercially farmed tracts of land.

Private ownership in this model is opposed to social or state ownership. There are a number of difficulties that we can avoid by clearly defining the components of our model. Some people claim that there is a variant called *state capitalism,* in which the state carries on all the functions generally attributed to private owners in a non-state capitalist system. For our purposes, state capitalism is a different model. In our model, ownership by the state is not private ownership; private ownership is contrasted with state ownership. Private ownership is also contrasted with social ownership; but private ownership is not to be contrasted with public ownership. A firm may be owned outright by an individual or by a small group of individuals. Such ownership is private ownership. A firm may, however, be owned by many people, each of whom owns a small portion of it, represented by shares of stock in the firm. The owners of the stock may be individuals or perhaps other firms, or they may be groups investing pension-plan money, or the like. Such firms, whose stock is publicly sold and held, are publicly owned. But because the public members hold their shares privately, such firms are also private property. Social ownership, for our purposes, would mean ownership by members of the society in general, insofar as they are members of the society. Co-ops, or firms owned by the workers, are for our purposes privately owned, but, because of the second ingredient of private ownership, they are marginal cases; they do not represent the dominant mode of ownership.

The second ingredient of private ownership characteristic of capitalism is that not everyone owns the means of production. The majority of people in our model of capitalism do not individually own the means of production that they use; they are employed by others and work for wages. Wages are the dominant source of income for the vast majority in our capitalist model. Workers sell their labor in order to earn money to keep themselves and their families alive, and to buy whatever else they wish with their disposable income.

Private property in our model is compatible with both private and professional management of firms. A firm that is privately owned may be run by those who own it. They may both own and manage the company or business, whatever it may be. The owners, however, may hire professional managers to run their businesses. The separation of ownership from management raises special problems for moral consideration. But in looking at the model in general, we need make no hard and fast decision on this issue. If, for analytic purposes, it would be helpful to distinguish the two cases, we could simply use two models. In one of them, ownership and management would go together; in the other, they would be separate. Our model is a third alternative and includes both of the others.

Private ownership of the means of production raises several moral issues. One is whether private ownership of the means of production is itself moral. By what right, some ask, do some people, either individually or collectively, claim the right to natural resources? The world is the home of all mankind. Its goods—coal, iron, copper, oil, and other resources—should be available to all, and used for the good of all. Is it fair for certain people, simply because they or their forebearers happened to have settled in an area, to claim the exclusive right to the resources of that area? Such questions form one part of the moral analysis of private property.

A second group of questions regarding private property concerns the social nature of knowledge and culture. Each people inherit a store of knowledge—knowledge of how to make iron and glass, or how to make engines and tools, and so on. Industry depends on a large store of accumulated information and know-how, inventions and discoveries that no individual owns because they have been socially developed. The modes of production are also social. No individual produces cars by himself, or with knowledge he individually developed. Private ownership uses for private profit what society has developed. The knowledge, techniques, and processes are all social. By what right are they individually appropriated and used for individual rather than for social good?

A third group of questions relates to the workers in our model. In our capitalist model, the vast majority of people do not own the means of production, and they earn their living by working for others. Their livelihood is dependent on others. By what right do some have such power of life and death over others? The workers work for a wage. What constitutes a fair or a just wage? What constitutes exploitation? If goods are exchanged at their real value, does profit for the owner of private property come from stealing from the worker by not paying him what is his due? How is the owner-worker relation to be construed? We have already seen that the slave-master relation is immoral. What is the moral status of the owner-worker relation?

A Free-Market System

The third characteristic of our capitalist model is a free, competitive market system. A market-type system can be shared with other types of economic models. In our model, the free-market system is the dominant type operative within the system.

A free market is one that is not controlled either by government or by any small group of individuals. In a free market, government does not set the price of any goods. It controls neither prices nor wages. It also does not control production. Absence of government control and intervention is matched by absence of control by any small group. This rules out monopolies (exclusive ownership or control of supply) and monopsonies (exclusive control of demand, i.e., only one buyer).

Competition is a necessary component of our model. Free competition involves the possibility of any who so choose to enter into the market structure as buyers or sellers. Access is not artificially limited by any power, government, or group. Free competition is driven in part by the profit motive. In order to achieve greater returns on investment, resources must be free to move from within the system to whichever portion of it will bring the greatest return. This is true of natural resources, capital, and labor. Workers are free to move to whatever employment they choose, and to seek to earn as much as they can.

Prices and wages in our model are determined by the mechanism of the market. They are a result of supply and demand. Skilled labor, if it is in short supply, will bring higher wages than if it is not in short supply. In general, unskilled labor will be in greater supply than skilled labor, and skilled labor will be paid more. Prices are also determined by supply and demand. Competition encourages many people to produce products in great demand, because there is a ready market for such products. Buyers prefer to pay less rather than more for goods of the same quality, therefore competition encourages efficiency among producers, and competition encourages competing firms to lower their prices to acquire a larger share of the market.

The free-market system, in our model, can claim several virtues. It promotes efficiency—the efficient production and use of resources. Even more importantly, it values freedom. Each individual within the system makes free choices in each transaction into which he enters. Competition tends to lower the cost of goods to consumers, who decide what will be produced by how they spend their money. The market responds by not producing what is not sold and by producing what is in demand. As demand changes, the market mechanism responds by encouraging the appropriate changes in the allocation of capital and resources. Workers are free to negotiate the conditions of their employment and the kind of work they will do. If the conditions under which each individual transaction takes place are fair, then each party freely enters into such a transaction to achieve his own good and his own ends. All benefit thereby.

Many moral issues arise in considering a free-market system. Each transaction entered into must be fair and free. What constitutes fairness? And to be free, what are the prerequisites of a transaction? One condition of fairness is that both sides have all the appropriate knowledge. Only if both parties know what they are doing can they properly evaluate the transaction. Is the doctrine of *caveat emptor* (let the buyer beware) a part of our system? Does freedom involve the possibility of one party taking advantage of the other party, or of one party gaining advantage of another party? If fairness is built into the system, then only fair transactions are allowed in the system. But efficiency or initiative, the willingness to take risks, or some other quality, may well give one party an advantage over another. Can a worker be said to enter into a wage contract freely if, other than starving, he has no alternative but to accept the wages offered? Do consumers, acting as individuals, enter into transactions on an equal footing with large corporations?

In addition to questions about the fairness and freedom of transactions, some people ask what, from a moral perspective, competition does to people. Does it treat them as ends in themselves? Does it undermine their inclination to be helpful? Does it divide them opposing classes and groups? Does it impede social cooperation? Does competition make people selfish, self-serving, mean, and inconsiderate of others?

Are there natural tendencies of the market that push it toward monopoly, or that encourage people to attempt to gain unfair advantage in order to improve their chances for success? If there are such forces, can they be remedied within the system, or must they be handled by other forces, for instance, by the political and legal system with which the model is joined?

Capitalism and Government

The structural components of capitalism and the end-state produced in a capitalist society can be morally evaluated, but to attempt to do so in a vacuum would be unrealistic. For capitalism is always found embedded in some cultural and political setting. The basis for determining the legitimate relations of business and government from an ethical point of view are contained in the end of government and business and in the conditions necessary for both to be morally justified. Yet the limits that morality sets for the business-government relation are loose enough to allow a great variety of different types of governments, operating in rich and poor societies, with educated or uneducated populations, and with a variety of different kinds of enterprises. We cannot fruitfully speak of the relation of business enterprises and government in the abstract because there are too many variables that must be taken into account in discussing this relation. Yet historically there have been at least six types of relation between government and capitalism, which produce six variants of our basic model of capitalism. In any given society a mix of several types may be present. Looking at each of the six separately will help us get some clarity on the relations.

1. The first is the model of laissez-faire capitalism. It is the version of the basic model of capitalism that was defended by nineteenth-century liberals. Today it is defended in the United States by libertarians and by some anarchists of the right. According to this view, the proper function of government is to preserve the peace (and hence protect business from external and internal threats) and to adjudicate disputes among those engaged in business transactions. These are the only morally legitimate activities of government. Neither taxation nor any kind of regulation of business by government is morally justified. The resulting model assumes that, in Adam Smith's terms, some "invisible hand" will make individual transactions, done for the purpose of private gain, benefit society as a whole more than any attempt to directly benefit society could. It also assumes, if it is to be morally justified, that competing enterprises will act morally and that where they do not the mechanism of the market will act as a corrective.

The model, however, has serious defects. It fails to take into adequate account the good of society as a whole, as opposed simply to the good of those who enter into economic transactions. There is much evidence as well against the two foregoing assumptions. Hence, if a system based on this version of the model is to be morally justifiable it must adequately address the issue of how those members of society who cannot take part in business activities will receive at least the essentials for their survival and well being, and how business activities can be kept fair and honest despite the temptations and tendencies toward profitable, unfair practices.

2. The second model depicts government as the protector of capitalists at the expense of the other members of society. Under this version of the model, if government is not actually run by the capitalist class, it is run by their representatives for the benefit of the capitalist class. The function of government in this view is the protection of the vested interests of the owners of the means of production against the members of the working class. Government protects profits, regulates what labor is allowed and not allowed to do, taxes enterprises at a lower rate than workers, guarantees profits through subsidies and contracts, and does whatever else is necessary for the benefit of business. In some instances the members of government are the entrepreneurs. Whether or not this is the case, the aim of government is to foster the interests of business—frequently big business—at the expense of the rest of society.

Marxist critics claim that this is the true relation of government and business under capitalism, despite attempts by both groups to camouflage the relation. If government in fact acts in the way described, its actions vis-à-vis business cannot be morally justified. The proper function of a legitimate government is to foster the interests of all the members of the society. To protect and promote some at the expense of others is a violation of its basic purpose.

This version of the model is undoubtedly implemented by some governments in some capitalist societies. In these cases the relation can be morally condemned. Anyone defending capitalism as morally justifiable must be able to show that this relation of government and business is not the dominant one in the society.

3. The third version of the model is one of governmental protectionism. According to this model, a proper function of government is to help business by protecting it from foreign competition through the imposition of quotas, import taxes, or other similar means. The function of government is also sometimes to help industries financially if they run into difficulties. From a moral point of view, the rationale for such government activity is that such industries benefit the society by producing goods and supplying jobs, or in other ways, such as making the country independent in time of war. It is therefore appropriate that government support such industries. Although the defense is plausible, such action is truly morally justifiable only if in fact the members of society do benefit by it, and if they are not the victims of industries that are protected from competition for the benefit of those who own the industries. This answer, however, is made from the point of view of only the society whose industries are protected, and ignores the effect of such protection on other countries and peoples.

4. The fourth version of the model assigns to government a variety of different tasks vis-à-vis business, all of which are responsive to the general interests of the citizens. One is to make sure that competition is fair and that all businesses operate according to the same rules, established in law. In this version, government acts to define the rules of the capitalist system, and it acts as an umpire with respect to those engaged in the system. It also raises, by taxes, the money it needs to provide such common goods as roads and schools. In addition, government takes on the responsibility of caring for those in need who are unable to take part in economic activity and who are ignored by the classical economic model.

Each of these activities requires moral defense. They are all plausibly legitimate and widely accepted. The difficult question is to determine the extent to which actual governmental actions are in accordance with them in fact as well as in appearance.

5. In the fifth version of the model government and business cooperate for the sake of both business and the society as a whole. The role of government is not one only of external umpire but also of internal helper. The best example of such a model is contemporary Japan. This model directly acknowledges the benefit of society as the proper moral end of both business and government, and the two work together to achieve that end. The model allows fierce competition within all industries and allows efficiency and innovation to operate. It allows businesses to fail as a result of competition. But government helps support successful large businesses, whose success it sees as being closely tied to the general welfare of the society as a whole. A proper function of government with respect to business in this model is to help successful businesses, especially in the area of foreign exports and competition. Such cooperation of business and government, if it truly leads to the benefit of all the people of the society, is compatible with the legitimate aims of both government and business. Whether it is fair with respect to international competition depends on how that competition and the international system in which it operates are envisioned.

6. The sixth version of the model comes closest to socialism. It allows government to take over and run those industries that private enterprise cannot handle successfully, or industries in areas where competition would be inefficient, where economy of scale is important, or where compatibility of equipment is a necessity. Thus, frequently government will run the transportation system, often at a loss. It will operate the telephone and telegraph lines; sometimes it will run radio, TV, and other communication networks, and so on. This is compatible with private industries of other kinds and is also compatible with government assuming, vis-à-vis those industries, any of the other approaches of the other versions of the model. There is no reason why a government's running an industry need be any more moral or immoral than private entrepreneurs doing so. What counts is how the running is done.

All six models illustrate possible and actual relations of government and business within a capitalist framework. In differing circumstances, exactly what a government justifiably allows or prohibits depends on a variety of factors. In a rich country, whose workers have a rather high standard of living and whose business enterprises are well established, a government might morally demand better working conditions in factories than is possible in a poor country with marginally profitable enterprises. This general principle applies in all cases: government should protect the worker from injustice and exploitation. But how this is translated into actual practice depends on many specific aspects of the concrete social and economic situation. Once the basic safety of workers is ensured, it is appropriate to ask, for instance, whether requiring one more safety device will in the long run cause more benefit or more harm to society as a whole. The same is true with respect to consumers. There is much room for reasonable, moral people to disagree about exactly how much government regulation, and exactly what kind of regulation, is morally justified in a specific situation. There is, similarly, much room for reasonable, moral people to disagree about the proper relation of government and business, and many different kinds of relations may well be justifiable.

A Socialist Model

There is no classical model of socialism as a purely economic system. Historically, we have a number of very diverse societies that have been, or are called, socialistic. To the extent that socialism involves government ownership, it is very difficult, if not impossible, to separate socialism as an economic system from socialism as a political system.

A partial model of socialism which is restricted to socialism as an economic system could be characterized by three features, each of which parallels to some extent our model of capitalism. The three features are an industrial base, social ownership of the means of production, and centralized planning. This is only one of many models; it does not correspond to all socialist societies, but it does correspond in part to some of the more important ones.

An Industrial Base

Socialism as a modern phenomenon appears later on the historical scene than capitalism. In Marx's writings, it is the stage that follows the stage of capitalism. The French socialists of the nineteenth century saw it as an alternative to capitalism. It is possible to speak of socialism in an agricultural society, but the model we shall use restricts socialism to industrial societies. This means that the major form of production is industrial. All the problems of industrialization must therefore be faced by socialist economies as well as by capitalist ones. With industrialization come problems of waste and pollution, which must be handled. For some problems the solutions may be the same as under capitalism; in others, the solutions may be different. Worker dissatisfaction, tedium and boredom at work, and other problems resulting from the productive process, from specialization, and from the division of labor are problems which must be solved in socialist as well as capitalist economies.

Social Ownership of the Means of Production

Social ownership of the means of production is the most frequently mentioned characteristic of a socialist economy. Such social ownership does not deny private ownership of personal goods; personal property is compatible with socialism. The form of social ownership in our model may be either state ownership or worker ownership. A model may be constructed with only state, or with only worker, ownership. Both are allowable in our model. Social ownership in the sense that the means of production are owned by all the people is not part of our model. The reason for excluding it is that there is no socialist society to which such ownership is applicable. Neither is it clear what such ownership would mean, nor how it would function on a large scale that would be applicable to a whole society. State ownership involves control by the government. The government of the society may represent the people, and it may act in their name; but the government, even if legitimate, is not the people.

The relation of government to people is the central moral question of socialism. The government is the employer of all. Is it possible for the government to pay people less than the value they produce? Is it possible for the government to exploit people? Is it possible for government to be inequitable in its allocation of goods, and to give preference to some at the expense of others? It is certainly possible for all these things to happen. Government ownership does not preclude them. Equality of opportunity is not necessarily guaranteed, nor will people's desires necessarily be fulfilled or weighed seriously. On the other hand, their desires may be weighed, their needs may be taken care of, and they may be treated fairly and equitably. There is no guarantee that government ownership will necessarily produce such a society, however, unless we build such virtues into the system. The difficulty with building these virtues into the model is that the model will not apply to an actual society unless the virtues are also present. Socialism as a model is frequently presented with such benefits built into it; our model, however, is neutral on this score.

Worker ownership is a relatively new phenomenon and is usually joined to some extent with government ownership. Worker ownership is comparable to co-ops. What makes them different is the total system or model in which they are found. If factories, for instance, are all owned by the workers, are they run competitively or not? Is competition between worker-owned factories to be considered a part of socialism or not? Because worker-owned factories are possible under capitalism, what would differentiate this portion of the socialist model from the capitalist model is that worker ownership would be the dominant form of ownership rather than a marginal one.

Centralized Planning

Centralized planning is a necessary part of our model of socialism, at least with respect to heavy industries, transportation, and communications. Total centralized planning is of course allowable under the model, but it is not a necessary component. Without centralized planning, at least in essential sectors, it would be difficult to distinguish the model of socialism from the model of capitalism. If worker-owned factories, for instance, were allowed to compete freely for resources, and in what and how they produced, they would not differ significantly in most respects from similar factories in the capitalist model.

Centralized planning involves government. It is the government that typically does the planning in a socialist society. The task might be done by some other group, but that group would in the final analysis be equivalent to a government. Its job is to allocate resources and to guide the production and allocation of resources and goods. Its ideal is to end the anarchy and wastefulness of the marketplace.

Centralized planning precludes free-market decisions of many types, though not of all types. The market might still be the indicator of what people want. Central planners can take into account such information as unfulfilled demand and a supply that exceeds demand. The point of centralized planning, however, is to replace competition. Hence, the competitive aspects of the market would not be allowed. For the system to work, the central planners obviously need an enormous amount of information, and in time to use the information in making decisions about the allocation of resources and the goods to be produced and distributed. Planners need some way of knowing the needs of the people and of the society, some way of determining which goods and needs must be given preference over others. Typically this involves a large government apparatus, usually of a bureaucratic nature.

Can government know all it needs to know successfully to operate such a system? The more centralized and encompassing the control, the more difficult it is to succeed. The fewer industries controlled, the more likely the success.

The Comparison of Models and Systems

Although we have raised some of the moral issues involved in the capitalist and socialist models we have not determined whether either one is (or both are) inherently immoral. If analysis revealed that there were structural elements in either model that were immoral, then the system depicted by the model would be immoral. To the extent that the model was instantiated in a society, people of that society would have to see what was necessary to remove the immorality, what other system might be adopted, and how the change might be best achieved.

We have not yet discussed how the economic models intertwine with political and legal systems. Do particular legal and political systems mitigate the negative tendencies of capitalism or of socialism? Do they interfere with the positive tendencies? Can the mix be modelled and morally evaluated? Specific cases, of course, require specific analyses.

In the abstract, the proponents of capitalism frequently enumerate the following values: it promotes individual freedom; it promotes and rewards initiative, innovation, and the taking of risks; and it results in the efficient production of multitudes of goods, increasing the productivity of society and so benefiting all members of the society. Capitalism is attacked for exploiting the workers, for producing false wants, for waste, and for allowing gross inequalities.

Champions of socialism emphasize equality, security, and the absence of exploitation. Gross inequalities of wealth and income are mitigated under socialism, though some differences in both still exist. Workers are guaranteed work and all are guaranteed that their basic needs will be taken care of—food, shelter, medicine, clothing, education. The lack of exploitation is premised on the fact that no individual employs other individuals. The state is the major if not the sole employer, and the state does not exploit its workers for profit, as private employers are tempted to do. The absence of complete equality, the difficulties of proper allocation of resources and markets, and the lower productivity on the whole, to the extent that they exist, are seen not as defects of the system but as remediable deficiencies.

During our century different countries have opted for different models. The newly emerging countries of Africa have frequently followed the model of socialism that is found in China, which is a primarily agricultural socialist model. Other countries have followed the model of socialism in the Soviet Union. Others have taken Sweden as the socialist model to follow. Still others, for instance Japan after World War II, have followed something like the model of the United States. In each case the economic models have been joined with a variety of political systems; they have been adopted by people with a particular history and tradition, with particular natural resources, and with specific international friends and enemies. Though the moral problems in each case vary to some extent, some basic problems are common to all. Some of these are a function of the economic systems with which they operate.

Economic Systems and Justice

We cannot be moral and choose or espouse an inherently immoral economic system. But on the assumption that there is more than one economic system that is not inherently immoral, there is no moral imperative mandating that we choose one rather than another. If we assume, for the sake of an example, that neither the capitalist nor the socialist model presented is inherently immoral, the choice of one rather than the other involves a choice of certain values over others. The mixture of freedom, security, and risk is very different in the two models. Which is the best mixture, from a moral point of view? Because neither is immoral, either one, if it is freely chosen, is morally acceptable. Immoral practices might develop in either system, however. If they do develop, such practices should be avoided and if possible rooted out. Each society can improve, and should attempt to do so. There is no one best society.

Yet any economic system as well as any political system should embody justice to a considerable degree. Distributive justice, that is, justice in the social allocation of benefits and burdens, is frequently thought to be the most important moral component of any economic system. Is justice a function of each system? Is there a capitalist conception of justice and a socialist conception of justice, each appropriate to the system? Is there an eternal, or system-neutral, conception of justice in terms of which we can evaluate any economic system?

In our earlier discussion of justice we noted that it consists in giving each person his due, in treating equals equally and unequals unequally. We also saw that distributive justice could be formulated in a variety of ways.

In the capitalist system, justice demands equality of opportunity; it does not demand equality of results. The best way to tell who is the fastest runner is to have all runners compete under the same conditions. Someone will finish first, someone will finish last, and the others will finish somewhere in between. The capitalist system rewards some people who take risks and penalizes others. That is what risk-taking involves. The rewards are frequently proportional to the risk. Capitalism also rewards a number of other attributes—work, initiative, energy, intelligence, and similar qualities applied in the marketplace. Within the system, some may be lucky and others unlucky. But so long as there is equality of opportunity, and so long as rewards are sufficient to generate productive activity, justice has been served. If we need a formula, we might say that each is rewarded in accordance with his input into the economy. "From each as he wishes to participate, to each as his participation is successful," might be its slogan.

Justice in a socialist system consists not only in equality of opportunity; it also allows proportionality of differential rewards. It guarantees that all receive some reward, but it tends to limit the amount of the reward anyone may get. A common slogan used to describe socialism is, "From each according to his ability, to each according to his work." Lenin, among others, noted that this was not the social ideal. The social ideal that embodies justice is the slogan descriptive of communism, "From each according to his ability, to each according to his need."

We have already discussed the suggestion of John Rawls that we choose our principles of justice behind the veil of ignorance. The two principles of justice thus derived, he claims, are compatible with both capitalism and with socialism.

Obviously, a view of justice that demands equality of results will not be compatible with capitalism, nor will a view of justice that requires that differential rewards according to merit, work, or input be compatible with a system requiring equality of rewards. A variety of formulations of justice are possible and appropriate for various circumstances. For instance, in a race, it would be inappropriate to require that everyone be given first place. If we want a race, then the honor of first place should go to the one who wins. If we are not interested in seeing who is fastest, but we feel that other conditions should be taken into account, then we may assign handicaps, equalizing weight, size, training, or other differentials. But once these are established, we will still expect one person to win. Justice does not preclude our playing that game, nor does it require that when we play it we not reward the winner. However, it may, for a variety of reasons, require that we not award the winner certain kinds of prizes, prizes out of proportion to the fact that the race is a game or a sport. But the consideration of justice here is different from the consideration of justice when all the runners run under the same track conditions, or when some run with a handicap.

A similar approach can be taken with respect to justice in economic systems and the justice of economic systems. There is not just one notion of justice that is applicable; there are several different formulations, and one of them may be appropriate for one purpose and kind of activity and another for another kind of event and activity. Each formulation of justice may be taken as a prima facie formulation. If its application is appropriate, it should be applied. If two or more different approaches seem to apply, and if their application is mutually contradictory, then we must determine which arguments can be mustered in defense of each. What are the claimed injustices? How do they compare with the other claimed injustices? Is there some way to reconcile the differing claims? How are the claims supported? Which arguments prevail in the given case?

This solution may be unsatisfactory to some, those who claim to have the final, true, or applicable view of justice. But faced with competing claims, we can resolve the conflict in this instance only by trying to sort out the claims and arguments in support of them. We may not reach a solution with which everyone agrees, and the debate may not be settled. All this is true. But this does not mean that we should not continue to strive to achieve justice in our economic systems, or that we should rest content that the view of justice we have is the last word on the topic. We should be constantly prepared to recognize injustice where we did not previously perceive it, and we should be ready, if the argument demands it, to reevaluate the justice of the economic system in which we find ourselves.

Further Reading

ACTON, H. B. *The Morals of Markets: An Ethical Exploration.* London: Longman Group Limited, 1971.

ARTHUR, JOHN, and WILLIAM H. SHAW, eds. *Justice and Economic Distribution.* Englewood Cliffs, N.J.: Prentice-Hall, Inc., 1978.

BENNE, ROBERT. *The Ethic of Democratic Capitalism.* Philadelphia: Fortress Press, 1981.

BOULDING, KENNETH E. *Beyond Economics: Essays on Society, Religion, and Ethics.* Ann Arbor: The University of Michigan Press, 1968.

BRANDT, RICHARD B., ed. *Social Justice.* Englewood Cliffs, N.J.: Prentice-Hall, Inc., 1962.

DALTON, GEORGE. *Economic Systems & Society.* Baltimore: Penguin Books, 1974.

HARE, R. M. "What Is Wrong With Slavery," *Philosophy and Public Affairs*, VIII (1979), pp. 103–121.

HARRINGTON, MICHAEL. *Socialism.* New York: Saturday Review Press, 1972.

MARX, KARL, and FRIEDRICH ENGELS. *Basic Writings on Politics and Philosophy.* Ed., Lewis Feuer. Garden City, N.Y.: Anchor Books, 1959.

NOVAK, MICHAEL. *The Spirit of Democratic Capitalism.* New York: Simon & Schuster, 1982.

NOZICK, ROBERT. *Anarchy, State, and Utopia.* New York: Basic Books, Inc., 1974.

RAWLS, JOHN. *A Theory of Justice.* Cambridge, Mass.: Harvard University Press, 1971.

SEVEN

American Capitalism: Moral or Immoral?

$\mathbf{A}$merican capitalism, from its inception to the present day, has grown, developed, and changed. An attempt to reduce it to one of the models described in the last chapter would be a gross oversimplification. Although it continues to contain the general features of capitalism, its varying relations to government are central to the changes that have taken place in the development of American capitalism. The American economic system is closely tied to the political, cultural, and social system of the United States, and an adequate moral evaluation of it must take these relations into account. The American economic model we examine, therefore, must include government's action with respect to it.

Government intervention is part of the American economic system, therefore a complete justification of the entire politico-economic system would involve a defense of the American system or government as being legitimate. For our purposes, however, a sufficient moral justification of government intervention is that it keeps the economic system internally fair, and that its intervention has as its end the protection and enhancement of the welfare of the people governed, while violating no basic rights and inflicting no unjustifiable injury. If government intervention benefits only the leaders of a country, only the official bureaucrats, or only the wealthy, or if it benefits these groups at the expense of the general population, it is not morally justifiable. A corrupt government that milks its own people for the enrichment of the leaders of the country might adopt either a capitalist or a socialist economic system. In either case the resultant politico-economic system can be morally condemned; but it would not follow that all capitalist or socialist systems are inherently immoral. In evaluating the morality of the American economic system we shall need to examine the structural components of the economic system, the legitimacy of government intervention, and the total effect of the system on the people in general. For the system to be morally justifiable it must contain no inherently immoral components, and the system—including the part played by government—must benefit the people as a whole as well as the individuals who carry on economic activities within it.

Because we hold that each human being is a person and as such has certain basic rights, and is worthy of respect, there is no morally legitimate reason for treating those subject to government simply as a means to an end (the enrichment of the rulers), as slaves, or as objects. The legitimacy of government consists in the fact that the people accept the rule of government not because they are forced to do so by the government but because it is in their interest and welfare to do so. The proper end of government coincides with the reason for its acceptance by the people.

But, it might be objected, if free enterprise is the result of the legitimate activity of free citizens within a community, their activity has as *its* end the good of those who engage in it. Why must that activity benefit society as a whole? The answer is that business is possible only within a certain social context of institutions, agreements, understandings, shared values, and other social-background conditions. Those who engage in business activity must, of course, expect to benefit directly, otherwise they would not engage in such actitity. A society can reasonably be expected to endorse, sanction, and support business as a private activity only if it in turn benefits from such activity; to do otherwise would be irrational. Society and all its members clearly need not benefit directly by each business transaction; but all its members must benefit somehow, either directly or indirectly, by the business structure. Otherwise it would be rational for the members of society to restructure economic activity so that they do benefit from it, because it is possible to do so. The typical benefit the society receives is the rising standard of living for all, even though typically some people benefit more than others. The point of including government within the economic system is to make sure that those who cannot compete successfully are nonetheless guaranteed protection of their rights as human beings, including their right at least to subsistence and provision of their basic needs.

The American economic system is sometimes called a free-enterprise system. Like the classical model of capitalism, free enterprise involves the absence of government ownership, control, regulation and planning, and the freedom of individuals to enter into transactions of their own choosing. This freedom is significant from a moral point of view. The American version of free enterprise postulates maturity, intelligence, and responsibility on the part of those operating within the economic system. It assumes that each person wishes his own good, and that each person knows, better than anyone else, what he wants. The system claims to respect each person as an autonomous adult and a responsible moral being when it allows him to make his own decisions and choose his own way of life. It further assumes that each person desires maximal freedom, and that as a competent, adult, moral being he or she deserves it, providing it is compatible with like freedom for all.

Adam Smith, in his classical defense of capitalism, claims that each person, in pursuing his own good, indirectly and unknowingly also promotes the public interest. The general good is better served in this way, he contends, than by any group directly attempting to promote the general welfare through some means of overall planning and control. American free enterprise adopts a modified version of this view.

Free enterprise, which prizes efficiency, insists, moreover, that the transactions between adults must be fair. Fairness can here be specified in procedural rather than substantive terms. A transaction is fair if both parties to it—usually the buyer and the seller—engage in the transaction freely (without coercion), and if both parties have adequate and appropriate knowledge of the relevant aspects of the transaction. If one of the parties hides relevant information, misrepresents the transaction in some way, or intimidates the other party, then the transaction is not a fair one. In such transactions one party takes unfair advantage of the other. A transaction is not defined as fair in terms of the value of the product or service that is transferred, because some people may value some product or service more than others do. If they are willing to buy a product at a higher price—providing they know what they are doing and are not coerced—the transaction is not unfair. This is the way the market works.

The Relation of the American Government to the American Economic System

What is the relation of government to the system? The economic system can operate only in a broader social system of reasonable security and stability. Government has traditionally provided security and stability for the people of a country by arranging for the means of common defense; protecting the person and property of the members of a society from incursion by other members; enforcing contracts; and by facilitating conditions for the exchange of goods and services. Thus, a national government typically provides armed forces for the protection of the country, making the people secure from outside invasion. Through its laws, police force, court, and penal system, it protects individuals in the society in their person and property. People can thus feel secure in acquiring goods and feel safe in their use of them. A nation's laws and courts make possible and enforce legally binding contracts, and make available acceptable procedures for the peaceful adjudication of disputes. The government also prints and mints money, the generally acceptable medium of exchange which facilitates transactions within the economic system.

The relation of government and the economic system in the United States, however, did not stop with these minimalist functions. At least five other needs arose, which the government sought to meet.

Development of a Welfare Safety Net

Even if the system of free enterprise works as its advocates argue it should, it rewards only those who contribute to the economy, and only in proportion to their contribution. It does not reward those who make no contribution to the economy. If someone cannot contribute, he is simply ignored, or left out of the activities of the marketplace. No one is forced to enter the marketplace, and those in the marketplace are not forced to consider those who do not enter it. But what does the free-enterprise system do for the sick, disabled, and incapacitated, those unable to take care of themselves, or those who fail disastrously? From the point of view of the classical economic model of capitalism, they are simply not considered. Yet, clearly, a nation should not ignore the plight of some of its citizens. They should not starve or die from lack of care simply because they cannot contribute to the economy. The other members of the society, from their largesse and kindness, might help such people through charity. But historically, such charity has been both inadequate and frequently demeaning. Hence, the government has been called upon, or has taken upon itself, to provide a safety net for everyone, and to help those unable to care for themselves. Has governmental aid been administered wisely, and has the aid been sufficient? Have people taken advantage of the systems of welfare that the government has set up? These and similar questions can be investigated, debated, and possibly answered. But it seems clear that a society has a moral obligation to prevent its members from starving and dying from lack of basic needs when the wherewithall to provide them is available. If free enterprise as a system does not consider those who do not contribute to the economy, society as a whole clearly must in some way make up for this deficiency; it acts immorally if it does not.

Provision of Common Goods

Government entered the marketplace to provide common goods that perhaps could not be (and in any event were not) provided adequately by the participants in the economic system. The United States highway system is an example of a type of common activity undertaken by the government. As in so many other areas, however, the United States government does not actually build the roads; it finances their building by private contractors. In the past, it assisted in the development of railroads, rather than building, owning, and operating them itself. It limited the liability of those who wanted to build nuclear power plants, enabling private producers to undertake a venture they felt involved too much risk to pursue otherwise. National, state, and local government has provided public education, public parks, reservoirs, and dams. Government has sought to consider and protect the common good where it was threatened by the transactions of private individuals and firms.

Control of Economic Cycles

Capitalism historically suffers from cyclical crises. In the United States, the economic system has experienced periods of great expansion and productivity, followed by periods of recession and depression. The cyclical nature of capitalism seems to be part of its natural tendency. But the periods of decline and depression result in great pain and distress for many. As demand decreases, factories produce less. As they produce less, they need fewer workers; people are laid off and are unable to find work elsewhere. Unemployment grows and with it comes misery for the unemployed and their families. Such a situation may be one that defenders of a capitalist system are willing to accept as part of the natural mechanisms of the market, which tends to be self-correcting. But such booms and busts take their toll on the members of a society, who clearly would prefer a system with more security and less drastic cycles. The United States government entered the economic realm both to alleviate the plight of the unemployed and to help set limits on the cycles through which the free market tends to go. It has attempted to keep the cycles from rising or falling too sharply. The task is complicated, and is one which government has not yet mastered. But it attempts to do so through its fiscal and monetary policies, through control of its spending, and similar devices. In fulfilling this function, government in America has become substantially involved in the economic system.

Correction of the Unfair Tendencies of the Free-Enterprise System

A premise of the free-enterprise system is that each party enter transactions freely and with adequate knowledge appropriate to each transaction. Several tendencies of American free enterprise, however, have historically tended to undermine the fairness of transactions. In each of these cases government has been called upon to regulate the conditions of the transaction, in an attempt to keep the transactions fair.

Antitrust legislation is one example of such an attempt. In any form of capitalism, capital tends to accumulate in the hands of a few who become rich and powerful. If they can successfully dominate an industry, they can prevent free entry into that industry and thereby set the conditions under which goods will be sold and persons hired. Such power clearly changes the conditions of a transaction; it is no longer a transaction between equals who freely enter into it for mutual gain. The one holding the monopoly is able to restrain trade and free enterprise in the area he dominates, and is able to set the conditions for the transaction. The other member, if he wants the product, has no alternative but to enter into the transaction with the monopolist, on the latter's terms. If the former needs the product or the job to live, the transaction is not free. To prevent such a situation from occurring, to preserve the conditions of a free and fair market, antitrust laws make restraint of trade illegal.

Regulated industries, such as communications and the electric power industry, provide a second example. In many countries these industries are owned and operated by the government and are seen as a common good. In the United States, power companies are privately owned. It has been considered to be in the general interest not to have many small competing producers of electric power. Large producers of electricity in a given area, tied in with other producers, can achieve economies of scale and efficiency. Monopolies are allowed in this area. But the government regulates power companies, to prevent them from taking unfair advantage of their customers.

Government also operates in a third area—that of food and drugs. In many transactions a buyer can decide, upon inspection, whether he or she wishes to buy a product and whether or not to pay the price asked. But the ordinary person can hardly be expected to know the effects of many drugs (one would need a chemical laboratory of one's own, in order to analyze a drug before taking it. Individuals are therefore at a great disadvantage when engaging in a transaction involving the purchase of pharmaceuticals. A transaction is fair only if both sides have adequate appropriate knowledge. The buyer can easily be taken advantage of, much to the detriment of his or her health. People have sought, therefore, to protect their interests and to guarantee the fairness of the transaction by having the government intervene. The government tests the effects of drugs, or forces drug firms to test the effects, and then regulates the sale of drugs. It also regulates the contents of food products, mandates clear labeling, and determines what other information the manufacturer must supply to the purchaser in order to make the transaction fair.

Taxation

The fifth type of government intervention in the system is a function of the four just mentioned, and of other similar activities. Through taxation, the government redistributes income, regulates business activity, and finances its own activities. It funnels money to the private sector through welfare-type programs and through contracts. It is also a giant employer in its own right, supporting vast numbers of people in the armed forces and in the large government bureaucracy required to run its many programs.

The free-enterprise model of American capitalism is not a static one. The intermingling of business and govenment has been justified, at various stages, in order to keep the conditions of the market's operation fair and just, to make up for deficiencies of the system, and to supplement the system. We can expect the continuing involvement of government in the economic realm even though we cannot predict the exact nature of this involvement.

Taking all of this into account, what moral evaluation can we make of the present-day American free enterprise? Is it inherently immoral? If not, does it contain any immoral aspects that can and should be remedied? Many Marxists claim that capitalism is immoral, and we shall look at their charges first. A number of non-Marxists have also condemned capitalism and its American instantiation as being immoral, and we shall investigate their claims next. We shall then look at the positive defense of the American free-enterprise system. Finally, we shall consider, from several points of view, the moral alternatives to American capitalism as proposed by critics.

The Marxist Critique

Karl Marx analyzed nineteenth-century capitalism, primarily as he found it in the England of his time. Though Marx frequently uses the language of morality in describing the ills of capitalism, commentators disagree about whether he actually condemned capitalism from a moral point of view. Capitalism, for Marx, was a necessary stage of economic and social development, but a stage that was to be superseded by the higher stage of communism. Yet many of Marx's followers have put his condemnation of capitalism into moral form, and have thus claimed that capitalism, in all its variations, is inherently immoral.

We shall examine three of the major claims of these Marxists: (1) Capitalism is inherently immoral because it cannot exist without robbing the worker of his due; (2) capitalism is inherently immoral because it necessarily involves the alienation of human beings; and (3) capitalism is inherently immoral at the present time because it protects the vested interest of the few and prevents the many from achieving a better, more just, more equitable society.

Exploitation of the Work Force

The first charge states that capitalism is based on exploitation of the worker, that is, not paying him what he truly deserves. Slavery, we have already seen, is inherently immoral. According to the Marxist critics, capitalism involves wage slavery. Capitalism cannot exist without exploiting the worker. Hence, there is no way of remedying this evil while preserving the system. Because capitalism is inherently immoral, it should be replaced by socialism, and eventually by full communism.

The basis for the claim of necessary exploitation is Marx's *labor theory of value.* According to this theory, commodities are exchanged at their real value. If this were not the case, then what one gains as a seller, one would lose as a buyer. Because commodities are exchanged at their real value, the question that must be answered is where profit comes from. Profit, in Marxist terminology, is called *surplus value,* or the money a commodity brings a seller, over and above its cost of production. Profit is accumulated as capital and allows the producer to expand and produce more. The producer would not produce if he did not get profit. But if we assume that all commodities are sold at their real value, there will be nothing left over, and therefore there will be no profit. We are then forced to conclude that something is not sold at its real value. That something is human labor.

What all commodities have in common, according to the Marxist analysis, is that they are the products of human labor. Human labor finds raw materials and, by further human labor, makes them available for transformation into commodities. If I wish to trade what I have for what you have, I also wish to know the comparative value of each item. The basis for comparison is that which is a common measure for both: the labor embodied in each. The total human labor that goes into a commodity is the basis for determining its value. For comparative purposes, moreover, we use as our least-common denominator the socially necessary unskilled labor time required to make a product. Once again, if I trade my product for yours, and if we trade equally, there is no profit left over. Profit must come from someone not being paid the value that he contributes to a commodity. Profit comes, according to the Marxist analysis, from workers not being paid the value that they contribute. The owner of the means of production systematically exploits his workers, or steals from them, by paying them less than the value they produce. The difference between the value the workers produce and what they receive as wages is surplus value or profit, and is taken by the employer. Unless he did, he would get no profit and have no capital to invest.

But why do workers sell their labor for less than it is worth? The answer is that they are forced to do so in order to live. This is why the system is said to be a type of wage slavery. Workers do not own the means of production. They have no choice but to sell their labor power, unless they wish to die of starvation. Nor are they free to seek employment where they will be paid the full value they produce. Every employer exploits his workers; he must in order to make a profit. If a worker does have a choice of jobs, it is simply a choice of whether he will be exploited by employer *A* or employer *B*. The system makes all employers exploiters, and exploits all workers.

Because an employer makes his profit by paying his workers less than the value they produce, he will tend to increase his profit by paying them as little as possible. If he pays them by the day, he will wish them to work twelve rather than ten hours, and ten rather than eight hours. If he pays them by the hour, he will wish them to produce during that hour five rather than four objects, or four rather than three. So long as there is not enough work for everyone who wants it, there will be a buyer's market, and workers will have to work for lower wages than they would otherwise. It is in the interest of the owners of the means of production to have a surplus work force, or for there to be a pool of unemployed. A high unemployment rate, rather than a low one, or no unemployment at all, is to their advantage. The worker, on the other hand, will seek to work shorter hours, or to work less hard during the hours he does work. He will also seek more pay rather than less, so that he can improve his standard of living. The war between management and labor stems from the fact that management wishes to pay as little as possible for labor in order to increase its profits, and labor wishes to receive as much as possible of what it deserves.

In the nineteenth century, Marx perceived certain trends in capitalism. He described the tendency of the owners to pay workers less and less, forcing women and even children to enter the labor force in order to help support their families. He described a growing army of the unemployed, and foresaw more and more blatant exploitation, until the workers finally would be forced to seize the means of production, take over the factories, put an end to exploitation and capitalism, and form a new social order—communism (the first stage of which he termed *socialism*).

The scenario according to the Marxist script has not taken place. The workers united and formed unions, in part, ironically, because of the efforts of Marx. As a result, the workers were able to gain more pay, shorter hours, and better working conditions. The impetus for them to revolt and seize the factories diminished. Their interests became identified with the continuation of the system rather than with its overthrow. Later Marxists asked how this was possible, and whether it meant that capitalism was no longer immoral.

Lenin gave an answer to both questions. According to him, the workers in the West were appeased by the increases they received in higher earnings and the goods they were able to buy with those earnings. Their standard of living rose, so that the American worker lived better than any large number of people in human history. But, said Lenin, this does not mean that the worker is no longer exploited. He is still exploited, even if he does not realize it. Profit still comes from paying the worker less than the value he produces. But productive capacities have increased to such an extent that the worker can enjoy the fruits of productivity even while being exploited. Furthermore, the worker is no longer as grossly exploited as he was in the nineteenth century. This is not a result of the generosity of management; it is a result of capitalism's advance to the stage of imperialism. American corporations can pay their workers well because the corporations are able to exploit people in other countries, primarily in the underdeveloped countries of the world.

The upshot, for Marxists, is that capitalism still involves exploitation and therefore is still inherently immoral. The American workers are still exploited, even though they have achieved a high standard of living. They could be better off than they are. Part of the reason they enjoy the standard of living they do, moreover, is the fact that American companies are exploiting other peoples of the world. Capitalism, the Marxists claim, necessarily involves exploitation.

What are we to say of the claim? The claim depends on the validity of Marx's labor theory of value. This economic theory attempts to explain not only profit but also prices, wages, economic cycles, and the variety of economic phenomena with which economics deals. Most Western economists have not accepted Marx's version of the labor theory of value. It does not give due weight to knowledge, creativity, and initiative in the productive process, nor to the place of invention and efficiency in expanding the economic pie which is to be divided. It fails to take into account the role of risk and the entrepreneur. It is inadequate as an analysis of contemporary American capitalism because that system is vastly different from the system Marx described. Through pension plans and insurance policies, American workers are in fact, to a considerable extent, the owners of the means of production. The workers are not oppressed. There may be some exploitation, but exploitation consists of paying the worker less than the productivity of a worker at the margin. It is not built into the system.

The claim that the worker deserves all the value he produces is neither obvious nor in accord with Marx's own ideal of just distribution, which requires that each give according to his ability and receive according to his need. Whatever notion of justice we use, moreover, the Marxist analysis of exploitation cannot be applied because, except in a very few cases, we cannot determine the exact value of what each worker produces.

Nor does the claim that American capitalism survives because it exploits the underdeveloped countries carry much weight. There was a time during which many European countries had colonies, however, this time has past. There are also many countries now that are not capitalist—they are socialist, and some of them have communist governments. But the underdeveloped countries do not sell the United States goods or raw materials at lower prices than they sell the same items to socialist countries. American firms also look to the Third World countries to supply large markets as well as resources, and this means that those in the Third World must have the disposable income to buy U.S. goods. Workers must therefore receive more than subsistence wages. American companies pay workers of a country with a lower standard of living than ours less than American companies pay American workers. Is this exploitation? The question is a complex one, involving comparisons of buying power, skill, and comparative wage structures. We shall examine it in a later chapter. We should note in passing, however, that American multinational corporations are sometimes criticized for paying workers more than the going rate in Third World countries. But the major point is that there are alternatives for underdeveloped countries. They can refuse American industry, and they can deal with other countries if they think it is not to their advantage to deal with the United States.

The conclusion we can draw from this brief analysis is that there are plausible replies to the Marxist charge of exploitation. The replies have not satisfied the Marxists; nor have attempts at updating Marx's theory satisfied most Western economists. The attack is at least inconclusive, if not definitely false.

Alienation of the People

The second Marxist claim is that capitalism is inherently immoral because it alienates human beings. It does not treat them as ends in themselves; it separates them into antagonistic camps and sets one against another; it stultifies the workers; it involves domination of some by others; and it produces other negative effects on all those who live within the system.

Alienation is a negative term. It describes the state of a person who is wrongfully separated from something to which he should be united, or who is dominated by something of his own making. The state or condition of alienation may be a conscious one, as when a person feels alienated; but someone may be alienated without feeling so.

There are various kinds of alienation. People may feel alienated from their government. Government is something created by people to serve their needs. When they have no control over it, and when government dominates them instead of responding to them and serving them, they are alienated from it. Religious alienation might be described by a believer as being separation from God through sin; by an unbeliever, as man being dominated by the idea of God, a creature of man's own imaginative making. Marx claims, however, that basic to all the other kinds of alienation is economic alienation. He describes it as the alienation of the worker from the product of his labor, from the productive process, and from other men.

Under the capitalistic system, Marx observes, objects come to dominate men. People are judged by what they have, not by what they are. People work and live for possessions. The possessions come to dominate them, rather than being objects which they use to satisfy their needs.

Under capitalism, Marx claims, work is typically stultifying, noncreative, and routine. Instead of expressing oneself through one's work and developing all the sides of one's personality, work limits, cramps, and dulls the worker. People live when they are not working, and when they are working they can hardly be said to be living. They look forward to their leisure time, weekends, vacations, and coffee breaks, times when they can be themselves. They are separated from their labor, which they have sold to their employer. They are alienated from their labor, which they must sell in order to live.

Finally, the capitalist system, built on competition, divides men from each other. Instead of all mankind living together in harmony and peace, capitalism pits workers against employers. It pits competitors against each other, just as it forces workers to compete against each other for jobs. Capitalism is built on the division of society into classes, the owners of the means of production on one side and the workers on the other. The society is divided, and the state, laws, courts, police, schools, churches, and the media are all controlled by the ruling class. The ruling class uses all these social institutions to dominate the workers, keep them subservient, and insure the continuation of the institution of private property. The workers are thus alienated in many aspects of their lives. The owners of the means of production also live in an alienated society; they are also evaluated in terms of what they have, and they are also separated from other men and dominated by what they have.

Marx maintained that capitalism necessarily produces alienation because it is a function of private property and of the division of labor. Alienation cannot be eliminated without eliminating private property, and this cannot be eliminated without at the same time eliminating capitalism. Therefore capitalism is inherently immoral.

Defenders of capitalism have given various replies. One claim is that the picture Marx drew is a caricature of capitalist society. In America, they say, the worker is freer than in any other society in the world. He has a strong voice in government, which frequently protects his rights and defends him against employers. Though there is still dull work to be done, automation has taken over much of it and has freed people to do more creative work. The dull work that is a function of manufacturing, moreover, is not peculiar to capitalism; it is present wherever there is industrialization. A second response points out that Marx's description of capitalist society as a society of class conflict may have been true of nineteenth-century England. The history of the United States, however, has been one of great class mobility. In fact, it is sometimes difficult for people to know to which class they belong. Classes are not obvious, and the division of people into proletariat and bourgeoisie is not clearly applicable to the people of the United States. Marx's description also ignores the spirit of cooperation that is present in many aspects of American life. The emphasis on goods undoubtedly characterizes many Americans. Yet even this emphasis has been somewhat tempered in recent times by large numbers of young adults who revolted against the emphasis on goods that typified their parents' values.

A third approach to the Marxist charge of alienation has been to see whether alienation has actually been eliminated in those countries that have done away with private property. The Soviet Union is the prime example of such a society. But clearly, the defenders of capitalism argue, during the reign of Stalin the Soviet people were more oppressed and alienated from their government than Americans have ever been. The claim that private property is the cause of alienation is therefore disproven.

There are other answers in defense of American capitalism; the ones we have given exemplify the line they take. The rebuttals have not convinced the Marxists; nevertheless they have a certain validity. Marx's description of the alienation of the worker in the nineteenth century is not an accurate picture of the worker in present-day America. There are, however, aspects of the Marxist attack that are valid. Many people in America complain that government is out of control, and that they have no real say in how they are governed; others complain about the emphasis of Americans on material goods; and some speak in terms of alienation. Still, no one has produced an analysis that satisfactorily shows that these ills are inherent in contemporary American capitalism. Once again, then, the claimed inherent immorality of capitalism remains an open question.

Vested Interests

The third Marxist charge is that capitalism defends the vested interests of the few and prevents the vast productive forces of society from truly serving the masses. The natural tendency of the productive process is toward social ownership instead of private ownership of the means of production. Those in the capitalist class, however, defend their own position and interests by preventing the transformation from private ownership to social ownership. In so doing, they delay the inevitable and prevent the people from enjoying that satisfaction of their needs which, given the great resources and productive capacity of our country, is possible. According to this critique, capitalism may not always have been inherently immoral. But it is immoral now, because it prevents the development of a morally better stage of social development. This analysis can be given a utilitarian interpretation. The consequences of protecting the vested interests of the rich at the expense of the workers produces less good on the whole than would the adoption of socialism or communism.

The reply of the defender of capitalism is to deny that the American system protects the rich at the expense of the worker. It protects and benefits all in the society, even if some benefit more than others. The defender of the system then usually refers to socialism as it exists in the world today, whether it is democratic socialism, such as in England, or communistic socialism, such as in the Soviet Union. Both are examples of highly productive societies. Yet neither society seems superior to American society, either morally or materially. Therefore, the reply continues, the claim that the American system prevents the development of a better society is a claim without adequate foundation. Moreover, the workers of the United States (the ones whom the Marxist critics say would benefit most by a change to socialism) show no signs of developing a Marxist revolution.

The third criticism, that of inherent immorality, has therefore not been convincingly demonstrated. Capitalism may be inherently immoral, but the Marxists' attacks fail to prove this.

Non-Marxist Moral Critiques of American Capitalism

Though Marxists have tended to be the most vocal, systematic, and thorough critics of capitalism, they are not its only critics. The non-Marxist critics do not always speak with one voice. Nor is it always clear whether the ills to which they point are inherent evils of capitalism or remediable by-products. We will now consider three criticisms which are symptomatic of others: (1) capitalism creates waste and false needs; (2) capitalism feeds the military-industrial complex at the expense of the general population; and (3) capitalism creates gross and unjust inequalities.

False Needs and Overproduction

The charge that American capitalism is wasteful takes a variety of forms. It is of course true that Americans have grown up with comparative abundance.

138

We have large expanses of land, a wealth of natural resources, and a high standard of living. As a result of our competitive system, we have worried little about conservation of our natural resources, or about the resources that we could buy from the rest of the world. The waste is evident in many areas. Our use of energy and of gasoline is particularly profligate. We have extended our cities into suburb after suburb without providing adequate public transportation, and then relied on large fuel-inefficient automobiles that are rarely fully occupied. We have tended to build obsolescence into most of our products. We have preferred disposable products to ones with replaceable parts. The list is endless.

In many instances, the claim goes, we could have done much better. Competition has frequently led to duplication of wasteful effort. Manufacturers have built obsolescence into their products to protect their future markets, not to serve the consumer. Our cities and suburbs grew without plan or adequate forethought. Our waste is a national disgrace.

The attack is in large part true. We are paying the price for mistakes we made in the past. But our past waste was not the result of capitalism, nor is waste a necessary ingredient in capitalism. For instance, many European countries with capitalist economies have not fallen prey to the vice of waste. Nor is it clear that centralized planning eliminates waste; that waste is frequently of a different kind. The chronic shortage of goods in some socialist countries is sometimes a result of producing a surplus of the wrong goods (e.g., too many pairs of size 13 shoes), rather than of having too few materials for the production of goods. Duplication of effort is part of the price of competition. But with some justification, its defenders claim that on the whole, competition is more efficient than centralized planning.

The second part of the criticism strikes at the creation of false needs. Entrepreneurs create a product (e.g., an electric toothbrush) for which there was not an antecedent need or desire. Through a high-powered advertising campaign the manufacturer convinces people that they need the product to clean their teeth. The result is that a false need is created and filled, consuming resources that could be better used for other products.

Defenders of the free-enterprise system have argued that the notion of false needs is an arbitrary one. Who is to decide what a real need is and what is a false need? Consumers, they claim, should decide for themselves how they want to spend their money. They are not forced to buy one product rather than another. Nor is it true that manufacturers can sell anything they make simply by advertising it. Many products fail to gain a market because consumers resist the ads and ignore the product. The attack assumes that someone knows best what the people of the country should have. The counterclaim is that people should be free both to produce and purchase what they wish without direction from some group with supposedly privileged knowledge.

The criticism, whatever its validity, is not central enough to make the judgment that capitalism is inherently immoral. It may, however, indicate an area in need of control, attention, or reform.

The Military-Industrial Complex

The second critique attacks the military-industrial complex, and takes a variety of forms. One view claims that the government drains the people of the country through taxation in order to support industries that produce materials for war. Another view is that the system can in the long run exist only if it is periodically sustained by war and the destruction and need for rebuilding that war produces. If the latter were the case, then the charge of an inherently immoral element could be sustained. A third claims that the military-industrial complex controls the government and has taken power out of the hands of the people, if it did indeed ever reside there.

To such charges no easy answer is possible, but a few observations are in order. First, war did not start with the appearance of capitalism. It has existed since the beginning of recorded history. Capitalism is not the only root of war, if it is a root at all. Second, the communist-run countries (such as the USSR) spend as much as, and sometimes proportionately more than, the United States on arms. Expenditure for war is not an exclusive characteristic of capitalism as found in the United States. Both the Soviet Union and the United States plausibly claim, moreover, that their major effort is in defense spending because of the threat posed by the other country. Each side has its hawks and its doves. Third, the United States does spend large sums on its military establishment, but it is not clear that its economy would topple if its defense budget were reallocated to peaceful pursuits. There is even reason to believe that the opposite might be the case. Finally, the claim that the people have no voice in the political process because of the military-industrial complex is an overstatement. They have less voice than many would like; however, they have some voice and have achieved some gains at the expense of the military-industrial complex, and there is no inherent reason why, within the system, they cannot make further strides in this direction. The trick is to preserve democracy and prevent a slide toward a dictatorship.

Inequalities Inherent in the System

The third attack charges that capitalism creates gross and unjust inequalities. The disparity between the very rich and the very poor in the United States is enormous. A small percentage of the population controls a large proportion of the nation's wealth and income. The tax structure that is supposed to tax the rich progressively is so full of loopholes that the tax burden is borne primarily by the middle class. Many of those with the largest incomes pay no or very little tax. No human being, the argument continues, is so much better than another that the vast discrepancy in income—$1,000,000 a year compared with $10,000—can be justified.

According to Rawls's principles of justice, differences in income are justifiable only if opportunities are open to all, and if the least advantaged group benefits by the difference. It is not clear that the least advantaged group does benefit by the large differences in income; nor is it clear that even if they did, the benefit they receive is in any way proportional to the benefit that the rich receive. The poor not only obtain little improvement in their material conditions, but by comparison with the luxury of the wealthy they suffer a loss of self-respect. To compound the difficulties, many of the wealthiest families of our country amassed their fortunes in questionable and unethical ways. The history of the robber barons is a notorious period in American history.

The drive toward greater equalization of wealth and income has many supporters. The charge that the tax structure needs overhauling is widely recognized. The claim that the discrepancy between the wealth of the very rich and the poverty of the very poor is excessive carries a good deal of weight. Yet the question remains whether all of this, though a result of capitalism, is a necessary feature of American capitalism. Differences in income are to be expected in a competitive system and in a system in which monetary reward is a prime incentive for creativity in production. Yet the overall system can reduce the differential between the highest and the lowest paid, or it can, through a different tax structure, equalize the two considerably more than it presently does. Such injustices can be handled within the system. The charge, therefore, does not necessarily require a change of system, although that is one way of achieving the equalization many seek.

The Moral Defense of the American Free-Enterprise System

Can a moral defense of the American version of capitalism be mounted? Although none of its defenders would claim that it is morally perfect, all would argue that it is not immoral. For those who believe the Amoral Myth of Business this suffices. Yet some defenders of free enterprise go further and claim that it is inherently moral; and a few even claim that it is the most moral of the available systems.

We have already shown some of the arguments in defense of American free enterprise, in the answers given to those who claim it is inherently immoral. A sketch of a positive defense is nonetheless in order. Typically, a defense of the American free-enterprise system includes (1) emphasis on its values, especially freedom and efficiency; (2) its historical record in the production and distribution of wealth; and (3) its preferability to actual socialist societies.

Freedom and Efficiency

Defenders of the American free-enterprise system place their greatest emphasis on the importance and value of human freedom, which they claim the system presupposes, develops, and enriches. From a moral point of view the importance of human freedom scarcely needs defense. Each person is an end in himself, and worthy of respect. The free-enterprise system starts by recognizing this, and then attempts to give it substance. The system allows the greatest freedom of action and choice to each person, compatible with a like freedom for all. This is guaranteed not only in the legal and political system but effectively in the economic realm. Consumers are allowed to buy what they want and to vote for products with their purchases. Producers are allowed free entry into the marketplace, where they compete under conditions kept fair by government. Some fare better than others, but that is a morally acceptable result of competition. The system, they say, fulfills its moral obligation by providing a safety net for all and caring for those unable to care for themselves.

Political freedom, the defenders of free enterprise insist, is only possible when economic freedom is its concommitant. Without individual economic freedom government not only makes all the economic decisions but also makes them as it pleases. If the government controls both the economic and political realms it has broad scope for unrestricted action. The concentration of power is more likely than otherwise to corrupt those who possess it. Political freedom is meaningful only when we can lead our lives as we ourselves determine—this is part of what political liberty means. Political freedom requires limiting the sphere of government intervention in our lives, as well as providing the freedom to vote or express our views on what government should do.

Because recognition of human freedom is an essential ingredient in treating people morally, the free-enterprise system is morally based. It values and enhances human freedom in all its aspects, and makes this the centerpiece of its moral justification.

This defense of freedom leads in turn to a moral justification of private property. Because human beings are by right and nature free, they are free to take the necessary means for their survival and development. This involves the proper use of the resources of the earth. Effective use, however, involves the right to exclude others from use, as well as the right to the produce that one derives from such use. But these claims to the right to exclusive use are what constitutes the essential ingredient of private property. Hence freedom and the human right to self-development yield the moral basis for private property.

The other value, efficiency, also has a moral defense. Efficiency involves the use of the resources of the earth, including human labor, in such a way as to be least wasteful and most productive. To the extent that we consider needless waste immoral because it deprives us or others of potential good, at least in the long run, efficiency is moral. Capitalism, its defenders claim, values and promotes efficiency. The American experience is less than perfect, and there are aspects of the economy and of everyday life where efficiency is not evident and waste clearly exists. But on the whole, the argument goes, the competitive process, which is imbedded in American free enterprise, is in the long run more efficient in the allocation and use of goods than any other system. This is true, they say, because suppliers respond to demand. Unless the market is used to indicate demand, goods are produced or talents are valued by a central decision-making agency—usually government—with much less information and with much less accuracy than that provided by a free market.

The Production of Wealth

Even its critics will not deny that under capitalism mankind has made enormous strides in its ability to produce goods. With the introduction of the machine and the rise of the industrial age there has been a manifold increase in human productivity. The result was that many more of the goods necessary for life became available in great quantity and at prices that could be afforded by the masses. From the seventeenth to the twentieth centuries, the rise in the standard of living of Americans dwarfs that of any other period in history. The ordinary person has come to have and expect what not even the wealthiest persons of previous centuries had. Mass production has increased the goods available, both those necessary for life and those simply desired for the ease, comfort, or enjoyment they produce.

The dramatic development of the machine age, moreover, has continued up to the present. The industrial revolution has been matched by the technological developments of the second half of the twentieth century. Infant mortality has decreased and life expectancy has increased. Health care has improved. The possibilities for universal education have been realized. People have more time for leisure and cultural development. The list of areas in which progress has been made, knowledge developed, and pain relieved is almost endless.

All this, its defenders claim, is the result of free enterprise. Historically no one can deny that the productive forces of human beings were multiplied and developed through capitalism. Even Karl Marx acknowledges capitalism as a necessary stage in the development of the productive resources of mankind, and evaluates it positively in that respect. Its defenders go further. Not only did capitalism help free humans from drudgery in the past; it continues to help improve the standard of living today. Nor is it only the rich who profit from it. Even the poorest members of American society live incomparably better than a great many Americans just a few generations—not to mention centuries—ago. The quality and availability of safe drinking water, the conditions of sanitation, and the presence of roads are just a few of the common benefits that all enjoy and that help make for a higher standard of living.

From a moral point of view, we can evaluate the result of the United States's economic system over time. It has unquestionably enhanced human life and welfare, not only for Americans but also for many people in other lands, through the export of its know-how and technology, its goods, and its example, as well as providing a refuge for people from a great many different lands. All this must certainly be to its moral credit. Moreover, its defenders claim, its positive contributions far outweigh its negative aspects and the undeniable negative side effects.

Preferability to Actual Socialist Systems

The third prong of the moral defense of American capitalism begins with the admission that it is not perfect. No system is. Every system can be improved, and the moral task of American free enterprise requires that its immoral aspects be constantly fought and that human welfare be further enhanced. Its defenders claim that the freedom inherent in the system makes it possible to reform it. And the checks and balances provided by the diffusion of power in a variety of hands makes it more likely that positive changes will be made than would be the case if power were centralized in government. If democracy is the worst system of government, except for all the other systems of government humans have known, then American free enterprise might be called the worst politico-economic system, except for all the other systems humans have known. Nor, claim its defenders, is there a better system waiting on the horizon.

Ever since the days of Marx, socialism has been touted as the next stage of human development and one that is morally preferable to capitalism. As a theory, socialism has a strong moral appeal. Who can deny that a society in which all live harmoniously together, in which each contributes what he can and gets what he needs, and in which wealth flows abundantly, is a desirable society? This is what socialism preaches. But the defenders of American free enterprise ask us to compare the American system not with the ideal of socialism but with the real socialist societies that those who have fought revolutions in the name of socialism have produced. Socialism is no longer an ideal waiting to be fulfilled, say the defenders of free enterprise. We have over fifty years of the results of the great socialist experiments. Compare conditions in the United States with those of the USSR or of the socialist countries of Eastern Europe, or with China, or Cuba. The higher standard of living of the American people cannot be denied. But look further, at the political freedom enjoyed by the people of the United States in comparison with the people of any of those countries. Once again its defenders claim there is no comparison. In all the historical instances we have, socialism has brought with it enormous human suffering, and the lot of ordinary people is not demonstrably better than it would have been otherwise. The conclusion drawn is that the American system, despite its defects, is morally preferable to the models of socialism offered by existing contemporary societies. Furthermore, the experiences of the socialist countries give most Americans no incentive to follow the road the socialist countries have taken. Whether a different kind of socialism—a democratic socialism with a human face and a nontotalitarian government—is possible is still an open question. It is not so certain, however, that the risk involved is worth the price America would surely have to pay to try the experiment. The conclusion drawn is that the American free-enterprise system, though not perfect, is morally justified.

Non-Socialist Alternatives to Contemporary American Capitalism

Defenders of the American free-enterprise system feel there is no need for a radical change. Though they may admit the system is not perfect, they argue it is the best history has yet known. It has provided wealth for the masses, a great variety of goods, inventions, scientific and technological advances for all people, and a degree of human freedom unparalleled in previous history. Not everyone agrees, however, that ours is the best of all possible systems. Some look at American cities, at the poor, and at many business practices and see what might be improved, and suggest ways of improvement. Others dream of radical change, of a new and better system, and still others fear the dreams of the radicals—whether of the right or of the left.

Neither Hitler's Germany nor Stalin's Soviet Union hold much appeal for most Americans. The dictatorial right is as much feared as the totalitarian left. From a moral point of view both involve a restraint on individual freedom incompatible with America's traditional value system. The moral arguments in support of our turning to either of these as real alternatives carry little, if any, weight. Rather, those two cases have become models of what most Americans feel we must guard against. They are imaginable alternatives to our present system, but they are models which are more feared and fought than pursued.

Nor is a radical revolution likely within the foreseeable future in the United States. The workers have not formed a proletariat of the type Marx thought would arise, and have not seized the means of production. Modern-day Marxists have sought revolutionary forces in the intellectuals, students, unemployed, and in the outcasts of society, but none of these groups is sufficiently unified, numerous, or motivated to carry out the revolution in America of which some Marxists still dream.

There are three other alternatives to our present American system, championed by various groups. The three are not necessarily mutually exclusive. One is libertarianism, a movement of the right. A second is workers' democracy, a movement of the left. The third is piecemeal change, wherever and however possible, with no overall blueprint. The first two are in some ways compatible with the third. Both the libertarians and the proponents of workers' democracy complain about the power and influence of government. The libertarians seek to diminish the role of government in business. The defenders of workers' democracy—whether or not they call themselves socialists—seek to end the collusion of big business and government, and to bring democracy into the marketplace. In the American context, neither group seeks violent revolution; both pursue dramatic change within the system.

The Libertarian Alternative

The libertarians, as their name indicates, put great emphasis on liberty. They not only consider this the major virtue of the free-enterprise system, but they believe only a minimalist government is compatible with liberty. They therefore complain that government has entered the marketplace with its laws, regulations, and taxes to the detriment of the freedom of the American citizen and businessman.

The attack takes several forms and involves not only a view of economics but also a view of government. The typical libertarian, although not an anarchist (someone who advocates the absence of government), is a minimalist concerning the role of government. The legitimate function of government, he maintains, is to protect people and property from foreign attack and internal violence, and to provide for the adjudication of disputes and the enforcement of contracts. Thus, armed forces, police, and a legal and penal system are allowable, but governmental activity beyond these is inappropriate.

In particular, libertarians attack the redistributive function of government. Government, according to this position, should neither tax people nor redistribute income through welfare and other similar programs. The attack on taxes is especially vociferous. Taxation by government, they claim, is theft. If someone at gunpoint stopped you in the street and forced you to hand over 25 percent of your earnings so that he could give it to the poor, you would certainly protest that you were being robbed. Government does the same thing in taxation. Moreover, the libertarians continue, government does not simply turn over the money it takes in taxes to the poor. It uses a significant percentage of what it takes in taxes simply to keep its own machinery and giant bureaucracy operating. Not only does government take money from all of us, but it uses it in ways that many of us do not sanction. It wastes, squanders, and misspends enormous amounts. That it does so should come as no surprise. You and I are careful in how we spend our money because we have to make do on limited funds. Government spends not its own money, but yours and mine, and overspends with impunity—raising taxes, if it needs more money, or printing or borrowing more. The resulting inflation further diminishes our real income, already cut by taxes.

The second strenuous attack by the libertarians is on government regulation of business. They see the capitalist system as one based on free competition. If allowed to operate as it could, they claim, there would be no need for government regulation. Competition would remedy the evils that government unsuccessfully and inefficiently tries to correct. Government has a penchant for overkill and overregulation, even when it operates with good intentions. Moreover, many regulations intended for big business slowly drive the small businessman out of business. There are so many government regulations, and they are so complicated that the small businessman must spend more time and money than he can afford, just keeping track of them and fulfilling their reporting requirements. The government guarantees loans to giants such as Lockheed and Chrysler when they are faced with bankruptcy but provides no help for the small businessman. The libertarians do not advocate that the government help the small businessman; the government should stay out of the business sector entirely, helping neither big nor small business.

The libertarian view is based on the notion of the sanctity of private property. Private property belongs to an individual. If he has worked for it, he deserves to keep what he has earned. If he has taken risks, if he has been lucky, if he has worked especially hard, if he has been innovative, the market will reward him. The rewards he fairly receives rightfully belong to him; they do not belong to government. The truly needy will be taken care of through charity and insurance plans; the lazy and unworthy poor will be forced to change their ways or suffer the consequences of their own actions.

The libertarian view has, therefore, a moral thrust. It champions liberty as a moral virtue worthy of human beings. It faults government as acting immorally in view of taxation, welfare, and many of its other programs. It demands changes. Yet libertarians emphatically defend democracy in the political realm, just as they defend free enterprise in the economic realm.

The libertarian position has not received widespread support, but some of its claims have struck a responsive chord in a number of people. The contemporary American revolt against excessive taxation is one instance of this response. California's rebellion against unlimited property taxes has spread to other parts of the country. Rising inflation and an unreformed tax structure are leading more and more people to adopt the European practice of cutting their own taxes, gambling on not being caught.

Historically, business has not been libertarian. Businesses sought and received protection from government in the way of tariffs and limitations on certain types of imports. They argued that the United States had to be self-sufficient. Its industry had to be protected against the possibility that war might prevent imports. Farmers sought and received governmental support for the prices of their crops. They argued that such support was necessary if farming was to continue successfully. In these and other areas business accepted the protection and help of government. Libertarians maintain that business has paid the price in regulation.

Yet, to be consistent, the libertarian cannot complain if people choose to be governed in certain ways (e.g., if they vote for taxes and for government spending) and if they freely choose security over freedom. He claims, however, that government is not truly responsive to the people; that people have not freely chosen that government act as it does; and that those who do not choose certain practices should not be bound by them. The practical matter of how to accomplish the ends libertarianism proposes is yet to be resolved. As an alternative to the present system, it is at best an indicator, an arrow pointing in a possible direction of change. It is not a ready-made alternative, just waiting in the wings as a panacea for the problems and immorality of the present system.

Workers' Democracy

The other alternative to the present system goes under a variety of names. It is sometimes called workers' democracy, sometimes socialism. But the kind of socialism advocated follows neither the Soviet model nor the British model, for the claim is not that government should take over and run industry. The advocates of these systems attack government as strongly as do the libertarians, but for different reasons.

Workers' democracy sees government as inextricably intertwined with big business. Our elected leaders do not necessarily or consciously aim at supporting business interests at the expense of the interests of the ordinary citizen, but the structures of society are such that the interests of government and the interests of business are most often the same. Government has an enormous budget. Because it does not own industry, the government spends a good deal in contracts, which it gives to private industry. America's interests abroad are predominantly business interests. We protect these interests in foreign countries and support them at home; we fight wars over natural resources in distant lands; and growing numbers of people move easily from the halls of government to the offices of big business, changing hats with little difficulty.

Capitalism has produced for the American worker a better life. American workers have more goods, comfort, and luxury than workers in any other part of the world and in any other period of history, but the American free-enterprise system has become more oppressive than liberating. Yet it can be liberated. True democracy is now possible, if we extend democracy to the economic realm and revivify it in the political realm.

Defenders of workers' democracy point out that many of the decisions made by the major corporations in America affect all of our lives more than the decisions made in Congress. We elect our representatives in Congress, but we have no say at all in what the board of directors of General Motors or Exxon or any other large corporation decides. The allocation of resources, the building and closing of plants, the creation and termination of jobs are all decisions that directly affect large numbers of people who have no voice in these decisions. Nor is government regulation the answer, because government is intertwined with big business.

The appropriate reply of the American people has been slow in coming. Consumer groups have grown up to protect their interests and to provide some sort of response to big business. Environmentalists have also organized to oppose business projects they consider harmful to the environment. Unions have, of course, represented workers vis-à-vis management, and have fought for better wages and working conditions. But because they have been wed to their adversarial role with respect to management, they have not typically sought worker participation in management, worker control of the productive process, or workers' democracy. It seems unlikely that workers' democracy in the United States will be anything other than a peripheral movement for a long time to come.

Piecemeal Change

If the basic aim of libertarianism is the liberty of the businessman, the basic aim of workers' democracy is workers' control over their own destiny. In some ways the two positions are similar. Both want greater freedom for members of society than they have today. Both attack government and the interrelation of government and business. But the means they advocate are dramatically different from one another.

The worker in a workers' democracy would have a say in what is produced and how it is produced. The division between workers and managers would give way. The workers would share directly in the profits of the firm. The adversary relation between employer and employee would be replaced by a cooperative effort of all those engaged in the same enterprise. An effective voice in business decisions would mean as much as an effective voice in government decisions. The democracy we have cherished in the political sector must be recouped and extended to the productive sector, in their view.

The separation of management from ownership has already taken place in most large firms. Managers are as truly employees as are assembly-line workers. Peter Drucker has written about the unseen revolution, in which workers, through union pension funds and insurance funds, are the largest owners of business.[1] Management works for them in their role as shareholders, and this relation should now be translated into fact. There should be an end to domination of the worker, his exploitation, and his alienation.

The movement toward workers' democracy has been slow in developing, although consumerism and environmentalism have grown rapidly. The demand for worker representation on boards of directors has been adopted in Germany, but such representation is rare in the United States. Ironically, the workers themselves have been slow to respond to the call for workers' democracy.

Both libertarianism and workers' democracy are straws in the wind. They are indicative of dissatisfaction with many aspects of big government and big business. They are rallying points for the expression of this dissatisfaction and for proposals for change. Both movements are wedded to change within the system, which may eventually lead to change of the system. They do not espouse violent revolution, or sudden, drastic change. Their gradualism is consistent with a piecemeal approach to the correction of the immoral practices within the system.

A small minority claims that the American system is free of immorality, is sufficiently just, and should not be tinkered with. But most people realize that we do not yet have a completely just society, that our structures can be improved, that the war on poverty has not yet been won, that we still have to solve the problems of the appropriate use of energy, and that we have barely begun to face the moral demands made on us by the poor and underdeveloped countries of the world. Yet the consensus in America is that we do not need another system. No other system is morally preferable, or waiting to be adopted. We can and should make the morally necessary changes in American capitalism, improve it, and work toward a yet unattained maximal mix of freedom and justice. The real alternative to our present American system does not consist in holistic change. What is most likely to succeed is piecemeal change: correcting ills where possible, outlawing immoral practices, and implementing structural changes that promote moral conduct. American capitalism can be made more moral than it is, and the task for all of us is to make the required changes where and how we can. One of the functions of business ethics is to scrutinize, from a moral point of view, the practices and structures within the

---

[1] Peter F. Drucker, *The Unseen Revolution* (New York: Harper & Row, Publishers, 1976).

American economic system, to identify immoral ones, and to propose preferable moral alternatives where possible.

Further Reading

ACTON, H. B. *The Morals of Markets: An Ethical Exploration.* London: Longman Group Ltd., 1971.

ARTHUR, JOHN, and WILLIAM H. SHAW, eds. *Justice and Economic Distribution.* Englewood Cliffs, N.J.: Prentice-Hall, Inc., 1978.

BECKER, LAWRENCE C. *Property Rights.* Boston, London: Routledge & Kegan Paul, 1977.

BENNE, ROBERT. *The Ethic of Democratic Capitalism.* Philadelphia: Fortress Press, 1981.

BOULDING, KENNETH E. *Beyond Economics: Essays on Society, Religion and Ethics.* Ann Arbor: The University of Michigan Press, 1970.

BRANDT, RICHARD, ed. *Social Justice.* Englewood Cliffs, N.J.: Prentice-Hall, Inc., 1962.

CHAMBERLIN, JOHN. *The Roots of Capitalism.* Indianapolis: Liberty Press, 1959.

DALTON, GEORGE. *Economic Systems & Society: Capitalism, Communism, and The Third World.* Harmondsworth: Penguin Books, 1974.

DRUCKER, PETER F. *The Unseen Revolution: How Pension Fund Socialism Came to America.* New York: Harper & Row, Publishers, 1976.

EDWARDS, RICHARD C., MICHAEL REICH, and THOMAS E. WEISSKOPF, eds. *The Capitalist System: A Radical Analysis of American Society,* 2nd ed. Englewood Cliffs, N.J.: Prentice-Hall, Inc., 1978.

FRIEDMAN, MILTON. *Capitalism & Freedom.* Chicago: The University of Chicago Press, 1962.

HARRINGTON, MICHAEL. *The Twilight of Capitalism.* New York: Simon & Schuster, Inc., 1976.

HEILBRONER, ROBERT L. *Between Capitalism and Socialism.* New York: Vintage Books, 1970.

MARX, KARL. *Capital.* Moscow: Foreign Languages Publishing House, 1959.

NOVAK, MICHAEL. *The Spirit of Democratic Capitalism.* New York: A Touchstone Book, Simon and Schuster, Inc. 1982.

NOZIK, ROBERT. *Anarchy, State, and Utopia.* New York: Basic Books, Inc., 1974.

OLAFSON, FREDERICK A., ed. *Justice and Social Policy.* Englewood Cliffs, N.J.: Prentice-Hall, Inc., 1961.

ROTHBARD, MURRAY. *For a New Liberty.* New York: Macmillan Publishing Company, 1973.

SCHUMACHER, E. F. *Small Is Beautiful.* New York: Harper & Row, Publishers, Inc., 1973.

SILK, LEONARD. *Capitalism: The Moving Target.* New York: Quadrangle, The New York Times Book Co., Inc., 1974.

STERBA, JAMES. *Justice: Alternative Political Perspectives.* Belmont, Calif.: Wadsworth Publishing Co., 1980.

EIGHT

Corporate Responsibility and the Social Audit

At the heart of the American economic system lies the large, publicly owned corporate manufacturer of goods. Such corporations are a prime target for those who attack immorality in business. Any piecemeal approach to remedying immorality in our system must pay special attention to the role and functioning of the large corporation.

We have already seen that the corporation can be held morally liable for its actions, and that within the corporation, moral responsibility can be held collectively or individually in a variety of ways and on many levels. But we have not yet looked at what corporations and those within them are morally responsible for. Some of the topics will require detailed investigation and will be discussed in later chapters. This chapter will present an overview of the moral responsibility of the corporation as a whole and of the people within it, without trying to examine any particular aspect in great detail.

Businesses can be organized as proprietorships, partnerships, or as different types of corporations such as family, closely held, not-for-profit, public, holding-company, conglomerate, and multinational. We shall focus on the American publicly held, manufacturing type corporation, postponing for later discussion the complications that arise if it is part of a multinational operation. Often the focus of moral and social criticism, this is the kind of business that manufactures possibly dangerous products, that opens and closes plants employing large numbers of workers, that tends to become monopolistic, that creates products sold through high-pressure advertising campaigns, that pollutes the air, poisons the rivers, and harms people through its chemical and toxic effluents. At least, this is the kind of enterprise that can do all of these things, and has done so in the past. Holding-companies pose special problems. Family-owned and closely held businesses, even if incorporated, tend not to divide ownership from management, control, and responsibility. Service and retail corporations in part depend on manufacturers and often deal directly with consumers, posing particular moral problems. The large, publicly owned manufacturing corporation is the typical target of moral critiques and is seen, with some justification, as a center of the capitalist system, a position it shares with banks and other financial institutions.

In dealing with the corporation from a wide perspective we shall discuss four broad topics. We shall first consider the status of the corporation and its moral significance. Second, we shall outline the kinds of moral responsibility appropriate to each of the groups that make up the corporation. Third, we shall investigate the structure of the corporation from a moral point of view. Last, we shall differentiate the social responsibilities from the moral responsibilities of the corporation, and illustrate the difference by considering some problems of pollution and the environment.

The Status of the Corporation and Its Moral Significance

The corporation is a special kind of entity. In 1819, Chief Justice Marshall, in *Dartmouth College* v. *Woodward,* defined it as follows: "A corporation is an artificial being, invisible, intangible, and existing only in contemplation of law. Being the mere creature of law, it possesses only those properties which the charter of creation confers upon it, either expressly, or as incidental to its very existence. These are such as are supposed best calculated to effect the object for which it was created." It can act, hold property, and be sued. A major aspect of corporations, and one of the primary reasons for which they are established, is that they have only limited liability. This shelters corporate shareholders or owners from personal liability. Those who invest in a corporation can only lose the amount of money they invest. Their personal assets cannot be attached.

We saw in Chapter Five that insofar as corporations act intentionally they can be held morally responsible for their actions. They are thus moral agents. But because they are not human beings, they are not moral persons. The moral obligations of corporations are therefore different from the moral obligations of human beings. The difference hinges on the fact that corporations are limited, organized for only certain purposes. They are bound, as all other moral agents are bound, not to harm others. This negative injunction is a major restraint on corporations. The ends for which they are formed can be judged from a moral point of view. But the positive obligations of corporations depend on their ends, their particular situations, their legal status, and the sociopolitical environment in which they are organized and operate.

In the American free-enterprise system, we can morally evaluate the corporation and its activities in terms of its place within the system and the values of the system. To the obligation to avoid harm we can add the obligations not to impair the freedom of economic activity on which the system is based, to be fair in its transactions, and to live up to its contracts. If it acts within these moral limits, the justification of the publicly held manufacturing corporation consists in the benefits it brings to society. It is for these benefits that it is granted limited liability and other privileges. The corporation provides remunerative work for the members of a community, it produces goods for social use, it pays taxes for public needs, and it generates the investment capital needed for development and economic growth.

Because corporations are not human persons, the injunction to produce the greatest amount of good applies differently to an individual person with a full range of activities open to him and to a corporation with very great restrictions on its purpose and its appropriate activities. Because corporations are not moral persons, it is doubtful whether we can expect them to act from moral motives. What we can expect is that they not do what is morally prohibited. We can praise them for doing what is in accord with the moral law, and blame them for what is a violation of it. Corporations lack the interiority characteristic of human individuals, therefore their actions, not their motives, are the proper object of moral evaluation.

The legal status of the corporation in the American free-enterprise system is firmly established, but the theory grounding the corporation is somewhat controversial.

There are two major views of the corporation. One—the *legal-creator* view—sees it entirely as a creature of law, existing only in contemplation of law. According to this view, the corporation is created by the state and does not exist without it. The state and the law are themselves creatures of society, therefore the corporation is a creature of society. It has special qualities, privileges, and liabilities as a result of social decision and action. The corporation is made by society for its benefit. When the corporation no longer benefits society, society may modify or do away with it. Corporate structures vary from society to society, and corporations are not necessary for society, even if industrial productive enterprises are necessary for modern societies. How corporations are structured, owned, and operated varies greatly. According to this view, the corporation exists by public license. If and when corporations are found to harm the public good, they can be legitimately restricted, changed, and even, if necessary, eliminated.

The second view—the *legal-recognition* view—focuses not on the legal status of the corporation but on the corporation as a free, productive enterprise. Individuals have the moral right to do what they choose so long as they do not harm others thereby. They can, among other things, produce goods and join together with others to produce goods. If they choose to organize their productive capacities, one of the ways open to them is incorporation. According to this view, a corporation is formed by its members, who organize themselves in certain ways. The state does not create the corporation. It simply registers and recognizes the existence of the corporation, similar to the way it registers a marriage or the birth of children, for legal purposes. The corporation is a freely formed organization. Those who buy shares in the corporation provide money for its operation in the hope of increasing their capital through the productive success of the firm. They take the risk of losing the money they invest in a corporation, even though their risk is limited to the amount of money they invest. Their gain is proportional to the percentage of the firm they own and to the profit of the corporation. The limitations of the liability of the corporation are set by law, but this again is simply an affirmation of an accepted practice freely entered into. Creditors know the status of the corporation; they realize that in dealing with it they cannot attach the property of the shareholders, and that their claims are limited to the assets of the corporation.

The legal-recognition view emphasizes that the corporation is a result of a free activity on the part of those who form it and on the part of those who deal with it. It is not a creation of the state or of society. It may be limited by society if it harms society, just as an individual may be restrained in his actions if he harms society. But because a corporation is not a creature of society, it sets its own ends and operates for its own purposes. It makes profit by serving society, but its end is not primarily to serve society; its end is to produce and sell certain goods, thereby earning a desired return on its investment. Because its end is not directly to help society, in evaluating it from a moral or social point of view it is inappropriate to fault it for not helping society in any way other than by doing what it is formed to do.

The two views of the corporation lead to different approaches to its moral and social obligations. According to the legal-creator view, society can legitimately demand that it do certain kinds of activities, even if the corporation itself, or those running it, do not wish to do those things. According to the legal-recognition view, the corporation is an autonomous entity, an entity owned and run by a freely constituted group; and, simply because it is organized in a certain way, does not mean it has special obligations. Because it is not the creation of society, society can regulate its free activity only to the extent that it rightly and justifiably regulates the free activity of individuals whose proper antecedent freedom the state should protect, and who do not receive their freedom from the state. Proponents of both views must acknowledge, however, that there are activities in which the corporation is not allowed to participate because they harm others, and that the law provides a necessary backdrop without which the corporation could not function as it does.

We need not settle the dispute between the two views here. In either view, providing its actions do not harm anyone, and providing its transactions are fair, the corporation as an institution is a morally acceptable kind of entity, a morally acceptable mode of organizing business, and a morally acceptable way of mediating the business relations among people. We shall examine the moral responsibilities of the corporation that are compatible with both views. This involves a discussion of shareholders, the board of directors, management, and labor.

Moral Responsibility Within the Corporation

The relation of the corporation to its investors requires careful analysis. What is the relation of those who own stock in the corporation and the corporation itself? Why is their liability limited, and is this morally justifiable? For what, if anything, are the shareholders of a corporation morally responsible?

The moral status of the shareholder is ambiguous. Moral responsibility involves a causal connection to an action or result that is morally evaluated, and moral responsibility is properly ascribed and assumed only if the action in question was done knowingly and freely, and if there were no excusing conditions. We have seen that the corporation can correctly be said to act, even if it acts only when those within it act. In a family-owned or closely held corporation the owners of the corporation and the principal managers are usually the same people. Hence the owners, as managers, have responsibility for what the corporation does. Limited liability shields the personal property of the owners, not only from creditors but also from those who file suit for damage of a negligent or criminal type. The shareholder of a large, publicly held corporation is a part owner of the corporation. He may own a very, very small part indeed. His ownership, moreover, is usually separated from management; he is in no sense a manager, and has no direct voice in the management of the corporation. He has a vote proportional to the number of shares he owns—a vote that he can exercise at the annual shareholders' meeting, on the issues presented for a vote by management. But the small shareholder has no say in what is put on the agenda, nor does his vote carry much weight. Even large shareholders may own a very small percentage of the stock of a giant corporation.

Can the shareholder in such a situation be held responsible for what the firm does? According to our earlier analysis, the shareholder is in fact very distant from the causal relation between an action of the corporation and its effects. If a corporation is established for an immoral end, then no one can give moral support to its activities through the purchase of stock. But the ordinary public corporation does not have an immoral end. If those who hold stock in a corporation know that the corporation acts immorally, then they should do what they can to change the practices of the corporation, and failing that, should sever their connection with the firm by selling their stock. The relation of shareholder and management, however, is a morally fuzzy one. The managers, strictly speaking, work for the shareholders, who are the owners of the corporation. The managers act as agents for the shareholders. Yet any individual shareholder has in fact little, if any, control over the managers. It is therefore farfetched to hold shareholders responsible for what the managers do, because the usual rule is that responsibility falls on the person or persons who start a causal chain of agency.

Both the legal-creator and the legal-recognition views of the corporation ignore the separation of ownership from management, which is the rule for large corporations. It is not clear exactly what a shareholder of a large corporation contracts into by purchasing a share in a company. Frequently, one simply invests in a company as a result of a broker's suggestion. The concept of being responsible for what the company does because one owns a share of a company is not part of the consciousness of many shareholders. The situation is magnified when someone owns stock through a pension or retirement plan, through a life insurance policy, or through a mutual fund. Though his money is invested in certain stocks, and he owns a certain portion of these stocks, he frequently has no idea what stocks his money is invested in, or how much of each stock he owns. Hence, he can hardly be responsible for what the corporation of which he is a part owner does. He is, however, penalized for what the managers do, and for which the corporation is sued. When the corporation pays a suit, the shareholders in effect pay it, even though they had nothing to do with the action in question. But they also gain by actions management takes, which, even if immoral, add to the profit of the firm.

Corporations are the result of free agreements, even if most owners do not know what management does. They purchase stock, knowing that they will not have control and knowing that they will gain or lose, depending on how effectively management runs the corporation. They know that the corporation may be sued, they know it may make a profit or suffer losses, and they know in general how such things happen. Shareholders agree to invest money, and they understand what this means. The corporation in turn acts under the direction of management. The corporation owns property, produces and sells goods, is liable for what it produces, and for its commitments.

There may be some things for which the corporation as a whole is responsible. But because the corporation acts only through the agency of those who work for it, we can often identify who within the corporation has responsibility for what. The shareholders and the owners of the corporation are legally represented by the board of directors, whose job it is, among other things, to look out for the interests of the shareholders. The board of directors oversees management. Management has the task of organizing the corporation in such a way that it can effect its end—make and market a product, profitably. Management is responsible to the board for what it does. In a large firm there are usually levels of management. Top management sets policy; middle management implements the broad policies by breaking them down into components and devising a strategy for achieving them; lower management implements the decisions made by middle management, by organizing and hiring the workers who actually engage in the production of the goods. Management is responsible for what is produced and for how it is produced. It is responsible to the workers for the conditions under which they work, and to the consumers for the quality of goods produced. The workers are responsible for doing the jobs for which they are paid.

The corporation as a whole is responsible for fulfilling its contracts to the other firms with which it deals, that is, for delivering what was promised when and as promised, for paying the debts it incurs in its operation, and so on.

The corporation is responsible to the consumer for the goods it sells. The corporation is also responsible to the general public, or to society, for the actions it takes which affect the public or society in general. All of these obligations can be deduced from the rule that every rational agent is responsible for his actions, and is responsible to those whom his actions seriously affect. Each such agent is morally responsible for wrongful injury done to another. To the extent that the corporation acts, it is responsible for its actions, although it is the people within the corporation who must act, in order for the corporation to fulfill its obligations. Let us look a little more closely at each level of the corporation, and at the kinds of moral responsibility of each.

In a large corporation, responsibility falls primarily on the board of directors. The board members are the legal overseers of management. The members of the board are responsible to the shareholders for the selection of honest, effective managers, and especially for the selection of the president of the corporation. They may also be responsible for choosing the executive vice-president and other vice-presidents. They are morally responsible for the tone of the corporation and for its major policies; they can set a moral tone or they can condone immoral practices. They can and should see that the company is managed honestly and that the interests of the shareholders are cared for instead of ignored by management.

Board members are also responsible for agreeing to major policy decisions, and for the general well-being of the corporation. The members are morally responsible for the decisions they make, as well as for the decisions they should make but fail to make. To be effective in their roles as protectors of the interests of the shareholders and judges of the performance of management, they should be separate from management. Members of the board cannot be objective in their evaluation of management if they are also members of management. If the president and the chairman of the board are one and the same person, for instance, we can hardly expect the board to be as objective as it should be in fulfilling its responsibility vis-à-vis management. Nor can we expect impartial evaluation of management if the board is composed of people appointed or recommended by management because of mutual ties. We can also not expect a board to be effective if it is not informed by management of what management is doing; if the board does not have access to all information about the firm it thinks necessary; and if its members do not have the time to investigate what should be investigated.

The increasing incidence of corporate takeovers raises special problems for boards of directors. When one company takes over another, no productive resources are increased, no jobs are created, and, from the point of view of society, there is no net increase of any kind. One company might take over another in order to diversify its holdings and so hedge against a decline in any portion of its operations. Or it might take over a firm that produces an item that it usually purchases from external suppliers. Sometimes one firm might take over another firm because its physical assets are greater than its market price—a good investment. Or it might take over a smaller competitor. Sometimes takeovers are friendly, and in the best interest of all parties; but sometimes takeovers are unfriendly, and are fought by the board or management of the firm being acquired.

Although board members are required to act in the best interests of the shareholders of the firm, in takeovers, there is often controversy over whether the members are acting for the benefit of the shareholders or for their own personal interests. The situation becomes especially acute when the president and other top executives on the board of a firm will lose their jobs as a result of a takeover. Matters are sometimes further complicated by competing bids by different companies for the same firm. Whatever the complications, the board is morally and legally responsible for the interests of the shareholders, and must resist the temptation to act out of personal interest and advantage, which might be to the detriment of the shareholders.

Management is responsible to the board. It must inform the board of its actions, the decisions it makes or the decisions to be made, the financial condition of the firm, its successes and failures, and the like. Management is responsible, through the board, to the shareholders. It is responsible to the shareholders for managing the firm honestly and efficiently, but management is not morally responsible for maximizing profits, for increasing the worth of the company's stock, or for higher quarterly sales or profits. Although these are all reasonable goals at which management may aim, shareholders have no right to any of these; if management acts as best it can within its proper moral and legal bounds, it cannot, strictly speaking, be faulted for not achieving them. If managers fail to produce as the board thinks it should, they may be fired or replaced. But that is different from their fulfilling or not fulfilling their moral obligations. Shareholders know that a corporation's stock may decrease as well as increase in value, that profits may increase or decline. They should also know that profit maximization cannot morally override a firm's moral and legal obligations. Although shareholders may desire short-term profits, they have no right to them, and managers should manage for the long-term benefit of the firm as well as for short-term results.

Management is also responsible to the workers. It both hires them and provides for the conditions of work. In hiring workers it has the obligation to engage in what have become known as fair employment practices. These include following equitable guidelines and not discriminating on the basis of sex, race, religion, or other non-job-related characteristics. Once hired, there is a continuing obligation of fairness in evaluation, promotion, and equitable treatment. These are moral matters, which may or may not be specified in contracts but which are implied in the hiring of one person by another. It is not moral for management to ignore unsafe working conditions. For instance, it should not endanger workers by failing to provide screening from dangerous machines, where appropriate; by not supplying goggles for work where fragments may cause blindness; by not supplying adequate ventilation; and, in general, by ignoring the needs of workers as human beings.

Employers are not free to set any terms they wish as conditions of employment. They have a moral obligation to employees even if these are not spelled out in contracts or by government regulations. Government regulations, such as those imposed by the Occupational Safety and Health Act (OSHA) make explicit many of the conditions employers are morally as well as legally obliged to fulfill with respect to the safety and health of their employees. The OSHA regulations are sometimes inappropriate for certain firms, or are based on codes inappropriate to particular enterprises. Where inappropriate, the regulations can and should be changed. But if employers had lived up to the moral obligation to provide adequate conditions of safety and health for their employees, there would have been no need for OSHA regulations.

The corporation is responsible to the consumer for its products. The goods produced should be reasonably safe. This means that the ordinary user is exposed to only a certain acceptable risk level which is known by the user, when using the product. For example, people do not expect to get shocked or electrocuted when they plug in an electrical appliance. They do not buy such appliances expecting to take that risk. A product that shocks or electrocutes them when plugged in is defective, causes harm to the consumer, and violates the contract involved in the purchase of the product. Goods must be as advertised or labeled, and the labeling should be adequate, so the buyer knows what he is buying. Adequate knowledge is one of the ingredients of a fair transaction, therefore it is the obligation of the manufacturer to inform the purchaser of those significant qualities that the purchaser cannot observe for himself. For instance, the kind of material a garment is made of is pertinent, as is the horsepower of a vehicle. And goods should be reasonably durable; they should not fall apart on first use. Warranties should be clear and honored. The customer buys a product for a certain price. He should know what he is getting, and he has a moral right to have certain expectations fulfilled. Obviously there are various grades of goods. Some are more expensive than others and may be correspondingly safer, more durable, more reliable, more attractive, and made of better-quality components than cheaper products. For any transaction to be fair the consumer must have adequate information and his reasonable expectations must be fulfilled by a product, or there must be adequate notice that the ordinary expectation in the given case will not be fulfilled. Damaged goods can be sold if marked as damaged. "Seconds" may be sold as seconds, but to sell them as "first quality" is immoral.

These few examples do not exhaust the responsibilities of corporations to consumers. We have not questioned the morality of built-in obsolescence; of purposeful lack of standardization, which locks a consumer into a certain line of products; of failure to develop certain products; or of preventing the production of items that would benefit the consumer but hurt a particular industry or manufacturer. But we have illustrated enough of the moral responsibilities of a corporation to consumers to indicate where its moral obligations in this area lie, and how they can be ascertained.

Finally, the corporation is morally responsible for its actions to the general public or to society in general. In particular, it has the moral obligation not to harm those whom its actions affect. We can group these obligations under three major headings. The first can be called its obligation not to harm the environment that it shares with its neighbors. It has the obligation not to pollute the air and water beyond socially acceptable levels, and also to control its noise pollution. It is obliged to dispose of toxic and corrosive wastes so as not to endanger others. It must reclaim and restore the environment to a socially acceptable level, if its operation despoils it.

The second group of moral obligations to the general public concerns the general safety of those who live in an area affected by a company's plant. A company has no right to expose those people living near it to a health risk from possible explosion or radiation. Some jobs involve a high risk, and those who take this risk are paid accordingly. But a plant has no right to expose its neighbors, even its distant neighbors, to dangers without their consent. Similarly, a corporation has an obligation to the general public for the safety of its products. For instance, substandard tires endanger not only those who purchase them but those whom the purchaser may kill or injure in an accident that the tires may cause.

The third set of responsibilities to the public concerns the location, the opening, and the closing of plants—especially in small communities and one-industry towns. These actions affect not only the corporation and its workers but also the communities in which the plants are located. Plant openings can affect a community positively or negatively, just as closings can. A corporation must consider, from a moral point of view, the impact of its actions on the community in these matters. This is not to say that plants can never morally be closed or opened. In both opening and closing a plant, a corporation has the obligation to minimize the harm, and so to consider a variety of strategies to achieve this end.

The opening of a plant may involve a large commitment on the part of the community in which it is located. The community, for example, may have to add sewer lines, increase its fire and police department staff, and add to its social services personnel. Developers build houses for the increased employment the plant makes available. Businesses spring up to provide support services. Schools may be built to educate the children of the workers. The city or county begins to count on the increased tax base the plant represents. All of this results from the new plant. The corporation does not always ask that all this happen; but it at least expects that its workers will be provided housing and services in response to market demand.

The community may thus be said to provide indirect support to the plant. The corporation should, therefore, not ignore the community's contribution to its operation when it considers closing the plant. It may have no legal duty to consider the community with which it has been associated; but morally, it does have an obligation to consider the effects of its action and to minimize the harm its closing will cause the community.

If we ask who has the obligation to do all this, the answer is, the corporation. Management has the major role to play. Yet both the members of the board and the individual workers may find, on occasion, that they have the moral responsibility to take certain actions to satisfy the corporation's responsibility to the general public.

Morality and Corporate Structure

Corporations should act morally. Equally important from a moral point of view, the corporate structure should be such that people who make up the firm are encouraged to act morally. Some structures encourage immoral behavior; others tend to preclude it. Organizational theory is only beginning to turn its attention in this direction. Yet a number of innovative organizational changes have been tried, both in the United States and in Europe, and deserve serious consideration.

We have already noted the tendency of moral responsibility to be ignored in corporations. Those at the top give orders and never see the specific results of the implementation of those orders on people far down the line. Managers tend to deny responsibility for results they never intended. Those near the end of the line, who execute orders given by those above them, frequently feel they are simply doing their job when they obey orders, no matter what the results. They deny responsibility for the results because they did not set the policies—they simply obeyed orders. They did not will to do harm or evil; they willed only to do their jobs.

Another structural aspect of many large corporations that undermines the acceptance of moral responsibility is a particular decision-making procedure, in which decisions are not made by individuals but by committees, or even worse, by sets of committees. Therefore, a corporation's actions, in some instances, can be traced to no one. Many people had some input into a policy or decision. One person suggested it, another added something, a third person deleted a portion of it; then a committee agreed to one version, which was altered by another committee, and finally, a modified version of that was adopted, albeit slightly changed as it went from organizational level to organizational level.

Structures that encourage morality and facilitate the assigning of responsibility are possible, however, for corporations that wish to operate morally. The moral tone is set by those at the top. Unless those at the top insist on moral conduct, unless they punish immoral conduct and reward moral conduct, the corporation as a whole will tend to function without considering moral questions and the morality of its actions. A corporation may by accident rather than by intent avoid immoral actions, though in the long run this is unlikely. We list here some specific suggestions for structurally implementing morality in a corporation.

1. If a board of directors is to be morally responsible it cannot simply rubber-stamp management. The board members must be informed of the activities of the corporation and must have access to all the information they want concerning the corporation. They are responsible to the shareholders, the public, and the government. They can fulfill their responsibilities only if they spend adequate time investigating the company's activities, and if they hold management accountable. Members of such boards will have to spend more than a few days a year on their board activities. If the position of board member is a demanding one, business executives will not be able to serve on more than one or two boards of other firms. Hence:

The board of directors of a firm should actively and conscientiously oversee management's running of a firm.

2. Management is responsible to the board. But it can obviously be held responsible only if management is different from the board. Executive compensation and perquisites, such as stock options, are notorious areas for conflict of interest. Management cannot be expected to evaluate its own performance objectively, or to compensate itself without prejudice. The pattern of outside board members has been established in Europe and is a pattern followed by many large (but few of the smaller) corporations here. The board might include chief stockholders, workers, or people entirely unconnected with the corporation. They must all, of course, be competent to fulfill their obligations as members of a board. There might be training courses run by the corporation, or by schools of business, to teach potential board members what they need to know. Hence:

More than half the board, including the chairman of the board, should not be from management.

3. Responsibility on lower levels should be assigned; but assumption of responsibility should be not only required but taught by example. A difficulty in many large corporations is that managers are able to make decisions and implement policies that are detrimental to a company in the long run, but profitable in the short run. By the time the negative aspects of policies or decisions become evident, the manager responsible for them has moved on to another position, leaving his successors to face the consequences of policies they inherited but did not initiate. In this way, managers on the rise can avoid responsibility for their actions. Hence:

Responsibility for policies and decisions by management at all levels should be tracked for at least five-year periods, and those responsible should be held accountable for policies and decisions they made in previous positions in the firm.

4. Responsibility and responsiveness are a corollary of accountability. Accountability requires not only a response to those to whom one is responsible, but it also requires access to information and the giving of reasons for decisions that have been made. One way to preserve one's power is to monopolize information so that others have to assume that the decisions taken were proper, in the light of all the information. Accountability under such conditions is impossible. Thus, accountability requires disclosure. There are certainly areas of business, such as legitimate trade secrets, which should be protected by law. But these areas are probably fewer than most corporations are willing to admit. If people are to be held responsible for their decisions, those affected by a decision have a right to know at least something of the rationale for it. To supply information about a decision, and reasons for making it, does not mean that the person who made the decision had no right to make it. But knowing that one may be called on to explain or defend decisions helps keep one from making them arbitrarily. Hence:

At each level, a determination should be made about how much disclosure is appropriate, and to whom. The determination should be made not unilaterally, but through reasoned discourse with those seeking information and those to whom one is rightly accountable.

5. Accountability is not simply hierarchical. Management should be accountable to the workers as well as to the board, and the workers should be accountable to each other as well as to management. The board should be accountable to the stockholders and the public, but it should also be accountable to management, and should provide reasons for the decisions it makes. The rationale is that the corporation is composed of people and not simply functions or positions on an organizational chart.

Accountability is at the heart of both the demand for responsibility and for responsiveness, and to achieve accountability may require significant organizational modifications. Hence:

There should be channels and procedures for accountability up, down, and laterally.

6. Workers should be able to make known their demands and concerns, without fear of prejudice, and should be given explanations for decisions that affect them. Clearly, to speak of channels and procedures goes well beyond the suggestion box. An ombudsman has been tried in some corporations; special departments have been established in other corporations. The public also needs the chance to tell corporations their concerns, to indicate what moral factors they feel should be considered, and to present the reasons for the demands they make. The American public does not expect corporations to act from moral motives. It does expect them not to violate basic moral rules and to consider the social ramifications of their actions. Hence:

Corporations should develop input lines whereby employees, consumers, stockholders, and the public can make known their concerns, demands, and perceptions of a corporation's legitimate responsibilities.

7. Clearly, obtaining information is only part of the task. Nor is it appropriate simply to react to pressures. Active concern and procedures for initiating action are necessary. Hence:

Corporations should develop a mechanism (possibly a department) for anticipating the various demands, for seriously considering and weighing them, and for proposing appropriate action.

8. The mechanism for weighing various moral demands is crucial. Many of the demands cannot be handled in cost-accounting terms. Where they cannot, then the arguments in defense of one set of actions and a consideration of the consequences are typically pitted against similar considerations for other sets of actions. But the only way to make the discussion fair is to have advocates for each side. The advocates should be within the corporation, even if they represent demands made by those outside the corporation. In at least one office or department it should be proper to ask, not "what can the corporation get away with?" but "what is the right thing to do?" That decision will have to be weighed against cost and other factors. But unless someone is paid to argue against the company's position, unless that person's position and advancement are dependent on his properly and strongly presenting the case of those outside the company, and unless he has some likelihood of winning, outside demands will not get an adequate hearing. A progressive company would demand even more, namely, that some people within it be responsible for anticipating moral demands so that the company can respond to them before outside forces have to be marshalled. The development of a group, office, or department within a corporation, which argues against the company's short-term interest in the light of its larger responsibilities, is a major organizational modification.

Some firms are already living up to their moral responsibilities, but firms usually do not justify their actions on moral grounds unless attacked. This is in part a function of accepting the Myth of Amoral Business. Making known the moral basis for decisions can, however, be socially useful, and can raise the appropriate expectation of corporate moral consciousness on the part of other firms and of society in general. Hence:

Corporations should develop techniques for disseminating to those interested the basis for decisions affecting the general good.

9. Responsibility without sanctions for improper behavior is empty. The demand for responsibility requires that sanctions be developed and enforced for those who fail to meet their moral responsibilities. If responsibility is personally assignable, then there is little difficulty in knowing whom to sanction. Kickbacks, foreign bribes, the use of insider information, and so on, are everyday fare in newspapers and magazines. The deceit, deception, and dishonesty of a few tarnish the image of the many. Yet very few corporations have been willing to admit blame for their wrongdoing; fewer still take any effective measures against their blameworthy managers or board members; and even fewer cast stones at fellow businessmen. It is difficult to believe that businessmen do not know when others are acting immorally, however that is defined. Yet rarely does any businessman publicly bring charges of impropriety or immorality, and even more rarely do any self-policing mechanisms result in the imposing of severe sanctions. Hence:

Responsibility should be enforced with sanctions within an organization, and, where compatible with antitrust laws, throughout an industry. The price for executive irresponsibility or immorality should be as severe as that for lower-level employees.

10. A corporate policy or action may come into conflict with the moral obligation of the corporation. There should be some mechanism for dealing with a discrepancy of this kind without endangering the position of the person raising the objection. There are a number of famous cases of whistle blowing in industry, and in most cases the whistle blowers have fared poorly after taking their moral stance. Hence:

A corporation that wishes to preclude the necessity of whistle blowing should provide procedures, mechanisms, and channels whereby any members of the organization can file moral concerns of the kind that lead to whistle blowing, and can get a fair hearing, and possible action, without fear of negative consequences.

11. To have procedures for handling conflicts of corporate policy and for employee morality does not mean that anything that anyone claims to be immoral is immoral. But there should be organizational procedures to insure that such charges get a full and fair hearing from those who will ultimately be responsible. Those who raise such issues should be able to do so without threat of negative consequences. Contrary to the traditional model, people at every level should be held responsible for seeing and reporting such issues and should be penalized for failure to do so. If industry were responsive to legitimate complaints by those who see product dangers, employees would not have to go outside the company to get corporate action. To give weight to the concern for precluding the necessity of whistle blowing:

The corporation should hold some highly placed official in the corporation responsible if insufficient attention is paid to a legitimate claim of product safety and the like.

The changes we have mentioned here, taken as a whole, fall far short of socialism and workers' self-management. Because of this, some may construe the foregoing suggestions as a means of defending the status quo. But it is not clear that worker participation increases morality on the part of firms, even though it may increase productivity or reduce feelings of alienation. Nor is there yet an American mandate to go very far in that direction. Others, enamoured of the traditional model and unwilling to give up any of the traditional privileges and autocracy of management, will argue that the foregoing suggestions call for an end to free enterprise and capitalism. Clearly, they do not.

The changes outlined are not original; most have been tried somewhere in some way. But they do form a whole, are a valid conception of what a moral corporation can be, and are in line with what is being legitimately demanded of business.

Morality and the Social Audit

In examining the moral responsibility of corporations we noted the obligation not to produce harm. If pollution causes harm, then a corporation is morally required not to pollute. But the moral obligations of a corporation can and should be distinguished from what have been called its "social obligations."

In one sense, a socially responsible corporation is one that abides by the law, and so fulfills its legal obligations. This is analogous to the socially responsible individual who does likewise. But sometimes, a "socially responsible individual" is one who not only obeys the law but also takes active part in social causes, social reform, and the political and civic life of society, and some people have come to use the phrase "corporate social responsibility" in an analogous sense. "Social responsibility," then, is ambiguous. Sometimes it goes beyond the legal obligations and refers to a corporation's responsibility to fulfill its social obligations. And sometimes it refers to the obligations themselves as imposed by society. Often, it refers to a corporation's concern for society, or for the impact its actions make on society, whether or not its concern corresponds to society's demands.

Human beings are multifaceted individuals, but corporations are formed for limited ends and are structured for certain purposes. We have seen that although both humans and corporations are morally bound not to do harm, the amount of good they can be expected to produce varies. In particular, it is not clear that an appropriate end of every corporation is the improvement of the general welfare, except by its productive activity. This is true if, by improvement one means that the corporation must engage in changing society directly, in changing the distribution of wealth within the society, or in improving the life of the inner cities, in addition to or instead of achieving its own ends. There is a difference, however, between claiming that a corporation does not have the moral obligation to engage in good works and social welfare—which are the proper province of individuals and of government—and claiming that it has no moral responsibility to society for what and how it produces, or how it treats its workers, its customers, and those affected by its actions.

In Chapter One we noted a changing mandate for business, and saw that this is given not only in law but that it arises from the general public and is expressed in many ways. Because the decisions of large corporations affect our society and the individuals in it in so many ways, it is no longer sufficient simply to demand that corporations provide a plentiful supply of high-quality goods at reasonable prices, despite the fact that some firms believe that merely doing this fulfills their moral responsibility. Concern for the ecosystem, worries about the limited supply of natural resources, and interest in the quality of employee life have all come to the fore. As we attempt to determine the nature of the changing mandate for business, however, we can distinguish three different sorts of claims or demands. They are not mutually exclusive, and in fact overlap to a considerable extent.

Moral demands stem from the moral law. The obligations not to steal, not to cheat, not to lie are all examples. We must also treat people as ends in themselves, not harm them, and if we are in positions of authority within a corporation, we must see to it that working conditions are safe. Such moral obligations remain whether or not they are enacted into law and whether or not they are socially mandated. When companies do not adequately protect the safety of workers, sometimes a social mandate develops in the form of newspaper campaigns, protests at board meetings, calls for legislation, and the like. If firms react to such public demands, they can be said to be reacting to a *social demand* which is also a moral demand. If the legislature passes laws requiring certain standards of safety, then the social demands are spelled out as *legal demands* and corporations are forced to comply. We can distinguish moral demands, social but not legal demands, and legal demands, which are also of course social demands. Some social demands may be neither moral nor legal demands; and some social demands may be moral but not legal demands. Some social demands may be both moral and legal demands. Moreover, some demands may be couched in terms of social responsibility but may be only the demands, or statements of interest, of a small portion of society.

Moral obligations are sometimes correctly put forth as social obligations because they can and should be demanded by a moral society. Such moral demands as the obligation not to harm (e.g., in the case of pollution) may be handled in various ways by a society. What society demands of firms in this instance are actually social demands. They are morally justifiable both because they implement a moral demand and because society has the right to impose particular demands on corporations as a condition for doing business, providing the demands are in the interest of the common good.

Society may also impose on business certain demands that are not moral demands. Morality, for instance, requires that corporations be run honestly. But it does not require that a certain percentage of a board of directors be from outside the company. A corporation is not immoral if it has mostly internal board members (even though having a majority of outside members precludes some conflicts of interest, as we have noted). Yet there has been, over the past years, a growing *social* demand for changes in the composition of corporate boards. This has been expressed by petitions at board meetings, by motions at shareholder meetings, and by newspaper editorials and articles, among other means. As a result, by 1980 over 90 percent of *major* American corporations had a majority of outside board members, as compared to less than 66 percent in 1970. This is not required by U.S. law, although the New York Stock Exchange requires a majority of independent outside directors on audit committees of listed companies. In Germany, corporations are required by law to have a majority of outside directors. This does not necessarily mean that German boards are more moral than American boards, for there is no guarantee that outside directors make a board act more morally. But the fact that Germany has such a law shows that German society as such feels more strongly about the issue than does American society. Although moral demands are similar across national boundaries (e.g., all corporations have the moral obligation not to cause harm) social and legal demands may vary greatly.

Social demands may begin as demands made by one individual or by a small group. But not all such demands are social demands; only some of them express the interests of a major sector of society, and only some of those are independent moral obligations. Societies vary, for instance, in the safety they demand in automobiles or on the job. There are trade-offs of cost in most safety decisions. American society for a long time has demanded great safety in commercial airplanes, but for an equally long time has tolerated private automobiles that are less safe than the state of the art makes possible. Those who voiced demands for safer automobiles initially did not seem to speak for society, even though they were concerned with the social good. The American public has been slow in demanding the automobile safety that is technically possible but expensive. The social demand for greater safety is, however, increasing.

It is often difficult to distinguish between the vested interests of certain groups, which are presented as social demands, and the legitimate but not legally mandated demands of society. The growing literature on the social obligations of corporations includes a grab bag of obligations, some of them moral and some not. The social obligations that some people would like to have corporations undertake include taking care of the poor, rebuilding the inner city, fighting illicit drug traffic, giving to charity, endowing universities, and funding cultural programs. None of these is a moral obligation of corporations. People from a variety of quarters demand lower prices, increased profits, higher wages, more job security, more disclosure from corporations about their operations, and corporate programs to help solve the problems of poverty, discrimination, and urban blight. Some of these demands negate or contradict other demands. Which are moral, which are only social, and which are simply statements of vested interest? Businesses have frequently not known how to react to this plethora of demands, and some firms have decided to proceed with business as usual until forced to change by legislation. Some corporations have indicated they would like to comply with legitimate demands, if only they knew how. But, they complain, the demands are vague, sometimes at odds with one another, and no one except government spells them out clearly. Moreover, many indicate that they would modify their actions only if all their competitors also did so, for otherwise they would suffer a competitive disadvantage.

The term *social obligation* suggests that society requires the corporations to act in the specified way. The term also implies a threat—that unless corporations fulfill these obligations society will force them to do so through legislation, or possibly terminate their existence. The threat may be a real one. But as a society we should try to determine exactly what it is we are asking of corporations. We should clarify the issues: which social demands are morally required; which are not morally required but are seen by the majority as appropriate; which might be nice for corporations to act on, if they are able; and which represent vested interests.

In the United States, the rebuilding of cities, caring for the poor, and the provision of welfare are social ends that traditionally have been socially implemented. Corporations may donate money to such projects if they choose. They would do so presumably to enhance their public image, to gain free publicity, or for some other such reason. The government encourages such donations by making many of them tax-exempt. But social welfare and social projects are appropriately the domain of government, not of business. Businesses are taxed, and such taxes may be used for social purposes. The purpose of the corporation, however, is profitable production and distribution, not social welfare. The manufacturing corporation is not structured to achieve social welfare. Moreover, there is great danger in expecting corporations to take upon themselves the production of public welfare, because they already have enormous power and are not answerable for its use to the general public. Politicians are elected by the public and are expected to have the common good as their end. We should not expect corporations to do what they are neither competent nor organized to do, but we should insist that they fulfill their *moral* obligations.

If as a society we decide that corporations should be forced to rebuild the inner city, should not be allowed to close down unprofitable plants, or should be made to train the hard-core unemployed, these demands should be thought through, discussed in the political forum, and then clearly legislated. They are controversial social demands, and should not be confused with what is morally required.

Some corporations have begun issuing social audits to inform the public as to where they stand on some social issues, and to explain their policies and their impact on society. Some people have suggested that social audits be made mandatory. However, we should keep in mind the distinctions we have already made between what is morally required and the meaning of the phrase *corporate social responsibility*. There is at present no consensus about what a social audit should contain, or how it should be constructed and presented. Greater clarity of purpose could be achieved if society were to impose on corporations not only a social audit but a moral audit as well, even though the content of the two audits would overlap. The social audit, in its broad sense, now includes charity and welfare (which are not moral obligations) and generally lacks any principles for determining what the audit properly includes and what it does not. Therefore it is often either arbitrary or merely a self-serving public relations document. A moral audit would concern that portion of the social audit that can be generated from moral principles and listed as responses to moral obligations. The moral audit should be distinct from other aspects of a social audit, which would include charitable contributions and not morally demanded actions of interest to environmentalists, conservationists, or other groups.

Why should there be a moral audit, and how can it be implemented? Morality governs the interaction of rational agents. The actions of corporations affect people. The general public, as well as actual and potential investors, has the right to know the moral as well as the financial position and record of a corporation. The techniques of reporting the moral quotient of a corporation are similar to techniques for implementing the social audit; but the attempts thus far have been rudimentary. The government already requires reporting on injuries, pollution levels, handling of toxic waste, and other data pertinent to a moral audit, hence much data are already available.

We have seen that corporations have the moral obligation not to harm people. This obligation is reasonably clear when it comes to many products. If pollution causes harm, then corporations are morally obliged not to pollute. This is a moral, not only a social obligation. It is a moral requirement, not a supererogatory act—that is, an act that is morally commendable but not required. How the corporation is to fulfill this obligation, however, is a social decision.

The moral audit with respect to pollution would include information about emission levels, the levels allowed, and other pertinent information, on the basis of which someone could tell whether the corporation was or was not fulfilling its obligations with respect to pollution. Its accident record would indicate whether it was providing adequate safety protection for its employees; its recall record would indicate its quality control and the safety of its products; its legal suits and its out-of-court settlements would indicate how it fulfills some of its moral obligations with respect to its customers. For each category of moral responsibility some method of reporting could be devised that would constitute an appropriate moral audit.

Corporations have moral obligations whether they wish to have them or not. Some firms attempt to fulfill these obligations; others are better at evading them. The free market allows the consumer to cast its vote for a company by buying its product, and to cast a vote against a company by not buying its product. If the moral audit were part of the public record of each company, people could take this into account when casting such votes. At the present time there are several mutual funds that invest only in companies that the managers of the fund judge to be morally and socially responsible. Some mutual funds do not invest in companies that operate in South Africa, or that make munitions; some eschew liquor and cigarette companies as well; and still others attempt to determine the employment and other practices of a company before deciding whether it is sufficiently moral to permit investing in it. As of 1983, *The Concerned Investor's Guide* reports on some of the relevant safety, labor, and other practices of firms listed on the New York Stock Exchange. Those interested in considering the morality of the firms in which they invest are thus beginning to have a practical means of getting this information with relative ease. More such data, including routine moral audits, would be extremely useful. The publication of such data would also be an incentive toward more morally responsible corporate activity.

People may, of course, buy a company's product if it is the best available, even if they know the company acts immorally. However, it is unlikely that they will ignore the immorality of a company if the immorality hurts them. But even that is possible. Defenders of a free market should have no reluctance about instituting a moral audit, for it would require a publicly owned firm to supply its potential customers and shareholders with information that they may appropriately wish to have before making their decisions about whether or not to deal with that firm.

In the first chapter of this book we examined the Myth of Amoral Business. The myth tends to obscure the moral obligations of corporations. The myth should be put to rest. Corporations *have* moral obligations, and they *can* and *should* be held morally accountable for fulfilling them. The moral audit is an innovation whose time has come. If it were required of all large corporations, it would go a long way toward replacing the Myth of Amoral Business with a clear and open approach to corporate moral obligations.

Pollution and Its Control

Because pollution can involve harm to others, it has a moral dimension. But because it can be controlled or handled in a number of ways, it has a social dimension that may vary from city to city, state to state, or nation to nation.

Consider the following case. Jason City, a community of 150,000 people, has five factories in an industrially zoned section on the east side of the city. One of the factories is much older than the others, and emits three times more sulphur into the atmosphere than the newer plants, each of which emits about the same amount of sulphur. The atmosphere can absorb a certain amount of pollution and carry it away without ill effects to either people or property. Therefore, the city has had no need to do anything about the emissions from the factories, and the factories have not invested in any pollution-control equipment. A sixth factory is built. It emits the same amount of sulphur as the other four new factories. But it adds just enough so that now a possibly dangerous level of sulphur is discharged into the air. The pollution may now cause harm. We have said that corporations have a moral obligation not to cause harm to people or property. Who is morally responsible to do what? The oldest factory claims that it was in the town first, and although it causes the most pollution it caused no harm until the sixth factory arrived. The other four claim that they are minor polluters and would cause no harm if either the sixth factory had not opened or if the first factory lowered its sulphur emissions to the same rate as the other factories. The sixth plant claims that it has as much right to emit sulphur into the atmosphere as the other plants, and therefore should not bear any special burden. By itself, it claims, it does no harm.

Clearly, the six plants together cause the harm, even though each one by itself would not cause harm. For purposes of a moral audit we would want to know how much sulphur each factory emits. But this information alone tells us nothing about whether the sulphur is causing harm. We also have to know what procedures have been adopted for handling the sulphur pollution problem in Jason City, and whether each factory is doing what, in this context, it is supposed to be doing.

There are many ways that Jason City can handle the problem of pollution. The city might decide that the amount of pollution is low enough, and the harm done to residents and property slight enough that nothing need be done about it. The city might decide that if anyone claims damage from the pollution, that individual should sue one or all the plants for compensation. The city could impose a limit on the amount of sulphur any plant can emit. It could prevent the construction of any more plants. It could allow more plants to be built only if they emit no sulphur whatsoever, keeping the emission level at its present rate. The city might even take it upon itself to supply emission-control devices to the plants, thereby controlling pollution at the source, at city expense. It might also tell the six companies that they are causing the pollution, and that they must lower the level or face a series of fines, thus leaving it up to the plants to arrange among themselves how to lower the sulphur to an acceptable level.

There is no one right and best way for Jason City to solve the problem of sulphur pollution, but there are many ways of approaching the problem.

It is appropriate, however, that the plants emitting the sulphur control their emissions, because the sulphur belongs to them. They have been allowed to use the air to get rid of their wastes, when doing so injured no one. But when such a procedure threatens to harm others, the action can be rightfully curtailed. The claim that the air belongs to all of us, and therefore any of us can discharge what we want into it, cannot be successfully defended.

Wastes belong to those who produce them. Just because people do not want their wastes does not relieve them (or firms) of the responsibility of disposing of their wastes in a way that does not harm others. The principle is recognized with respect to garbage. Individual households in some cities pay to have their garbage disposed of; in other cities this is a service provided through tax funds; and in rural communities people are sometimes allowed to dispose of it by burning it or carrying it themselves to the town dump. Air and water pollutants are industrial wastes, which belong to the plants that produce them as truly as a household's garbage belongs to the household. The method of disposal of such wastes varies with communities. But the principle that the wastes belong to the producer, and that producers have no right to harm others by their wastes, is a sound moral basis for imposing limits on what pollutants are admissible, in what amounts, and how the rest is to be controlled or disposed of.

A moral or social audit of each company in this case would require reporting both how much pollution is being produced, how much harm this causes, what the relevant regulations are, and how the company is handling its relevant obligations, both moral and social. To what extent does it cause harm? To what extent is compensation made for the harm done? To what extent does it comply or not comply with regulations? As with a financial audit, a moral audit would be more believeable if it were carried out by an independent auditor than if it were developed entirely by the firm.

Jason City exemplifies some dimensions of the problem of pollution. But the problem has many facets and dimensions; it is often extremely complicated, and involves conflicting principles. There is also much uncertainty about facts, the dangers posed, and the probable effects of proposed solutions. The term *pollution* is used in general to cover contamination of water, air, and land. There are many varieties of pollution, and varying degrees of damage done by it. *Pollution,* moreover, is sometimes a relative term. Certain gases and chemicals are not dangerous in very small amounts but are dangerous in large amounts. When present in small amounts, they are not usually considered pollutants, and they become pollutants only when they reach a certain, dangerous level. Other substances are noxious in even minute amounts and are considered pollutants in whatever amounts they are present. What is considered to be a pollutant in drinking water may not be considered a pollutant in river water. Moreover, pollution is defined not only by the substance but also by the source. The term is usually restricted to products produced by human action. In the air, sulfur that results from a volcanic eruption is not considered pollution, even though it is the same chemical substance as that introduced by some chemical plants. The reason, of course, is that we can control what human beings produce but we cannot control volcanic eruptions. For instance, if we are monitoring air to see that it has only a certain amount of sulfur in it, we consider it to be polluted by only that portion of sulfur produced by humans, even though naturally produced sulfur is included in the overall clean-air index.

Pollutants produced by many chemical and manufacturing processes are highly noxious. If improperly disposed of they can find their way into drinking water or the food chain, resulting in cancer or other extremely serious diseases; other effects range from malformed babies to serious intestinal disorders. Such chemical by-products clearly cause harm. Those who produce these substances have the moral obligation to dispose of them in safe ways; otherwise they are morally guilty of the harm they produce. Their obligation to dispose of them properly and safely was a moral obligation, even prior to government regulation of such waste disposal. After a number of widely publicized reports about improper disposal and the sad effects thereof, the federal government passed a law requiring a "paper trace" that covered the handling of such wastes, from the producing plant through the final disposition in a proper facility. Just before the law went into effect, a number of companies—both originators of the waste and haulers—dumped toxic wastes along open roads, to save the cost of hauling the waste to the proper disposal locations. Clearly, such acts threatened the health and safety of people who would be affected by the run-off and seepage into their drinking water supplies. The action was immoral, a blot on the record of the firms involved.

Pollution, we noted, can be morally handled in many ways. One way is for those who produce harm to reimburse those harmed for the harm done. In this way compensatory justice is brought into play after the fact. Where the harm done is serious, and preventable, pollution is not usually morally justifiable, even though reimbursing those harmed is preferable to not reimbursing them. In some cases, however, the harm done is not serious and recompense is a satisfactory remedy. The involved parties may even agree, prior to the harm, to a fee that is to be paid those who are damaged for the damage done. This is a form of licensing the harm done by compensating those harmed. This might be the procedure, for instance, in the case of noise pollution produced by airport traffic as it affects those living near the field. The owners of the airport might buy from the neighbors affected the right to produce the noise. (Property values decrease, and they suffer from the disturbance of noisy airplanes flying overhead.) One approach to pollution, as these examples show, is to allow it, but to compensate, either before or after the fact, those who are adversely affected.

A second approach allows a firm to pollute but attempts to eliminate the pollution, or clean it up before it damages anyone. The cleaning up might be done by the firm that produces it, or the firm might hire someone else to handle the clean-up process. Or the clean-up might be carried out by some governmental agency or body. In the latter case, the clean-up might be done at public expense (in which case the taxpayers are subsidizing the polluting industry) or at the expense of the polluting firms.

A third approach to pollution is to prevent it at the source. This means that the pollution will not be allowed to develop. Government might mandate this, or firms might decide on their own that it is preferable to prevent the damage rather than pay for it afterward. If government mandates the prevention of pollution, it may either specify the means to be taken to prevent the pollution, or it may simply require that there be no effluents of a certain type produced, and allow the firms involved to take whatever measures they wish to achieve the mandated end. Many firms prefer the latter approach, because they claim it offers them greater incentives to find cost-effective means of preventing pollution. Government-mandated procedures are usually not individually tailored to particular needs and so are not cost-effective. A variant of this approach is to set certain limits on the pollution to be tolerated, requiring that it be kept at or below a certain threshold level.

The case of pollution caused by motor vehicles raises several interesting aspects of the general problem of pollution. One is the decision about how much pollution, and what kind of pollution, from cars is to be tolerated. This is a social decision, to be made by society as a whole. It is not appropriately made only by the automobile industry, or only by drivers, because the ill effects of pollution are suffered by all, even though some (e.g., those with emphysema or asthma) suffer more than others. Clearly, the amount of air pollution that produces ill effects is a technical question. But the amount of pollution that a society wishes to tolerate is a social question and should be decided socially via the political process.

What makes the question of vehicular pollution different from the pollution caused by factories is that the actual pollution is caused not by a company or firm, but by individual cars, and hence by individual drivers. One way to cut down pollution is to prevent cars from spewing pollutants into the air. Another way is to prevent people from driving more than a certain amount, or taxing them for the right to do so. Cars driven in a small town might pose no threat to anyone. The same cars driven the same amount in Los Angeles add to the air pollution of Los Angeles, and that pollution, if uncontrolled, would do serious harm to many. Therefore, neither the amount of pollution produced by an individual car nor the number of miles driven can be equated with unacceptable levels of pollution. Why should all car drivers have to pay more to buy cars that reduce pollution when the problem exists only in certain areas? On the other hand, how can one prevent people from driving where they wish? California did in fact introduce stricter pollution-control laws than the other states in the United States: It chose to impose stricter regulations on car manufacturers than others, and hence raised the cost of cars made according to those specifications. Should all the cars in the United States be made according to the standards set in California? Clearly, many would think not, and they would not be obviously wrong.

The national standards regarding car-manufacturing are a matter of public policy and should be determined in accordance with the procedures set up for deciding such issues. Some countries have come up with standards different from those in the United States. We cannot say, without thorough investigation, that either of the standards is morally preferable. It may be that each is appropriate for the country involved. In all countries there will be a trade-off of allowed pollution against the expense of pollution control. In this situation it is not immoral for an automobile manufacturer to comply with the standards set by government rather than deciding on its own to make the standards more rigid for its cars, at increased cost to the buyer. Manufacturers may, of course, take the latter course, but this is not a moral requirement. The moral obligation in this case would be to fulfill the socially mandated standard, and, in this instance, the manufacturers' moral and social responsibility would coincide.

In America, some moral responsibility also falls on the individual car user. All new cars are made with catalytic converters that require the use of lead-free gas. Such gas is more expensive than regular gas. But the converters are effective in controlling pollution to the allowed limit only if lead-free gas is used. For an individual to intentionally pollute by using regular gas is to intentionally contribute to harming people and property. The harm any individual will do is of course small, but the principle of not harming is violated nonetheless. If many people acted in this way the harm done would be serious, and each guilty person would share in the blame for that harm.

The problem of pollution is complex and open to a variety of solutions. There is controversy about acceptable levels of pollution, the necessity for producing certain kinds of wastes, the relative benefits involved with producing nuclear wastes for which there are no agreed upon disposal procedures, and so on. These issues involve corporate, social, and moral responsibility. But the problems are not always as easy to solve as some of those who attack corporate policy claim. In dealing with pollution, as in dealing with other issues of social responsibility, it would be helpful to distinguish what is morally mandatory, what is desirable but not mandatory, what is to be decided by the political process, and how goals are to be achieved. A moral audit—or a social audit, of which a moral audit is a clear part—can be constructed to include an evaluation of corporate actions with respect to pollution. We would all benefit if such instruments helped make clear what the problem is, what the variety of solutions are, and which companies are fulfilling their moral, legal, and social responsibilites in this area.

Further Reading

ACKERMAN, ROBERT W. *The Social Challenge to Business.* Cambridge, Mass.: Harvard University Press, 1975.

ANSHEN, M., ed. *Managing the Socially Responsible Corporation.* New York: Macmillan Publishing Company, 1974.

BAUER, R. A., and D. H. FENN, JR. *The Corporate Social Audit.* New York: Russell Sage Foundation, 1972.

BERLE, A., and G. C. MEANS. *The Modern Corporation and Private Property.* New York: Macmillan Publishing Company, 1932; rev. ed., 1968.

CHAMBERLAIN, NEIL. *The Limits of Corporate Responsibility.* New York: Basic Books, Inc., 1973.

HESSEN, ROBERT. *In Defense of the Corporation.* Stanford: Hoover Institution Press, 1979.

HURST, JAMES WILLARD. *The Legitimacy of the Business Corporation.* Charlottesville, Va.: The University Press of Virginia, 1970.

JACOBY, N. H. *Corporate Power and Social Responsibility.* New York: Macmillan Publishing Company, 1973.

KNIGHT, SHAREN D., and DEBORAH KNIGHT. *The Concerned Investor's Guide: Non-Financial Corporate Data.* Arlington, Va.: Resource Publishing Group, Inc., 1983.

LUTHANS, FRED, RICHARD M. HODGETTS, and KENNETH R. THOMPSON. *Social Issues in Business,* 3rd ed. New York: Macmillan Publishing Company, 1980.

NADER, RALPH, and MARK J. GREEN, eds. *Corporate Power in America.* New York: Grossman Publishers, 1973.

SETHI, S. PRAKASH. *Up Against the Corporate Wall,* 3rd ed. Englewood Cliffs, N.J.: Prentice-Hall, Inc., 1977.

STONE, CHRISTOPHER D. *Where the Law Ends: The Social Control of Corporate Behavior.* New York: Harper & Row, Publishers, 1975.

WALTON, CLARENCE, ed. *The Ethics of Corporate Conduct.* Englewood Cliffs, N.J.: Prentice-Hall, Inc., 1977.

Workers' Rights: Employment, Wages, and Unions

The American free-enterprise system is possible not only because of the presence of capital and entrepreneurs, but also because of the presence of a diverse and available labor pool. Workers employed by a corporation have rights they can exercise against their employer. We shall consider these in the next chapter. But even prior to employment in a particular job, workers have rights against the system because of their place within the system. As opposed to specific rights concerning conditions of employment, these are general rights against the society or the system as such, and therefore have a special status. To the extent that they are human rights, they are held by all human beings, no matter what the politico-economic system in which they live. The appropriate implementation of these rights varies with the resources, level of development, and politico-economic structure of different societies. The rights we shall consider in this chapter are the right to employment, the right to a fair wage, the right to organize, and the right to strike. Consideration of these rights will also involve us in a discussion of unions and of collective bargaining.

The Right to Employment

A right to employment is not a right that is recognized in the United States, where unemployment is both expected and accepted. The right can be derived from the right to work, another right not recognized in the United States but one that is listed in Article 23 of the Universal Declaration of Human Rights, and one that is recognized in a great many countries. Whether there is truly a right to employment, which should be recognized in the United States, depends on whether it is a justifiable claim. We shall therefore look at the argument that supports it, and look as well at alternatives to the recognition of that right, which do exist in the United States.

In those countries in which the only employer is the government, each able-bodied person can exercise the right to employment directly against the government. In such countries the right is frequently joined with a correlative obligation to work—an obligation that government enforces against the able-bodied. In the free-enterprise system, the right to employment is not a right that can be exercised against any particular employer. In the United States, no one has a right to any particular job or position. Even the fact that one is the most capable person for a position does not give one the right to it.

Because the right to employment is derived from the right to work, we should start with this. As a human right, the right to work applies to all human beings, merely by virtue of their being human. But the right is appropriately implemented differently, both in different societies and for people of different ages and circumstances. Infants as well as all other human beings have the right to work; but because they are physically and mentally incapable of working, it is not a right they actively exercise. Adults in primitive societies exercise the right differently from those in advanced industrial societies.

We can roughly divide the population of the United States into four groups. One group is composed of children too young to work, or at least considered too young to work full time in our society. Either they are incapable of working because they are infants or very young children, or they are required to go to school and so are legally precluded from working full time. After a certain age they may be allowed to work part time. A second group consists of retired workers. They have worked for a certain period of time and have now left the work force. A third group consists of those unable to work—whether because of sickness, injury, or other infirmity. The fourth and largest group consists of adults who are able to work.

The group of able-bodied adults can be further subdivided. The largest subgroup consists of those actually in the work force, those who are self-employed, employed by government, by someone else, or by a firm. The second largest subgroup consists of those who work at home but who are not employed. These include housewives, mothers of small children, and others with no outside employment, who do not seek employment. There is clearly a difference between *work* and *employment*. A woman who raises a family and "keeps house" works but is not employed. A person who sculpts, writes, or makes his or her living in a similar way, works but is not employed. Children who work at home or for the family are not employed, but they work. Consider a small family on a farm: the husband and wife work in the fields, care for the animals, and work in the house; the children do chores in the morning and evening, and go to school between times. All the members of the family work. None are employed, but none are unemployed either.

The third largest group are the unemployed. This group can be further subdivided. It includes young adults who want to work but are unable to find their first full-time job, as well as those who work at home but want outside employment. It includes seasonal workers, young or older, for instance, fruit pickers, who work in certain seasons and are unable to find work in other seasons. It includes the hard-core unemployed, who do not have work and who have given up looking for a job. It includes the structurally unemployed, that is, those who had work in a certain industry but who are unable to find that sort of employment, are unable to relocate, and have no other skills to sell. It includes as well the cyclically unemployed, that is, those who are unemployed because of a cutback in the number of workers employed by firms, owing to recessions or depressions; and the fractionally unemployed, that is, those who are temporarily out of work, for a short period while changing jobs.

Employment usually implies both an employer and a wage. Work implies neither of these. Defining work is notoriously difficult. We can, however, determine what the right to work involves without deciding precisely what is and is not work, or how we distinguish work from play or from other kinds of human activity.

The right to work as a universal, human right, is itself a derived right. Defenders of the right have attempted to derive it from the right to life, the right to development, and/or the right to respect. In each case the derivation hinges on certain assumptions and background conditions. Thus the right to work can be derived from the right to life to the extent that access to work is necessary to obtain the wherewithal to preserve life. The right to life carries with it the right to engage in those activities, compatible with the exercise of the rights of others, necessary to sustain life. To the extent that work is the typical means by which adults produce the goods they need and want to sustain themselves and those dependent on them, the right to work is a derivative of the right to life. The right so derived is a negative, not a positive right. The derivation hinges on the assumption that if one is deprived of work, one is deprived of the means of sustaining one's life and the lives of one's dependents. In a society in which preventing people from working threatens their lives, the right to work is easily derived from the right to life.

Although the assumption that people in general produce the means of their subsistence is correct, it is not necessarily the case that each adult person able to engage in productive labor must be allowed to do so to prevent him from dying. For society can so arrange what it produces to sustain not only those who work and those dependent on them, but others as well. In the United States, for instance, a variety of welfare programs are justified on the basis of a recognized right to life, which can be sustained without recognizing a right to work.

The derivation of the right to work from the right to development, despite a certain plausibility and appropriateness in some societies, is also tenuous. If work or productive activity is a means by which human beings develop themselves physically and mentally, then to the extent that one has a right to such development, and to the extent that work is necessary for such development, one has the right to work. But at both critical junctures the link is weak. For even granting the right to development, such a right could be implemented by education, leisure activity, and other non-work-related means. Furthermore, many kinds of work do not develop one either physically or mentally. Thus a frequent charge brought against much industrial work is that it is stultifying and prevents rather than fosters development.

The derivation of the right to work that hinges on the right of all human beings to respect provides its most solid basis. Human beings belong to human society. An able-bodied, competent member of society has and plays a role in it. Each has a right to do so. No adult is "excess" or "expendable," and the recognition of this fact is part of what it means for people to have the right to respect. Work is the typical way by which human adults assert their independence and are able to assume their full share of responsibility in a community. Work involves the taking of one's place in the community, whether it is work in the home, in the fields, or in the factory or office. One's self-respect as well as the respect of others is closely linked with what one does, how a person expresses himself through his actions, and the extent to which one assumes the full burden and responsibility for one's life and one's part in the social fabric. If one is not allowed to work, one is not allowed to take his or her rightful place in society as a contributing, mature, responsible adult. The right to work is in this way closely related to the right to respect and is derived from it, for every society.

For this reason, to deprive a person of a productive role in many societies is a form of ostracism, tantamount to punishment, and justifiable only for a serious social offense or crime.

The right to work can be interpreted as both a negative and as a positive right. As a negative right, no one, including the government, may legitimately prohibit someone who wishes to work from doing so, that is, within the normal restrictions for negative rights, such as not infringing the similar, equal, or more important rights of others. As a positive right, it requires at least that one's society accept one, and give one the opportunity for full membership, including the opportunity for participation in the productive activity of society.

The relation of respect and the right to work is implied in Article 23 of the Declaration of Human Rights, which insists on the "free choice of employment" (thus precluding forced labor, slavery, or gross exploitation), and on "just and favorable remuneration ensuring for himself and his family an existence worthy of human dignity."

As with most rights, the right to work rises to consciousness only at a certain historical time. In the idyllic society of an imaginary tropical island where needs are few, food is plentiful, and the population is small in comparison with the land and resources available, the right to work would not arise. It is not explicitly raised, although it is implicitly implemented in a traditional society, for in such a society everyone has a place in the social order—whether that society is one of hunting, herding, or agriculture, and whether it is organized on tribal, feudal, or other similar lines. Each adult is accepted into the community and participates in the activity of the adults of that community. Nor would one tend to invoke the right in a country where land is plentiful and where there are many alternative ways to keep oneself and one's family flourishing with dignity. The right to work was not an issue when there was always an alternative to the jobs available. Finally, the right to work would tend not to arise in a society that had a chronic shortage of labor. If the demand for labor always exceeded the supply, the notion of the right to work would have little, if any, importance, except in its negative sense.

The right to work typically arises when the supply of labor exceeds the demand, when large numbers of people have no available alternative to earning their living by working for others, and when the social fabric characteristic of tribes and extended families, where all share in whatever is available, breaks down. Historically, the right to work became an issue with the advent of industrialization, in which the means of production was owned by only a few and the typical worker earned his living by working for a wage.

In an industrialized society the line between the negative and the positive interpretation of the right to work often blurs. Preventing one from working in a traditional society involves depriving one of access to work or to a place in the society. In an industrial society, those who depend upon employment for wages can be kept from working by being kept from employment. One might actively be kept from employment, by some action or intervention—blackballing, or the like—or passively, when no employer needs workers. Unemployment might, in this latter sense, result from the system. It is not the active result of employers discriminating or refusing, out of malice, to employ people. No individual employer has the obligation to employ others, and employers, acting individually in their own interests, cannot be blamed if collectively they cannot provide work for all who want it. The system is to blame, not individual employers within it.

In such a situation the right to work is equivalent to the right to employment for those able, willing, and desiring work and unable to engage in productive work if not employed. Properly speaking, the right to employment is not itself a human right but becomes a specification of the human right to work appropriate in industrialized society. The right to employment is properly exercised by the unemployed against the society with such a system, because it is the system that is responsible for preventing them from working. Americans have come to accept the system because of the goods and wealth it produces, and have provided welfare as an alternative to employment. But welfare, critics claim, has masked the right to work and has kept its violation from general consciousness. For although welfare does indeed preserve life, it does not allow the able-to-work who receive it to take an active, productive part in their society, with the concomitant respect and self-respect that go with having work or employment.

To say that the right to work is exercised against the system or society does not mean that it is exercised only against government. For just as business benefits from the system adopted by society, business appropriately shares in meeting the obligations of society to those members who suffer as a result of the system. Government, however, would have to enforce the right. It might use tax incentives to motivate firms to retain employees they might otherwise fire. Government might require, and help, firms to retrain or relocate workers when plants are shut down. It could give businesses tax benefits or subsidies to provide training for the unemployed. It might mandate cuts in the time worked by all workers in a firm—with a corresponding cut in salary—rather than allowing layoffs when these are economically necessary. Government can also directly serve as a clearinghouse for openings and applicants, aid in relocating the unemployed, supplement insufficient wages through a negative income tax, or, finally, serve as a temporary employer of last resort.

These and other similar requirements placed on business may seem like interferences with their freedom. And of course they are. But the freedom of business is, and has always been, legitimately circumscribed by the rights of the individuals in society. Such interferences perhaps seem severe only because as a society we have not considered seriously the right to employment.

To the extent that the right to work has received any attention in labor law in the United States it has been in the sense of a negative right. Thus, for instance, some have claimed that union shops (in which union membership is required for employment either on or after the thirtieth day of beginning employment) prevent those who do not want to join the union from working, or at least from working where they choose. Legislation on the union shop has varied from state to state in the United States, ever since Section 14(b) of the Taft-Hartley law allowed states to outlaw such shops. Right-to-work laws in this context mean laws that outlaw union shops and thus preserve the right of all workers to work without the obligation to join or belong to a union. But although the legislation and debates surrounding union shops have been couched in terms of right-to-work laws, such laws touch only a small portion of what the human right to work covers. Whether such laws are truly for the benefit of the worker is a hotly debated issue. The existing right-to-work laws, therefore, do not implement the human right to work we have been considering; and having preempted the terminology, they make discussion of right-to-work laws (in the sense of positively implementing the right) confusing and difficult.

Yet the right to employment is compatible with the best in the United States tradition of free enterprise and peaceful and productive labor relations, and implementation of that right does not necessarily lead to socialism or to disruption of the free-enterprise worker-management relation.

In the United States, the failure to recognize and address the right to employment has to some extent been mitigated by a variety of public programs, from unemployment insurance to welfare programs. Unemployment insurance, as the name implies, is a type of insurance program. It is available only to those who have such insurance, and the minimal requirement is that one have been previously employed. It is thus not available to those leaving school who have not been previously employed on a full-time basis. Nor is it available to women, for example, who have been working in the home raising a family and who wish at a certain time to join the work force. And it is not available to those who have been out of work for a longer period than that covered by the insurance. As a stopgap measure for those temporarily unemployed or for those between jobs, it is on the whole adequate and serves an obvious need. For the others, however, it does nothing.

Welfare programs come to the rescue for some of those not eligible for unemployment insurance and in need of help. Such programs serve another obvious need. But there is a difference between providing support for those who cannot work outside the home because of disability, or the need to care for children, or some other similar reason, and providing support for those who both can work and wish to do so. For the latter, the absence of work can be and very often is demoralizing and, as we have noted, leads to loss of both self-respect and the respect from others. The reason for their unemployment is not theirs, but in some sense the society's or the system's. That failure is only partially made good by charity or by welfare payments. And what is not made good marks the difference between welfare and recognition of the right to employment.

In the United States, the notion of full employment is often equated, for practical purposes, with the right to employment. The right to employment, however, is not identical with full employment. Full employment is an aim or goal that, if reached, would go a long way toward implementing the right to employment for all those seeking it. But *full employment* is usually defined, in the United States, as being compatible with a certain level of unemployment (some have even suggested that 10 percent unemployment in the United States might constitute full employment). Moreover, unemployment figures ignore the discouraged or hard-core unemployed, who have given up looking for work. Full employment, moreover, is a societal goal, not a right. It is a goal properly adopted by a society in which unemployment is a result of the socioeconomic system. But there is an important difference between full employment as a *goal* and the *right* to employment. As a societal goal, full employment is appropriately balanced against other societal goals, such as control of inflation. The right of individuals, however, is different from societal goals and should not be weighed simply as one good against another. A right is an entitlement that should be respected even at the cost of some other good. (For instance, there is no right to single-digit inflation, even though that is desirable.) Government might attempt both, implement rights and control inflation; but the difference between considering full employment simply as one goal among many, and considering the right to employment as a valid individual claim against society, is fundamental.

If the *right* to employment were taken seriously, American society, American business, and the American government would all have to take a different approach to problems of unemployment and welfare than they have. A new approach would require imagination and experimentation. As a nation we lack neither the means nor resources to implement the right. But as a society we have not yet been either forced or willing to recognize it.

The Right to a Just Wage

The right to a just wage, sometimes called a living wage, is a right derived from the right to life, the right to employment, and the right to respect. For some people the problem of what constitutes a just wage is a pseudoproblem: a just wage is whatever the market determines. For them, there is no sense in taking any other approach. The market matches buyer and seller with respect to labor, as with anything else. But clearly that approach, if it claims to be not simply a statement of how wages are set but of how they should be set, demands justification. If setting wages by the market is indeed just, then it should be possible to spell out the reasons why it is just. And once spelled out they can be carefully analyzed to see if they are sound.

Fairness can be taken to mean several equally plausible things; and what is fair according to one justifiable principle may be unfair according to another.

We have already seen that according to Marx's labor theory of value, a just wage is a contradiction in terms. Wages cannot be just because all wage labor involves exploitation. The way to achieve justice is to do away with wage labor and replace it with some other form of distribution. But we have also seen that this analysis has not convinced many Americans or West Europeans or Japanese. Except for a small number of Marxist critics, we do not hear workers complaining about being exploited because they receive wages.

We can, however, do without the notion of exploitation and substitute for it less controversial concepts that will enable us to state clearly the problems of wage differential and its justification. The need for a theory of a just wage is not eliminated by doing away with theories of exploitation, but its focus is shifted. A system that allows "anything the market will bear" is not acceptable from a moral point of view. A pure market approach to labor—and to wages as the price of labor—will not do. For an unrestricted free-market approach leads historically and potentially to a variety of injustices. Yet a theory of a just wage can include the market as one of the determinants of wages. A theory that does so must place limits on the market through social institutions acceptable to the rational participants in the system, each armed with appropriate knowledge.

The solution provided by the Marxist approach suggests, in some ways, the need for proper institutions. It misplaces its criticism, however, by focusing on private property. The marginal-productivity approach to wages ignores background institutions and often sees such institutions as restrictions on free contracts and markets rather than as necessary prerequisites if they are to be morally defensible.

We can talk meaningfully about a just wage only in relation to a system. A just legal and political system must at least provide an income floor, and must keep desperation out of the market by providing alternatives to forced acceptance of any wage offered, regardless of conditions. Only within a set of what can be called fair background institutions can the market be allowed to determine wage differentials. This approach makes no attempt to set wages according to some scale of worth, social usefulness, or need, and allows all of these to enter in, if those engaged in the process so choose. Hence, adopting this approach, we can say that what is just is whatever the market produces within the confines of a just system, in the way of wage differentials. If we claim that the results are not just, then we must argue that the background conditions are defective, that additional background institutional limitations are necessary, or that the market is defective. This approach also allows us to judge the morality of excessively low wages in Third World countries, where charges of injustice can often be sustained because of the lack of appropriate background institutions, with the result that the labor transactions are not free but forced.

Exploitation and discussion of what constitutes a just wage are not issues of vital concern among American workers because our system of background institutions has been developed and modified so as to be generally acceptable to them. The market system in the United States is severely restricted; the labor market operates only within certain parameters. Minimum-wage laws put a floor on the lower limit, and unemployment insurance and a variety of welfare programs provide an alternative to employment at starvation wages. Such legislation helps keep desperation out of the market. Unions helped to equalize the wage-negotiation process by equalizing the power of both parties in the transaction. An effective full-employment bill or legal recognition of the right to employment at an adequate wage would do even more to equalize the bargaining process for all. But at the lower limits, where the charge of exploitation is most likely to occur, there are floors; thereafter the market allows for wage differential. At the upper limits of management, if morality enters, it is not because of claimed exploitation, according to some theories, but because the multiple of minimum to maximum wages is too great.

Although in general the approach to wages in the United States is both morally justifiable and acceptable to most Americans, and although exploitation is not a burning issue in American labor relations, it does not follow that the notion of a fair or just wage is absent from the American scene. But the locus of the discussion of fairness has come to center on equality and discrimination rather than on exploitation or minimum wage. Thus, the argument is that the market needs further restraints. And some people have argued for correction of the market by other norms, as we shall see.

Before looking at the contemporary scene, however, we can usefully cast a glance at the historical development of fair-wage theory. Some of the present charges of unfairness stem from the prior implementation of a criterion of fairness we no longer use. If we are not fighting against habitual unfairness, but are moving toward a changed version of fairness, the means by which we move might well appear in a somewhat different light than otherwise.

If we go back to the nineteenth century, we find a doctrine of a just wage spelled out, for instance, in some of the papal encyclicals. In general, a fair wage was one sufficient to keep a family at a reasonable level of life beyond bare subsistence. This notion contains several assumptions and allows a great deal of variation from society to society. It assumed that there was one primary wage earner, who was typically male and typically the head of the family. A fair wage, therefore, was by definition a wage sufficient for a male head of a family to raise his family and support its members at a level comparable to that at which the other members of his society—or more particularly, his social class—lived. It was expected that as one's family grew one's expenses increased. Therefore seniority was to count toward an increase in wages, even if one's work and productivity were comparable to those performing a similar job at an entry level. Women had a full-time job at home keeping house, cooking and cleaning, raising children, and managing the household. They were sometimes forced by economic need to work; but they would not have to work outside the home, and certainly not full time, if the male head of the household were paid a fair or living wage. Thus Pope Pius XI, in his encyclical *Qadragesimo Anno* (1931), called the necessity of a woman's working to help support a family "an intolerable abuse," which was "to be abolished at all cost."[1] When they did work outside the home, women were marginal contributors to a household income, and because their wages were typically supplementary, it was considered fair to pay them less than men. It was also considered fair if single men were paid less than married men because they needed less. And children, if they worked part time, could be paid very little, because whatever they received was gravy for themselves and the family.

Fairness was thus to a large extent connected to need, and a judgment was not made on the basis of individual need but on the need of classes of people—male heads of households, single males, females, and children, in that order. Part of Marx's fierce attack on the capitalist system was its tendency to pay less than a fair wage to the male head of a household, forcing women, and finally even children, to work. This state of affairs was in part rectified by laws that limited child labor and then limited female labor.

To our contemporary ears such a view of a just wage seems strange. But the principle is a defensible one: namely, that wages should be proportional to classes of need. We have now substituted several other principles for that one, the main one of which is that equal work deserves equal pay. Thus it makes no difference whether the work is done by a male head of a household, by a single male, or by a female—single or married. Need is beside the point, except at the bottom, where it is handled by minimum-wage laws and welfare programs. What one deserves is equal recompense for equal work.

According to this principle, many of the old, customary practices are prejudicial and discriminatory. The change in the criterion of fairness that was to be used in wage distribution took place during and after World War II. During that war, American women entered the work force in large numbers, and many remained there. And with the increase of divorce, one can no longer assume that males rather than females are the heads of households. One's family situation is no longer a pertinent consideration, and now fairness demands that each person be considered on the basis of the work he or she does

---

[1] *The Papal Encyclicals*, ed. Claudia Carlen (Wilmington, N.C.: McGrath Publishing Co.), Vol. III, p. 426.

rather than on one's need, family status, or other considerations. Women have fought for equality in the labor market and have attempted to have the old customs replaced by new ones. The fight has been a long one, and women still make less than men. But the general principle of equal pay for equal work has been adopted in legislation, and it is a principle to which there is no vocal opposition.

Equal pay for equal work, however, is not a simple principle, nor an unambiguous one. It admits of at least five levels of initial interpretation: (1) on an international level, across an occupation or position; (2) on a national or regional level, across an occupation or position; (3) on an industry level; (4) on a company level; and (5) on an individual or interpersonal level. Thus, some claim that U.S. multinationals should pay all their personnel in similar positions at the same rate, regardless of whether they are in the United States, in Europe, or in Third World countries. This position is not required by justice. Wages should always be considered in the context of background institutions as well as that of cost of living. Nor has the case been made that equal pay for equal work demands that people holding similar positions anywhere in the United States receive similar pay, or even that a given company pay all its people at the same rate, wherever they are in the United States. For the cost of living varies, and the labor markets are different in different parts of the country. There is no reason why a company must pay everyone in its employ what it must pay in the sector where the cost of living is highest, and where the supply of people it needs to employ is not plentiful.

The principle of equal pay for equal work has been used successfully in uncovering and uprooting discrimination (on the basis of race and sex) within a particular firm in a given location. In such cases it has been used either in class-action suits or on the basis of interpersonal comparisons. If a man and a woman are performing similar tasks, and have equal training, seniority, and competence but are paid different wages in the same firm at the same location, there is certainly a prima facie case for claiming discrimination.

Equal pay for equal work, however, does not quite mean what it might be interpreted to mean if taken literally, even within a given firm. Consider a college or university.

Professors of computer science, engineering, business, or medicine receive a considerably higher salary on entry and thereafter than do professors of English, history, or philosophy, at the same college or university. Why is this not a violation of the principle of equal pay for equal work? And if an assistant professor teaches the same number of students and courses as does a senior professor, publishes the same number of articles or books in a given year, and serves on the same number of committees, why should the assistant professor not receive as high a salary as the senior professor? The answer in the latter case is seniority, a system superimposed on the principle of equal pay for equal work. It is not without justification, because although the assistant professor (the junior person) receives less upon entry, he or she can expect to receive comparable increases over time, as did the senior member. And in the long run, they will have received comparable, if not necessarily equal, pay for equal work. The practice in universities, moreover, parallels the seniority system in the private business sector, and is justifiable if the system is justifiable.

In the former case, the only justification for the difference in salaries between the pay of the professor of computer science and the professor of English is that of the marketplace. The market, if fair, is blind concerning sex or race. But discrimination on the basis of skill is permissible. The skill of the computer scientist is not greater in his domain than the skill of the English professor. But the computer scientist's skill is in shorter supply than the skill of the English teacher; the computer scientist therefore commands higher pay. The justification is that in the long run the market, by differential reward, will signal the need for more computer scientists and for fewer English professors. Students interested in income will pay attention to these signals and act accordingly. Those who refuse to do so and take their chances on receiving appointments as English professors, should realize that they will receive less than computer scientists with comparable training. Such wage differentials help allocate human resources to where they are most needed, and are justifiable because of the efficiency they thus promote.

This justification takes into account the system, as any justification should. Those who knowingly choose poorer-paying positions cannot legitimately complain that their positions are poorly paid. No one is forced to take a particular position, and those willing and able to prepare for the skills for which there is most demand will receive the best returns. Professors of some subjects may receive less pay than people with similar training in industry, but presumably there are attractions in the teaching profession that compensate for less pay. If this were not so, there would be a shortage of qualified people in academia, and the pay for professors would have to be increased as it has increased for professors of computer science. Because professors of the humanities are in less demand outside of academia, the pay sufficient to attract and hold professors of the humanities is less than what is necessary to attract and hold professors of computer science. Therefore they are paid different wages, even though both a professor of English and a professor of computer science may teach the same number of students, serve on similar committees, and teach a subject that is just as important to society.

A similar argument justifies paying college teachers less than those with similar education who perform tasks of equal social importance. But something very close to this has been challenged under the new claim of equal pay for comparable work. That principle is presented as a principle of justice, in terms of which we can judge that some wages are unfair and demand rectification. Implicit is the claim that the market fails in certain areas, and therefore changes in background institutions need to be brought in. The impetus, as in the case of equal pay for equal work, is claimed discrimination.

Some traditionally female jobs—nursing, elementary-school teaching, and secretarial work, among others—have remained low-paying positions. Women continue to be the major group of people attracted to these positions, for reasons that are not altogether clear. The question that has arisen is whether the pay for these positions is low because of the nature of the work or whether the pay for these positions is low because women are attracted to them. If secretaries were primarily men, would secretarial pay be as low as it is? The contention of some people is that the positions would not be low-paying if they were filled primarily by men. Hence, they consider the low pay for such positions to be discriminatory. The case was difficult to make under the principle of equal pay for equal work, as written into law and as generally interpreted, because the small percentage of men in such jobs received the same pay as women. This, then, is the reason for the more recent claim, that the principle of equal pay for equal work implies the principle of equal pay for comparable work; and if the law does not include this latter principle, new legislation is needed that does embody it.

The issue was raised explicitly in a case in the State of Washington, which will probably be appealed to the U.S. Supreme Court. In the Washington case, Judge Jack E. Tanner ruled that women employees of the State (members of the State's public colleges and universities excluded) had been underpaid and deserved compensation. He based his ruling on Title VII of the Civil Rights Act of 1964, which bars paying women less than men performing "comparable" jobs. Judge Tanner based his decision on a "comparable skills" study adopted by the State of Washington. According to the study, points were attached to various factors, such as responsibility, knowledge, skill, working conditions, and accountability. The results showed that occupations in which women dominated received about 20 percent less than occupations that ranked in the same place on the scale but in which men dominated. Thus, a ranking of 97 points was given to both laundry workers and truck driver I's. But truck drivers, who are mostly male, received a maximum of \$1,574 a month, and laundry workers, who are mostly women, received only \$1,114. A secretary II received \$1,324 for a 197-point job but an electrician received \$1,918. In making his ruling, Judge Tanner claimed he was simply applying standards that the State had determined. Implications of the ruling for other states without a commitment to such a study, or for the private sector, therefore, may be nil.

The State of Kansas, for instance, has a 93-year-old law requiring the State to pay the "prevailing wage," as determined community by community, for various services. It thus determines its wages by the market as it operates in the private sector. The determination of wages in the public sector is notoriously difficult, because there is often no measurable product, and the determination of productivity in the various sections is fairly arbitrary. One solution is the adoption of a step system, according to which those who supervise others are to receive more pay—a principle that operates in a great many firms and that leads to very high salaries in the more complex and very large firms.

If we prescind from the Washington study, however, and the determination of state salaries on the basis of that study, we can ask whether the principle of equal pay for comparable work is a morally justifiable one.

There are three arguments against it, which are serious enough to make it a questionable principle.

First, the argument of equal pay for comparable work assumes that some fair determination of comparable work is not only possible but morally justifiable. There are many measures of work and of comparability. One of the arguments for the market is that different people weigh the various factors differently. The market gives priority to no one set but considers them all, the end result being a mix of all the factors with their various weights. Secretaries may have as much responsibility, and need as much skill and knowledge as electricians or truck drivers. The conclusion that therefore they should be paid at the same rate does not follow, for a great many other factors enter into these jobs. If women, as some do, prefer the pay of a truck driver to the pay of a secretary, they should be able to enter that market. If entry is denied them, then that is where the injustice lies and where remedy is needed, rather than in adjusting salaries elsewhere. The comparable work argument cannot be used fairly if it is used selectively, that is, only in the instances where women are paid less and dominate the occupation. Such selective use of a principle is not an application of a morally justified principle, and such use of the principle seems only a rationalization for what is perceived for other reasons as unjust. If there is discrimination—and we cannot deny that there is—then discrimination should be addressed. The attack in this instance misses its proper target.

Second, the approach of comparable worth, if accepted, will not help to reduce discrimination; it will help to reinforce it. If it is true, as some claim, that women are discriminated against by being forced into secretarial jobs, nursing jobs, and so on, raising their pay in those jobs may well increase, not decrease, the likelihood that those jobs will remain filled predominantly by women. The incentive for women to go into other fields will be diminished and the incentive for them to enter those fields will be increased. If there is discrimination in those areas, the best solution would be to remove barriers to the entry of women into other areas, and to change the incentives that push them into those areas. If there are truly alternative opportunities, and if women still choose those occupations, despite lower pay, then their choice may call for social analysis; it does not call for compensatory justice.

Third, the claim of equal pay for comparable work undercuts the market mechanism and raises more problems than it solves. We have argued that if we have proper background institutions, the market is the best determinant of wage differential, above the minimum. This leads to the most efficient use of talent, and results in talent being drawn to where it is most needed—in the long run. To introduce a scale of comparable work into government would imply that the scale is morally justifiable (and if in government, then also in the nongovernmental sector). This in turn would ultimately lead to the imposition of pay scales and wage determination by government.

In the private sector, a rating service would generate competing and conflicting rating services, with different scales; then government would be required to set norms and determine the salary scale to be used. The result would be grossly inefficient and ultimately arbitrary. We need not only speculate that it would be so. Numerous countries have tried to do away with the market, and wages or remuneration have been set by government—the USSR is a case in point. The results have not been perspicuously just or rational. An assumption that things would be different in the United States seems unwarranted.

If equal pay for comparable work is a justifiable principle, it has not yet been shown to be such. Consideration of the principle does illustrate, however, how discussion of the justice or fairness of wages can and does take place within the system of American free enterprise.

Finally, although we have discussed the necessity for a bottom for wages, we have not addressed the question of the justifiability of upper limits. What is the proper maximum multiple of highest to lowest wages? Within a company, is a multiple of seven to one high enough, as some socialist countries maintain and have enforced? Is a thousand to one too high? If the lowest-paid worker gets $3.35 an hour, should management at its highest levels make no more that $335.00? Or no more than $3,335 an hour? Is there a proper multiple? There seems to be no way to decide that a multiple of five or seven or ten or one hundred is the proper upper multiple. If this is true, we should not attempt to set one. Rather, we should ask what background institutions are appropriate to keep income differentials from skewing our society in undesirable ways, robbing those less well off of their dignity and personal or social esteem. One solution available, which we already use, even if we do not use it as well as we might, is taxation. In Japan, for instance, multiples are kept low because large incomes are taxed at such high rates (e.g., up to 83 percent) that there is little to gain by increasing the multiple. But it would not make a great deal of difference if the multiple of one person's earnings was considerably more than another's if there were a fair method of progressive taxation. One solution to high incomes, therefore, is to judge not the fairness of the wage or income but the proper and fair rate of taxation on that income.

The Right to Organize: Unions

In a just society, among the institutions necessary to achieve a system of fair wages, unions have played an important role.

The gross annual income of such corporate giants as General Motors, Standard Oil, and Ford is larger than the gross national product of Austria, Norway, Finland, or Greece, not to mention that of many Third World countries. An individual facing the corporate colossus is no David standing before Goliath. The individual who takes on a large corporation is more like David facing a whole army.

We have already seen several times that an agreement between two contracting parties is fair if each of the parties has adequate, appropriate information, and if each enters into the transaction freely, without coercion. But what of contracts between an individual worker and a giant corporation? Can such a contract be fair, and can the worker deal as an equal in negotiations with the corporation?

Individual workers, of course, are no match for large corporations and are in a very weak position with respect to negotiation. Individual workers are most often given the choice simply of accepting employment on the terms offered by a firm or of not accepting such terms and conditions. If the number of firms is fairly small and the number of employees in search of work comparatively large, then the firms are clearly in a position of superiority in any negotiation and they can offer employment on terms that favor themselves. Even if they do not offer the lowest wages possible, it is in their interest to offer lower rather than higher wages whenever possible. The system of competition, in theory, should offset this advantage. But when the labor supply exceeds the demand for labor, this does not happen. Hence workers have found it to their advantage to organize into workers' associations, or unions, in order to deal with managers on more equal terms. By forcing management to deal with workers as a group rather than individually, the workers are in a better position to make the terms of any labor contract fair, at least in the sense that it is freely accepted by both sides.

How is the claimed right to form unions justified? The justification in the free-enterprise system stems from the prior right of individuals to the greatest amount of freedom compatible with a like freedom for all. This includes the right of individuals to pursue their own ends, and the right to associate with others to achieve common ends. The free association of workers to achieve common ends leads to the organization of labor unions. Because labor unions are the product of united workers, the unions have the same rights as the workers. The derivation and justification of unions parallels the derivation and justification of corporations. Unions are thus as morally legitimate as corporations. Unions, moreover, have no special rights beyond those of the individual workers, except those that are due organizations under their legal status. Union activity may be justly limited by government, for instance, if the workers in a field create a monopoly of labor in that field. Monopoly power goes beyond the rights of individuals and therefore of unions. Just as a government can legitimately regulate or preclude monopolies in industry, it can also do so with unions. But this does not mean that government can legitimately outlaw unions, for workers have the right to free association. Workers in unions can also do what they are allowed to do as individuals—jointly provide insurance for members, build up savings in case of need, establish funds to carry on strikes or civil suits in defense of workers, and so on.

Unions and their activities can be morally evaluated, just as corporations and their activities can be morally evaluated. Charges of corruption within unions need little discussion here. If union leaders use union money illegally, or for their own private purposes, such actions are clearly immoral.

Is it fair for unions to restrict membership in certain trades so that the number of members will be kept lower than the demand for them? Such a device obviously makes each member more valuable and therefore able to command a higher wage. But he is able to do so at the expense of those who would like to enter the marketplace and are prevented from doing so. If it is unfair for businesses to restrict trade and gain monopolies, it is unfair for some workers to restrict other workers from pursuing their interests and engaging in the type of work they prefer. Both are attempts to curtail competition for the benefit of the one restricting entry.

Although workers have the right to form and join unions, workers have no *obligation* to do so. What then is the moral status of union shops? In a union shop the union typically does not restrict union membership; often, the point of a union shop is to encourage membership. But a union shop allows only union members, or those who join the union within thirty days of employment, to work in the plant or industry. The argument given in defense of a union shop is twofold. If a plant is allowed to hire nonunion labor, then it can hire such labor at nonunion rates. Once a plant is able to hire people at less than union rates, it will find it to its advantage to do so. As a result, it will tend to replace union labor with nonunion labor, and the success that unions have achieved will thus be undercut. The second argument claims that if a plant hires both union and nonunion labor and treats them both equally, workers will have little incentive to join the union. Why should they, if they receive the same benefits without having to pay union dues? The result in this case is once again to undercut and weaken the union, deplete its coffers, and make it financially impossible to fund its activities.

Although both arguments carry a good deal of weight, they are not conclusive. For there is no obligation that everyone who benefits by the actions of others must somehow support those actions, or contribute to the activities of the group from whose actions they benefit. If a particular enterprise agrees to hire only union labor, however, it does not thereby violate the rights of potential nonunion workers because the latter have no right to work for that enterprise. The right of union members must be balanced against the right of an individual worker to seek a job and to have the option of not joining a union. He should not be forced to do so if he does not wish to do so. He should not be prevented from working or have his options narrowly restricted because he prefers not to join a union. Therefore we have a conflict of rights. The controversy has been resolved in various ways in the United States. Because the Taft-Hartley Act has left the decision of whether there should be union shops to the individual states, the decision becomes one of law and public policy. Such a policy may be written into a contract between a union and a given enterprise. The issue in some states has been decided at the polls. Right-to-work laws that guarantee the right of a worker to seek employment without joining a union have been passed in some states. If this means breaking up the union shop, it robs unions of one of their key implements. The last word on the controversy has not yet been spoken.

Unions have a specific constituency—their members. They do not claim to serve directly the larger society, or to have the good of society as their primary aim. Their goal is to protect and promote the interests of their members. They typically take management as their adversary. Unions have championed the right to strike and have used it as an effective weapon. They engage in collective bargaining and press the demands of the workers as forcefully and fully as possible. They have achieved a good deal of success.

Can unions properly be faulted for ignoring the public good and for sacrificing it in order to achieve their own ends? The union practice of feath-erbedding, for example, preserves the jobs of those employees who would otherwise be laid off because of technological improvements. A frequently cited case—during the transition from steam to electric trains—was the re-quirement that each train have a fireman, even though the train was run by electricity and did not need a fireman. The fireman was carried on each run, although he had no work to do. He continued to be paid, and this pay even-tually came out of the pockets of those who used the train. Unions have also been accused of fueling inflation by seeking higher wages in an unending spiral—each demand fueling other demands that in turn raise the demands of the first group. Each raise increases the cost of the products produced, and in the long run may lead to unemployment and recession.

Unions, like businesses, sometimes act in terms of vested interests, to the detriment of the general good. Union leaders claim, however, that in the long run (even in the particular instances cited), their actions lead to more good than harm, not only for their own workers but for all workers and for society in general. Such claims are a shorthand version of a utilitarian argument and can be properly evaluated only by considering particular cases and by at-tempting to evaluate the good and bad done to all those affected by the actions in question.

Individual workers are legally bound by the contracts entered into on their behalf by their union representatives. Yet we can legitimately ask whether workers are morally so bound, and whether they are bound even if they have voted against a contract supported by a majority. There is room for moral disagreement, for instance, about the justifiability of strikes by workers that are not called or sanctioned by union leaders. Whether these "wildcat strikes" are morally justifiable depends on the facts and circumstances of the case, the nature of the organizations involved, the agreement made by members with their unions, the degree of trust the workers have in their leaders, and similar considerations.

To have said this much, however, seems to have assumed the right to strike on the part of unions, and we should ask whether this is in fact a right, and if so, how it is justified.

The Right to Strike

In relations between labor and management there are four major groups in-volved, not merely two. The four are labor, management, government, and the general public. From a moral point of view it is essential to remember that all persons who make up these groups are human beings, and they do not stop being human beings by becoming workers, managers, a part of gov-ernment, or a part of the general public. Workers and managers are persons, beings deserving of respect, who have the moral obligation to do what is right and to avoid doing what is wrong. They thus have both moral rights and responsibilities that take precedence over their role-related rights, duties, or positions as workers or managers. Hence, despite the adversary relation of workers and managers in the American free-enterprise system, both deserve respect from the other and deserve to be treated as human beings, regardless of their differences. This general background truth, though simple, obvious, and powerful, is often ignored.

Government, the third party, has the task of providing all the members of society—and so, both workers and managers—a reasonable degree of security from both internal and external violence. It has the obligation to provide for the adjudication of disputes, and it also has the duty to safeguard the common good and protect the rights of all its citizens. The fourth participant in labor relations is the general public. By *general public* we usually mean all the people considered, without regard to their particular roles. The general public as such has no rights, but each of the persons making up the general public has rights. They have the right, for instance, not to have violence done to them by another. Each person has the right not to be killed arbitrarily and without just cause, even if such killing would somehow produce good for the rest of society. To speak of the rights of individuals means, we have seen, that there are certain claims that each individual has against society that cannot be overridden by some calculation of the good to be achieved. If their rights are to be respected they can only be overridden by the stronger rights of others, not simply by a claimed maximization of good.

Given this background of worker-management relations, do workers have a right to strike? If a strike is seen as an extension of an individual worker's freedom to refuse employment, or to refuse to accept employment on certain conditions, then it seems clear that workers—workers in associations or unions—have a right to strike. One obvious exception is in a nonvolunteer army, in which soldiers are drafted and required to serve for the common good. But if employment is freely engaged in, then, whether the employer is private industry or government, the right of the worker to choose not to work carries with it the right of workers, collectively, not to work. Nonetheless, the right is morally restricted by at least two considerations. One consideration is respect for a valid contract. Inherent in valid contracts is the moral obligation to live up to them unless there are seriously overriding moral reasons not to do so. These reasons must involve conflicts of serious moral obligations, not simply the desire to achieve greater good or welfare. Hence, if a contract includes a no-strike clause, it should be respected for the term of the contract. The second restriction is consideration of the rights of the general public to protection, medical care, and other necessities of life. Strikes by public-sector employees—police, firefighters, hospital workers—thus pose serious problems.

The right to strike has been widely accepted. The discrepancy between the power and resources of big business and the resources of the individual worker historically put the latter at the mercy of the former. Workers have had to unite to gain a position of equality from which to bargain with management about higher wages, shorter hours, vacations with pay, safer working conditions, retirement plans, and other similar benefits. Management has frequently passed on some of the cost of these benefits to their customers, in the form of higher prices. But increased productivity has often made it possible for companies to retain the same rate of profit despite paying higher wages to workers. The unions have also helped the plight of nonunion workers by bargaining for standards that have become the norm for all.

Once we have granted the right to strike, however, a question arises about management's right to hire other workers in the place of striking workers. The right of management to hire whomever it wishes at whatever conditions they mutually agree on undercuts the effectiveness of unions and strikes. Management in some industries is not able to do this. In the United States, for instance, the baseball players went out on strike for higher wages. Because there are a limited number of baseball players of the quality of the professional players, and because one cannot form a team simply by hiring people willing to play, the strikers did not worry about others being brought in to replace them. In other industries, however, unskilled laborers have sometimes been brought in by management to replace strikers. This has often led to violence against those who chose to work under those conditions, who are called strikebreakers. Violence against strikebreakers, however, violates the rights of those people. Moral considerations here demand solutions other than violence. Striking employees are usually considered employees of a firm unless fired, even though they have no contract governing them if the strike occurs after a contract has terminated. Strikebreakers are either temporary replacements or employees hired to replace those who have been fired and those on strike. Unions, however, have learned to deal with management's right to hire strikebreakers, and have often become strong enough to preclude this practice. One effective technique involves the solidarity of workers, both the skilled and the unskilled, within a firm. If all the workers in a firm refuse to work when any strikers are fired, and until they are rehired and a contract signed, the possibility of a strike being broken by imported workers is lessened or precluded. Other techniques have also been used. The point is that there *are* methods of achieving the aim of a strike while respecting the rights of all involved. Consciousness of the rights of all persons will help keep strikes, as well as other forms of dispute settlement, within moral bounds.

But what of the harm done to the public by strikes?

Here it is necessary to distinguish between rights and good. If the workers of a particular industry, the auto industry for instance, go on strike, then a certain amount of harm is done to the general population. Those who ordered cars or who wish to buy cars may not have them available for purchase. Steel mills may suffer from lack of orders from the automotive industry and may have to lay off workers. Such harm may produce public pressure on automobile manufacturers to settle the strike. It may also prepare the public for the higher prices that they will have to pay for cars as a result of the settlement of the strike. But the harm done to the public in this instance does not violate any of its rights. People do not have a right to be able to buy a car whenever they have the money to do so. It may be their desire to be able to do this, and we might say that their ability to do so helps the general welfare. But no one's rights are violated when this is not the case. Hence the harm done to the public in this case does not override the right of workers to refuse to work, or to refuse to accept certain terms in a negotiated contract. Nor does the public have a right to buy cars at a certain price, so that consideration cannot be used to offset the workers' right to strike.

There may be times, however, when the public's rights *are* violated by a strike. And in such cases the *right* of the public must be weighed against the *right* of the workers to strike. A frequent example is public-sector strikes. The general public has the right to protection by police and firefighters. Does its right to such protection override the right of police and firefighters to strike? Clearly, the considerations here are different from those in the auto industry, for in these cases we are weighing competing rights and not rights versus good.

The right of workers in the public sector to strike is controversial. In the United States, public-sector strikes are strikes by federal, state, and municipal employees. Should teachers, firemen, policemen, municipal hospital employees, and members of the armed forces be allowed to strike? Enough strikes by public school teachers have taken place that a precedent for their right to strike has been established. The claimed harm to children has not been as great as feared. Firemen, policemen, and municipal hospital employees have also gone on strike in various parts of the country. When they do, they harm not only the city, state, or federal bureaucracies or departments that hire them, but they also endanger the lives and safety of ordinary citizens who have no say in the settlement and no responsibility for the negotiations. Is this fair? A strike by employees against an employer aims at forcing him to suffer greater damage by failure of the workers to work than he would suffer by giving in to their demands. Is the same true of public-service strikes? Firemen, policemen, and municipal hospital workers work for the city, state, or nation, and they are paid from money raised by public taxes. If their demands are not totally unreasonable, if the wages or other benefits they seek are in line with what others in the private sector are making, then by striking they apply pressure on the members of society to bear an increase in taxes or take cuts in the services they receive. The pressure is appropriately placed on the public, because these people work for the public.

But what of the lives threatened by such strikes? The problem is a difficult one, and one that has been handled in a variety of ways. Sometimes the supervisory personnel in the organization take over the basic jobs; sometimes police are called upon to man the firehouses; sometimes the state militia or the army are called in to handle the jobs of those on strike. Sometimes, also, if a true emergency arises, those on strike—or at least some of them—pitch in to help.

Members of the armed forces have recently raised the question of their right to strike, but they have won little support. The qualities that are important in battle are immediate response to authority and trust in one's commanders. Soldiers are no more permitted to do what is immoral than anyone else. Yet within those bounds obedience is essential to their survival and to their effectiveness. Is such obedience undermined by the development of a strike mentality? Some people argue that it is. When, after all, would a strike by the military be most effective? When the military is most needed, is the reply. Yet that is precisely the time when a strike is most inappropriate, from the point of view of those who wish to be defended by the military. What about strikes in peacetime by a peacetime army? The case justifying the military's use of the strike technique has yet to be forcefully and convincingly made; but that does not mean it cannot or will not some day be made.

The justification for public-sector strikes is that strikes are the only effective way such workers can make their plight known and can apply pressure to achieve some of the benefits enjoyed by the workers in the private sector. Whether strikes are the only way, and whether mandatory arbitration is not an acceptable alternative, are at the heart of the issue.

The adversary relation of workers and management in the American system is not in itself unethical or immoral. Yet simply because workers have the *right* to strike does not mean that workers *ought* to strike. The exercise of a right to strike is often shortsighted, and from an economic point of view may in the long run as well as the short run not be in the interest of the workers, the management, or the general public, whose lives are disrupted in one way or another.

Are there, however, no other moral restrictions on the right of workers to strike? Are there no moral considerations that should be fulfilled before a strike is undertaken? Is there no moral obligation to seek negotiation rather than confrontation? Is it not better from a moral point of view to give up the right to strike and to enforce impartial negotiations to which both unions and firms must submit?

It is not a violation of a right to require that it not be exercised capriciously. It can be legitimately circumscribed. Although labor and management at the time of negotiations have adversarial roles, they need not act out those roles to their detriment. In a given firm, workers and management can function together. If workers benefit when the enterprise is successful, then the fate of both management and of the workers is bound up with the success of the firm. If management alone benefits, then workers have less incentive to contribute to the success of the firm. But their welfare is associated with the firm's continuing to operate, and so continuing to provide them employment. Neither side benefits when workers do not work, therefore neither side benefits more from a strike than they would from a negotiated settlement. A negotiated settlement, moreover, would tend to disrupt the public served by the firm less than would a strike. A negotiated settlement, therefore, is in the best interest of all concerned, providing that the negotiations yield fair results.

This consideration of the general good is not sufficient to override the right of the workers to strike, but it is sufficient to provide the basis for legislation requiring attempts at negotiation prior to a strike. There are difficulties with any such law. Such negotiations are fruitful only if both parties negotiate in good faith and make reasonable demands and concessions. A party that enters into negotiations by setting demands that must be met without change is not really entering into a negotiation. Good faith and goodwill are difficult, if not impossible, to mandate by law. But even when good faith is lacking, a forced period of negotiation prior to a strike does provide what is sometimes called a cooling-off period. If such a period is legally mandated and a good faith effort at negotiation is required, there is at least a chance for a settlement. Such legislation is morally legitimate. Though such legislation cannot morally take away the right of workers to strike, it can legitimately delay the exercise of that right.

What of legally mandatory arbitration by a third party acceptable to both labor and management? If the industry is one that protects the public (e.g., police) or serves it in such a way as to fulfill its rights, then we weigh the right of the public to protection, for instance, against the right of the police to strike. In given circumstances and conditions, it is possible that the public's right will override the right of the police to strike. In such a case, binding, legally mandatory arbitration is permissible. The condition for its being morally justifiable is that the arbitration be truly impartial. In industries that provide goods or services to which people have no right, then we once again are forced to weigh good against rights. If our previous analysis is correct, we cannot outlaw strikes on the basis of an argument in favor of the public good, even though the government may mandate attempts at arbitration before a strike. The threat of a strike, in this instance, is an inducement to management to negotiate in good faith. If, to preclude wage increases, a government temporarily suspends the right of workers to strike for higher wages, it must, in justice, also preclude the right of industry to increase prices that place workers at a disadvantage.

Despite all of this, many settlements in labor relations that come about from voluntary negotiations (which is the ideal, and therefore the preferable approach to labor relations) are shortsighted. And many settlements from mandated negotiations or from strikes are also shortsighted. This is because the negotiators frequently look only at the interests of labor and management. They do not consider the long-range impact on society or on the industry itself, or, in the long run, on the workers and management. Society would profit if labor and management were to take a long-range view, would consider the good of society, of which they are a part, as well as of their own short-range good. If labor and management would cooperate with each other and with other industries, they would probably help to serve the common good by arriving at socially helpful solutions to disputes, and also help to control inflation. The problem is that no one has the answer to the question of what is the proper way for all industries to act. In those countries where the government makes all the decisions, the results are not demonstrably better than in those in which the various sectors and individuals are allowed to negotiate for their own good.

In the United States, labor and management have traditionally seen themselves as adversaries, and most American labor law has developed from this premise. There are, however, two indications of possible future change. The first is the placement of union representatives on corporate boards. The first time this happened was in 1980, when Douglas Fraser, president of the

United Auto Workers, took a seat on the board of directors of the Chrysler Corporation. There was some worry at the time about possible conflict of interest, because the board of directors negotiates the labor contract with union representatives. Not all directors need to be present at all meetings, however, and where conflict of interest is a danger or an issue (as in the board's negotiation with labor over contracts) a member can be excused. Labor has not been anxious to join boards, and management has not been anxious to have designated representatives from any area, unions included. But at least a dozen companies added union representaives to their boards in the three years following the Chrysler precedent, and others may do so. If they do, this will signal a significant change in the adversarial relation of management and labor.

The second indicator of change is the significant decline in the number of union members in the United States, which in part reflects the changing composition of the American labor force. By 1984, only 22 percent of American workers belonged to a union. The traditionally unionized occupations—factory workers—have declined significantly, and the number of white-collar workers has increased. Whether unions have served their function and will be replaced eventually with government guarantees of workers' rights and negotiated contracts, remains to be seen.

Morality cannot supply the concrete solutions to labor disputes or to the specific agreements to which negotiations must lead. But morality can provide a general framework within which labor disputes can be negotiated. It can specify the conditons of justice under which such negotiations should proceed. And it can clarify the right of the parties, which any solution must respect. In the long run, only by observing moral norms and constraints can we expect that solutions to labor problems will be truly accepted and so lead to general long-term social peace and stability. The attempt to make all our actions—including our actions as workers or industrialists—conform to moral norms is simply an attempt to act as true human beings in all our relations with others.

Further Reading

BATT, WILLIAM L., JR. "Canada's Good Example with Displaced Workers." *Harvard Business Review*, *83*:No. 4 (July–Aug., 1983), pp. 6–22.

BROWNLIE, IAN, ed. *Basic Documents on Human Rights*, 2nd ed. Oxford: Clarendon Press, 1981.

CARLEN, CLAUDIA, ed. *The Papal Encyclicals*. Wilmington, N.C.: McGrath Publishing Co., 1981.

COOPER, ELIZABETH A., and GERALD V. BARRETT. "Equal Pay and Gender: Implications of Court Cases for Personnel Practices." *Academy of Management Review, 9* (1984), pp. 84–94.

FREEMAN, RICHARD B., and JAMES L. MEDOFF. *What Do Unions Do?* New York: Basic Books, Inc., 1984.

KERR, C. *Labor Markets and Wage Determination*. Berkeley, Calif.: University of California Press, 1977.

LIVERNASH, E. R., ed. *Comparable Worth: A Symposium on Issues and Alternatives.* Washington, D.C.: Equal Employment Advisory Council, 1981.

ROEMER, JOHN. *A General Theory of Exploitation and Class.* Cambridge, Mass.: Harvard University Press, 1982.

SULTAN, PAUL. *Right-to-Work Laws: A Study in Conflict.* Los Angeles: Institute of Industrial Relations, University of California, 1958.

TREIMAN, D. J., and H. I. HARTMAN, eds. *Women, Work and Wages: Equal Pay for Jobs of Equal Value.* Washington, D.C.: National Academy Press, 1981.

WOOD, ADRIAN. *A Theory of Pay.* Cambridge: University Press, 1978.

TEN

Workers' Rights and Duties
Within a Firm

Free enterprise allows capital, resources, and labor to flow freely, and, ideally, where they flow is determined by the market. But labor is significantly different from capital and resources. Labor is not simply a commodity to be bought and sold, even though we have argued that wages are defensibly determined by the market, in a system with proper and just background institutions. For by labor we always mean the labor of human beings, and human beings have rights, which they do not give up by becoming employees. They also have obligations.

What of the transactions between worker and employer? Can we subsume these into a contract or agreement and treat them as we would any other contract? Are there aspects of an employer-employee relationship that cannot be negotiated? Are there certain assumptions about workers' rights and obligations, and about employers' rights and obligations that form the background for worker-employer contracts, and are these assumptions justifiable? In this chapter we shall look at the rights of employees within a firm, at the loyalty and obedience appropriate for employees, and at employee obligations to an employer.

The Rights of Employees Within a Firm

A simple approach to the rights and duties of employees states that employees as employees have all those, and only those, rights and duties that they negotiate with their employers as conditions of employment. This approach, however, is too simple and is seriously misleading. Employees and employers are not mere abstractions. A potential employee is first of all a human being and a rational agent, an end in himself and worthy of respect. As a moral being he carries with him in all his endeavors and undertakings the moral obligation to do what is right and to avoid doing what is wrong. Neither on the job nor in any other aspect of his life is he free to do whatever he chooses. He remains bound by the moral law in all his activities. An employer—whether we mean by employer the corporation as a legal entity or the actual persons who act for the corporation—is also bound by the moral law. Hence, neither side in the hiring process has the moral right to set whatever terms it wishes. Both sides are bound not only by law but also by morality. For instance, if someone wishes to sell himself into slavery to raise money to give to his family, he is legally and morally prohibited from doing so, and everyone else is legally and morally prohibited from making him a slave.

The background conditions for any contract between employer and employee are the conditions set by morality, law, local custom, and by the existing social circumstances in which the contract is made. Most people who start out in the employment market would like to earn as much as possible. Usually they have no work experience. If they also have no work skills, what they can offer is their time, their labor power, their ability to learn, and their intelligence, developed by however much schooling and training they have had. They offer these to the employer, who in turn has work of some kind available, for which he promises a certain compensation. A wage laborer works for wages—a certain amount of money per hour, week, month, or per piece.

The development of industry in the nineteenth century taught us many lessons. Workers fought for and secured legislation that protects them and their interests in many areas. Many workers in the past had to face the problem of how to live if they were laid off, fired, injured, or retired. Unemployment insurance, workman's compensation, and social security have helped alleviate the worst of those problems for large numbers of employees.

Employees have bargained collectively as well as individually for certain rights and privileges and have committed themselves to fulfilling certain obligations. Some employees have more to offer employers than others. Some people have special skills, much accumulated experience, and character or other traits that are in short supply and therefore in great demand. Such people can bargain better than those with no special skills, experience, or traits. Hollywood movie stars, stellar baseball, basketball, or football players, and top executives of large corporations all command handsome salaries or compensation for their work. Teenagers often work at jobs that pay the minimum allowable by law, and they are happy to find even those jobs. The range of pay is enormous, as is the range of other types of compensation. The tasks required—from menial to professional to entrepreneurial—are also extremely diverse. Yet we can make some general statements about the rights of all workers.

Employment-at-Will: Rights in Hiring, Promotion, and Firing

In the United States, the traditional legal view of the employer-employee relationship has been known as the doctrine of "employment-at-will." According to this doctrine, individuals are free to work for whomever they choose, and employers are free to hire whomever they choose. Because the agreement is a mutual one, and both are free to enter an agreement, the employment agreement can be terminated at will, unless there is a contract that precludes it. If a worker wishes to move to another job, the worker may do so. If an employer wishes to fire an employee, the employer may do so. Both parties therefore work "at will."

Although the doctrine sounds fair and symmetrical, we have already seen that the relation of individual worker to large corporation is not an equal relation. Because the ordinary worker must work to get the wherewithall to live, he is both forced to work (and often must accept work not of his preference) and lives in fear of losing his job if he has no contract guaranteeing him a secure position. The employer, on the other hand, rarely suffers more than some inconvenience when an employee leaves; and if the firm wishes to keep someone who is leaving to take a better position, the firm can make its own position more attractive than the competition's. Employment-at-will, therefore, is not a symmetrical relation.

To offset the disparity, unions usually have contracts with employers, guaranteeing employment at a certain level for a certain period of years, and requiring that a firm terminate an employee only for "cause." This precludes arbitrary firing, or firing at will or at whim. Civil service also provides job security for government employees who also can only be fired for "cause." The same is true for educators who have been granted tenure at their institutions. But there remain a large number of people who are subject to the doctrine of employment-at-will. This includes both high-level executives and nonunionized beginners in many occupations, as well as those workers not covered by union contracts, civil service regulations, or tenure systems. Do they have any rights with respect to their jobs? Although the employment-at-will doctrine says no, there are good arguments in defense of the right to job security, at least of a certain type.

People are fired for many reasons. A common one is an economic recession, which forces a firm to cut back on production and so decrease the number of people it needs to work for it. But there are other reasons as well. Inefficiency, immorality on the job, chronic lateness or absenteeism, lack of ability to perform at the level expected, are all common reasons, and are also examples of reasonable cause. Other reasons are less clearly justifiable, such as incompatibility with management or with other workers, lack of respect or deference to superiors, poor attitude toward work, voicing of dissent, or an employer's belief that he can find someone who can do the job better. In some instances, an employer fires an employee simply because he dislikes him for personal

204

reasons, or because the employee refuses the sexual advances of the employer, or because the employee knows of an irregularity in the firm and cannot be trusted not to expose it. Has the employee no right in these instances?

Fairness requires that workers not be fired arbitrarily. Arbitrary firing violates the ordinary expectations assumed by workers when accepting employment. They properly expect to be treated as persons deserving of respect; they are not objects to be discarded or replaced at whim. But exactly what rules should govern the termination of employment is a controversial issue. Two general principles are often applied, however. One states that the longer one has been employed by a firm, the greater the obligation of the firm not to fire, except for cause. Thus a beginner is seen as being on probation. Although even a beginner should not be fired on a whim, the reason for termination can be less substantive if the term of employment is short. The reason given in favor of that principle rests on what a probation period means. Another consideration is that unless a firm is allowed to fire beginning people whom, for one reason or another it does not want, it becomes chained to employees simply by virtue of having initally hired them. Even civil service regulations allow for probation periods; and academic tenure is not usually awarded manditorily except after six years of full-time teaching.

The second principle states that the employer should inform the employee of the reason for the termination of employment. This principle is derived from the obligation to treat persons with respect.

Some people argue that respect for persons requires more than simply being informed of the reason for one's dismissal, because the reasons given may be false, inadequate, or unjustifiable. One may be told that one is fired for refusing the sexual advances of one's superior, for instance, but being told this is not sufficient to make the firing morally justifiable. The reason for the firing is itself morally unjustifiable. Hence, some argue, respect for persons requires that one should be fired only for legitimate cause, and that employees who dispute the legitimacy of the stated cause should have recourse to due process, such as that available in law (and under a system such as the civil service). The reasons stated for the firing, if challenged by the employee, must be considered adequate by an impartial judge, arbitrator, or other third party. Evidence must be produced in case an employer's charge against an employee is denied by the latter, and a chance for the presentation of a defense must be allowed the employee. Such procedures are in fact followed by some large firms. They are not as likely to be implemented by small employers, who work closely with their employees. Small employers do not have the facilities or personnel to carry out such formal procedures; moreover, the closeness of daily contact makes it unlikely that an employee who is kept on— under what the employer considers duress—will find any satisfaction on the job.

The extent to which an employee has a right to due process in the case of firing is still being debated. But there is ample precedent in the areas of civil service, union contracts, and tenure systems to show that due process is practicable in cases of firing. There are laws that preclude the firing of whistle blowers in government positions, and many have suggested that such laws be extended to cover the private sector as well.

When firing is done for cause, and the reason is financial exigency, union rules require that layoffs be made under rules of seniority, according to which those last hired for any kind of position are those first fired. This rule has been affirmed by the courts even when those fired have been hired for affirmative-action reasons.

Although we cannot decide here exactly what restrictions should be placed on the employment-at-will doctrine, in addition to the limitations just mentioned, two observations are worth making. First, those firms with a policy of not firing employees who have been with the firm beyond a certain probation period, even when the firm is in financial difficulty, tend to enjoy greater employee loyalty than other firms. It is not hard to understand why. Delta Airlines and IBM are two companies with such policies and records. According to such policies, both lower-level and management-level employees are kept on. If an individual has risen to the level of his incompetence, he may be shifted laterally or moved to another position, or helped to improve. Concern for one's employees is a function of good management, and also implements the moral injunction to treat people as ends in themselves.

Second, if job offers are to be truly fair, employees have the right to know the real conditions under which they are hired. If the position is only a temporary one, they should be so informed. If there is a probationary period, they should know the length of it, and what is expected of them if they are to be kept on. If they are expected to fulfill conditions beyond those stated in a job description, these should be stated. If employees might be terminated simply because the employer feels someone else might do the job better, that too should be made clear from the start. Some people would not accept a position under these conditions; others would. If the employer does not volunteer all of this information, the potential employee has the right to ask, and to have his or her questions answered honestly. The clearer the conditions of employment—including promotion, salary increases, and possible termination—before a person is hired, the more likely it is that the employment agreement is truly fair.

Employees have no right to promotion unless promotions are automatic, or are generally expected or promised. But employees do have a right to fair and regular evaluation and consideration for promotion, and they have a right to be informed of the reasons for lack of promotion when it might usually be expected. Similarly, they have the right to cost-of-living increases periodically, and to fair consideration for merit salary raises, and should be given the reason for lack of such increases if they might usually be expected.

The rights to rest periods, vacations, holidays, and work days of reasonable length are all generally acknowledged in American society. Because Social Security payments are usually an insufficient replacement for salary, workers also have a right to some sort of retirement or pension plan after completing a certain number of years with a firm. Such plans are usually part of a contract and have become a legitimate expectation of workers. To fire an employee shortly before he retires, so the firm will not have to pay him a pension, is clearly unjust and violates the employee's right to the pension he has earned.

Employees, from the lowest-paid employee in the corporation to the president, do not have the right to continuance in their jobs if they do not perform adequately or if the firm is not able to continue employing them. But they do have the right to be told the reason for their termination. Those who give many years of acceptable service deserve more consideration than those who are new on the job, and should be helped, encouraged, and given a chance to improve; they should be transferred to less demanding jobs where possible. This is minimal recompense for employee loyalty.

The doctrine of employment-at-will does not require that either employer or employee give advance notice of termination of employment, although this has become a common custom in many fields. It constitutes acknowledgement that the termination of employment on the part of either party causes some inconvenience to the other party, and the advance warning gives them both a chance to make alternative arrangements. When an employer fires an employee for reasons of financial exigency, some firms either by contract or unilaterally give the employee a certain amount of severance pay to provide a financial cushion until he or she finds another job. When executives are fired, some firms allow them to continue to use the firm's address, or to look for a job from an office in the firm, where telephone and secretarial services are available. Even when firing is morally justifiable there are various ways of softening what is always a blow, and a firm that truly treats its employees as persons will do what it can to soften that blow—especially when the firing is for financial reasons, rather than for what the employee did or failed to do.

Employees who are being laid off, or those whose appointments will not be renewed, deserve as much advance warning as possible. Whether this is, strictly speaking, a moral right is debatable. But it is clearly the morally preferable way of acting when an employer has an option, and advance notice, of periods ranging from several months to as much as a year or longer, is a contractual agreement in some fields.

Plant closings raise these issues in a dramatic way; four states have already passed plant-closing bills. Similiar bills have been proposed in Congress and in forty other states. Such bills typically require advance notice of a factory's closing (e.g., 90 days), continuation of health insurance (e.g., for three months after being laid off), unemployment compensation, counseling, and retraining. In states that do not have such laws, laid-off workers have turned to litigation in an attempt to get legal recognition of what they consider their rights. They have met with mixed success, because many employers still firmly defend employment-at-will as their right. Erosion of the doctrine has clearly taken place, however, and more restrictions to it, based on workers' rights, seem likely.

Employee Civil Rights and Equal Treatment

There are many kinds of rights. Civil rights are legal rights that entitle each person covered by them to certain treatment, or that guarantee noninterference in their acting in certain ways. The right to equal employment regardless of race or sex makes it illegal for employers to discriminate in their hiring practices with respect to these. The right to freedom of speech allows each citizen to express his views publicly, and prevents others, especially government officials, from interfering in such expression. A moral right does not depend on positive law, but a moral right might also be a civil right. Not every moral right is written into law, nor is the state the source of moral rights. People have such rights simply by virtue of being moral agents and worthy of respect. The rights to life, liberty, and the pursuit of happiness are among these moral rights.

By contract and position, one can secure other special rights. A business executive of a certain level may earn the right to eat in the executive restaurant; other employees have the right to eat in the company lunchroom. Those not employed by a firm have no general right to eat in the firm's lunchroom or restaurant, or to use facilities of the firm. Special rights are not moral rights. However, if such special rights are extended under certain regular conditions and are then denied to a particular individual for no defensible reason, failure to extend them may be a violation of a moral right to equality of treatment.

Civil Rights on the Job

Many disputes have arisen about whether an employee is allowed to exercise his civil rights, either on or off the job, if the exercise of such rights is in some way perceived by his employer as being detrimental to the good of the firm. Does a worker have the right to criticize his company, its management, or some of its decisions, either on or off the job? Many managers complain that workers who criticize the company on the job sow disaffection, unrest, and discontent among other workers. This clearly hurts the company and affects its productivity. Hence, they argue, it is right to fire such people. Some companies go so far as to claim that speaking or writing against the company and its policies during off-hours is disloyal and harmful to the company, and that people who so act are rightly open to censure and dismissal.

The right of an employee to freedom of expression on his own time is a civil right that his employer cannot morally deny him. Employers have the right to demand work of a specific kind from their employees, and while they are working they can be expected to do certain tasks assigned to them. But no employer has the right to deprive his employees of their civil rights off the job. Because freedom of expression is one of their rights, they are free on their own time to say what they choose. This includes criticizing their em-

208

ployer, but not, of course spreading lies about him. Also not defensible as a right are verbal abuse, divulging secret or confidential information learned in one's capacity as an employee, or revealing of the legitimate plans or activities of the firm.

Employees, as members of society, have the moral right, moreover, to the most extensive liberty compatible with a like liberty for all. They have the right to belong to the church of their choosing, to live their private lives as they wish, and to engage in political or social activities as they desire. An employer violates these rights if he penalizes his employees for what they do on their own time. Employees are properly evaluated for their work on the job, but this evaluation should not extend to their non-job-related activities so long as these do not adversely affect their job performance. There are borderline cases, of course. An employee who is an alcoholic should not be fired for drinking off the job, but his drinking may affect his performance on the job. The latter is the only proper criterion for job evaluation.

Whether employees have a complete right to freedom of expression on the job is not a clear-cut issue. They do not have the right to sow disaffection and foment employee unrest during their working hours. But they do have the right to organize, form unions, raise grievances, and so on, on their own time at work—whether on coffee breaks, lunch breaks, or before or after hours. Fairness requires procedures whereby workers can register their complaints against those above them and receive a fair hearing. Their right to complain about grievances to those above them, and to go higher up the managerial ladder than their immediate superior, is, moreover, not considered to be sowing disaffection. Their right to free speech at work cannot be legitimately taken from them, but the right cannot be so exercised as to interfere with one's regularly assigned tasks, or in such a way as to be disruptive of the orderly functioning of the firm.

On the job, workers have the right to equality of treatment. They should receive equal pay for equal work, regardless of sex, race, or religion. They should all have equal opportunity for advancement. They should be evaluated fairly, and only on job-related criteria. They have a right not to be fired for non-job related matters or for registering legitimate complaints. Established procedures for hiring, promotion, layoffs, and firing should guarantee that the worker's right to fair treatment is respected.

The Right to Treatment with Respect

The right of an employee to be treated like a human being is a moral right. It is an extremely broad and, in many ways, a vague right, nevertheless it is a central right. Its foundation is straightforward: each person is a human being, a moral agent deserving of respect. We saw in our study of the Categorical Imperative that to treat a human being only as a means is immoral. Thus an employer who treats his workers *only* as a means to his profit, or *only* as a way of getting done what he wants done, treats them immorally. They are not machines or objects. What does this imply about their treatment? Can we translate the notion of respect for human beings into specific conditions of labor?

Because workers are human beings worthy of respect, they should not be treated like slaves, nor can they morally contract into such treatment. Their work should not be demeaning, nor the conditions of work unsafe, or unhealthy, and in general not suitable for human beings. These vague statements are translated into different work conditions, depending on the country, the standard of living, the kind of work, and the availability of safety and other equipment. The right to be treated with respect also means that workers should not be made to work in stultifying jobs, or to be considered replaceable parts in the productive process.

The Right to Privacy

Employees have a moral right to privacy. They work for their employers for a certain period of time each day, and the rest of their time does not belong to the company but to themselves. They should be allowed to do what they want during that time, free from company interference. When they are employed, they do not surrender the right to privacy in their personal lives. Nor does this privacy end when they enter the corporation's walls. Some aspects of their lives do not affect their capacity to do the work expected of them. Consequently, corporations have no right to inquire about such things, nor to keep such information on record in personnel files. Workers have a right not to answer personal, non-job-related questions, and have a right to know that no such material is kept in their files. They have a right to know their evaluations, and other information in their personnel files, as well as to enter rebuttals about such information if they believe it to be erroneous. They have a right, if they have personal lockers or desks, not to have them searched without good cause, and then only by those authorized to do so for job-related reasons. The conditions of privacy of lockers and desks should be clear, and should be made known to employees. Workers also have the right to refuse to submit to polygraph tests after they are hired, even if they agreed to them prior to hiring; and workers can refuse to answer personal, non-job-related questions.

The Right to Freedom from Sexual Harassment

Employees have the right not to be sexually harassed, and, as in other areas, they have a right to get a hearing on such complaints. Office romances are not uncommon, and drawing the line on what constitutes sexual harassment is sometimes difficult. But in general it consists of *unwelcome* sexual advances or requests for sexual favors, sexual jokes or verbal abuse, and physical or verbal conduct imposed on an employee, and submission to which is either explicitly or implicitly a condition of continued employment or advancement. Words or actions of a sexual nature or with sexual overtones that interfere with one's work or make an employee uncomfortable also constitute sexual harassment. Complaints made to the individual responsible for such conduct are sufficient to show that the words or acts are unwelcome. If they persist, this becomes a violation of the employee's right to freedom from sexual harassment.

Quality of Work Life

In addition to concern with workers' rights is growing concern for the quality of work life—a relatively new arrival on the American social scene. Quality of work life is a reflection of the affluence and level of technological development present in American society, which has become concerned with the general quality of life. American society has found that the blessings of advanced technology have brought with them certain dysfunctional aspects, of which pollution and the deterioration of the quality of air and water are the clearest examples. The general concern with the quality of life has been carried over into the workplace as concern for the quality of work life. The concern also reflects the changing conditions of American work and the changing attitudes toward work. American labor is no longer dominated by nineteenth-century concerns, and work itself has changed since then. In the United States, by 1980, only 16 percent of the workers were employed in manufacturing—the traditional kind of work that dominated trade-union concerns and formed the focus of analyses of the condition of the working class. Forty-six percent of the American work force is now employed in the service sector of the economy. The concerns of these workers are not necessarily the same as those of factory workers.

Although there are still disputes over wages, vacation, retirement, and safety, workers have begun to turn their attention to qualitative rather than quantitative aspects of their work life. These are not yet stated in terms of rights, and the demands are still to some extent unfocused. But they are growing concerns to which management will eventually have to respond.

The following are four aspects of the quality of work life, which will throw some light on what is meant by the phrase. The components can be scaled, though not always quantitatively, for analytic purposes. The first concerns the conditions of labor; the second, the organization of the work performed; the third, the relations of workers among themselves, with those above them, and with the tools or machines with which they work; and the fourth, the attitude of the worker to work.

Conditions of Labor

Workers have traditionally focused on the number of hours worked, the amount of pay received, the number of days of vacation and sick leave provided, and the level of seniority accruing to length of service. They have also been somewhat concerned with safety on the job, for example, with screens around dangerous machines, adequate ventilation, sufficient light, noise levels below certain decible ratings, protection from radiation or noxious chemicals and gases, ladders of a certain strength, and so on. Some of these concerns have been translated into industry codes that specify minimum levels that must be met. Each of the foregoing items is quantifiable and specifiable, and one can plausibly argue that the quality of work life is significantly improved when these are met at a high, as opposed to a low, level. However, all of these considerations, although necessary for a high quality of work life, are not sufficient to insure it.

Conditions of labor also refer to the atmosphere in which work is done. Pleasant surroundings are preferable to grim, dirty, or unpleasant ones, even if strictly speaking one has no particular right to pleasant surroundings. Adequate space rather than cramped quarters, and air-conditioning where appropriate, are two other examples of improved working conditions. A change in dress codes, so as to minimize the distinction between labor and management, is another subtle aspect of changing work conditions. At IBM, technicians wear jackets and ties, just like management. At the GM Fiero plant, managers go tieless, just like the assembly-line workers. The improvement in working conditions at other companies involves the breaking down of what are perceived as invidious distinctions, and no longer are there separate restrooms, restaurants, and recreational centers for workers and managers.

Improving the conditions of labor requires that one start from the existing conditions. The better the existing physical condition, the more concentration on other conditions—aesthetic, psychological, and personal. But improving these conditions, even more than improving physical conditions, requires consultation with, and input from, workers. The improvement of working conditions cannot be done only from above and then imposed on workers; workers should not only be considered but consulted as to what improvements they desire and which ones they value more than others.

Improvement of working conditions thus includes a variety of concerns.

The Organization of Work

The division of labor leads to greater and greater repetition of tasks. At its worst it consists of doing one mechanical task (e.g., tightening a certain bolt, on an assembly line). Such work is inherently dull and stultifying. Many such tasks could be done as well, and probably better, by robots. Increasing the quality of work life involves lessening the division of labor, allowing workers to carry on more complex or more diversified tasks. This is true as well with respect to office and secretarial work, which can be either mechanical, routine, and dull or more varied and diversified. If the goal is quality of work life, then work should be as interesting and fulfilling as possible to those engaged in it. Some people may well be comfortable with jobs that are not very demanding and are fairly routine, but it is difficult to image anyone being satisfied with deadening, stultifying work.

Although worker self-management has not received much support from most American workers, what has received support is greater worker participation. Workers frequently can contribute to improvement in the work they do if allowed to have input. Grouping workers into teams that handle a variety of different tasks, holding weekly worker meetings to discuss improvements in the productive process, and allowing workers to take part in some of the planning and policy sessions of a firm are all techniques that have been tried, and they have helped to improve the quality of work life for the workers affected.

Lessening the division of labor by the use of teams of workers and worker participation in general are not yet recognized rights, but workers are expressing these wishes more and more frequently.

Worker Relations

The relation of workers to others, and to their tools, is an area difficult to quantify. We can speak of cordial and less cordial relations, competitive and cooperative, supportive and destructive ones. We can also speak of arrangements that produce certain types of relations—hierarchical as opposed to collegial, arbitrary as opposed to rule-governed. We can speak of treating people with respect or treating them like things, and this can be specified in greater detail. The tone of voice in which directions or orders are given may reflect the relations between the person in a superior position and the one in a subordinate position. Some may argue that there should be no distinction between superior and subordinate, and that everyone should be on the same level. The initial implausibilty of this claim in any large-scale operation leads one either to press for only small-scale operations or to try to rethink organizational structures.

Any suggested changes can be measured against productivity. Changes may lead to greater or lesser productivity. If they lead to less, then this is a cost that must be considered. Whether the cost is too great depends on how much difference the changes make to those involved. A number of innovations have been adopted, at least on a small scale, for example, flexible time, when employees set their preferred schedules rather than being bound by the traditional eight-to-five day. This can be very convenient. Some people have children who come home after school and they wish to be home by three to greet them. Others might wish to drive home after six to avoid the traffic jams they would otherwise encounter. Some people are early risers, others are night people, who prefer to sleep late in the morning. All these considerations can be taken account of in a flexible approach to work schedules, in many operations. In some, they are not possible. The point is that thought can and should be given to workers and their needs and preferences, when at all possible—and it is possible more often than many managers believe. Day-care centers for the small children of workers are another innovation some firms have adopted to improve the quality of work life. Workers can spend their lunchtime or breaks with their children. The increase in productivity may be worth the cost of providing the centers. Whether or not it is, such centers certainly help the morale of the parents involved.

The relation of workers to tools and machines is a subtle but important area. Craftsmen consider tools an extension of themselves, and, in a sense, become one with their tools, but this is not the typical relation of industrial workers to the machines they work on. Machines should be kept subordinate to workers, and the structures of a plant or firm should build machines around people rather than people around machines. Technology has made possible the reduction of drudgery in many jobs, but new technology is sometimes introduced without consideration of the people who will use it. Computer-terminal screens that are difficult to read and cause eyestrain are one example; and computer operators who are virtually chained to their screens can easily replace the nineteenth-century picture of workers chained to their machines. Work networks must be not only efficient, from a technological point of view, but should enhance rather than diminish concern for the people who use them. It is unlikely that many people will feel toward their computer terminals what craftsmen felt toward their tools; but it is possible to keep the terminals from becoming tyrants.

Worker Attitude

What attitude should workers and society take toward work? Is work punishment for the human condition, or is it a means of self-expression and development? Technology opens up possibilities not previously available. Will we use technology for the benefit of people, or will we use it to repress them and their energies? The change in work from manufacturing to service, and from machine-operating to machine-tending, is bringing about a search for a new conception of work and an attitude that fits the new reality. How can alienation be diminished and worker dissatisfaction lessened? The answer is not always clear, although various experiments are being tried. But concern for the quality of work life seeks answers to these questions as it seeks to make work meaningful and fulfilling.

Worker attitude is often related to worker involvement—the more involvement the better the attitude. But workers have reacted negatively to attempts at worker involvement, which they see as being aimed merely at increased productivity. They perceive such programs as being ultimately manipulative. Worker involvement can involve more worker autonomy, more worker responsibility, and more worker interaction with management than is ordinarily the case, but this may require the breaking down of strict hierarchical lines. However, as quality of work life improves, workers' attitudes toward work will change; they may see it not as something one must do to live but as an activity that is part of one's life, growth, and self-expression. That is the ideal.

The changing conditions and forms of work are forcing a rethinking of work and its place in workers' lives. Discussions of quality of work life are a sign of the change and will play a role in the change. We can expect concern for the quality of work life to be translated into more and more specific demands that are in better accord with the realities of changing work conditions. Such changes will eventually come to be expected and will be considered entitlements and rights, just as the concept of worker rights and the specification of those rights have developed up until now.

Worker Loyalty and Obedience

Do workers owe loyalty to their firm, as well as an honest day's work? The question is an ambiguous one. While they work for a particular firm, workers should not subvert it or sabotage its activities. But loyalty to a firm does not require that employees be unwilling to change employers, or that they do not criticize their employer. What can a firm legitimately expect from an employee, in addition to what it can command or demand?

Consider the following three hypothetical cases:

- CASE A: Susan Monroe works for ABC Construction Corporation. Her immediate superior has drawn up an estimate for a project, and on the basis of the resulting bid, the company has received the contract. Though the contract has already been signed, Susan's boss asks her to verify her calculations, which is part of Susan's job. In doing so, Susan discovers an error. The result is that there will be a slight loss for the company rather than the anticipated profit. Susan points this out to her superior, who tells Susan to forget the error and mention it to no one, otherwise she will be fired. Her superior does not report the error to her own superior.
- CASE B: Sam Jones works for XYZ Printing Company. He is in charge of ordering high-quality paper for the firm. A salesman from O. Good Paper wishes to land a large contract from XYZ Printing and offers Sam a new Ford, as a gift, if he gives him the contract. Sam refuses the car. The next day he learns that Tom Brand, who is in charge of ordering lower-quality paper for XYZ, placed an order with O. Good Paper; he also knows that Tom is driving a new Ford.
- CASE C: Lewis Cage is director of personnel at a large firm. He is in charge of hiring new personnel, keeping records, and issuing notices of dismissal. His firm has just hired a new president, from a competitor. On his first visit to Cage's office, he tells Cage that he (the president) is not prejudiced. He believes in hiring the best people for a job. But, he goes on, he does not like to work with Jews. He tells Cage that if there are any Jews working for the firm, he should keep his eyes open for any excuse to have them fired. He also tells Cage that he should also not consider Jewish people for any future opening in the firm. Cage, unbeknownst to the new president, is Jewish.

The three cases raise a variety of issues dealing with worker obedience and worker loyalty. Before analyzing the cases, we shall state a few general principles. Many firms expect obedience, and in fact many employers regard it as a prime virtue. Employees are to do what they are told, how they are told, and when they are told. They are frequently not asked to think originally, or to inquire too deeply into the workings of the company. They need only follow orders. Some people are paid to be leaders; others are paid to be followers. When a worker accepts a position he agrees to do what the position requires, including what those above him tell him to do. This view makes of obedience a blank check, to be filled in by the employer.

Though obedience can be morally justified, there are clear moral limits to obedience. No one can be morally obliged to do what is immoral. This statement needs little defense; it is essentially a statement of self-consistency. If we were morally obliged to do what is immoral, we would be morally obliged to both do, and not do, the action in question. Every command by an employer to an employee has two parts. One is the fact that the employer tells the employee to do something, or gives him an order, which he expects will be obeyed. The second part constitutes the action he is told to do. If the action falls within the area of work of the employee, and if it is not an immoral act, then the employee is rightly expected by the employer to obey the command. For instance, if the vice-president for finance tells his secretary to type a letter to the auditors before typing the letter to the accounting department, he can rightly expect the secretary to follow his instructions. If he hands his secretary his personal Christmas shopping list, with instructions to spend the weekend buying the items on the list for him, the secretary may well protest that doing his shopping is not part of a secretary's job. If the vice-president tells the secretary to come to his apartment that evening to spend the night with him, the secretary clearly has no moral obligation to do so, and if the secretary reads his intent correctly, the secretary may have a moral obligation *not* to do as the vice-president commands.

Loyalty is also a quality expected and demanded by many firms. A worker for such a company does not merely give it minimal time and effort. The employee is part of the enterprise, a member of the team, and is expected to show loyalty to the company in a variety of ways. If the company has a vacancy in a branch office, company loyalty may demand one's being willing to move to the branch office. An offer by another company, at somewhat higher pay, is to be refused because of loyalty, even if the other offer is not matched. If the company is sued or maligned, the loyal worker defends the company. In these and in many other ways, an employee can show loyalty. Being loyal in these ways is morally permissible, but it is not morally obligatory. One has no general moral obligation of loyalty to one's employer, even though employers would like to have loyal employees.

We can now turn to Case A. What, if anything, should Susan Monroe do in the situation described? She is told by her immediate superior not to say anything about the error to anyone. If she does as she is told, she will be obeying her immediate superior. Does she owe anything more to the company?

Suppose that by going over her superior's head, to the vice-president, she can bring the error to the company's attention and some adjustments can be made so that the company does not lose money on the project. Does she have an obligation to the company to do so? If she does go to the vice-president, perhaps nothing can be done, and she will simply get herself fired for disobeying her superior. Sooner or later the company will find out that it will lose money on the project. Will Susan be made the scapegoat, because she was supposed to verify the calculations? These and similar considerations are likely to come to Susan's mind. The approach she is implicitly taking is a utilitarian one. What are the consequences for all concerned if she does go over her superior's head? What are the results for all concerned if she does not?

Another approach is to try to weigh the obligation to obey her superior against her obligation to inform the company of facts that may adversely affect it. The latter is an obligation of loyalty. The former is one of obedience. Each is prima facie defensible. Which carries more weight in this situation?

The first thing Susan should do before going above her superior's head is attempt to reason with her superior, thusly: If there is a mistake, it will be found out sooner or later. Will it be better for all concerned to find out sooner rather than later? How will the superior try to remedy the situation, if at all? Will she take the blame when the error is found, or will she put the blame on Susan?

The case is not clear-cut; but because it is internal to the company it reflects a difficulty not only for Susan but for the company. Susan can argue that she owes obedience to her superior, and that in doing as she is told she also shows loyalty to the firm. She does not know what will happen, and is not responsible for what does happen. If the firm suffers a small loss, the firm will not be ruined. Susan is not being asked to do anything immoral. If she had been asked to falsify a record, or to sign a statement that the figures were correct, she could not morally do so. But she is simply being told not to report a mistake, and unless it is her duty to report it (i.e., unless it is a part of her job to do so) she is not doing anything immoral.

Companies might learn from such cases. A company should have a mechanism by which to protect those who have something to report to higher echelons of a firm, but who are threatened with dismissal by those immediately above them if they do so. A firm should also not tolerate attempts by anyone to cover up mistakes or immoral conduct by threatening to fire those subordinates who report the mistake or conduct.

Case B raises somewhat different problems. Sam Jones acted properly in refusing the car offered by the O. Good salesman. Does he have a further obligation to find out whether Tom Brand received his new Ford from the O. Good salesman? If he finds out that Tom did receive it from the salesman, should he report it to the appropriate person in his own firm? Should he, or should XYZ Printing also report the incident to O. Good Paper?

In the absence of any written guidelines, does one have an obligation to investigate and report wrongdoings in one's firm? To what extent is one one's brother's keeper in a firm, and does loyalty require that one report wrongdoings in the firm by others? Does a company or its employees have an obligation to report the wrongdoings of other firms' employees to their employers?

Once again the situation could be clarified if XYZ Printing Company had a policy on these issues. If it were policy not to accept any gift, or any gift worth more than $25, for example, Sam would certainly know that he should not accept the car. But he did not accept it. Does he have an obligation to report that the salesman offered him a car? If there were a company policy that such offers be reported, then he should do so. Those to whom he reported could then watch other areas of the company dealing with that salesman; or they could stop dealing with that salesman altogether, and let O. Good Paper know what they were doing, and why.

In the absence of such guidelines, however, Sam is not morally obliged to investigate Tom's conduct. He is not Tom's supervisor and has no responsibility for his actions. If he does investigate, and if he finds out that Tom took the car, he is not morally obliged to report it to their superior. He might talk to Tom about it; or he might report that he was approached by the salesman and let those above determine whether Tom was similarly approached. If they choose not to investigate, that is their decision. Loyalty to one's firm does not imply that one should be on constant watch to make sure that those over whom one has no authority are acting morally.

Case C involves discrimination and injustice. One can never morally do what is immoral. Hence, the order to find a pretext to fire people because of their religious beliefs, and the order to practice discrimination based on religion in hiring, are both orders that Lewis is morally prohibited from carrying out. The irony is that if Lewis obeyed the order, he would have to find a reason for having himself fired. That reason would be found easily: Lewis should not follow the order of the president, and because he disobeys the order to have Jews fired, Lewis gives the president grounds to fire him.

Does a company not have the right to hire whom it pleases? Can anyone rightly force a company to hire people it does not want working for it? Does the president not have the right to issue the order he gave Lewis? The answer is that although no one can force a company to hire certain people, companies are obliged, both by morality and by law (Title VII of the Civil Rights Act of 1964), to hire on the basis of job-related characteristics and should not discriminate on the basis of sex, race, color, religion, or national origin. To refuse to hire qualified people because of religion is discriminatory, and firing people because of their religion is also discriminatory. Neither practice is morally justifiable.

Lewis could report the order to the board of directors of the company. If they agree that the president's policy should be followed, Lewis could then report the situation to the appropriate government agency.

Lewis could take another approach—tacitly ignore the order, and wait until he is called to task, or fired for not obeying orders. This, however, puts an excessive burden on him—a burden that loyalty to the company cannot legitimately demand. There are times when injustice within a company can be rectified only by forces outside a company, and recourse to them is morally justifiable.

Obedience can be demanded of employees, so long as what is commanded is job-related, and neither illegal nor immoral. Firms may wish their employees to be loyal, but loyalty cannot be demanded. It must be developed, encouraged, and, ultimately, earned.

Employee Obligations

The list of a worker's obligations depends in part on his or her job or position, but we can specify in general some obligations that hold true for all employment.

Workers are morally obliged to obey the moral law, and they are legally obliged to obey the civil law at work, just as during all other times. Hence, they should not steal from their companies, even in little ways—taking stamps, pencils, paper, or other materials. If they feel they are underpaid, they should let this be known, bargain for more pay, or find other employment. They have no right to adjust their pay by taking things they want from the company.

They are obliged not to lie, not to spread false information, not to sexually or otherwise abuse or harass others. They are morally obliged to treat their fellow employees, whether above or below them, with respect.

They are also obliged to fulfill the terms of their contracts. If they are hired to work an eight-hour day, they should work that amount of time. They should work conscientiously at their jobs, and live up to the terms of their contracts. This is an obligation of justice.

The obligations of workers are sometimes spelled out in contracts and job descriptions. The latter are often extremely vague, and exactly what a person in a particular position is obliged to do may be unclear. A person in such a position has no obligation to do the maximum, although if he or she wants a promotion, he or she may choose to do more than is expected or required. Workers have the obligation to perform adequately; they do not have the obligation to break records, work overtime, or do jobs other than those that come with the position. Conversely, however, there is no moral objection—at least in most cases—to their doing more than can be legitimately expected of them.

Employees are obliged, in addition, to consider the interests of the firm for which they work. For instance, they should not work part-time or consult for a competitor. Nor is it appropriate either to undercut their firm or to help a competitor do so by solicited public statements. Unsolicited public statements concerning their private, but negative, opinion of their employer are also inappropriate.

Managers are in most cases employees of the firm for which they work. Their obligation is to manage efficiently and fairly. This includes respecting the rights of their employees and creating an ambiance in which all can work together for the benefit of the firm.

Management usually emphasizes the obligations of workers much more frequently than it mentions the rights of workers. Therefore, it is often easier to learn what is expected of one than to know when one's rights are being unjustly ignored or violated.

The moral concerns of workers, as well as their moral rights, have received little attention from corporations. A firm that takes morality seriously will set a moral tone from above, and will pay close attention to the moral concerns of its employees. It will make sure that its structure facilitates the expression of employees' concerns regarding their moral and civil rights.

Further Reading

BENDIX, REINHARD. *Work and Authority in Industry.* Berkeley, Calif.: University of California Press, 1974.

EWING, DAVID W. *Freedom Inside the Organization.* New York: McGraw-Hill Book Co., 1977.

———. *"Do It My Way or You're Fired!"* New York: John Wiley & Sons, Inc., 1983.

GIBSON, MARY. *Workers' Rights.* Totowa, N.J.: Rowman & Allenhead, Publishers, 1983.

NADER, RALPH, MARK GREEN, and JOEL SELIGMAN. *Taming the Giant Corporation.* New York: W. W. Norton, & Co., Inc., 1976.

O'NEILL, ROBERT. *The Rights of Government Employees.* New York: Avon Books, 1978.

WESTIN, ALAN F., and STEPHAN SALISBURY, eds. *Individual Rights in the Corporation.* New York: Pantheon Books, 1980.

ELEVEN

Whistle Blowing

We have seen that corporate disobedience is required when one is commanded to do what is immoral. We have also seen that loyalty to the corporation may morally allow, and sometimes demand, breaking the chain of command by going over the head of one's immediate superior. In many companies, breaking the chain of command is considered a form of corporate disobedience. Another form of corporate disobedience is whistle blowing.

Kinds of Whistle Blowing

Whistle blowing is a term used for a wide range of activities that are dissimilar from a moral point of view. Sometimes the term refers to disclosures made by employees to executives in a firm, perhaps concerning improper conduct of fellow employees or superiors who are cheating on expense accounts, or are engaging in petty or grand theft. Students are sometimes said to "blow the whistle" on fellow students whom they see cheating on exams. In these cases, whistle blowing amounts to reporting improper activities to an appropriate person. This can be called *internal whistle blowing,* for the disclosure or allegation of inappropriate conduct is made to someone within the organization or system. Generally, one believes an investigation will follow and a sanction will be imposed. In the classroom situation, if the students are on the honor system, they have agreed to report cheating and are morally obliged to do so. If they are not on the honor system, such reporting may be morally permissible, but is not usually required, from a moral point of view. A similar analysis applies on the job, as well.

Internal whistle blowing is frequently not an act of either corporate disloyalty or disobedience. In fact, it is more often than not a form of corporate loyalty. But it does involve disloyalty or disobedience to one's immediate superior or to one's fellow workers. If done from moral motives, the intent of such whistle blowing is to stop dishonesty or some immoral practice or act, to protect the interests and reputation of the company, or to increase the company's profits. For these reasons, it is in the company's interest to encourage such whistle blowing, so long as it does not turn the firm into a sort of police-state, where everyone watches and reports on everyone else.

Someone who reports sexual harassment is also sometimes said to blow the whistle on the offender; this is often because simply speaking to the person has no effect. In this case, the charge is about an offense not against the organization or system, but against oneself; the whistle blowing might be called personal, as opposed to impersonal whistle blowing, in which the potential or actual injury is to others or to the organization rather than to oneself. *Personal whistle blowing* is, in general, morally permitted but not morally required, unless other aspects of the case show that there is immediate danger to others.

We have discussed the fact that workers have a right not to be sexually harassed, therefore they should have a means by which to report such harassment if simply speaking to the harasser proves ineffective. Similarly, workers who have other rights violated should also have channels through which to get their legitimate complaints heard and acted on. Acts of personal whistle blowing are usually within the organization. But if serious enough, the whistle blower who gets no satisfaction internally might have to report to someone outside. Only a shortsighted firm would force external whistle blowing; a well-managed firm would be so structured as to take care of such cases internally. This is in the best interests not only of the firm but also of the workers and their morale.

Whistle blowing sometimes refers to government employees who divulge to a governmental regulatory or investigative bureau unethical practices in their division or office. It sometimes refers to reporting such things as cost overruns to Congressional committees or to the media. (The former is still considered external whistle blowing, because one goes outside the division or office to alert someone in another part of the government system.) Sometimes whistle blowing refers to leaks by government employees to the media, such as those revelations of classified material made by Daniel Ellsberg. We can call all these kinds of disclosure *governmental whistle blowing*.

This sort of whistle blowing is different from private-sector whistle blowing, which is by employees on their employers. The obligations one has to one's government are considerably different from obligations to a nongovernmental employer. The reason is that government employees are related to their government, both as citizens and as employees, and the harm done by governmental employees may have effects not only on the particular division in which they are employed but also on the government and country as a whole. The law recognizes this difference, and Congress has passed special legislation governing and protecting certain kinds of governmental whistle blowers. The laws do not protect those who break the law by revealing classified information, but they protect from dismissal those who reveal waste, overspending, or illegal or corrupt activity within the government bureaucracy. The legislation has been enforced only sporadically, and those who have blown the whistle have usually not fared well in terms of promotion or career advancement, even if they have kept their jobs. No Administration has yet signalled that such people, if they have the best interests of the country at heart, are to be rewarded and made examples to be emulated.

We shall restrict our discussion to a specific sort of whistle blowing, namely, *nongovernmental, impersonal, external whistle blowing*. We shall be concerned with (1) employees of profit-making firms, who, for moral reasons, in the hope and expectation that a product will be made safe, or a practice changed, (2) make public information about a product or practice of the firm that due to faulty design, the use of inferior materials, or the failure to follow safety or other regular procedures or state of the art standards (3) threatens to produce serious harm to the public in general or to individual users of a product. We shall restrict our analysis to this type of whistle blowing because, in the first place, the conditions that justify whistle blowing vary according to the type of case at issue. Second, financial harm can be considerably different from bodily harm. An immoral practice that increases the cost of a product by a slight margin may do serious harm to no individual, even if the total amount when summed adds up to a large amount, or profit. (Such cases can be handled differently from cases that threaten bodily harm.) Third, both internal and personal whistle blowing cause problems for a firm, which are for the most part restricted to those within the firm. External, impersonal whistle blowing, is of concern to the general public, because it is the general public rather than the firm that is threatened with harm.

As a paradigm, we shall take a set of fairly clear-cut cases, namely, those in which serious bodily harm—including possible death—threatens either the users of a product or innocent bystanders because of a firm's practice, the design of its product, or the action of some person or persons within the firm. (Many of the famous whistle-blowing cases are instances of such situations.) We shall assume clear cases where serious, preventable harm will result unless a company makes changes in its product or practice.

Cases that are less clear are probably more numerous, and pose problems that are difficult to solve, for example, how serious is *serious*, and how does one tell whether a given situation is serious? We choose not to resolve such issues, but rather to construct a model embodying a number of distinctions that will enable us to clarify the moral status of whistle blowing, which may, in turn, provide a basis for working out guidelines for more complex cases.

Finally, the only motivation for whistle blowing we shall consider here is moral motivation. Those who blow the whistle for revenge, and so on, are not our concern in this discussion.

Corporations are complex entities. Sometimes those at the top do not want to know in detail the difficulties encountered by those below them. They wish lower-management to handle these difficulties as best they can. On the other hand, those in lower-management frequently present only good news to those above them, even if those at the top do want to be told about difficulties. Sometimes, lower-management hopes that things will be straightened out without letting their superiors know that anything has gone wrong. For instance, sometimes a production schedule is drawn up, which many employees along the line know cannot be achieved. Each level has cut off a few days of the production time actually needed, to make his projection look good to those above. Because this happens at each level, the final projection is weeks, if not months, off the mark. When difficulties develop in actual production, each level is further squeezed and is tempted to cut corners in order not to fall too far behind the overall schedule. The cuts may be that of not correcting defects in a design, or of allowing a defective part to go through, even though a department head and the workers in that department know that this will cause trouble for the consumer. Sometimes a defective part will be annoying; sometimes it will be dangerous. If dangerous, external whistle blowing may be morally mandatory.

Producing goods that are known to be defective, or that will break down after a short period of time, is sometimes justified by producers, who point out that the product is warrantied and that it will be repaired for consumers free of charge. They claim it is better to have the product available for the Christmas market, or for the new-model season for cars, or for some other target date, even if it must later be recalled and fixed, rather than have the product delayed beyond the target date.

When the product is so defective as to be dangerous, the situation, from a moral point of view, is much more serious than when only convenience is at stake. If the danger is such that people are likely to die from the defect, then clearly it should be repaired before being sold. There have been instances, however, when a company, knowing that its product was dangerous, did a cost-benefit analysis. The managers of the company determined how many people were likely to be killed, and what the cost to the company would be if a certain percentage of the deceased persons' families successfully sued the company. They then compared this figure with the cost of repairing the defect, or of repairing it immediately rather than at a later date, through a recall. They also estimated the cost to the company if they were not only sued but also fined. If the loss from immediate repair substantially exceeded the probable cost of suits and fines, they continued production.

Such a cost-benefit analysis might seem, at first glance, to resemble a utilitarian calculation. However, a utilitarian calculation would not fail to consider the effect on all parties. The cost-benefit analysis is made exclusively from the standpoint of the company. How much, we have to ask, is a human life worth? If a defective part will probably cause fifty or sixty deaths, can we simply calculate the probability of a certain number of people suing, and then weigh that cost against the cost of replacing the part? An adequate moral utilitarian calculation would include the deaths and the injuries, plus the inconvenience for all the purchasers, and weigh these factors against the dollars saved. The equation is not difficult to solve. We know that we all have a moral obligation not to harm others, when we can prevent it. In such cases, the equation of deaths to dollars is an equation which, from a moral point of view, will always balance out in favor of lives saved. This realization often provides the moral motivation for whistle blowers.

The reply of some defenders of the cost-benefit analysis just described is that every product carries some risk. When driving an automobile, for instance, there is some risk that people will die. We cannot make cars absolutely safe, because we have to trade off some safety features against cost. Some very expensive cars are safer than many inexpensive cars. Everyone knows that. There is nothing immoral about making cars less safe than is technically possible, they may say.

Now, we all know that less expensive cars are frequently less safe than more expensive cars, but this is different from knowing that a part in a car is dangerously defective. A new car, for instance, is expected to have working brakes, even if it is an inexpensive car. If the brakes are defective, and likely to give out under pressure when going down a steep incline, this is a danger that no one purchasing a new car expects. If a car dealer were to explain what was wrong with the car, and what might happen, it is unlikely that many people would purchase it. Thus, even when the argument is that the immorality is not in selling a defective product but in selling a defective product without informing the purchaser, one must ultimately conclude that the sale is immoral. The argument does not justify the cost-benefit analysis in which profits are compared with lives.

Other corporate activities have led people to disclose publicly the internal actions of their companies. In some cases, companies were dumping toxic wastes into a water supply, knowing that it would harm the people who lived near the supply. In other cases, papers were signed by employees, certifying that a dangerous defect had been repaired, when in fact no repairs had been made. In the Bay Area Rapid Transit case three engineers saw a dangerous defect in the system. When their warnings were systematically ignored, and they were told to keep quiet, they felt it was their moral duty to make the danger known to the public.

The whistle blower usually fares very poorly at the hands of his company, as we mentioned before. Most are fired. In some instances, they have been blackballed in the whole industry. If they are not fired, they are frequently shunted aside at promotion time, and treated as pariahs. Those who consider making a firm's wrongdoings public must therefore be aware that they may be fired, ostracized, and condemned by others. They may ruin their chances of future promotion and security; and they also may make themselves a target for revenge. Only rarely have companies praised and promoted such people. This is not surprising, because the whistle blower forces the company to do what it did not want to do, even if, morally, it was the right action. This is scandalous. And it is ironic that those guilty of endangering the lives of others— even of indirectly killing them—frequently get promoted by their companies for increasing profits.

Because the consequences for the whistle blower are often so disastrous, such action is not to be undertaken lightly. Moreover, whistle blowing may, in some cases, be morally justifiable without being morally mandatory. The position we shall develop is a moderate one, and falls between two extreme positions: that defended by those who claim that whistle blowing is always morally justifiable, and that defended by those who say it is never morally justifiable.

Whistle Blowing As Morally Prohibited

Whistle blowing can be defined in such a way that it is always morally permissible, or in such a way that it is always morally obligatory. Initially, however, we can plausibly consider as morally neutral the act of an employee making public a firm's internal operations, practices, or policies which affect the safety of a product. In some cases whistle blowing may be morally prohibited, in some cases it may be morally permissible, and in some it may be morally mandatory.

Each of the two extreme positions on whistle blowing, although mistaken, is instructive. The view that whistle blowing is always morally prohibited is the more widely held view. It is held not only by most managers but also by most employees. There is a strong tradition within American mores against "ratting," or telling on others. We find this to be true of children, in and out of school, and in folk wisdom: "Don't wash your dirty linen in public." There is ample evidence that when someone does blow the whistle on his or her company—even for moral reasons, and with positive results for the public—he or she is generally ostracized, not only by the management of the firm but also by his or her fellow employees. The whistle blower is perceived as a traitor, as someone who has damaged the firm—the working family—to which he or she belongs. In so doing, he or she has hurt and offended most of those within the firm.

Rarely are whistle blowers honored as heroes by their fellow workers. A possible explanation might be that, by his or her action, the whistle blower has implied that because fellow workers did not blow the whistle, they are guilty of immorality, complicity in the wrongdoings of the company, or cowardice. The whistle blower did what the others were obliged to do but failed to do. His or her presence is therefore a constant reminder of their moral failure. Such a scenario may describe some situations, but whatever the scenario, the evidence is overwhelming that the whistle blower is not considered a hero by his fellow workers.

How can we justify this feeling of most workers and managers, that an employee ought not blow the whistle on the firm for which he or she works? Are they not operating under a double standard if they themselves wish to be preserved from injury caused by other firms, even if the means of achieving that protection is the result of someone in another firm blowing the whistle?

The most plausible, and most commonly stated, rationale for not blowing the whistle is given in terms of loyalty. When people join a company, it is claimed, they become part of an organization composed of fellow employees. They are not simply automatons, filling positions. They are people with feelings, who are engaged in a joint enterprise. In accepting employment, employees at every level owe something to the employing firm as well as to those with whom they work. Employees owe not only a certain amount of work but also a certain positive attitude toward that work and to their fellow workers. Without such a positive attitude (which we can characterize roughly as loyalty), a worker is either indifferent or disaffected. An indifferent or disaffected worker is clearly not a team player, and typically contributes only enough work to keep from being fired. Given the chance, such a worker would gladly leave the firm for a job with another company. Such an employee lacks loyalty to his or her employer.

Now, if the indifferent or disaffected worker were to blow the whistle on his or her employer, one might doubt that he or she did so from noble or moral motives. One might be mistaken in assuming ignoble motives; but the natural tendency would be to see the whistle blowing as stemming from the worker's indifference or disaffection. Therefore, it is unlikely that those workers who feel a sense of obligation or loyalty to the firm will look kindly on the whistle blower or the whistle blowing.

This leaves us to consider the loyal worker. What is the basis of this loyalty, and to what extent is it owed the company or employer? In one view, loyalty is based appropriately on gratitude. The firm or employer, after all, gives the worker a job, which is no small consideration in a society in which 4 percent unemployment is considered normal, and in which unemployment for some groups in the society has recently reached 18 percent. To be disloyal to one's employer is to bite the hand that feeds one—hardly an admirable or praiseworthy action. But even if the worker feels no gratitude, both the worker and the employer profit from their mutual contract, because if the worker is to be more than a cog in an impersonal machine, he or she comes to see the company as his or her company. The worker, in any event, has a stake in the firm for which he or she works. The stake is appropriately translated into positive concern for the firm, if not full identification with it—a concern that is in part what people mean by *loyalty*.

But even if we concede that an employee appropriately feels loyalty to a firm or to those within it, we cannot agree that such loyalty involves or demands that a worker engage in immoral activities for the firm. Nor need we admit that loyalty is always the overriding consideration in an employee's actions. The flaw in the argument of those who claim that whistle blowing is always immoral is that they make loyalty to a firm the worker's highest obligation, and consider it to be always overriding.

On the other hand, those who argue that whistle blowing is always at least morally permissible typically approach such acts from the point of view of the right of free speech. Workers do not give up the right of free speech—a civil right—by taking employment. They usually make no pledge of loyalty; and any claim that employers make regarding an employee's obligation to be loyal to their firm is wishful thinking, or self-serving ideological hogwash which they try to foist on naive employees. There is no obligation of employee loyalty, either as a result of a contract or as an implied condition of employment. But there is the right of free speech.

The right of free speech, of course, is a limited right. One is not free to yell "Fire" in a crowded theater when there is no fire. One is legally prohibited from making libelous statements. But one is not prevented from making true statements, whether they be about one's employer or about others. American citizens freely criticize their government and their elected leaders. It would be strange if they did not have a similar right to criticize their employers. Moreover, the argument continues, if the actions of their employers, or of some members of the firm, are morally suspect, or if actions of the firm may in some way damage consumers, workers, or innocent bystanders, or if these actions threaten the interests of shareholders or of other interested parties, then workers clearly have the right to speak out in whatever way, and in whatever forum, they desire. By doing so they violate no commitment to loyalty, because there is no such commitment; they are simply exercising their right to free speech. It may be imprudent at times to speak out, and they may suffer from the often unjust reactions of others, but whistle blowing, or speaking out about a company's practices, is not immoral; it is always a morally defensible act.

This extreme position has much to recommend it. But it is extreme because it makes the right of free speech always overriding, and it fails to consider the harm done to one's firm or fellow workers by the usual kind of whistle blowing. In denying any obligation of loyalty, it implicitly denies any consideration of the harm that one's actions may do to those with whom one is associated, and fails to consider whether there are morally preferable alternatives—or perhaps even morally required alternatives.

Each of the two positions we have described as extreme suffers from the same defect. Each makes absolute one aspect of a complex situation and fails to consider the conflict of obligations, rights, and responsibilities that usually arise in the conditions that lead to whistle blowing. If neither loyalty nor the right to free speech is always overriding, and if neither always determines the morality of a case, it is sometimes possible for loyalty to be overriding, sometimes for the right of free speech to be overriding; and it is possible therefore that at times neither be overriding, and that both may give way to some other consideration. This suggests that sometimes whistle blowing may be immoral—as when loyalty is overriding; and that sometimes it is morally justified—as when the right to free speech is overriding.

On whom is the onus of justification? Should we assume that whistle blowing is generally morally justifiable, and require that anyone who claims that a given act of whistle blowing is immoral make out that case? Or should we assume that whistle blowing is generally immoral, and require moral justification for those acts that are morally permissible or obligatory? Tradition has placed the onus on those who justify whistle blowing, the common assumption being that it is morally prohibited. We have already noted the general attitude of most workers to whistle blowing, and their negative reaction to the whistle blower. Moreover, unless we are to indict most workers as moral cowards, the relatively rare incidence of whistle blowing indicates that most workers do not feel it is their moral obligation to blow the whistle. Although these considerations do not by themselves show that workers feel it is immoral to blow the whistle, they at least tend to put the onus on those who would claim it is morally obligatory. Finally, the literature on whistle blowing has developed in such a way that those who justify it have assumed the need to do so.

That whistle blowing needs justification makes sense, moreover, if it is seen as an instance of disobedience to the corporation or organization. Frequently the whistle blower is in fact told by his or her superiors to mind his or her own business. To blow the whistle is to go beyond what he or she is paid to do, and is to fly in the face of orders given to one by a legitimate superior within the firm or organization. Disobedience typically requires justification if it is to be considered moral—whether it is a case of civil disobedience, disobedience to the corporation, or a child's disobedience to its parents. Under the appropriate conditions, obedience is the expected and required moral way to act. Disobedience may be morally justified; but if it is, the onus is on the disobedient or his spokesman to make out the case.

To admit that whistle blowing is often an instance of disobedience to the corporation, and that at least sometimes one (i.e., the corporation) is owed obedience, leads us to the conclusion that at least sometimes whistle blowing is morally wrong. That it is sometimes morally wrong seems the general consensus in American society, and there is no reason to challenge the consensus. But sometimes whistle blowing is morally permissible, and sometimes is even morally obligatory; therefore it is appropriate to accept the onus of spelling out and justifying the conditions that render it such.

Whistle Blowing As Morally Permitted

The kind of whistle blowing we are considering involves an employee somehow going public, revealing information or concerns about his or her firm in the hope that the firm will change its product, action, or policy, or whatever it is that the whistle blower feels will harm, or has harmed others, and needs to be rectified. We can assume that when one blows the whistle, it is not with the consent of the firm, but against its wishes. It is thus a form of disloyalty and of disobedience to the corporation. Whistle blowing of this type, we can further assume, does injury to a firm. It results in either adverse publicity or in an investigation of some sort, or both. If we adopt the principle that one ought not to do harm without sufficient reason, then, if the act of whistle blowing is to be morally permissible, some good must be achieved that outweighs the harm that will be done.

There are five conditions, which, if satisfied, change the moral status of whistle blowing. If the first three are satisfied, the act of whistle blowing will be morally justifiable and permissible. If the additional two are satisfied, the act of whistle blowing will be morally obligatory.

Whistle blowing is morally permissible if—

1. The firm, through its product or policy, will do serious and considerable harm to the public, whether in the person of the user of its product, an innocent bystander, or the general public.

Because whistle blowing causes harm to the firm, this harm must be offset by at least an equal amount of good, if the act is to be permissible. We have specified that the potential or actual harm to others must be serious and considerable. That requirement may be considered by some to be both too strong and too vague. Why specify "serious and considerable" instead of saying, "involve more harm than the harm that the whistle blowing will produce for the firm?" Moreover, how serious is "serious?" And how considerable is "considerable?"

There are several reasons for stating that the potential harm must be serious and considerable. First, if the harm is not serious and considerable, if it will do only slight harm to the public, or to the user of a product, the justification for whistle blowing will be at least problematic. We will not have a clear case. To assess the harm done to the firm is difficult; but though the harm may be rather vague, it is also rather sure. If the harm threatened by a product is slight or not certain, it might not be greater than the harm done to the firm. After all, a great many products involve some risk. Even with a well-constructed hammer, one can smash one's finger. There is some risk in operating any automobile, because no automobile is completely safe. There is always a trade-off between safety and cost. It is not immoral not to make the safest automobile possible, for instance, and a great many factors enter into deciding just how safe a car should be. An employee might see that a car can be made slightly safer by modifying a part, and might suggest that modification; but not making the modification is not usually grounds for blowing the whistle. If serious harm is not threatened, then the slight harm that is done, say by the use of a product, can be corrected after the product is marketed (e.g., as a result of customer complaint). Our society has a great many ways of handling minor defects, and these are at least arguably better than resorting to whistle blowing.

To this consideration should be added a second. Whistle blowing is frequently, and appropriately, considered an unusual occurence, a heroic act. If the practice of blowing the whistle for relatively minor harm were to become a common occurence, its effectiveness would be diminished. When serious harm is threatened, whistle blowers are listened to by the news media, for instance, because it is news. But relatively minor harm to the public is not news. If many minor charges or concerns were voiced to the media, the public would soon not react as it is now expected to react to such disclosures. This would also be the case if complaints about all sorts of perceived or anticipated minor harm were reported to government agencies, although most people would expect that government agencies would act first on the serious cases, and only later on claims of relatively minor harm.

There is a third consideration. Every time an employee has a concern about possible harm to the public from a product or practice we cannot assume that he or she makes a correct assessment. Nor can we assume that every claim of harm is morally motivated. To sift out the claims and concerns of the disaffected worker from the genuine claims and concerns of the morally motivated employee is a practical problem. It may be claimed that this problem has nothing to do with the moral permissibility of the act of whistle blowing; but whistle blowing is a practical matter. If viewed as a technique for changing policy or actions, it will be justified only if effective. It can be trivialized. If it is, then one might plausibly claim that little harm is done to the firm, and hence the act is permitted. But if trivialized, it loses its point. If whistle blowing is to be considered a serious act with serious consequences, it should be reserved for disclosing potentially serious harm, and will be morally justifiable in those cases.

Serious is admittedly a vague term. Is an increase in probable automobile deaths, from 2 in 100,000 to 15 in 100,000 over a one-year period, serious? Although there may be legitimate debate on this issue, it is clear that matters that threaten death are prima facie serious. If the threatened harm is that a product may cost a few pennies more than otherwise, or if the threatened harm is that a part or product may cause minor inconvenience, the harm—even if multiplied by thousands or millions of instances—does not match the seriousness of death to the user or the innocent bystander.

The harm threatened by unsafe tires, which are sold as premium quality but that blow out at 60 or 70 mph, is serious, for such tires can easily lead to death. The dumping of metal drums of toxic waste into a river, where the drums will rust, leak, and cause cancer or other serious ills to those who drink the river water or otherwise use it, threatens serious harm. The use of substandard concrete in a building, such that it is likely to collapse and kill people, poses a serious threat to people. Failure to x-ray pipe fittings, as required in building a nuclear plant, is a failure that might lead to nuclear leaks; this involves potential serious harm, for it endangers the health and lives of many.

The notion of *serious* harm might be expanded to include serious financial harm, and kinds of harm other than death and serious threats to health and body. But as we noted earlier, we shall restrict ourselves here to products and practices that produce or threaten serious harm or danger to life and health. The difference between producing harm and threatening serious danger is not significant for the kinds of cases we are considering.

2. Once an employee identifies a serious threat to the user of a product or to the general public, he or she should report it to his or her immediate superior and make his or her moral concern known. Unless he or she does so, the act of whistle blowing is not clearly justifiable.

Why not? Why is not the weighing of harm sufficient? The answer has already been given in part. Whistle blowing is a practice that, to be effective, cannot be routinely used. There are other reasons as well. First, reporting one's concerns is the most direct, and usually the quickest, way of producing the change the whistle blower desires. The normal assumption is that most firms do not want to cause death or injury, and do not willingly and knowingly set out to harm the users of their products in this way. If there are life-threatening defects, the normal assumption is, and should be, that the firm will be interested in correcting them—if not for moral reasons, at least for prudential reasons, viz., to avoid suits, bad publicity, and adverse consumer reaction. The argument from loyalty also supports the requirement that the firm be given the chance to rectify its action or procedure or policy before it is charged in public. Additionally, because whistle blowing does harm to the firm, harm in general is minimized if the firm is informed of the problem and allowed to correct it. Less harm is done to the firm in this way, and if the harm to the public or the users is also averted, this procedure produces the least harm, on the whole.

The condition that one report one's concern to one's immediate superior presupposes a hierarchical structure. Although firms are usually so structured, they need not be. In a company of equals, one would report one's concerns internally, as appropriate.

Several objections may be raised to this condition. Suppose one knows that one's immediate superior already knows the defect and the danger. In this case reporting it to him or her would be redundant, and condition two would be satisfied. But one should not presume without good reason that one's superior does know. What may be clear to one individual may not be clear to another. Moreover, the assessment of risk is often a complicated matter. To a person on one level what appears as unacceptable risk may be defensible as legitimate to a person on a higher level, who may see a larger picture, and knows of offsetting compensations, and the like.

However, would not reporting one's concern effectively preclude the possibility of anonymous whistle blowing, and so put one in jeopardy? This might of course be the case; and this is one of the considerations one should weigh before blowing the whistle. We will discuss this matter later on. If the reporting is done tactfully, moreover, the voicing of one's concerns might, if the problem is apparent to others, indicate a desire to operate within the firm, and so make one less likely to be the one assumed to have blown the whistle anonymously.

By reporting one's concern to one's immediate superior or other appropriate person, one preserves and observes the regular practices of firms, which on the whole promote their order and efficiency; this fulfills one's obligation of minimizing harm, and it precludes precipitous whistle blowing.

3. If one's immediate superior does nothing effective about the concern or complaint, the employee should exhaust the internal procedures and possibilities within the firm. This usually will in-

volve taking the matter up the managerial ladder, and, if necessary—and possible—to the board of directors.

To exhaust the internal procedures and possibilities is the key requirement
here. In a hierarchically structured firm, this means going up the chain of
command. But one may do so either with or without the permission of those
at each level of the hierarchy. What constitutes exhausting the internal procedures? This is often a matter of judgment. But because going public with
one's concern is more serious for both oneself and for the firm, going up the
chain of command is the preferable route to take in most circumstances. This
third condition is satisfied of course if, for some reason, it is truly impossible
to go beyond any particular level.

Several objections may once again be raised. There may not be time enough
to follow the bureaucratic procedures of a given firm; the threatened harm
may have been done before the procedures are exhausted. If, moreover, one
goes up the chain to the top and nothing is done by anyone, then a great deal
of time will have been wasted. Once again, prudence and judgment should
be used. The internal possibilities may sometimes be exhausted quickly, by a
few phone calls or visits. But one should not simply assume that no one at
any level within the firm will do anything. If there are truly no possibilites of
internal remedy, then the third condition is satisfied.

As we mentioned, the point of the three conditions is essentially that whistle
blowing is morally permissible if the harm threatened is serious, and if internal
remedies have been attempted in good faith but without a satisfactory result.
In these circumstances, one is morally justified in attempting to avert what
one sees as serious harm, by means that may be effective, including blowing
the whistle.

We can pass over as not immediately germane the questions of whether
in nonserious matters one has an obligation to report one's moral concerns
to one's superiors, and whether one fulfills one's obligation once one has reported them to the appropriate party.

Whistle Blowing As Morally Required

To say that whistle blowing is morally permitted does not impose any obligation
on an employee. Unless two other conditions are met, the employee does not
have a moral obligation to blow the whistle. To blow the whistle when one is
not morally required to do so, and if done from moral motives (i.e., concern
for one's fellow man) and at risk to oneself, is to commit a supererogatory
act. It is an act that deserves moral praise. But failure to so act deserves no
moral blame. In such a case, the whistle blower might be considered a moral
hero. Sometimes he or she is so considered, sometimes not. If one's claim or
concern turns out to be ill-founded, one's subjective moral state may be as
praiseworthy as if the claim were well-founded, but one will rarely receive
much praise for one's action.

For there to be an obligation to blow the whistle, two conditons must be met, in addition to the foregoing three.

4. The whistle blower must have, or have accessible, documented evidence that would convince a reasonable, impartial observer that one's view of the situation is correct, and that the company's product or practice poses a serious and likely danger to the public or to the user of the product.

One does not have an obligation to put oneself at serious risk without some compensating advantage to be gained. Unless one has documented evidence that would convince a reasonable, impartial observer, one's charges or claims, if made public, would be based essentially on one's word. Such grounds may be sufficient for a subjective feeling of certitude about one's charges, but they are not usually sufficient for others to act on one's claims. For instance, a newspaper is unlikely to print a story based simply on someone's undocumented assertion.

Several difficulties emerge. Should it not be the responsibility of the media or the appropriate regulatory agency or government bureau to carry out an investigation based on someone's complaint? It is reasonable for them to do so, providing they have some evidence in support of the complaint or claim. The damage has not yet been done, and the harm will not, in all likelihood, be done to the complaining party. If the action is criminal, then an investigation by a law-enforcing agency is appropriate. But the charges made by whistle blowers are often not criminal charges. And we do not expect newspapers or government agencies to carry out investigations whenever anyone claims that possible harm will be done by a product or practice. Unless harm is imminent, and very serious (e.g., a bomb threat), it is appropriate to act on evidence that substantiates a claim. The usual procedure, once an investigation is started or a complaint followed up, is to contact the party charged.

One does not have a moral obligation to blow the whistle simply because of one's hunch, guess, or personal assessment of possible danger, if supporting evidence and documentation are not available. One may, of course, have the obligation to attempt to get evidence if the harm is serious. But if it is unavailable—or unavailable without using illegal or immoral means—then one does not have the obligation to blow the whistle.

5. The employee must have good reason to believe that by going public the necessary changes will be brought about. The chance of being successful must be worth the risk one takes and the danger to which one is exposed.

Even with some documentation and evidence, a potential whistle blower may not be taken seriously, or may not be able to get the media or government agency to take any action. How far should one go, and how much must one try? The more serious the situation, the greater the effort required. But unless one has a reasonable expectation of success, one is not obliged to put oneself at great risk. Before going public, the potential whistle blower should know who (e.g., government agency, newspaper, columnist, TV reporter) will make use of his or her evidence, and how it will be handled. He or she should have good reason to expect that the action taken will result in the kind of change or result that he or she believes is morally appropriate.

The foregoing fourth and fifth conditions may seem too permissive to some and too stringent to others. They are too permissive for those who wish everyone to be ready and willing to blow the whistle whenever there is a chance that the public will be harmed. After all, harm to the public is more serious than harm to the whistle blower, and, in the long run, if everyone saw whistle blowing as obligatory, without satisfying the last two conditions, we would all be better off. If the fourth and fifth conditions must be satisfied, then people will only rarely have the moral obligation to blow the whistle.

If, however, whistle blowing were mandatory whenever the first three conditions were satisfied, and if one had the moral obligation to blow the whistle whenever one had a moral doubt or fear about safety, or whenever one disagreed with one's superiors or colleagues, one would be obliged to go public whenever one did not get one's way on such issues within a firm. But these conditions are much too weak, for the reasons already given. Other, stronger conditions, but weaker than those proposed, might be suggested. But any condition that makes whistle blowing mandatory in large numbers of cases, may possibly reduce the effectiveness of whistle blowing. If this were the result, and the practice were to become widespread, then it is doubtful that we would all be better off.

Finally, the claim that many people very often have the obligation to blow the whistle goes against the common view of the whistle blower as a moral hero, and against the commonly held feeling that whistle blowing is only rarely morally mandatory. This feeling may be misplaced. But a very strong argument is necessary to show that although the general public is morally mistaken in its view, the moral theoretician is correct in his or her assertion.

A consequence of accepting the fourth and fifth conditions stated is that the stringency of the moral obligation of whistle blowing corresponds with the common feeling of most people on this issue. Those in higher positions and those in professional positions in a firm are more likely to have the obligation to change a firm's policy or product—even by whistle blowing, if necessary—than are lower-placed employees. Engineers, for instance, are more likely to have access to data and designs than are assembly-line workers. Managers generally have a broader picture, and more access to evidence, than do nonmanagerial employees. Management has the moral responsibility both to see that the expressed moral concerns of those below them have been adequately considered and that the firm does not knowingly inflict harm on others.

The fourth and fifth conditions will appear too stringent to those who believe that whistle blowing is always a supererogatory act, that it is always moral heroism, and that it is never morally obligatory. They might argue that, although we are not permitted to do what is immoral, we have no general moral obligation to prevent all others from acting immorally. This is what the whistle blower attempts to do. The counter to that, however, is to point out that whistle blowing is an act in which one attempts to prevent harm to a third party. It is not implausible to claim both that we are morally obliged to prevent harm to others at relatively little expense to ourselves, and that we are morally obliged to prevent great harm to a great many others, even at considerable expense to ourselves.

The five conditions outlined can be used by an individual to help decide whether he or she is morally permitted or required to blow the whistle. Third parties can also use these conditions when attempting to evaluate acts of whistle blowing by others, even though third parties may have difficulty determining whether the whistle blowing is morally motivated. It might be possible successfully to blow the whistle anonymously. But anonymous tips or stories seldom get much attention. One can confide in a government agent, or in a reporter, on condition that one's name not be disclosed. But this approach, too, is frequently ineffective in achieving the results required. To be effective, one must usually be willing to be identified, to testify publicly, to produce verifiable evidence, and to put oneself at risk. As with civil disobedience, what captures the conscience of others is the willingness of the whistle blower to suffer harm for the benefit of others, and for what he or she thinks is right.

Precluding the Need for Whistle Blowing

The need for moral heroes shows a defective society and defective corporations. It is more important to change the legal and corporate structures that make whistle blowing necessary than to convince people to be moral heroes.

Because it is easier to change the law than to change the practices of all corporations, it should be illegal for any employer to fire an employee, or to take any punitive measures, at the time or later, against an employee who satisfies the first three aforementioned conditions and blows the whistle on the company. Because satisfying those conditions makes the action morally justifiable, the law should protect the employee in acting in accordance with what his or her conscience demands. If the whistle is falsely blown, the company will have suffered no great harm. If it is appropriately blown, the company should suffer the consequences of its actions being made public. But to protect a whistle blower by passing such a law is no easy matter. Employers can make life difficult for whistle blowers without firing them. There are many ways of passing over an employee. One can be relegated to the back room of the firm, or be given unpleasant jobs. Employers can find reasons not to promote one or to give one raises. Not all of this can be prevented by law, but some of the more blatant practices can be prohibited.

Second, the law can mandate that the individuals responsible for the decision to proceed with a faulty product or to engage in a harmful practice be penalized. The law has been reluctant to interfere with the operations of companies. As a result, those in the firm who have been guilty of immoral and illegal practices have gone untouched even though the corporation was fined for its activity.

A third possibility is that every company of a certain size be required, by law, to have an inspector general or an internal operational auditor, whose job it is to uncover immoral and illegal practices. This person's job would be to listen to the moral concerns of employees, at every level, about the firm's practices. He or she should be independent of management, and report to the audit committee of the board, which, ideally, should be a committee made up entirely of outside board members. The inspector or auditor should be charged with making public those complaints that should be made public if not changed from within. Failure on the inspector's part to take proper action with respect to a worker's complaint, such that the worker is forced to go public, should be prima facie evidence of an attempt to cover up a dangerous practice or product, and the inspector should be subject to criminal charges.

In addition, a company that wishes to be moral, that does not wish to engage in harmful practices or to produce harmful products, can take other steps to preclude the necessity of whistle blowing. As we noted in Chapter 8, it can establish channels whereby those employees who have moral concerns can get a fair hearing without danger to their position or standing in the company. Expressing such concerns, moreover, should be considered a demonstration of company loyalty and should be rewarded appropriately. The company might establish the position of ombudsman, to hear such complaints or moral concerns. Or an independent committee of the board might be established to hear such complaints and concerns. Someone might even be paid by the company to present the position of the would-be whistle blower, who would argue for what the company should do, from a moral point of view, rather than what those interested in meeting a schedule or making a profit would like to do. Such a person's success within the company could depend on his success in precluding whistle blowing, as well as the conditions that lead to it.

Unions and professional organizations should become concerned with the problem of whistle blowing. They should support their members who feel obligated to blow the whistle on a company; they should defend and support the member in his or her endeavor, and prevent him or her from being fired or abused on the job. They can also establish channels of their own, to which members can report concerns, and then follow up such concerns and force appropriate action.

Although we have concentrated on a specific type of nongovernmental, impersonal, external whistle blowing that threatens serious physical harm to the public, the analysis provides a model for dealing with other kinds of whistle blowing as well.

In all cases, because whistle blowing involves disloyalty or disobedience at some level, we start by requiring that it be justified, rather than assuming it needs no justification. If the action needs no justification, it is probably not an instance of whistle blowing. To distinguish the various kinds of whistle blowing, listing conditions that make it morally permissible and those that make it morally required is useful as a guide. In personal whistle blowing, there are many instances in which it is permitted but not obligatory. Many people may prefer to change employers rather than blow the whistle, and this may be perfectly justifiable. In all cases, one must weigh the harm done to individuals against the good to be achieved and the rights to be protected.

Whistle blowing is a relatively recent phenomenon in the workplace. It is one more indication of the falsity of the Myth of Amoral business. Whistle blowing should also alert corporations to what can and should be done if they wish to be both moral and excellent. When corporate structures preclude the need for whistle blowing, they protect both workers' rights and the public's good.

Further Reading

ANDERSON, ROBERT M., ROBERT PERRUCCI, DAN E. SCHENDEL, and LEON E. TRACHTMAN. *Divided Loyalties: Whistle-Blowing at BART*. West Lafayette, Ind.: Purdue University, 1980.

BAUM, ROBERT J., and ALBERT FLORES, eds. *Ethical Problems in Engineering*. 2nd ed., 2 vols. Troy, N.Y.: Center for the Study of the Human Dimensions of Science and Technology, 1980.

EDDY, PAUL, ELAINE POTTER, and BRUCE PAGE. *Destination Disaster. From the Tri-Motor to the DC-10: The Risk of Flying*. New York: Quadrangle, New York Times Book Co., 1976.

NADER, RALPH, PETER J. PETKAS, and KATE BLACKWELL, eds. *Whistle Blowing: The Report of the Conference on Professional Responsibility*. New York: Grossman, Publishers, 1972.

PETERS, CHARLES, and TAYLOR BRANCH. *Blowing the Whistle: Dissent in the Public Interest*. New York: Praeger Publishers, Inc., 1972.

RAVEN-HANSON, PETER. "Do's and Dont's for Whistleblowers: Planning for Trouble." *Technology Review*, May 1980, pp. 34–44.

U.S. MERIT SYSTEMS PROTECTION BOARD. *Whistle Blowing and the Federal Employee*. Washington, D.C.: U.S. Government Printing Office, 1981.

WALTERS, KENNETH D. "Your Employee's Right to Blow the Whistle." *Harvard Business Review*, July-August, 1975.

WESTIN, ALAN F., ed. *Whistle Blowing! Loyalty and Dissent in the Corporation*. New York: McGraw-Hill Book Co., 1981.

TWELVE

Discrimination, Affirmative Action, and Reverse Discrimination

Discrimination

The term *discrimination* is usually used in a pejorative sense with respect to employment. But there is also a morally neutral sense of the term. We discriminate between those things we want and those we do not want. We can discriminate between good apples and bad ones in a fruit market, and we are allowed to choose those we wish. We can also discriminate between people on the basis of qualifications. If a position requires the ability to type, that ability will serve to discriminate between those who have the ability and those who do not. What we are not morally allowed to do when discriminating between people with respect to work is to use improper criteria. Improper criteria in the job market are non-job-related criteria. Discrimination in the job market has come to mean discrimination in the pejorative sense.

Workers have the right to equal treatment, therefore discrimination on the basis of non-job-related characteristics when hiring, firing, or promoting people is immoral. Few dispute this statement, which is fairly easy to demonstrate using a utilitarian, a Kantian, or a Rawlsian approach.

Consider the practice of discrimination from a utilitarian point of view. We see, immediately, that harm is done to those who are discriminated against. If the practice is widespread and repeated in successive job situations, the harm done is serious and long-lasting. It affects not only the individuals but also their families. Those who do get the positions and promotions they would not get under conditions of fair competition do benefit. The good done to them, however, is probably not as great as the harm done to those discriminated against. But let us assume that the good is equal to the harm. In this case, the morality of the practice hinges on the results to others and to society in general. We can first consider the companies in which discrimination is practiced. If they did not discriminate, but hired and promoted only on the basis of merit, they would undoubtedly hire and promote some of those they discriminate against. Hence they are not getting the best people possible. To that extent they suffer some harm and experience no benefit. What about society as a whole? It also suffers. Systematic discrimination produces a class of people who are treated unjustly. They cannot help but feel anger against society, an anger that will show itself in many ways—from violence to seething ill will. Other groups in the society will also have cause to worry about whether they will be the next group to be discriminated against. On the whole, more harm than good is gained by following the practice of discrimination than by not following it. Discrimination is therefore an immoral practice.

We can reach the same result by a Kantian-type analysis. Can discrimination be made universal consistently? In fact, it can. People might not like the kind of society in which they were to live if discrimination were made universal; but the action is not self-contradictory. It passes the first of the three Kantian tests, but it fails the next two. Discrimination does not treat people as ends in themselves. They are not considered as persons; they are treated as members of a class with a certain characteristic. As a result of that characteristic, they are not given equal treatment, and they are not treated with respect. They are made means to the ends of the dominant class's desire to maintain its superiority and its class prerogatives. And if we were to ask whether rational human beings would be willing to live in a society that discriminates rather than in one that does not, could we expect anything other than a negative answer?

Using a Rawlsian-like approach, we should consider the decision that rational people would make if they were behind the veil of ignorance. If they did not know where they would end up, would they prefer to live in a discriminatory society or in a nondiscriminatory one? Clearly, the least advantaged would be better off in a nondiscriminatory society than in one that discriminates. Therefore the rational person, not knowing where he would end up, would see that the morally preferable, the morally just society is the one that does not practice discrimination. Discrimination, moreover, directly violates Rawls's principles of justice, because it does not allow either equal freedom to all or equality of opportunity.

Because it seems so clear that discrimination is immoral, we should pause to consider why discrimination has been so widely practiced in our society. Part of the reply comes from historical circumstances. To understand why people discriminate is not to justify their doing so; and although condemning the practice, we can at least understand the human motivation for it.

Blacks have been one chief group against whom discrimination has been practiced for a long period of time, and in a systematic way. The reason for the discrimination stems from the fact that, with but a few exceptions, blacks in the United States were slaves until freed as a result of the Civil War. Many whites did not even consider them human beings. This attitude toward blacks enabled the whites to live with the immoral institution of slavery. The Emancipation Proclamation could not instantly change the attitude of those who considered blacks slaves, inferior to whites, and nonhuman. Neither amendments to the Constitution nor legislation granting the blacks the rights of citizens could change the views and attitudes of such whites—Southern or Northern. Attitudes are not easily or quickly changed. Moreover, the blacks were uneducated, and were used to living in extremely poor conditions. When they were freed, they could leave the plantation and seek employment elsewhere. But they were not trained to work in factories or to run their own affairs. They were easy prey for entrepreneurs, who hired them for a pittance. After they were freed, the standard of living of many blacks was little, if at all, improved over the slave days. Some were even worse off. The whites in both the North and the South, who had felt superior to the slaves, continued to feel so. The well-to-do felt superior because they lived better, had more money, and could hire the blacks cheaply; and the poor whites felt superior simply because they were white. The color of their own skin was all they had to feel superior about, but it was enough. The blacks were forced to live in segregated areas, and were discriminated against in schooling, opportunities to gain advancement, employment, and in almost every aspect of social life.

Women are another group against whom discrimination in employment has been practiced. The historical situation with respect to women is more complicated and more controversial than that of blacks. During the nineteenth century and the early part of the twentieth century, other than the movement for women's suffrage, little was said or written concerning discrimination against women. The majority of women did not seek employment outside of the home. The man in a household was considered the head of the family and the breadwinner. We have already seen, in Chapter 9, that men were paid more than women for the same work because it was assumed that men had to support their families whereas women either had to support only themselves, or had to contribute to the support of a family in which the man already worked. The allocation of pay was based on a combination of both work and need, a criterion that many people in former times considered appropriate. Women who did not work, or who worked to supplement their husband's income, benefited from the fact that their husbands were paid more than women. With hindsight, we can now see that the women who were underpaid for their work were actually being discriminated against. As women joined the work force in greater numbers, as divorce increased, as more women became heads of households, and as it became clear that single men were also paid more than single women, a movement gradually formed. Women demanded equal pay for equal work, equal opportunity for women, and an end to discrimination against women. Old habits die hard, however, and much discrimination, often in subtle forms, continues to the present day. Its historical roots are nonetheless important to remember.

Ethnic groups have also been the object of discrimination: the American Indian, Orientals, Hispanics, Italians, Irish, Poles, Czechs, and so on. At one time or another, members of religious sects, including Jews, Catholics, and Mormons, have been discriminated against. In each case, the people in question were different from the majority of Americans, in that they lived on reservations or in ghettos, or were immigrants or migrant workers. Eventually, most of them were assimilated, but sometimes only after two or three generations. And before assimilation, they suffered discrimination in the job market as well as in other areas of life.

Discrimination is unjust and causes harm to those against whom it is practiced. Compensatory justice demands that restitution be made to those harmed. The compensation should be equivalent to the harm suffered, and it should be paid to the one harmed by the one who caused the harm.

If a black or a woman working for a company has been receiving less pay for the same work done by white males, then compensatory justice requires that the company pay the black or the woman the amount he or she did not receive during his or her tenure with the company. Few cases, however, are that simple. Those who were discriminated against and have since died cannot be compensated by payment. Should their children or their heirs be compensated? Those who were never hired by any of the firms to which they applied cannot easily say which ones turned them down because of discrimination. Even if they could say which firms were guilty of discrimination, for what amount should they be compensated? Should they be paid a certain sum by all the companies that turned them down, or by all the firms that would have turned them down had they applied to them? None of these questions is easy to answer.

Some people have urged that certain groups or classes of people who have been discriminated against should be identified. The members of that group deserve compensation of some form from the group of people and companies who have discriminated, or who have been the beneficiaries of discrimination. In concrete terms, the class of all blacks, women, Chicanos, American Indians, and Orientals are considered to be the major bearers of the burdens of discrimination. If an individual in any of those groups has not been personally discriminated against, it is very likely that his or her parents have been, or that some other ancestor or relative has been. If by chance a few who bear no scars of discrimination receive compensation, that is better than large numbers never receiving any compensation.

Who is to pay the compensation? Those who have benefited from discrimination are said to be American corporations and American white males. Even if some individual white males did not benefit directly, they benefited indirectly as a result of the systematic discrimination which has favored them throughout their lives. Similarly, even if a particular company did not discriminate, it took advantage of the climate of corporate life which discrimination fostered.

Of what should compensation consist? It could not, in justice, consist of monetary payments, for there would be no way to determine these in an equitable way. The only sort of compensation possible, the argument goes, is that the class of people who were previously discriminated against be given special privileges and opportunities to make up for the absence of such privileges and opportunities in the past. A variety of target goals have been proposed. Some urge that every firm have represented in it the same proportion of women, blacks, Chicanos, and Orientals as is found in the general population. Others favor the idea that proportions in each type of position should be equal to the proportion of each group in training for that position. But this is considered to be unsatisfactory by those who feel that fewer women and blacks, for instance, are in engineering schools than should be because discrimination has steered them away from such professions.

At what rate should those previously discriminated against be taken into companies and given promotions? Some would set targets and quotas for each year until the proper proportion is reached. Some simply advocate an affirmative approach, that is, making sure that places are open to those qualified. Others seek preferential hiring—a term that can be interpreted in several different ways—of women and minorities.

Before we look into the specifics of some of these proposals, we should examine carefully the approach to compensation in terms of classes. Is such an approach fair, just, and proper? In arguing that discrimination was immoral, we saw that harm was done to the one discriminated against, that benefit was provided to the one chosen, and that harm was done to society and to the companies that engaged in the practice. Suppose we follow the class or group approach. If people from the previously discriminated-against groups were chosen in favor of more qualified white males, we would have an instance of discrimination, even though the discrimination was against white males and in favor of blacks and females. Less qualified people would still be chosen over more qualified people. Harm would be done to the group and to the individuals discriminated against, as well as to the companies and to society. If discrimination was wrong because of these results in the first instance, it cannot be right when the results are similar in the second instance. After years of this practice, we would have a group of white males who had suffered discrimination, and we would have to start the cycle all over again. The argument that white males are the group that had previously benefited will not be convincing to the individual white males presently being discriminated against. They will rightly claim that they are not guilty of past discrimination, and that it is unjust to punish sons for the sins of their fathers. The children of immigrants from Italy or Poland or Ireland will cry out even louder for justice. Their parents were discriminated against, just as blacks and women were. Do they not deserve compensation too? But under the proposed system, they are the ones threatened with direct discrimination, after having suffered indirectly from the discrimination against their parents.

Other objections have been raised against the class approach to compensation. How much black blood is necessary for one to be considered black and therefore eligible to belong to the class of those to get recompense? How much American Indian blood, or Mexican blood, and so on, is necessary? This is not an insuperable obstacle, because the number of borderline cases may be small in proportion to the number of clear cases. Yet it does raise some problems. Are those who have succeeded, despite discrimination, to receive compensation? There are, of course successful and prosperous blacks and women. Some are in the professions; some are in business. Some were born in middle-class communities; some were born well-to-do. Some were born in the slums and worked their way up the ladder to success, however *success* is defined. Their children may not have suffered discrimination. Should they be recompensed? Many women now in college have lived their lives during the period of the rise of the women's movement. They have not been discriminated against in school. They frequently come from families supported by their fathers. If their fathers are white, they probably benefited from the discrimination against blacks and women, which aided their fathers' success. Should these young women be compensated for discrimination?

The class approach to discrimination and recompense suffers from many forms of inequity. One assumption is that without discrimination no white male would have been successful in the competition of the marketplace. This seems unlikely. Further, it assumes that all white males somehow make up a class that can and should be penalized. Discrimination, however, was practiced by those now at the senior levels, not by those who will suffer the cost of reparation. In our earlier discussion of responsibility, we saw that, for someone to be responsible, and to be properly censurable and punished, a causal connection is necessary. But those being punished in the class approach to discrimination are not those who are causally responsible for discrimination; and those who benefited most are not those who will suffer the major effects of this new discrimination.

The conclusion to which we are reluctantly brought is that the class approach to discrimination and compensation itself involves discrimination, produces harm to those who did not cause it, does not solve the social problems of discrimination, and is immoral. Yet we saw that the individual approach is not sufficiently extensive, and that it ignores many who still suffer indirectly from the discrimination practiced against their parents. Is there any way to satisfy the demands of compensatory justice without continuing discrimination in another form—frequently called *reverse discrimination?*

We suggest four answers. First, the problem is not simply one of individuals, classes, or groups; the problem involves all members of society. Past discrimination was a result of social structures; therefore, these have to be changed, and some beneficial structures must be built that give at least some compensation for those still suffering from the effects of discrimination. Second, in an attempt to change existing conditions, the government has mandated equal employment opportunity for all. Although morally proper, some claim it is not enough. Third, affirmative action can be taken to insure that members of those groups previously discriminated against are not further ignored by the system. Fourth, preferential hiring can be implemented to achieve affirmative-action goals. Each of these deserves further discussion.

Changing Social Structures

Discrimination against women, blacks, and other minority groups was not necessarily done consciously or with personally malicious intentions. It was an effect of certain ways of doing business, certain patterns of thinking and acting, and certain social structures. These must be changed. A necessary first step has been the raising of the consciousness of the ordinary citizen and of those people holding responsible positions in business. Discrimination is now illegal. But legislation cannot change people's attitudes and their old habits. These have been changing slowly, under constant pressure from both minority associations and women's groups, as well as from individuals who push for their rights, sue when appropriate, and jostle those who tend to revert to old habits.

People who, as individuals, have been discriminated against can bargain or sue for compensation; but those who suffer the effects of discrimination in a less specific manner cannot. In many ways, society as a whole is to blame for past discrimination. So society should bear the burden of compensation when direct individual reparation by a business or individual is not available. Though the claim is plausible, its implementation raises questions. For instance, what is to count as evidence of suffering from past discrimination, either directly or indirectly? Similarly, what is to count as evidence of having profited, directly or indirectly, from past discrimination? Who should bear the cost of compensation? What form should the compensation take? There are no easy answers to these questions, but we suggest some approaches.

No specific condition is evidence of past discrimination: neither poverty, nor a poor education, nor failure to get and keep a good job, however *good job* is defined. All of these are often the result of discrimination. But other causes also contribute to poverty, poor education, and failure to get a job of one's choosing. From a social point of view, need we distinguish between the help given to the poor or to the poorly educated, which is called compensation, and the help we give to the poor and the poorly educated simply because they are poor and poorly educated? There is little to gain in attempting to make such fine distinctions. If one of the results of racial discrimination is poverty and poor schooling, then justice requires that attempts be made to get rid of poverty and to improve schooling. But it is also appropriate for society to do these things for all the poor and the poorly educated. Society should make available the opportunities for people to rise above the poverty level, to take part in the mainstream of social activity if they wish, and to have available the schooling and more advanced educational opportunities that allow them to better themselves and to compete on an equal footing with others.

The attempts to make black schools equal to white schools have not been successful. Obviously, more must be done in this regard. The problem of how to achieve the desired end of equal educational opportunities for all has not been satisfactorily solved. It is a problem that requires more work, thought, experimentation, and money. Society should supply all of these in greater quantity than it has thus far.

Improving education for blacks by improving their schools is a slow approach. It will take several generations of people to produce any real effect. We first have to provide good, basic schooling at the elementary level, then improve the junior high and high school levels, so that blacks can compete on the college level and then go on to professional schools. The process is obviously long and drawn-out. What of the blacks and other minority members who have had poor elementary school training and are now in high school, or those who have had poor high school training and are having difficulty in college? Thus far, the best that can be done is to provide remedial help wherever possible. Those who earn engineering degrees or medical degrees must have mastered the requisite knowledge. They are not passed through because they are the victims of past discrimination, nor do many advocate that they should be. No one would want to consult a doctor who was not properly trained, nor entrust his life to a building designed or built by an incompetent engineer.

Industry, however, can provide special training, financed by business as well as by public funds. Business can appropriately be asked to take the lead in such programs, and to make some contribution to them, for two reasons: because businesses in the past have practiced discrimination, and because businesses, once they hire them, will benefit by the training they give such people. Government can appropriately be asked to contribute because such programs represent society's effort to make restitution for past social injustice.

The situation with respect to women is in some ways easier and in some ways more difficult, because it is more subtle. It is easier because at least white women have in recent years gained access to as good schools as men, and have had the opportunity to receive adequate education for a variety of jobs and professions. They have been discriminated against, however, in the hiring process and in the promotion process. But these are both remediable, and important first steps have been taken. Obviously, however, not many women have made it to the top of their professions and firms, considering the number of women in them. Proportional representation at the top takes time; women have to compete with men, and have had the opportunity to do so for too short a time. Those impatient with this approach want more women at the top, now. Those with more patience claim that promoting women to the "level of their incompetence" too soon will not help but hinder the cause of women in general. There are admittedly still too many barriers to and at the top, which must come down, and which will come down with time and with steady pressure.

On the other hand, the situation of women is more difficult than for blacks and minorities because women are a majority. Some of them feel they are oppressed by language, which gives dominance to men, and by culture, which stereotypes them and forces them into certain roles. There is less agreement about whether there is such discrimination and oppression of women by men. Nor is it a matter of males against females on these issues; a significant number of women are unsympathetic to the radical position of the women's movement, but there are men who sympathize with it. The social problem of stereotyping women and men in textbooks, in the media, and in business has been persuasively raised. Some change has been made; however, less of a change has been made than many think is appropriate. But change does continue, and society is surely, if slowly, moving in the direction of greater equality of treatment for women.

Racial, sexual, religious, and other kinds of discrimination have always been immoral. Discrimination is now illegal in many areas, and is under attack in areas that are beyond the reach of the law. We must still provide equal access to all, making up for past discrimination by improved schooling for those who have suffered from poor schooling, improved training for those who have not had access to training, and improved chances for advancement through affirmative action and preferential hiring. Changes in our social structures are essential.

What we have not suggested is that either businesses or individual white males be directly penalized unless they can be identified as perpetrators or direct beneficiaries of specific discrimination in the past. There are some who claim this permits the guilty, or at least those who have benefited from discrimination, to remain without censure or penalty. However, just because a white male has been successful in business, we cannot know whether his success is owing to discrimination. Presumably, if there had been no discrimination, some white males would be successful. Unless we have evidence to determine which are which, we do some an injustice by condemning or seeking retribution from all. One solution may be for society to appropriately tax all people who do well financially, in order to help those who need financial assistance. Society taxes businesses for the social good. Such taxation can be defended as justifiable, even though we cannot say exactly which company benefited from discrimination, to what precise extent it benefited, which company practiced it, to what extent, and whether wittingly or unwittingly.

Equal Employment Opportunity

Since 1963, the United States Congress has passed a series of laws that attempt to implement the right of each person to equal treatment with respect to employment. The Equal Pay Act of 1963 guarantees the right to equal pay for equal work, and is aimed especially at wage discrimination against women. In 1964 a Civil Rights Act was passed, and was amended in 1972. It prohibits all forms of discrimination based on race, color, sex, religion, or national origin. The most important section of the Act, known as Title VII, prohibits discrimination in employment. It applies to all employers, both public and private, with fifteen or more employees. The purpose of the Act is to target the major employers. Non-job-related discrimination is, of course, morally prohibited no matter how few workers one employs. But the Act's reporting and other requirements are onerous enough to impose unreasonable cost on small businesses that employ only a few people. In 1967 the Age Discrimination in Employment Act was passed (amended in 1978). In particular, it protects those between the ages of 40 and 70 from discrimination because of age. All of these acts are enforced through the Equal Employment Opportunity Commission (EEOC). In addition, there have been several acts and Executive Orders that regulate government contractors and subcontractors, and that require equal opportunities for the handicapped, disabled veterans, and veterans of the Viet Nam War.

Taken together, these form a solid basis for implementing equal opportunity. But laws alone cannot in fact extend equal opportunity to all. The laws provide an incentive not to discriminate, and they specifically provide legal recourse for those who suffer discrimination in employment. But as with any legal procedure, filing charges requires time and energy, and the victims of discrimination are frequently loath to pursue the matter, especially if another job is available.

Equal Employment Opportunity (EEO) places certain responsibilities on employers of fifteen or more people, and these begin with the specification of a job requirement. In making employment decisions, employers are to consider only job-related criteria. Sex and race are not job-related criteria for the vast majority of jobs. One result of EEO has been to prohibit the stereotyping of jobs. Before the EEO laws, it was common practice to list jobs in the newspaper under either "male" or "female." It was expected and accepted, for instance, that a secretarial job would be listed in the "female" column, and a truck driver's job would be listed in the "male" column. This is no longer allowed or done. Although most truck drivers are still males and most secretaries are females, a company can no longer advertise its positions in this way, nor should it consider applicants on the basis of sex. Males can be secretaries as well as females, and females can be truck drivers as well as males. There is nothing in the nature of either job that requires one to be of a certain sex. Hence, sex is a non-job-related characteristic for both jobs—as well as for most others.

The EEO laws require an employer to give greater care to writing the job description for a position than many employers did prior to the laws. The descriptions should state the actual qualifications needed for the job. Only if the job description is clearly and accurately written can prospective employees know if they are qualified, and only if the description is clear and accurate can employers both make and defend unbiased judgments concerning who the best applicant is.

Once a clear and accurate job description has been drawn up, EEO laws preclude the asking of non-job-related questions on application forms and during interviews. The list is not exhaustive. But the types of questions that should not be asked include age, marital status, race, religion, sex, plans to have children, and arrest (as opposed to relevant conviction) record. Of course, some non-job-related characteristics, such as sex and race, may become immediately apparent in an interview. But they should not be the basis for the final decisions of whom to hire.

Laws can, however, only go so far. If someone refuses, without saying so, to hire women and blacks, the laws do not force them to do so. More is required than simply equal opportunity laws, and this is part of the purpose of affirmative action and some Executive Orders.

From a moral point of view, equal opportunity is a moral right of all people. It is built into the two principles of justice developed by John Rawls. But equal opportunity has several dimensions, and equal employment opportunity is only one of them. Although people now have the legally guaranteed right to equal consideration for a job regardless of race, sex, and national origin, applicants must be qualified for the jobs in order to compete for them. Is there equal opportunity to get the education, training, and experience that jobs require? We certainly cannot assume that each person has the equal opportunity to develop his or her talents to an equal extent. Children raised in a ghetto have many fewer opportunities for development than do children in affluent communities. Sex stereotyping still persists in many schools, where girls are subtly led into some courses and boys into others. Because the schools of our country are not equal, there are differences in the quality of education that children receive. There are also native differences in human beings: some are more intelligent than others, some are stronger than others, some are more energetic. Family also makes a difference. Some families are nurturing and help children develop, providing them with values and support which sustain them throughout life. Others provide little support, encouragement, or positive values. The law does not take upon itself the remedying of all these differences—nor can it. Does morality demand that equal opportunity take all these differences into account, and that those who have greater advantage in the natural lottery of talents be somehow handicapped so as to make everyone equal? Some people believe so. But that is not demanded by law, nor is it clearly a moral demand.

The demands for equal opportunity have as their aim overcoming discriminatory practices. However, they do not do anything to overcome the disadvantages of people who have been discriminated against in the past. The network of information concerning job availability, for instance, was developed in such a way that minorities and women were ignored. In order to make up for such subtle and indirect discrimination, many believed that postive, affirmative action had to be taken. The result has been a program of affirmative action, some aspects of which are mandated and implemented by Executive Orders and government regulations.

Affirmative Action

The promise on the part of businesses not to engage in discrimination is not enough to offset the effects of past discrimination. Nor is it enough for them simply to refrain from discrimination. An active rather than a passive approach is required. An approach mandated by government and advocated by many groups has become known as *affirmative action*. Affirmative action can operate on four levels: (1) active recruiting of women and members of minority groups; (2) equalization of criteria so as not to give preference to any group; (3) adequate training for senior positions; and (4) promotion of women and members of minority groups to senior positions.

Who should practice affirmative action? Those firms and institutions that have a small number of minorities and women in proportion to the general population (or in proportion to the number of persons qualified for the positions in the firm or organization) are prime candidates for affirmative action. Though the small percentage of women and minority members does not prove active discrimination in the past, it presents prima facie evidence of either active discrimination or of cooperation in discriminatory conditions in other parts of society. The head of a scientific laboratory that has no women may plead that he has never had good women candidates. The question then becomes why have so few women gone into science? Is there any reason other than that sexual stereotyping took place from infancy on? But if indeed there is a shortage of women in a certain field of science, it would be ridiculous to demand that, within the next two or three years, all laboratories add women scientists. The patterns that lead to women choosing scientific fields must be established if women are to be represented in adequate numbers in all laboratories.

Business has less excuse for not hiring women. Many women are eligible for executive traineeships, just as they are eligible for other kinds of work in business. The training is neither so long nor so specialized in many cases that it may justify long delays in hiring women in appreciable numbers. Though the same case cannot be made for all minority groups, because of the fact that a smaller percentage of minorities go on to college, growing numbers of minority members are available for managerial jobs. The problem here is why more minority members do not go on to college. What forces of discrimination have to be overcome to change that pattern? It seems justifiable to assume that more members of minority groups would choose college and the kinds of jobs it can lead to if they had the chance.

Active Recruitment

The first level of affirmative action involves the active recruiting of women and members of minority groups. This represents a change from the way many positions were filled in the past. Probably no woman or minority member was ever turned down in competition with a white male because no woman or minority member *knew* of the opening. Openings were filled by the "old boy" network. If one employer had an opening for a good job, he would call up his friends and ask whom they recommended. Or one would write to a few select universities and hire one of their best graduates. Affirmative action requires that jobs be advertised publicly, and not simply by word of mouth to one's friends. It also requires adequate advertising in the outlets commonly used by those interested in certain kinds of positions. If in addition there are special publications that are more likely to be read by women and minority members, then the opening should be listed in these. Affirmative action goes even further, if a reasonable number of women and minority applicants do not apply. In such cases, active soliciting of applications from members of these groups may be in order. Affirmative action, as the name suggests, consists of actively seeking applicants from the previously discriminated against groups rather than waiting for them to take the initiative. This is not too much to demand. Typically, those who have been discriminated against by a certain firm or kind of business tend not to apply there, on the assumption that the future will be like the past. Those who have discriminated, or who give prima facie evidence of having participated in a discriminatory social syndrome, should take the initiative to contact groups whom they have previously ignored. This may be more costly in time and money than the old way of hiring. The extra burden is part of the cost of compensation, and an appropriate form of reparation.

Equalization of Criteria

Discrimination is often subtle. If for a position one chooses criteria in terms of what skills white males are typically good at, one can write a job description that can be filled only by white males. If standard tests are skewed in such a way that white males excel at them, and if these tests are used to screen candidates, then white males will appear as the most qualified. Hence we must ask, are the criteria themselves free of bias and prejudice? Are they fair? Are they relevant to the position advertised?

The fairness of criteria and tests has taken many strange turns. Some claim that blacks should not be discriminated against for using "black English" and for not writing standard English fluently. The argument may hold if the command of standard English is not necessary for the job, but it does not hold true for a job in which a person must write memos, letters, and reports for a range of American readers. This does not constitute prejudice, any more than not hiring a Mexican who cannot write English would constitute prejudice, if the job called for such a skill. More plausible are the claims that many of the objective tests designed to test intelligence or work skills are culturally slanted in favor of middle-class white males. The problem is a difficult one. Research has so far proved to be inconclusive; and even where the result seems to bear out the claim, it is not clear how to devise a test that will be fair to all, or how to weigh the built-in bias in favor of a certain group.

Other sorts of bias are built into job criteria. Frequently, a position calls for a college degree. The reason for demanding a college degree is not because one needs to know a particular subject that was taught in college. Any degree in any major will do. The assumption is that anyone who had the discipline to work for four years for a degree is a better candidate than someone who does not have that sort of background. But in many cases a person who has worked for four years shows as much discipline as the person who attended college, and perhaps even more.

Discrimination that is built into job criteria is difficult to root out by law. Employers are free to draw up their own job descriptions, and no government bureaucrat can presume to know better than an employer what qualifications an employer needs in an employee. But pressure can be brought to bear, by those within a firm as well as by unions and professional associations, to free job descriptions from built-in discrimination.

Adequate Training

We have already noted that many women and minority members have only in the past decade or two entered a large number of firms and institutions. They are still poorly represented in top positions. To remedy this situation, affirmative action has been taken by a number of firms. They have established training internships for women and members of minority groups, in which they become apprenticed to a senior executive, for six months or a year. They learn what executives do and how they do it. The firsthand apprenticeship has served as an effective means of advancing those who have taken part in them. This is affirmative action. Instead of letting the natural process work, this technique has advanced people faster. The internships are usually available only to women or minority members in the firm, those who have been there a certain length of time and who compete for the positions. Does this mean the internships are discriminatory against white males? The answer seems to be clearly no. When vacancies occur for regular positions, white males are eligible for them and compete with women and minority members. The best person for the job should be chosen. Women and minority members need such internships to compete adequately with many white males, who for years had access to special privileges not available to them.

Promotion to Senior Positions

Affirmative action in hiring is not significant unless those hired have a chance to compete fairly for advancement and raises. In these areas, just as in hiring, many firms have had built-in prejudices and bias in favor of white males. Their background assumptions have frequently favored the white male. Managers have usually assumed that married women would not accept a promotion that involved transfer to another city, whereas they have offered such positions to men and later found out whether they would accept the transfer. Managers have assumed that single women would soon get married, or leave to have and raise children. Minority members were stereotyped as blue-collar workers, and racial prejudices about intelligence and ability were prevalent, even when proved false by performance. These and other assumptions were not spelled out in promotion criteria.

Affirmative action in promotion means that higher-level positions are truly open to competent women and minority members. It means searching through personnel records and inviting women and minority members to apply for positions that they may otherwise feel would not be open to them. It involves counseling them (if in fact they are passed over) as to how they can improve their chances for the next opening. Once again, what may seem like favoritism is justifiable, in order to equalize the predispositions in favor of the white male that still linger consciously or unconsciously in the system.

Affirmative action does not mandate quotas. If quotas mean hiring unqualified people, it is difficult to see how they can be morally mandatory. The unqualified will be let go after a short while or will remain at their entry level indefinitely, be passed over by those qualified, and eventually will lose their self-respect. Quotas will not supply role models for women and minority members, nor will it improve their image among managers in general. Quotas, however, can be distinguished from the expectation that firms will make reasonable progress toward hiring members of those groups grossly underrepresented, if the pool of applicants is sufficiently large. Making such progress is a reasonable moral expectation.

Hiring token women and members of minority groups is not affirmative action. Tokenism is not an adequate way to fulfill the moral responsibility to break the pattern and system of discrimination. The moral obligation to take affirmative action goes beyond satisfying the letter of the law.

Preferential Hiring

Preferential hiring is the hiring of one person rather than another, on the basis of some non-job-related characteristic, such as sex, race, or religion. Is preferential hiring a form of discrimination, and is it therefore immoral?

A standard way of seeking someone to fill a job is to announce the opening, with a description indicating the qualifications necessary for the job. The implied agreement between those who advertise job openings and those who apply for them is that the best person for the job will be chosen. The criteria to be used in making the selection are understood to be job-related criteria. It is unfair to use non-job-related criteria, because the use of such criteria breaks the implicit conditions of seeking and granting jobs. It is unfair to raise expectations when hidden criteria are being used, which, if known, would let some people know that they will not be seriously considered for the job. To use criteria other than those stated or those that are obviously job related, is to mislead, deceive, raise false hopes, and violate an implied practice governing hiring. If a person is denied a job solely because of sex, race, or religion, that person is a victim of discrimination.

Is preferential hiring in this category? We can simplify our inquiry by rejecting two interpretations immediately. One might claim that preferential hiring is not a form of discrimination because it *chooses* someone on the basis of sex, race, or religion rather than *denying* someone a position for these reasons. The distinction, however, will not stand up to scrutiny. If a white male is hired because he is white and a black male is not hired, and we are told that the black male was not discriminated against, the white male was simply preferred *because* of the color of his skin, we would certainly call the choice one of racial discrimination.

In the second interpretation, one might claim that it is permissible to use preferential hiring if the announcement indicates that preference will be given to women or minority members. This, the claim goes, would indicate the rules of the game, would not deceive, and hence would be morally permitted. Consider, however, an ad for a job that included these words: "Women and minority members need not apply." Or an ad that indicated preference would be given to white males, even though one need not be a white male to do the job described. Surely we would say that such ads were discriminatory, as would be the practice. The same can be said of the reverse situation—when preference is given to women or minorities. If employers use non-job-related criteria, such as sex, race, or religion to hire people, they discriminate, whether they announce openly that they are or whether they do so without making it public.

To clarify the moral status of preferential hiring, consider the following job announcement with respect to each of the situations listed:

WANTED:
Computer programmer. Must have knowledge of Fortran and Cobol, plus at least two years programming experience. Salary: open, depending on experience. An equal opportunity employer. Call 938–7625.

SITUATION 1
Sally Hanson and Tom Byers both apply for the job. Sally knows Fortran but does not know the program language, Cobol. She has had only one year of experience as a programmer. She applies, figuring she has nothing to lose. Tom knows Fortran and Cobol, and has three years of experience as a programmer.
(a) Tom gets the job. He is the more qualified of the two.
(b) Sally gets the job. The employer needs to add women to his work force, to meet affirmative-action goals.

SITUATION 2
Sue Jones and John Green apply for the job. Sue fulfills all the listed requirements. John knows Fortran and Cobol but has only one year of programming experience.
(a) Sue gets the job. She is the more qualified of the two.
(b) John gets the job. The employer prefers to hire males.

SITUATION 3
Sandra Hopkins and Henry Thompson apply for the job. Both Sandra and Henry know Fortran and Cobol, and both have had two years of programming experience.

(a) Sandra gets the job. The employer wants to add women to his work force, to meet affirmative-action goals.
(b) Henry gets the job. Henry is a veteran, and the employer gives extra credit to veterans.
(c) Henry gets the job. The employer prefers to hire males.

SITUATION 4

Sarah Hall and Peter Brock apply for the job. Sarah knows Fortran and Cobol, and has had two years of programming experience. Her former employers stated that she was only adequate on the job. Peter is a computer whiz. He knows Fortran, Cobol, and three other computer languages. He has had four years of programming experience, and is rated as outstanding by his past employers.

(a) Sarah gets the job. The employer wants to add women to his work force, to meet affirmative-action goals.
(b) Peter gets the job. Regarding job experience, he is the better of the two applicants.

In Situation 1, it is appropriate that Tom rather than Sally get the job because he has the specified qualifications, which she does not have. If Sally gets the job because she is a woman, and the employer wishes to meet his affirmative-action goals, then the employer has achieved his purpose in a way that does an injustice to Tom. If the qualifications listed are not the qualifications required for the job, and if the employer is going to consider someone with lesser qualifications, if that someone is female, then he should write the job description differently.

Clearly, if the situation with respect to qualifications were reversed, as they are in Situation 2, we feel that it is inappropriate for John to be hired rather than Sue. Sue has all the stated qualifications. John has only one year of experience. The reason the employer gives, in Situation 2(b), is that he prefers to hire males. Hiring John, who does not have the stipulated qualifications, rather than Sue, who does, is a classic case of discrimination. The employer's only criterion for choosing John over Sue is that John is male. Is there a difference between Situation 2(b) and 1(b)? In both cases, a person who does *not* meet the stated qualifications for the job is chosen over a person of the other sex who *does* meet the qualifications. In both cases, the person is chosen on the basis of sex, a non-job-related characteristic. The difference in the two cases is that in 2(b) the reason is personal preference, and in 1(b) it is a desire to fulfill an affirmative-action goal, with or without personal preference for hiring women. Does achievement of the goal outweigh the injustice done to Tom?

In order to answer this we might try a utilitarian approach to the question. Consider the following rule: Managers should hire women who do not meet stated job requirements, rather than men who do, when the choice is between two such people and when the firm should make progress toward fulfilling affirmative-action goals. If we calculate the good and bad effects of the rule on all concerned, we can decide whether the practice is morally justifiable.

The good effect for Sally, at least initially, is that she gets the job. The bad effect for Tom is that he does not get the job. Would the results be equal if Tom got the job rather than Sally? The answer is no. If Tom got the job rather than Sally, Sally would not feel that an injustice had been done, because she knew she did not have the stated qualifications. Tom, however, would feel that an injustice had been done to him because, despite his qualifications, he did not get the job and someone unqualified did. Therefore, just by considering the two people directly affected in the first instance, more good overall would be done by hiring Tom than by hiring Sally.

Next, consider what happens after the person hired is on the job. If the job actually requires knowledge of Cobol, Sally will not be able to perform that portion of her job. She could, of course, learn it. But this takes so much time that, if it were really necessary for the job, she might be fired for lacking this knowledge, before she would have had time to learn it. This would not happen if Tom were hired.

How does the practice affect the company? Hiring Sally helps the company achieve its affirmative-action goal; but if she cannot perform adequately in the job, her performance hurts the firm. Hiring Tom helps the firm do its work but does not help it achieve its affirmative-action goal. What is the effect on the other workers? If they feel that Sally was hired because of affirmative action, she will probably not be treated well, or thought well of, by her fellow workers. This will have an adverse effect on Sally. And because she cannot do what the job calls for, the other workers are likely to resent her being hired. They would have no such feelings toward Tom.

The practice of hiring women who do not meet the stated requirements rather than hiring men who do, results in more harm than good. Hence it is immoral and should not be adopted as a practice.

In the analysis, certain assumptions were made, one of them being that Sally could not learn Cobol quickly enough to be able to carry out her job well. If she could learn Cobol quickly enough, then the job description was not an accurate statement of the qualifications needed for the position. The real qualifications would then be knowledge of Fortran and one year experience as a programmer, together with the ability to learn Cobol quickly. But if those were the real qualifications needed, we would have an entirely different situation, the kind described in Situations 3 and 4.

In Situation 3, both Sandra and Henry have all the required qualifications. Assuming that those are the only qualifications needed for the job, both candidates are equally qualified. Hence, there is no job-related criterion on the basis of which the employer can choose one of them rather than another. He could with justice make his decision in a random way, for instance, by tossing a coin. Situation 3(c) is puzzling. Is this an instance of discrimination? The employer chooses Henry only because Henry is a male. Is it proper for him to do so when he could choose either of them, indiscriminately, by tossing a coin? Is it wrong to choose one of them because of sex when it is right to choose either of them? The answer is yes. To choose a male applicant rather than an equally qualified female applicant, simply on the basis of sex, is discriminatory. It would be better to choose between them by the toss of a coin rather than on the basis of sex, because the toss of the coin gives them each an equal chance at the job.

What of situations 3(a) and 3(b)? In each case the employer uses a criterion other than job-related qualifications. Is this fair? The answer is yes. But this answer requires some defense. Situation 3(a) is a classic case of justifiable preferential hiring. It is justifiable because in hiring Sandra rather than Henry, the employer is able to meet another need of his firm, namely, making progress toward its affirmative-action goal. The need of the firm is not identical with a job-related qualification. But, in a broad way, it is an employment-related criterion; it does not spring from a prejudice. It does no injustice to Henry, because he is not being turned down in favor of someone unqualified. The job could properly go to either of them. If an employer can serve affirmative-action goals by hiring a qualified woman over an equally qualified man, this is a step, even if a small one, in the direction of making up for past discrimination by the firm.

Government jobs allow a certain amount of credit to an applicant who has served in the armed forces and has been honorably discharged. This is considered both a reward for past service to the government and to the country, and perhaps an incentive to others to join the armed forces. Such service credit is not inappropriate in private employment, though it is not required by law. By giving military-service credit, the employer helps the country achieve certain goals. But the fact that the company gives such credit should be made known in advance. It should not be used as a criterion after the fact. If the policy is to give government-service credit, then it should be given consistently. If, in Situation 3(b), giving Henry credit for military service is part of the firm's policy, it is justifiable. If giving Henry credit for military service is just a device used to decide this case, then it is an inappropriate device. If the firm has the policy of giving military-service credit, the problem then becomes how one is to balance military-service credit against affirmative-action goals. Both policies are governmentally and socially approved. Which takes precedence is not clear, and to decide it requires more information. For instance, how close to meeting its affirmative-action goal is the firm? How much weight does it give for military service? However the manager finally makes that decision, he should be able to defend it, giving reasons for his weighting of the various factors. If they are equally weighted, then we are back to tossing a coin.

Situation 4 demonstrates another aspect of preferential hiring. In 4(a), Sarah gets the job. In 4(b), Peter gets the job. Both outcomes are morally justifiable. Preferential hiring is morally justifiable to achieve affirmative-action goals and to make up for past discrimination. But so long as a firm makes reasonable progress toward affirmative-action goals, it is not required in any specific case to hire a woman or a minority member rather than a white male. As in 4(a), the company may properly decide to hire Sarah. She satisfies the job qualifications. The qualifications, we shall assume, are appropriate to the job she will fill. She will be able to handle the job and will in no way harm the company. Someone else has stronger credentials in the field, but this does not make her any less qualified for the job. By hiring her, the company gets a qualified person and helps achieve its affirmative-action goal, which is an employment-related criterion.

In 4(b), the company hires an excellently qualified worker. He has more skills than the job requires. Even discounting his additional knowledge, his past ratings are higher than Sarah's. As far as job qualifications go, he can be shown to be the stronger candidate, on the basis of job-related qualities. The firm cannot be blamed for choosing him, and no injustice is done to Sarah if he is chosen. No injustice is done to him, however, if Sarah is chosen.

We can generalize from our discussion of these varied situations.

1. Affirmative action does not justify hiring unqualified women or minority members in preference to qualified white males.
2. Qualified women and minority members can morally be given preference, on the basis of sex or race, over equally qualified white males, in order to achieve affirmative-action goals.
3. Qualified women and minority members can morally be given preference over better-qualified white males, in order to achieve affirmative-action goals.
4. Preferential hiring is not mandatory in any given case, though overall, a firm must make adequate progress toward achieving affirmative-action goals.

These generalizations can be applied to promotion as well as to initial hiring. Firing raises a special problem. Many companies use the rule: "last on, first off." Unions generally support this rule and often agree to it in contracts. The rule protects seniority rights. Senior people, under this rule, have more job security than junior people. Older people usually have a harder time finding a new job than do younger people. Older people have put down roots, which are more difficult to pull up than newly planted roots. Older people usually earn more than beginners, and therefore may be prime candidates for a firm that wants to save as much as possible by laying people off during a recession. This is why unions favor the rule. Supporters of the rule argue, moreover, that it does no injustice to the young, because in the natural course of events the young grow older. What they lose in their youth they gain in their older age.

The rule is compatible with the foregoing four principles, when properly modified to apply to firing instead of hiring. Where two workers—for instance, a woman and a man—have comparable jobs, have worked the same amount of time, and have performed equally well in their jobs, then the woman can be given preference, in order to help the firm achieve affirmative-action goals. But because affirmative action and preferential hiring are of recent vintage, many of the people most vulnerable to layoff under the seniority system are those hired under affirmative-action guidelines. Hence, a period of recession and the resulting layoffs tend to undo most of the good done by affirmative-action programs. Is the seniority rule sacrosanct? Or would more good be done by violating it and giving preference to achieving affirmative-action goals? (This would mean keeping on junior women and minority members and laying off white males senior to them.) An argument has not yet been mounted to support a breach of seniority rules in favor of affirmative action, at least, none that is adequate to convince the Supreme Court, union leaders, or many members of the general public.

The Supreme Court has moved very slowly and carefully in deciding cases that involve reverse discrimination. It has chosen to rule narrowly rather than broadly in such cases as Bakke, De Funis, and Weber. The issue, however, is amenable to moral analysis and argument.

Three Cases: Bakke, Weber, and Stotts

Three cases stand out as landmark decisions by the Supreme Court with respect to issues of affirmative action and reverse discrimination. The cases were all decided on legal grounds. But the decisions have been argued in moral terms as well. Each of the cases, moreover, has reflected public sentiment and each has influenced public sentiment with respect to these issues. The Bakke case set limits on reverse discrimination. The Weber case defended affirmative action. The Stotts case gives preference to seniority over affirmative action. No one believes that special preference should be given to any group, whether minority or majority, indefinitely. The ideal is for all people, regardless of race, sex, or national origin, to have truly equal opportunity and freedom, and to be allowed to develop as fully as possible. Those who believe that the Stotts decision marks the beginning of the end of affirmative action are probably overreacting to the decision. But at some time in the future, the need for affirmative action and preferential hiring will no longer exist, and at that time these programs will no longer be necessary. But the process will require time, and the dismantling of the programs will undoubtedly occur slowly.

The Bakke Case

In the case of *Bakke* v. *Regents of the University of California*, Allan Bakke applied for admission to the Medical School at the University of California at Davis. The University had set aside sixteen places for minority students out of a class of one hundred. Minority students could request to be considered by a separate admissions committee, which applied less stringent admission criteria than the regular admissions committee. Mr. Bakke, a white male, applied for admission to the Medical School twice, and was twice rejected. Yet his grade-point average, his Medical College Admission Test (MSAT) scores, and his overall "benchmark" rating by the University were considerably higher than those of some of the minority students who were admitted.

Bakke sued for admission, and won. The court decision was upheld by the Supreme Court of the State of California. The United States Supreme Court, on June 28, 1978, ruled that Bakke had been unlawfully denied admission, and that race could be considered in admissions criteria. Exactly how that was to be done was not clear. But we can look at the moral issues involved nonetheless.

The Supreme Court of California indicated that either increasing the number of people admitted in order to allow minorities, or the admission of all disadvantaged persons, regardless of race, on some special criteria, would be legally acceptable. From a moral point of view, either of these alternatives would also be morally acceptable. For what was unfair in the Bakke situation was depriving Bakke, simply on the basis of his race, a chance to gain admission to medical school on an equal footing with all other applicants. If we agree that each person has a right to an equal opportunity for such admission, then having a standard based on race is unfair.

The counter arguments are that the standard admission procedure is skewed in favor of whites because of the nature of the MSAT, that whites have access to better colleges; and that blacks have restricted opportunity in many areas of society. But the proper response to this argument is to change the criteria so that it is fair for all, rather than change it only for certain applicants from minority races. What was unfair at the Davis Medical School was not the changing of the rules to encourage more minority candidates to apply, but the way the rules were changed.

The question of quotas was also at issue in the Bakke case. There was not simply affirmative action to encourage more minorities to apply, or a change in the requirements so they would be fair to all. There was a quota—a certain number of places which were set aside for minority students. If that number had been added to the one hundred places originally available, then there would be less basis for charging injustice, although there might still be some. But because the sixteen places were subtracted from the original one hundred, Bakke legitimately claimed an injustice had been done to him; his chances were lessened because of his race.

Quotas, as we have already seen, cannot be morally defended as a means of achieving racial balance; they cannot remedy the injustice of past discrimination. What the Bakke case helped to underline was the need for policies that are fair to all, yet geared, in some affirmative fashion, to help right the wrongs of past discrimination. The same is true in the area of employment. Finding such policies requires imagination and ingenuity. It requires, especially, a readiness to rethink one's procedures objectively and honestly, and a willingness to change them as necessary so they are truly fair.

The Weber Case

Justice William J. Brennan, Jr. wrote the majority decision in the case of *United Steelworkers of America* v. *Brian F. Weber et al.* Brian Weber, a member of the United Steelworkers Union and an employee of Kaiser Aluminum & Chemical

Corporation, complained that he was being treated unfairly as a result of an affirmative-action plan that Kaiser and the Union had agreed upon. The Kaiser plant was in Gramercy, Louisiana. Until 1974, Kaiser hired as craft workers for the plant only persons who had prior craft experience. This almost precluded blacks from such positions, because they had been excluded from the craft union. Prior to 1974, only five out of 273 (1.83 percent) of the skilled craft workers at Gramercy were black. Because 39 percent of the work force at Gramercy was black, there was basis for at least a prima facie claim of past discrimination, either in the Union or in the plant, or both. As a result of a collective-bargaining agreement between the Union and Kaiser, an affirmative-action plan was adopted at fifteen plants—including the Gramercy plant—and black hiring goals for craft positions were set. In the Gramercy plant, the goal was eventually to have 39 percent of the skilled craft positions filled by blacks. In order to reach this goal, an on-the-job training program was set up to teach craft skills to nonskilled workers. The program was open to both whites and blacks. At least 50 percent of the openings were to be reserved for black workers. In the choice of both whites and blacks, selection was based on seniority.

In the first year of the program at Gramercy, thirteen workers were chosen for the program—six whites and seven blacks. The most junior black selected had less seniority than several of the white applicants who were rejected. On behalf of himself and the other rejected whites with more seniority than the last-appointed black, Weber claimed that he and the others had been unjustly discriminated against. The District Court decided in favor of Weber; the Fifth Court of Appeals for the Fifth Circuit upheld the decision; but the Supreme Court overturned it. The Court acted on the legal aspects of the case. We shall consider the moral aspects.

Was the setting up of the program by Kaiser and the United Steelworkers Union morally justifiable? The program was part of a collective-bargaining agreement, and so both management and labor were represented. The program was not one that was established unilaterally by Kaiser. Moreover, both Kaiser and the United Steelworkers Union were, at least in the Gramercy situation, prima facie guilty of past discrimination, as reflected in the small number of blacks among their skilled workers. Clearly, the policies of both organizations had to change. But simply changing the policies would not be enough, because the pool of black skilled craft workers was extremely small, and there was no clear way for that number to increase. The policy adopted was one of affirmative action. It had as its aim the training of workers already employed at Kaiser; it did not bring workers in from the outside. The benefit of such a program was that it not only helped increase the percentage of blacks in the skilled positions, but it also gave those black workers—who had possibly been discriminated against by the system—a chance to improve their position. The intent of the program was morally justified. Were the details? Weber did not claim that the Union and Kaiser did not have the right to establish a program. He argued that the program established was unfair to him and others. Was it?

Remember that if there had not been the need for affirmative action with respect to blacks at the plant, the new training program would not have been established. When there was no such program, no one, including Weber, could claim that he had a right to one. Moreover, as a result of the affirmative-action program, whites, who did not need any special program to gain entrance into the Union and the craft positions, were also to be given the opportunity for special training. Hence, white workers could not argue that as a class they were being discriminated against. Furthermore, this training program was just that—a training program. No whites were displaced from their jobs; no blacks were given jobs automatically because of the training program. Presumably, when a position had to be filled, it would be filled with a qualified applicant. The training program supplied blacks as well as whites to the pool from which craft positions could be filled. So far, there seems to be no injustice for anyone to complain about.

The complaint of Weber was not that whites as a class had been discriminated against, but that a small class of whites, namely those with more seniority than the last black accepted into the program, had been discriminated against. One must assume that, because the agreement specified that at least 50 percent of the trainees were to be black, if there had been only twelve trainees—six whites and six blacks—there would have been no complaint. The basis for the complaint was that in choosing the thirteenth trainee, seniority did not count. But it is not at all clear why it should have counted. If seven whites had been chosen, and only six blacks, then at least 50 percent of the trainees would not have been black. This would have violated one of the conditions of the program. Weber and the others seem to have claimed that the seniority rule was to take precedence over the 50 percent rule; that if there was to be a 50 percent rule, and an odd number of trainees were to be chosen, it was unfair that the rule should read, "at least 50 percent blacks" rather than simply "50 percent blacks," with the last person of an uneven number being either black or white, depending on seniority.

Now, if this is the issue, what argument can be given that the latter is the only fair way for the agreement to have been written? As we saw, prior to its being formed, no one had a right to a training program, and it was formed for affirmative-action purposes. Hence it does not seem unreasonable that the agreement should call for at least 50 percent blacks. This would allow for seniority to count in favor of blacks, of course, and in any given training group there might be more blacks than whites if more blacks with more seniority applied than did whites. But whites were not excluded.

In the Supreme Court decision, Justice Brennan concluded that, from a legal point of view, Title VII precludes requiring preferential treatment because of race, but it does not preclude permitting voluntary affirmative-action programs to correct racial imbalance. Chief Justice Burger, dissenting, said that as a member of Congress he would be inclined to vote for an amendment to Title VII, permitting such a program, but that under the law as written, the program was illegal. They differ, therefore, over the law and its application.

But those Justices who affirmed the program and those who disagreed seemed to support the program as morally justifiable.

The Stotts Case

The *Firefighters* v. *Stotts* case involved black firefighters in Memphis, Tennessee, who were laid off prior to whites with more seniority. Carl Stotts was a black District Fire Chief in Memphis. In 1977, the black firefighters filed a class-action suit charging the Memphis Fire Department with hiring and promotion discrimination. In 1980, the city and the black firefighters agreed on an affirmative-action plan, which was approved by a federal judge. Under the plan, the percentage of blacks rose from 4 percent to 11.5 percent. When financial difficulties forced the City of Memphis, in May 1981, to lay off firefighters, it followed the seniority rules negotiated with the Union. The last on were the first off. The blacks protested, and the federal district court mandated that the same percentage of blacks be kept in the department. As a result, seventy-two whites with seniority were laid off or demoted, but only eight blacks.

The city of Memphis and the Union appealed the ruling. A federal appeals court upheld the ruling. The U.S. Supreme Court overturned the lower court, indicating that bona fide seniority systems were protected by Title VII of the 1964 Civil Rights Act; that class-action suits could not be filed for such cases; and that only individuals who can prove they are victims of discrimination can sue for protection under affirmative action. Once again, the legal grounds need not concern us. Is the last-on-first-off rule morally justifiable?

The argument against the rule is that the blacks were hired under affirmative-action programs. If the last hired were the first fired, then the good accomplished by the affirmative-action plans would be defeated. If it was appropriate for blacks to be hired in preference to whites, providing both were qualified for the job, then it should be right to keep blacks on in preference to whites, providing both are qualified. Seniority refers to length of time on the job. But people with different amounts of seniority may do essentially the same jobs and be equally qualified. If one must terminate people, to be in accord with affirmative action plans (which are allowed, encouraged, and sometimes mandated by government), one should not terminate only on the basis of seniority if goals of racial balance will be adversely affected. The attainment of such goals has at least as much social and moral merit as seniority. To use only seniority rules as a basis for determining who will be laid off is to institute a revolving-door policy for women and minorities. They will be hired, only to be fired. In the interim, firms will claim to be exercising affirmative action, but in fact, little will change in the composition of the permanent work force in these firms. The argument seems reasonable. But it did not persuade the Supreme Court.

The Court held that seniority takes precedence over affirmative action, and that only individuals who have been the victims of direct discrimination have the right to claim preferential treatment. A moral argument in support of this decision is that both minorities and white males earn seniority. The seniority principle is blind when it comes to race, sex, or any other characteristic. Using this principle is therefore fair, because it allows all to compete equally. It may, in some cases, interfere with the progress made toward affirmative-action goals. It does not necessarily do so, and will do so even less as more and more women and minorities find positions in companies in which they were previously underrepresented. Moreover, the seniority system establishes certain *rights* of employees. These cannot be violated even to achieve good ends.

The decision in this case has been called ambiguous, and to some extent it is. In none of the three cases we have considered have there been clear defenses of principle. The Supreme Court has preferred to make narrow rulings rather than clearly endorse or clearly curtail affirmative-action programs. In this way the Court reflects the ambiguity with which affirmative action is greeted by the general population. Although it is clear that past injustice must be rectified, it is also clear that no individual's rights should be violated to achieve racial balance in all areas of the workplace. The attempt to balance the rights of both minorities and of white males has led to excesses on both sides. There is no easy way to achieve the necessary and just balance. Therefore society must keep trying to achieve the balance until the problem eventually recedes because a reasonable approximation to a just situation has been achieved. Until that time arrives, both law and moral reasoning must be constantly invoked to find the best solutions to an extremely difficult problem.

Further Reading

BITTKER, BORIS. *The Case for Black Reparations.* New York: Vintage Books, 1973.

BLACKSTONE, WILLIAM T., and ROBERT HESLEP, eds. *Social Justice and Preferential Treatment.* Athens, Ga.: University of Georgia Press, 1977.

COHEN, MARSHALL, THOMAS NAGEL, and THOMAS SCANLON, eds. *Equality and Preferential Treatment.* Princeton, N.J.: Princeton University Press, 1977.

DAVIDSON, KENNETH M., RUTH B. GINSBURG, and HERMAN H. KAY, eds. *Sex-Based Discrimination: Text, Cases, and Materials.* Minneapolis: West Publishing Company, 1974.

EPSTEIN, E. M., and D. R. Hampton. *Black America and White Business.* Belmont, Calif.: Dickenson Publishing Co., Inc., 1971.

GLAZER, NATHAN. *Affirmative Discrimination.* New York: Basic Books, Inc., 1975.

GOLDMAN, ALAN H. *Justice and Reverse Discrimination.* Princeton, N.J.: Princeton University Press, 1979.

GROSS, BARRY R., ed. *Reverse Discrimination.* Buffalo, N.Y.: Prometheus Books, 1977.

VITERITTI, JOSEPH P. *Bureaucracy and Social Justice: Allocation of Jobs and Services to Minority Groups.* Port Washington, N.Y.: Kennikat Press Corporation, 1979.

THIRTEEN

Marketing, Truth, and Advertising

Once products are made, they must be sold. Marketing covers this process. The process actually begins before production, in order to determine such factors as need, feasibility, cost, projected market share, profit margin, and sales strategy. Some products are produced only when ordered; others are first produced and then sold. The techniques that are used to determine a market and the goods to be sold are frequently complex; the specific means chosen depends on the nature of the product, the potential buyer, the cost, and similar considerations. Some goods are sold primarily by salespersons, others through store displays. Advertising is the major method by which consumer goods are sold. If truth is the major virtue governing advertising, honesty is the major virtue governing marketing. We shall start with a brief look at marketing and then concentrate more fully on advertising.

Marketing

Marketing techniques seek to solve a variety of problems in order to sell the product or service that a company produces or provides. Marketing research attempts to determine customer demand and the most efficient and profitable means by which this demand can be met. Often the desired data are not available or not reliable. There are also competitors, who may possibly be interested in the same market, and their actions and potential actions must also be considered. Although many in the business of marketing and marketing research would like marketing to be or become a science, it falls far short of that. Markets can only rarely be predicted with certainty, and the ability to manipulate markets and market demand is much less than many critics claim. Yet the temptation to try to manipulate markets, to lessen one's chances of failure by illegal or immoral means, is often present. We shall examine just a few of the areas where the temptations to act immorally are significant, and where some practices are morally questionable. These areas are competition, pricing, bidding, and consumer sales.

Competition

We have already seen that competition is part of the free-enterprise system. Competition tends to produce efficiency in the market and benefits the general consumer by resulting in a variety of goods at the best prices. But the competitive market works to the advantage of the buyer only when the competitive process is fair. The government plays a role in trying to keep competition fair. But government regulation is not enough. Unless those engaged in the competitive process operate fairly and honestly, the system itself is undermined. Moral standards have a role to play, and play it daily. But the temptations to violate the standards of honesty and fair competition for one's personal benefit or that of one's firm are also constantly present.

One major way of undermining competition is through the creation of monopolies. If a firm is able to create and maintain a monopoly in any area, then it has no competitive restraints on its prices. It may consequently charge what it wants, so long as there is a market willing to purchase its product or service at the price it sets. But how does a firm gain a monopoly? Several techniques, some of them questionable, are common. One scenario begins with a large producer of a product coming to dominate the field. Frequently, the producer is the best in the field and wins its market share honestly. It then proceeds to either buy up or undercut the competition. Buying up other firms is in itself not immoral. But if the intent is to eliminate competition, then the intent is at least questionable, because such action tends to undermine the market system. Undercutting the competition might be done in several ways. One way is simply to price one's product lower than the competition. If this is possible because a firm is more efficient, more productive, and is able to operate at lower cost, or is satisfied with lower profit margins, the process is fair. It is part of the competitive system and leads to the efficiency the system promises. But a large producer may undercut a smaller competitor by selling products for less than they cost to produce, absorbing the loss for a short time, with the intent of capturing the market. It thus forces the competitor also to sell at a loss or lose its market share. If the smaller competitor is unable to operate at a loss, or to match prices, it will eventually go under. A large corporation can target its areas of competition; it will keep up its profits in one geographical or product area, and use these profits to subsidize its loss in another area, where it wishes to drive out the competition. An alternative to driving out the competition (in the sense of its failing), is to buy up the competing firm just before it fails, at a better price than would have been possible before. Is this morally justifiable? Is it simply part of the competitive market process?

If we admit that monopolies constitute a restraint on the market, which is detrimental to the general public, and are therefore not morally justifiable, then practices done with the intent of producing monopolies are also not morally justifiable. In the United States, takeovers by large companies must often be approved by government to preclude the formation of monopolies. The forcing out of competition by selling products below cost, without taking over the competitors, although not illegal, is at least morally questionable.

A second way of controlling competition is for a small group of producers of a product to collude for their common good. They may agree, for instance, not to compete against one another in certain areas, dividing up the market among them. Or they may agree on the prices to charge—a practice known as *price-fixing*. Such collusion is generally illegal, because it undermines the competitive system to the detriment of the buyer. It is also immoral. The collusion may be done so subtly that it cannot be proven to be collusion. This may preclude legal prosecution, but it does not change the immorality of the action.

The growth of giant corporations has tended to make competition in many areas very costly. The growth of supermarkets, which began in the 1940s, has forced most small grocers and vegetable and fruit markets out of business. The prices the supermarkets were able to charge were lower than those the small operators could charge for equal-quality goods. The large chains were able to eliminate middle men, buy in large quantity at better prices, and, through self-service, reduce the cost of labor. They were also able to operate at a lower profit margin because of their large volume. A consequence was the gradual elimination of most small grocers. This was neither illegal nor immoral, because the chains did not force out the small competitor and then raise their prices to the disadvantage of the consumer; they continued to operate as they had before. Consequently, the small grocer gave way before the more efficient supermarket. Nor has competiton been eliminated. The competition is now between large food chains. The small business cannot compete with them on prices, and to survive they must offer service, credit, or something the large chains do not offer. Some people question the morality of a system that allows competition only among the wealthy, or those able to finance large operations. But so long as the general public benefits from the system, there seems no valid moral objection to it.

The ways in which a company can attempt to stifle competition are numerous. Many are part of the system and are morally justifiable, so long as the aim is not to establish a monopoly. Some involve clearly dishonest practices, and therefore need not be discussed here. Lying, stealing corporate secrets and plans from a competitor, corporate espionage and sabotage, violation of contracts, dumping products on a market, paying bribes and kickbacks, and so on, are dishonest practices that are part of the competitive system. However, they are not an essential part of it; they tend to undermine it, and are not morally justifiable.

Pricing

Pricing is an important part of the marketing process. A producer wishes to sell its product at a profit, and must price its product appropriately in order to do so. The producer must be able to control its costs. But competition, if it is fair, will force the producer to price its product at its true worth. If the price is set too high, the market for it may shrink so that its sales are less than required for it to make a profit. Or it may not be as attractive to a buyer, who can purchase from a competitor a similar product at a lower price. Unless one is in a monopolistic position, setting prices is in part a result of the market, and one's success depends in part on knowing the market conditions.

We shall deal with only two issues in pricing: overpricing, and mark-up and mark-down.

Overpricing is a special issue in marketing. In general, the competitive system should preclude the possibility of overpricing, where this means charging much more than the producer knows the product is worth, thus yielding an excessive profit. There are some who might claim that overpricing is a misnomer, because there is no specific limit of justifiable profit. But this claim assumes that prices are competitive, and they are not always competitive. We have already mentioned the possibility that a producer in a monopolistic position can charge more than it would otherwise be able to do. There are other ways, however, that overpricing can take place. In each case they involve either a monopolistic position, force, or ignorance on the part of the buyer. One of the claims made about merchants in poor areas, ghettos, and slums, for instance, is that they overcharge their customers. They are in effect in a monopolistic position; their customers are not mobile enough to go to other parts of the city to buy, at competitive prices, what they want. They need the goods available at the only source available to them—the local store. The store is thus in a position to charge more than it would otherwise do, to the disadvantage of the consumer. Some store owners in such locations admit that they charge higher prices for goods than stores elsewhere, but they claim that their insurance costs, including rates for fire, robbery, and personal-risk, are higher than elsewhere. These factors, they claim, justify their higher prices. Whether they do depends on the relation of these costs to the increase in the price of the goods they sell.

A second area in which excessive rates arise is in the lending of money. For those unable to borrow money in the conventional, competitive way, loan sharks can charge usurous rates. Although they may claim that they are simply providing a service that people need and cannot find elsewhere, they are in fact taking advantage of the need of others, and usually the transactions cannot be described as fair.

In addition to cases of forced need and no other supplier, ignorance on the part of the buyer often provides the occasion for overpricing. This is possible primarily among poorly educated people, but it is possible even with the well educated. Techniques of overpricing vary. They range from simply charging more for goods than they usually sell for, to charging more than an item is worth, on the assumption that the buyer will think that because it costs more it must be better than a lower-priced competing product. In all these cases, the seller counts on the ignorance of the buyer. To do this is to take advantage of the buyer, and that is not morally justifiable. The practice, in the long run, undermines the system, sows distrust of all products and prices, and fails to treat people with the respect they deserve.

Mark-ups are a specific form of pricing. Instead of simply determining the price at which to sell to wholesalers, a manufacturer may calculate all the mark-ups for all the middlemen and the retailer and set, or suggest, a retail sales price. This price is a guide to the retailer regarding the price at which the item is to be sold. Unless the item is sold at the same price at all outlets, defenders of the practice maintain, the purchaser will be confused as to the real value of the item. For some years, in the United States, the manufacturer's suggested retail price was defended as the fair market price, and attempts were made to declare discounting illegal. But the difference between this practice and price-fixing did not withstand the scrutiny of the courts. Competition has led to discount houses and mail-order dealers, who sell products at lower prices than those at which the same goods can be found in traditional retail stores. The suggested price set by a manufacturer takes into account many things: the mark-ups of the wholesaler, the jobber, and the retailer, as well as the various mark-downs that the retailer may make in the way of end-of-season or other sales. Setting such a price is allowable. But if by eliminating some of the middle markets a seller can reduce the final price on an item and still make a profit, he cannot be prevented from doing so. It remains in the interest of many sellers to sell items at their suggested retail price in order to maintain their profit margins. They may also apply pressure on the producer not to sell the same goods to discount dealers. But if the discount dealer pays the same price to the manufacturer as the regular retailer, the manufacturer frequently has no incentive to yield to the pressure. Although calculating and suggesting a retail sales price are not immoral, trying to enforce such a price stifles competition and is not in the best interest of the consumer. The step from these observations to declaring it immoral is a short one.

We have assumed that the various mark-ups were at least justifiable. A clearly immoral practice, because it is deceptive, is setting a higher price for a product than that at which it is ever sold, so that it can always be sold at a discount. This is deceptive, because to sell at a discount implies a discount from its real price, not a discount from an artificially inflated one.

Bidding

Bidding is a commonly used practice. It is sometimes used by a seller, as at an auction, to get the highest price. More often, it is used by a buyer, to get the lowest price. It is used in construction projects, it is used by government and large firms in seeking supplies purchased in quantity, and by firms in seeking subcontractors and suppliers. Bidding is a morally justifiable procedure, providing it is fair. Keeping it fair is not always easy.

Not all bidding is secret, as the case of an auction illustrates. But much of it is. How does one justify secret bidding? Why should bidding not be an open process? The answer is that secrecy tends to produce fairer bids and lower prices for the purchaser. This happens in two ways. If the process were open, and the seller—for whatever reason—was able to make a profit by accepting a contract for X, and that price was considerably less than that of the competition, to get the contract, the firm would bid just enough less than the lowest competitor. This bid might well be higher than the lowest bid he would offer if he did not know what the competition was, and simply operated on his cost plus what he considered an acceptable, competitive profit.

Second, if the competition were open, a firm might start out at a bid low enough to scare off others from bidding, even though the bid is not the lowest he would offer if forced to make a secret bid. Therefore, secrecy per se is not morally unjustifiable. But if the bidding process is to be secret, then in fairness to all parties it must be kept secret. Any violation of secrecy by any of the parties violates the fairness condition of bidding. Often a government or company will not accept bids above a certain amount. If no bids are lower than that amount, it will not proceed, and will restudy its options. But it may hope to get a bid lower than the highest it is willing to pay. Clearly, the figure it is willing to pay must be kept secret if the bidding is to be fair. Any leaks violate the procedure.

In addition to fraud, using materials inferior to those specified in the bid, and other obvious violations of justice, honesty, and fairness, bidding has led to other questionable practices. Two that involve government contracts are common enough to deserve some discussion. One deals with road-building and large construction projects; the other with defense and similar government contracts.

One difficulty many of the states in the United States encounter is that there are only a few construction companies capable of handling the state's large construction needs, whether for roads or large buildings. Some states, moreover, are committed by state law to using only companies located in their state for state projects. Assume that a state wishes to build a new road and there are only three construction companies in the state capable of building it. How does the state get the best price for the construction job? Usually, a secret bidding procedure is used. But in a state with only three large construction companies, all the managers or owners of the three companies know each other. The temptation is for the executives of the three companies to agree, for instance, on which one of them will get the road job, with the understanding that the second gets some other job they know of, and the third gets the job following that. It would be to their advantage not to compete; to divide up the contracts, agree on what their respective bids will be, and make sure that the lowest bid submitted is sufficiently high to make a handsome profit. Such collusion would in fact be both illegal and immoral. But because such an arrangement would be so easy, so tempting, and so difficult to prove, this might easily take place. How can a state protect itself?

The secret bidding process is one way, but it is open to the defects just described. The state, however, usually gets from its own engineering experts an independent estimate of what the cost of the project should be, and then only accepts bids that are at or below that figure. However, because the costs for large projects are sometimes only guesses (e.g., they have to include unknown inflation rates), there is a great deal of leeway in the process. The need for fairness is obvious, but legal and completely effective ways to control abuses are difficult to formulate.

A second area involves government contracts, for instance, in the defense industry. Two aspects have raised questions of morality. One is cost overruns; another is the locking in of government to a single supplier. Let us assume that a government contract for a new airplane is given to the lowest bidder in a fair, secret procedure. The lowest bidder, however, may not in fact be able to deliver the contracted airplane at the quoted price. Once engaged in the process of developing the plane, however, the government cannot change the manufacturer because of these cost increases, simply because it has already invested considerable time and money in the project. Nor can it allow the company to go bankrupt and not complete its work. Thus, government has seemed to be forced to live with cost overruns, paying more for projects than it contracted for, or making do with delayed production schedules. The limited number of suppliers available to bid is also a factor here. If companies deliberately bid low to get contracts, knowing that cost overruns will be necessary, then their bids are not fair bids, and they get contracts by misrepresentation. This practice is immoral, but again, often difficult to prove, and so difficult to prosecute legally.

The technique of locking in a buyer can be practiced with individual consumers as well as with governments. It consists in pricing a major item or contract bid lower than the manufacturing cost of the product, with the assurance that the cost of spare and replacement parts, or the cost of the supplies needed to run the product, can be priced sufficiently high to guarantee a profit in the long run. Thus an airplane manufacturer might enter a bid on an airplane contract that is less than its projected development cost, knowing that, on spare or replacement parts, it can overcharge to such an extent that it will make a profit overall. The buyer is locked into purchasing from the company, if that company is the only one that makes the spare parts or the other items needed to use the product. Immorality enters in the form of an overcharge on parts. In government contracts, this has led to some scandals. For example, fifteen dollars were paid for screws worth a few cents, and hundreds of dollars were paid for parts worth just a few dollars. In an attempt to preclude this, government may require that the price of parts is included in the original contract, or that specifications for spare parts be made available to other possible suppliers.

A third kind of case involves the purchase of goods by a government or large firm. Consider the firm or agency that wishes to buy typewriters. How does it write its specifications for bidding? Several pitfalls are common. There is always the possibility of leaking information to a potential supplier—an unfair practice. This is sometimes done as a result of bribery, or offers of a kickback. Both are clearly immoral. There is also the possibility of writing specifications in so detailed and narrow a way that only one supplier can fill the order, thereby undermining the purpose of the bidding procedure. Direct negotiation with that supplier would make more sense, and would probably yield better results than bidding because the supplier has no incentive to make his bid low when he knows he is the only bidder.

Bidding is a morally defensible practice in businesss. But it is open to many abuses, and it must be carefully controlled if it is to be kept fair.

Consumer Marketing

The opportunities for fraud, deception, and unethical practices are endless. But most such practices are clearly immoral and so raise no ethical problems. Advertising poses special problems, which we shall deal with separately. A few of the issues of current concern, however, include truth in lending, unit pricing, and labeling and dating. All of these have become items of consumer concern and the focus of attention by the consumer's movement. The consumer's movement can be seen at least in part as a reaction to marketing practices perceived as unfair or as less fair than they could or should be.

Truth-in-lending concerns the true amount paid by those who purchase items on the installment plan, who get loans to finance purchases, or who buy with credit cards. One sales technique is to state how much an item bought on time or credit will cost in terms of monthly payments. If little or no mention is made of the actual total cost of the purchase, the terms of the loan, or the true annual interest rate, consumers enter into legally binding contracts without full knowledge of what they are agreeing to. Some find out too late that their goods can be repossessed if they miss a payment, or that they are actually paying two or three times more than the original price of an item because of interest and other payments.

These practices were not illegal, and a prudent and cautious buyer could have found out the exact nature of the contract into which he or she was entering. But this frequently requires a good deal of investigation and fig-uring—more than the average consumer is used to. Truth-in-lending therefore became a consumer demand, justified as a means of making transactions fair. The moral demands have been translated into legal obligations as well.

Unit pricing is an attempt to enable buyers to make accurate comparisons based on price. Most consumers would expect, for instance, to pay less per ounce for a soap powder bought in volume than the same brand packaged in a small box. But this is not always the case. If both the contents of each box and the prices are not stated in round numbers, it is sometimes difficult to know which is the better buy. The same is true regarding competing brands. Yet one of the ways in which competition is supposed to take place in our system is based on price comparison. Pricing techniques that make it difficult to compare prices are not deceptive or immoral, but they do not help the consumer judge on the basis of price. Unit pricing consists in indicating (e.g., what one ounce of soap costs in each of the packages for each of the brands the store carries). A consumer who wishes to make a choice based on price is helped to do so. The demand for unit pricing is a demand to make transactions fair, and is morally justified. Although marketing techniques may justify packaging in fractions of an ounce, such practices are clearly not adopted to help comparison shopping or competition on the basis of price.

Labeling and dating are other demands that have been made by consumers, to make the transactions into which they enter fair. When one buys a garment it is often difficult to know exactly of what it is made, whether it is a synthetic fabric, a natural fiber, or a mixture, or what are the proportions of each fiber. In effect, one buys blindly, unless the information is supplied. Adequate information on both sides is a necessary condition if a transaction is to be fair. Hence, demanding such labeling is morally justifiable.

Unless the ingredients of processed foods are listed, in descending order, according to the quantity of each contained in the package, the purchaser does not know exactly what he or she is buying. In the case of perishable goods, unless there is stamped on the product a date by which an item must be sold, there is no way for a buyer to know how fresh the product is and how long it can be kept before it spoils. Consumer demands in all these instances are legitimate; these practices not only preclude deception and misleading marketing techniques, but they help to keep transactions fair, and so help the free-market system to operate as it should.

Advertising

Although moral issues arise in other aspects of marketing, public and governmental concern has tended to focus on the advertising of consumer products to the general public. Corporations are thought capable of handling their own wants, and of being qualified to determine on their own what they need. Although they are legally protected against fraud, they are less likely than the ordinary consumer to be taken in by misleading advertising, or to be sold what they do not want.

Once a producer makes a commodity, his object is to sell it. To do so he must inform potential buyers that the product is available, what it does, and why it might be a product they want or need. Advertising provides this information to large numbers of people. A product might be advertised through a direct-mail campaign or through use of the media—newspapers, magazines, TV. Advertising, therefore, is part of the process of selling one's products. Because any sale is a transaction between a buyer and a seller, the transaction is fair if both parties have adequate, appropriate information about the product, and if they enter into the transaction willingly and without coercion. From a moral point of view, because advertising helps achieve the goal of both seller and buyer, it is morally justifiable and permissible, providing it is not deceptive, misleading, or coercive. Advertising can be abused, but it is not inherently immoral.

Before we examine in detail some of the abuses of advertising, we should put aside three morally irrelevant charges brought against advertising. The first charge, that advertising is not necessary in a socialist economic system, and that it is an immoral part of capitalism, is vague and for the most part untrue. In every economic system there must be some way of letting potential buyers know of the existence of goods. Any producer must make known that a product is available if people are to know that they can buy it. Displaying an item in a window, so that people can see it, is a form of advertising, as is displaying it on a shelf. In a society of comparative scarcity, where only essentials are available, people may constantly be on the lookout for products they want, spotting them when they arrive on a shelf. They may then, through word of mouth, transmit the information that the product is available. Before long there are lines of people waiting to purchase the item, and soon it is sold out. Those who did not get the item then wait for it to appear again. Or if an item is a staple, and generally available, people know where it can be purchased and simply go to that store when they need it. In such a society, advertising plays a comparatively small role.

American society is not a society of comparative scarcity, it is one of comparative wealth. There are many items available to the consumer. Competition, moreover, encourages producers to enter a market in which there is consumer demand. If a company had a monopoly on an item, then it would have little need for advertising, once people knew of its availability. Competition, therefore, accounts for the amount of advertising we have in the United States, as opposed to that in the Soviet Union. The American automobile industry, for instance, produces a great many different kinds of cars—different styles and makes, with different accessories and price ranges. If there were only one kind of car made, clearly there would be less advertising by the automobile industry. Would it be better if there were only one car manufacturer—perhaps the government? The typical American answer is no. Once we allow competition—which has not been shown to be immoral—then advertising is a reasonable concomitant, and as such it is not inherently immoral.

A second charge against advertising which we can dismiss from a moral point of view is its frequent poor taste; it is offensive to one's finer sensibilities. The charge can hardly be denied. But poor taste is not immoral. As members of society we can make known our displeasure at such advertising, either by vocal or written protest, or by not purchasing the item advertised. However, we should distinguish between that which is in poor taste and that which is immoral.

A third charge claims that advertising takes advantage of people, either by forcing them to buy what they do not want, or, more plausibly, by psychologically manipulating them to buy what they do not need. According to this view, people are not able to resist the lure of the vast resources available to producers for advertising campaigns. Manipulation and coercion through advertising are immoral, as we shall discuss in detail. But the charge is clearly an overstatement if it asserts that all members of the public are gullible, unsophisticated, and manipulatable by media advertising. Advertising would be immoral if it always and necessarily manipulated and coerced people, but it does not. The difficulty is in deciding what is manipulative and what is not; who should be protected from certain kinds of advertising, and who does not need such protection. The notion of protection from advertising is closely linked to government paternalism. To what extent are people to be allowed to make their own decisions, and to what extent should government protect them against themselves because of its superior knowledge of their real needs and wants? The Federal Trade Commission (FTC) and the Food and Drug Administration (FDA) are the two American agencies with major responsibility for policing advertising. The standards they adopt are frequently more restrictive and paternalistic than morality requires. They have sometimes ruled that advertising is misleading if only 5 percent of the population would be misled by it. Whether morality demands this much protection is among the topics we shall investigate.

We shall consider five areas in which the moral dimension of advertising is of central importance: (1) the immorality of untruthful, misleading, or deceptive advertising; (2) the immorality of manipulation and coercion through advertising, including the question of audience; (3) the morality of paternalism with respect to advertising; (4) the immorality of preventing some kinds of advertising; and (5) the allocation and distribution of moral responsibility with respect to advertising.

Truth and Advertising

A major function of advertising is to sell goods. But this is not its only purpose, nor does it accomplish this only by supplying information. Advertising may educate the public or mold public opinion. Propaganda might be considered a form of advertising for a political party, a religious sect, or some special social group. Let us, however, limit this discussion to advertising in business, with the aim of selling a product. Informing the public of an item's availability is only part of the task of advertising. A manufacturer also wants to influence people to buy the product. Hence, ads are not only informative but persuasive. Through advertisements, some companies wish to achieve public notice and recognition; they feel that people tend to buy products with a familiar name. The purpose of some advertising is the building of goodwill for the producer, who assumes that public goodwill will eventually help sales.

The approach to advertising which sees the function of advertising only in terms of supplying information takes too narrow a view of its objectives and tends to evaluate it from too narrow a moral perspective. If its proper function were exclusively the giving of information, and if information were always given in declarative sentences, then we could concern ourselves exclusively with the questions of truth in advertising. If what an advertisement says is true, it is morally permissible; if what it says is false, it is immoral. We shall initially approach advertising in this way. In doing so, we shall also see the shortcomings of this approach.

Let us start with some distinctions that will be helpful in clarifying the complex question of truth in advertising. With what is truth in advertising contrasted? It can be contrasted with either falsehood or lying. Lying is immoral; stating falsehoods is not necessarily immoral. Suppose, for instance, someone were to tell a story. He could make a number of statements that were not factually true; yet he would not be lying.

The terms *true* and *false* are properly predicated of sentences or propositions. Only a proposition can be true or false. An exclamation, a question, or an interjection cannot be true or false. A statement or a proposition contains a subject and a predicate. The subject has the property, or is related to something else stated in the predicate. A statement or proposition is true, roughly speaking, if the relation stated to maintain between subject and predicate actually corresponds to the same relation in the world between what is designated or referred to by the subject and predicate. Hence the sentence, "This page of this book has words printed on it," is true if the page of this book does in fact have words printed on it. Obviously this page does have words printed on it. Therefore the sentence is true. The sentence, "This page is colored green," is false if in fact this page is not colored green. This rough characterization of truth and falsehood will suffice for our purposes.

Lying consists, however, not simply in making a false statement. From a moral point of view, lying is an activity. Lying consists in making a statement, which one believes is false, to another person, whom one has reason to think will believe the statement to be true. Lying consists of my saying what I believe to be false, and of my intending that another will believe to be true what is actually false. I not only say what I do not believe, but I also intend to deceive or mislead the one to whom I make the statement.

Using this definition, falsehood is not a necessary part of lying. Suppose, for instance, that Tom believes there are four pints in a quart. A friend, who is baking a cake, asks him how many pints are in a quart. Tom replies, "There are four pints in a quart." Actually, there are only two pints in a quart. What Tom said is false. But he has not told a lie; he has made a mistake. Conversely, suppose, as before, that Tom believes there are four pints in a quart and the same person asks him the same question in the same situation. Tom wants the cake to fail, so that his friend will not spend any more time making cakes. So, intending to give false information, Tom says, "There are two pints in a quart." Morally speaking, Tom is guilty of telling a lie, even though, by accident, what he said was a true statement. It is a lie because Tom thought that what he was saying was false; he said it with the intent to deceive, and with the expectation that what he said would be believed.

Whether a statement or proposition is true or false depends on the world; whether a statement is an instance of lying depends on the intent of the speaker.

Not all false statements that someone makes, believing that they are false, are lies. Suppose, for instance, a friend says during a chilling wintry day, "I'm as cold as an iceberg." What he says is literally false. His body temperature is about 98.6 degrees, even if he feels cold. But his statement is not a lie. He had no intention of deceiving anyone when he made that statement; nor is it likely that anyone will be deceived by it. We use language in many ways. Part of the normal person's use of language enables one to distinguish by context, phrasing, intonation, and other subtle techniques the difference between a sentence that is literally true and one that is figurative, exaggerated, or not to be taken literally. Metaphor, simile, and hyperbole are all accepted figures of speech. We do not speak only in declarative sentences, and when we do speak in declarative sentences we do not always speak literally. When someone says, "I'm so hungry I could eat a bear," he does not expect people to point out that an average bear weighs much more than he does, that he could not possibly eat a whole bear, or that he probably would not even like bear meat. All that is true, but it is beside the point. He is simply saying, in an expressive way, that he is very hungry. There is no moral reason why we should not use expressive language when we do not intend to deceive, and when there is little or no likelihood that we will deceive, even if our statements are not literally true.

We now turn to advertising. Some advertisements contain sentences—express propositions—that are appropriately evaluated in terms of truth and falsity. If an ad makes a false claim, which the advertiser knows to be false, for the purpose of misleading, misinforming, or deceiving potential customers, then the ad is immoral. It is immoral because in the ad the advertiser is lying, and lying is immoral. An advertiser might also be morally guilty of lying if what he said in an ad was accidentally true, but he believed it to be false and intended to deceive. This problem, however, need not concern us, because it is of only peripheral interest.

The problem of truth in advertising, however, does not end here. For it is possible to deceive and mislead without making statements that are false; and it is also possible, as we have seen, not to deceive or mislead while making statements that are not literally true.

Consider the following slogan, used by Esso a number of years ago: "Esso puts a tiger in your tank!" The statement, of course, is not literally true. But did anyone think it was literally true? Do we really wonder if, after some customer had put Esso gasoline into his car, he worried about whether it had turned into a tiger? Exactly what Esso meant to convey by its slogan is to some extent a matter of speculation. It clearly did not want its slogan to be taken literally, but rather figuratively. The semantics of advertising properly allow for use of figurative language. To restrict ads to statements that are literally true is to fail to understand the semantics of advertising or of language in general. There is, however, no neat line between allowable figurative language and lying. An obvious exaggeration is not likely to be taken literally. But what is obvious to most people may not be an obvious exaggeration to everyone. Must we protect those who might be deceived by exaggeration by forcing advertising to be literally true in the statements it makes? From a moral point of view, it seems sufficient that the vast majority of those at whom the ad is directed not be misled by it. When discussing responsibility, we used the rule that people are morally responsible for the foreseeable consequences of their actions. The test of what is foreseeable is what the ordinary person of goodwill would foresee in those circumstances. A similar approach can be taken to advertising. An advertiser will know whether he intends his ad to deceive. If he does, then the advertiser acts immorally in placing the ad. But if he does not intend to deceive, and we are to judge the ad on its merits and not on the advertiser's intent, then the ad is morally permissible if the ordinary person at whom the ad is directed would not be deceived. Some ads directed at car owners might be misunderstood by children. This is not a matter of moral concern, however, because the ad is not directed at them but at car owners.

The Better Business Bureaus, the FTC, and the FDA are all concerned with accuracy in advertisements. Advertisers are not allowed to make false statements. Moreover, if challenged, advertisers must be able to document statements that make factual claims which are taken literally. These government agencies sometimes go beyond what is morally necessary, according to our analysis. Even if a very small percentage of people might be misled, the ad is not allowed. The action of government agencies in these cases, if morally justifiable, depends not on the question of lying, but on the legitimate extent of governmental paternalism. We shall consider this question later.

Without making any false statements, an ad might be misleading or deceptive. A misleading ad is one in which the ad does not misrepresent or make false claims but makes claims in such a way that the normal person, or at least many ordinary people, reading it quickly and without great attention and thought, will make a false inference or draw a false conclusion. Those who attempt to justify such ads claim that the mistake is made by the reader or viewer of the ad and that the responsibility for drawing the false conclusion rests with the reader or viewer and not with the advertiser. Strictly speaking, this is correct, but clearly, often the intent in such ads is to mislead. They are written or presented in such a way that their effect is predictable. Such ads are immoral because they intend to deceive, even if they do not literally state what is false. The same is true of packaging. If a large box is only half filled, a consumer may erroneously think he will get more in a big box than in a smaller one. If no claim is made that the box is full, no false statement has been made. The mistake is the consumer's. But the maker of the product is morally at fault.

A deceptive ad is one that either makes a false statement and therefore lies, or that misrepresents the product without making any statement. Deception of the eye and mind may take place not only through sentences or propositions but also through pictures, through individual words, or through certain juxtapositions of objects. Such deception trades on a background of ordinary expectations. We are accustomed to having the contents of a box pictured on the box. We expect the pictures to be reasonably close to the product within, and when this is not the case, the picture is deceptive. If an item is called "chicken soup," and it contains no chicken and was not made from chicken, the name is deceptive, even if no statement is made that the soup contains chicken or is made from chicken. If an item is advertised as being at half price, and the item was never sold at full price but is always sold at the price indicated, the ad is deceptive.

The semantics of advertising, however, allows a certain leeway in some products. The cosmetics field provides some examples. We expect cosmetics to be packaged in pretty bottles, boxes, or containers. Perfumes would smell as sweet if they were packaged in mustard jars, but they would not sell as well. Face creams without perfume would cleanse and soften as well, but they would not sell as well. Cosmetics are a luxury item, and they are packaged as such. They are sold as much for their promise as for their chemicals. Shampoo, hair rinse, conditioners, and other hair products will not make the ordinary person's hair look like the hair of the models who claim in ads to use these products. Nor will the use of other beauty products make the average person look like the models using them. Is this misleading advertising? Do people actually believe that a product will change their looks, their personalities, their lives? Most people know that the semantics of cosmetics advertising is puffery and do not take the pictures or the implied claims literally. They hope the product will make them more attractive, and the products sometimes *do* make their users more self-confident. This is what the customer is paying for. Repeat sales for such products is an indication that the customer is not being deceived.

Advertisements do not only make statements; their purpose is to try to persuade people to purchase the product advertised. Persuasion may take the form of making statements, but it need not. Many ads simply create associations in the mind of the purchaser. An ad for an expensive scotch whiskey might simply show a couple in evening clothes, sipping a drink, in an elegant room, together with a picture of the bottle of scotch. The association of the scotch with elegance and class is all the ad wishes to convey.

Some ads simply show a picture of the product; the aim of these ads is only recognition of the product—when the consumer sees it on a supermarket shelf, together with eight other brands of the same kind of item. Name recognition has an effect on purchasing. This is not inappropriate. A customer who knows little about the nine items on the shelf knows that at least one of the nine items is advertised. This is at least some information about the product. An item that did not sell would not be advertised for very long. An item that depends on repeat purchases for success must have a fairly large number of users if it is continuously advertised. All this does not mean that the product is the best of its kind, but it is information that makes the choice of products less than random.

The final aspect of truth in advertising that we will consider is the question of half-truths. A statement made about a product may be true, may not mislead, may not deceive, but it may be morally objectionable nevertheless. Sometimes, what the ad does *not* say is as important as what the ad does say. It is immoral to advertise and sell a dangerous product without indicating its dangers. If, for a certain product, the background assumption of the ordinary person is that products of that kind are safe, and the given advertised product is not safe, then the ad and/or the box should include the appropriate caution. We expect lye to be caustic, therefore if ads for lye emphasize its caustic property, these ads may not have to specify that it burns the skin, although that information should be prominent on the can. But we do not usually expect hair dye to contain lye, or to be caustic; therefore if an ad for such a product does not indicate its unusual potential danger, it would be immoral.

General rules concerning truth in advertising can be summarized in the following way: It is immoral to lie, mislead, and deceive in advertising. It is immoral to fail to indicate dangers which are not normally expected. It is not immoral to use metaphor or other figures of speech if these will be normally understood as the figurative use of language; nor is it immoral to persuade as well as to inform.

Manipulation and Coercion

Advertising not only informs, it frequently also aims to persuade. Persuasion in itself is not immoral. We all attempt to persuade others to do what we wish—to go with us to a movie, or go out to dinner. If what we persuade another to do is not immoral, and if we do not use immoral means to persuade them, persuasion is not an immoral activity. Persuasion, however, is different from manipulation and coercion, although all these are ways of getting others to do what we wish. But manipulation and coercion are at least prima facie immoral. They are immoral in business and advertising. The reason is not difficult to state. In Kantian terms, both coercion and manipulation treat another person only as a means to my end, and deny respect for his freedom. Coercion involves force or the threat of force, either physical or psychological. Manipulation does not use force; it involves playing upon a person's will by trickery or by devious, unfair, or insidious means. Both take unfair advantage of a person, and the use of either renders a transaction between the two parties unfair or unjust. Coercion and manipulation in advertising are therefore immoral.

But what constitutes coercion or manipulation in advertising? Can an advertiser truly coerce or manipulate consumers?

A clearly coercive form of manipulative advertising is *subliminal advertising*. An advertiser can insert a message in a music track which is played in a store, in a film shown in a theatre, or on TV, in such a way that the viewer is not consciously aware of the advertisement, even though he or she is subconsciously picking it up. It is possible to do this because a certain threshold of perception must be exceeded before we consciously see a motion picture. The film must be run at a certain number of frames per minute. By inserting a message between the frames below the threshold of conscious perception, we do not consciously see the message. Despite the fact that we do not consciously see it, tests have shown that we do perceive the message without being conscious of it. Such ads are called subliminal because they are projected below the limit of our conscious perception.

Subliminal advertising is manipulative because it acts on us without our knowledge, and hence, without our consent. If an ad appears on TV, we can tune it out or change stations if we do not want to be subject to it. If an ad appears in a magazine, we are not forced to look at it. In either case, if we do choose to look and listen, we can consciously evaluate what we see and hear. We can, if we wish, take a critical stance toward the advertisement. All of this is impossible with subliminal advertising, because we are unaware that we are being subjected to the message. The advertiser is imposing his message on us without our knowledge or consent. We cannot tune it out, because we do not know it is there. Nor can we be at all critical of it. A subliminal advertisement may simply flash on the screen the name of a product, or a simple message, such as "Buy X brand of soap." The messages are not complex. Yet they have been shown to have an effect. They are manipulative, and to use them is immoral.

Some department stores and supermarkets have inserted in their music tracks the message "Don't shoplift" or "Don't steal." Studies have shown that stores that use this device have a lower rate of shoplifting than comparable stores which do not use it. Even though the message may advocate moral behavior, the use of the subliminal technique is still immoral. Because we do not know the content of the message or messages we are being subjected to, there is no way of guaranteeing that the message is moral, rather than one that is objectionable in some way, or to some people. Because we have no control over the content of a subliminal message, the practice is manipulative; it tends to produce more harm than good, and is, from a moral point of view, unjustifiable.

Advertisements aimed at preschool children are another fairly clear case of manipulation. At this age, children tend to be very impressionable. They believe most of what they hear and see, are unable to distinguish clearly truth from fancy, and have very little critical skill or experience. They are very susceptible, therefore, to TV advertisements. What is the point of advertisers aiming messages at preschool children? Clearly, they do not make purchases, but they can put pressure on their parents to make the purchases they want. For instance, if a certain children's vitamin is successfully advertised to children on TV, they may be anxious to take that vitamin pill rather than any other. A parent interested in having a child take vitamins may find the job made easier by having the child anxious to take a certain brand, and may buy that brand for that reason. Children may also pester their mothers and fathers to buy certain sugar-coated cereals or other products advertised for children. Is this manipulation?

Two replies have been given. One is that the adults in the family make the purchases. If they feel that the product should not be purchased, they should exercise their best judgment. They, and not the children, make the final judgment. If they cannot stand up to their children's demands, that is not the problem of the advertiser; it is the parents' problem. The other reply is that if the parents are the purchasers, the ads for children's products should be aimed at the parents and not at the children.

Ads aimed at children are inappropriate because they create a desire in children for products they do not understand (e.g., vitamins). The intent of the ads is clearly to manipulate the children into applying pressure on their parents to make such purchases. Though the parents make the final decision, the children are still being manipulated for the advertiser's purposes. Such ads take advantage of children, and those who advertise in this way are morally culpable of manipulation, and of treating children only as means to their ends.

The situation with respect to adolescents is more difficult. Many ads aimed at this group play on their social insecurity. They are told that unless their breath is sweetened by a certain product they will not be popular; that if they want to attract that certain boy or girl they should use brand X deodorant; that the key to their making friends is using a certain shampoo or soap. Each of the products does something: reduces bad breath or body odor, or cleans hair and skin. And each of these may to some extent make one more attractive, or less offensive. But it is extremely unlikely that any of them, or all of them together, are the basis for making a teenager popular, or for winning friends. Adolescents know this; yet they are frequently so insecure socially that the ads play on their fears, worries, hopes, and dreams. Do such ads coerce or manipulate? Only a case-by-case examination can answer this question. The potential for manipulation is present, though not all such ads are manipulative.

The question of audience is relevant. Certain products—alcohol and cigarettes, for instance—are restricted for sale to adults. These and similar items should not be advertised in children's magazines or in magazines aimed at young teenagers. A more difficult problem involves the small minority, such as those people who are gullible or those with a lower than average intelligence, who may be manipulated by ads that are not manipulative to the average adult. From a moral point of view, a general rule would be that it is immoral to gear ads to that group in order to manipulate them, but that for ads aimed at the general public, the usual appropriate moral criterion is whether the ad is manipulative for the average reader or viewer. Society may take a stronger line; the FTC has done so. The arguments for a stronger line, however, have to do with paternalism.

Paternalism and Advertising

The United States Surgeon General has determined that smoking is dangerous to one's health. We know that drinking intoxicating alcoholic beverages can sometimes lead to alcoholism, to many automobile accidents while driving, and to other ills. Should the United States government and American society allow the spread of the use of these products through advertising? Should we prohibit the advertising of pornography? Should we allow the advertising of marijuana and other illegal drugs? What of "Saturday night specials" and other guns? Are there any limits to what can be morally advertised?

Although there are clearly limits, there is much dispute about where to draw the line. Anything that is illegal to manufacture and sell to the general public cannot legally be advertised to the general public. This poses no real problem because it would be self-defeating for anyone to advertise what is illegal. If someone is selling illegal drugs, for instance, to advertise would be inviting the police to arrest him. We have also seen that it would be immoral to advertise to children what they are prohibited by law from buying. Beyond these clear cases, however, there is little consensus. If an item can be legally sold, why can it not be advertised? What is the proper role of government in protecting people against what will harm them? The question is a political one. In a democracy such as the United States, the answer is that the proper paternalistic role of government should be decided by the people through their representatives, and with a majority rule, limited by the rights of individuals and minority groups.

The Food and Drug Administration (FDA) acts in the people's interests when it requires by law that packaged foods list on the package the ingredients in order of the decreasing quantity. Such information allows the purchaser to know what he is buying and makes the transaction a fair one. With respect to drugs, the FDA also acts to protect the consumer. It prohibits the sale of certain drugs, allows other drugs to be sold only with a doctor's prescription, and demands a testing period before approving drugs. It sets high standards, standards which some people and some drug companies claim are too high.

The Federal Trade Commission has prohibited the advertising of tobacco and alcohol on TV. It has not prohibited the advertising of such items in journals and newspapers, though in the case of cigarette ads, the Surgeon General's warning must be included. Some people claim that drinking alcoholic beverages is immoral, and that smoking, because it harms the health of the smoker, should be prohibited. They claim that even if such items can legally be sold, the producers of them should not be allowed through advertising to encourage people to smoke and drink.

The philosophy of liberalism, defended eloquently by John Stuart Mill in the nineteenth century, in *On Liberty,* defends the principle that government should not interfere in the actions of individuals if the results of their actions fall mainly on themselves. In both smoking and drinking, the results fall mainly on the agent, hence the government should not interfere with their use by individuals. The government does more than required by insisting that packages of cigarettes carry the Surgeon General's warning. The liberal position can be extended to the question of advertising these products: if they are legal and publicly sold, then those who wish to purchase them should be allowed to do so. Those who do not wish to purchase them are not forced to do so simply because they are advertised. Each person can weigh the good and bad effects for himself and make his own decision. If the smoker feels that he gets more enjoyment from smoking a pack of cigarettes a day for twenty-five or thirty years, even if it cuts four or five years off his life, the government cannot legitimately say he is mistaken. Other people will consider that the four or five years of extended life are preferable to the enjoyment of smoking. Neither answer is right or wrong; each is simply a matter of choice or preference. The question allows for a difference of opinion.

The extent to which the FTC has restricted any kind of advertising that might mislead even a very small percentage of the population goes beyond what morality requires of advertisers. The FTC perceives its paternalistic mandate to extend that far. We have no indication yet that the general public feels the FTC has gone too far. Because the amount of paternalism government exercises is a political as well as a moral question, we can distinguish what is morally required from what is politically required without expecting that the two will always coincide.

One further attack on advertising should be discussed before we leave the role of government and paternalism. Some people claim that advertising creates false needs in people. Producers decide not what the people want or need, but what the *producers* want to produce, based on which products will bring the most profit. The producers then manufacture those items, create demand through a high-powered and expensive advertising campaign, and in effect, take advantage of the general population. Because we can correctly call this taking advantage of people, it is immoral.

The attack is not entirely without merit. American producers sometimes do choose to produce what they want instead of what the general public wants. When they do so, it is not always possible to convince people to buy what is produced. Sometimes it is. It is difficult to imagine that people really needed electric toothbrushes. It seems more likely that a manufacturer decided to produce them and then advertised the product. It is also doubtful that Americans really wanted large cars with built-in obsolescense, but for many years they had little choice. Detroit decided what cars would be produced and Americans picked from what was available. Only when foreign manufacturers entered the market in significant quantity did American car manufacturers switch to producing smaller cars.

What conclusion can we draw from this? The conclusion that advertising can sell anything is much too strong; it cannot. But it can sell some products that people had not thought they needed or wanted before the item was produced. It is difficult to imagine, however, an appropriate solution to this kind of problem—if it *is* a problem. People can purchase what they want. If they do not want to buy electric toothbrushes, advertisements do not force them to do so. If they do not want to buy an Edsel car, an expensive ad campaign will not make them buy one. But if they want small cars and only large cars are available, they may prefer to buy a large car rather than no car. Even here, however, the possibility of free entry into the market by foreign-car makers seems to show that the system of the free market tends to correct itself in the long run. The alternative would be some type of centralized decision-making apparatus, either governmental or private. This body would, presumably, decide that electric toothbrushes should not be made, or that small cars rather than large cars should be produced. But how will this group know what should and should not be produced? Will they know better than the individual consumer what the consumer wants? It seems unlikely. In countries where there is such central planning the consumer is generally more poorly served than in the United States.

Our system may be wasteful to some extent. It may produce goods that are not necessary. It may needlessly duplicate effort. All this is true. But a better system, to replace the present one, has not been sufficiently articulated or defended. Nor is advertising the culprit. We have seen that government can restrict advertising to some extent, in cases where harm to people will result. But the harm must be more clear and present than simply the advertising of what some people think is unnecessary. This sort of governmental decision goes far beyond the kind and extent of paternalism mandated to government by the American people.

The Prevention of Advertising

The prevention of advertising, in some cases, comes up against the First Amendment's right of free speech. We have seen that in some instances the government can, with the consent of the people, exercise a certain amount of paternalism. Can it do so by violating the rights of advertisers? Do advertisers have the right, by virtue of the First Amendment, to advertise? The question is a legal, not a strictly moral one. First Amendment rights, as well as other civil rights, can be restricted under certain circumstances. However, government restriction of advertising, in the case of cigarettes and liquor, has not been successfully challenged in the courts.

Another area of advertising presents a different moral issue. Is it moral to prohibit advertising by doctors, lawyers, and other professionals? Obviously, no individual doctor or lawyer is morally obliged to advertise. But is it appropriate for the American Medical Association (AMA) or the American Bar Association (ABA) or other professional organizations to prohibit advertising by their members? Until recently, many professionals were restricted from advertising by their professional associations. Advertising was considered to be in poor taste, vulgar, and unprofessional. Moreover, many professionals claimed, it was not possible to advertise adequately. Reasons given were that the services professionals perform vary from client to client or patient to patient; the relations they develop are personal; and they do not sell a product at a certain price.

The prohibition of advertising by doctors and lawyers, however, has been attacked as being self-serving and harmful to the general public. It has been determined to be a prohibition that tends to hinder competition and free trade. Recently, therefore, these portions of the AMA and ABA codes of professional conduct have been declared illegal, and they have been changed.

The arguments in favor of changing them were several. One can be put in utilitarian terms. Essentially, the good gained by the lawyers and doctors and their respective professions was less than the evil suffered by their potential and actual clients and patients. Potential clients and patients were not able to compare doctors or lawyers, as they could compare plumbers and carpenters. The latter could compete through their ads, making known their specialties, rates, and other pertinent information. In picking a doctor or lawyer, one usually had only a list in the Yellow Pages. Store-front lawyers who wished to serve lower-income groups at very low rates, frequently in ghetto areas, were prevented, by the old code, from advertising. This was not in the best interests of people who might be able to use their services but could not afford the services of the typical law firm.

Another argument rests on the right of the individual practitioner to make known his services, and to compete, in price and in kinds of services provided, for the business of potential clients. Preventing the individual practitioner from advertising, if he so chose, was a violation of his right to free speech, restricted not by government but by his professional organization. The right of a professional organization to do this has been successfully challenged.

Under the new guidelines, lawyers are still supposed to insure that their ads are in good taste, so as not to harm the reputation of the profession. "Good taste," however, is broad enough to include a wide range of ads.

The important principle underscored by the ruling on professional advertising is that to prevent advertising is, in many instances, harmful to the public, because it withholds information the public wants and can profitably use; thus, it protects the interests of members of the professions at public expense. Monopolies do not have to advertise, simply because they control the market. A market that allows free entry appropriately allows advertising, so that each of the competitors can make known its product or service, inform the public of its availability, and attempt to persuade the public to purchase the product or service.

We therefore conclude that in some cases it is immoral to prevent advertising, just as in other cases, morality demands that certain advertising be restrained or prohibited.

The Allocation of Moral Responsibility in Advertising

In each of the preceding sections we have seen that certain advertising practices are immoral. Who is morally responsible for advertising, and who has moral responsibility with respect to it? We can identify five groups: (1) the producer or manufacturer; (2) the advertising agency; (3) the media in which or through which the advertisement appears; (4) the general public; and (5) government and governmental agencies.

1. Prime responsibility for advertising rests on the one who initiates and directs the advertising. In most cases, this is the producer or manufacturer of a product. The manufacturer decides what and how to advertise. The decisions may be made by the chief executive officer, by the marketing, publicity, advertising, or public relations departments, or by some combination of these and others. In whatever way responsibility for the decision on advertising is made internally, the company is responsible for the advertising it does or commissions; the company is responsible for its content and accuracy, the medium it chooses, and the like. If it aims ads at preschool children, it is responsible for doing so; if it misrepresents or misleads, it is responsible for doing so. Although primary responsibility is held by the company or manufacturer, it does not hold exclusive moral responsibility.

2. Advertising agencies handle the promotion of a great many goods. They frequently produce ideas for advertising campaigns, which are submitted to and approved by their customers, the manufacturing or producing companies. What is their responsibility?

Because ad agencies do not manufacture the product, they are not responsible for the product as such, but they must be informed of the product's qualities and selling points. Advertising people often work closely with their customers. They frequently know what is true about a product and what is not, what is misleading or deceptive. Sometimes it is the ad writer rather than the manufacturer who comes up with a promotion that is deceptive or misleading in a way that will benefit the manufacturer. The temptation, in such cases, is for the ad writer to feel that responsibility for the ad rests with the manufacturer. The ad writer is simply an agent paid to do what the client asks. The manufacturer feels that the responsibility is that of the ad writer. He, after all, is the specialist. Actually, both are responsible, and neither party can escape moral responsibility.

Frequently, neither the manufacturer nor the ad agency has difficulty with the initial advertising of a product. A good product that serves a need will sell if it is attractively presented. However, as competition increases, the pressure builds. As a competitor's product resembles one's own more and more, the need to find something distinctive as a selling point becomes more difficult. If a company's number one position in the field is threatened, or it slips to number two, the temptation is to keep or regain first place by more noticeable advertising. The temptation to exaggerate, write misleading copy, or consider immoral approaches becomes strong. One is tempted to think in terms of the good of the company, protecting the interests of the shareholders, keeping up profits, protecting one's job, and thereby justify practices that one would not ordinarily consider or condone.

Advertising agencies have the moral responsibility not to lie, mislead, or misrepresent products. They also have an obligation to investigate when they suspect that they are being asked to lie, mislead, or misrepresent a product. Ignorance is no excuse, if the typical advertising specialist knows something is amiss in what he or she is told about a product to be advertised. Advertising men and women should not take part in lying or misleading the public; they should try to convince their clients not to push for that approach. Even if they cannot convince their clients, they still have the responsibility not to take part in lying or deception. A good ad agency should not have to resort to unethical practices to sell a product.

3. Once an advertisement or an advertising program has been produced, it can be presented to the public in a variety of forms. The major ones are TV and the print media (newspapers and magazines). Specialized products are usually advertised in specialized journals, trade journals, or through direct mail. General products are usually advertised through TV, magazines, and newspapers.

All TV stations, magazines, and newspapers have the moral responsibility for what appears in their shows or in the pages of their publications. They receive copy or film submitted by the manufacturer or ad agency. Do they have the right to question, censor, or prohibit something they are paid to show or print? Yes, they do. Moreover, they have the moral responsibility not to show or print an advertisement that they know to be false, misleading, or deceptive. They may go even further and choose not to air or print an advertisement they feel is offensive or in extremely bad taste. If they feel that running a particular ad will offend their readers, then they may refuse the ad, though they are not morally required to refuse it. They are morally required to refuse an immoral ad, however.

To show or print an immoral ad would be to take part in an immoral action. We are neither allowed to act immorally nor to take part in immoral conduct by acting as agents for others. But the obligation must be kept within the bounds of reason. We cannot expect every magazine editor to check up on every ad submitted for publication to see whether it is in fact false or misleading. The primary responsibility rests with the manufacturer and the advertising agency that produced the ad. But even if the ordinary professional working on the magazine were to suspect that a given ad is false or misleading, then the ad should be questioned and some evidence sought to show its moral legitimacy. The general principle is that it is immoral for those in control of TV advertising or of advertising in newspapers or magazines to air or print what they know to be immoral. Once again, the temptation will be to claim that the responsibility falls on the manufacturer or ad agency, especially when the account is a big one. But TV stations, newspapers, and magazines cannot cast aside their moral responsibility so lightly.

4. What of the public? Members of the general public do not act immorally when they look at misleading ads (how would they know they were misleading if they did not look at them?). They also have no moral obligation to take any positive action about them. But if they are concerned about the truthfulness or accuracy of an ad, if they feel an ad is misleading or deceptive, they can perform a public service by making their feelings and perceptions known. They can write to the manufacturing company and complain about the ad, or if they know the responsible ad agency, they can appropriately write to it. They can write to the TV station, newspaper, or magazine that carried the ad. They can write to the local or national Better Business Bureau, the FTC or FDA, or to the National Advertising Review Board (NARB). The NARB was formed in 1971 and is sponsored by the American Association of Advertising Agencies, the American Advertising Federation, the Association of National Advertisers, and the Council of Better Business Bureaus. The NARB's aim is self-regulation by advertisers. It investigates complaints, asks advertisers for substantiation, and reports the results to the one who files the complaint and also prints the results in a monthly press release.

Public pressure can help keep advertising responsible. If advertisers know that the public will not only complain about misleading or immoral advertising, but will also cast their vote against a product so advertised, by not purchasing it, they would have a strong incentive to keep their advertising moral.

5. Government has taken an active role in regulating and monitoring advertising. The FTC and the FDA enforce only legal standards, however. They do not and should not enforce moral standards if these differ from legal ones. Government is not empowered, in our political system, to be the final arbiter of morality, but, through law, it can sometimes legally settle issues about which there is moral controversy. But government does not make actions, policies, or practices moral or immoral by its legislation. Legislators and administrators can certainly listen to moral arguments. Moral arguments, prudential arguments, and legal precedents are all appropriately considered. Government and its agencies should not act immorally, but they are neither capable of, nor empowered to, legislate morality.

The role of government in the area of advertising is to protect the public interest. It does this in a variety of ways, some of which we have seen. To the extent that advertisers regulate their own behavior, legislation is not needed. When advertisers seek to achieve their own good at the expense of the general public, however, then government plays a legitimate regulatory role.

The role of government as regulator is not without its temptations. Regulatory agencies have sometimes been staffed by people who have worked in the areas being regulated, or who hope to work in the areas regulated. The possible conflict of interest is fairly clear. Who regulates the regulators? Regulators also sometimes take it upon themselves to interpret legislation very broadly, even if this was not the legislative intent. Regulatory agencies can become minor legislators on their own, by writing the regulations that implement the laws. They may, if so inclined, attempt to impose their own moral standards on an industry. They may misinterpret the degree to which the general public wishes or needs paternalistic protection. Regulators, Congress, the President, and the people should be aware of the dangers inherent in governmental regulation.

Advertising is a pervasive activity in the United States. Most people learn the semantics of advertising as they grow up. They learn to discount certain claims as puffery; they learn to read fine print in ads, to see if an ad may be interpreted in more than one way. They learn that advertisers make associations but that some associations tell us nothing about a product. Whether or not a movie star or a baseball hero claims to use a beauty product or eat a breakfast cereal tells us more about the star and the hero than it does about the product. Inherent in the semantics of advertising are the notions of lying, misrepresentation, deception, manipulation, and other questionable practices. Those that are immoral should be labeled as such. Public pressure, even more than government regulation, is likely to be effective in curbing the major excesses of advertising.

Further Reading

BAIRD, CHARLES W. *Advertising by Professionals*. International Institute for Economic Research. Ottawa, Ill.: Green Hills Publishers, 1977.

BOK, SISSELA. *Lying: Moral Choice in Public and Private Life*. New York: Pantheon Books, 1978.

GALBRAITH, JOHN KENNETH. *The Affluent Society*, 3rd ed. Boston: Houghton Mifflin Company, 1976.

KOTLER, PHILIP. *Marketing Management*, 4th ed. Englewood Cliffs, N.J.: Prentice-Hall, Inc., 1980.

LUCAS, JOHN T., and RICHARD GURMAN. *Truth in Advertising*. New York: American Management Association, Inc., 1972.

MILL, JOHN STUART. *On Liberty*. New York: Appleton-Century-Crofts, 1947.

PRESTON, IVAN L. *The Great American Blow-up: Puffery in Advertising and Selling*. Madison, Wis.: University of Wisconsin Press, 1975.

SANDAGE, C. H., and VERNON FRYBURGER. *Advertising Theory and Practice*, 9th ed. Homewood, Ill.: Richard D. Irwin, Inc., 1975.

STUART, FREDRIC, ed. *Consumer Protection from Deceptive Advertising*. Hempstead, N.Y.: Hofstra University, 1974.

Truth in Advertising: A Symposium of the Toronto School of Theology. New York: Harper & Row, Publishers, 1972.

FOURTEEN

Trade Secrets, Insider Information, and Corporate Disclosure

If one company were to hijack a truckload of TV sets from another company, or if an employee were to embezzle funds from his employer, we would have no hesitation in calling the acts immoral. We know what it means for a company to own TV sets or money, and what it means for someone to take these wrongfully. When it comes to knowledge and information, however, our concept of proprietorship is less clear. If I take information or knowledge from you, I do not physically deprive you of it. We may both have it and have it equally. My taking it from you does not leave you without it, because knowledge and information are different from physical objects. If, furthermore, we lived in a society in which all goods were shared, knowledge and information would be among those items that would be shared most freely, because each person could enjoy the benefit of the knowledge and information without depriving anyone else of their use.

Information and knowledge are vital aspects of many businesses, and special information may give one business an advantage over another. Hence, in a competitive situation, one business may not wish to share its knowledge and information, although doing so would not lessen its own knowledge and information. Information and knowledge, moreover, often represent a financial investment by a firm. Some knowledge is costly to obtain or develop. A marketing study, for instance, may represent a great deal of time and money, and a company's desire to keep such information secret is understandable.

To whom do knowledge and information, which have been developed by people in a corporation, belong? To whom do knowledge and information about a corporation belong? From a moral point of view, what may be kept secret and what must be disclosed? In a broad sense, trade secrets refer to all knowledge developed by a firm, which it guards as proprietary; in a narrow sense, trade secrets designate an alternative to patents and copyrights as a means to protecting inventions, formulas, and the like. Trade secrets, insider information, and disclosure are three aspects of questions pertaining to knowledge and information in business. They have generated much discussion. Many people are demanding and receiving more and more disclosure of information from corporations, and, at the same time, computer theft is rising, and corporations are trying to devise ways of keeping corporate information both secret and secure.

Trade Secrets

Let us start our discussion of trade secrets by looking at three typical, though hypothetical cases.

- CASE 1. John Knosit was head of a research team of CDE Electric. His team was working on developing a cheaper and more effective filament for light bulbs. Six months ago, a rumor circulated in the industry that the team had made a breakthrough, and all that was required was final testing. This would put CDE Electric far ahead of its competitors. Five months ago, X Electric hired John away from CDE, offering him $25,000 a year more than he had been getting. No mention was made of his work on the new filament. After being in his new position for three months, his superior approached him and said that X Electric had hired him because of his work on the filament, and that he would have to develop the filament quickly for X Electric or be fired. John knows how to develop the filament. Is he morally justified in developing it for X Electric?
- CASE 2. Jane Berry works as Sales Manager for Pretty-Good Refrigeration. She is hired by Even-Better Refrigeration to fill a similar position in their firm, at a sizable raise in salary. Before she leaves Pretty-Good Refrigeration, Jane makes a copy of the customer book, which contains the list of Pretty-Good Refrigeration's customers, the contact person in other firms, the kind of equipment each purchased, when it is due for replacement, and other similar information. She brings the list with her and then systematically contacts the people on the list at the appropriate time, promoting the products of Even-Better Refrigeration. She

believes that Even-Better Refrigeration products are superior to Pretty-Good Refrigeration, and because she knows both products she is able to mount a convincing sales pitch. Does she act morally in doing so?

• CASE 3: Henry Mangel is Assistant Personnel Manager of Dirt-Brown Construction Company. He has worked for the company for five years. During that time he has learned a good deal about personnel-management techniques, which were implemented and proved to be successful. Partly as a result of his innovations, the workers have been content and their productivity has increased. He is hired by Grass-Green Construction Company as their Personnel Manager. At his new job, he immediately introduces a series of changes based on his experience at Dirt-Brown Construction, and uses some of the techniques he learned as well as those he introduced there. Is he morally justified in doing this?

The three cases share a common feature. In all three cases, a person goes from one company to another, bringing with him certain knowledge from the first company. He uses that knowledge in the second company. Is it appropriate to do so? Does the knowledge belong to him or to the firm at which he worked? What kind of knowledge belongs to a company, and how can it be protected?

Consider the first case. John Knosit was the head of a research team. He was appointed to that position, presumably because of his leadership ability and because of his knowledge and skill. These belong to him. He takes with him his own knowledge, skill, experience, and personal qualities wherever he goes. But while employed by CDE Electric, he works on a specific project. The company pays his salary while he works on the project. It also pays the salaries of his fellow teamworkers. The company provides the laboratory in which they conduct their experiments; it supplies all the materials they need. When they develop the new filament, the company will take out a patent on it. Clearly the filament belongs to the company. But John knows how to develop the filament. Is that knowledge his?

To get some perspective on the question: Suppose that while working for CDE Electric John went to X Electric and offered to sell them, for $50,000, the process he had developed. Most people would readily admit that to do so would be immoral. The reason it is immoral is that the process belongs to CDE Electric. Even though John knows the process, it does not belong to him. He is morally restricted in what he can do with that information, and giving it or selling it to others is not morally allowable. His being hired by X Electric does not change the status of his knowledge of the filament. That still belongs to CDE Electric. Hence, he cannot, morally, develop the filament for X Electric as he is commanded to do. John's superior at X Electric acts immorally in commanding it, and if John does as he commands, John also acts immorally.

A short utilitarian analysis will help us see why it is immoral to develop the filament for X Electric. Consider the consequences for all those involved. John benefits because he gets to keep his job and his handsome increase in salary. X Electric benefits because they get the filament quickly and cheaply. They will therefore be able to compete easily with CDE Electric. In order to get around patent laws, they may have to make minor modifications so that the filament is not identical. But the cost of doing that will not be anything like the cost of developing the original filament. Because they do not have to recoup research and development costs, they will even be able to market the new bulbs more cheaply than CDE Electric. CDE Electric is the loser. It still has the filament, but it has lost its competitive edge; it will lose to X Electric part of the market it would otherwise have had to itself. And because of the research costs, it will make less profit.

The harm that CDE suffers, however, is offset by the benefit that X Electric reaps. If we then add in the benefit John receives, John's action seems morally justifiable. This, however, is not the case. For we have not yet considered the result or effect of the practice on the rest of society. Suppose that hiring team leaders in order to gain trade secrets from them becomes a practice. Any firm that spent money—perhaps millions of dollars—to develop a new product or idea would expect to lose that investment to a competitor, who would obtain the information by hiring away its developer. In each case, the second company would benefit at the expense of the first. Clearly, every company would see that it is not in its best interest to develop any product or idea. They would all be better off waiting for someone else to develop a product or idea. In the end, no one would develop products or ideas. The result of the practice in the long run, therefore, would be very serious, not only for society as a whole but for the companies—all companies—that now benefit from research and development. Taking the broad consequences into account, we see that the practice is an immoral one.

What can we draw from this consideration? If the analysis is correct, we can legitimately claim that at least some trade secrets are justifiable. A company is allowed to protect the products and ideas it develops in its research and development programs, for at least a certain amount of time.

However, the analysis, though plausible, is not universally accepted. There are some who argue that John Knosit is the real inventor of the product because it is the result of his genius or ingenuity, and it rightfully belongs to him. He developed it while working for the company, therefore the company has the "shop right" to it, that is, the company has the right to use the invention for its own ends. But it has no right, this view maintains, to prevent John from taking that knowledge with him and using it for the benefit of his new employer, if he so chooses.

Because of controversies of this type, certain practices have become more or less standard in industry, and laws have been developed to help regulate the use of information and inventions. Patent laws are one obvious device that help companies achieve some protection in the use of products developed by those in their employ. A company can protect its interests in other ways as well. It can, for instance, fragment its projects so that very few people know the total project. It is also typical for a firm to require that people who work for it in development areas keep sensitive information they acquire as em-

294

ployees of the firm (including information on products the employees themselves develop) confidential for a certain length of time, even if they leave the company. This is specified in a contract, which details what an employee may and may not reveal. Employees must often sign such agreements before they are given access to the company's research and development. Should an employee break this contract, he can be sued for the damages incurred. The contract itself, in such cases, sets not only the legal but also the moral framework within which to decide the morality of a given act of disclosure. In general, the practice is morally defensible, even though some companies abuse the practice. Abuse occurs when the contract violates an employee's rights by imposing unreasonable limitations on what the employer assigns to an employee in terms of his or her knowledge. Firms will sometimes subtly coerce the employee to sign unreasonable agreements. For instance, the employee will be asked to sign a condition of employment *only after* leaving his or her other position and is ready to work for the new firm.

The right of the company to be the first to use and profit from its research is nonetheless in general morally defensible. This does not mean, however, that it has the exclusive right to what it develops forever. Nor does this mean that if it develops a product that would benefit society, it can for its own reasons indefinitely prevent it from ever becoming known. Knowledge is not something that one can keep locked up for as long as one likes. Patents, appropriately, do expire. Long before they expire, any new idea that can be reverse-engineered may be so engineered, and copied with just sufficient changes so as not to infringe on the patent laws. Competition thus enters the field. However, the delay that such copying requires after the original item appears is sufficient for the originator to recoup his research expenses. Interestingly, the formula for Coca-Cola has never been patented precisely in order to keep it secret. Chemical analysis has not yielded the formula. The formula for Coca-Cola is one of the best-kept trade secrets in history. From a moral point of view, there is no objection to that secret remaining a secret of the company indefinitely; no demonstrable harm would befall society even if the secret eventually died with its keepers.

If a cheap substitute for gasoline was found, however, oil companies might consider it to be in their own interests to keep such a product from being developed. If the product was discovered in their laboratories, they might prefer to lock up the process in their company safe until it was necessary to use it, rather than compete with their own oil interests. Could they morally do so, and could they morally keep those employees who developed it from divulging the formula *forever*? No. The good that society would reap from the oil substitute would far exceed the damage done to the oil company by the substitute's appearing on the market. The developer has the right to be the first to market the product, and to protect its investment in development so as to recover its cost. But this right is a limited one.

The argument necessary to show why this is a limited right hinges on the nature of knowledge. Whatever new knowledge a company produces is always an increment to past knowledge which has been developed by society in years past, and passed from one generation to the next. Any new invention is made by people who learned a great deal from the general store of knowledge, before they could bring what they knew to bear on a particular problem. Though we can attribute inventions and discoveries to particular efforts of individuals or teams, they are also the result of those people who developed them and passed on their knowledge to others. In this way, every advance in knowledge is social, and belongs ultimately to society, even though for practical purposes we can assign it temporarily to a given individual or firm.

Case 2 raises a somewhat different issue. Jane Berry makes a copy of the customer book, a list of Pretty-Good Refrigeration's customers. She does not take the original, therefore the information is still available to Pretty-Good Refrigeration. To whom does the list belong? The list is in the company's book. It does not contain simply a list of purchasers, such as might be obtained from an industry trade list. It was generated by employees of the company, and they were paid for their services while it was generated. The list therefore belongs to Pretty-Good Refrigeration. By taking the list with her, Jane is stealing information that does not belong to her. She uses it, moreover, for her own ends and at the expense of her former employer. As in the previous case, the information rightfully belongs to the company, and in taking it, Jane acts immorally.

What if instead of taking a copy of the customer book Jane goes to her new employer with the list memorized? Does this make a difference? The answer is clearly no. What is immoral is not the fact that she took a certain amount of paper from Pretty-Good Refrigeration but that she took its annotated customer list. That list belongs to the company. Whether she takes it in her head or on photocopied paper does not matter. The information is not hers, and she uses it immorally when she uses it to take away the customers from her former employer.

Case 3, however, is different from the other two. In Case 3, Henry does not take what does not belong to him. He steals no secrets from the company. What managerial skill he learns while working for the company belongs to him. It is not patentable information, and it is not guaranteed by copyright or any other law. A person who works for a firm earns his pay by discharging the duties of whatever position he holds in the firm. As Personnel Manager, Henry performed his duties. In doing so, he gained experience. He had ideas for improvement, and these were implemented in the firm, to the firm's advantage. But managerial techniques and organizational structures that one develops do not belong to the firm for which one works.

Let us test this claim. Suppose that while working for Dirty-Brown Construction Henry went to Grass-Green Construction and offered to sell them his managerial ideas for $50,000. What would we say of the morality of that action? A proper first reply is that it is unlikely that Grass-Green Construction would be interested. Managerial ideas are not the kinds of things one can simply take and implement; each firm has a particular structure and dynamism. A consultant might come in and do a study of how to increase the efficiency of a firm, but no consultant would simply offer an idea regarding management and expect to receive much, if any, money for it.

If Henry's ideas are good, could he legitimately consult on the side? The answer, of course, depends on the firm he is working for and the nature of his agreement with the firm. His employer could make it a condition of his employment that he not consult; and of course he should not consult for the company's competitors. His consulting, however, is different from his selling information that belongs to the firm. The skill that one develops and the experience that one attains on a job belongs to the employee, not the firm. If he can sell his experience and skill for more to another employer, the employee is entitled to do so. Each company, unless it hires only unskilled labor and does all its training and hiring from its own ranks, hires people who have acquired knowledge, skill, and experience working for other employers.

The distinction between the information and knowledge that belong appropriately to the employer, and the information and knowledge that belong appropriately to the employee is not always an easy one to draw. Several guidelines may help. Information that is available in the public domain is not secret. Even if a firm independently develops information in its own laboratory, and the identical information is available in technical or popular journals, the firm cannot claim proprietary rights to it. If such material is publicly available, an employee violates no trust or obligation of loyalty if he uses that knowledge in a new position. Similarly, if the information can be easily generated by those competent to do so, then the restriction on an employee's using such information in a new position is minimal, if it exists at all.

Three indicators are useful in determining what information is appropriately secret, what information belongs to a given firm, and hence what information an employee has a moral obligation not to reveal to his original firm's competitors. A first indication is the amount of security the company employs to maintain the secrecy of the information. A company may treat the information—techniques or inventions, or consumer and/or supplier lists—as highly confidential, that is, it takes measures to insure that the information is not available routinely, it restricts access, and takes other comparable measures. If such measures are taken, then the employees with access to that information know that it is considered secret by the firm. Usually, the employees are not only cautioned about the secrecy of the data or information to which they are given access, but they must sign an agreement not to divulge the information.

A second criterion is the amount of money that a firm has spent in developing the information. Strict security regulations for information that is in the public domain, or that can be easily developed, make no sense. Elaborate safeguards make sense only where the information is costly to produce and

297

important to the financial future of the firm. A third criterion is the value of the information to a competitor. Again, it unlikely that a firm will initiate great security to protect information valuable only to the firm itself. If, however, the information could be used by a competitor to gain a competitive edge, then it is reasonable that the originating firm be permitted to protect its investment.

From the foregoing analysis we can conclude that firms have the right to protect certain kinds of information if it belongs to them; and that they can legitimately impose restrictions on their employees not to divulge such information. The analysis provides some rough guidelines. But the conclusion should not be taken to be stronger than it actually is. In particular, we should note two points. First, the obligation on the part of an employee not to sell or give to another what properly belongs to the firm is a moral obligation. Attempts to reinforce the moral obligation through law have been only minimally effective. Some employers have attempted to restrain their employees from working for competing firms for a period of two years after they leave their own company. Such agreements, even if signed, have generally not held up in court because they violate the right of the employee to change jobs. The attempts of firms to issue injunctions against competitors who are pursuing research with the help of a former employee have usually been unsuccessful. Some companies have emphasized the ethical obligations of employees both before they begin work on certain projects and just prior to their leaving the service of the company. They have also attempted to keep them loyal by offering consulting fees for a period of one or two years, and by giving them retirement benefits, or other benefits that they would not normally receive, in return for not revealing trade secrets.

The second point again concerns the information that a company can appropriately keep secret. Some, it seems, would prefer to keep all aspects of their operation secret. They have been reluctant to disclose any information at all, unless forced to do so by law. The foregoing guidelines concern only certain kinds of information, namely that which is closely guarded, expensive, and which, if divulged to a competitor, would cause serious harm. However, a great deal of company information is not of this type. There are some interesting borderline cases. Many firms have claimed, for instance, that the salaries of their top executives were trade secrets. If the competition knew what these salaries were, they could more easily lure top executives to their own company. But clearly, what a top executive makes is not something he is required to keep secret from others who might want to employ him. His total compensation is also of interest to stockholders. Such information is now a matter of public record. Companies' claims to secrecy have to be balanced against claims of the employees to freedom of speech and movement; against claims of the government, stockholders, and the public to information that concerns them, and which they have a right to know. Lastly, claims to secrecy must be balanced against the right of society in general to benefit from socially useful information and knowledge.

Insider Information

Insider information is information that someone within a company has but which is not available to those outside the company. This includes not only trade secrets, which we have already discussed, but company strategy and plans. The moral problems connected with insider information concern the use that individuals may make of such information while they are still members of a firm. Two aspects of the question raise special problems. One is that of someone within the firm using information for his or her own private gain, at the expense of the firm. This is called conflict of interest. The other is the use of insider information by someone within a firm, to secure personal advantage over those not in the firm. In both cases the individual seeks his or her own gain rather than the firm's. Is this morally justifiable?

We have seen that some information belongs to a company and and some information belongs to the employee, who may use it in another firm. In our discussion of the corporation and of the responsibility of employees within it, we distinguished between an employee as a person and the role he plays or the function he performs within a corporation. We can also distinguish between information belonging to an individual, which he can use as he wishes, and that which does not belong to him and which he cannot use as he wishes.

An employee of a firm fills a certain position within the firm. We saw that no employee can morally do what is immoral, even if he is expected or commanded to do so as part of his job. While filling any position in a firm, an individual remains a moral being and a person. He cannot compartmentalize himself into person and employee. Hence, any information he receives or absorbs in his capacity as an employee he retains in his capacity as a human being. As a human being he has certain interests, and a private life. He is interested in advancing his own good as well as advancing the good of the firm for which he works. Of all the information and knowledge he receives in his capacity as an employee, what can he morally use for his own benefit?

Consider the following fairly obvious case. A vice-president of a railroad company is involved in planning the expansion of the railroad. He and others work on the most desirable route for the railroad to take. He has access to the plans of the company and knows well in advance where the railroad expects to put its new line. The company does not disclose to the public its plans. It tries to keep the route secret until it can purchase or negotiate the right-of-way. If it were to divulge its intent, the price of the land would rise significantly. The vice-president, knowing the route, purchases as much of the land along the projected route as he can. He intends to buy the land as cheaply as possible from its present owners, who of course do not know the railroad's plans, and then sell the land to the railroad at as high a price as he can get. He knows in advance the amount of money the railroad has projected for purchase of the land, and therefore knows how much he can hold out for. Does he act morally in doing this?

The company will certainly not look kindly on his action. He is increasing the cost of the land to the company and profiting at the company's expense. Such action will probably result in his being fired. But is he not free to exercise his private right to buy and sell land, to look after his personal finances, and to invest as he wishes? What, if anything, is wrong with his action? The crux of the situation is that he used information that he received in his corporate capacity—in his position as the company's vice-president—for personal gain in his private capacity. The information was not available to him in his capacity as a private individual. It was not public knowledge, and it was knowledge available to only a few persons within the company. The basis for calling this immoral is that he used information that was not his. He used it for his private gain at the expense of the company. The company might call that a breach of loyalty. More serious is his use of information to which, as a private individual, he had no right.

The distinction between the information one has as occupant of a certain position in a firm and that which one has as a private individual has wide application. In casual conversation, employees frequently emphasize their importance by dropping information they have gained because of their position in a firm. They do this to impress the people to whom they are speaking—a form of one-upmanship. Frequently, no harm is done. But sometimes great harm is done. Those who have access to personnel files, for instance, have no right to divulge what they know about employees if the information is learned only through their work and is not otherwise available. Morality demands confidentiality of records, whether or not one signs a contract not to divulge such information. Similarly, many plans, discussions, or memos that pertain to a company's business, and to which the employee has official access, do not belong to him in his private capacity. From a moral point of view, one is not free to divulge such information casually, for personal profit, monetary gain, or even to feel important.

The second case of the illegitimate use of insider information also concerns personal gain, not at the company's expense but at the expense of those not connected with the company. This typically occurs in trading the stock of the company for which one works. What is morally allowable in this respect, and what is not?

Those who work for a company are in a position to know it better than those who do not. They can judge the efficiency of management, on a daily basis. They can estimate worker satisfaction and productivity. They can sense whether the company is developing, and whether management is dynamic and anxious for expansion and growth. On the basis of this information, they may be in a better position than others to decide whether or not to invest in the company by buying its stock. Such information is not privileged; it is generally available. This sort of information lacks the specificity of the sort of insider information that would make its use immoral when deciding whether to buy the company's stock.

Consider the following two cases, however. The management of Company *A*, in its private planning sessions, decides that buying Company *B* as a subsidiary would be a profitable move. Such takeovers frequently result in the stock of Company *B* rising to the price that Company *A* will offer for the stock in its purchase offer. Adam Agile of Company *A* buys stock in Company *B* before any news or rumor of the takeover gets out. He makes a handsome profit. In the second case, Nick Nimble, an officer in Company *B*, buys a large block of stock in his own company, as soon as he sees that the takeover is likely to occur. He too acts prior to any news or leak of the takeover, and reaps the reward of a sizable profit. Are their actions morally justifiable?

In both cases the two men act on inside information. Neither one harms either company. If their action is inappropriate, it must be because it harms someone. Whom do they hurt? As a result of their inside information, they are able to act upon knowledge not available to the general public or to other traders in the stock market. Any charge of immorality must be based on the fact that to buy and sell stock, both parties to the transaction have access to the appropriate information. Their interpretation of that information, or their diligence in analyzing the information available, as well as their personal situations, make some people buyers at the time others are sellers. But the use of inside information makes the transaction an unequal one, and hence an unfair one.

In these cases, Adam purchased stock in a company other than his own. Officers, board members, and large shareholders of publicly owned corporations are legally required to disclose the purchase of stock in their own company. They do not have to disclose their purchase of stock in other companies. Construed strictly, Adam's action was not insider information, when this is taken to mean knowledge of the actions of one's own company and the purchase of that company's stock. But in a broad sense, it was insider information. Nick used the same information to purchase stock in Company *B*. From a moral point of view, the two cases are similar. If one acted immorally, so did the other. Both took advantage of special knowledge to make a profit, which they would not have been able to do without inside information.

In the foregoing cases, however, there was no manipulation of the stock and no other unfair practice. Corporations are required to disclose or release information promptly, to avoid special privilege to an insider. But clearly those on the inside frequently have access to the information before it is disclosed. Because they have that information in their capacity as corporate agents and not as private individuals, they inappropriately use it to achieve personal gain at the expense of members of the general public. This, of course, does not mean that they cannot buy and sell stock in their own companies. It simply means that morally, they cannot take unfair advantage of their special insider information.

The Securities and Exchange Commission (SEC) has in recent years attempted to crack down on insider trading, which it claims is stealing. It has urged increasing the penalties for those convicted of such criminal action from $10,000 to $100,000, and in civil suits it urges that government be able to recover 300 percent instead of the present 100 percent of the gains insiders make by their illegal trades. It has also started prosecuting about twenty cases a year—

far more than in the past. The Commission considers an "insider" anyone who has pertinent information that is not publicly available, and that gives the trader an advantage over the public. Thus secretaries, lawyers, consultants, and others who might be considered outsiders become insiders because of their knowledge—as do all others who are told the pertinent information, or who overhear it. Many companies go to extreme lengths to keep takeover and similar plans secret. They use code words for the companies involved, shred memos, and guard against tapped phones and electronic surveillance. But to prove successfully the case against accused insiders is not often easy. Moreover, those who have access to foreign currencies (e.g., a Swiss bank account) can buy stock from abroad without fear of their activities being detected.

The SEC argues that insider trading will lessen the public's interest in investing in what people feel is an unfair market, one in which insiders have all the advantages. But the SEC has its critics. They claim that the practice of insider trading is so widespread that the SEC investigations barely scratch the surface and are not worth the money or effort poured into attempts to stop such trading. Furthermore, they claim, insider trading has not discouraged investor interest in the stock market, and hence the SEC's fears are unfounded. A few economists go so far as to claim that insider trading helps make the market efficient by taking into account all information about a firm. Who, they ask, is actually hurt by insider trading?

The critics claim that no one is hurt by insider trading. Those who sell their stock do so for reasons of their own. There is always a market for stocks, which means that there are always both buyers and sellers. Because sellers are willing to sell at the price they get, how are they hurt? The reply is that they would not sell if they knew the stock was sure to go up. But the insiders buy with that knowledge. Hence the transaction is not fair, and harm is done to the seller, who does not make the profit he would make if the insider's knowledge were public knowledge. The critics, believing the Myth of Amoral Business, view the stock exchange as an impersonal market for impersonal transactions. Winners and losers are beside the point, because the market is simply an efficient means of matching buyers and sellers. Even though the stock market acts impersonally, it mediates transactions between people. And transactions between people are properly subject to moral rules.

Insider trading is difficult to control. But because insiders use for their personal gain knowledge they have acquired as corporate agents, because the transaction is based on unequal knowledge, and because harm is done to those without the inside knowledge, the argument against the justifiability of insider trading is stronger than the justification thus far given for it.

A closely related issue concerns not insiders but investment advisories. One such advisory service, for instance, run by Joseph Granville, is so influential that it is able to influence the market—at least in the short run. In January 1981, a recommendation by Granville to "sell everything" led to a dramatic drop in the stock market. Granville knew that this would happen, as did those who work for him, because they had this information before others. Those who buy Granville's investment service got the information and were able to act on it before the general public. It was their action that led to the precipitous drop in the market. Knowing that this would happen, they could also have sold short, making a profit when the market declined. Is acting on such information comparable to acting on insider information? In both cases, one party has information that is not public information. But the cases are different. Insiders trade on knowledge that will be appropriately public, and they know it only by virtue of their corporate position. The advice of an investment advisory is based on generally available information. The advice is paid for by subscribers to the advisory, and that advice is therefore proprietary. No one else has a right to such knowledge, even if having such knowledge can at times help one make a better investment than otherwise. If any advisory were found guilty of trying to manipulate the market, the situation would be different; any such activity is immoral. There may be cases in which the SEC is uncertain whether manipulation is actually intended. But investment advisories do not have shareholders to protect, as members of a board are required to protect the interests of their shareholders. Their knowledge can be more appropriately characterized as guesses, even if their guesses are sometimes shrewd, and following them leads to financial gains. The issues here are borderline and require individual analysis. Although the issues are in part similar to insider trading, they are not the same and should be kept distinct.

Corporate Disclosure

Trade secrets include those items of information and knowledge to which a firm has proprietary right, which it can legally and morally protect and refuse to reveal. At the other end of the information spectrum is a large amount of information that a public corporation must, by law, reveal. The information that a corporation is morally obliged to disclose coincides with much that is legally required, though pressures for increased disclosure are based for the most part on moral arguments.

The moral basis for disclosure of corporate information rests primarily on two second-order, substantive moral principles: (1) each person has the right to the information he needs to enter into a transaction fairly; and (2) each person has the right to know those actions of others that will seriously and adversely affect him or her. Each of these requires some defense.

We have discussed the first of these principles several times. A transaction is fair if those who are a party to it have the appropriate information and freely enter into it. They cannot fairly participate in a transaction if they are denied pertinent information. On the other hand, it is not necessary for each party to make sure that the other party is properly informed. What is necessary is that each party have access to the appropriate information. A transaction is fair even if one of the parties does not take advantage of information that is available to him, and which he could use profitably. This principle probably requires no more explanation here, even though it can be defended by using a utilitarian, a Kantian, or a Rawlsian approach.

The second principle can be derived from our earlier analysis of moral responsibility. We saw that each person is morally responsible for his actions and their effects. He is responsible to those whom his actions affect, and he is morally bound not to harm others unless there is some overriding reason for doing so. Respect for persons, a contract formed behind a veil of ignorance, and a utilitarian calculation all lead to the conclusion that, if we are going to engage in some action that endangers others, then we are morally bound either to warn them or not to perform the action. Though we are not morally permitted to harm others, we are permitted to do some things that might cause others harm, providing we take the precautions necessary to prevent harm to them, including warning them. For instance, if a road crew is authorized to dynamite a pass, it is morally allowed to do so only if the crew takes proper precautions to assure that no one gets hurt. The obligation not to hurt others involves the potential victim's right not to be hurt, and his right to be warned of actions that could hurt him, even if they are legitimate. If a company intends to build a nuclear power plant in a certain location, those in the vicinity of the site have a right to know this. If such a plant potentially endangers them, they have the right to this information. They may have further rights as well. But a basic right, and the one in virtue of which they can rationally take other action and exercise other rights, is the right to be informed.

In our discussion of disclosure, we shall deal with three questions: to whom must disclosure be made available; morally, what must be disclosed; and what form should disclosure take?

1. Based on the two principles stated previously, a corporation has the moral obligation to disclose appropriate information to those with whom it enters into transactions, and those whom its actions affect seriously and adversely. In broad terms, those affected are (a) the shareholders and potential shareholders of the corporation; (b) the board of directors; (c) the workers; (d) government; (e) the corporation's suppliers and agents; (f) the consumer of the corporation's product; and (g) the general public, whether or not they are consumers of the product. A different kind of disclosure is appropriate for each of these groups.

The actions of a corporation may seriously and adversely affect its competitors. Yet if the harm results from legal and moral activities, such as producing a better product, making a technological breakthrough, pursuing an aggressive marketing strategy, or increasing efficiency, then the corporation owes the competitor no special information. If a competitor's plant is adjacent to that of another corporation, however, and an explosion may cause harm to the competitor's plant, then the competitor has the right to be informed of the danger, just as every other neighbor does.

2. What morally must be disclosed? Because each group relates differently to the corporation, that which is to be disclosed will vary from group to group. In each case the two principles apply.

a. Disclosure of information to stockholders and to potential stockholders has caused a great deal of debate. Corporations have argued that in disclosing information to these groups they were making information available to their competitors—information which by right the corporation should be allowed to keep secret. The argument in favor of secrecy, however, conflicts with the right of these groups to information. A partial solution has been effected by the Securities and Exchange Commission. It requires the disclosure of certain information by all corporations to shareholders and to potential shareholders. Disclosure to the latter group in effect means disclosure to the general public. Because the same information is required from all competing corporations, the conditions of competition are kept fair.

Those who own stock in a corporation are its legal owners. It would seem that they have the right to know everything about a corporation that they choose to know. Yet because disclosure of trade secrets, for instance, would compromise those secrets to the detriment of the owners, shareholders do not have the right to be informed of everything, nor are they routinely informed of everything. What they have a right to know includes information on the management of the corporation, its financial position, and its general plans for the future. They are routinely informed, in some detail, of these matters through the corporation's annual report to the shareholders, given during the annual shareholders' meeting. They are informed of the net sales of the company, net earnings, return on shareholder's equity, earnings per share, dividends, working capital, and the assets and the liabilities of the corporation. The annual report usually includes an overview of the corporation's activities, possibly something about its research and development, a list of the members of the board of directors and the corporate officers, a financial balance sheet, information on the corporation's debts and taxes, and possibly some information on its retirement plan and similar pertinent information. This information is necessary if a shareholder is to evaluate how his investment is being managed. Because he has a right to vote for members of the corporation's board of directors, he is also informed about them: who they are, what position they hold, either in the corporation or in other companies, and how many shares of the corporation's stock each one owns. If new members of the board are to be elected, shareholders are informed of who they are. For many years, the salaries of a corporation's top officers were considered a trade secret. This information is now, by law, reported to the shareholders; this is appropriate because the shareholders are owners of the corporation.

Once information of this sort is disclosed to the shareholders, it also becomes a matter of public record with the SEC. The information is therefore available to a corporation's competitors. More important, it is available to potential purchasers of the corporation's stock. Before someone invests his money in a corporation—if the transaction is to be a fair one—one has the right to know something about the company one is investing in: its assets, the dividends it pays, its growth or lack of growth, the price/earnings ratio of the company's stock, its assets and liabilities, and its management.

The information disclosed to shareholders and to potential shareholders has for the most part been financial. Those who defend this policy argue that the financial details of a corporation are the pieces of information that are necessary to judge its management, and also to judge whether one is making a sound investment. But there are some who feel that other kinds of information are of interest to shareholders and potential shareholders. The proposed Corporate Democracy Act, for instance, desires "To increase the flow of information to consumers, shareholders and workers about employment patterns, environmental matters, job health and safety, foreign production, directorial performance, shareholder ownership, tax rates and legal and auditing fees."[1] The Act spells out in detail a great deal of information about distribution of the work force by sex and race, about records submitted to the Environmental Protection Agency, and about overseas operations. In some cases it would require such information be included in the annual report; in others, it would require only that a corporation make such information available on demand to its shareholders.

The right of shareholders to information about the company is a right that no one denies. But exactly what they have the right to, in addition to what is already required by law, is a matter of debate. Corporations have argued that investors are interested only in financial information, and they claim that they already supply much more than the vast majority of investors are interested in having. They also argue that, beyond a certain point, the increase of information results in a decrease in understanding on the part of all except the expert in accounting. An investor who is interested in whether the corporation is acting morally, however, may well be interested in how the corporation operates from the point of view of hiring women and minorities, how often its employees have blown the whistle, whether the corporation is operating in South Africa, and, if it does, whether it follows the Sullivan Code (see Chapter 17). These and other issues are not irrelevant if one wishes to evaluate the corporation from a moral point of view. If shareholders and potential shareholders demand such information, they have a right to it. Uniform disclosure by all large corporations, however, can only be achieved by making such disclosures legally mandatory. A moral audit would, of course, provide this information.

Shareholders are legally represented by members of the board of directors of a corporation. Shareholders, therefore, should be informed about the operation of the board and the actions of its members. Shareholders have a right to know not only for whom they are voting but how the nomination procedure for board members works; how the board functions; who sets agendas; how often the board meets; what the committees of the board are and who serves on them; the number of meetings each board member has attended in the previous year; and the reasons for the resignation of any board members. If a board member resigns in protest to board or corporation action, such in-

[1]Mark Green and Robert Massie, Jr., eds. *The Big Business Reader: Essays on Corporate America* (New York: The Pilgrim Press, 1980), p. 592.

formation is of direct and pertinent interest to shareholders. At the present time, this information is generally not disclosed.

b. The members of the board of directors are the legal representatives of the shareholders, therefore they owe the shareholders appropriate information, as well as honest service in their interests. Yet board members need not make public everything they learn. Because they are legally and morally bound to look after the interests of the corporation, and to evaluate the corporation's activities and the performance of management, they have the right to independent access to the information they desire. The owners' right of access is exercised through the members of the board, and this access cannot be appropriately restricted by a decision of management.

c. What must be disclosed to the workers? We have already seen that they have a right to know the conditions of work, including their rights, benefits, and obligations. This follows simply from the fact that this information is necessary if the contract between employer and employee is to be fair. The worker must know in advance what he is contracting into. He must also be informed of any danger to his health the work he performs might produce. If a corporation learns that a certain substance with which employees have been working is dangerous to them, it has the moral obligation to inform the workers of this. Such information not only directly affects them but also changes the background conditions of their employment. Workers may choose to work in a dangerous or unhealthy environment for extra pay; but they must be informed of such conditions.

Workers also have a right to know the general policy of the corporation in the areas in which they have moral concerns. If they do not wish to work for a company that practices discrimination, they should be able to find out whether their company does engage in such practices. The other items of moral concern we have previously discussed may all be of moral concern to workers. If so, they have a right to such information.

Workers also have the right to know, in ample time, about decisions made by management which will directly and adversely affect them. The decision to close a plant and to dismiss all the employees working there, we have seen, is a decision that they have the right to know about in sufficient time to make alternative plans, especially if the corporation does not intend to help them relocate or find other jobs.

d. Government has the right to know that corporations are complying with the law. Despite the fact that government receives a great deal of information from corporations concerning their activities, it is still very difficult for the Federal Government to obtain adequate information on the activities of mammoth conglomerates. The information required of small and middle-sized corporations raises few problems from the point of view of adequate disclosure. The information reported by the large conglomerates and multinational corporations tends to be aggregative rather than broken down into the activities of each of the subsidiary units. The difficulty of mandating adequate reporting from these giants makes control difficult. In some cases, the government needs more information than it has before it can even get an idea about what specific additional information it must have. Ralph Nader, among others, has proposed federal chartering of corporations, rather than the present system of state chartering, as a means of gaining greater govern mental control over large corporations and their operations. Information about their operations is a necessary prerequisite to adequate control, and adequate information is not now available to the Government.

e. The corporation, from a moral point of view, should disclose to its suppliers whatever is necessary to make the contracts between them fair. The same general principle applies to a corporation's disclosure to its agents. They should know enough to fulfill, in turn, their responsibilities of disclosure to their customers.

f. The consumer should be informed of any dangers posed by the use of the product he purchases. He properly expects that the item he buys will be reasonably safe if properly used. If a product is caustic, he should be so informed. If it is poisonous, he should be warned. If it is defective, he should be notified in some way before it is purchased. He should know what a food or a drug contains, what an article of clothing or upholstery material is made of, and so on. Government regulations have been passed, frequently as a result of consumer pressures, mandating the disclosure of information about consumer products, for example, the estimated gas mileage of a new car, or the efficiency of air conditioners.

A customer cannot usually obtain information about such things as the morality of the corporation's employment practices, or its overseas operations. Such information, of course, should not be carried on every box of cereal a company sells. But if customers, by their purchases, wish to vote for companies that behave morally, and, by withholding purchases wish to vote against companies that engage in immoral practices, customers should have some way of determining a company's policy. Obviously, we cannot expect any company to assert that it is engaging in an immoral practice. But we can expect that customers will have access to information about a company's employment policies, overseas operations, suits successfully brought against it, government fines it has paid, and similar details, from which customers can draw their own conclusions about its morality.

g. The term *general public* includes more than simply a corporation's customers or potential customers. The potential customers of an airplane manufacturer, for instance, would be airlines, governments, and possibly individual firms. Yet the location of an airplane manufacturing plant, the closing of such a plant, and its operation have a large impact on the area in which it is located. Those directly affected by such a plant include not only those employed by it but those who live near it.

The closing of a plant may seriously and adversely affect not only the workers in the plant but also the shops and stores that have opened to serve the workers of the plant. Communities frequently have zoning regulations and negotiate the terms under which a plant can locate in a community. They rarely negotiate any conditions for the plant's closing. Certain conditons, such as a specified amount of advance warning of a closing, as well as specifications about closing procedures, similar to opening procedures, would be appropriate.

Information concerning environmental impact, pollution, and the possible dangers of the operation to the surrounding population would also be of interest to the general public. The building of nuclear-powered electric plants poses particular problems. The dangers of radiation are greatest to those nearest the plant. Morally, such plants cannot be built without informing those in the vicinity of the danger. But if the dangers are considered low enough by the licensing authorities, this information is all that is required. Presently, the consent on the part of those who will be directly affected, in case of an accident, is not required. Nor is there agreement on whether it is possible to state meaningfully what the chances of an accident occurring are. The moral issues here go beyond the question of appropriate disclosure. But it is agreed that public disclosure is appropriate where the actions of a corporation seriously and adversely affect the general public.

3. What form should disclosure take? We have already touched indirectly on some of the appropriate forms of disclosure. Shareholders are informed of a corporation's activities through the annual report and the annual shareholders' meeting; government is informed of a company's activities through legally mandated reports, and, where appropriate, through on-site investigations and inspections; and workers are informed of the conditions of employment prior to their employment. In some of these cases the information required is disclosed routinely, through reports. In other cases it is supplied only on direct request from a party authorized to receive it. Information that is a matter of public record is available to the general population. If some action will directly endanger certain people, then that information must be conveyed directly to them.

The appropriate channels for reporting information concerning the moral dimensions of some of a corporation's actions have yet to be decided upon, much less standardized. The moral audit to which we referred in Chapter 8 fits into the question of disclosure at this point, and will, if developed, be an appropriate vehicle for such information.

Problems arise when a corporation engages in an activity that is immoral, illegal, or dangerous to the public. We cannot expect the people engaged in such activities to disclose the fact that they are acting in that way. We have already seen the conditions under which an employee is morally allowed and morally required to inform the public of conditions that will seriously injure people. But some questions still remain concerning disclosure of such activities.

Problems arise with respect to members of the professions who work in one way or another for a corporation. Lawyers, engineers, accountants, and sometimes doctors and nurses, fall into this category. They owe a certain loyalty to the corporation that employs them, or pays them. However, they are also professionals. As such, they are expected to maintain certain standards of conduct in the exercise of their profession. Suppose an accounting firm conducting an independent audit turns up a discrepancy in the company's books.

It reports it to the president and perhaps to the chairman of the board. Suppose the discrepancy involves bribery or embezzlement, and the company decides simply to take the loss. Should this be reported to the shareholders? If the company does nothing about it, does the accounting firm or the individual accounting firm or the individual accountant have any obligation to make known the facts of the case?

Suppose the corporation's lawyers are asked how to cover up some illegal procedure or act. Do they have any responsibility to make that fact known, and also the procedure or act? Should they go to the board? And if the board does not take action, should they go to the shareholders or the government? If health measures are enforced only when there is danger of governmental inspection, or if the company doctor finds that more and more workers show signs of a work-related disease, does he fulfill his responsibilities by simply reporting this to management? If management takes no remedial action, and does not inform the workers, does the doctor have any obligation to inform them?

These questions are related to disclosure, within the firm, to shareholders, management, the board, and the workers. Some of these questions are covered by codes of professional conduct of the individual professions, and some are covered in individual firms by the firm's policy statement of its ethical code of conduct. Where neither is the case, then the rules that apply to whistle blowing can be modified to handle these questions.

Confidentiality raises another set of problems. Some of what a professional learns about his client or patient is confidential and is not a proper matter for disclosure. The rule with respect to lawyers was once so severe that even if a lawyer learned, in his professional relation with a client, that the client was going to commit a felony, it was considered improper for the lawyer to disclose that information. That rule has recently—and appropriately—been changed. Journalists claim the right not to have to disclose their sources, but this does not mean that they are not required to document their stories. Investigative reporters often seek information about the wrongdoings of a firm, a group, or an individual and make this information public. They have no right to lie, but they do have the right to make known wrongdoings where they discover them, especially if they involve a cover-up by those who should appropriately disclose them.

Not all wrongdoings by members of a firm need to be publicly disclosed. But if members of a corporation have engaged in bribery, taken kickbacks, or covered up defects in a product, such information should be reported to the board of directors and possibly to the shareholders, together with a report of any action taken against such persons. A moral firm does not reward immorality with raises and promotions. One way shareholders can judge the morality of a firm is by knowing how it deals with those who are guilty of wrongdoing, even if done in the name of, and for the sake of, the company.

Corporations have typically been reluctant to disclose information about their activities. If left to themselves, some of them would consider all their internal operations trade secrets. However, if they wish to remain within the law, they must disclose that which is legally required. Should they disclose more, and if so, how much more? The analysis we have given indicates the basis for deciding what should be disclosed. Corporations frequently see the issue of disclosure in an adversarial context—a struggle between their desire not to disclose and the unreasonable demands of environmentalists, consumer activists, and the enemies of capitalism. The relation need not be an adversarial one. A corporation that wishes to act morally and to fulfill its moral obligations will be amenable to discussion of the demands made upon it. It will, moreover, establish channels to hear those who have claims to press and demands to make. This does not mean that every claim for information is justifiable. Either the board, the officers of a corporation, or both must in the final analysis decide what disclosure, beyond what is legally required, is appropriate. But they should base this decision on what the corporation's customers, share-holders, or the general public wish, and the arguments they give in defense of their demands. Shareholders' meetings are only one forum for raising and discussing these questions. Such meetings are more and more frequently used, often because this is the only channel available to those who have concerns about corporations, their policies, and their activities. It is possible to find other channels, and they are needed; they are certainly not beyond the organizational capacities of most large corporations.

Information plays a central role in modern business. Information is vital for adequate evaluation of business activities, from the point of view of law, economics, and morality. The tension between a corporation's urge for secrecy, and the right to know of those affected or involved, can strain a corporation's relations with the public. But if a corporation responds to this tension creatively and openly, it can lead to the exercise of more responsibility on the part of a corporation, and to greater acceptance of corporations on the part of the general public.

Further Reading

BENSTON, GEORGE JAMES. *Corporate Financial Disclosure in the UK and the USA*. Farnborough, Hants, England: Saxon House, 1976.

DeMOTT, DEBORAH A., ed. *Corporations at the Crossroads: Governance and Reform*. New York: McGraw-Hill Book Co., 1980.

Executive Disclosure Guide: SEC Compliance: Corporations, Directors, Officers, Insiders. Chicago: Commerce Clearing House, Inc., 1976.

FLOM, JOSEPH H., BARRY H. GARFINKEL, and JAMES C. FREUND. *Disclosure Requirements of Public Companies and Insiders*. N.Y.: Practicing Law Institute, 1967.

GOLDSCHMIDT, HARVEY J., ed. *Business Disclosure: Government's Need to Know*. New York: McGraw-Hill Book Co., 1979.

GREEN, MARK, AND ROBERT MASSIE, JR., eds. *The Big Business Reader: Essays on Corporate America*. Rev. ed. New York: The Pilgrim Press, 1983.

KINTNER, E. W., AND J. L. LAHR. *Intellectual Property Law Primer: A Survey of the Law of Patents, Trade Secrets, Trademarks, Franchises, Copyrights, Personality, and Entertainment Rights*. New York: Macmillan Publishing Company, 1974.

KRIPKE, HOMER. *The SEC and Corporate Disclosure: Regulation in Search of a Purpose.* New York: Law & Business, Inc., 1979.

LIEBERSTEIN, STANLEY. *Who Owns What Is in Your Head?: Trade Secrets and the Mobile Employee.* New York: Hawthorn Books, Inc., 1979.

NADER, RALPH, AND MARK J. GREEN, eds. *Corporate Power in America.* New York: Grossman Publishers, 1973.

STEVENSON, RUSSELL, B., JR. *Corporations and Information: Secrecy, Access, and Disclosure.* Baltimore: The John Hopkins University Press, 1980.

FIFTEEN

Computers, Ethics, and Business

Businesses have adopted computers in their daily activities, and computers are quickly transforming the way office work is organized, communication takes place, and business done. The computer revolution has accordingly raised a number of moral issues in business.

Some moral issues deal with computer hardware, for example, with the morality of its production, sale, and abuse. Many of these problems—such as the question of whether it is moral to sell computers to the secret police of an oppressive regime in a foreign country—raise issues that are not peculiar to computers. Computers may help oppressive regimes control a country's people; but so do radios, cars, and guns. Everyone is morally bound not to aid and abet criminals or those engaged in immoral activity. Producers and distributors of computers fall under this general rule, just as all other producers and distributors do. Computer manufacturers make products that are, or might be, sensitive, and are covered by special governmental restrictions as to selling them to certain foreign countries. But aside from such restrictions, no special moral issues are raised by the sale of computers. Nor are any special moral issues raised by the theft of terminals, or willful damage to computer centers. It is immoral to steal computer terminals, just as it is immoral to steal anything else.

The social impact and use of computers raise other moral issues. Issues related to the displacement of workers by computers are partially questions of business ethics, partially questions of social practice. Whenever an employer considers the introduction of new equipment or new technology, he should consider the impact of that equipment or technology on his employees. Will the new equipment replace employees, require that they be retrained, or necessitate additional employees? If it will mean laying off employees, then this is a factor that should be carefully considered before the equipment is purchased. Also, adequate attention should be paid to the terms and conditions under which the employees are to be terminated, giving full consideration to their rights. Once again, however, no special moral problems are raised by computers in this respect.

There are, however, some areas in which the introduction of the computer into business either raises familiar problems in a somewhat different way, or raises new problems. We shall consider four such areas: (1) computer crime; (2) responsibility for computer failure; (3) protection of computer property, records, and software; and (4) privacy of the company, workers, and customers. Three basic concepts emerge in many of the cases in these areas, and will require special attention: information, privacy, and property.

Computer Crime

The notion of computer crime has become fairly common. It is simple enough to understand in its gross aspects. We know that it is immoral to steal from others. And whether we do so physically, by stealing cash from a drawer, or electronically, by transferring money into our account from the account of others, makes little difference. We know that harming others is immoral, and whether we produce that harm with a computer or by other means makes little difference, from a moral point of view.

Stealing via computer is immoral, just as is stealing by any other means. But stealing by computer has raised a number of problems for businesses. The computer theft plaguing business is of three types. One is the actual stealing of funds or assets. A second is the stealing of information. A third is the stealing of computer time.

Computer Theft of Funds

The stealing of funds or assets by computer has resulted in the loss to business of what is conservatively estimated to be three billion dollars annually. The thefts carried out by computer are of many kinds. If the theft is by an outsider, it requires breaking into the firm's computer system. If it is by an insider, it requires the surreptitious introduction of appropriate commands into the firm's computer system.

The incidence of such crimes is rising. Yet many firms, banks included, are reluctant to report computer crimes, and, if they find the culprit, are loath to prosecute. They do not wish to publicize the fact that their computer system has been compromised and is not entirely secure; this would create doubts about the firm, which would possibly result in losing customers or depositors. So the firms have either written off the losses or tried to collect the amount of the loss from insurance companies. It is not uncommon for an employee who is found guilty of computer theft to be made to restore whatever money he still has, be dismissed, and then let go, unprosecuted. The thief would be fired, but soon hired by another firm anxious to use his computer skills. Many are not caught. Insurance companies have begun refusing to pay unless the guilty party, if found, is prosecuted. And some states have passed, or are considering, laws that make it illegal not to report computer crimes. But reporting them and pressing charges are two different matters. Nor do the media report such crimes, even though they report bank robberies.

Those reluctant to prosecute, in addition to the reasons just stated, sometimes argue that there *is* a difference between computer crimes and other crimes—a difference that makes them no less crimes, but that, insofar as punishment is concerned, changes the punishment that is appropriate. Consider the difference between the James gang robbing a bank and a computer operator stealing the same amount of money from a bank by setting up a special account into which he siphons off any fractional part of a cent in the daily interest due to each account. That fractional part of a cent is not usually credited to the depositors; it remains with the bank. The thief thus steals from the bank what may only dubiously belong to the bank. But there is no face-to-face confrontation. There is no overt violence. There are no threats made, no guns fired, no physical harm either threatened or done to people. In crime by computer, there is a physical distance—the yards or miles of space between the computer operator and whatever is being manipulated; a psychic distance, because the operator sees no human being face-to-face, perhaps trembling in fear. The operator may imagine that he or she is faced with impersonal electronic and bookkeeping challenges—a game—rather than with human beings who may be harmed. Crimes by computer are intellectual crimes rather than crimes of force. They require work and imagination of an intellectual sort, which has traditionally inspired respect. They are crimes committed by white-collar workers—and white-collar crime has always been treated as less serious, as deserving of less severe punishment (if any punishment at all) than physical, violent crime.

Although this states the view both of many culprits and of many employers, it carries little moral weight. White-collar crime is still crime, even if it is not violent. The fact that banks and other firms do not wish to prosecute despite losses is an indication that perhaps they are not entirely blameless. They have adopted a technology that they cannot completely control, and security measures that fall short of what they wish the public to believe or know. They can be morally faulted on both counts. Reluctance to prosecute simply compounds the offense, making further losses because of computer theft more likely. If the worst that can happen to the thief, if caught, is that he or she must return the stolen money, the deterrent to computer crime is almost nonexistent.

The incidence of computer crime, therefore, raises special problems for management.

Unauthorized Computer Entry

In addition to money, one can steal, by computer, a company's trade secrets, its corporate data, and anything else the firm stores or files in its computer.

Corporate espionage by computer theft is easier than before the widespread introduction of computers; it is more likely to occur, and is on the rise. Such theft once again raises no special problems. It is clearly immoral. But the vulnerability of computers to outside intrusion requires at least some brief discussion.

In the present stage of computer development, we have not even developed rules of computer etiquette, much less of computer ethics. Over the years locksmiths have guarded their art with great care. Only a select few are taught how to pick locks and gain entry to areas protected by locks. The same is not true of computers and computer locks. It is illegal to break into another's home or office; there is no question about the immorality of the practice. Is it immoral—or illegal—to break into another's computer file? The law is not always clear, nor are the moral intuitions of many people, including those in the business world.

Some university computer instructors encourage their students in computer courses to try to break into the university's secured computer operations. Some seem to condone attempts to break into other computer networks and systems as well, to compromise them. This is done for fun, or as a means of testing the students' skill, developing their proficiency, or uncovering weaknesses that can be remedied to make the systems or networks secure. Other universities frown on any such attempt to enter files or systems to which one is not given direct access. Is surreptitious entry, even when not illegal, immoral? Is such entry a violation of privacy or a violation of property? Is it legitimate to "look around," providing there is no change made in data or commands, and no copying? What are the proper limits to protection of knowledge, data, or information? Our intuitions are clear about entry into homes and offices. Is entry into someone's computer system or file comparable? If not, why not?

It is not surprising that our intuitions differ on a number of questions relating to computers in business. Because the questions are new, we have not had the time to develop our moral intuitions in this area. Intuitions concerning the morality of murder, theft, and perjury are the result of a great deal of social thought, practice, and experience which have been distilled into maxims or principles that are accepted by society and passed onto children as the accepted moral norms to follow. We have not yet reached consensus on the morality of many aspects of computer use.

In August 1983, one or more young men using a home computer broke into the computerized radiation-therapy records of cancer patients at Memorial Sloan Kettering Cancer Center in Manhattan. This was not the first such entry, and the hospital had left messages in the computer asking the culprits to stop. There have been reports of similar entries at the nuclear weapons laboratory at Los Alamos.

The boys who broke into Sloan Kettering changed the master program so that anyone entering the system would reveal his or her password. Hospital officials asked the intruders via the computer to call them so they could determine whether the intruders had changed any records that would endanger the patients. A boy phoned, apologized, but refused to say how he had broken into the system. The hospital offered him free access to its computer if he would stop his break-ins. But he did not need it. Twenty other illegal entries were recorded, some of which gave false leads to the culprit's identity.

Was the intrusion morally wrong? After all, what harm was done? If the intruder simply exercised his skill in entering, and did not change any records, what is wrong with that? The reply is that there are at least three things wrong with it. First, it involves entry into another person's file, which is an invasion of property. One of the senses of property involves the right to exclusive use. Entering another's file is a violation of that right. The intruder might claim that no harm was done by entry, that is, that no changes were made in any records. But how is one to be sure of that? The fact that someone who is unauthorized enters a file or system means that the owner of that system cannot be sure that no changes were made. Changes made in computer records can be made so as to leave no trace. Even if there were backup records, one could only be sure that no change had been made in a record by checking the record with the backup—a costly and time-consuming procedure. Moreover, which records should be checked, and how often? What of the programs themselves? Have they been altered? Has a logic bomb—a command programmed to be activated at a certain date and time, or when certain entries are made—been planted? Unauthorized entry causes all these concerns, costs, and damage. This is the first basis for claiming that unauthorized access is immoral. The second is the potential violation of privacy. Patient-doctor confidentiality is a clearly recognized principle. Hospital records are privileged information, access to which is allowed by morality and law only to certain people. The same is true of the records of a business. To intrude into these records is at least a violation of privacy. Once again, damage is done, whether one actually looks or not, for once it is known that someone has gained illegitimate entry, no one knows what has been seen and what has not. This undermines the confidentiality of the records and of the process, and so of the doctor-patient or employee-employer relation. Third, the system is itself compromised. The Sloan Kettering computer system was part of Telenet, a large computer network. If the boys were able to break into part of that system, then there is worry that they can break into other parts. Hence harm is done not only to Sloan Kettering but also to the other sixty subscribers to the system and to its owners and operators.

There is a counter argument to this line of reasoning. It claims that if nothing is changed by a hacker, and the system is not secure, by violating it the operators of the system are given an inducement to build in more safeguards against those intruders who might do damage. In the Sloan Kettering instance, this was not a motivation for the break-in, because the perpetrator did not reveal how he managed to violate the system. But even if he had, the argument in defense of hackers is defective. Computer hacking is like using a plastic credit card to open an office door so that the owner will put a better lock on it. The usual assumption is not that we can enter wherever we are able to penetrate, but that we are not allowed to penetrate except where authorized. The latter principle is the one that we follow in the other areas of our lives. The principle that more good will be done by penetrating, wherever we can do so electronically, does not hold up under scrutiny. If teachers wish to teach their students how to safeguard systems, and if they wish them to have practice breaking codes, they should set up the codes to be broken. We do not teach students of locksmithing how to pick locks by telling them to see how many locks they can pick, or how many banks they can successfully enter simply to "look around."

The possibility of surreptitious computer entry, and the safeguarding of computer systems and the data they contain, raise special problems for corporate managers.

Theft of Computer Time

What of stealing computer time? This can be done either internally or externally. Surreptitious entry into a system does not mean that automatically one has access to private files. One might simply break into a system in order to use the computer for one's own purposes. The fact that the entry is surreptitious is enough to make the act morally suspect. Use of a computer by an unauthorized user either steals time, which is usually sold, or involves unauthorized use. There is no general rule that allows someone, for instance, to use another person's typewriter when the typewriter is not in use by the owner. Simply because one can gain access without physical trespass does not change the morality of the act. But the morality of use of computer time by a firm's employees who have authorized access is less clear. May they use the computer for their personal use on their own time if the computer is not in use? The firm pays the same amount for the computer whether or not it is in use. The employee has authorized access and does no harm to any company records or files. Why is using a computer not like using a blackboard, which one erases when one is finished? Do we really believe it is immoral to use a blackboard in an office after hours, providing one is allowed to be in the office after hours? Is use of a computer any different?

There is no consensus on the use of computer time by employees when a computer is idle. IBM does not allow any personal use of its computers; General Electric allows employees to use the computer for personal purposes during their own time, when the computer is not in use; Equitable Life encourages employees to use its mainframe from their home terminals, and allows family use as well. In such a situation it is impossible to say that one should not use a company's computer for one's personal use. One must say that one can use a computer to the extent that the owner allows. Because company policies differ, it is in the best interest of companies and employees for each company to determine its policy on the private use of the company's computer, and to notify its employees of the policy. Without a policy, numerous conflicts can arise, and have arisen.

Who, for instance, owns the job-related results that an employee develops on his own time although with the allowed use of the company's terminal? If the terminal was used without permission, then the employee's claim of individual proprietorship could be challenged. But with company permission the case becomes more difficult. This situation is the one that obtains at many universities as well as in businesses. Stanford, Cal Tech, MIT, and Yale are all involved in trying to set policies on intellectual property. Stephen Wolfram, when at Cal Tech, developed a program to manipulate complicated algebraic expressions, and it turned out to have commercial applications. Cal Tech felt it had a right to some of the royalties Wolfram receives, because the program was developed while he was on the staff, using Cal Tech's materials. Yet Cal Tech does not claim the royalties of those who write books while on the staff, even if they do so on the computer. If Wolfram had quit his job and taken none of his data with him, then reproduced the program on his own computer, would the program have been his, or would it still have been partly owned by the university?

The solution found by many universities and companies is to enter into signed agreements, stating what the rules of computer use are, who gets rights to what, and how royalties are divided, if there are any.

Although the fact that computer systems are so vulnerable raises special problems for businesses, most companies have not yet adequately considered them.

Computers and Corporate Responsibility

We have already seen that corporations can be held morally responsible for their actions which affect others. Because ultimately the corporation acts only through human individuals who act for it, the individuals are morally responsible for what the corporation does. They must assume the responsibility for actions attributable to the corporation, if it is assumed at all. The same is true with respect to computers. Computers, no matter how sophisticated, are simply machines. They are incapable of assuming responsibility, and responsibility cannot be correctly ascribed to them. Anything they do can be traced back to human beings, who are ultimately responsible.

Because human beings are the ones who must accept moral responsibility, no one can legitimately blame a computer, in a moral sense, for anything. The computer does what it is programmed to do. If it is poorly constructed, it may not do what one expects it will do; if a program is defective, it will not give the anticipated results; and if the data fed into it are faulty it cannot be expected to correct them. Hence whatever mistakes the computer makes are the fault of human beings; and whatever harm is done to human beings by computers is the fault of human beings. Computers have become a means for human beings to attempt to avoid responsibility. We commonly hear the excuse given that the computer malfunctioned, or that the mistake is a computer error. Mistakes, however, are human mistakes, not computer mistakes, and responsibility for mistakes rests with human beings, not with computers.

The development of computers, which have many different aspects, raises the question of human moral responsibility—and in law of liability—in some new ways. How much responsibility does a programmer have for checking a program before selling it or marketing it? If the program is defective, or if it does not do, under some unusual conditions, what the company purchasing or ordering it thought it would do, who is responsible for harm caused employees or customers? How much responsibility and liability appropriately falls on the programmer, and how much on the user? If a system is unable to handle a payroll properly, is it the fault of the programmer, of the engineers who overload the computer, or of those who are in charge of the overall operation? Assigning responsibility may sometimes be difficult; but the fault can always be placed at the feet or on the shoulders of human beings. And if they perform their actions in their official capacity, the results of their actions are attributable to the company for which they work. If a company wishes to operate morally, it will accept the responsibility for attempting to foresee and preclude any harm through the use of its computers, and it will also make good any harm it does through computer use or failure.

Just as human beings are morally responsible for the harm done other human beings by computers or through their use, so human beings are responsible for the use to which computers are put. Computers, like other areas of modern technology, are not good or bad in themselves. They can be used to benefit or to harm human beings and mankind, and whether they are used to benefit or harm is up to human beings.

Firms that utilize computers are responsible for safeguarding them from misuse. Banks, for instance, take great precautions with the physical security of their vaults. But billions of dollars are sent electronically across the country every day, with much less security. Many firms do not know for certain whether their computerized networks and systems are secure, not only from those seeking illegal entry but also from those wishing to sabotage the systems physically. The firms nevertheless have responsibility for safeguarding their funds.

As we move from communicating with mainframes by telephones and terminals to communicating by radio waves, problems will increase. It will be more difficult to safeguard transmitted data from interception because the legal status of data so transmitted is not protected by law, as are data transmitted by telephone lines or computer linkages. There are laws against wiretapping. But there are no laws against picking up radio waves. Are data in the air, in the form of radio waves, a thing that one can claim one owns? Or is air use free to all? When someone has a conversation with someone else and they are overheard, no one steals their property. If someone purposely listens when others speak in a low voice he may be invading the speakers' privacy, but simply overhearing does not.

Listening to radio messages or CB chatter violates no one's rights, and senders assume others may be listening. Why is sending business information between computers by radio waves different? Many such messages are scrambled or coded; but is intercepting them wrong? Is it either a violation of privacy or of property? To some extent, what constitutes property is a social matter, and a social decision is required to determine what is legitimate and what is not. As a society we have not yet decided how to treat the contents of radio messages and the data they may carry. Until we do, the morality of various practices cannot be definitively determined.

Technology makes possible great speed in transmitting messages. But unless those businesses that use computer networks consider the possibility of theft and interception and take adequate measures against them, they fail in part of their responsibility. How can managers guarantee shareholders that funds sent electronically are secure if managers do not know that they are in fact secure? Consideration of this aspect of computer use puts a burden on management, which managers often are not technically competent to handle. But ignorance is not an excusing condition here because the responsibility for such security includes the obligation to determine possible breaches. The obligation to protect a firm's funds falls on managers, and they cannot shift this responsibility to computer departments. Managers will undoubtedly have to work with and rely on computer specialists; but the managers retain ultimate responsibility. How to adequately fulfill this responsibility remains an unsolved problem for many managers.

As we search for legal means of protection, and applicable moral norms, we, as a society, must look at the implications of computers for our ordinary definitions of property and privacy—both of which are being stretched beyond their ordinary meaning.

Property: Information and Software

The notion of property is best analyzed as a bundle of rights. The exact nature of the bundle varies from society to society and from one kind of property to another. The status of intellectual property is different from real property (i.e., real estate), and the status of tangible property is different from intangible property. If Tom has a hundred dollars of his money in his wallet, he has the right to the exclusive use of those particular bills. He may exchange them for other bills or for products they buy. If Tom has a hundred dollars in a bank account, he does not have a right to the exclusive use of any particular bills. Rather he has a right to the use of a hundred dollars that he can demand the bank to produce. The bundle of rights that constitute his ownership of a hundred dollars is somewhat different in the two cases. The right-to-use that one has of a house one rents to others is different from the right that one has to a house that one uses oneself. Although in both cases one owns the house, one's rights to the use of it differs in the two cases. Usually ownership rights include the right to exclusive use, the right to divest oneself of what is owned, and the right to the income from what is owned, as well as liability for the misuse of what is owned.

With respect to computers, we can raise questions of property rights regarding programs, data, and, as we have already seen, computer time. Does a program developed by an employee belong to the employee or to the employer? Does the algorithm used to solve a problem constitute general knowledge or proprietary knowledge? Does reproducing a program in a different computer language constitute new knowledge, or should it be compared to translating an article from one natural language to another? Are computer languages properly proprietary? What constitutes intellectual property must be determined before we can make valid judgments about who, if anyone, properly owns such property, under what conditions, and for how long. Property interests and claims of privacy often overlap in this area, and both can clash with claims of the "right to know." Some of these clashes are being raised in the courts. Yet the issues are not only legal but also moral. We shall first look at data and information as property; next, at the protection of computer software; and then at some cases involving the ownership of programs by employers and employees.

Data and Information

One difficulty with many discussions of computer cases is that the term *information* is used all-inclusively. People speak generally of "information systems" and of "processing information." But to get clarity in many cases, we should distinguish facts, data, knowledge, and understanding. Another difficulty is that we use the word *program* to cover a great variety of different things, all of which have in common the fact that they are in some sense the product of the incorporation of a sequence of commands, and these commands will result in the electronic machine, which we call a computer, performing certain operations. Similarly, we use the word *computer* to refer to a wide variety of machines and parts of machines, ranging from silicon chips to parts of automobiles to personal computers to mainframes. Just as Eskimos have many different words to describe kinds of snow, so we can use a variety of different words to characterize the different kinds of information, computers, and programs.

Let us, then, start by defining some terms. By *fact* we shall mean a statement of the way the world is. The way the world is is independent of our knowledge of it. Nor does the individual appropriation of facts deprive anyone else of them. Facts, knowledge, and information are all infinitely shareable. We can all know the date of the discovery of America, or that five times five equals twenty-five. This knowledge on the part of one person does not prevent its being known by others, and no harm is done the first person if someone learns from him—at least no harm is done *qua* knowledge. But the discovery of some facts, as well as the collecting and storing of facts, often involves time and expense, and this provides a basis for claims to some facts as proprietary, at least for a short period of time.

Knowledge can be of facts, and in part knowledge consists of facts as known. Understanding consists of knowledge that is integrated in some unified way, and evaluated. The word *information* is sometimes used to include data, facts, and knowledge, as when we speak of information systems. But though information systems might include knowledge in the sense of interpreted facts informed by theories, systems strictly speaking do not know. They simply contain symbols that can be interpreted by those who can know, just as books might contain written words that when read by others transfer knowledge to the readers.

What computer systems can be properly said to contain and manipulate are data. What is entered into a computer are data. The entered data can represent either words or letters or numbers, and so the data can represent facts in coded fashion. So far as computers have developed, they do not know anything in the sense that humans do, nor do they understand anything. But computers can handle data and manipulate them with great speed. Data may represent falsehoods as well as facts, and the two should not be confused.

Although facts available to all cannot be owned, data representing facts can be owned. Data entered into a computer can be owned, at least in some of the senses of ownership. Suppose we enter into a computer the distance between one hundred major American cities, and a table of one hundred square roots. The distance between cities is a fact of the world, given certain conventions. The distance between cities has been measured and is available; it is knowledge that no one owns. The fact that New York and Boston are 190 air miles apart does not and cannot belong to anyone. The square root of a number also cannot belong to anyone. This is not a fact about the world but a mathematical fact—which, given most theories of knowledge, is a fact about numbers and mathemtical operations. The square root of four is two. No one can own that. If no one can own the individual facts, can anyone own the collection of one hundred distances and one hundred square roots? The answer is again no. The combination can no more be owned than the individual facts. But the facts can be entered as data into a computer. The facts cannot be owned, but the data can be owned. For the data entered into the computer belong to whoever owns the computer and entered the data into it. In saying that the owner of the computer owns the data, all we mean is that he owns the computer and whatever is put into it. They are his in some of the important senses of ownership. Data cannot be possessed as objects can, and hence data cannot be owned in this way, even though printouts of data can be owned in this way, as can tapes and floppy discs. But data can be owned in the sense that the owner has the right to exclusive use of the data as put into the computer. The same facts can be stored as data in other computers. The data in each of the computers may be similar, as tokens of the same type. But each owner has the exclusive right to the use of the data in his computer. If he uses the data to produce something else, that product in turn also belongs to him. As his property, he has the exclusive right to manage the data, the right to the income from the use of the data, the right to replace or erase it, the right to keep it indefinitely, and the right to transfer it to other computers. No one other than the owner, therefore, has the right to erase or tamper with that data; nor to copy them without permission. For copying them, although that does not violate the original owner's use (because the data will still be in his file), does violate his *exclusive* use.

If the data in a person's computer are his and he has exclusive right to their use, then it makes no difference what the data are or represent. The data are his. But part of the notion of property also involves liability for its use. One cannot use one's property in any way one wishes. If, for instance, one owns a gun, one cannot legitimately use it to harm or threaten harm to others. The same is true of data. Someone's owning data does not give him the right to use them any way he wants. But providing he harms no one and threatens no harm, then the data are his to use as he wishes.

We shall use these definitions and distinctions to help solve a number of cases and answer a number of questions later in this chapter.

The Protection of Computer Software

If we have a problem we wish to solve by a computer, we can start by thinking through the steps necessary to solve it. This logical process might be first diagramed in a flowchart. In some cases an algorithm—a logical statement (or formula) of how to solve a problem—is involved. This is then translated into a high-level computer language, such as BASIC or FORTRAN. The result is a program that will direct a machine either to perform certain actions or to manipulate special data entered into it in certain ways. Such a program is called a *source code*. This in turn is translated by a compiler or assembler into an object code, in machine language of ones and zeros, which controls the passage of electrical impulses.

Japan has decided to protect both computer software and hardware through the use of patents. In the United States, we have decided to cover software with copyrights and hardware with patents. But neither patents nor copyrights were originally developed with computers in mind, and numerous difficulties have arisen. The line between software (programs used to run computers) and computer hardware (the physical computer) is becoming less and less clear, as is the line between physical and intellectual property. Some programs are of the "read only" variety, and these may simply control a certain activity, for instance, the working of part of an automobile engine. Such a program is not read, in the usual sense, by a human being. It may be on a silicon chip. It is simply instructions to a machine.

Copyrights were originally intended to protect the written word. They were extended to cover works of art, films, and records. And they have been further extended to cover some computer programs. To be eligible for copyright in the United States, an item must be intelligible to human beings, and the medium in which it is carried must bear an indication of copyright. The courts have decided that because a source code is understandable by human beings, it can be covered by copyright; but they have been reluctant to grant copyrights to object codes—which are written in machine language consisting of ones and zeros, and which are probably not intelligible to human beings. Yet the object code is simply a translation of the source code. Nor can computerized instructions to a machine (e.g., governing fuel injection) be copyrighted. Exactly what can and cannot be copyrighted is being decided by the courts on a case-by-case basis. But the issues involving the protection of software raise moral as well as legal questions.

324

Although a program that is not readable in any ordinary sense by human beings cannot be copyrighted, we can still ask to whom it belongs. If we buy a car with a silicon chip that governs the injection of fuel, we own the chip as well as the other parts of the car. We have the right to the exclusive use of the chip as part of the car, in the sense that no one has the right to take it. But do we thereby have the right to the program embedded in the chip? Is it ours to duplicate as we wish—whether we are private individuals or competing car manufacturers? The program cannot be copyrighted and cannot be patented, but if it can be reverse-engineered, it can legally be copied. If legally it can be copied, is it moral to copy it? We have seen that reverse engineering—a topic that is not unique to computers—can be defended as morally justifiable, so copying that chip is morally justifiable.

Some troublesome cases involve the right to the object program, in instances when this is not put into a chip but placed on a disc. Although copyright may apply only to a source code, we can clearly raise the question of whether by right the translation into an object code or into electronic impulses changes the right to ownership. The question of copyright is a question about the means of protection, and this question is distinct from the question of ownership rights.

If the data and the programs—insofar as they are considered data—are the property of the owner of the computer, then clearly a program that one generates for one's own use belongs to oneself and cannot morally be copied, anymore than it can be erased by another person without permission. This does not answer the question of whether a program that is sold can be copied. But to answer that we need to know the background conditions governing sales and the rights to reproduce what one has. Here law is pertinent, because it sets the public rules of commerce, which are necessary in order to determine the morality of transactions made possible by them. This is true both within and outside of firms, as we shall see.

Attempting to solve moral issues related to computers is often complicated by the lack of any established and agreed-upon practices. Many computer programmers for example, feel no proprietary claim to the programs they write; they trade them with others, or allow others to copy them freely. Others claim proprietary rights even if they do not copyright their programs. Therefore the question of how to handle programs is often not clear. Should one treat all programs as if they were the property of others, or should one treat them all as common property, unless they are copyrighted?

Another difficulty is knowing exactly when enough changes are made in a program to make it a new program. If Company A commissions a computer service to write a program to handle its payroll, can the computer service, after completing the job, simply modify the program and sell it to Company B, to handle its payroll? Or does the original program belong entirely to the original purchaser? Must the computer service start from scratch with each program? If Company A paid for all the time involved in producing the first program, is it fair for Company B to pay considerably less because the program had been basically developed, and paid for, by Company A? Is it fair for the computer service to charge both companies the same amount, even though it spent a great deal of time—for which it was paid—in the first case, and considerably little time in the second case?

The logical process or algorithm constitutes the heart of a program. Because mathematical equations and logical processes cannot be copyrighted, the algorithm cannot be copyrighted. But then the protection one gets for one's program is protection for the particular string of commands one writes to implement the algorithm. In a very complicated program involving thousands of steps, this may be enough. But frequently the difficult task is not writing the steps but solving the logical problem. Why is it fair for someone to take that algorithm and write a program based on it, when simply translating a program from one high-level computer language to another is considered a violation of copyright? There is fertile ground for many disputes over whether a program is a slightly changed copy of a copyrighted program or an original program based on the same algorithm as another program. The issues are perplexing to computer and software manufacturers, as well as to businesses and individual users.

Program Property Rights Between Employer and Employee

Let us now consider the following set of cases:

- CASE A: Joan Collins works for a large firm, Company Z, in the marketing department, and does most of her work on computers. During several weekends and evenings, working on her home personal computer, she writes a program that will facilitate her work and make her more efficient. She transfers the program to the office computer, and uses it daily. After several months she gets an offer from another firm. When she leaves Company Z, she takes her program with her, and erases it from Company Z's computer.
- CASE B: This is the same as Case A, except that Joan develops the program, on her own time, using Company Z's computer during weekends and evenings. Her company allows her access to the computer during these times.
- CASE C: This is the same as Case B, except that Joan leaves the program in Company Z's computer and only takes a copy of the program with her when she leaves.
- CASE D: This is the same as Case B, except that Joan takes neither the program nor a copy with her when she leaves. She rewrites the program when she goes to her new job.
- CASE E: This is the same as Case D, except that Joan develops the program on company time.
- CASE F: This is the same as Case B, except that Joan does not write her own program. Instead, she modifies a copyrighted pro-

gram that Company Z has purchased from a commercial supplier of software. When she leaves, she takes her modified program with her, leaving behind the original.

Case A poses no serious moral problem. Joan takes a program that she developed on her own time, using her own computer. The fact that she used it on the job was of benefit to her employer. But she is the only one who used it. Although it makes her more efficient, and its use by her replacement might make that person more efficient, she does not owe the program to the firm. It is hers, and she can rightly take it with her.

In Case B, Joan writes the program on her own time, but with the computer facilities of her employer. Who owns the program?

To answer this, consider Cases D and C first. In Case D, Joan rewrites the program at her new job. She does not take the program from Company Z. Does she take anything from Company Z that belongs to it? No, she leaves the program with the company. The program in her head does not belong to the company, even though she developed it while working for the company, for it was not a program she was paid to develop, or told to develop, or one that she produced on company time. Nor was it a trade secret of the company's. If it had been a trade secret, then she could not legitimately reproduce it for a competitor. But her experience is her own, including in this case the knowledge of the program she developed. She can legitimately rewrite the program to help her in her work for her new employer.

In Case C, Joan takes a copy but leaves the original program. As a result, the employer does not have exclusive use of the program. But because Joan developed the program on her own time, what could be the basis for a claim to exclusive use by the company? Because Company Z allowed employees to use its computer, it has no claim to exclusive use of the products they develop. Yet because the program was written and stored in the company's computer, and since it was job related, is there not some weight to the claim that because the company's facilities were used, the company has some right to the product? Because there may be a dispute here, we can see how helpful it would be if agreements were reached about ownership of programs before disputes arose.

How much of the company's resources were actually involved in producing the program? If the proportion of assets of the company and of the employee's time are reasonably matched, then the claim of the company is potentially greater. If, in monetary terms, the amount of computer time is very small, the claim of the programmer is much greater. Because the employer did not prohibit Joan's use of the computer, and because she wrote the program on her own time, Company Z cannot support the claim that the program belongs exclusively to the company. Joan may therefore take a copy of it. Nor would it be wise for the company to establish a contrary policy. Consider adopting the principle that no programmer should ever make any program to improve his or her own work unless he or she is willing to sign it over to the company. What would the results be? The programmer's incentive to produce such a program on his or her own time would be killed. The effect on the company would be to get poorer work performance from its workers. Hence the overall effects of adopting that principle are neither in the interest of companies nor in the interest of employees. The only possible reason for adopting the principle is to keep one's competition from getting the use of programs. But what one loses by losing an employee to the competition, one gains in getting new employees from other companies. Hence that principle, if adopted, would clearly produce less good for all concerned than would its opposite.

Providing, therefore, that the cost of getting the copy is minimal, taking a copy is morally permissible. To assume that the cost is minimal, and that Joan gets the program while still an employee of the company, are small enough assumptions to raise no serious moral problems. If while an employee of Company Z Joan uses a few sheets of company paper to write notes of ideas she does not wish to forget when she gets to her new job, she does not act immorally. In such an instance, paper is considered by most companies to be an expendable item, and such use should not be confused with an employee's routinely taking paper and other items home in any quantity, for his or her strictly personal use. For someone who works with computer programs, a printout or a floppy disc is comparable to other items of an expendable kind. The main issue in the case is not the use of expendable supplies but the copying of the program. And on that point, because exclusive use by the company cannot be justified without a prior policy to that effect, Joan's copying her program is legitimate.

A related issue is whether Joan owes Company Z anything in addition to leaving the program in the computer. No one will know it is there unless Joan tells them. If the program appears by name on a list of programs in the computer, no one will know what it is or does. Unless Joan lets Company Z know that the program is in the computer, indicates what it is for, and provides documentation about its use, the company gains nothing. But if Joan is required to provide documentation—which can be an onerous job—this might well be a disincentive to producing the program in the first place. Once again, clear guidelines would help. In their absence, Joan has no obligation to provide the documentation.

In Case C, she may take the program; may she also take it in Case B? The difference in the two cases is that in Case C she leaves a copy of the program, but in Case B she does not. Is she required to leave a copy of the program? If it is correct that Joan does not have to leave documentation, even if she leaves the program, there is little reason to stop her from taking the program out of the computer entirely. Not only does it do no good without documentation, but its presence might actually cause confusion, or at least take up storage space.

Joan might have asked her superior whether the Company wanted her to leave the program; or she might have asked permission to take a copy of the program. If taking the program represented any significant amount of expense, permission would be required. But if her superior did not even know she had developed and used the program, asking permission is more than is required. Once Joan asks, moreover, she implies that her superior has the right to refuse permission. If she does ask, then she is required to abide by her superior's decision.

We might ask whether a company should adopt one of these policies: whatever employees produce on the company's computer, on their own time, belongs to the employee; belongs entirely to the company; belongs in part to the company. A company can morally choose any of the three alternatives. But it should choose one, and so inform its employees. In the absence of any stated policy, it is not implausible to assume that what one produces on one's own time is one's own. Some companies, we noted, even allow families to use the company's mainframe for personal computing.

Case E is more difficult. In this case Joan wrote the program on company time. It is not only job related but can legitimately be considered as part of her job. The program therefore belongs to Company Z. When she goes to her new job and recreates the program, is this copying a program (and so morally prohibited) or is it using an algorithm (and so morally permitted)? For her to rewrite the program, she would most likely remember the algorithm rather than have memorized all the specific commands that constitute the program. Algorithms cannot be copyrighted or patented. The program Joan wrote may not be copyrighted either. Still, it belongs to her employer. Can the same be said of the algorithm? The moral basis for such a claim is weak. One may not take a program directly; nor may one directly reproduce for a competitor the identical program. But because an algorithm is a logical formula (like an idea), one cannot own it. The distinction between data and the ideas represented by the data here becomes crucial. The exception would be if the algorithm could be defended as a trade secret. But we have discussed the rules for trade secrets in Chapter 14, and this case does not fall under them.

Case F raises another set of issues. In this case, the program belongs neither to Joan nor to her employer. What one buys when purchasing a program is the program's use. Company Z cannot copy the program to sell or give to another user—assuming the program is covered by a copyright. When Joan changes the program, she adds something to it. Does she thereby make it her program? How much change must be made before a program is no longer the original program is a difficult issue, as we have noted. But if we assume that the basic program is one of considerable complexity, and Joan modifies it only somewhat, then the basic program is not hers, even though the final program she works with is not identical to the original. Hence she does not have the right to take either the program or a copy with her. But she may remember how to alter the program and use that knowledge to alter the same, or a similar, program at her new place of employment.

These examples demonstrate a few of the complexities involved in program use. The wise firm will establish guidelines and ground rules governing computer use and programs before problems arise.

Computers and Privacy

The fears of many people concerning computers and privacy can be described as the Big Brother syndrome. We know that computers are capable of assembling large amounts of data, making the data assembled easily and readily available. We know that much data on each of us is assembled. Our bank keeps a record of our financial transactions—our checks and deposits—on computer tapes; our credit is filed in computers; hospitals keep our medical records in computers; Master Charge and Visa keep our records on computer; the IRS keeps all kinds of information on us, in computers. It is, moreover, possible to assemble and collate all of this information. Someone—Big Brother, the Government, someone else—can at least in theory assemble all the information about us and use it for a variety of purposes. There may be errors that we do not know about, have no way to correct, and yet are used to make decisions about us. Some fear that their privacy is invaded in the process. The capacity for collecting, storing, and retrieving information far exceeds anything generations prior to ours had to face. The capacity to assemble such information raises questions about whether our privacy is in fact invaded by the collection of such information, whether our rights are in any way violated, and whether we are threatened with potential damage. There are moral issues in the collection and use of information that require some reflection, and which may yield moral problems for which we have no ready answers.

Let us extend the distinction between data and facts or information in several ways. If we cannot own facts, then we cannot own facts about ourselves, any more than we can own other kinds of facts. Consider the implications in the following ways.

First, suppose that the statement, "John had an operation ten years ago," is a fact. John cannot own that fact. It is a fact known by those who knew John was in the hospital, by the doctor and nurses in attendance, by those to whom John told that fact. That fact is entered as data in the computers of the hospital, in the computers of the insurance company that paid for the operation, and perhaps elsewhere as well. The fact belongs to no one, although the data belong to the owners of the various computer systems. Do they have the right to sell that data? Does John have any rights because the data represent facts about him? There are also other facts about John that others know. If they can use their data as they wish because the data are theirs, and if no one owns facts, might not all sorts of threats to John result from the improper use of the facts or data?

We should be careful of our distinction. Facts are statements about the way the world is, and hence, by definition, true; *data*— as we have been using the term—are neither true or false. When interpreted, data may yield falsehoods. This may be because falsehoods rather than facts were entered into the computer as data; because mistakes were made in entry; because the program was defective; or for a variety of other reasons. Hence, although one owns one's data, there is no guarantee that the data represent facts. One is responsible for the interpretation and use one makes of one's data—for mistakes, harm done, and so on. The issue of responsibility is not solved, but is perhaps more clearly defined by distinguishing facts from data. The term *information,* when used to cover both facts and data, tends to obscure the issue and location of truth. In its broad sense, information, unlike facts, can be false; but in a common, narrow usage, information is considered equivalent to facts, and by definition true. Keeping data and facts distinct helps us state, and so resolve, a number of issues.

The definitions we gave of *fact* and *data,* moreover, are compatible with several restrictions on use of data and on the method of learning facts. Although the fact that John had an operation is owned by no one, it does not follow that it is properly common knowledge. For ownership is not the only way of preventing use or dissemination of facts. Nor does the statement that no one owns facts mean that everyone has a right to know all facts. Society can—and our society does—for good reason, recognize certain areas of privileged communication, of secrecy, and of privacy.

Patient-doctor confidentiality, priest-penitent confidentiality, and lawyer-client confidentiality are all instances of privileged communication. Society recognizes that statements that patients, penitents, or clients make are appropriately kept confidential. The facts revealed in such disclosures may not be freely repeated; and any records kept of them are confidential as well. That the records are kept on computers changes nothing in this respect. The data belong to the lawyer or doctor, but the facts they represent may not be disclosed except under certain conditions, and anyone who has legitimate access to the data is also bound by the same strictures of confidentiality. If this were not the case, the practice of law and medicine would be seriously impaired. There are restrictions, therefore, on the use that one can make of one's data, even though the data are owned. Confidential data may not be sold or otherwise transferred, copied, or divulged to outside parties without authorization.

Does the circumstance that the facts are about us give us any special right to them? The answer seems clearly no, because we have no right to facts. But we have no obligation to make known personal facts about ourselves, and if we make them in confidence, we have the right to insist, and expect, that they will be kept confidential.

Are the facts that John subscribes to a certain magazine, that he pays bills on time, and that he buys certain products, facts to which John has a right? The answer again is no. These are, at least in part, facts about John that are not confidential. The fact that he subscribes to a certain magazine is known by him, by the magazine and some of its employees, the postman, and others along the way who might see the magazine in his mailbox, or the secretary who distributes the mail in his office. His name is on a list of all the subscribers to that magazine. He knows that it is. Does the owner of the list have the right to sell a list with John's name on it? Unless the relation is confidential, the owner of the list does have the right, because John's subscription is a fact, and because the data are the owner's—unless by selling it he does John some harm. For he has no right to use his data to harm John or anyone else. The owner's selling his list to another magazine, to be used for promotional purposes, or to some other advertiser, in general does not harm John, even if it increases the amount of mail he gets. But if the list were to be used in ways that did harm John, he would have the right not to have his name given to others. The reason is not that John owns facts about himself, but that he has a right not to be harmed. The same is true of his credit rating. If information about the way he pays his bills is to be given to others and used for some purpose that may harm him, then he should at the very least know that this is being done, and should have access to that information so that he can correct it if it is in error. This again is in virtue not of his owning the facts but of his right not to be harmed.

What of one's right to privacy? This is ground for keeping confidential facts about people. Our society recognizes areas of privacy for the individual, into which others have no right to penetrate, unless serious harm is threatened to others. Each person's thoughts are his own, as are his beliefs. We have no obligation to reveal them, even though it is a fact that we are thinking certain things and have certain beliefs. There are other private areas in our lives that we have no obligation to divulge any information about. We have the right to keep these secret; and if anyone tries to find out about them, they may violate our privacy. Hence, surreptitious surveillance, wiretapping, bugging, and so on are violations of privacy, which are allowable under law only in very special circumstances.

The argument that, although having records about us in various places is allowable, the ability to gather all of this data, through the use of computers, somehow violates our privacy, is mistaken. Facts about us do not belong to us; therefore, if those who have facts about us, stored as data, own that data and have the right to sell it or give it away (providing it does not harm or threaten to harm us), then collecting that data in one place does not violate our right to privacy. But such a collection may be used to harm us—if we have no opportunity to verify what it contains, to correct errors, or to rebut false statements. The right of workers to inspect their files is an instance of a general right that applies to all people—against credit agencies, governments, and any others who maintain and use such files in ways that directly affect, and harm, us. Clearly, we should be notified of any such files kept on us, and rules governing their use should be established and enforced. Such mandatory notification and enforcement obviously require appropriate legislation.

In addition to the Big Brother syndrome, the computer makes invasion of privacy possible in other new ways.

Employees, we noted, have a right to privacy. When employee records are kept in computer files rather than filing cabinets, employers are bound to secure that information at least as well as they secure filing cabinets. Yet many managers have no idea how safe such files really are, or how open to compromise. They know the usual means of protecting physical files by lock and key; but they often simply trust their computer department to do what is necessary to safeguard computer files. Obvious passwords are sometimes used, and compromise is easy, especially for workers in the firm with access to other files.

As more and more personal data are kept on computer, more and more people will have authorized, as well as easy unauthorized, access. The rules for handling this data are often left unspecified, and different companies differ in their rules. But every company has an obligation to determine that any system containing confidential records is secure, and that employees with access to such files are informed of, and trained in, security procedures. They should also understand the importance of confidentiality. Computer access is much easier to compromise and more difficult to control than physical access. Keys to doors can be made such that duplication is difficult, if not impossible. Employees are not likely to give a key to others, because when they do so they no longer have the key. But they can give an access code to others and still have it themselves. Access codes, moreover, can often be easily used to gain entrance into other parts of a system. Unless due care is taken, this is much easier than getting from one room to another when one has the key to the first. Computers have been adopted by many companies so quickly, and in such numbers that insufficient care has been taken about security. But privacy is an obligation that managers owe to their employees, just as they owe security of funds to shareholders. Employees have the obligation to respect the privacy of files, to control their curiosity when it is possible for them to gain unauthorized access to files, and to protect the confidentiality of records and files to which they have authorized access. The problems of providing privacy and and of providing security in the age of the computer are related and demand a corporation's serious thought and effort.

The computer, in these and other ways, raises new problems for business and places new responsibilities on corporate managers. The major difficulty is that change in this area is taking place so fast that inadequate thought has been given to the moral implications involved in the changes. Not only is there no consensus on many issues, and on the legitimacy of many practices; many managers do not even know there are issues about which they should be concerned, or that they should be establishing practices to preclude future difficulties. Because there often is no consensus on issues, and because the intuitions of different people differ on the propriety of practices involving computers and their use, the need for clear moral thinking and moral argument is especially important in this area.

Further Reading

BEQUAI, AUGUST. *Computer Crime.* Lexington, Mass.: Lexington Books, 1978.
Committee on Government Operations. *The Computer and Invasion of Privacy.* New York: Arno Press, 1967.
Computer Crime: Criminal Justice Resource Manual. Washington, D.C. U.S. Department of Justice, 1979.

HOLOIEN, MARTIN O. *Computers and Their Social Impact.* New York: John Wiley & Sons, Inc., 1977.

PARKER, DONN B. *Crime by Computer.* New York: Charles Scribner's Sons, 1976.

————— *Ethical Conflicts in Computer Science and Technology.* Arlington, Va.: AFIPS Press, 1979.

WESSEL, ANDREW E. *The Social Use of Information: Ownership and Access.* New York: John Wiley & Sons, Inc, 1976.

WESTIN, ALAN F. *Freedom and Privacy.* New York: Atheneum Publishers, 1967.

————— and MICHAEL A. BAKER. *Databanks in a Free Society: Computers, Record-Keeping, and Privacy.* New York: Quadrangle Books, 1972.

WHITESIDE, THOMAS. *Computer Capers: Tales of Electronic Thievery, Embezzlement and Fraud.* New York: Thomas Y. Crowell Company, 1978.

SIXTEEN

Professions, Business, and Ethical Codes of Conduct

The professions are inextricably inter-twined with business. Corporations, for example, in 1977 spent $24 billion on legal services. Lawyers sometimes are employed directly by corporations; others form partnerships and sell their services. Still others have independent practices. The health professions form an important part of social life. Drug companies are among the corporate giants; hospital, doctor, and medical insurance bills take a significant part of the average worker's salary. Engineers build our roads, skyscrapers, bridges, and plants. They are hired in great numbers by corporations, to design cars, airplanes, washing machines, electric toothbrushes, and the other many mechanical and electronic objects that form part of our daily life.

As modern society becomes more complex, it requires greater specialization and specialized knowledge. In the United States, automation has taken over many of the routine jobs formerly performed by unskilled labor. The need for advanced training and the growth of the service professions have encouraged more people to go to college and to professional schools. Schooling has in turn provided business and industry with a pool of trained workers to take on the jobs that require communication skills, computer programming knowledge, engineering expertise, and accounting procedures, legal practices, and a variety of specialized information.

The trend toward specialization has led groups to identify themselves as a profession, and to seek the prestige and wealth that have become identified with professions. Professionalism and the professions raise special problems

335

from the point of view of ethics. Their rapid growth makes the problems more pressing.

In dealing with the professions and professionalism, the first problem is to identify what we mean by a profession or by professionals. What is a profession? Typically, professions have been self-governing, and society has allowed them a large amount of autonomy. Is such autonomy justifiable? And does it carry with it special moral or ethical responsibilities? A second topic for investigation follows from these questions: professional ethical codes. Our discussion of professional codes can provide a basis for the evaluation of other ethical codes, for instance, those issued by some corporations to their employees. Professional codes make demands on members of the professions, demands that are not always compatible with the loyalty and obedience expected by many employers. The role of the professions in business therefore requires examination, as do the activities of professional organizations. Because the members of many professions are self-employed, we should also look at the professions as independent businesses.

Whatever fields are characterized as professions, and whatever roles are played by professions, it is always people who fill professional roles and are members of professions. Members of a profession are people first and members of a profession second. Hence, there is no special ethics that allows people in a profession to do as professionals what it is immoral for others to do. Lawyers, for instance, have no right to lie or cheat or mislead in order to help or to defend a client. Doctors in their role as doctors may not for the good of medicine experiment on their patients without the patient's informed consent, nor may they lie to patients for the patient's good. Those in professions do have a special relation to ethics because of the roles they fill as members of a profession. But *more* is appropriately expected of them because of their roles, not less. In order to get straight the proper moral obligations of members of a profession, we must understand the role of professions in society.

Professionalism and the Professions

The history of the professions is still being written. How it is written depends on whether one identifies the professions first and then writes their history, or whether one specifies certain criteria that must be met for a group or field to qualify as a profession, and then investigates which groups or fields have met those criteria. The trend toward specialization has led more and more groups to identify themselves as professions, and to seek the prestige and the wealth that have become identified with professions.

The confusion about what constitutes a profession is reflected in the linguistic confusion between the terms *profession* and *professional*. We have no single, unambiguous term to refer to a member of a profession; *professional* is the term we use. But many people who are, in one sense, professionals do not belong to professions. Professionals in this sense do full time, for pay, and with considerable expertise, what others do occasionally, without pay, and as amateurs. Thus, a professional is someone who earns his living by practicing some skill or engaging in some activity that requires expertise, but which others do as a hobby, for pleasure, or in their spare time. Members of the various trades are professionals. There are professional carpenters, plumbers, auto mechanics, bricklayers, barbers, and so on. A professional knows his craft, devotes his full working time to it, usually is paid for what he does, and takes a certain pride in doing his job well. We speak of professional actors and actresses, writers, painters, gardeners, and athletes—people who do professionally what many other people do at an amateur level. Many activities are professional activities in this sense. But not all these activities constitute professions.

With some justification, the witch doctor has been proposed as the paradigm of a member of a profession. A witch doctor has arcane knowledge; he controls access to that knowledge and initiates his successor to his role; he performs an important service to his society; he commands respect and prestige. These are characteristics that tend to designate professions. In the West, two occupations have served as exemplars of the professions. The doctor, from ancient times to the present, has performed a needed service for society, has controlled and had access to specialized knowledge, and has been given status and prestige, though not necessarily wealth. In the Middle Ages, priests made up an acknowledged profession. They had special powers and knowledge, controlled entry into their ranks, exercised a large degree of autonomy, and served an important social function. They were the educated members of society and professed the faith from the pulpit. By extension, other scholars came to be considered members of the scholarly professions. They too had access to and controlled knowledge, performed a service to society, and had something to profess. They were called professors, and formed a profession. Two other groups that had some early claim to being members of a profession were professional soldiers, especially officers, and engineers—those who designed and built aqueducts, cathedrals, palaces, and roads.

In the contemporary world, the paradigms of the professions are the medical and legal professions. Other occupations often considered professions are engineering, pharmacy, architecture, and nursing. Some people consider journalism a profession, as well as accounting. University teaching is probably a profession, though high school and grade school teaching are probably not. Many other groups claim professional status: actuaries, insurance underwriters, school administrators, public administrators, social workers, and paramedics, among others. The professions traditionally carry with them prestige, respect, social status, and autonomy. In recent times they have also been regarded as well-paid occupations. Hence the desire of more and more groups to have their activity recognized as a profession is understandable.

Does it make any difference whether or not society considers a group to be a profession? Would plumbers do better work if they were a profession instead of a trade? Would doctors perform less well if they were a trade rather than a profession? The answer depends on what society allows members of a profession that it does not allow others, and what it expects from members of a profession that it does not expect from others. Traditionally, society has allowed professions greater autonomy than it allows the trades, arts, or business. Members of a profession set their own standards, regulate entry into the profession, discipline their own members, and function with fewer restraints than others. They frequently set their own tasks, are not closely supervised, and do not punch time clocks. In return for such increased autonomy, however, they properly are expected to serve the public good, to set higher standards of conduct for their members than those required of others, and to enforce a higher discipline on themselves than others do. The trade-off granted by society is less social control, on the condition that the profession be self-regulating and self-disciplinary. The standards to which members of a profession are to hold themselves are usually expressed in a professional code (most often called an ethical code) of conduct, promulgated and enforced by a professional organization. Those groups wishing to gain the status of a profession frequently organize into a professional association and promulgate a code of professional ethical conduct.

Professional Ethical Codes

The argument in favor of allowing a profession to govern itself is based on two claims. The first is that the knowledge that members of the profession have mastered is specialized, useful to society, and not easily mastered by the layman. The second is that the members of the profession set higher standards for themselves than society requires of its citizens, of unskilled workers, and of business men and women. The profession, therefore, is, appropriately, in a position to know how its members should behave, to be alert to violations of the standards it sets, and to censure or dismiss from its ranks those who do not live up to the profession's standards.

Doctors and lawyers are two groups that plausibly make both claims. Doctors have a large body of specialized knowledge. They study for four years beyond college, do an internship, and then sometimes go on to further specialized study. The knowledge that they have is clearly useful to society, and though some knowledge of health care is accessible to the layman, much is not. The medical profession has developed a specialized vocabulary and an impressive technical jargon. Mastering the vocabulary and jargon is part of a doctor's knowledge and expertise. Doctors perform a service that laymen need and want. Moreover, people wish to be able to trust their doctors. They want to be assured that those to whom they entrust their health and lives are competent. Hence it is reasonable for society to demand that only those competent should be allowed to practice medicine. Society reasonably requires proof of training, knowledge, and competence, and identifies those qualified to perform medical services by requiring a licensing procedure.

Who does the licensing? The state does. But the state is not competent to decide what a doctor must know, nor to grade the tests of those who wish certification. Because the knowledge is technical, only those already trained, that is, doctors, or representative doctors, make up the medical examinations, set requirements for entry into the profession, and certify those who pass. The profession, therefore, decides what knowledge a person must have to practice medicine legally; it sets the curriculum of medical schools. Because doctors decide how many students the medical school can handle, they control entry into the market. They decide not only how many people will be trained, but also who will be admitted to medical school, what these people must learn, and who will be allowed to practice medicine. They set the standards for the practice of medicine. Lawyers similarly control legal education, bar examinations, and the standards of the legal profession. Because both groups control entry into the field, and set policy for remaining in the field, both groups act, in many ways, like monopolies. Why should society allow these groups to have so much power when it denies such power to business?

The reply is based on the second claim, namely, that the professions set higher standards for themselves than society sets for other groups. What exactly does this mean? Though originally the claim was best understood in moral terms, its present meaning is no longer clearly that of morality. What would it mean for members of a profession to hold themselves to higher moral norms than those applied to other members of society? Obviously, it would not mean that members of the profession were merely to refrain from cheating their clients, or to refrain from lying to their patients. Honesty is a moral requirement of everyone, as is telling the truth. The higher moral norms to which members of a profession were to adhere, in the past, were norms that went beyond the requirements of minimal morality. Doctors, for instance, were expected not to work only for money, but to serve patients even if they could not pay for medical services. Lawyers, too, were expected to put their thirst for justice above their desire for fees. They were expected, therefore, to be willing to defend some people who could not afford to pay for their services. Tradesmen, shopkeepers, and businesspeople are not expected to work without pay. To expect members of a profession to do so is to expect more of them than society demands of others.

Members of a profession were also expected to take a different approach to their time and commitments than ordinary workers. Doctors and lawyers were not expected to punch a time clock. They were expected to work as many hours as their professional duties required, which frequently amounted to more than the standard workweek of others. Doctors, especially, were expected to be ready to provide their services at inconvenient times of the day or night, when necessary.

A third way in which members of a profession were expected to follow a higher standard was in their personal as well as their professional conduct. They were expected to set an example of proper conduct, and be above suspicion. They were expected not only to refrain from improper conduct but also to be known to refrain. This is more than is expected of others.

In these and other ways the professions, at least in earlier times, were expected to adhere to higher moral standards than other people. They were in turn given more respect.

The benefits that accrue to members of a profession are legitimate to the extent that they live up to a higher moral code than others.

An individual can only be a member of a profession if he or she is part of a constituted, self-regulated, properly defined group. The group as such, moreover, has moral obligations that each of its members shares by belonging actively to the profession. The moral status and responsibility of professions in many ways parallels that of corporations and corporate responsibility. We can correctly speak of the responsibilities of the medical profession. But the profession acts only through the actions of its members, who are the ones who must assume the responsibility of the profession. Thus, if the medical profession is entrusted by society with the regulation of the profession, then each of its members has the obligation not only to live up to proper standards but also to make sure that other members of the profession do so. If society allows the medical profession to control access to the profession, the profession has the moral obligation to make sure that medical care is available to all, not only to the well-to-do or to those who live in urban areas. That is the responsibility of both the profession and, necessarily, of those within it.

This leads to professional ethical codes. If the argument given so far is valid, members of a profession, both individually and collectively, have special moral obligations. How adequately are they reflected in professional ethical codes?

Clearly, professions no longer set higher *moral* standards for themselves. But they do set professional standards, sometimes called *ethical standards.* These, to a large extent, have become substitutes for higher moral standards, and though not immoral, these frequently have little to do with moral standards. The standards are now professional, but not necessarily higher, from a moral point of view. Doctors and lawyers claim to know the proper role members of their professions should play in society. They claim to set high professional standards to protect society against incompetent practitioners, frauds, and quacks. They know the subterfuges to which members of their profession are prone, the means by which doctors or lawyers can be immoral or unethical without public awareness of their activities. Because they have virtually exclusive access to their specialized knowledge, some may be tempted to use it to achieve their own ends at the expense of the public. Such practitioners can best be restrained by those within the field who have comparable knowledge. Doctors and lawyers argue, accordingly, that they should be given autonomy, should be allowed to be self-regulating, not because they adhere to higher norms but because they are best equipped to know how their peers should act, and therefore best able to judge when they act improperly.

This argument in favor of self-regulation by the professions is plausible. If accepted by society, then society can allow these and similar professions more autonomy than other occupations. The standards to which members of the profession hold themselves are stated in their professional ethical codes.

Before we look at professional codes of conduct, however, we should note that the argument in defense of autonomy presents some difficulties. The ordinary person does not spend four years learning medicine. But he or she can learn something about medicine. The ordinary person can also tell to some extent when a doctor seems unsure of himself or herself; when the patient is not being given all the facts; when a diagnosis turns out to be wrong, or a treatment inappropriate. It is not true that only doctors can judge other doctors. The ordinary people who make up society can judge certain aspects of medical practice and the results of some medical activities. The doctors' expertise is not as exclusive as some doctors would like others to believe. The same observation is true of lawyers.

Nor is it always the case that doctors are better judges of doctors and lawyers of lawyers than are the laypersons untrained in these professions. Ordinary citizens serve on juries to judge evidence of crimes; the evidence, when technical, is made intelligible to the jury members. Similarly, laypersons could serve on trial boards, to judge the charges of unethical or immoral conduct on the part of doctors and lawyers. Laypersons could either master the knowledge necessary for a particular case, or could have the case explained in a nontechnical manner so that they could make an intelligent judgment on the issue.

Members of a profession know the pitfalls of the profession from the inside. But self-regulation by a profession is justifiable only if the general public is satisfied that a given profession is effectively policing itself; that its code requires higher standards than nonprofessional occupations; that its members are living up to the code; and that the profession is promoting the general good.

Does restricting entry to the medical profession, for instance, promote the general good? The extent to which doctors restrict entry to the profession may be justified by the absence of facilities for training more doctors. By restricting entry, however, doctors can protect their own positions. A potential conflict of interest clearly exists. The more that doctors restrict entry, the fewer doctors there are, and consequently they can demand more money for their services. Doctors were not always well paid. The old-time country doctor and the general practitioner received modest pay, worked long hours, were frequently called out at night, and did not complain loudly when someone could not pay. They were a service profession (somewhat like priests and ministers), and it was considered improper for them to charge or to receive high fees. As professions change, so should society's view of the professions and of their autonomy.

Although professional codes of conduct were once expected to state high standards, they now serve a variety of purposes. Some codes are simply used to indicate that the group is a profession. The code is brought out and referred to on ceremonial occasions, and is sometimes read by new members upon initiation to the profession. Some codes state a set of ideals that members of the profession should try to attain and by which they should guide their practice. But failure to attain the ideals is expected, and few members of the profession actually achieve the goals stated. Other codes or parts thereof are disciplinary. They state the minimum conditions that a member of the profession must satisfy. If he or she falls below that minimum, he or she is subject to sanction by the profession, the most serious of which is expulsion. Still other codes spell out the etiquette of the profession. A single code may include a statement of ideals, a set of disciplinary rules, and standards of professional etiquette.

If a professional code is to serve as a basis upon which a profession claims autonomy from the nonprofessional social control to which other groups are subject, the code should have the following characteristics:

1. The code should be regulative. The inclusion of ideals is not necessarily inappropriate. But the code should make clear which of its statements are ideals and which are punitively regulative. Unless a code actually regulates the conduct of the members of a profession, the profession has no public statement to which society can hold the profession. Society allows a profession autonomy on condition that it holds its members to higher norms than those to which others are held, therefore these norms must be publicly available, and must be perceived as being higher than other norms.

2. The code should protect the public interest and the interests of those served by the profession. Unless the public benefits by granting the profession autonomy, it should withdraw this privilege.

3. The code should not be self-serving. Codes can be used to serve the interests of the profession at the expense of the public. Certain regulations (for instance, those concerning the setting of fees or the restricting of advertising) protect the profession and are not in the public interest. Code provisions that prevent competition within the profession are generally not in the public's interest; they tend to emphasize the negative, monopolistic aspects of the profession.

4. The code should be specific and honest. A code that simply says that its members should not lie, steal, or cheat requires nothing of them that is not required of all others. If a code is honest, it deals with those aspects of the profession that pose particular and specialized temptations to its members. The profession is allowed autonomy because it knows the special pitfalls of the profession—its shady areas, and its unethical, though not quite illegal, practices. Unless these are addressed, the profession is not truly regulating itself.

5. The code must be both policeable and policed. Unless the code has provisions in it for bringing charges and applying penalties, it is no more than a set of ideals. Unless a profession can demonstrate by its record that it does police its own ranks, society has little reason to believe that it is doing so. In such cases, it has no justification for allowing special privileges to the profession.

Society should then, appropriately, legislate concerning the members of the profession and control their activities, as it controls those engaged in other occupations.

Recently, the codes of both the medical and the legal professions have come under attack. The provision that prevents advertising by doctors and lawyers has been successfully challenged as restricting trade and preventing competition. The setting of fees for professional work by the respective organizations has also been successfully attacked as artificially setting rates, serving the profession at the expense of the public, and preventing competition. Neither the American Bar Association nor the American Medical Association has been especially anxious to discipline its members. Frequently, they act only after a lawyer or a doctor has been found guilty of a felony. Such limited action hardly justifies special privileges.

Although professions can enforce their codes, they are not courts of law and cannot act as such. Violations of a code are subject to limited discipline. Expulsion from the professional association is typically the severest penalty that can be enforced, together with public exposure of the act. Censure is a more frequent penalty.

Professional codes are supposed to govern the professional activity of all members of the profession, whether working for oneself or for an employer. The codes may set higher standards than the employer wishes his or her employees to adopt, or than the company code allows.

Professional codes usually ignore such problems, which at least some members of a profession face. Professional codes often specify obligations to the client or patient, to the employer (if there happens to be one), the public, and the profession. What is a professional to do when he finds that these obligations conflict? For instance, what if a company's doctor is told not to release information about mounting evidence that the workers in the plant are suffering from an employment-related health hazard? Does his obligation to public health and to his patients (the workers) take precedence over his obligation to his employer?

The 1983 National Association of Accountants Code of Ethics for accountants working within a firm suggests (does not require) that accountants report improper activity (bribery, fraud, false accounting) to top management and the board of directors. But rather than require whistle blowing if no remedial action is taken, the accountant is advised to resign. The guide for these accountants is what is required by law. If law requires public disclosure, the code requires it. If the law does not require public disclosure, the code counsels silence. Because the code requires no more than the law does, the code does not satisfy the conditions for a profession's autonomy, and this is partial grounds for not considering accountancy a profession.

The professional codes give no indication of what action to take when the profession itself acts inappropriately. Professional codes do not consider this possibility. Nor have the professions adequately considered their collective responsibility to society, or how it is to be met. Our discussions of corporate responsibility and accountability can be fruitfully applied to the professions. Work along these lines is still in its early stages. But unless professions both acknowledge and live up to their collective responsibilities, society has no moral warrant for not tightly controlling them through legislation.

Corporate Codes

Ethical codes have proliferated in recent years. Not only are they issued by professions, but they have often been adopted by corporations, by businesses, and by industries across corporate lines. Not all such codes are ethical codes. None of them are *moral* codes, because no individual or group can make actions moral or immoral by fiat. Every code, therefore, can and should appropriately be evaluated from a moral point of view. Some corporate codes simply specify the legal requirements of which employees may not, but should, be aware. Some codes reflect specific concerns, such as bribery and illegal political contributions. Some firms have drawn up codes that serve as guidelines to what is accepted practice within the organization. Some companies feel that no gift from a supplier should be accepted, and others allow accepting gifts of up to $25 or $50. Some firms prohibit giving gifts to suppliers or customers. Others limit contributions to political parties, the purchase of stock from companies with which the firm does business, and other practices that may cause or give the appearance of causing conflict of interest.

Industry-wide codes attempt to set standards of fair competition within an industry. Although sometimes effective, they are limited in what they can control, for they must not restrict trade or competition. Codes that place a lower limit on the price of a good, for instance, violate the antitrust act, as do industry policies that standardize the hours of work.

Codes can nonetheless serve an important function and can help in resolving specific issues faced by members of a profession or by workers within a firm. If there is a company policy, for instance, about how large a gift can be accepted, then an employee knows not only that bribery is immoral and to be avoided, but also what his employer considers a bribe to be.

Even when intended to set moral standards, a typical defect of codes is that they give the professional or worker no insight into how the code was formulated, what moral principles it exemplifies, or how to resolve issues of interpretation or of conflicts not covered by the code. The codes are usually promulgated by some board or committee of the profession or company in question; many seem like a form of the Ten Commandments. The Ten Commandments, however, came from God, Who many people thought and still do think has either the knowledge or the authority to dictate what is morally right and morally wrong. Are ethical committees or boards of directors similarly placed and gifted? Most people think not.

The difficulty with many codes is not that they prescribe that which is immoral, but that they fail to be truly effective in helping members of the profession or company to act morally. To be moral means not only doing what someone says is right, but also knowing *why* what one does is right, and assuming moral responsibility for the action. How were the provisions of the code arrived at? On what moral bases do the injunctions stand? Faced with a serious moral problem, how can the code help a member of a profession or of a firm sort out issues? In corporate codes, it is sometimes suggested that any difficulties or uncertainties should be discussed with the corporation's legal office. The legal office, presumably, can give advice about the law and what is legally permitted or forbidden. Not every legal office is competent to give advice about the morality of an action, insofar as this may differ from the law.

Although corporate codes cannot be expected to contain a detailed presentation of moral reasoning, they can make reference to general moral principles. The injunction to employees (found in one corporate code) to act in such a way that they would not be ashamed to have their actions exposed to the public—for instance, in the headlines of the local newspaper—is a step in the right direction. A code could appropriately and helpfully refer to the principles from which the code flows, to principles of justice and fairness. It could also refer to these moral principles: objectively weighing the consequences to all those affected by one's actions; respecting the rights of others; and the like.

An objection might be that this is asking too much of a code. It cannot and should not provide general moral principles because these are assumed to be held by everyone. People should learn these from their parents, ethics teachers, and churches, and not from their professional organizations or from their employers. There is some truth to such an objection. But unless the code is understood in terms of moral principles, it will tend simply to be the expression of rules learned by rote, or even worse, of ideals never to be attained. If the members of a profession are to internalize the rules of their profession, or if workers are to internalize the rules of their firm, they must understand how the rules are derived, and how they implement moral principles. Only in this way can those persons subject to a code use similar reasoning to cover situations of conflict, as well as those situations not handled explicitly by the code. Ideally, each member who is covered by a code should understand its moral principles, as well as the nature of his or her profession or firm. Rather than memorizing a code, each could then derive the same code by thinking clearly and objectively about the moral issues typically faced by those covered by the code.

Professional and company ethical codes have a certain limited usefulness. They are frequently better than nothing at all. But they are inadequate as guides to moral conduct or as guarantees that a profession or firm is serving the public and preventing its members from acting in a way detrimental to the public interest. If this is the case, then why develop a corporate ethical code? There are several advantages to doing so. First, the very exercise of developing one is in itself worthwhile, especially if it forces a large number of people in the firm to think through, in a fresh way, their mission and the

345

important obligations they as a group and as individuals have to the firm, each other, their clients or customers, and society as a whole. Second, once adopted, a code can be used to generate continuing discussion and possible modification of the code. Third, it could help to inculcate in new employees at all levels the perspective of responsibility; the need to think in moral terms about their actions; and the importance of developing the virtues appropriate to their positions. Fourth, a code can be used as a document to which employees can refer when asked to do something contrary to it. Fifth, a code might be used both to reassure customers and the public of the fact that the firm adheres to moral principles, and to provide them with a touchstone against which they can measure the firm's actions.

At its best, a corporate code can not only guide the actions of employees on legal matters and conflicts of interests, but it can also enable workers and managers to evaluate in moral terms the *firm's* ends, practices, and actions, to be sure *the firm* measures up to the code. If management adheres to the code, the code can help develop a moral corporate ethos.

Professional Organizations

Members of a profession tend to gather and organize into professional organizations and associations, just as workers tend to gather into unions. The role of the professional association is to promote the profession's interests, to provide a forum for discussion, and to disseminate information concerning the profession. Professional associations also tend to be both the promulgators and the enforcers of professional codes. Although this is appropriate, some professional associations need policing.

A professional association has the de facto (if not always the legal) power to control entry into the field, dismiss certain practitioners from the field, set policy for its members, and restrict access to publication for those whose work it does not approve. Such organizations are sometimes asked for advice by government; publishers ask them for definitive texts; and others ask them to recommend consultants and experts. The power of the officers of professional organizations is often uncontrolled and sometimes excessive. Such power can be damaging to those members of the profession who disagree with the organization's leadership or policies. Professional organizations are often able to silence opposition to the organization's policies and prevent minority views from being heard on public as well as professional issues. Such cases have led to the suggestion that professional organizations should be subject to independent review by those outside the profession; that there be lay participation in hearing disciplinary cases under the code; and that an independent group serve as the recipient of complaints made by the public against members of the profession, and follow the handling of the complaint by the profession.

Professional associations have tended both to monopolize power in the area of the profession's prestige and to safeguard the vested interests of their members. The failure of those in the professions and professional associations to police their ranks erodes the basis for society's trust of the profession and for its autonomy. In professional codes, provisions for reprimand, censure, and expulsion are usually phrased so as to preserve secrecy rather than to publicize immoral activities by members of the profession. If a profession has higher moral standards than those required by law, the professional organization should not only make these standards generally known but should also reveal infractions of these standards by members of the profession.

Because the professions have access to and control over specialized knowledge, the public is dependent on them for the effective use of this knowledge. The members of the profession are in the best position to know how their fellow professionals can abuse this knowledge and how they can take advantage of the public. Yet professional organizations rarely inform the ordinary person of the ways to protect himself or herself against malpractice or unethical or immoral behavior by a member of the profession. Nor do professional societies ask for increased competition within professional ranks, greater disclosure regarding the activities of their members, lower fees, and so on. Changes that the professions could make that would be in the public interest would be a higher code of ethics, greater disclosure of their activities, active demystification of their jargon, and simplification of their language.

Professional associations should also provide a forum within the profession or industry, at which members can raise ethical issues, which the association can face and provide solutions—or work toward solutions—which can be morally justified to the general public. To ask the professionals in an industry to help the public achieve more disclosure about a profession or industry might seem like asking them to go against their own best interests. But it is in the general interest of the professions, and of industry, to foster and develop public trust. There is no better way to do so than by full, understandable, and proper disclosure.

Professional societies have in general failed to fulfill their obligations in the defense of members of the profession who lose their jobs or are otherwise penalized for following and living up to the code of the profession. Those who work for an employer (e.g., a corporation) are sometimes asked, or are required, to perform some action that violates their professional code. For instance, the typical engineering code states that the safety, health, and welfare of the public shall be held paramount in the performance of professional duties. Suppose an engineer for a tire company sees that the tires being produced are unsafe, reports this to his superiors, including the board, and gets no reaction except to be told to keep quiet and mind his own business. But he knows that the code of his profession requires that he hold the safety of the public paramount, and accordingly he informs the newspapers that the tires are unsafe. This leads to an investigation, to a recall of the tires, and to a penalty for the tire manufacturer. Typically, this engineer would be fired; perhaps he would be blackballed in the industry. And typically, no professional engineering organization would come to his defense for upholding its code.

347

Yet such a defense seems professionally and morally mandatory if professional organizations expect their members to take their codes seriously and to live by them.

The Professions in Businesses

The case of the whistle blower in the tire factory is a classic instance of a professional conflict between the demands of a professional code and the demands of an employer. Although any employee may have blown the whistle (e.g., on a tire manufacturer), the engineering code places a special, more stringent obligation on engineers than on others to be concerned with public safety.

A professional code of conduct appropriately demands more of professionals than of ordinary workers. If a professional is self-employed he may be able to live according to a higher standard of conduct. But what if he is employed by a corporation that demands he conform to the letter of the law? Does he have special obligations because of his role as a member of a profession, and does a company act immorally if it does not respect these higher obligations?

The situation is especially difficult for engineers, nurses, and others who work for large corporations, hospitals, or firms. Engineers and nurses are often treated as if their only duty is to obey orders—do what they are told. What does a nurse do when hospital rules require doctors to scrub before an operation but one doctor refuses to do so, and tells her to mind her own business? What does an engineer do when he believes that the safety of some design is questionable, advises against using it, and is told that for cost reasons the company refuses to change the design? What if an actuary sees that what he has produced is used in a way that he did not intend, or that it may be misleading, even though in his report he took pains to make sure his methods and assumptions were clear? Perhaps in none of these cases will the danger to the public be serious enough to mandate whistle blowing. But in each case, a professional would rightly feel that his or her professional code demands that he or she take some action. Does loyalty to one's professional code take precedence over loyalty to one's employer?

There is no agreement on the appropriate answer. The typical professional code is not written to handle this problem, nor do the professional societies insist that employers respect the right of professionals in their employ to follow the letter and the spirit of the professional codes.

Members of the professions, just as everyone else who works for a firm, have the obligation *not* to do what is *immoral*. They have the obligation to employ their knowledge as they deem appropriate, to warn of unsafe products, illegal activities, and dangerous work conditions. But they do not have the responsibility to make final judgments that appropriately belong to management. Typically, an engineering judgment, a legal judgment, and a medical

348

judgment are only part of the relevant information that goes into a managerial judgment. Professionals should make their professional views and concerns known. They should insist that public safety be protected when it is clearly threatened. But they have no obligation to insist that their way of doing things be observed, or that their fears carry the day in a disputed area. The special obligations of those in professions require them to do more than others, be more sensitive to how their work is used, and be more alert to violations of ethical standards in their firms. Yet even here we can distinguish between what they are morally required to do as individuals from what they are professionally required to do. The limits on what they are professionally required to do are set not only by the code but also by the extent to which the profession as a whole is willing to support them.

Journalists have long fought for the right to preserve the secrecy of their sources. In their fight against the courts, they have generally been supported by their fellow journalists, their newspapers or TV stations, and the news media in general. Such support is an indication of a profession's commitment to a principle. The right to preserve the confidentiality of one's sources is a right that journalists have insisted on and convincingly defended. A right to confidentiality is claimed and generally given to priests in the confessional, to lawyers and their clients, and to doctors and their patients.

Members of the various professions may have special rights and duties that outweigh their obligations to corporate loyalty and obedience. But until the profession as a whole—its members and its professional organizations—stand up and defend those professionals who strive to live up to the higher code by which they are supposed to live, neither the public nor most employers will take such rights and duties very seriously.

We can draw several conclusions concerning professional rules and moral obligations.

1. Professions and members of professions deserve more autonomy in their actions than do others, providing they impose upon themselves, and live up to, higher moral demands than those required of others. The specific nature of these higher moral demands will vary from profession to profession. But in general they will concern serving and protecting the welfare of society—the general public, and their clients or patients in the realm of their professional expertise.

2. When one becomes a member of a profession, one incurs not only individual moral obligations insofar as he or she fills an individual professional role, one also shares in the collective moral obligation of the profession.

3. The moral obligation of the members of a profession thus extends beyond each one's own individual activities. A member of a profession has the obligation to police one's professional peers, to help change professional structures if they need changing,

and to be concerned with the impact of the profession on society. (This aspect of professional moral obligation, we have noted, is ignored by professional ethical codes.)

4. Members of a profession sometimes encounter special moral problems in business, because of conflicts of interest and conflicts between one's professional obligations and the demands of one's employer.

Because members of professions are moral beings first and only secondarily professionals, professional ethics cannot appropriately relieve one of the general moral obligations that apply to all people. To choose to be a member of a profession is to choose greater not lesser moral obligations; and it is only to the extent that its members fulfill these moral obligations that the professions deserve respect.

The Professions As Business

To contrast the professions and business is to give only a partial picture, for many members of the professions are also businessmen. Lawyers and engineers frequently move up the corporate ladder to management positions. Lawyers, doctors, accountants, consulting engineers, and members of many other professions are in business for themselves. As more and more groups claim the status of a profession, the line between the professions and business blurs even more.

In considering the professions as businesses, we shall focus only on a few aspects that tend to distinguish them from other businesses: restriction of entry to the field, restrictions on competition, and service to the public.

We have already seen that the medical profession has practical control of most aspects of the health industry. For many years there has been a shortage of doctors—at least in certain portions of the country. Rural areas and ghettos, for instance, are poorly served. Doctors as a profession set the standards that must be attained to practice medicine. They control the degree requirements for the M.D.; they also decide how many doctors should be trained in their medical schools, and how large the medical schools should be. They set up the testing and other procedures required before one is allowed to practice medicine. All of these practices can be justified. Yet when doctors trained abroad have difficulty being licensed, and when the shortage of doctors remains chronic despite a large pool of applicants for medical school, the profession is open to the charge of restricting entry. The charge is reinforced by the fact that doctors now are typically among the more affluent members of society, whereas in previous eras they were among the less affluent. The responsibility for supplying doctors for all sectors of society is a responsibility held collectively by the profession. It is, moreover, a responsibility that individual members of the medical profession cannot simply ignore as being not their concern or their moral obligation.

Entry into the legal profession has also become more difficult than it once was, even though the supply has kept up with, and at times even exceeded, the demand.

Would society be better off if it were de-professionalized? Have the professions become too strong? Have they won protective legislation that makes their services necessary, without reason? Could midwives and paraprofessionals perform some of the services that are now the exclusive right of doctors? Are lawyers really needed to draw up wills, file for divorce, and defend those charged with minor offenses? Can the law be simplified so that the intelligent layman could adequately handle these and similar tasks? The answer to these questions is still hotly debated. Yet a comparative study in the United States and other countries provides evidence that we are overlegalized and over-doctored.

What of the other professions? The techniques of licensing and claims to specialized knowledge have made entry into certain areas difficult, as we have noted. When used to keep fees up and to keep competition out, such techniques are clearly not in the public's interest.

Restrictions on competition among those already in a profession affect two areas in particular: professional limitations on advertising and the setting of fees.

The prohibition on advertising by doctors, lawyers, architects, and members of other professions has a long history not restricted to the United States. The prohibition, moreover, has frequently been included in codes of professional conduct and backed up by law. Many reasons are given for the prohibition. Some point to the outrageous claims made by quacks and peddlers of patent remedies for diseases ranging from the plague to cancer. Others claim that if doctors, lawyers, and similar professionals could advertise, the public would be poorly served. The best advertisers rather than the best practitioners would probably get the most patients and clients. Furthermore, the personal relation of doctor to patient and lawyer to client is developed and not just promoted. Such relations are neither fostered nor established by advertising. A third claim is that advertising undermines the dignity of the profession. Clearly, though the arguments carry some weight with respect to some advertising, they do not make a very strong case for the total prohibition of it.

The prohibition against advertising by the professions has been found to be unconstitutional—an abridgement of First Amendment rights of freedom of speech and the press. The professional codes have been changed to reflect this. Yet we have not seen a rash of advertising by doctors, lawyers, architects, and others. Why not? There are two possible answers: One is that the members of these professions have been raised on the prohibition against advertising, are unaccustomed to advertising, and are therefore not advertising from past habit. The other is that the absence of advertising has always benefited the professions and not the public. Lack of advertising reflects a lack of competition. By restricting entry, doctors have all the patients they can handle. Why seek more through advertising? Removing the law against advertising and removing the statement in the codes against advertising have had little effect on actual practice.

The second area of concern is the setting of fees by the professions. Is this unfair restraint of trade? Members of the professions, it is claimed, should not haggle over fees. To do so would be demeaning, undignified, and, in a word, unprofessional. A second argument claims that a sliding-fee schedule would give the professional an upper hand when faced with a desperate individual who needs his help, but put a professional in a poor bargaining position vis-à-vis a large firm. The same service would cost the individual who could least afford it more than it would the rich corporation. The claim is that the setting of fees assures equal access and guarantees equal fees for equal work. However, this does not justify the reluctance to reveal fees, or the lack of competition in setting professional fees. The ordinary person rarely shops around to inquire how much the various doctors in a town charge; nor is this part of general knowledge. The ordinary person's approach to medical and legal service is strangely removed from consideration of the fees that members of the profession charge. There is no obvious competition on the basis of fees. Some professions have even recommended minimum fees to be charged for certain services, a practice clearly in the interest of the profession and not in the interest of the public.

The practice of payment by results further protects the self-interest of the professional at the expense of the public. It is rarely practiced by doctors. They do not charge only if the patient gets better, or only if the patient survives the operation; they charge for the use of their skill and their time. The practice of charging by results is more common in civil suits, in which lawyers take a certain percentage of the amount awarded their clients if they win the suit and nothing if they do not. However, the temptation is to sue for a larger amount than otherwise justifiable, so as to collect higher fees.

The dual role of businessman and professional involves many potential conflicts of interest in which making money is opposed to serving the client or patient as best one can. Such conflicts make disclosure all the more necessary. Those professions that prefer to work under a veil of tacit secrecy must be more open to the public scrutiny of their business practices.

The professions are an important aspect of the American business scene. Actions of the professions and their members can and should be evaluated from a moral point of view as objectively and critically as the actions of business.

Further Reading

American Bar Association. *Code of Professional Responsibility and Code of Judicial Conduct.* Chicago: American Bar Association, 1977.

ASHLEY, JO ANN. *Hospitals, Paternalism, and the Role of the Nurse.* New York: Teachers College Press, 1976.

BAUM, ROBERT J., and ALBERT FLORES, eds. *Ethical Problems in Engineering,* 2nd ed., 2 vols. Troy, N.Y.: Center for the Study of the Human Dimensions of Science and Technology, 1980.

BAYLES, MICHAEL D. *Professional Ethics*. Belmont, Calif.: Wadsworth Publishing Company, 1981.

BENNION, F. A. R. *Professional Ethics: The Consultant Professions and Their Code*. London: Charles Knight & Co. Ltd., 1969.

BRILOFF, ABRAHAM J. *The Truth About Corporate Accounting*. New York: Harper & Row Pub., Inc., 1979.

CLAPP, JANE. Professional Ethics and Insignia. Metuchen, N.J.: Scarecrow Press, Inc., 1974.

GOLDMAN, ALAN H. *The Moral Foundations of Professional Ethics*. Totowa, N.J.: Rowman and Littlefield, 1980.

HAZARD, GEOFFREY C., JR. *Ethics in the Practice of Law*. New Haven, Conn.: Yale University Press, 1978.

LARSON, MAGALI SARFATTI. *The Rise of Professionalism: A Sociological Analysis*. Berkeley, Calif.: University of California Press, 1977.

MARTIN, MIKE W., and ROLAND SCHINZINGER. *Ethics in Engineering*. New York: McGraw-Hill Book Co., 1983.

MOORE, WILBERT. *The Professions: Roles and Rules*. New York: Russell Sage Foundation, 1970.

PIRSIG, MAYNARD E. *Cases and Materials on Professional Responsibility*. St. Paul, Minn.: West Publishing Co., 1970.

SEVENTEEN

The International Free-Enterprise System, Multinationals, and Morality

Thus far, we have considered the morality of the free-enterprise system in the United States and the morality of a variety of business practices within that system. But the American system is not an isolated one. The United States is a world power; just as its political interests extend far beyond its borders, so do its economic interests. Lenin called the last stage of fully developed capitalism "imperialism." He claimed that the developed countries were able to reduce the level of exploitation of their own workers by shifting the worst aspects of exploitation to their colonies. However, this colonial theory had to be modified once the European industrial powers lost their colonies. The United States, moreover, was never a colonial power in the sense that England and France were. The present-day version of the Leninist charge is that the capitalistic, advanced industrial nations of the world are able to prosper because they exploit the people and resources of the less developed countries (LDCs) of the world—those countries often referred to as the Third World. The brunt of the attack on the developed industrial countries often falls on the activities of their multinational corporations (MNCs).

354

Multinational Corporations and the International System of Free Enterprise

The international system of capitalism or of free enterprise is not simply an extension of the American system. Involved in the system are a great many other countries, each with its own system of capitalism, together with its own political system and its own social and historical background and institutions. The total international capitalist system is a result of the extension and interaction of all of these. It operates in a world where socialist countries exert various influences, and compete with capitalist countries for markets, resources, and capital. Multinational corporations have their parent headquarters not only in the United States, but increasingly in Japan, Germany, and other industrialized countries as well. Even some of the Third World countries, such as Brazil, have developed multinational corporations that operate in many countries. For purposes of simplicity, however, we shall focus on the American extension of the capitalist model as it projects into the rest of the world. Critics fault the United States government with supporting American-based MNCs and exerting political influence for the benefit of the American companies at the expense of the LDCs.

Multinationals are corporations that operate extensively in more than one country, usually through branches or subsidiaries engaged in production, marketing, or both. They pose special moral problems. Because their activities are not confined to a single nation, no one nation can effectively control them. National law can circumscribe the activities of national firms, and government action can offset the ill effects of certain activities of a firm. But there exists no supranational state which can confine or control the many varied activities of multinationals. Among some nations there are agreements that restrict, to a limited extent, the activities of such firms. But that control is far short of what can be imposed on firms operating in only one country. Critics of multinationals loudly proclaim that the multinational corporations operate to benefit themselves and their interests, with no moral or legal constraints on their activities.

Multinational corporations are not immoral in themselves. The fact that Japanese firms operate in the United States, either independently, as Sony does, or in cooperation with an American corporation, as Toyota does (with General Motors), is no reason to call them immoral. Nor is the fact that Ford has factories in Germany a reason to feel that it operates immorally. But when large multinationals operate in Third World countries, critics claim that although they do not *necessarily* operate immorally, often they do *in fact* operate immorally. Developed countries are able to control foreign firms. Less developed or developing countries are not able, or are less able, to do so, especially when the firm has greater total sales than that country's gross national product.

When we examined the capitalist system in the United States, we noted that government fulfills many necessary functions, such as keeping competition fair and protecting the interests of workers and consumers. On the international level, however, there is no effective way to prevent firms from forming cartels and controlling prices and production. We see this clearly in the case of OPEC (Organization of Petroleum Exporting Countries). Critics charge that the large international oil corporations (the seven largest have been called The Seven Sisters) have conspired to limit the production of oil, creating false shortages, and driving up the price without any regard to whom they hurt by such action. Because these companies operate internationally, it is not possible for any government to check their books, worldwide, or to prevent such collusion. Other multinationals are charged with supporting repressive governments which serve the interests of the MNCs, exploiting workers in underdeveloped countries, marketing dangerous drugs and unsafe equipment, and disrupting the culture and traditions of other nations. We shall start by looking at some of the general attacks on American multinational corporations. We shall then examine some particular charges and cases.

The following are three general, major charges: (1) MNCs operate immorally in the less developed countries by exploiting workers, by exploiting natural resources, and by reaping exhorbitant profits; (2) MNCs compete unfairly in the LDCs, to the detriment of the host countries; and (3) MNCs are a major cause of the impoverishment of the LDCs, and of the unrest found there. Each of the charges has some basis in fact and history.

Multinationals and Exploitation

Multinational corporations operate in less developed countries for a variety of reasons. They seek cheap labor; they seek available resources; they seek tax shelters and relief; and they seek markets. If they did not think they could make a profit in a less developed country, they would not establish subsidiaries there. In seeking cheap labor, they operate just as they do in the United States. Many textile factories, for instance, moved from New England to the South, to take advantage of cheaper labor there. Were the Southern workers exploited because they were paid less than Northern workers? One cannot conclude that they were, simply because the workers were paid less; the charge of exploitation requires more than the existence of a comparatively low wage scale. In discussing a fair wage, we saw that this requires background institutions that are just, which include minimum-wage laws and welfare programs as alternatives to workers having to accept any wage offered in order to live. In many Third World countries, fair background institutions of this sort are woefully lacking. Under such conditions, it is difficult to speak meaningfully of a fair wage set by the market. For without the restraints imposed by background institutions, the market does not guarantee fair wages; the market inclines firms to go in the direction of paying the lowest wages possible. Sometimes this is lower than what is required for subsistence. To the extent that this is the case, the wage is not a living wage; it does not allow the worker to live in dignity as a human being, and it can be morally faulted. Some MNCs

356

are guilty of paying such wages, and that practice can be morally condemned. But the situation is more complicated than a blanket condemnation would warrant.

In many situations, multinationals pay the same rate as the local employers. If the other employers fail to pay a living wage, they are as guilty as the MNCs. But in other cases, local businesses criticize the MNCs for paying more than the going wage. The businesses complain that the multinationals thus attract the best workers, leaving the less skilled or less productive workers to work in the locally owned firms. Furthermore, they say that the multinationals force up the wages that workers in general expect, in some instances to more than local firms can afford. The MNCs are thus caught between contradictory demands. Some critics demand that they pay more, others demand that they pay less than they do.

The solution is to pay a living wage, even when this is not paid by local firms; and otherwise to pay only as much as necessary to get competent workers, given the competitive situation of a particular region or country. Although most people would not expect the MNCs to help in the development of labor unions or to lobby for the passage of minimal wage or other laws, the MNCs should not work against any such developments. And to the extent possible, they should foster an atmosphere in which the development of fair background institutions can develop.

The exploitation of resources raises a different problem. Mineral resources represent one of the assets of a country. The resources, however, do little good unless they are removed from the earth and sold or used. There is no moral demand that resources extracted from one country be used only in that country. If that were the case, oil-poor countries would be precluded from buying the oil they need. The complaint against multinational corporations, therefore, cannot be simply that they extract minerals and ship them outside the country. The complaint is that the MNCs buy the mineral rights for a very low price, and sell the minerals abroad for a much higher price. The natural-resource wealth of the LDCs is thus being extracted and diminished. Those who are profiting by the extraction are not the less developed countries but the MNCs. The complaint is well taken. It was just such a situation that led to the OPEC nations' raising the price of oil, insuring a large return on their diminishing assets. Oil-depletion taxes in the United States are a means by which states seek to be repaid by those who extract oil, thereby making the state that much poorer in resources. Once a state's nonrenewable resources are used up, it has lost that portion of its wealth. Taxes reaped from the depletion, however, help offset the loss.

LDCs can take measures to offset exploitation of their resources by MNCs, and more and more are beginning to do so. MNCs are morally bound not to take advantage of the LDCs, and governments are morally permitted to impose regulations or taxes on the extraction of minerals. The United Nations has drafted a "Charter of the Economic Rights and Duties of States," which includes a chapter on multinationals and the rights of states with respect to them. The UN has also established a Commission on Transnational Corporations and an Information and Research Center to monitor multinationals and to draw up a code of conduct for MNCs. These are all steps in the direction of helping the less developed countries to control the blatant abuses of multinationals. The LDCs can tame the MNCs and ensure that their presence helps the host country, by providing employment, transferring organizational knowledge and productive techniques, and paying their fair share of taxes.

If American MNCs pay workers very low wages, pay little for natural resources, and sell in the United States at the regular prices the products they produce in LDCs, they clearly have the opportunity to make significant profits. They can also price their products somewhat lower than the going price for similar products produced in the United States. They thereby gain a greater share of the market, without reducing their profit margin by more than is necessary to undersell the competition.

Those Americans who felt the LDCs were being treated unfairly complained; those in the United States who felt they were losing jobs to cheap labor abroad complained; and those who felt they were faced with unfair competition complained. The complaints were often justified, and various remedies have been suggested or tried. Import taxes on some of these goods have forced up the price and reduced the profit; export taxes imposed by the LDCs have helped the LDCs share in some of the profits of the multi-nationals. Competition has developed among the MNCs themselves, so that the profit margin has been driven down—to the benefit of the consumer. But international background institutions are still not adequately developed, and codes cannot be effectively enforced.

MNCs try to play one less developed country against another in an attempt to get the most favorable conditions possible. Only slowly are LDCs learning that they can play one company against another, as well. They can establish laws governing the allowable growth of MNCs; they can require companies to hire a certain proportion of a firm's managerial staff from the local population; they can demand that profits be reinvested in the host country instead of being sent to the parent country; and they can renegotiate initial conditions of operation to their own benefit, after a firm has developed an expensive plant in the host country and is unable to move elsewhere.

The Unfair Competition of Multinationals

The charge that MNCs compete unfairly in the LDCs has two major components. One is that the MNCs are able to operate on especially favorable and uncompetitive terms. The MNCs can borrow money from local lenders at favorable rates, because they are sound and competitive. The result is that little local capital is left for local firms, and the rates for that capital which is left are often higher than for the MNCs.

The second charge is that MNCs do not carry their fair share of the cost of social development, which imposes greater burdens on local industries. MNCs frequently utilize advanced technologies, which local companies do not have or cannot afford. The MNCs are thus able to be more productive. The result is that they not only pay higher wages but they also hire fewer people than the local firms who produce the same product. They are thus able to underprice the competition, and often force local firms out of business. The MNCs also negotiate low tax rates, and by manipulating transfer payments among their affiliates worldwide, they pay little tax anywhere. The overall result is unfair competition. The MNC hence does the host country little good. These charges are often well-founded. But at least some of the LDCs have found ways of countering the dominant position of the MNCs, as many policies adopted by Latin American countries show.

Capital formation is a crucial issue for developing countries. Capital is often in short supply. Under such conditions LDC national policy can restrict the amount that a multinational corporation can borrow; and it can require that MNC profits be reinvested or loaned within the host country. The difficult situation many Latin American countries find themselves in, however, results more from external borrowing by the country or local firms than from MNCs tying up all the local capital—even though that is sometimes a contributing factor. The national debt of some Latin American countries is so large that the country must use a major portion of the money it receives from exports merely to pay the interest on its loans. The moral blame, if blame is to be assessed, falls on MNCs, on the lending banks, on the borrowing countries, on oil-exporting countries, and on the policies of the developed countries. Except for purposes of determining instances of compensatory justice, however, determining blame is less important than finding solutions to the debt and to the capital-development problems of LDCs. Latin America faces a worse debt problem than many African countries, which were too poor even to qualify for loans, or to attract MNCs.

The charges that MNCs use advanced technology, are more productive, and undercut local firms are in part true. Some people urge MNCs to utilize more labor-intensive productive processes and thus equalize competition with local firms and increase employment opportunities for the local population. However, competition in itself is not unjust. Some less developed countries have taken a more positive approach to the problem. They have allowed foreign companies to establish only firms that do not compete with local firms. A country gains little or nothing by allowing a foreign company to operate to the detriment of a local producer of the same product. But a country can gain if a foreign enterprise establishes a plant that produces and sells locally a desired product not produced locally.

The less developed countries give multinationals tax advantages in order to attract them. But this makes sense only if the multinational in other ways contributes to the wealth, development, and good of the country. Transfer payments are related to taxes. Transfer payments are payments made by a multinational to its various divisions or affiliates. Where profits are highly taxed, it is to the benefit of the MNCs to put low prices on products sold to other parts of the firm, thus claiming low profits. Where profit taxes are low, they put high prices and claim higher profits on products sold abroad to other affiliates. This in turn lowers the profit and taxes paid by the affiliate in the receiving country. A multinational is able to change prices from country to country to suit its needs, transferring prices at intervening countries where necessary, prior to selling a product in the United States. The UN code proposes that MNCs engage in "arm's length" pricing, that is, it proposes that prices among an MNC's affiliates be figured as if each affiliate or division were truly independent. LDCs can demand this.

The attacks on MNCs have not been misplaced. But the age of the multinational robber baron is slowly drawing to a close. The financial crisis in many countries makes them unattractive places in which to invest, and in other countries governments are learning from one another how to use MNCs to their own advantage. Abuses still take place, but as government controls increase, firms have more reason to adopt policies that do not grossly exploit a host country. The more responsibly MNCs behave, the less likely that a host country will impose restrictive legislation upon them.

Multinationals and Third World Impoverishment

The charge that MNCs are the cause of the impoverishment of the Third World and of the unrest found there is partly correct. Colonialization was a mixed blessing for most nations. To some extent the substructure of the countries was developed. Roads were built where none existed before, water was made safe to drink, schools and hospitals were built, as were airports and railroads. Industry was imported and work and capital provided. But in the colonies and in general, the people of all LDCs were poor before colonization. Hence, the sense in which they were impoverished is not in the ordinary sense of the word. They were impoverished culturally. Their cultures were disrupted; Western ways were imposed on the people, and if not imposed then imported, and made attractive, so as to seduce many of the local population. Division, unrest, and raised expectations that could not be fulfilled were the results. Some responsibility falls on the more developed countries for enticing people with goods and products they could not afford and did not previously want or need. Secondly, people of the less developed countries were impoverished in a comparative sense. Poverty is not only an absolute condition; it is also relative. When all are poor, people do not feel as poor as when they are poor and others have much more. By increasing their wealth, the rich make the poor relatively poorer. In these two senses, the industrial countries are in part responsible for the poverty and unrest of the less developed countries.

There is a third sense in which the developed countries are partly responsible for the impoverization of the LDCs; paradoxically, this is related to the gains made by the LDCs. The more developed countries have helped eradicate some of the diseases—such as smallpox—that ravaged some countries; through medical technology they have decreased the infant mortality rate and increased the average life expectancy of the people of many countries. At the same time, this has contributed to the population growth in many LDCs, which poses enormous problems and leads to increasing poverty and starvation.

Fourthly, several MNCs have directly helped produce starvation in some countries. The typical scenario is this: an MNC goes into a country and buys up large portions of the productive land. It then grows cash crops for export, whereas before, local farmers grew food for local consumption. The best land is thus taken out of production for local consumption, people are no longer able to grow their own food, and the result is frequently increased malnutrition or starvation. MNCs have played this role, and continue to play it. Multinational corporations, just as do other corporations, have an obligation not to harm, and must consider the consequences of their actions. They cannot act with moral impunity. Some LDC governments, moreover, are learning to control the actions of multinationals in the agricultural sector. They are requiring cooperation with local farmers; limiting the amount of land that can go into cash crops; and taxing profits for the benefit of the people. All of this requires governments that are not corrupt, that do not benefit by colluding with MNCs at the expense of the people, and that are strong enough and stable enough to control and restrict MNCs. The number of countries in which these conditions prevail is growing. But unfair practices have by no means been eliminated.

The abuses of multinational corporations in Third World countries need not, and should not, be denied, ignored, or excused. But even taken at their worst, and as a whole, they do not establish the case that the American free-enterprise system rests on the exploitation of Third World countries. That the Third World offers potential markets cannot be denied. That continued expansion by American companies is made easier by such markets is obvious. But the claim that the developed countries depend on exploiting less developed countries does not follow from the claims we have examined. The arguments do show that there is a tendency on the part of MNCs toward injustice, which must be controlled. Some practices are immoral and should be changed. The advantages that the system brings to Third World countries at least offset the costs imposed by it on them. As in our analysis of the free-enterprise system in the United States, the arguments that critics mount do not show that the extension of the system through American-controlled multinationals is inherently immoral.

The role of the multinationals is not, however, the same as the role of the United States in international economic affairs, even though they are related. The United States, because of its size, wealth, and global importance, intervenes in the economy of many nations even if it does nothing to them directly. Its internal monetary and fiscal policies, for instance, affect the interest rates other countries must pay for loans, and influence inflation rates. Its import and export policies also influence what happens in many MNCs. Does the United States have obligations toward other countries? It has at least the obligation not directly to harm them through its practices. Where it has knowingly and willingly done harm, it owes reparations. Furthermore, the United States has sometimes acted benevolently, but despite its good intentions has caused harm. This happened, for instance, when it sent sugar to Bolivia for humanitarian reasons. The distribution of the sugar required all the distributive resources of the country. As a result, the local wheat growers were unable to transport their wheat to market, and were forced out of business. Although the United States intended no harm, it was causally responsible for it. In this case the United States is more guilty of paternalism than of exploitation. The United States can help avoid unintended harm by working more closely with local governments, and by replacing paternalism with cooperation. If the United States wishes to help a country, it can support programs developed by the country itself, especially when these help the poor, provide employment, and lead to self-improvement. Whether the United States has obligations to other countries, based not on charity, reparations, or self-interest but on the rights of other countries, we shall investigate in the next chapter. Its obligation not to harm other countries, however, is not necessarily violated by its adherence to a free-enterprise economy and the extension of that system into the international domain.

Although multinational corporations are not inherently immoral, we can fruitfully evaluate, from a moral point of view, the activities of individual multinationals in specific countries. The less developed countries are not all the same; nor are all multinationals. In each case we can ask of a multinational: Does it contribute to the host country by hiring local workers at all levels; by transferring its technological and organizational expertise; by paying reasonable wages and producing goods that the local population needs and wants? Does it pay its fair share of taxes? Does the MNC help improve the quality of life of the country, more than by simply importing the goods the company produces? If the answers to these questions are affirmative, and the MNC obeys the laws and does not engage in unethical practices, the operation of the MNC is prima facie morally justifiable.

We can now turn from a consideration of multinationals in general to a moral evaluation of some particular practices and cases. We shall continue to concentrate on American-based firms. Many moral issues are involved in the charges made against American multinationals. We can illustrate and sort out some of these by discussing three controversial situations: the marketing abroad of drugs that are prohibited in the United States; the transfer of dangerous industries to underdeveloped countries; and the operation of U.S. firms in South Africa.

Before we do so, however, we should put to rest two questions. First, in dealing with multinational activities the question is often raised: Can we really apply our morality in evaluating a firm's activities abroad? This is a pseudo-question. As we saw in Chapter 2, there is not a U.S. morality, a French morality, and a Korean morality. Laws in various countries differ, as do customs and mores, conditions and standards of living. But if we mean by morality a normative system of overriding rules applicable to all human beings, then there is no such thing as national moralities. The basic normative principles apply universally, even if their application in differing circumstances leads to the proscription of different specific actions. Nor do we need to wait for a morally justified world order or for morally justified governments and institutions in all countries before morally evaluating specific actions of individuals or of multinational corporations.

The second question, although in some respects similar to the first, is a valid question: If corporations in the United States are required to live up to social demands, must they live up to the same social demands when they operate in foreign countries? Here the distinction between social and moral obligations is especially relevant. An MNC must live up to its moral obligations abroad just as it does in the United States. But the social, nonmoral obligations that it must fulfill vary from country to country. In each country, a MNC is appropriately bound by the social and legal obligations imposed by that country rather than by U.S. norms. If Americans demand that American multinationals follow U.S. norms abroad, this demand is itself an additional social demand; but it should not be confused with moral demands.

Multinational Drug Companies

The control of drugs in the United States is probably more restrictive than in any other country in the world. The Food and Drug Administration (FDA) has adopted stringent requirements for testing drugs, and any drug allowed on the market in the United States must pass long and comprehensive testing. The FDA also determines which drugs require a doctor's prescription.

The argument in defense of the FDA's actions is that lives and health are at risk in the taking of any drug. Unless a drug is found to be safe it should not be sold. If a drug is known to have certain dangerous side effects, it should be sold only under certain conditions, for people under a doctor's care. If the drug is known to cause cancer or some other serious illness, it should not be sold at all, or only under rigidly controlled conditions. The drug thalidomide was not authorized for sale in the United States but was prescribed by doctors in Europe. Its use by pregnant women resulted in large numbers of seriously deformed babies. Such disasters explain the FDA's insistence on high standards.

American drug companies, however, often feel that the FDA standards are too rigid, that the testing required is too expensive, cumbersome, and long, and that it is inappropriate to impose U.S. standards on the operation of U.S. companies in other countries. They claim that so long as they do not act illegally in those countries, there is no reason why they should not market whatever is allowed.

The morality of the action of these companies is not settled by determining whether what they do in other countries is legal. But, on the other hand, the morality of their actions abroad is also not settled by simply determining whether they live up to American standards abroad. The standards may be appropriate for Americans but inappropriate for people of some other countries, because of special circumstances in those countries. We can distinguish several typical cases and investigate them from a moral point of view. Consider the following three hypothetical cases.

- CASE 1: Drug Company XYZ produces a drug that relieves the symptoms of migraine headaches. It is marketed in the United States, and was initially thought to be safe enough for sale over the counter. After it is widely used, however, it is determined that one of the side effects in a significant number of patients is severe depression, sometimes leading to suicide. The drug is therefore considered too dangerous for sale over the counter in the United States, and is allowed only for use by those under a doctor's care. Doctors are warned of the dangerous side effects and are cautioned to be alert to signs of depression in their patients. The drug is sold in many countries besides the United States. After the U.S. action, some other countries take similar action. Others do not. Drug Company XYZ continues to market the product in these other countries. It is sold over the counter, and no information is provided about its possible dangerous side effects.
- CASE 2: Drug Company MNO develops and tests a drug that is slightly more effective than insulin for diabetics. After some use, the drug is found to produce cancer. It is forbidden in the United States. Drug Company MNO continues to market it where it is not forbidden to do so.
- CASE 3: Drug Company ABC develops a drug that helps cure glaucoma. There is no other effective drug for this ailment on the market. After some extended use, the drug is found to produce cancer in a significant number of cases. The drug is taken off the market in the United States. The drug company continues to market it in those countries in which it is legal to do so.

The three cases raise a number of different issues.

Is the action of Company XYZ morally justifiable, and if not, why not? In trying to decide, consider two substantive second-order principles that might apply. Principle 1: A drug company should not sell any drug that it knows to be harmful in any way. Principle 2: A drug company should not sell any drug that it knows to be harmful without informing the purchaser of the harmful effects.

The first of the principles is too strong. In Case 1, Drug Company XYZ was allowed to sell the drug in the United States to those who had a doctor's prescription for it. It is morally justifiable for the FDA to allow some drugs, which have possibly harmful side effects, to be sold. The reason is that the side effects are usually less serious than the illness that is being treated; the risks involved are worth taking, providing the patient and the doctor know about them and decide to take the risks, exercising due caution. The second principle is morally sound. We can justify it in a number of ways. If we consider the purchase of the drug as a free transaction, such transactions are justifiable if both parties have the relevant knowledge concerning the transaction, and freely enter into it. If the drug company knows of the drug's ill effects but does not disclose these to the purchaser, the latter does not have the information necessary to make a competent decision concerning the transaction. To keep this information from the buyer is morally inappropriate, because the buyer will assume that the product is safe. The transaction is thus not morally justifiable. We can reach the same conclusion by asking whether the drug company is treating the purchaser as an end rather than simply as a means of earning profit. It does not warn him of the dangers of the drug, therefore the company treats him only as a means, and hence treats him immorally.

Adopting the second principle, Drug Company XYZ therefore can be morally faulted, not for selling the drug but for selling it without informing the potential purchaser of the dangers of its use. Note that if this analysis is correct, it is morally permissible for Drug Company XYZ to market the drug as an over-the-counter product in the countries where this is allowed—even though it is not allowed to do so in the United States and other countries—providing its side effects are clearly indicated and users are properly warned. The argument does not claim that the U.S. standards are the only appropriate ones, that all countries must adopt them, or that drug companies must adhere to them wherever they operate. This is not morally required. Standards other than those adopted by the FDA may be appropriate in other countries. But some standards are necessary. It would clearly be wrong to sell drugs that did little good and were known to be harmful, even if the selling of such drugs were legally permitted in some countries. It would also clearly be wrong to sell drugs without adequate warning of possibly harmful side effects. Drug companies are morally bound not to inflict harm on others knowingly. To the extent that they do, drug companies act immorally even if they act legally.

In Case 3, there is no other drug for the disease, whereas in Case 2, an alternative drug is available. The argument for marketing the drug (in Case 2), which is only slightly more effective but more dangerous than insulin, is difficult to make. We might argue that if the company makes the risks known to the public, then it may sell the drug to those who wish to buy it. But why anyone would wish to buy it is not clear, because the harm significantly outweighs the benefit of using it instead of insulin. Thus, if we assume that only those who really do not know what they are doing would use this drug instead of insulin, we can conclude that, despite its issuing a warning, the drug company is trading on the ignorance of the consumer. To so trade at the consumer's expense is to take unfair advantage and hence to act immorally. The case, however, is not as clearly immoral as it would be if the drug were marketed without any warning of its dangers.

The drug in Case 3 helps cure glaucoma but tends to produce cancer in some people. There is no other drug on the market for this ailment. Once again, the drug can be morally sold only if those who buy and use it are informed of its dangers. But even when informed of the risks, people may choose to use it, preferring to chance getting cancer rather than suffer blindness. That the drug is not allowed in the United States indicates that the FDA does not think the risk is worth the cure. But others may feel differently and weigh the odds differently. If a person is relatively old, and if the drug takes many years to produce cancer, the person may feel the risk is worth taking. His or her doctor may agree.

A principle implicit in this analysis is the principle of informed consent. In order for the transaction to be morally permissible, the purchaser of the drug must be truly informed. A warning sentence, in small print, on page three of a technical information sheet inside the box is hardly adequate notice of the danger. The purchaser should be informed of any danger before purchasing the drug, and the information (e.g., on the box) should be readily visible and understandable.

If adequate information about the ill effects of the drug is not supplied to the potential purchaser, the practice is immoral. If adequate information is supplied, if there is no alternative drug, and if the risk is reasonable, the sale of the drug is still justifiable, whether or not its use is allowed by the FDA in the United States . However, if there is a similar or better product available, one that does not have the ill effects of this particular drug, the latter should not be marketed at all. The principles apply to drug companies, wherever they operate.

Some countries are unable to fund the kind of extensive testing operations that are conducted by the United States government or required by it. These countries have passed laws, however, that prohibit a drug company from marketing a drug that has been prohibited for sale in the country of origin. Some drug companies, wishing to market their drugs but also wishing to abide by the law, have adopted a number of practices for which they have been morally condemned. Some have added an inert substance to a drug so that, technically, it is not the same item, even though it has all the same effects. Then the drug has been marketed in the foreign country, but under a different name. Others have produced the drug that has been outlawed in the United States in some third country, where it is not outlawed, and then they have shipped it elsewhere. Both of these practices are within the letter of the law in the countries where the drugs are finally sold, even if they are clearly outside the spirit of those laws. The morality of *these* practices depends not on whether the law has been circumvented but on whether the companies that act in this way are doing harm to the people who take the drug, and whether they are supplying adequate and appropriate information. Their critics claim the drug companies frequently fail to supply such information. If this is so, then the companies act immorally.

These cases illustrate some of the the difficulties of dealing with multinationals. How laws can be rewritten to prohibit the sale of drugs outlawed in the country of origin is an unsolved problem. Some solutions might be that all nations adopt similar rules and standards; that an agency, such as WHO or UNESCO, set minimal standards. Some nations might then adopt more stringent regulations. Until international standards are adopted, the temptation of drug companies to abide only by the legal minimum in each country will remain. Succumbing to the temptation will benefit the drug companies, mainly at the expense of the poorer and less developed countries—those who in the long run will be least able to cope with the negative effects of such drugs on their people.

The Transfer of Dangerous Industries to Underdeveloped Countries

Consider the following case: Asbestos USA (a fictitious name) produces asbestos products for the United States market. It competes with asbestos products made in Mexico. It is able to compete, despite the fact that Mexican labor is so much cheaper than labor in the United States, because it operates more efficiently and with more advanced equipment than do the Mexican companies. Recently, the United States government determined that asbestos causes cancer. Those exposed to it for long periods had a significantly higher rate of cancer than others. The rate was especially high for people who worked in asbestos plants. The United States therefore passed legislation requiring the introduction of a series of safeguards for people working in asbestos plants. Asbestos USA calculated the cost of implementing the safeguards and decided it could not implement them and still stay in business. Rather than close down completely, however, it moved its plant to Mexico, which has not passed comparable safety legislation. Asbestos USA continues to market its product in the United States, even though it manufactures its products in Mexico. There, it operates its equipment in the same way (i.e., without safeguards) as it did in the United States; however, it has to pay its workers only the going wage for the industry in Mexico.

By moving its plant to Mexico, is Asbestos USA acting immorally?

Exposure to asbestos tends to produce cancer in a significant number of people. This is the overriding consideration to which the American government reacted when it passed legislation requiring safeguards. No company, it has ruled, has the right to expose its workers to cancer if this can be prevented. The ruling is a defensible one. It applies to all industries and to all asbestos manufacturers. But obviously the U.S. rule applies only in the United States; it does not apply to asbestos factories in other countries. The United States government could protect its home industries by passing duties on imported asbestos products, making it possible for U.S. companies to produce asbestos products under safe conditions and also compete with foreign industries. If Asbestos USA's imports were subject to an import duty, it would have little incentive to move to Mexico. But because the safety requirements were passed without the concomitant protection against imports, it moved its plant. This move is better for its shareholders than if the company had gone out of business. The asbestos products would be bought from Mexican firms anyway, so why not have an American company selling asbestos products to the United States, as well as Mexican companies? These considerations, however, fail to respond to the major issue: is it moral to expose employees to the danger of cancer when this can be prevented? If the answer is no, then it is not moral to so expose Mexican workers.

Which second-order principle is applicable to this case? One possible principle: It is immoral to hire anyone to do work that is in some way dangerous to his or her life or health. But the principle, as stated, is too strong. Any job might be dangerous in some way; therefore, if it were immoral to hire someone to do work that was in any way dangerous, no one could be hired to do many jobs that seem perfectly acceptable. But we must also acknowledge that some jobs are more dangerous than others. A fireman is paid to put out fires, but he knows he risks his life in doing so. Policemen are also paid to risk their lives. Yet most people would be reluctant to say that hiring people to do these jobs is immoral. The immorality, therefore, does not come from hiring people to do work that involves risk to life or health. But we can defend the principle that it is immoral to hire someone to do work that is known to the employer to involve significant risk without informing the prospective employee of that risk. This application of the principle of informed consent is defensible, as guaranteeing a fair exchange between consenting adults.

If we adopt this principle, then Asbestos USA could be morally right in hiring workers in Mexico, with working conditions that would not be allowed in the United States, if the potential workers were warned of the dangers. We can assume that once warned of the dangers, the workers would agree to work in the plant only if they received more pay than they would for comparable work in a factory in which they were not exposed to the danger of cancer. If this were not the case, it would be an indication that the people who were hired were in some way being forced into the jobs, were not free agents, contracting freely and knowingly to do dangerous work at pay they considered appropriate to make up for the increased risk. A contract between employer and employee is fair if both parties enter into the contract with adequate appropriate knowledge, and if both freely agree to the terms of the contract.

The critics of Asbestos USA contend that the Mexican workers, even if they are informed of the dangers, and are paid somewhat higher wages than other workers are paid (Brazil requires triple pay for dangerous work), are forced because of the lack of work in Mexico to accept employment in asbestos plants, at less than adequate pay. Hence, the critics contend, despite protestations regarding informed consent, the workers are forced to take such jobs and are exploited in them.

Informed consent is *necessary* if the the action is to be moral, but it is not *sufficient*. There are some things (e.g., selling oneself into slavery) to which no one can morally consent. There are also some conditions that are immoral for an employer to impose on his workers, even if the latter agree to work under those conditions. Consent is not enough, because people who desperately need money may agree to work under almost any conditions. Built into capitalism is the tendency of employers to pay workers as little as possible, and to spend as little as possible on a safe work environment. In the United

States, this tendency has been offset by unionization and government legislation. In countries where it is not offset, employers can take unfair advantage of workers and engage in immoral practices. If Asbestos USA wishes to operate its plant in Mexico, it can morally do so only if it informs the workers of the risk, in terms they can understand; if it pays them more for undertaking the risk; and if it lowers the risk to some acceptable level. It need not be the same level demanded by the Occupational Safety and Health Act (OSHA) in the United States, but morally, it cannot be at a level so low that risk is maximized rather than minimized. It would also be immoral not to eliminate risks that could be removed without extravagant cost. If, in Mexican plants, asbestos particles float freely through the air, collecting like cobwebs, and if workers are not even given paper masks, it is clear that minimum safety standards are not being observed.

Why does the Mexican government not pass laws similar to those in the United States concerning safeguards for workers? Why do not all nations pass such laws, so as to preclude such moves as that made by Asbestos USA, because it would be unprofitable? The answer is that not all countries are as affluent as the United States. A wealthy country can afford to spend more to protect the health of its people than can a much poorer country. The standards of cleanliness and safety that the United States can enforce by law are much higher than businesses in many countries could afford. Traditions also vary from country to country. There is no reason to think that the traditions of the United States are the only right ones, and that all the world must become like us. This attitude is itself condemned by many, because it is considered a form of U.S. imperialism. We are a democratic country, and our people enjoy a large measure of freedom. Some other countries are not democratic, or are much less so. The literacy rate and the level of education of the average person are much higher in the United States than in many other countries. We must be careful not to set our standards as the model of what every nation should do if it wishes to be moral. Our standards do not constitute the moral norm. Although morality is universal and does not differ from country to country, conditions do differ from country to country, and therefore, what morality demands in different countries may well vary. What may be required by the principle of utility in one country may not be required by the same principle in another country, because the consequences of adopting the practice in each of the two countries may differ significantly. What may be prima facie right in both countries may be the proper thing to do in one country but not in the other, because of conflicts with other duties or rights, owing to differing circumstances.

We return to our example of Asbestos USA. The Mexican government sometimes passes laws concerning health and safety, which are different from those passed in the United States. We cannot conclude that the Mexican government cares less for the welfare of its people than does the American government for its citizens. United States industry is more technologically developed than Mexican industry. Mexican industry is more labor-intensive, on the whole, than U.S. industry. Mexico seeks to attract foreign industry to help develop its potential, to train its people in work skills, and to bring in tax and other revenue. Imported industry also provides work for Mexicans who would otherwise be unemployed. Suppose that for these and similar reasons the Mexican government decides that it gains more by allowing somewhat unsafe factory conditions than by setting standards that would preclude the development of industry in the country. Suppose that the workers prefer working in Asbestos USA to not working at all. We can complain that it is unfair for people not to have work, or that the contract of employment with such people is not free and hence morally marred. But granting all of this, it might still be true that Mexico and the Mexican people benefit more by Asbestos USA locating its plant in Mexico than by its not being there. If this were the case, then the move of Asbestos USA would not be immoral, providing it fulfilled the foregoing conditions.

Does this mean that it is moral to export cancer-producing industries to Mexico and other countries, where the regulations are more lenient than in the United States? The argument so far has considered Asbestos USA an isolated case. What will be the effect on Mexico and its people twenty years hence, if such industries move there in significant numbers? Are the country and the people better off without such industries? How will the cancer cases be treated? What will happen to families of workers who get cancer? Are health provisions and pension plans provided for the workers?

Companies that wish to act morally must consider and attempt to answer these questions.

Ideally, there should be international agreements on minimally acceptable standards of safety in industry. In the absence of such standards moral sense and pressure must function until law can equalize the position of the worker vis-à-vis the employer. But moral sense and pressure seem to play little role in the policies of many international corporations. Paradoxically, some underdeveloped countries see the conditions for moral action, which have been discussed here, as impediments to the development of their countries, as requirements that keep them underdeveloped, and as the moralizing of Americans who are basically well off and do not understand other situations, including the aspirations of other people. The difficulty of knowing what will benefit the people in such countries most, and of knowing what the people truly want—as opposed to what some governmental leaders say—is enormous. The difficulty forces us to be careful not to confuse what is morally right with what is proper for Americans. But American companies who are operating abroad and wish to be moral should not ignore the moral dimension of their actions; they should not simply follow the letter of the law in the countries in which they operate.

Is Asbestos USA immoral if it does not pay its Mexican employees the same wages that it paid its U.S. employees? The claim that it is immoral if it does not is a difficult one to sustain. Justice requires that people who do the same work should receive the same pay. A Mexican could rightly complain of injustice if he were paid less than an American for doing similar work in the same factory. But the principle applies only within the same factory, plant, or office.

The desirability of international minimal wage standards is obvious. But there is no visible movement in this direction, and multinational corporations on the whole have not attempted to promote such standards.

Finally, is it immoral for Asbestos USA to produce products in Mexico for sale in the United States? Suppose a German company made cars in the United States exclusively for export to Germany. Would we claim that the German company was exploiting the United States? It is difficult to apply a principle under which we would make such a determination. Earlier, we suggested the principle that unless a foreign company benefits the country in which it operates, it exploits that country for its own advantage, and so acts immorally. This rules out as immoral exploitation of one country, A, by another, B, that dominates A in such a way that B can force A to act contrary to A's own best interests. But if we consider the building of plants in sovereign states by firms from other countries, the host countries are able to prevent and prohibit such exploitation. If Asbestos USA were to force the demise of Mexican asbestos companies, it is difficult to see why it should be tolerated. But if it does not, there are many ways Asbestos USA might help the economy other than by producing its products for the Mexican market. It supplies work for its Mexican employees, teaches skills to the people it employs, pays taxes to the government, provides work for those who must build the plant in the first place, and purchases materials it needs locally to the advantage of the local economy. The workers in turn use their wages to buy goods, food, and shelter and so help support others in the economy. The Mexican government might well consider the trade-off to be to its advantage.

This analysis does not exonerate Asbestos USA on all counts. It has argued that Asbestos USA is not automatically guilty of the immoral practices attributed to it by typical critics.

We have not touched on the question of what the moral obligations of a multinational are in a country in which the government is repressive, and in which the leaders care more for their own good and benefit than for the good of their people. If a government itself exploits its people and encourages foreign exploitation of its people by foreign firms that pay taxes to the government, or pays government officials directly, the government acts immorally. If a firm knowingly and willingly exploits its workers, even if it is legal to do so, it also acts immorally. But whether a particular firm is exploiting its workers often requires detailed investigation.

The critics of multinationals will have little patience with the analysis we have given of Asbestos USA. Even if multinationals *can* operate morally, they would assert that multinationals typically do not act morally. By outlining the conditions under which multinationals might act morally, the critics would maintain, we have given the impression that multinationals do act morally, and that attacks on them are unwarranted. Such was not the intent. The temptations to act immorally are great in the international arena, and it would be surprising if many companies did not succumb. If moral restraints are ineffective, then the restraints on such activity must be international restraints. The abuses of multinationals underscore the need for effective international controls—controls, however, which the present international climate has not strongly fostered.

U.S. Firms in South Africa

The situation in South Africa illustrates a third aspect of the morality of multinationals, and one of the major difficulties in multinational operations.

The Union of South Africa practices a policy of racial segregation, discrimination, and oppression known as *apartheid*. The practice is condemned as immoral by many in the United States and in other countries throughout the world. It is justified and defended by many whites in South Africa as the morally allowable lesser of two evils.

Under apartheid, the blacks in South Africa suffer extreme repression. Although they constitute the overwhelming majority of the population, they are allowed to live on only 13 percent of the land. The other 87 percent is reserved for the whites, who constitute only 17 percent of the population. The whites control the gold and diamond mines, the harbors, and the industrial areas. Blacks who wish to work in these areas are required to live in townships outside of the major cities. Because only males are allowed in the townships, the workers are separated from their families for the major part of the year. The blacks cannot vote, own property, organize politically, or join unions. They are systematically paid less than whites for the same work. They are not allowed to hold managerial positions of even the lowest kind. They are forced to use segregated eating, dressing, and toilet facilities.

United States companies began moving into South Africa as early as the 1880s. At that time, these firms employed only whites and sold their products almost exclusively to the white community. The white community was the economically advanced and productive sector of the country, and supplied the market for goods. The blacks lived in their own sections of the country, in their traditional tribal ways. The whites set up and controlled the government. The blacks did not take part in any governmental activities, were not educated, and were not considered able to run the government or to have any impact on it. A colonial type of paternalism was exercised by the whites over the blacks.

Whatever one considers the morality of such colonial paternalism, it is understandable how and why companies from the United States initially saw their market as the white community, and their employees as coming from that same community. The intent of these companies was to expand their markets and make a profit, and South Africa was a ripe market to develop. With time and the changes of over half a century, colonialism fell out of favor in other parts of Africa; the native inhabitants took over the reins of power in country after country, and ran their own affairs. In South Africa, however, blacks did not succeed in gaining power and have been kept from doing so by the legal enforcement of apartheid. Some changes, however, did take place finally. Factories, as they expanded, found that there were not enough whites to fill the jobs available, and blacks were found able and willing to work in these factories. Fear of their achieving control was, in part, what motivated the government to draw up and enforce the apartheid laws. But as blacks entered the labor market, they also had money to buy goods and so represented a potential market for goods.

American-controlled multinationals moved into South Africa in greater numbers, to take advantage of the low wages they could pay blacks and the large market that South Africa represented. The profits earned by American South African subsidiaries were often twice as much as the profits earned by the home-based mother company. Many black-dominated countries in Africa have placed embargoes on goods manufactured by U.S. companies operating in South Africa. But the local market is sufficient to make operation of subsidiaries in South Africa profitable for IBM, Ford, General Motors, Goodyear, Firestone, Exxon, Mobil, Kellogg's, Eli Lilly, Kodak, Control Data, and over 300 other U.S. companies.

Despite the protestations of the whites in South Africa, most people acknowledge that apartheid is immoral. It is blatant racial segregation, discrimination, and oppression. Let us assume the majority view (i.e., apartheid is immoral). The moral issues that have surfaced have been of two kinds, related though separable. One is the question of whether it is moral for U.S. multinationals to operate in South Africa. The other is whether U.S. investors, especially university endowment associations and churches, should invest in companies that operate in South Africa.

U.S. Multinationals in South Africa

U.S. multinationals would not open subsidiaries in South Africa unless it were profitable to do so. South Africa has four conditions that make it attractive to U.S. companies. First, it has a stable government. U.S. companies are reluctant to open plants in countries with unstable governments, for fear of losing their investments because of nationalization or constant domestic turmoil. U.S. companies therefore have an interest in helping preserve stable governments. They tend not to care whether the government is repressive or dictatorial. That, they claim, is a local, political matter. And from a business point of view, a strong, stable government is a guarantee of the safety of their investment. Second, South Africa has a large potential market. Its population is 28 million people. Even though only 17 percent of the population is white, that represents a market of close to 5 million people; and the other 23 million form a pool that can be increasingly tapped. The U.S. companies are the chief suppliers of consumer goods and of advanced technology. Third, South Africa has a large and cheap supply of labor. The standard of living of the blacks is extremely low, and the scale paid them by South African firms is about one-fourth the wages paid to white workers. As more blacks are brought into the work force, the market for manufactured goods grows. Fourth, South Africa is rich in minerals. It can provide from within its own borders, the materials necessary for manufacturing, as well as ship to the parent U.S. companies raw materials needed for production in the United States.

All four conditions supply both the reasons why multinationals want to locate subsidiaries in South Africa and the reasons why critics of such firms charge them with immoral exploitation and with supporting repressive regimes.

United States firms have not been unaware of the charges of immorality. A few of them have responded to the charges by withdrawal. Polaroid is one such company. Citibank and the First Pennsylvania Bank no longer give loans to the South African government. But most of the other companies have not moved out. They have felt the moral pressure from stockholders and from other vocal groups in the United States, however, and have responded in a number of cases by adopting a set of principles drawn up in 1977 by Leon Sullivan, a black Philadelphia minister and a director of General Motors. The principles, known as the *Sullivan Code,* aim to end apartheid in the companies that adopt the code. The code calls for desegregation of eating, toilet, and work facilities; equal pay for all people doing comparable jobs within the plant; equal opportunity for advancement regardless of race; apprenticeships and training of nonwhites; promotion of blacks and other minorities to supervisory positions; improvement of living conditions; and support of unionization by nonwhites.

The Sullivan Code, its supporters argue, works to break down apartheid from within and so is more effective than simply casting moral stones at the system from outside the country. It helps nonwhites get training they could not get without the multinationals. It serves to increase the pay of the nonwhites to the level of the whites doing similar work. All of this is illegal; it violates South African law. But the South African government has not complained or sought to prevent the adoption of the Sullivan Code by American companies.

The critics of the Sullivan Code claim that it is not an effective way of breaking down apartheid. If it were, it would not be allowed by the South African government. The American firms pay taxes, and so provide revenue essential to the government to support and enforce its practice of repression throughout the country. The Sullivan Code, its critics claim, serves as a smoke screen behind which American companies can hide. They can sign the Code and claim to adhere to it, but in fact not do so, or do so only in token fashion. The Code, moreover, takes pressure off the companies to withdraw from the country, and gives them a moral excuse for continuing their profitable and exploitative operations.

The Sullivan Code was proposed in 1977. The fact that many U.S. firms adopted the Sullivan Code so readily, at least in principle, indicates two things: such companies respond, to some extent, to moral pressure applied in the United States, and they can operate profitably (even if less profitably) while observing the Code. But if we admit that U.S. companies act immorally when following the apartheid laws, are they morally permitted to operate in South Africa even if they follow the Sullivan Code? The question is not whether an American company follows the Sullivan Code completely; but rather, *if* a company diligently enforced the Sullivan Code in all its detail, would its continued operation in South Africa be morally justifiable? If we assume that the Sullivan Code negates all of the immoral aspects of apartheid, then a company that implements the Code would not be guilty of racial segregation, discrimination, or exploitation (unless white employees were also exploited). To that extent its operation would not be immoral. But through its taxes, the company helps support the government, which in turn enforces apartheid in the South African firms and in all other aspects of life within the country. Is such support of a repressive government morally justifiable?

Let us attempt to analyze the question from a utilitarian point of view. What are the consequences of the American firms operating within the country as opposed to withdrawing from the country? The critics of the American firms claim that if the firms left South Africa, much of the revenue needed to support the government would disappear. Furthermore, a wholesale withdrawal of American firms would leave the country in chaos. The government would not be able to keep the peace or run the economy. Because of the subsequent turmoil, blacks would have the opportunity to stage an effective revolution; they would seize control of the government and put an end to apartheid. As a result, they claim, the repression of the blacks would be ended. The 23 million nonwhites would benefit incomparably more than the 5 million whites would suffer. The whites would suffer loss of their special position; but the blacks would gain respect as persons, which they have been denied for a century. The American firms would not be substantially harmed by withdrawal, and after the revolution they might even return to South Africa to operate within a moral rather than an immoral context.

The foregoing scenario, however, is disputed by those who are in favor of continuing American operations in South Africa. In the first place, they say, consider the benefits to the South African blacks and other minorities. The U.S. firms are the only places where they can get work at wages comparable to whites. They are the only firms at which they can learn skills and rise to supervisory positions. Hence, those who work for American companies that follow the Sullivan Code gain much more by working in American-owned plants than they would if these firms left South Africa. Second, a wholesale U.S. withdrawal would not bring the results claimed by the critics of the U.S. companies. As the American companies left the country, they would be replaced by firms from other countries, most likely by Japanese or German firms. And these firms are less likely to follow the Sullivan Code. The South African government would continue to receive from these firms the revenue it needs. Hence, the government would not be affected, but the workers would be harmed. Therefore, by withdrawal of U.S. companies, less good would be achieved than by their continued presence.

A third reason they give is that the violation of the apartheid laws by U.S.

companies is the first step in the process of abolishing these laws. It is admittedly a small step, but it is a first step. It sets the stage for a gradual change in the laws. Breaking down the laws from within the country is more effective than simply condemning the laws from outside the country. The spokesmen for an American presence also claim that if (counter to what they predict) a revolution does take place, there is little reason to believe that such a revolution would produce more good on the whole than a continuation of the present system. The blacks have not been educated or trained in the skills required to run the economy or the country. There is little reason to believe that a stable black government would be formed, or that whatever government is formed would be less repressive than the present government, even though the repression might express itself differently. They also say that many black leaders fear what might happen if the American companies were to leave. Defenders of a continued American presence argue that, on utilitarian grounds, more good is achieved by the U.S. firms remaining in South Africa, and following the Sullivan Code, than would be achieved by their departure.

Which scenario is the more likely? Which side's predictions of what would happen as a result of U.S. withdrawal should be believed? The evidence is not sufficiently clear to make a dogmatic judgment of the morality of American companies in South Africa. What is clear, however, is that any company operating in South Africa without adopting and fully enforcing the Sullivan Code practices apartheid, and hence acts immorally.

Investing in Multinationals

Thus far we have focused on the morality of practices of multinationals which are outside of the control of the United States government. But American-controlled multinationals are not beyond control of the American parent company. These companies are controlled by their respective boards of directors, which are in turn subject to the interests of the shareholders. American shareholders could, at least in theory, determine the practices of the U.S. multinationals.

Concerning those U.S. multinationals that operate in South Africa, we can raise two moral issues: (1) Is it morally permissible for people or groups to hold stock in corporations that engage in immoral practices? And (2) Should churches and universities, in particular, divest themselves of the stock of corporations that operate in South Africa?

The answer to the first question is that every person has a moral obligation *not* to engage in immoral practices. Is it, then, immoral for anyone to own stock in a company that engages in immoral practices? The simplest answer would be a flat yes. By owning part of a firm, a shareholder supplies the capital for its operation. If it operates immorally, the shareholder is helping it to do so. The answer to the foregoing question would apply clearly to a company that had as its end some immoral purpose. For instance, no one could morally invest in Murders, Inc., if its purpose was to provide excellent hit men for those who wished to kill people they did not like. But few if any companies have as their purpose something that is outrightly immoral, and the typical investor would not invest in such a firm if it did exist.

What makes a firm immoral? Is it enough that someone within the firm acts immorally? Is a firm immoral only if it habitually acts immorally? Is a firm immoral if one of its practices is immoral? The questions cannot be answered with a simple yes or no. Clearly, a firm is not immoral simply if someone within the firm acts immorally. If an employee of a firm, for instance, were to embezzle funds from the company, we would say that the employee and not the company was immoral. If a company made it a practice to exploit its workers, to discriminate against women and blacks, to overcharge its customers—and if it did all these things as a matter of ordinary practice—we could well say the company was immoral. It would therefore be immoral to invest in such a company because such an investment would help promote the company's immoral practices.

But what are the moral responsibilities of an investor? Must he investigate from a moral point of view the activities of a company in which he is interested in investing? Is such a rule practical and reasonable, or does it ask too much of the typical, small investor? It is not always easy to obtain information about the immoral activities of companies. If a company's activities are questionable, it is unlikely to publicize this or include it in its annual report. No moral audit is required of companies to help potential investors. The Council on Economic Priorities, and a few other groups, monitors corporate performance on social issues. Those who do not want to purchase stock in munitions firms can learn which firms make munitions. Those who do not wish to purchase stock in firms that operate in South Africa can find out the names of those firms. And those who wish to purchase stock in firms that operate in South Africa only if the firms follow the Sullivan Code can learn which firms do so. But this sort of information is not always easily available to the small shareholder, and in the absence of such information, an investor must make do with information that is available to him in the newspapers—legal suits, and the like. A moral investor should not support a firm that engages in immoral practices. But the lengths to which one must go to determine which practices are immoral and which companies engage in the immoral practices are matters of judgment, with much room for discretion and disagreement.

We come now to the second question: Should churches and universities, in particular, divest themselves of the stock of corporations that operate in South Africa?

Individuals should not support firms that engage in immoral practices; it therefore follows that institutions also should not invest in such firms. Because corporate bodies usually make larger investments than individuals, they have a correspondingly greater responsibility concerning the investments they make. Critics have claimed that churches and universities should take the lead in ethical investment practices because they are appropriate models for moral behavior.

The critics of multinationals operating in South Africa have focused primarily on church and university investments. They have attempted to persuade these groups to divest themselves of their investments in American companies operating in South Africa. Their arguments are based on two premises. The first is that companies operating in South Africa are engaged in immoral practices, even if they follow the Sullivan principles, because they help the government through their taxes. Secondly, they argue that the churches and universities can force the U.S. companies out of South Africa by selling their stock in protest.

We have already seen that those firms that do not follow the Sullivan Code principles act immorally. Because it is immoral to support apartheid, both institutional and private investors who own stock in such companies should divest themselves of it. Many universities have done so by eliminating from their portfolios investments in banks that grant loans to the government of South Africa. Such banks do not help to break down apartheid by hiring blacks, promoting them, or by doing any of the things the Sullivan Code requires; the banks help the government without attacking apartheid in any way, and thereby help to support apartheid. Because this is immoral, many universities have protested this action by divestiture of their stock.

Two arguments that oppose such action have been raised, but neither is very convincing. One argument claims that no investor can be sure that a company in which he is investing is not engaged in immoral practices. No one can investigate all companies, therefore it is unreasonable to expect investors to be guided by moral considerations. The argument is not convincing. We grant that no one is required to find out what he cannot in practice determine; however, when it is clear that a company is engaging in an immoral practice, and when this is brought to one's attention, then one should act on that information. For instance, to refuse to act on information concerning company A simply because one may not know whether company B is acting immorally is to choose, knowingly, to participate in an immoral practice.

The second argument is that, for most American companies, their South African operations constitute a very small part of the company's total activities. Hence, if on the whole the companies operate morally, a small immorality in a minor portion of their operations should not be blown out of proportion. The companies, the defenders say, are on the whole moral. The corporate investors also claim that they have obligations to their respective institutions, that is, to invest their funds to produce the greatest return. They must weigh this obligation against the obligation not to support a company that engages in an immoral practice but only in a small area of its total operation. The equation, they claim, often comes out in favor of retaining their invested shares. The counter claim, however, is that they would lose so little if they did divest themselves of the shares of those companies that not to do so is to condone the immoral practice.

The situation is far less clear, however, when we consider those firms that follow the Sullivan Code. Nor is it clear that the universities and churches could effect the withdrawal of these companies from South Africa by selling their stock in protest. If they were to sell their stock and drive the price of the stock down, it would simply be purchased by traders who would be de

378

lighted to get it at a lower price, confident that it will soon rise again, in line with its actual worth. Some of the institutional shareholders claim that they are more effective voting from within the company than they would be if they voiced their disapproval as outsiders. But the fact is that they have not been effective as insiders when they have sought to force a company to leave South Africa.

During the 1970s and the early part of the 1980s, and to the present time, groups on campuses around the country have sought to get their local endowment associations to divest themselves of companies operating in South Africa. These groups have in some cases been successful and in others unsuccessful; and they show how pressure might be brought to bear on university endowment associations. But they have not accomplished much in the way of effecting withdrawal of companies from South Africa. One reason is that their protest has been in some ways too broad and in others too narrow. It has been too broad because they have tarred with the same brush all U.S. corporations operating in South Africa, instead of concentrating on those corporations that do not adopt the Sullivan Code principles. Their protest has been too narrow because it has focused only on divestiture by university endowment associations, groups which even together could not force a change in policy. If Ford Motor Company and IBM are immoral, then the attack should not stop with refusal by a university to own stock in the company. Ford is helped more by millions of students and their families, who buy Ford cars, than by some endowment associations owning Ford stock. IBM is helped more by universities buying or renting IBM computers, and by offices and individuals buying IBM typewriters, than by endowment associations owning IBM stock. If a practice is immoral, there are more effective ways to influence a company than by symbolic divestiture. But what are we to do if all the major car makers operate in South Africa, or if we prefer IBM computers or typewriters to those of other companies? This question gets to the crux of the issue. Those seriously interested in stopping immorality, and who wish to protest the immoral practice of a company, should not only urge other people to make sacrifices and take action, but they themselves should be willing to do the same.

Multinationals can be held accountable by their shareholders if the shareholders are truly interested in holding them accountable. Shareholders can demand to know what practices the companies follow in their subsidiaries abroad. If immoral practices are discovered in an operation abroad, and if enough people in the United States refuse to purchase the product of the manufacturer in question until the immoral practice is stopped, then it is safe to assume that the practice will be changed when the economics of the situation demand it.

The structures for controlling multinationals and for preventing practices that harm people have been slow in coming. They require international cooperation both on the part of governments and people—organized either as workers or as consumers. Multinationals are helping to bind the world closer together. As they do so, they help prepare the way for collective efforts by those affected by their actions. Those interested in morality on the international level can be effective only if they act collectively. Morality is not a matter of individual activity only. Our obligations expand, as our effective role in the world expands. But moral issues on the international level, though complex, are amenable to careful analysis from a moral point of view.

Further Reading

BARNET, RICHARD, and RONALD MUELLER. *Global Reach: The Power of Multinational Corporations.* New York: Simon & Schuster, Inc., 1974.

BARRATT-BROWN, MICHAEL. *The Economics of Imperialism.* Harmondsworth: Penguin Education, 1974.

BROWN, PETER G. and HENRY SHUE, eds. *Boundaries: National Autonomy and Its Limits.* Totowa, N.J.: Rowman and Littlefield, 1981.

FELD, WARNER J. *Multinational Corporations and U.N. Politics: The Quest for Codes of Conduct.* New York: Pergamon Press, 1980.

MEAGHER, ROBERT F. *An International Redistribution of Wealth and Power.* New York: Pergamon Press, 1979.

POWERS, CHARLES W. *The Ethical Investor.* New Haven, Conn.: Yale University Press, 1972.

SCHWAMM, HENRI, and DIMITRI GERMIDIS. *Codes of Conduct for Multinational Companies: Issues and Positions.* Brussels: European Centre for Study and Information on Multinational Corporations, 1977.

SILVERMAN, MILTON. *The Drugging of the Americas.* Berkeley, Calif.: University of California Press, 1976.

——, PHILIP R. LEE, and MIA LYDECKER. *Prescriptions for Death: The Drugging of the Third World.* Berkeley, Calif.: University of California Press, 1982.

TUGENDHAT, CHRISTOPHER. *The Multinationals.* New York: Random House, Inc., 1972.

TURNER, LOUIS. *Multinational Companies and the Third World.* New York: Hill & Wang, 1973.

United Nations Department of Economic and Social Affairs. *Multinational Corporations in World Development.* New York: United Nations, 1973.

WILBER, CHARLES, ed. *The Political Economy of Development and Underdevelopment.* New York: Random House, Inc., 1973.

EIGHTEEN

Famine, Oil, and International Obligations

A wealthy society that allows some of its members to die of starvation could hardly be called a moral society. In America, government supplements the capitalist system to provide for those unable to contribute to the economy and unable to care for themselves. The American economy, however, is intertwined with much of the rest of the world. When we move beyond our borders and look at the rest of the world, we see that many people die of starvation and that millions of people in the world suffer from chronic malnutrition. Is it just or moral for Americans to stockpile surplus food or to cut back on the acreage planted while people in other countries starve or live on the edge of starvation? Do our moral obligations stop at our borders? It is immoral to let people in our own country die of starvation; is it therefore immoral to let people in other countries die of starvation? Can our society be a moral society if it does not respond to the needs of others? Starvation and malnutrition present one set of problems; the use of natural resources presents a second set.

America, as a nation, possesses great material wealth but some other countries of the world are pitifully poor. By what right do some countries and people have so much wealth, and use so much of the world's resources, yet others have so little? To whom do the natural resources of the earth belong? The sun, moon, and ocean belong to no one. By what right do land and the natural resources on or under it belong to those who happen to inhabit the land, or who happen to find the resources? By an accident of birth, people born in an arid, barren country are doomed. They have no free access to better land, no equal opportunity for improvement, and no chance for a decent life. Is it fair for others, who happen to be born in lands of rich soil, and with minerals, oil, and gold to enjoy the exclusive use of these natural resources? The people of "have-not" nations are saying—more clearly and more often— that it is not fair. They are calling more and more strongly for an international plan of redistribution.

If once there seemed to be an inexhaustible supply of land and natural resources, this is now known not to be the case. We can foresee the complete depletion of the world's oil supply, and we know other minerals are exhaustible. This knowledge raises a third set of problems. Do we have the right to use as much of these as we wish, and in any way we desire? Do we have an obligation to save any of these resources for future generations? Do Americans owe more to the poor of other countries or to their own descendents, if we must choose between them?

All of these questions are extremely complex, controversial, and difficult to answer. The moral intuitions of most people falter when they are faced with questions of this scope. It is easier to ignore them than to face them. But both as a nation and as individuals we would be immoral if we chose to ignore our moral obligations simply because they were difficult and new, and concerned people far away in space or time. Because businesses, large and small, are the major users of resources—and, some claim, the perpetrators of exploitation—as well as the chief mediators between the economies of rich and poor nations, they are centrally involved in the moral issues.

Famine, Malnutrition, and Moral Obligation

The basic approaches of utilitarianism and deontology can be used to handle any type of moral problem. But it is also possible, using these approaches, to develop second-order principles or rules. These rules, we saw, are typically substantive rather than formal, and thus have specific moral content. We can use them in solving complex moral problems. Frequently, the application of second-order principles is clearer than the application of the general, basic first-order moral rules or principles.

The most fruitful approach to complex moral problems is to divide them into smaller, more manageable parts. As we develop clarity in each of the parts, we develop greater clarity with respect to the problem as a whole. In dealing with the general problems of famine and malnutrition, therefore, we should see if we can reduce them to manageable pieces. We should also see if we can find some appropriate second-order moral principles that are applicable. Questions of famine and malnutrition concern our relations to food and to other human beings. We can start with ourselves. Each of us needs food in order to live. We need a certain amount and quality of food to do more than just survive, that is, to develop fully, maintain our health, and work and act efficiently. When there is food enough for all, it is morally permissible for me to satisfy my need for food. It is moreover a prima facie moral duty for me to preserve my health, under normal conditions, and so it is a prima facie moral duty for me to eat adequately.

What about an obligation to others with respect to food? Most people would readily agree that parents are morally obliged to feed their children if they are able to do so. Parents have a special responsibility with respect to their children because the children are theirs. It would be inappropriate in a family of meager means for the parents to eat well and let the children starve. They are not required, however, to feed the children well and to starve themselves. How, in the long run, would the parents' resulting death benefit the children? As a general principle, no one is obliged to sacrifice himself for others. To do so may be morally praiseworthy, but it is not morally required because, as a moral agent, each person is an end in himself, as worthy of respect as any other person. We can also argue that each person has a greater obligation to feed those for whom he is responsible than to feed those for whom he is not so responsible, because of this special relationship.

We can push this a step further. In general, everyone is obliged to help others in serious need, if he can do so at little cost to himself. Suppose we are in a boat when we see another boat turn over. We see that the occupant of the other boat is drowning. We could easily extend an oar, let him grab it and then climb to safety in our boat. Most people would readily admit that we have the moral obligation to do so, because to adopt this rule would be to promote the greatest good of all concerned. In the case of the overturned boat, the good the drowning man gains is weighed against the minimal effort required for us to extend an oar. It is equally clear that we, as rational beings, would all will such a principle to be a universal law; it can be universalized without contradiction, and would show respect to people as valuable ends in themselves. Applying the same principle, if one person has plenty of food and sees someone else starving, and if he can save that person at little cost to himself, the person with food is obliged to do so.

We used similar reasoning to arrive at our collective obligation to help those in our society who are in serious need. Each of us has an obligation to help, if we can do so at little cost to ourselves. If all those who are able to do so contribute a little, those in dire need can be helped. As a society, we collectively organize to fulfill this as well as other common ends. We achieve the redistribution of income through taxation and welfare programs.

But why help the needy in our own society rather than those in other societies? Are they not all people and therefore have equal claim on us? By following a line of reasoning analogous to that we just used, we find that we have a special relation to those with whom we form a society. We are bound to each other by common laws, share common burdens, and jointly pursue common goods within our society. Just as we have a greater obligation to feed those for whom we are responsible, so we have a greater obligation to feed the hungry in our own society than we do the hungry of other societies, if the need of each group is equal.

383

Suppose that as a nation all of us are adequately fed, and that we have surplus food, or resources to produce it. There are starving people in other countries. Do we have a moral obligation to feed them? We saw that each of us has an obligation to help a person in serious need, if we can do so at little cost to ourselves. Is the principle applicable here? Starvation constitutes dire need. Individually, someone in the United States can do little to help someone starving in a remote area of Africa. But collectively, that is, through a united effort, or through governmental action, one may be able to do a great deal. If this is the case, then the principle applies and the person has a moral obligation. An individual discharges this obligation by paying taxes or donating to Care, the Red Cross, or some other relief fund. Obviously, those within our country who have barely enough for themselves cannot help others without significant cost and sacrifice to themselves. But those who can do so have the obligation to help others. They can discharge their obligation through the government, which acts for them and uses the money they pay in taxes in the way they authorize. The obligation of the government is to act as the people authorize; the obligation of the people is to help those in need. The distinction is an important one.

Thus far we have argued using a weak second-order moral principle. Can we justify a stronger principle, for example, each person has an obligation to help another seriously in need, even at considerable cost to himself? We argued that no one is morally obliged to sacrifice himself for another. But if we consider that principle as being at one end of a continuum, and, at the other end, the obligation of helping another at little cost to oneself, we see there are many alternatives between the extremes. Where do we draw the line of obligation? How much cost must we bear in order to help others in dire need? Rather than attempt to answer that question directly, we can answer it indirectly. We can join our weak second-order principle to this principle: to those for whom we are directly responsible we owe more than others; and we owe more to those with whom we have a special relation than we owe to those with whom we have no special relation. Therefore, no matter where we draw the line concerning the trade-off of the other's good and one's own cost, we have greater obligations, and should be willing to suffer a greater loss to benefit those with whom we have a special relation and ties.

Up to now, we have been dealing with the responsibility of Americans, assuming that on the whole Americans have enough to eat and the wherewithal to help others. The argument, however, can be applied equally well to all other people. It can apply to the Japanese, the Germans, the people of the Soviet Union, and many others as well. This consideration leads to two questions. Does each individual have an obligation to help up to a certain point, or do individuals have an obligation equal only to the total amount necessary to relieve starvation, divided by the total number of people on earth able to help? Are people in countries that are not organized for such purposes relieved of their responsibility?

In answer to the first question, our principle assigns an obligation to help if we can do so at little cost. What is little cost to someone who is rich is different from what is little cost to someone of very modest means. Hence, the obligation is proportional. If we chose to have the government discharge our obligations, we equalize the burden if we tax people in proportion to their income. If the people of some countries of the world do not fulfill their obligations with respect to starving peoples of other countries, does that affect our obligations? The first obligation is to help if it costs us little. The amount is initially determined by dividing what is required by all those capable of giving. The failure of some to give what they ought increases the amount the others must give if the lives of those in need are to be saved. We are obliged to give that greater amount if we are able to give it at little cost.

The reply to the second question is that people are not relieved of their responsibility if their countries are not organized to serve these ends. The obligation remains, even if it cannot be directly discharged. It then leads to the obligation to so organize that they can discharge their obligations. But the situation is by no means simple. People who do not know of the starvation of others may be excused from fulfilling their obligation to the starving if they are invincibly ignorant, or can satisfy some other excusing condition. For instance, at little cost to themselves, they may not be able to organize the country to satisfy this obligation.

How moral responsibility and blame for failure to fulfill one's responsibility should be assigned in all these cases is far from clear. The starving people of other countries are to us unknown, unseen people whose presence and plight do not impress themselves upon us as do the needy of our own society. If we feel an obligation to help the starving in other lands, it is usually an obligation not first and foremost on the list of other pressing obligations we have. If the share of each of us is ten cents, it does not seem to be a major moral obligation, even if the ten cents is part of the $2 million required to save the lives of the people in question. If no one helps, and thousands die, is each of us responsible for the death of all these people, or only for a very small part of the death of one person? In the latter case, is a small part of the death of one person a reasonable concept, or is each of us, together with some others, fully responsible for that one death? The answer, though not clear, is worth pondering.

There is a difference between a country suffering from a temporary famine because of an unusual and devastating drought and a country whose people suffer from chronic malnutrition. Are the obligations of those able to help the same in both cases? Many argue that they are not, and we can consider the cases separately.

People live in countries; they are organized into societies within certain geographical boundaries. Each of these nation-states has a government that, with only periodic exceptions, other governments recognize as exercising sovereignty within their domain. Recognition of sovereignty demands that no state physically violate the territorial integrity of another state. Each government rules its own people and represents them in the international arena. This in some ways simplifies, and in some ways complicates our problem. If the people of one country are starving, the system of nation-states makes it possible for other countries to make the plight known to other countries. The governments of these other countries can in turn respond with food or aid.

Suppose, however, that some people of a country are starving. The government of the country does not wish foreign aid and would prefer to have some of its people die; or suppose the starving people are a dissident, rebellious sect, who are being starved into submission by the government; or suppose food delivered free to the government of a country is not freely given to the starving but sold by the government to those able to purchase it. Or suppose that the government wishes to distribute the food it received from abroad to the starving, but because of inefficiency on its part, it is unable to deliver the food to those needing it, and the food rots on the docks.

Is the moral obligation to help the starving greater than the obligation to respect national sovereignty? As with many cases that involve the clash of prima facie obligations, the question cannot be answered a priori. We are using the weak principle of little cost, therefore, if the violation of sovereignty might lead to war, to a break in diplomatic relations, or to something else that may be viewed as more than a little cost, the principle does not apply. The fact that such difficulties frequently arise, moreover, makes it difficult for individuals to know what the actual situation is, and whether they actually have a moral obligation to supply aid.

What is the difference between cases of famine and cases of chronic malnutrition? We can distinguish cases: famine through no fault of the people versus famine through the fault of the people; and malnutrition through no fault of the people versus malnutrition through fault of the people. Does it make any difference whether people starve through no fault of their own or through their own fault? We might get a better perspective by making the fault versus no-fault distinction with respect to people in our own country. Suppose someone is able to work, work is available, but he prefers not to work; he chooses to sleep and idle away the hours. He runs out of money and still refuses to work. He comes close to starvation, announces that he is starving, and claims it is the obligation of others to feed him. Do they have this obligation? Each person has the obligation to care for himself if he is able to do so. If he does not, must others care for him? Several principles seem to apply here, in addition to the one concerning helping others. One is that it is not unjust to let people suffer the evil consequences of their freely chosen deliberate actions. A solution to the problem, which can satisfy both principles, would be not to feed the person indefinitely but to make it possible for him to work, and to make his receiving food contingent on his working. Suppose he has children. Assuming they are starving through the fault of their father, and no fault of their own, theirs is a no-fault case, which is governed by our weak principle concerning aid to the needy.

Let us now return to a starving country. Suppose a people were warned not to denude their forests, and they did so nonetheless. This resulted in floods, loss of topsoil, and destruction of their farmlands. They are now starving and ask for help. By analogy with the prior case, only some of the people are at fault—those who cut the forests. The others suffer as a consequence

386

of the actions of a few. Help should be given in accordance with earlier principles. But because the land is barren, help might appropriately include not only food but fertilizer, saplings for planting, and technical aid necessary to prevent future failure. As in the case of the individual, the willingness of a country to help itself is an appropriate condition for continued aid.

The cases of malnutrition are in some ways parallel to the cases of starvation, and in some ways different. Let us assume the malnutrition is serious, and so the harm to those who suffer it is serious. Though the harm is less than in the cases of starvation, the same principles apply. We have not yet considered one principle, however, which some people claim is applicable, viz., we should not help others if giving such help will produce more harm than not giving it. This is a simple application of the general principle of utility. It can also be defended from a deontological perspective.

Suppose that by supplying food to a country whose people chronically suffer from malnutrition we alleviate that malnutrition for a given year. If we did not supply them with food, some of them would die from their inability to fight off disease, but some children would still be born and the population would remain on the whole stable. If for one year we supply them with food, fewer people would die. Let us further suppose that being healthier, the population increases faster than it would otherwise. The result is a larger population than before. If there was not enough food for the smaller population, there will be even less food per person with the increase in population. By giving aid we thus render a larger number worse off than the number of people that would originally suffer without our help. In fact, our help produces more harm than good. If we alleviate the harm that would follow by helping them a second year, we postpone, but multiply, the harm of helping them the third year, and so on. If they can be helped to become nutritionally self-sufficient through technological aid, then that is our moral obligation. But if despite advanced agricultural techniques the land is unable to support their numbers, then the numbers must be reduced by decreasing the fertility rate. This, however, may not be what they choose to do. Then the principle of accepting the consequences of their freely chosen actions is applicable. A difficulty, of course, is that frequently the people involved do not freely and knowingly choose a course of action, and the situation is unclear.

We have argued thus far from the weak principle of help at little cost. We did not attempt to draw the line at some greater cost, except that it is higher for those for whom we are responsible and with whom we have special relations. If we defend and adopt a stronger principle, the analysis will proceed in much the same way: Our moral responsibility for helping those in need will increase in direct proportion to the increase in cost we are to bear, and inversely as the need of the other is less serious.

We did not claim that governments have the obligation to help people in foreign countries except insofar as government is the medium through which the people of a country discharge their obligations. The reason for making this distinction is that the government of a country has obligations to the people of the country which it governs. Its obligations to feed the hungry of its own country are a result of the structure of the society. The members of the society contribute to the government and, as members of that society, receive benefits and bear obligations. We are not subject to governments other than our own. We owe no duties to them, and deserve no benefits from them. Our government properly takes the initiative in helping the starving in other countries, to the extent that that action is one that has been authorized by the people, through their representatives.

Nation-states are not moral beings. The international arena is not one of total anarchy, because there is cooperation and there are some agreed-upon rules of interaction. And although all peoples of the earth form a moral human community, the nations of the world form an ambiguous moral community. Although each of us has the obligation to help people in dire need, governments come and go, and national boundaries change. Agreements may obligate one nation to help another. Nations per se do not starve, however. People do. The moral obligation to help the starving is an obligation to people, and so the obligation is not dependent on the type of government under which a people live. Nonetheless, we have a special relation to the people of those other countries with which our country forms special communities; we have a greater obligation to help them than to help those with whom we do not form a community. The absence of a world government precludes the kind of redistribution—through taxation, for instance— possible within a nation-state. This often makes it difficult to give effective and equitable aid to people in need in other countries.

Although individually we have some obligation to answer the legitimate claims of people to subsistence, when their governments are unable to satisfy this right, there are many impediments to our individually fulfilling this obligation. There are fewer impediments to our fulfilling an obligation collectively, however, through our government. The major responsibility, therefore, falls on government. We can rightly demand that our government take an active role in helping us collectively meet our obligations. We can legitimately demand that our government take an active role in developing and supporting effective international structures capable of meeting these obligations. If our government so acts, it will mean increased taxation and possibly some loss of sovereignty. But as participants in a world economy, these are costs we cannot morally refuse to bear.

What of businesses? Do they have obligations with respect to the starving in other lands? Do farmers and those in the food industry have special obligations? On the basis of the second-order principles we have been using, the answer is that businesses in this regard have no special obligations, providing they have no special relations to the country in question. But they have the obligation to bear their fair share of taxes, including their fair share of increased taxes.

An American-based multinational corporation has increased obligations because of its international activity. It is more closely tied to foreign peoples and nations than are businesses that operate only in the United States. Multinationals are citizens of more than one country and hence have obligations to the people of all the countries in which they operate. The obligation to pay their fair share of taxes in each country is clear. The obligation not to harm is also clear. Agricultural multinationals have the obligation not to contribute to starvation and malnutrition by buying up farmland for export crops with no concern for the effect of this action on the local population. The general principles of morality will require different specific actions by particular corporations in particular countries. But the obligations of these corporations directly involved in a foreign country are greater to that country than are the obligations of corporations not so involved.

American farmers and businesses in the food industry, on the other hand, do not have greater obligations to feed the starving simply because they are food producers or processors. Because the food for starving people in other lands is paid for by the people of the nation giving the food, the burden should be equitably borne. No special responsibility falls on any group. The decision to increase crop production, or to grow enough to produce a surplus for the needy of other countries is a decision to be made within our system. Production can be increased in response to the government's placing orders for food. Farmers have no special obligation to help others, though it would be immoral for them purposely to hinder others from providing such help by refusing to increase production. Hindering others from doing what they ought is wrong for everyone, and farmers in this instance come under the general rule.

The foregoing analysis of starvation and malnutrition has assumed certain background conditions. It has assumed, for instance, that it is possible to feed all the people of the world at a level above that of malnutrition, and that each country is capable of doing so. If we change these background assumptions, we shall have to modify the analysis accordingly. Assume, for instance, that the world is not capable of supporting the number of people in it at a decent level of life. We might then argue either that the number of people should be reduced or that those with more than enough should change their diet, sharing more of what is available with others. The demand to share is already being pressed with respect to natural resources.

Property and Allocation of the World's Resources

In speaking of the resources of the world, and asking to whom they belong, we imply that the resources are property. But there is a good deal of ambiguity in the term resources. We can categorize resources in several ways. In one category we can place natural resources—air, water, minerals, land, fire. In a second category we can include natural but developed resources: cultivated fruits and vegetables, domesticated animals and their products (milk, meat, wool, eggs, etc.). In a third category we can place manufactured goods; and in a fourth, social, nonmanufactured goods—knowledge, technology, organization, talents, skills, and perhaps even language. People, of course, inhabit the earth. Should they be considered as part of its resources? A country with a large labor force, for instance, has an important resource that a country with few people does not have. A country with a skilled labor force, or with an industrious people, or with a cooperative, productive population has a resource other countries may lack. People, however, are not property. Are their properties (their intelligence, their skill, their strength) their own, or are they simply bearers of these characteristics, which should be used for the benefit not only of themselves but for the benefit of mankind or at least of their fellow citizens?

In answer to the question of ownership of the resources of the world, three answer are often given. One is the common-sense answer of business: The resources of the world have already been divided up. Corporations, governments, and individuals own them. This is the status quo position. The second reply acknowledges that the resources of the earth have in fact been divided up, but claims that *by right* the resources of the world belong to all the people, or to all the people of a given state or country or society. The third reply also acknowledges the fact that the division of resources has already taken place, but, like the second reply, it denies that the de facto division is necessarily morally justifiable. However, rather than claiming common ownership, it claims a universal right of access to the resources of the earth.

The Status Quo View of Resources

The common-sense view of natural resources is that we must start from where we are. The resources of the earth have already been divided up. It is futile to inquire about the original allocation of resources, or to deny the reality of present ownership. However resources are defined, property comes into existence only within a framework of recognized rights—typically, the right to use, the right to exclude others from use, the right to dispose of an object, and sometimes the right to benefit from that which is owned. It makes no sense to speak of property or ownership in the abstract. Property is the result of a social practice and is always defined within a social context.

The world is divided into countries, each of which makes territorial claims. Most of these are not challenged by others, even though a few areas and borders are in dispute. Each of the countries has within it a government and an economic order. Ownership means different things in different societies, and claims and rights are treated differently in different countries. In some, individuals or groups are allowed to own land, minerals, factories; in others, only the government owns these. In all systems, however, some food and some goods are produced and distributed; some services are available and enjoyed. Each system has a mechanism for deciding when the ownership rights it recognizes have been violated, and procedures for deciding how to allocate them when there is a dispute. Fairness, according to this view, means abiding by the rules and procedures governing those within the system. This is usually equated with legality.

Instead of asking who by right owns the resources of the earth, suppose we ask to whom do the large deposits of oil that have been discovered in Mexico belong? We know that the oil belongs to the human race, because it is of no interest to the other species on earth. All of mankind is richer because of the discoveries, because that much more oil is now available for human consumption. However, we refer, quite properly, to the oil as Mexican oil, because it is in Mexico. The Mexican government has control of it, and hence the oil properly belongs to Mexico, where that means, ambiguously, to the Government and to the people of Mexico. Within that country, the laws of the land determine to whom it belongs, more specifically. It belongs in part to those who discovered it, to those who own the land under which it lies, to those who extract it, to those who process it, and to those who buy rights to it. Mexico is richer because of the new-found oil. But the oil is not apportioned to each Mexican citizen, much less to all people of the world. Most of them would have no use for a certain quantity of crude oil. After it is processed, the oil is used by Mexicans, who no longer have to import oil. But it is also sold to other countries. Mexico is richer because it sells oil to other countries. If a glut on the market diminishes the foreign demand for its oil, Mexico is no longer able to profit from its oil as it did before.

Any attempt to claim that the oil did not belong to Mexico but to all the people of the earth would be met with immediate, fierce, and legitimate resistance. For according to the rules by which Mexico and the rest of the world abide, the oil is Mexico's. Notice, moreover, that the natural resources of a country are not only valuable to a country because they are available for the direct use of the population. They are also important because of the possibility of selling (e.g., the oil) to others who want it and are willing to pay for it. Therefore, those who make simplistic charges, that some people use too much oil or other resources because they buy them from other countries, fail to understand that natural resources constitute economic riches only to the extent that they are usable and desired by someone. This is compatible with an obligation not to waste natural resources, even if one can afford to do so.

In the United States, the allocation and use of resources are determined by the market, within limits set by the law. Individual firms buy the raw materials they need to produce their goods and services. Individual consumers buy what they need and want, to achieve their own ends. Defenders of the system argue that this allocation of resources is more efficient and entails less waste than allocation by government. The same is true, they claim, on a worldwide scale.

The reality of sovereignty is of significance, not only for how much any one country can do for another, but also for any discussion of the rights of countries with respect to the allocation of resources. The status quo view resists any claims by resource-poor countries on the resources of other countries.

The Universal-Ownership View

The status quo view is attacked, however, by those who claim that the present division of the world's resources is unjust. The distribution of resources is arbitrary; some countries have very few resources and others have a great deal. From a moral point of view, the natural distribution can be taken as the starting point; but it must be corrected so that the resources serve the good of all people, not only the good of the lucky and rich. Originally, the goods of the earth belonged in common to all, and all people retain a claim on the earth's resources, despite arbitrary divisions and allocations that some people have introduced.

But what does it mean, when one says that the resources of the earth belong to everyone? In one sense, something can belong to everyone if each person has a right to its use and no one has a right to exclude anyone else from its use. Thus, a public park might be said to belong to all the people. Anyone who wants to may use the park as a park; but there are limits on the use one can make of it, and the obligation to maintain it must somehow be assigned.

A second sense in which all land, resources, and productive property may belong to everyone is this: each has the equal right to appropriate and use (and in the process, consume) the item in question. If everyone in the society owns the wheat grown in the country, then everyone has a claim on an equal or fair share of the grain. The grain does not belong to the farmers who grow it or to the people who process it or to those who distribute it. It belongs to all, and all are entitled to a fair and—other things being the same—an equal share. This would also be true of the mineral resources of a land.

Yet it would be a vacuous right, or type of ownership, if the iron in the ground belonged to everyone, and this meant that everyone had the right to go to where it is, dig it up, and use it. Most people do not live near iron deposits, and do not need iron ore. What they need and want are products made from iron. Then, to be effective, their ownership of the iron in the ground must mean a right or claim on that iron such that they eventually get the iron products they need. In practice, this would mean that some people would have the right and obligation to mine the ore, to smelt it, to process it, to turn it into goods. At each stage, only certain people would have the right to access and to work on the material. It is unlikely that anyone, anywhere along the line, would be allowed to take what he wanted because everything belongs to everyone. Because there is scarcity, although everything would belong to everyone in the society, it would have to be apportioned so that each would get his fair share. To allow anyone to take anything at any time would interfere with the fair allocation. In this sense, saying that everything belongs to everyone means that each of us has a certain claim on a certain portion of what is available.

Clearly, if we were to have a society of any complexity, there would have to be rules and regulations about allocation, production, work, and the distribution of goods. How allocation, production, and distribution would be carried out in a society in which all property is socially owned is far from clear; thus far, socially owned property has been more or less equal to government-owned property. Whether, on a large scale, there would be any alternative, such as true social ownership without government, is at best problematic. But even if it were achieved, individuals would still have different bundles of rights with respect to different goods.

Defenders of the universal-ownership view have no clear plan for worldwide redistribution; but they defend the need for this redistribution nonetheless.

The existing division of mankind into sovereign states, each of which claims control of the natural resources within its borders, effectively divides up the resources of the earth. To a poor country it makes little difference whether the goods within some other country are privately or socially (government) owned. If a country has no oil, and it needs oil for the development that it desires, it has as little claim on Soviet oil whether the oil is owned by the Soviet government or the Soviet people, as it has on United States oil, whether the oil is owned by corporations or individuals. The internal structures of these societies, and the internal property relations in these countries result, in both cases, in outside countries having no independent claim on their resources.

Proponents of the universal-ownership view maintain that because every person has a legitimate claim on goods of the earth, and national sovereignty prevents the exercise of that claim, national sovereignty stands in the way of a worldwide just distribution of natural resources. Hence, sovereignty is to this extent morally arbitrary and should be superseded.

The argument, even if it could be made out to be valid, is not soon to be accepted by the people of any country today. Nor is it clear what would replace national sovereignty, and how a just allocation of natural resources would be accomplished.

The Right to Universal Access

Although the natural distribution of resources is arbitrary, from a moral point of view, what is done with the resources is not arbitrary. According to the proponents of the right to universal access, the riches of the earth should be used for the benefit of all. To this extent this third view agrees with the second, that of universal ownership. But the heart of the dispute between rich and poor countries, they claim, does not hinge on the ownership of land or resources. Basically, the moral concern of most people is related to the standard of living of those within a country, or in the world. Asking whether each has a right to a certain standard of living is more important than asking whether each has the right to a certain amount of land or resources.

The right to a certain standard of living is in turn linked with the right of development. The right of development is a right that is properly and primarily ascribed to individuals. But because individuals can develop fully only in society with others, and because their level of personal development is a function of the level of development of society, we can also speak of the

393

right of nations to develop. Therefore it makes sense to speak of the right of underdeveloped nations to develop. Such development may require access to and use of natural resources; but the question of the right to development can and should be kept distinct from the question of the ownership of the natural resources. The two issues are related, but they are not identical.

Because nations are not persons, a nation's rights—to the extent that it has any—are different from individual rights. Nations, for instance, have no right to continuance, simply because they happen to have been established; but people have a right to at least subsistence.

What is being claimed, when claiming the right of a nation to develop? There are three different, though related components, or three different sub-claims. First, by the right to develop is meant the freedom to develop; that is, the right to be allowed to develop and not be prevented from developing by other nations. To speak this way is to envisage each nation as a sovereign entity, claiming for itself the freedom each individual has in virtue of his personhood. Although nations are not human persons, the right to develop as they wish without being kept from their development by other nations is a right easily defended, if the nation is seen as the collection of people within it. Each nation legitimately exercises this right, providing it does not violate a similar right of other nations, and providing it does not violate the rights of the persons who make it up. This claim raises no special problems and is generally acknowledged in principle, if not always in fact, by proponents even of the status quo view.

Secondly, the claim to development may be a claim of one nation to receive from those nations that have them the wealth and resources that the first country needs in order to develop as it wishes. But this will clearly conflict with the right those others will claim to what they have justly appropriated, produced, or in other ways obtained. Although there is a generally acknowledged obligation to keep people alive and at least minimally nourished, the obligation to go beyond that is not generally acknowledged and needs more defense. The obligation within a given community or state may arise from the agreement among the members of that community or state, which leads to a certain amount of redistribution. This obligation does not clearly exist in the international arena, either with respect to individuals or with respect to nations. Proponents of the third view acknowledge this. What they claim nations can morally demand is equal access to what they need to develop. But without the money or resources to buy what they need, the right of equal access is vacuous.

The developed nations do not deny the right of all nations to equal access, and they have in fact developed institutions (e.g., the International Monetary Fund and the World Bank) that assist nations in their development through capital loans. These are funded by developed nations. As the undeveloped nations develop and their people achieve higher standards of living, they increase the market for more and more goods. The development of the less developed countries is thus in the interest of the more developed countries. Multinational corporations can assist in the development of many Third World countries, and can do so on conditions favorable to both the countries and the corporations. But none of these institutions or practices recognizes a *right* of less developed nations to loans, assistance from other governments, or help from multinationals. The third view insists on the right of access and the concomitant right to aid from developed nations. What is now done in the name of self-interest or charity, the view holds, should be recognized as a right.

The third component of the claim to development is the right to the knowledge—technological, scientific, social, and organizational—necessary for development. No one owns knowledge. It is no one's exclusive possession, with certain small exceptions, for instance, when, for a short period of time some proprietary or other right might protect the use and dissemination of certain types of information. Because knowledge is not used up by consumption, and is infinitely sharable, sharing does not diminish the amount anyone has—although it may increase the power of those who have it over those who do not. By its nature, knowledge is also social. It has been developed by mankind as a whole, and does not belong to any particular people or tradition or society or set of societies. The knowledge of high technology builds on centuries of earlier work; this knowledge properly belongs to all human beings, and is the common property of all. In this sense, it is the true common property from which no one can be excluded. And it does not fall prey to the tragedy of the commons, because all can cultivate it freely and fully without using it up or destroying it.

To some degree, the developed nations have raised the expectations of people in less developed countries and so bear some responsibility for helping them realize these expectations. This is especially true of the multinational corporations which have led the way in supplying the TV's, transistor radios, communication equipment, automobiles, airplanes, and other fruits of technology to the peoples of underdeveloped countries. Such corporations say that they have simply satisfied a demand, not created it; that on the whole they have helped such countries rather than hurt them, and that their responsibility ends with supplying the product paid for. In a situation in which a government provides adequate background institutions to keep the market fair, such a claim is plausible. In many developing countries this is not the case, and defenders of the universal-access view press on multinationals the obligation not only to refrain from causing harm as they pursue their profit, but also to contribute actively in helping countries develop.

Of the resources necessary for development, the most important is an educated, skilled, industrious work force. Governments wishing to educate their people can use the present communications networks already available. But even more can and should be done. Multinational corporations can provide an important means of transferring technical knowledge and training to workers of less developed countries. The obligation on the part of firms to help educate local populations, train workers, and transfer technological and organizational knowledge is one that we have seen can be made contractual, assuming that a government is interested in the development of the country and of the people, and not just in its own power, wealth, and survival. If education and training cannot be carried on profitably by a company, such training might be underwritten through tax incentives or subsidies from either the host country or the United States and other developed countries. The justification for such action would be self-interest, the morally justifiable aim of helping others, and the fulfilling of the rights of the people and nations of the Third World to socially developed knowledge. Little along these lines is now done.

Through prudence, rather than through moral obligation, the nations of the world already share their knowledge, to some extent. The developed nations through the UN and other agencies send teams to help apply their knowledge to local problems; universities accept students from abroad, even though such programs run the risk of acculturating the students to the way of life of the host country and may make them reluctant to return to their own lands. Both activities could be multiplied considerably.

Although knowledge is the key to development for underdeveloped countries, they also need capital to finance the substructure—roads, railroads, telephone lines, schools, hospitals, electric power plants and lines, and so on—and the development of home industries. Adam Smith (1723–1790) spoke of the wealth of nations. There is also the wealth of the world as a whole. Just as knowledge was not developed by any one person or people and belongs to all human beings, so there is a sense in which the wealth of nations is not the result only of individual enterprise and work, but is the result of the contributions of people as a whole. And each nation has some claim on that general world wealth. The universal-access view does not press these claims as strongly as the universal-ownership view does. But the right to access is not only a negative right. It is also a positive one that involves a right to aid on the part of those needing it.

Whether or not a fully defended moral claim can be made out for transferring some wealth to underdeveloped countries to provide capital for local development, it is prudent to extend aid. For extremes of wealth and poverty cause social disruption, and social disruption tends to hurt the well-to-do as well as the impoverished, who have less to lose. Such help can be made on terms acceptable to both sides, and not simply on terms dictated or demanded by either side. A match between what one country has to offer and what another country needs or desires might be made through individual negotiations, or through the mechanisms provided by the United Nations and other international organizations. Individual firms can play a significant role here. Multinationals have not entered the poorest countries, for they offer few markets and fewer resources. Government subsidies or government guarantees against loss for firms that enter marginal, unstable, or unprofitable markets would often be a better use of money than government attempts at direct aid. This presupposes more planning and thought than has sometimes been the case with the giving of aid in the past. Aid seldom involves simply the giving of money to be used in any way the receiver wishes. For the most part, developmental aid should consist not only of supplying goods but also of transferring appropriate technology, and building substructural or productive facilities. The ideal is to help each nation achieve productive development.

The claim of equal access to the goods one needs individually or as a nation can be justified in terms of justice or of the right to life and development. But the wherewithal to secure those goods separates those people who get the goods from those who do not. And the obligation to provide the wherewithal is a disputed one. The realization that all nations form part of an increasingly interwoven network, making each nation in some way dependent on a great many others, is slowly coming to the consciousness not only of world statesmen but of ordinary citizens in many lands. If this perception is correct, then the ultimate justification for the transfer not only of knowledge but also of wealth among nations is the same as that among people of the same nation, namely the promotion of the common good. The difficulty is that we still lack the necessary structures to make the analogy hold. Nor is it clear that even the recipient developing nations would be willing to give up the autonomy and sovereignty that such structures would demand.

We do not yet have a world society, or even the necessary background institutions for the common sharing of goods and benefits and for implementing global distributive justice. We have, however, an obligation to attempt to establish such structures. Multinational corporations have an opportunity to play a significant role in helping the developed nations meet these obligations.

Oil and the Depletion of Natural Resources

For many centuries, the goods of the earth seemed inexhaustible. Only in recent times have people come to realize that at our present rate of consumption and growth we can conceivably use up certain nonrenewable resources within the foreseeable future. This realization has raised many questions relating to the use of resources, to growth, alternative means of producing energy, and to other similar issues. For purposes of simplicity and illustration, we shall address only a few of the moral issues involved in our use of oil. How do we balance the present need for oil against that of future generations?

The Morally Justifiable Use of Oil

The United States today has approximately 6 percent of the world's population. Collectively, we use approximately 30 percent of the world's refined oil. Is our use of it just?

Until very recent times human beings lived without oil. Oil is not necessary for life as such, but it is essential to many aspects of modern life. Oil is used in the manufacture of gas for our automobiles and of fuel for our airplanes.

397

Oil is widely used to heat our homes and to run our factories. Oil produces 43 percent of our energy. In a modern society such as ours, oil is a present and practical necessity. Oil is also important for underdeveloped nations if they are to achieve a standard of living that will approach our own. And countries that produce no oil, such as Japan, are heavily dependent on it.

If we take the view that oil belongs to those who happen to own the oil fields, or to those who produce the oil, a number of questions arise. Can those who own the oil do with it whatever they choose? Can they morally choose to produce it or not? Can they morally refuse either to pump it out of the ground or to sell it? Can they morally charge any price they wish for it? The traditional free-market approach to all these questions would be yes, providing that the market is truly free. The oil belongs to those who find and develop it. They can do with it what they choose. They will be induced to develop and sell it by others who want the oil, and it will be in the interests of both parties for them to do so. Competition and the market mechanism will determine the price of oil and its use. When the price becomes too high, alternatives will be used. The answer is straightforward and simple: The transaction is fair, providing both parties enter into it freely and with adequate knowledge.

However, many people will say that the situation is not that simple. Saudi Arabia is one of the largest oil producers in the world. Suppose that tomorrow it decided to terminate its oil production. Even worse, suppose that the Organization of Petroleum Exporting Countries (OPEC) decided to stop producing oil. The effect on the oil importing countries would be devastating. It would be devastating to many of the highly industrialized countries, and it would also be devastating on oil-poor Third World countries. Can a producer, from a moral point of view, terminate its production in this way? It cannot if it has contracts that it has an obligation to honor. But suppose it honors those contracts but does not renew them, and does not sell what it has not contracted to sell? The results will still be disastrous. A scenario that would have almost as serious consequences involves the OPEC countries raising their prices so that the poorer importing nations cannot afford to import the oil they need. Is this moral?

A defender of free enterprise might argue that it is moral, but that neither scenario is likely to develop because both fail to take into account that it is in the interest of the oil-producing countries to sell oil. This is their chief source of wealth and income. If they do not produce and sell oil, they deprive themselves of the wealth they can use to modernize their countries and improve the standard of living of their people. If they wreck the economies of the industrialized countries, they kill off their markets, to their own detriment. But the assumption behind this reply is that the oil proceeds go to the country and not to individuals within the country, those who may have more money than they know what to do with and who therefore have no incentive to continue to produce and get more money. If they have reasons of their own for not producing oil, are they morally obliged to?

A utilitarian approach to this question considers the action and its consequences. Whereas the stopping of oil would produce very damaging results on large numbers of people, the action can be morally justified only if the damage is outweighed in the long run by advantages. One of the consequences to consider is the reaction of the industrialized countries to such a shut-off of oil. They would undoubtedly see the action as seriously detrimental to their life and not merely to their life-style. If this were in fact so, they could argue that they are justified in taking military action to secure for themselves the oil they need to survive, and thereby preserve themselves. It is difficult to imagine the positive benefits of terminating the production of oil, or to imagine them to be so great as to outweigh the evils that would result from such termination. To the extent that the action produces more harm than good, it is immoral.

Does the same line of reasoning hold with respect to raising the price of oil? Or to one country rather than all of the OPEC countries terminating the production of oil? Clearly, the consequences of one country's terminating its oil production would not be as serious as all of them doing so. Utilitarianism requires that we investigate the consequences of that particular action, or if it is an action based on principle, that we investigate that principle in terms of its consequences.

The free-market approach to prices depends on the market's being truly free. Within the confines of the United States, the political mechanism operates to preclude collusion and monopolistic action. Internationally, we have no such mechanism. Hence, the setting of prices by an international cartel is possible. If users are dependent on the product, they are forced to purchase it on the terms of the seller or not to purchase it at all.

Within the United States, the price of oil is dependent not only on the cost of oil imported into the country but also on the cost of domestically produced oil. If the free market is allowed to operate, American oil companies would find it profitable to charge the same prices as foreign producers. American producers could compete against one another. But if the supply is less than the demand, they have no incentive to do so. One result of letting the market set the price of oil is that it may price oil out of the reach of the poor. For instance, if the poor need oil to heat their homes but cannot afford it, they suffer extreme consequences. The earlier principle of helping those in our society through taxes and governmental redistribution of income would have to come into play. The money that is redistributed might come from the well-to-do, but many would argue that it should come from the profits of the oil producers, if they reap unusually high profits as a result of the operation of OPEC.

What of the poor countries of the world? We have no international mechanism to protect them from the effects of the rise in prices of oil owing to cartel action. If they are just beginning industrialization, they will be precluded from developing industrially and will be condemned to being poor and underdeveloped for the indefinite future. As we noted, there is a mechanism for redistribution from the oil companies to the poor in the United States; there is no similar mechanism for redistribution from the oil producers to the poor countries in the world. To the extent that their continued plight is a result of the cost of oil, they have a moral claim on the oil producers, a claim that the producers should weigh against the uses to which they put their profits. The moral claim of the poor countries is one, however, that they cannot presently press either by law, war, or economic sanctions.

If we start from the moral legitimacy of certain people owning and controlling the production of oil, then those who have a right to it are those who are able to purchase it. We adopt this general approach with nonessential as well as with essential resources. Because the people of the industrialized countries are dependent for their well-being on a continuing supply of oil, it would cause serious harm, and so be morally improper, for all oil producers to suddenly stop producing and selling oil. The price for oil is determined by the market, just as the price for other goods is determined. But when oil becomes very expensive, those who depend on it and cannot afford it must be taken care of by others.

The Needs of Developing Countries

The foregoing solution is plausible if oil is inexhaustible. We did not consider the fact, however, that the world's oil supply is not inexhaustible. Does this throw some special light on the fact that 6 percent of the people of the world use 30 percent of the oil? Does the fact that a portion of the human race can afford to buy up nonrenewable resources make it morally permissible to do so? We cannot find the answer by looking at statistics but by attempting to uncover the relevant second-order moral principles. Is there any reason to think that a principle is justifiable if it says that n percent of the people of the world should use n percent of the nonrenewable resources of the world? Might we derive it from a principle of equity, and might we defend that principle by saying that everyone has a right to an equal amount of the resources of the world? Is such a principle of equity reasonable? Suppose, for instance, we consider people in the sixteenth century. Did they have the right to the oil in the ground? It would have been a vacuous right. For they did not know about the vast deposits of oil, nor did they know what to do with oil. They had no need or use for it, given their knowledge and technological development. It only makes sense to talk about the equal right of people to oil if we mean by that, equal right of access to the oil they need. If someone does not need oil, it is hard to understand what his right to it means.

Suppose we adopt the principle that each person has an equal right of access to the oil that he needs. Suppose, further, that Americans, for a variety of historical reasons, have built their houses in the suburbs, have not developed their public transportation systems, and hence need far more gasoline than do their German or Japanese counterparts. They also need much more gasoline than do countries with very few roads and automobiles, or small countries in which the need to travel great distances is much less than in the United States. People who live in cold climates need fuel oil to heat their homes, and also need more oil than people who live in warm climates. There are a great many variables. If we consider need, therefore, the simple quotation of statistics is not necessarily morally significant.

There are several other principles, however, that are appropriate and that we can apply to the case of the use of oil. The amount of oil is limited. Oil is a natural resource available for the good of people. If we approach the use of oil either from a utilitarian point of view or from a deontological one, we can defend the principle that, other things being equal, we should not waste natural resources and hence should not waste oil. Stated positively, this is a principle of conservation. We should conserve natural resources to the extent possible, consistent with our needs.

Had we known that oil was limited and that we might exhaust it in the foreseeable future, we would not have built our cities as we did. But we did not, and perhaps could not, foresee the consequences of our actions. Therefore, as a nation, we can plausibly argue nonculpable ignorance. However, we can no longer make the same excuse. We are now morally obliged to conserve oil. This is a prima facie obligation, to be weighed against our other obligations. It is an obligation not only of individuals but also of those in a position to make it possible to conserve oil—automobile manufacturers, those who build factories, and others appropriately placed.

If, so far, this argument has been correct, there is no set amount of oil which, in principle, has to be saved for some particular people. If we Americans use more oil per capita than other nations, this is justifiable, providing we do not waste it. We should make efforts to conserve it, and, as the cost grows higher, we are now becoming motivated to save it. We are also now motivated to develop alternative energy sources.

Poor countries, according to this analysis, have as much right to the available oil to satisfy their needs as do industrialized countries. As underdeveloped countries develop, they will need more and more oil. This fact does not justify the industrialized nations preventing the development of the underdeveloped countries. Nor does it justify an arbitrary limit being placed on the use of oil by industrialized nations, on the grounds that a certain amount must be saved for use by developing countries after they develop. Once oil is no longer available, no one has any right to it. To have a right to what does not exist is to have a vacuous right.

The Needs of Future Generations

We have argued that people have a right to equal access to the oil they need. But how are we to deal with the needs of future generations? Do they have a right to oil? Do we have a moral responsibility to consider their future needs as well as our present needs? There are those who claim that future peoples have an equal right to the world's oil. This argument can be reduced to an absurdity. Consider the amount of oil that is in the ground. Call it x. If each person has a right to a certain amount of oil, then the amount to which each has proper claim is x, divided by the number of people with a basic claim, however that is measured. The question, then, is how many people in the future we wish to count. The denominator of the equation increases as we add more and more generations. The amount each person has a right to gets proportionately smaller as the number we consider increases. Each of us has a right to a barrel, a gallon, or to a thimblefull of gasoline, depending upon how far into the future we extend our calculations.

We do not know the needs of all generations in the future. But there are some things we do know, assuming there will be future generations. They will have certain needs, some of which will be similar to our own. We also know that generations overlap. One obligation that every generation has to the next generation is to pass on to it the common goods that it has received. The goods of knowledge, virtue, and culture do not belong to individuals; they are not used up, and they should be passed along, at a higher level, if possible, than that at which they were received. The passage takes place normally by one generation teaching the next. In this way each generation maximizes good, and each fulfills an obligation to the next generation.

What of goods that can be used up? There is no obligation to pass on these goods at the same level at which they were received. Such an obligation could not be discharged. Because each generation uses part of the nonrenewable resources available, it necessarily leaves less to later generations. If such resources are needed by one generation, the people of that generation have the right to use them. They also have an obligation not to waste them. They have no obligation to make sure that those who come after them will enjoy a higher standard of living than they enjoy. Because the good of each person is as important as the good of any other, no sacrifice of one's good for another is required. No particular generation must sacrifice so that the next generation will have a higher standard of living than it had. It may do so out of love, but it is not morally required to do so.

Yet this does not mean that generations have no obligations to take into consideration the needs of those who come after them. No generation has the right to endanger future people any more than it has the right to endanger present people. It should not, for instance, bury nuclear waste in such a way that it will not affect people of the present, but will be dangerous five hundred years from now, to people who live where it is buried. This obligation is one that applies not only to generations but to individuals, governments, and businesses, because it is through their agency that generations act.

Optimally, each generation should make it possible for all succeeding generations to live at a decent level of life, well above that of subsistence. But practically, we can only foresee a certain distance into the future, and can only provide for a few generations beyond us, if that far. Nor can we guarantee that some later generation will not selfishly endanger the good of later generations.

How does this relate to oil? One suggested conclusion is that, collectively, we have no obligation to save oil that we can profitably use. Our resources are not so low as to demand that; nor are alternative sources of energy unimaginable. They are already possible, and are likely to be developed. Nor would there be any justification for Americans, for instance, to try to guarantee future Americans access to oil by preventing developing countries from developing and using more oil than they presently do.

People are sometimes spoken of as stewards of the earth. If we are stewards, we should use the resources of the earth wisely. But such stewardship cannot justify any group's preventing any other group from legitimate access to fulfill its needs. Nor does it demand that we not use what we need, so that we may pass it on to those who come after us.

In discussing these broad questions, the moral obligations of each individual are difficult to pinpoint. Individuals should not consider the small amount of resources they waste as inconsequential; their combined waste mounts up to a great deal. Businesses also should not waste, even if they can afford to do so. Nor should governments. The difficulty, of course, comes in trying to specify exactly what constitutes waste and what constitutes need. There are clear cases of each, and there is a gray area. People may genuinely differ on these questions. But rational debate and discussion of the issues can help to clarify them, and an organized effort in these areas will make an important difference. By trying to think through the issues in moral terms, we may arrive at a course of action that will be just and maximally beneficial.

The problems of famine, of our obligations to people in foreign countries, and of our obligations to future generations to a large extent fall outside of the socioeconomic structures of our country. In our political process, future generations of Americans are represented only through those in the present who have an interest in representing and planning for them. The problems relating to people outside of our system are difficult to solve because of the absence of international structures necessary to make all the people of the world into a true community. Without a world community, and without structures for redistributing wealth, redistribution is haphazard, inequitably assigned, and skewed by a host of barriers. A truly worldwide application of moral principles requires a truly worldwide community.

Whether such a community can be formed while preserving national sovereignty and differing economic systems is a basic question, to which we have no clear answer. Without a true international community, however, it is difficult to form a clear idea of the extent of our duty—individually or collectively—to people of other countries, and it is even more difficult to fulfill our obligations. Paradoxically, the rise of multinational corporations, the targets of so much moral condemnation, may pave the way for increased contact and community, and so lay the basis for developing the structures we need if we are to relate morally to peoples throughout the world. We should be aware of this possibility, even while we help prevent such companies from exploiting other peoples. We have argued that our government has no direct obligation to other peoples. But we as individuals do. It is up to us to make known to our government our desire to fulfill these obligations collectively, through government action. We can come up with many rationalizations to ignore our moral obligations to the people of other nations. But we have no valid excuse for not attempting to determine our obligations in this area, and then do what we can to fulfill these obligations.

Further Reading

AIKEN, WILLIAM, and HUGH LA FOLLETTE, eds. *World Hunger and Moral Obligation.* Englewood Cliffs, N.J.: Prentice-Hall, Inc., 1977.

ARTHUR, JOHN, and WILLIAM H., SHAY, eds. *Justice and Economic Distribution.* Englewood Cliffs, N.J.: Prentice-Hall, Inc., 1978.

BARRY, BRIAN. "Do Countries Have Moral Obligations?" in *The Tanner Lecturer on Human Values, 1981, II.* Salt Lake City, Utah: University of Utah Press, 1981.

BEITZ, CHARLES. *Political Theory and International Relations.* Princeton, N.J.: Princeton University Press, 1979.

BLACKSTONE, WILLIAM T., ed. *Philosophy and Environmental Crisis.* Athens, Ga.: University of Georgia Press, 1974.

GOODPASTER, K. E., and K. M. SAYRE, eds. *Ethics and Problems of the 21st Century.* Notre Dame, Ind.: University of Notre Dame Press, 1979.

HEILBRONER, ROBERT L. *An Inquiry Into the Human Prospect.* New York: W. W. Norton & Co., Inc., 1975.

NARVESON, JAN. "Moral Problems of Population." *Monist,* LVII (1973), pp. 69–78.

PASSMORE, JOHN. *Man's Responsibility for Nature.* New York: Charles Scribner's Sons, 1974.

PENNOCK, ROLAND, and JOHN CHAPMAN, eds. *Property.* (Nomos XXII). New York: New York University Press, 1980.

REUTLINGER, S. and M. SELOWSKY. *Malnutrition and Poverty.* Baltimore: The Johns Hopkins University Press, 1976.

SCHUMACHER, E. G. *Small Is Beautiful.* New York: Harper & Row, Publishers, 1973.

SIKORA, R. I., and BRIAN BARRY, eds. *Obligations to Future Generations.* Philadelphia: Temple University Press, 1978.

TUCKER, ROBERT. *The Inequality of Nations.* New York: Basic Books, Inc., 1977.

Conclusion

NINETEEN

The New Moral Imperative for Business

"There is no free lunch." This adage, often quoted in certain business circles, means that for everything we get, we pay a certain price. The price is sometimes in money, sometimes in time, sometimes in convenience, sometimes in opportunities lost.

Business met the original mandate of the American people to grow, produce a rich variety of goods at as low a price as possible, provide employment, and help society achieve the good life. It met this mandate at a certain cost, which has varied with the times. As the service industries began to employ more people than did factories, the possibility of expanding output to cover increased wages diminished. Wage increases without increased productivity led to inflation. America's use of oil was profligate. People counted on this cheap energy source for inexpensive transportation, heating in winter, and industrial use. As the cost of oil rose dramatically, Americans faced, and will continue to face, decisions about the use of oil and of energy in general. Cost must be traded off against comfort.

The original American mandate to business has changed, as times and conditions have changed. The change in the mandate has been gradual, and it has not been sufficiently articulated. Many businesses still do not realize there is a new mandate, and struggle to maintain their old ways of doing things. They see increasing legislative controls on business not as a part of a changing mandate but as a personal affront and attack by antibusiness factions and minorities. The national concern with pollution provides an index of the new mandate. When industry was starting, a certain amount of pollution was

407

tolerated as a necessary evil. As automobiles came into popular use, again a certain level of pollution and smog was tolerated. But as industrial waste became more toxic, as lakes and rivers were threatened, as the air became dangerous to plants and humans, the general population came to see that something had to be done. Business was reluctant to change its ways, and was slowly forced to do so by the Environmental Protection Agency. Car manufacturers were ordered to find ways to lower the pollution caused from car fumes. Once ordered, the industry responded. Unless ordered, it is unlikely that any manufacturer would have spent the money necessary to modify its engines because the increased cost would tend to make its cars uncompetitive. The cost of cleaner engines, of course, is ultimately borne by the consumer, who, although breathing cleaner air, pays for it through increased car costs. Electric power plants pay for antipollution devices and pass on the costs to their customers. But manufacturers are reluctant to incur expenses that force them to raise their prices, for fear of losing some customers who are no longer able to afford their products. Though the cost of controlling pollution might be handled through taxes, our society has favored the technique of making the user of the product bear the additional cost.

The American people have not operated according to a plan in changing the mandate to business. It has been changed through legislation, through collective bargaining, and through the rise of a powerful new force—consumerism.

American business started with the businessman in the dominant position. He set the pace, took the risks, invested his capital, and sometimes made a financial killing. The marketplace provided an opportunity for the poor to improve their lot. Social mobility was possible in the marketplace, and the stories of Horatio Alger inspired many workers to try to strike it rich. Some succeeded. Most did not. Capitalism put the workers into a situation of inequality with respect to employers. The workers organized into unions to defend themselves and to advance their interests. Big labor soon matched big business; then big government became the third component of the system. A fourth component, the consumer, was long ignored, and has only recently gained the self-consciousness necessary to organize. Consumers now fight for their rights; they lobby government, and force management and labor to consider their interests.

The result is a new mix on the economic scene. Decisions are not as easy to make as they once were. Instead of aiming only at profits or at increasing production, managers must now weigh many factors and many interests. They must respect the rights of employees, consumers, and of society in general. Respecting these rights has an economic as well as a moral dimension. Faced with conflicting demands by different groups—some of which seem to be counter to the interests of business—many corporations have not known how to respond. Many of them do only what legislation forces them to do, evidently hoping that such things as consumerism and demands for social accounting will go away. Some corporations have indicated that they would like to comply with the new demands placed on them, but complain that the demands made on them by diverse groups are vague, sometimes at odds with one another, and not always clearly in the best interest of society as a whole. A few corporations have attempted to respond by taking positive action to preempt harsh legislation or by mounting public counterattacks, explaining and defending their views of the situation to all interested parties.

Frequently, a corporation has an outdated image of itself, that of an independent entity responding to the simple mandate of a former time, which precludes an effective response to current demands. We have seen that the attacks on the system of American free enterprise have not proven that capitalism is inherently immoral. But we have also seen that moral issues pervade business and society, and that they cannot be ignored or dismissed as irrelevant to business.

The new moral mandate to business can be found not only in such movements as consumerism, environmentalism, and conservationism but in public outcries over bribery and windfall profits, as well as in legislation. Business has opposed legislation dealing with environmental protection, worker safety, consumer protection, social welfare, affirmative action, truth in lending, fair packaging and labeling, truth in advertising, child labor, workmen's compensation, minimum wages, and pension reform. Legislation has been passed in all these areas, over the objections of business. Why has business been opposed to such legislation? In most instances, the legislation seems progressive, socially desirable, and in the public good. In each case, business decried the encroachment of government; and government claimed that business was protecting its profits. Nevertheless, all this new legislation has not prevented business from prospering and from making profits. The legislation has expressed social demands; it embodies a view of business that, when taken as a whole, is clearly different from the eighteenth-century view found in the writings of John Locke or in the Constitution. The present mandate is different from the simplistic mandate given to business in an earlier time.

The negative response of business to each such piece of legislation shows that it is less sensitive to popular demands than many people think it should be. As a result, the general public has labeled business self-seeking, narrowly self-interested, and socially blind. Some books, such as Silk and Vogel's *Ethics and Profits*,[1] show that even businessmen tend to have a low image of themselves. The fact that business has prospered despite such legislation demonstrates that it is more resilient and more able to face social demands than many of its leaders believe, or would have us believe. There may be a limit beyond which business cannot respond. But so long as the costs of such demands can be shifted to the consumer, who is the ultimate beneficiary, the costs represent social decisions. For instance, if air bags in cars increase passenger safety, and if the degree of safety that such bags represent is desired by the general population, then the car buyer will have to pay the cost. It is difficult to know whether any particular piece of legislation represents the

---

[1]Leonard Silk and David Vogel, *Ethics and Profits: The Crisis of Confidence in American Business* (New York: Simon & Schuster, Inc., 1976).

will of the people. If the proposed air bags are to be optional, car buyers would have a choice. Many Americans did not, and do not, want to wear seat belts. Do they want air bags? The issue has not been left to public choice. Should it be? The new mandate to business is more complex than it was in the past; but exactly what it includes and what it does not is still not completely clear.

What is clear in the new mandate is that business must now consider the worker, consumer, and the general public as well as the shareholder—and the views and demands of all four—in making decisions. The good of all must be considered. The key to responding positively to this moral requirement is to develop a mechanism for assuming moral responsibility. Business must find structures for doing so.

The solution to handling competing demands is not to be found in ethical codes, although these are important. Nor is it to be found in any other set of substantive guidelines. Sometimes the demands of workers will carry greater weight than the interests of shareholders; sometimes the opposite will be the case; and sometimes both will have to give way to environmental needs. And the demands cannot all be expressed in cost-accounting terms. The solution to handling these sometimes conflicting demands lies not so much in substantive as in procedural guidelines. This approach leaves the ultimate decisions concerning a business in the hands of management. But management can and should be held responsible for the decisions it makes, and for its mistakes, making management more vulnerable than it was under an older view of the corporation and of business. More importantly, this approach requires a restructuring of business and of the corporate organization itself. Codes and substantive guidelines superimposed on an organization will not significantly change the way the organization functions. Procedural guidelines call for internal modifications, therefore, in some ways, the corporation will no longer function as it did before.

By what right can anyone require such changes? The reply is that only organizational changes can enable the corporation to handle the many demands placed upon it and survive in anything like its present form. If corporations adhere to the traditional model, refuse to consider the social dimensions of a corporation's activities, and refuse to take positive action except when forced to, they invite increasingly harsh and restrictive legislation. Such legislation may eventually replace management of the corporation with governmental control, and may lead, finally, to government ownership. The creative genius of American business, if put to the test, can undoubtedly come up with better solutions to many problems than those forced upon it by procrustean legislation. But business must be willing to respond and willing to change.

In the past, consumers interested in buying a car have not been given the opportunity to vote on how much styling, as opposed to safety, they wanted to pay for. Car manufacturers assumed that the public was interested in the former. The automobile industry decided what would sell and what would not, and how much emphasis to put on safety. American car dealers have not usually emphasized safety features when selling their cars. Despite market surveys, American drivers have had little voice in the decisions. Typical surveys ask about consumer preferences among what the manufacturers wish to offer; they do not attempt to find out what consumers want.

Engineers are in a better position than anyone else to figure costs and risks; but they are not able to calculate the acceptability of risk, or the amount that people should be willing to pay to eliminate such risk. Nor are the managers of automobile corporations. The amount of acceptable risk is a public decision, which can and should be made by representatives of the public, or by the public itself.

What should be the roles of the manufacturers, government, and the public with respect to automobile safety? A proper role of government is to ascertain the minimum level of risk compatible with the state of the art of automobile manufacturing. Such a standard can be arrived at by an independent body of engineers, who should be invulnerable to lobbying by the automobile manufacturers. However, the engineers need not be government employees. A broad representation from engineers at university automotive engineering departments, from industry, and from government might be an appropriate mix. The automobile manufacturers should be informed of the minimum standards they must meet, in reasonable time for them to make the required changes. Thus far, the National Highway Traffic Safety Administration (NHTSA) has established and implemented only a few major safety standards, the two most important being the 1972 side, impact standard and the 1977 gasoline safety-tank standard. The NHTSA appropriately allows each manufacturer to determine how it will meet the set standard. The next appropriate step is for the automobile manufacturers to exceed the set safety standard and market additional safety features of their cars, as they would market other options and new models. Safety could become as much a component of competition among car makers as style now is. To enhance this feature of cars, the NHTSA might require auto manufacturers to inform the public about the safety quotient of each car, just as it now requires each car to specify the miles per gallon it is capable of achieving. Such an approach would put the onus for basic safety on the manufacturers, but it would also make additional safety a feature of consumer interest, competition, and choice. It is puzzling that manufacturers have not taken the initiative in this respect. The auto industry for years preferred to follow the patterns of the past rather than respond to the changing views of the public.

In the preceding chapters, we have seen a variety of suggestions for change, including ways of increasing input by those employees with moral reservations about a company's policy or product, ways of making the board more responsive to the shareholders whom it represents, and ways of assigning responsibility. A bill that has been proposed in Congress requires company managers to disclose the existence of life-threatening defects in their products to the appropriate federal agency. Failure to do so, and attempts to conceal defects, could result in fines of $50,000, or imprisonment for a minimum of two years, or both. The fine, in corporate terms, is negligible. But a prison term for corporate managers is not. The possibility of going to jail for one's corporate actions would make each manager more careful of his decisions. The president of a corporation could be held criminally responsible for life-threatening defects, unless he could show who in the company was causally responsible for the decision to proceed with a product known to be dangerous. This would supply strong outside pressure to reorganize the corporation so that responsibility would be individually assigned and assumed. Such a law would provide an incentive for corporations to listen to complaints by their employees about defective and dangerous products.

We must have moral persons if we are to have moral businesses. But that is only half the truth. We must also have structures that reinforce rather than place obstacles in the way of moral action.

Business ethics has as much to do with business as with ethics. The Myth of Amoral Business with which we began this book has not yet been put to rest in the business world. Many still believe business has no moral responsibility. The myth stands in the way of suggested changes which would reinforce moral action. Showing it to be a myth is not enough. Corporate organization must be changed so that it can respond to moral mandates, and so that those in business can act morally by design rather than by accident.

We may now briefly consider three topics: the role of government; corporate democracy; and the role of business ethics in building a good society.

The Role of Government

The government is involved with business at many levels. It is itself an employer and a purchaser of goods. It controls interest rates, regulates the money supply, and performs a great many other functions. Our central concern with respect to the new moral mandate is in government's relation to business through its regulatory agencies or through legislation. The question may therefore be asked: What is the proper role of government?

From a moral point of view, no government has the right to demand, through legislation, that which is immoral. And its proper function is not the legislation of morality. Through its courts, it settles disputes. Through its tax structure and social welfare programs, it provides for a redistribution of wealth and takes care of those for whom the market system does not provide. In supplementing the economic system of free enterprise, we saw that government fulfills a moral need.

A prime requisite for a moral government is that it act justly. It should treat its citizens as equals before the law; provide the conditions in which they can interact safely; and prevent gross injury by any individual or group against any other individual or group. It does this through its law and its law-enforcement system. Beyond this, its primary moral obligation is not to harm or cause harm to any of its citizens. This obligation is stronger and more important than the moral obligation to provide for the welfare of its citizens. The first is a demand of justice; the second a demand of welfare. A government has no right to harm its citizens. It has an obligation to help them to the extent possible. The first is an imperative by which it is bound; the second a task which it should try to fulfill. As a result, it should not attempt to weigh the harm it does to some and the benefits it brings to others—it should not simply act so as to produce the greatest amount of good on the whole. The government is not an individual. It is a servant of all the people, who have equal rights before it, and who have the right not to be harmed by it. If its laws do harm or are unjust to any citizen, its laws cannot be morally justified on utilitarian grounds.

Let us consider the income tax, which some say is stealing from the rich for the benefit of the poor. If it were stealing, it would indeed be immoral. We have already seen the moral obligation of people within the same society to help those in need. The justification for taxation, moreover, goes beyond that. It is the result of legislation which represents the majority will. The government has the moral as well as the legal right to take those actions that it is empowered to under the Constitution, with the consent of the majority, providing it violates no one's rights. The practice of majority rule is bounded by respect for the rights of the minority. But within that restriction, majority rule can be justified as productive of the greatest amount of good for all—even for those in the minority, assuming that the same group is not always in the minority on all issues.

If we follow this line of reasoning, the American government can protect the consumer through truth in advertising and labeling laws, through actions of the FDA and the FTC, and in many other ways, some of which we have discussed. The government is not morally obliged to interfere or to protect people in all their transactions. But it is entitled to do so to the extent that it is authorized to do so by the people. Hence, legislation that controls various aspects of business, and places demands of one kind or another on it, is morally justifiable providing the laws represent the will of the people and do not violate the rights of any citizen. In this sense, legislation represents the people's mandate to business. A tendency for legislation to move in the direction of greater free enterprise is in itself no more or less moral than the tendency for it to move in the direction of socialism. Both are morally justifiable, providing that neither violates the rights of any citizen or infringes norms of justice. We have seen no argument that satisfactorily concludes that one direction rather than another is morally preferable. How far we should go in either direction is therefore a matter for public debate.

Because the direction that government takes with respect to the control or lack of control of business is a matter for the public to decide, it is called a public policy issue. Such issues should be fully and publicly debated, even though frequently they are not. One of the difficulties of big government, however, is that decisions are often taken by agencies with limited vision. No one takes the time, or has the capacity to see, how all the different regulations impinge on those affected by them. Many small businesses, for instance, claim that there are so many government regulations with which they must now contend that they must hire more people than they can afford, simply to fill out the required government forms and keep up with the government requirements. When requirements become so burdensome that they force people out of businesses, there should be some mechanism by which government and the people can see if legislation and regulation are becoming counterproductive. The tendency of Congress to form administrative units to carry out supervision has also led to such units passing regulations that seem, to some, to go well beyond what Congress originally intended. These units are not carefully overseen, and therefore become self-perpetuating bureaucracies.

Issues that deserve careful scrutiny are the complaints about inefficient government regulation; about regulators being partial to the industries they regulate; about people moving back and forth between the regulating agencies and the industries that are regulated; and about overregulation. To the extent that these complaints are well-founded, government tends to harm some of its citizens, or treats some of them unjustly, and it thereby violates its primary obligation.

Immoral practices in business can be eliminated if those involved in it want to change. Governmental regulation and legislation have been used more and more frequently, and now have become the favorite and usual means of reform. Self-regulation and self-reform are possible alternatives. But unless they are used, increased governmental control is the direction in which the public mandate will continue to move.

Corporate Democracy

We have already seen that workers own a large part of industry, because of their pension plans and insurance policies, and that workers have rights that should be respected. We have also discussed the need for greater disclosure to shareholders by and about the boards of directors. The corporation is now being looked at in a fresh light; there is more public debate about its future, and concern about its power, than in previous decades. But we are still a very long way from corporate democracy.

Worker self-management is an experiment that is being tried with some success in Yugoslavia. Other forms of it have succeeded in Sweden. A few experiments, such as informing employees about a firm's entire operation, and the use of teams instead of individual stations on an assembly line, have proved to be moderately successful. As possible models for future development, they deserve careful study. But most American workers do not want to take over management or to run their own corporations. Legislation has been suggested that would require a company to offer to sell to its employees a plant that it intended to close. But the point of the legislation is not clear. If the corporation feels the plant is unprofitable, why should the workers feel any differently? And why should anyone assume that the workers could run it successfully if management could not? Workers have even been reluctant to have union representatives sit on boards of directors of corporations, because they feel that their representatives would take on management's view rather than that of the workers. Yet, the placing of union leaders on corporate boards, which has already taken place, may presage a direction that will be followed in the future. The practice of naming a majority of outside members to boards of directors is also growing in popularity.

The claim that political democracy demands economic democracy is ambiguous. In one sense, the freedom of individuals to form productive or service units, and to work together to carry out an enterprise, is democracy in the marketplace. The existence of private corporations, therefore, can be seen as an exercise of freedom in the economic realm. But when those corporations become giants, with a gross income as large as the GNP of some nations, critics claim that they should be subject to the same kinds of controls citizens have over governments. The argument is reasonable, if the shareholder is considered comparable to the citizen. It is less clear if the claim is that each person should have the right to some say in the operation of large corporations because such corporations influence all of our lives.

The movement toward some form of corporate democracy may be taking place. But if it is, it is taking place slowly and in a piecemeal fashion. No head-on movement for corporate democracy has as yet caught the conscience or the consciousness of the public at large. In a typically American way, the corporation is changing slowly as it meets new situations and encounters new problems. If our earlier analysis is correct, and if corporations are beginning to perceive the new moral mandate more clearly, they could move more quickly to accommodate themselves to that mandate. But where there is still too little consensus and too little articulation of the mandate, the corporation will develop together with the mandate, until, one day, some observer will bring to public consciousness what will then be readily perceived: that business has changed and that the corporation has responded willy-nilly to a new mandate.

Building a Good Society

A society without justice, at least without justice in its basic institutions, cannot be a good society. A good society must also have a sufficient amount of wealth, distributed in such a way that all its people have their basic needs satisfied and enough in addition for them to enjoy some of the goods of life. Beyond this, there is no single morally preferable mix of other goods in a good society.

One good society may have a certain amount of security for its people, together with a large amount of freedom of economic activity. Another good society may have less economic freedom and more security. Any good society probably has both freedom and security. But there is no one proper place to draw the line between them. Some societies desire and require a great deal of paternalism on the part of their leaders and government; some prosper with less.

And it is not necessary that a good society have no evil in it. A society that tolerates a limited amount of drunkenness among its citizens, for instance, might be preferable to one that has no drunkenness, but at the price of a lack of periodic governmental searches and a lack of privacy. The totalitarian society depicted in Orwell's *1984* is hardly the notion of what most Americans think of as a good society. But neither are the societies portrayed in More's *Utopia* or in Plato's *Republic*.

The freedom of the individual to choose his or her own life-style, to develop those talents the individual wishes, to engage in one type of labor or occupation rather than another—all of these are part of what most Americans would expect to be available in a good society. A welfare state is not the kind of society that Americans want; nor is a society run by and for big business. Equality of opportunity has long been treasured, rather than equality of results. But the opportunity must be truly equal and truly available to all.

We can describe no one best society. For each one we imagine we can always add more happiness, virtue, beauty, or knowledge. One of the tasks of ethics is to describe the goods worth seeking in life. Paramount among them is virtue, but it is not the only good. Happiness ranks a close second, and, for some people, happiness may be the same as virtue. A society whose people value virtue, respect each human individual, and think not only of themselves but of all whom their actions affect, is a good society, even if it does not enjoy luxury and ease. One of the greatest gifts any generation can give to the next generation is the wisdom to make the best of what is available, and the fortitude to overcome adversity.

Business is an activity in which human beings associate with one another to exchange goods and services for their mutual advantage. It is not an end in itself. It is a means by which people endeavor to attain a good life for themselves and their loved ones. Business is a central activity of society, and a type of human association. Too often it is seen in terms of dollars and cents rather than in terms of people. Although a firm may be established for profit, the profit earned is simply a means to an end and not an end in itself. When this fact is obscured and profit becomes an end, then people are poorly served because they are forgotten and ignored in the business process.

This volume has been a long argument in defense of the thesis that the Myth of Amoral Business should be seen for what it truly is—a myth. Ethics and morality have an important part to play in business. If morality is to pervade the marketplace, management must come to acknowledge the role of ethics and morality, openly and vocally. The central moral obligation of business is not to cause harm to any of those affected by its actions. This is the heart of the new moral mandate. It is not the obligation of business to reform society, but to reform that part of society which is business. Business has no mandate to take on government's responsibility for promoting the general good, for providing welfare programs, or for redistributing income. These are properly public policy matters, to be decided by the people. Business does have the obligation, however, to treat its workers and customers fairly, to give them adequate information, to control its toxic wastes, to provide reasonable safety in its products, commensurate with the state of the engineering art, and to give due weight to those with whom it interacts.

There are three stages in the process of overcoming the Myth of Amoral

416

Business. The first is to see it as a myth. The second is to raise the moral consciousness of those engaged in any aspect of business—managers, workers, shareholders, consumers, or simply people affected by what happens generally in business. The third is to change the structures that have been built under the guise of being value-neutral. The processes of business are all value-laden. The need for moral heroes in business is an indication of immoral structures in business. Moral heroes will appear from time to time. They are to be applauded. But we cannot and should not expect ordinary people to be moral heroes. They cannot be trained in school, or made heroic by courses in business ethics.

In recent years, we have had more moral heroes in the marketplace than we have had for many decades. Their appearance is an indication both of the changing times and of the need to change some of our social and corporate structures. Business ethics should have as a goal not only the teaching of moral reasoning and the presenting of moral arguments in defense of moral practices; it should also encourage thought among those in business, as well as among legislators and the general public, about the changes that are needed to promote morality. We have no moral blueprint for what has to be done, no panacea waiting in the wings, and no full-blown alternative system waiting to be adopted. But we are faced every day with moral problems, with immoral and unethical conduct, and injustice. If we look carefully, we can see what needs change and improvement, what will increase justice and fairness, and what will motivate people to act so as to benefit rather than harm others. This requires moral imagination. A better life, a better society, and a more moral society will not be achieved by a few people developing and presenting such a society to others. A moral society is the product of a joint endeavor, and can only be achieved jointly.

Business can cling tenaciously to the Myth of Amoral Business, and can refuse to respond to the new moral mandate. If it does, it will convince the public that business is business, that it condones and fosters immorality and injustice, and that it puts profit above people. Some businesses and some business people act in this way; but not all businesses do. Business will enjoy the moral respect of society only when it earns it. It can show that business ethics is not a contradiction in terms, not a myth, and not merely a body of theory. Ethics and morality can be a part of business. When they are built into its structure, when business lives up to its new moral mandate, it will deserve the public respect it will once again enjoy.

Further Reading

ACKERMAN, ROBERT, and RAYMOND BAUER. *Corporate Social Responsiveness: The Modern Dilemma.* Reston, Va.: Reston Publishing Co., Inc., 1976.

BELL, DANIEL. *The Cultural Contradictions of Capitalism.* New York: Basic Books, Inc., 1976.

HEILBRONER, ROBERT L. *Business Civilization in Decline.* New York: W. W. Norton & Co., Inc., 1976.

CONCLUSION

HERMAN, EDWARD S. *Corporate Control, Corporate Power.* Cambridge: Cambridge University Press, 1982.

HILL, IVAN, ed. *The Ethical Basis of Economic Freedom.* Chapel Hill, N. C.: American Viewpoint, Inc., 1976.

KAHN, HERMAN, WILLIAM MARTEL, and WILLIAM BROWN. *The Next 200 Years.* New York: William Morrow & Co., Inc., 1976.

LUTHANS, FRED, RICHARD M. HODGETTS, and KENNETH R. THOMPSON. *Social Issues in Business,* 3rd ed. New York: Macmillan Publishing Company, 1980.

MILLSTEIN, IRA M., and SALEM M. KATSH. *The Limits of Corporate Power.* New York: Macmillan Publishing Company, Inc., 1981.

PALUSEK, JOHN L. *Will the Corporation Survive?* Reston, Va.: Reston Publishing Co., Inc., 1977.

SILK, LEONARD, and DAVID VOGEL. *Ethics and Profits: The Crisis of Confidence in American Business.* New York: Simon & Schuster, Inc., 1976.

STONE, CHRISTOPHER. *Where the Law Ends: The Social Control of Corporate Behavior.* New York: Harper & Row, Publishers, 1975.

WALTON, CLARENCE C. *Corporate Social Responsibilities.* Belmont, Calif.: Wadsworth Publishing Co., 1967.

Index

A priori, as characteristic of reason, 68
Accountability, moral responsibility and,
    87–90
  corporation and, 162–163
Act utilitarianism, 49–52, 56
Action, moral responsibility lessened by
    precluding possibility of, 83–84
  See also Moral action
Active recruitment, affirmative action
    and, 250–251
Adolescents, advertisements aimed at,
    282
Advertising, 273–290
  coercion or manipulation in, 280–282
  deceptive, 278–279
  half-truths in, 279–280
  misleading, 279
  moral responsibility in, 286–290
  paternalism and, 275, 278, 282–285,
    289–290
  to preschool children, 281–282
  prevention of, 285–286
  by professionals, 285–286, 351–352
  protection from, 275
  subliminal, 280–281
  truth and, 275–280

See also Marketing
Advertising agencies, responsibility of
    for advertisements, 286
Advocates, moral responsibility of cor-
    poration and, 163–164
Affirmative action, 249–253, 263–264
  Stotts case and, 263–264
  Weber case and, 260–263
Age, discrimination because of, 248
Age Discrimination in Employment Act,
    248
Agent moral responsibility, 90–91
Alienation of the people, as Marxist cri-
    tique of American capitalism,
    135–137
All Nippon Airways, 62
Alternatives, absence of lessening moral
    responsibility for action, 85
American Bar Association (ABA), 285,
    343
American capitalism, 126–150
  government intervention and, 126–
    127, 128–132
    common goods provision, 129–130
    economic cycles control, 130
    regulation, 130–131

419

equal employment opportunity, 247–249
preferential hiring, 253–259, 260–263
reverse discrimination, 244, 259–260
utilitarian view of, 239–240
women and, 241–242, 246–247
affirmative action and, 249–253, 260–264
Distributive justice, 77–78
in economic systems, 123
Divine inspiration, theological ethics and, 65
Division of labor, quality of work life and, 212–213
Drucker, Peter, 149
Drug companies
American companies' regulating, 131
standards for as multinational, 363–367
Due process, firing and, 205–206

Economic cycles, control of by government under American capitalism, 130
Economic freedom, of American capitalism, 142
Economic systems
American. See American capitalism
justice and, 123–125
contemporary systems' morality, 108–110. See also Capitalism; Socialism
as games, 110–111
slavery and, 103, 104–108
See also Capitalism; Socialism
Education, discrimination against blacks lessened by improving, 246
Efficiency
of American capitalism, 141–143
as business value, 7
Employees. See Labor
Employment, 177
equal opportunity in, 247–249
full, 183
labors' right to, 177–183
See also Labor
Employment-at-will, 204–207
Energy problems, 4

Environmentalism, 4–5
growth of, 149
See also Pollution
Equal employment opportunity, 247–249
Equal Employment Opportunity Commission (EEOC), 248
Equal opportunity, as business value, 7
Equal Pay Act of 1963, 247
Equal pay for comparable work, 189–191
Equal pay for equal work, 187–189
Equal treatment, right to of labor, 208–211
See also Discrimination
Espionage, of corporations by computer theft, 316
Ethical codes
corporate, 344–346
professional, 338–344
Ethical formalism, 67–69
See also Moral action
Ethical pluralism, 42
Ethical relativism, 32, 34–38
Ethical theory, approach to, 41–42
Ethics
general, 16–17
special, 17–18
Ethnic groups, discrimination in employment against, 242
Eudaimonistic utilitarianism, 46
Excusable ignorance, moral responsibility lessened by, 84–85
Excusing conditions. See Moral responsibility
Exploitation of the work force. See Labor
Expression, freedom of. See Free speech
External coercion, moral responsibility for action lessened by, 85–86
External whistle blowing, 222, 224
See also Whistle blowing
Extravagance, in American system, 8

Fair wage, right to a, 184–191
Fairness
as business value, 7
in free enterprise, 128
False needs, as criticism of American capitalism, 138–139

Ownership
  classical capitalism and private, 113–115
  management dissociated from, 11

Papal encyclicals, just wage and, 185–186
Patents
  computer hardware protected by, 324
  trade secrets and, 294–295
Paternalism
  advertising and, 275, 278, 282–285, 289–290
  of business in Japan, 10
Personal whistle blowing, 222
Piecemeal change, as alternative to American capitalism, 145, 148–150
Pius XI, Pope, 186
Pluralism, moral, 39–41
Polaroid, South Africa and, 374
Political freedom, of American capitalism, 142
Pollution
  concern with as new mandate for business, 407–408
  moral responsibility of corporation and, 159–160, 169, 170–175
Positive rights, 79–80
Postconventional level, of moral development, 29–30
Poverty, in Third World and multinational corporations, 360–362
Pragmatism, as business value, 7
Preconventional level, of moral development, 28
Preferential hiring, discrimination lessened by, 253–259, 260–263
Preschool children, advertisements aimed at, 281–282
Presuppositions of business, business ethics analyzing, 18–19
Price-fixing, competition controlled by, 267
Pricing, marketing and, 268–269
Prima facie moral rules, 75–76
Principled level, of moral development, 29–30

Privacy, labor's right to, 210
  computers and, 330–333
Private ownership of means production, in classical capitalism, 113–115
Private property
  in American capitalism, 142
  libertarians and, 146–147
Procedural justice, 77
Production. See Means of production
Professional organizations, 346–348
Professionalism, professions and, 336–338
Professionals
  corporate disclosure and confidentiality and, 309–310
  definition of, 336–337
  moral obligations and rules of, 349–350
Professions, 335–352
  advertising by, 285–286, 351–352
  as business, 350–352
  in businesses, 348–350
  competition among, 351–352
  corporate ethical codes and, 344–346
  ethical codes of, 338–344
  fees of, 352
  organizations for, 346–348
  professionalism and, 336–338
Profit, 44–46
  Marx on, 132–133
  as value, 6
  See also Utilitarianism
Program (computer), ownership of, 324–329
Promotion
  affirmative action in, 252–253
  rights regarding, 206
Property, 142, 321
  foundation of, 13–14
  See also Computers; Private property; Resources, ownership and allocation of
Protectionism, by government under capitalism, 118
Protestant work ethic, 11
Public
  advertising scrutinized by, 288–289
  corporate disclosure to, 308
  labor relations and, 195

428